Litigating Across the Color Line

Litigating Across
the Color Line

*Civil Cases Between Black and White Southerners
from the End of Slavery to Civil Rights*

MELISSA MILEWSKI

OXFORD
UNIVERSITY PRESS

OXFORD
UNIVERSITY PRESS

Oxford University Press is a department of the University of Oxford. It furthers
the University's objective of excellence in research, scholarship, and education
by publishing worldwide. Oxford is a registered trade mark of Oxford University
Press in the UK and certain other countries.

Published in the United States of America by Oxford University Press
198 Madison Avenue, New York, NY 10016, United States of America.

Library of Congress Cataloging-in-Publication Data
Names: Milewski, Melissa Lambert, author.
Title: Litigating across the color line : civil cases between black and white
southerners from the end of slavery to civil rights / Melissa Milewski.
Description: New York, NY : Oxford University Press, [2018] |
Includes bibliographical references and index.
Identifiers: LCCN 2017023644 (print) | LCCN 2017026447 (ebook) |
ISBN 9780190249199 (Updf) | ISBN 9780190249205 (Epub) |
ISBN 9780190249182 (hardcover : alk. paper)
Subjects: LCSH: African Americans—Legal status, laws, etc.—Southern
States—History. | African Americans—Legal status, laws, etc.—Southern
States—Cases. | African Americans—Civil rights—Southern
States—History. | Race discrimination—Southern States—History. |
Courts—Southern States—History.
Classification: LCC KF4757 (ebook) | LCC KF4757 .M49 2018 (print) |
DDC 346.74/008996073009041—dc23
LC record available at https://lccn.loc.gov/2017023644

1 3 5 7 9 8 6 4 2

Printed by Sheridan Books, Inc., United States of America

CONTENTS

7. The Law of Bodily Injury

8. Fighting for Rights in the Courts

Epilogue

ACKNOWLEDGMENTS

I would first like to thank senior archivist Dale Couch of the Georgia Archives for suggesting that I examine the case files of state supreme court cases when I appeared at his archives as a young PhD student and told him that I was interested in studying race in the South. I am also hugely indebted to the many other archivists and law librarians who assisted me along the way. I appeared back at their archives and libraries again and again over numerous years and emailed them many times, and I always received helpful advice and invaluable assistance in locating sometimes difficult-to-find court cases.

I also profited from the guidance of many scholars at New York University. I am particularly grateful to my dissertation advisor, Martha Hodes, for her constant encouragement, keen insight, and careful guidance in this project. She was extremely generous with her time, and the content and language of my dissertation and book benefited enormously from her counsel. In addition, Michele Mitchell provided important assistance in my exploration of court cases involving Liberia. Linda Gordon encouraged me to explore the physical element of trials and think more about the role of women in these cases. Jeffrey Sammons encouraged and guided my first written chapter draft in a writing seminar. Finally, NYU law professor William Nelson offered important suggestions that vastly benefited my chapters on fraud, personal injury, and economic disputes.

I am also grateful to many historians and legal scholars who have given valuable suggestions and guidance along the way. The two outside members of my dissertation committee, Ariela Gross and Paul Finkelman, gave useful advice on the legal aspects of my dissertation and, more recently, provided extremely helpful feedback on my book manuscript. The members of my dissertation writing group—Lauren Gutterman, Lilly Tuttle, and Peter Wirzbicki—provided unfailing friendship and important comments on my dissertation. Laura Edwards encouraged me to think further about why African Americans were able to litigate certain kinds of cases, and Rebecca de Schweinitz urged me to explore the ways in which African Americans' legal action continued in the decades after 1920. Françoise Hamlin provided useful thoughts on my final chapter, encouraging me to more carefully consider how these cases fit into the black freedom struggle. J. Morgan Kousser was enormously encouraging of my project, reading my entire book manuscript at an early stage and providing important advice on the quantitative aspects of my research and on the process of disfranchisement. Walter Johnson encouraged me to think more about how these cases benefited white southerners, helping to develop a central argument that runs through my book. R. Volney Riser generously read my manuscript and offered encouraging feedback. Gregory Downs pointed out that moving beyond voting rights to analyzing African Americans' participation in civil suits has critical implications for our understanding of black political action. In addition, during my time as a postdoctoral scholar at the American Academy of Arts and Sciences, my two mentors, Patricia Meyer Spacks and Mary Maples Dunn, and the other scholars-in-residence—Benjamin Coates, Matthew Rubery, Chin Jou, Daniel Geary, Lisa Siraganian, and Benjamin Fagan—all provided useful feedback during workshops on my personal injury and fraud chapters.

An ACLS postdoctoral fellowship at Columbia University gave me the opportunity to further develop this manuscript. I am grateful to Celia Naylor, for her extremely collegial mentorship and friendship during my time at Columbia, and for the advice and encouragement of many Columbia faculty members, including Eric Foner, Karl Jacoby, Mae Ngai, Natasha Lightfoot, Samuel Roberts, Christopher Brown, and Frances Negrón-Muntaner. I also benefited enormously from my association with students and staff at the Center for the Study of Ethnicity and Race at Columbia. In particular, the students in the Race and the Law in US History course that I taught three years running at Columbia challenged me to think in a more nuanced way about the opportunities and limitations within the courts and to consider the ways in which African Americans pushed against injustice in multiple ways, based in part on which avenues proved successful. I am also indebted to my writing group at Columbia, including Małgorzata Mazurek, Laura Madakoro, Hidetaka Hirota, Dan-el Padilla Peralta, and Rebecca Woods, who workshopped multiple chapters and provided important support throughout the writing process.

My colleagues at the University of Sussex have been particularly generous with their time. I am especially grateful to Robert Cook, who provided detailed comments on my entire manuscript and encouraged me to highlight more how these cases reveal African Americans negotiating the system of Jim Crow. I am also indebted to my colleague Tom Davies, who provided invaluable feedback on my introduction and final chapter and pushed me to think more deeply about the role of white supremacy in this story. I would also like to thank the many other scholars and friends who commented on and vastly improved my manuscript.

The team at Oxford University Press have also played a key role in this book. I'm particularly grateful to my editor Susan Ferber, who believed in my book from the outset and was enormously supportive throughout the revision and publishing process. Her attention to detail and many important suggestions have made this a vastly better book. I'm thankful, too, to my production manager Maya Bringe and the many others at OUP who worked on this book.

I am grateful as well to my husband, Anthony Milewski, for his constant love and support throughout the many years that I worked on this project. Finally, I am grateful to my three children—Jack, Will, and Kate—who were all born during this project and brightened my days as I worked on it.

Litigating Across the Color Line

Introduction

In 1903, Isham Hodge had farmed his own land in Black River Township, North Carolina, for 23 years. Up until a few years before, 63-year-old Hodge had likely also cast his vote in local and state elections. But at the end of the nineteenth century, the balance of power in the state shifted. By 1900, North Carolina had managed to disfranchise most African American men like Hodge through a constitutional amendment and registration changes.[1] Perhaps with this in mind, in April 1903, an unfamiliar white man from a neighboring county appeared in Hodge's cornfield. The intruder claimed to have bought an old mortgage on the black landowner's farm and said he now owned the property. If Hodge didn't sign a document agreeing to pay him rent, the white man—a 55-year-old doctor named William L. Hudson—threatened to eject Hodge from the land and put him in the penitentiary. Hodge initially refused to be bullied. The mortgage in question was over 20 years old and he had paid it back—and then some—years ago. He told the doctor that before he would pay rent to him, "I would give the land up." Undeterred, the white man returned again and again, continuing to make threats, until finally Hodge signed a document. As Hodge was illiterate, he was unable to read what he signed.[2]

He soon found out that it had been a deed to all of his land. While the white man did not have a real claim to all the land before, now he had a signed deed for the land from Hodge. When Dr. Hudson attempted to take control of the property, however, Isham Hodge and his son-in-law Jim Woodward forbade him from stepping onto the land. When Hudson still appeared to try to collect rent, Woodward told him that they would "pay no rent." The white man replied that he would "get the rent." In response, Woodward told him that if he did so "it would be by law."

Indeed, both sides brought their claims to a court of law. Hodge and Woodward hired a prominent local white lawyer and filed suit against Hudson, claiming that he had obtained the deed to the land through fraud. Even though their political rights had been curtailed, the black farmers clearly believed that they still had legal rights and they might be able to regain the land in a courtroom.

Meanwhile, W. L. Hudson brought an action before a justice of the peace for the rent he claimed they owed him. When the justice dismissed his action, Hudson appealed to the Cumberland Superior Court. The white doctor likely felt optimistic that a southern court would uphold his claim against a black man.[3]

In many ways, the southern legal system appeared nearly impenetrable to people of color like Isham Hodge in the eight and a half decades after the Civil War. The juries who decided some of the cases were largely white until the 1890s and almost entirely white for decades after that. The judges who oversaw proceedings and decided other cases were even more likely to be white; only a very small number of black judges served in the South before 1950. Apart from during Reconstruction, judges were generally appointed by largely white, Democratic legislatures and governors or voted into office by typically Democratic-leaning electorates. And the vast majority of lawyers in the South were white. Many had served in the Confederate Army during the war and had owned slaves or were the children and grandchildren of slave owners and Confederate veterans. With almost exclusively white gatekeepers, it seemed unlikely that people of color could get very far through the system.

The legal system had played a central role in upholding and legitimizing slavery in the South. Then, from the moment the Civil War ended, African Americans were sentenced in criminal cases and put in southern jails in vastly disproportionate numbers. In a practice that rivaled slavery in its cruelty, many states hired out their largely black prison populations for profit. Moreover, in the decades after Reconstruction, southern state courts and federal courts largely allowed segregation to proceed in schools, parks, housing, and transportation. The courts also enabled massive constitutional disfranchisement throughout the South at the end of the nineteenth and the beginning of the twentieth centuries.

But African Americans' experiences with the judicial system in the nineteenth and first half of the twentieth centuries were deeper and more complicated than the courts simply denying them rights. For nearly a century after the Civil War, some black southerners continued to believe that there was a chance for justice in civil cases in southern courts. When the financial futures of their families were on the line, black litigants took on other African Americans in civil suits, and even more often—in cases that reached southern states' highest courts—litigated civil suits against white southerners.

Most often, these cases took place between black and white southerners over disputes that originated from their daily lives. The outcome of the case would usually have an immediate impact only on the families involved in the suit, but it was often life changing. The results of African Americans' litigation would determine whether they would have their own land under their feet, funds to replace missing wages when they were injured, or be paid for a year's work. Other cases decided whether they would be able to obtain property left to them in a will or if they had a legitimate claim to ownership of a horse or mule.

As they litigated these cases, African Americans operated within a system in which the actors making decisions often had very different interests than their own. Consequently, black litigants found that, in contrast to the broad range of civil cases litigated between whites, they had the most success bringing certain kinds of cases against whites. Frequently the cases they were able to litigate aided whites' interests in some way or did not threaten whites. The kinds of cases they could bring also shifted as the societal constraints they operated under changed.[4] Black litigants further found that presenting themselves in particular ways and making certain arguments made it more likely for whites to hear their suits and rule in their favor.

By carefully negotiating this system, black men and women found some of the justice they sought in both local and state courts. Former slaves brought cases against former masters and, at times, won. Sharecroppers gained justice from white landowners. Men and women who could not read successfully fought back when they were cheated out of their property by whites. Indeed, when civil cases between black and white litigants came before them between 1865 and 1950, eight southern state supreme courts decided in black litigants' favor more often than not.[5] Viewed another way, together these eight southern supreme courts upheld trial decisions in favor of black litigants and reversed decisions against black litigants more often than they did so for the white litigants in these suits. In a society in which almost everything was rigged against them, the rates in which state supreme courts reversed and upheld lower courts' decisions in these civil cases between black and white litigants were similar to appellate reversal rates throughout the nation.[6] In slightly over half of these civil cases that made it to their state's highest court, these black litigants had also won against whites at the local court level.[7]

Thus, in a tremendously constrained environment where they were shut out of other government institutions, seen as racially inferior, and segregated, African Americans found a way to fight for their rights. As they did so, they often displayed immense pragmatism and savvy in understanding how to get whites on their side. This book examines how African Americans adapted and made a biased system work for them under enormous constraints. It explores the types of civil cases that black litigants were able to litigate at different times and how they maximized their chances by working with their lawyers and testifying in court. At the same time, it considers the limitations of working within a discriminatory white-dominated system and the choices black litigants had to make to have their cases heard.

This is also a story about the white participants in these cases and about the operations of white supremacy.[8] While I initially focused on the black litigants,

I soon found that, to truly tell this story, I would also have to examine the actions and motivations of the white litigants, judges, lawyers, witnesses, and jury members who played central roles in these suits. Only through their dealings with southerners on the other side of the color line would the black litigants' suits gain traction in southern courts. These cases show white southerners seeking to use the legal system for their own benefit and to uphold white supremacy. At times, though, white men and women also treated certain individual African Americans with a measure of fairness, sometimes to uphold the very system of racial inequality.

Until now, these stories have been largely untold. Most legal analyses of the post–Civil War South have examined African Americans' experiences in the criminal justice system in which they had little choice in their participation in the court system.[9] In civil cases, by contrast, one or more of the litigants chose to initiate the case. But because it seemed so difficult for African Americans to access the southern legal system for their own benefit during much of this period, most scholars have assumed that individual African Americans litigated few civil cases in southern courts in the post–Reconstruction South and usually experienced stark injustice in the cases they were able to litigate. Scholars have reached these conclusions, in part, because when they have examined civil cases involving African Americans in the post–Civil War South, they have largely focused on cases in which the issue of race itself was central: cases over racial classification, sexual liaisons across the color line, and racial discrimination.[10] But these are only a small portion of all of the civil cases in which black litigants took part in the post–Civil War South and are often the types of suits in which African Americans fared the worst. In fact, African Americans litigated a range of cases that reflected their many concerns in addition to racial inequality—jobs, money, illness, custody, inheritance, property, and debt. Even though race was not at the forefront in most of these cases, the racism built into the structure of life in the South had a deep impact on these suits as well.[11]

Putting the pieces of this story together has challenges. Historians can determine what happened in the past only from the evidence that is left behind. In legal action, there is both too much and too little left behind to make putting the pieces of the puzzle together easy. African Americans first entered the court system at the local level, having their cases heard by local magistrates or justices of the peace and tried in county courts, presided over by judges. Many of the records of local courts survive in county and state archives and county courthouses throughout the South. Yet, while some local court records contain petitions and even testimony, large leather-bound minute books with summaries of the cases or microfilm copies of the minute books are often all that survive. Moreover, my examination of the post–Civil War minute books of two superior courts found that, even in a highly racially conscious time, the litigants in these records were rarely identified by race.[12]

There is another type of legal source available that is both more accessible and more problematic: the cases heard by the highest court in each southern state. Unlike local records that usually must be painstakingly pored through, I was able to search the summaries and opinions of these appeals cases through LexisNexis, a legal database created for modern legal research. Many of the summaries and opinions of these cases mention the race of the litigants, allowing a keyword search to find cases involving African American litigants in the records of eight state supreme courts.[13]

Because these cases reached their states' highest court, the full original lower- court trial record, including in most cases, the lower-court proceedings and testimony, lower-court petitions, and the lower-court decision, as well as the lawyer's appeals to the higher court and the higher-court opinion, have been frequently preserved together in case files. Instead of being scattered around the state like local case records, the original files from these cases are often preserved in one central state archive. Thus, after conducting research in legal databases, I turned to archives in each of the eight states, where I examined the surviving case files of suits involving black litigants that reached the eight state supreme courts. Fortunately, the vast majority of the case files have survived and are available in the state archives. As the case files normally include the full record of the initial trial, the files were often several inches thick and numbered 200 or 300 pages, or more. A number of the cases were still tightly knotted in faded ribbon and seemed to have gone untouched for generations.[14]

Although much easier to access, these cases that reached appellate courts are not representative of the full range of cases litigated by black southerners in local courts. The black litigants who were able to appeal were not completely typical: They may have been more knowledgeable about the legal system, better connected to whites in the community, more desperate, or had lawyers more willing to appeal.[15] Additionally, cases involving African Americans that reached appellate courts, like cases that reached appeals courts generally, often had strong legal claims and undoubtedly received greater consideration than most cases heard only in lower courts. Higher-court judges also likely gave heightened attention to factors such as precedent, as the decision in the case could set a precedent of its own.

Examining race in these records has challenges as well. With a few exceptions, I only found the state supreme court cases in which black litigants had been labeled by race in the court report. More civil suits involving black litigants undoubtedly exist in which the litigants' racial classification went unnoted in the official court summary and opinion.[16] Assigning racial categories to these

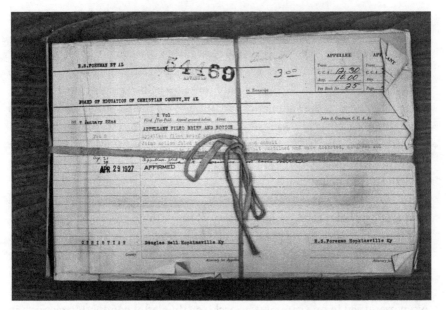

Fig 0.1 The case file of *Foreman v. Board of Education of Christian County*,
Kentucky, 1929. Courtesy of the Kentucky Department for Libraries and Archives.

participants based on the court record is also problematic. Lawyers, judges, and
witnesses labeled each other during the trial and in legal documents based on
their long-standing knowledge of one another, the reports of others, and observations about the person's appearance, companions, and behavior.[17]

Nevertheless, because working with appellate cases allows for an examination of a much broader and longer swath of cases from around the South and
the records are far richer, this book focuses on both the local trials and appeals
of cases that reached southern state supreme courts, while remaining mindful of
these suits' many limitations. I tackle the court records' subjective use of racial
categories by using the terms "black" and "white," based on how the cases and
the laws of the states characterized litigants and witnesses. I employ these classifications to show how the legal system—and southern society—labeled these
men and women during their legal action. The records of these appellate cases
are also more representative in certain ways than one might think. For one, the
backgrounds of black litigants in these suits are fairly representative of African
Americans in the South at the time—many of them were former slaves or the
children of former slaves and presented themselves as illiterate and poor. If they
did have any unusual quality, it was their ties with local whites that they leveraged
to hire lawyers and litigate suits. Perhaps even more important, during the nineteenth century, southern appellate courts heard a wide range of cases, including suits involving only small amounts of money. Not all cases were appealed,

but many of the cases that litigants attempted to appeal were taken up by state supreme courts during much of the period under examination.[18]

Examining legal sources has its own challenges. Most texts used by historians are unreliable in different ways, based in part on how they were created and the purposes behind their creation. In the case of trial testimony and petitions, lawyers and the litigants involved shaped their testimony to achieve a certain end—to win their cases. Witnesses, too, shaped their testimony based on their relationship with the person they were testifying about, financial consequences such as losing their jobs, their own personal views, and their actual knowledge of what they testified about. Because there are two sides to almost every case, two different groups of people were shaping their words for opposite ends. As a result, in many—if not most—cases, the statements of material facts by both sides contradict each other. But rather than rendering these cases useless as a historical source, the ways that litigants and lawyers shaped their cases provide important information. I plumb their testimony and petitions to examine how they sought to shape their cases to win their suits and to better understand their knowledge of the law and race relations in their communities. As I read legal decisions, I recognize too that, even as judges sought to give authority and legitimacy to one side in the dispute by drawing on precedent and couching their words in legal language, such decisions are subjective. The outcome of cases is based on the unequal resources of the two different sides and the judges' and jury members' ideas, experiences, and relationships as well as on the law itself.[19]

Because of the subjective nature of many court records, materials beyond the legal record assist in interpreting and contextualizing court transcripts. This book uses the records of white and black newspapers throughout the South to better understand attitudes toward the courts, illuminate responses to African Americans' legal action, and learn more about the trials and aftermaths of certain cases. In addition, I searched the records of the Freedmen's Bureau to discover how the Bureau helped set the stage for African Americans' access to southern courts and traced claims that were appealed to both the Bureau and state courts. I also studied records written by or about by the participants in lawsuits, including census data, local histories, letters, speeches, and wills. Finally, I used contemporary legal manuals, texts, and memoirs to better comprehend the legal process of the time and gain insights into the decisions of southern judges.

Through a search of the records of eight southern state supreme courts between 1865 and 1950, I unearthed the surviving trial records and appeals of 1,377 civil cases litigated by African Americans during this period.[20] Although this number is much higher than historians have assumed, these cases still only made up a small proportion of overall suits in southern appeals courts. In all, these civil appellate cases involving black litigants made up about 1 of every 162 civil and criminal cases in the state supreme courts in which they were litigated between 1865 and 1950.[21] The vast majority of these courts' business involved civil disputes between whites.[22]

Slightly less than one-third of these civil appeals cases involving African American litigants (397 suits) were litigated between two or more black litigants.[23] By far the greatest number of appellate civil suits between black litigants were disputes over wills and estates. For decades after slavery ended, a large number of these inheritance suits between black litigants dealt with the aftermath of the ban on slave marriage. If formerly enslaved men and women did not marry after the Civil War and died without wills in place, their partners and children struggled at times to inherit. Slave sales of fathers and mothers away from their families also resulted in some former slaves having more than one family who claimed an inheritance. Disputes over property formed another fifth of suits between black litigants, reflecting the importance of property ownership to black southerners throughout much of this period and southern courts' continuing respect for property rights. An additional fifth of suits involved black churches or black fraternal organizations, which played central roles in African American communities.[24]

The remaining 71 percent of civil cases involving black litigants in the eight state supreme courts (980 suits) occurred between white and black litigants. These suits are the focus of this book. Despite important differences among the states, what stood out most in these suits was how consistent the patterns in these cases were across eight widely varied southern states. Although all had been slave states, in many ways the states' contrasts were just as great as their similarities. One of the states—Mississippi—had a majority-black population throughout much of the period examined and several others, such as Alabama and Georgia, had almost as many black residents as whites. Other states, like Arkansas and Kentucky, had far more white than black citizens.[25] In states such as Virginia and Georgia on the Eastern Seaboard, white communities had been established for centuries before the Civil War. In contrast, states farther west like Mississippi and Arkansas were not part of the original thirteen colonies and did not achieve statehood until the first decades of the nineteenth century. While seven of the states fought for the Confederacy, Kentucky did not secede during the war. During the era of Reconstruction (1865 to 1877), Republican control ended earlier in some states than others, as Democrats gradually took back much of their power in state after state. Throughout the South, African Americans' political power also varied: In states like Georgia, their role in politics weakened far earlier than in North Carolina, where black voters continued to wield significant political power through the 1890s.[26] Even with these vast demographic and political differences, though, patterns of litigation by African Americans in southern state supreme courts were surprisingly similar and shifted over time as a region.

Throughout the eight states, many civil cases that reached appellate courts took place between former slaves and their former masters. In two-thirds of these cases during the Reconstruction era and about a third of cases in the two decades after Reconstruction, men and women who had been considered property sued the very people who had owned them or their former owners' heirs.[27] They brought into courtrooms their long histories together during slavery. Black litigants also brought suits against white employers, neighbors, city officials, landowners, speculators, and shopkeepers. In other civil cases, white southerners initiated the legal action, and black southerners fought back against whites' claims. At a time when white men dominated the courtroom, black women litigated 41 percent of these suits, at times explicitly using their gender to elicit sympathy from the court.[28]

Before entering the courtroom, black southerners had often sought other ways to settle their disputes with whites. One black plaintiff explained that he and other "colored citizens" in Louisville, Kentucky, had tried to settle the issue of segregated parks "in divers ways and means" before bringing it to court.[29] Black southerners also faced many barriers to entering a courtroom. Even if black men and women wanted to bring their dispute before a court, they often lacked the money to hire a lawyer or pay court fees. Certain kinds of cases were difficult to bring before white-dominated courts. And in the post–Civil War South, the threat of violent repercussions was ever-present.

Nonetheless, some black southerners continued to turn to the courts in their disputes because they saw them as a possible realm for justice. Throughout this period, African Americans were challenging inequality in the nation on many fronts, experimenting in diverse forums and with various strategies. They soon found that certain methods worked best at different times and places. Litigation, in particular, remained a viable strategy in the South even after many other political avenues had been closed to them.

Black southerners also were willing to take on the expense and risk of legal action because they saw civil cases as having hugely significant financial consequences for their families. Isham Hodge's and Jim Woodward's case could completely change their family's finances, turning them from landowners into renters.[30] Other suits could allow black litigants to gain thousands of dollars left to them in wills, funds to provide for their families in the wake of debilitating injuries, or money they were owed from a cotton crop.

Even as they held out a measure of hope in the courts, black litigants were realistic. Although Union occupation temporarily shifted the balance of power in the South during Reconstruction (in some states longer than others), the courts remained dominated by white lawyers and judges, and most jurors continued to be white. No doubt some black southerners noticed the difficulties they faced in litigating cases that appeared threatening to whites: Black men and women were being given much longer sentences than whites in criminal cases and were often unsuccessful in cases they litigated over racial discrimination.[31] Their cases over contracts, personal injury, and property were much less threatening to white southerners. But even in these suits, African Americans had to gain the support of white lawyers, witnesses, judges, and juries to have a chance at winning. In many kinds of civil cases, it was not possible to win whites' support at all, limiting the types of civil suits black men and women were able to litigate.

Instead of giving up on the legal system altogether, black litigants continued to pursue the kinds of cases in which they could participate. Clear patterns in what kinds of cases black southerners could litigate and the strategies they used to win their suits emerged across the South. In the 35 years after the Civil War, many cases centered around bequests left to freedpeople in a former master's will, appealing to white men's rights to leave funds and property to whom they wanted. Other cases between black and white southerners took place over transactions, contracts, and property (unrelated to white people's wills) and asserted black litigants' ideas of economic equality and independence. But as the decades passed, the ties between former slaves and former masters became more distant. By the end of the nineteenth century and the beginning of the twentieth century, segregation and disfranchisement had become entrenched throughout the South. As a result, in the first two decades of the twentieth century, the types of civil cases black southerners could litigate became even more limited. The vast majority of cases now involved cases of personal injury or fraud in which black southerners had to emphasize their ignorance and vulnerability to gain white support for their cases. Beginning in the 1920s, the types of cases that black southerners could litigate broadened once again. Between 1921 and 1950, more and more seemingly everyday kinds of suits over personal injury, property, contracts, and wills began to include challenges to the racial status quo.[32]

Along with litigating the kinds of cases that were acceptable to whites at different periods of southern history, the black litigants whose cases would make it to appellate courts frequently sought to make their civil suits as appealing to white juries and judges as possible. Although such pragmatic decisions enabled their cases to be heard, they narrowed the range of arguments and cases and at times reinforced white supremacy. Having a white lawyer was key to making their civil cases acceptable. Black litigants had white attorneys in almost every civil suit between white and black litigants that made it to an appellate court. Often these lawyers were prominent men in their communities. Isham Hodge's attorney, 40-year-old Neil Angus Sinclair, came from a respected local family and served as the state senator from Cumberland County the year he tried Hodge's case before the appeals court. Sinclair was well known for his oratorical skills, which he put to use in the courtroom and in political speeches around the state.[33]

During the lower-court trial, black litigants worked with their lawyers to shape their testimony and their case to appeal to white jurors and judges. In the decades immediately after the Civil War, this often meant emphasizing their ties with local whites, including the family of their former masters, and finding white witnesses to testify in their favor. As they testified, black litigants and witnesses also frequently shaped their words to conform with white jury members' and judges' ideas about race. At times, they asserted that they had acted the way they had because they had trusted whites. Isham Hodge, for one, testified that when the white doctor and another white man had read over the papers for him to sign, they "didn't say I was deeding away the land." Particularly in the first two decades of the twentieth century, declarations of ignorance and illiteracy by black litigants and their witnesses helped to give black southerners their day in court. Isham Hodge testified to the court, for instance, that when the white doctor had brought papers to his farm for him to sign, "a heap of it I didn't understand."[34] But even when they played to white expectations of black ignorance, some black litigants used legal knowledge to improve their cases' chances of being heard and to bolster their legal claims.

In the end, these cases continued in southern courts in large part because of a stark disjuncture in how many black and white litigants viewed them. Because black litigants saw their participation in civil cases as having life-altering economic consequences, they usually did all they could to win their suits. In contrast, white judges and jury members typically did not see the civil cases that black litigants were especially successful at litigating as dangerous or having the power to upset the status quo. To them, many of these cases appeared to support white supremacy. In their view, cases over white men's bequests to their former slaves and employees upheld white men's property rights. An occasional suit over a labor contract made little difference in the face of widespread violence and harsh economic realities within the southern labor system and could be used as evidence of legal elites' paternalism and benevolence toward poor black laborers. Suits over fraud and personal injury in which black litigants testified about losing their land or receiving grievous injuries reinforced many of whites' own ideas about black southerners' ignorance and dependence on them. This disconnect played a crucial role in allowing black litigants to continue to participate in—and sometimes win—civil cases, even after they had lost power in other areas of government in the South. By carefully calibrating their testimony and arguments, black litigants and their white lawyers played an important part in perpetuating this disjuncture.

The black individuals who held onto hope that the courts might change their lives for the better and the white judges and jury members who saw the courts as upholding the system of white supremacy both had valid points. On the one hand, white southerners were all too correct in their realization that these civil cases had enormous limitations. Even in states with majority black populations, these civil cases made up 1 percent or less of the total civil and criminal appeals during this period.[35] When black men and women could litigate civil suits, they almost always had to use white lawyers and make their testimony and claims in a way that white southerners found acceptable. By presenting themselves as vulnerable and ignorant in these cases, black litigants reinforced many white stereotypes about their race. The decisions themselves often reinforced the ideas of inequality manifested in white supremacy. In the opinion in one of Isham Hodge's 1905 cases, for instance, the justice began by noting the vast difference in knowledge between the two litigants. "The plaintiff was an illiterate colored man," he explained, while the white defendant was "an educated man and a physician."[36] These civil cases also exacted costs from black participants. During courtroom battles, black men and women at times found their sexual histories aired, their reputations questioned, and their bodies publicly exhibited.

The very dependence on precedents and formal procedures that allowed black litigants to sometimes prevail in civil suits gave the courts a misleading guise of impartiality. This lent a veneer of legality to a system based at its core on white supremacy. An apparently objective court was a powerful tool of social control: If ordinary citizens believed they might be able to gain justice in the courts, they might not turn to extralegal measures or take part in social unrest.[37] Because these cases made up only a small proportion of the overall cases heard by southern appeal courts, the benefits of allowing such cases to gain favorable decisions may have outweighed the losses to individual whites.[38]

In cases that had real potential to affect southern society, black southerners struggled to have their cases heard throughout much of this period or habitually ended up on the losing side. As a result, during most of the period between 1865 and 1950, black men and women were able to litigate only a small number of civil cases in the eight state appellate courts examined that directly challenged racial discrimination. When they could litigate such cases, they won them only 36 percent of the time across this period.[39] Criminal cases involving black defendants, on the other hand, seem to have come before southern state supreme courts more often than civil cases with black litigants. In the state supreme courts of Alabama and Georgia between 1865 and 1950, criminal cases made up two-thirds of suits involving African Americans, while civil suits accounted for one-third of black litigants' suits.[40] This was far higher than the proportion of criminal cases in state supreme courts as a whole.[41] But in appellate criminal cases, black defendants ordinarily received significantly less favorable decisions than in appellate civil cases involving black and white litigants. Between 1865 and 1950, black litigants won 59 percent of their civil cases on appeal in the eight state supreme courts examined, but only 38 percent of their criminal cases before the supreme courts of Georgia and Alabama.[42] For certain kinds of crimes, such as the rape of a white woman, the reversal rate for black defendants was even lower.[43] Moreover, in many of the criminal cases in which the higher court overturned the sentence, their cases were sent back to the lower court for a retrial, where in many cases they may have still received a hefty sentence.

The differing success in civil and criminal appellate cases was affected by trial court outcomes and who appealed. But these numbers also reflect that whereas black litigants' civil cases often seemed unthreatening, white southerners had long thought of African Americans as naturally inclined toward crime and saw criminal law as one of the few tools they had to control such tendencies.[44] The criminal justice system also played an outsized role in regulating the southern labor market. Laws that criminalized leaving before completing a labor contract, for instance, gave whites considerable control over black workers. Furthermore, black convicts made huge sums of money for southern states and local law enforcement, who sold their labor to private corporations and individuals for profit. As a result, black southerners often received vastly unequal justice in criminal cases, and the number of black convicts in southern prisons soared.[45]

Yet black southerners had valid reasons to turn to the courts in civil actions, even after losing the vote and seeing segregation written into law. After 1890, the courts were often more accessible to oppressed groups in the American South than other branches of government. In large part, this was because whites did not view the legal system, stacked with white judges, lawyers, and juries, as capable of upsetting the status quo. As a result, a black litigant was much less threatening than a black voter. The structure of the legal system itself also played a part in the courts' accessibility. Southern judges were more insulated from politics than popularly elected politicians. In some cases, they were appointed by the legislature or governor. Even elected judges rarely had to run in competitive elections in the South, and their terms often lasted a decade or more. The American legal system's reliance on precedent—the decisions of the past—could work in black litigants' favor, too. In civil cases that did not have the potential to shake up society, judges often decided cases involving African Americans just as they decided the other suits that came before them—relying on precedent and the merits of the case as well as their own personal opinions of justice. Even in jury trials, judges relied on these factors as they gave instructions to the jury.[46]

Thus, southern courts had some insulation from the changes that set in around the South during and after Reconstruction. Even as Democrats regained political power, the kinds of cases litigated by African Americans remained much the same. Only at the end of the nineteenth century, when it became nearly impossible for most black men in the South to vote, did the tenor of court cases involving black and white southerners dramatically change. Even then, civil cases involving black people continued and black litigants continued to win; only the types of cases and content of the testimony shifted. Clearly, the legal system did not operate completely in tandem with the politics of its time. Yet neither did it function entirely outside of politics; the black loss of the vote manifested itself in every trial heard before its courts.

Despite their limitations and costs, black southerners' suits had important economic and social consequences for the individuals involved and influenced other people who observed or read about them. Throughout their legal battles, black and white southerners worked out their new relations with each other. When black litigants won, direct actions followed, as they took possession of property, obtained a legacy promised in a will, regained custody of a child, or obtained damages. Even when black litigants lost, they had gained legal knowledge, exercised their rights as citizens, and stood up to local whites. Other black people in the community also recognized their own legal power as they watched and read about their black neighbors and acquaintances gaining favorable verdicts against local whites.

The case of Isham Hodge realized some of African Americans' hopes in the legal system. The two suits between Isham Hodge and Jim Woodward and W. L. Hudson—one brought by the white doctor and the other by the black landowners—were heard by a Cumberland County court in the spring of 1905 in Fayetteville, a midsize city in central North Carolina.[47] Although the county was almost half black, none of the jurors seem to have been African American. Black jurors were very occasionally called to juries in North Carolina in 1900, but, as one North Carolina court clerk noted, only rarely, "as talisman."[48] The outcome of the suit, then, would be decided by whites in a state where black men no longer had political power.

In a confusing move, juries decided in favor of the plaintiffs in both the white doctor's suit and in the black landowners' suit—deciding that the black litigants owed the white doctor $5 in rent and that the deed to the land on which the white litigant based his claim for rent had been fraudulently obtained and was invalid. Many members of the community likely heard about the case. The *Fayetteville Weekly Observer* devoted two paragraphs to the white doctor's suit, noting that the trial had "consumed the morning and afternoon sessions" of the local court. The newspaper noted, too, the race of the black defendants, and the fact that the white plaintiff and his lawyers were from another county. "Though the amount is small," the newspaper concluded, "much law is involved."[49]

Both cases were then appealed to the state's highest court, the Supreme Court of North Carolina. Located in an imposing courthouse in the state capital of Raleigh, the state supreme court was made up of five justices, who were elected every 8 years.[50] These white justices validated Woodward's hope that some fairness could be obtained through the legal system, as they dismissed the white doctor's claim to any rent and canceled the deed in which Isham Hodge had signed over his land to Hudson. Justice C. J. Clark explained in the opinion canceling the deed that "it appears from the defendant's evidence that he paid the plaintiff nothing." The white jury's decision for the black plaintiff also played a part in swaying the state justice. To support his decision, Clark cited the jury's finding in the lower-court trial that "the deed from plaintiff to the defendant was procured by the fraudulent misrepresentation of the defendant." Several newspapers around the state briefly noted the outcome of the cases.[51]

In the end, Isham Hodge's family would keep their land—although its ownership would remain embattled. Five years later, a 70-year-old and reportedly somewhat senile Isham Hodge would sell what he believed to be 10 acres of his land for $75, only to discover that the white buyer had misled him and the deed conveyed all 76 and 1/2 acres of his property. After his death, his heirs would turn to the state's highest court in 1914 to defend their claim against this fraudulent deed. As in 1905, they would prove successful in preserving their property rights through the courts.[52]

In addition to mattering to the people involved, these suits have important implications for African American history and the history of the US South. Court battles involving African Americans have often been seen as the battleground of elite civil rights lawyers, far removed from everyday people's lives.[53] These cases, however, showcase the central role that the courts played in many ordinary African Americans' lives and their active involvement in initiating civil suits and testifying in trials against local whites.

These cases also reimagine African Americans' ability to work within a white-controlled institution at a time when they lived under tremendous restrictions. In the past, scholars have largely dismissed African Americans' ability to participate meaningfully in any government institutions in the Jim Crow South.[54] This book shows that African Americans' participation in the southern legal system—limited as it was—was one exception to their larger inability to engage with white Southern institutions. African Americans negotiated the justice system by recognizing the interests of the people wielding power and framing their claims to appeal to such parties.

African Americans' civil litigation also connects earlier struggles for rights in the US South with later twentieth-century battles over rights. In the traditional narrative, black southerners worked within politics and the courts until the end of the nineteenth century, then largely turned inward to their own communities and began to move to the North or West before mobilizing once again in the mid-twentieth century. During the past decades, however, historians and legal scholars have begun to show a struggle for legal, political, and economic rights in the South in the 1920s, 1930s, and 1940s.[55] Recently, scholars have also started to unearth African Americans' challenges to the status quo in the

South at the end of the nineteenth and beginning of the twentieth centuries.[56] Taking black southerners' participation in civil cases into account further challenges a narrative in which the struggle for rights in the South stops and starts. Every case litigated by a black person against a white man or woman in a southern court had implications for African Americans' legal rights. Many cases also claimed African Americans' economic rights—the right to gain and hold on to property, the right to make contracts without being defrauded, and the right not to pay taxes for schools that their children were not allowed to attend. African Americans' civil litigation, then, shows a continuous grassroots struggle by individuals for rights in the South, from the Civil War to the civil rights movement.

Primarily litigated by individuals without support from any larger organizations, these cases contrast sharply with the group-based actions, such as boycotts, marches, voting registration drives, and civil rights test cases, that receive the lion's share of attention in the struggle for African American rights. This book builds on histories documenting both the opportunities and limitations of individual action.[57] Because these cases were litigated by individuals and ordinarily concerned only their own families, they were relatively unthreatening and could proceed when collective action often failed. In addition, such cases arguably involved ordinary African Americans more than test cases orchestrated by elites. At the same time, the plaintiffs were constrained by limited resources, lack of coordination, and narrower claims.

These civil cases also provide insight into a disadvantaged group's complicated relationship with the courts. In particular, they help clarify why, despite experiencing massive injustice in the criminal justice system, African Americans turned to the courts repeatedly to assert their rights and challenge inequality. As segregation set in at the end of the nineteenth century, black litigants challenged racial segregation in cases such as *Plessy v. Ferguson*. Multiple national organizations working for racial justice at the end of the nineteenth and beginning of the twentieth centuries, including the Afro-American League, Afro-American Council, and Niagara Movement, used litigation as a strategy to confront discrimination. From the beginning of the twentieth century through the civil rights movement, the National Association for the Advancement of Colored People (NAACP) focused much of its attention on assaulting discrimination through the courts.[58] Although criminal cases do little to explain these actions, the civil cases that flowed through southern appellate courts help show why African Americans often sought justice in courts.

These cases illustrate, too, the varied ways in which white supremacy operated in everyday southerners' lives. Not only could it be manifested as violence and election fraud, but white supremacy could underpin a court's decision in a black litigant's favor. White members of the community who had owned slaves and believed fervently in the inequality of people of color could testify in favor of black litigants whom they had known for years. Similarly, white lawyers at the height of their profession could take on landless black laborers as clients and represent them well. This complexity does not make the South any less violent or white supremacy any less harsh. Rather, it shows that, even as racial segregation set in, black and white southerners' lives remained entwined in relationships of unequal power.[59]

In addition to being a story about the US South and African American history, this is a story about law. Black litigants' stories have not been fully told because of the ways legal historians have defined their sources. For many years, scholars of legal history looked largely at the laws enacted by legislatures and at judges' decisions in appellate cases, leaving aside the litigants themselves and the many other participants in court cases.[60] But in recent years, with the rise of cultural and social history, there has been a sea change in how scholars examine the law. Many legal historians are now concerned with how the law played out in people's lives. Legal historians are especially aware that the law written down in statutes and proclaimed in higher-court legal opinions was not necessarily the law carried out on the ground in particular localities. The new cultural legal history also draws on ideas of performance and uses techniques of close reading when analyzing courtroom testimony.[61] In many instances, these works hone in on one case or a small number of cases to allow historians to examine the events in their larger societal context and analyze the multiple players within the courtroom.[62]

My work draws from both these older and newer approaches. Like scholars of previous generations, to see patterns across the South and across time, I examine a broad range of cases that reached appellate courts across multiple states. Unlike earlier legal scholars though, I am not just concerned with judges' opinions, but also pay attention to the lower-court trial records of these cases and the actions and words of the litigants, witnesses, jury members and lawyers, and the judges involved in these cases. When discussing key cases, I firmly place the trial participants in specific locations and within the politics and ideologies of their time. My work also examines the performative aspect of African Americans' testimony and considers why black litigants and witnesses framed their testimony as they did.[63]

The book begins by tracing how African Americans accessed southern courts during and in the wake of the Civil War and how they held on to some of these rights even after Reconstruction ended. Chapter 2 follows the legal journey of African Americans who succeeded in litigating cases against whites from the end of the Civil War to the end of the nineteenth century. I show how they hired lawyers, testified before crowded courtrooms, and appealed their suits to their states' highest courts. But to truly understand African Americans' participation in southern courts during the decades after the Civil War, we must look at the kinds of civil cases they were most frequently able to litigate against whites. Chapter 3 examines suits involving white men's wills, focusing on cases in which masters had set aside money in their wills for their slaves to be emancipated and sent to Liberia upon their owners' death. After the war, the chapter reveals, former slaves used these wills to go to court against their former masters' heirs over the funds. From Reconstruction to the end of the nineteenth century, African Americans throughout the South also litigated cases in state supreme courts that asserted their right to participate in the postwar economy on an independent, equal basis. Chapter 4 investigates suits in which black litigants disputed transactions of land or livestock that they had conducted with white southerners, battled over contracts, and demanded fair payment for their work.

A significant shift in black southerners' litigation occurred not as Reconstruction ended in state after state, but at the close of the nineteenth century. Part II examines African Americans' civil cases after this pivotal shift. Chapter 5 shows how the types of civil cases African Americans were able to litigate in southern courts narrowed as black men largely lost the right to vote in the South and segregation was increasingly written into law. In the first two decades of the twentieth century, for instance, almost three-fourths of their appellate civil suits involved particularly egregious cases of fraud in property dealings or personal injury claims and highlighted black people in dependent, vulnerable positions. Chapter 6 examines the fraud cases black southerners litigated, accusing whites of deception in property dealings. In case after case, black litigants testified about their diligence in attempting to understand the contract, their own ignorance and vulnerability to deception, and their trust in the defendant. As such testimony appealed to white judges' and jury members' ideas of racial superiority and paternalism, as well as the legal claims needed to prove fraud, their cases often proved successful. Chapter 7 explores their cases involving personal injury, noting that, although the racial discrimination and segregation of the Jim Crow South often influenced their cases, these black litigants largely sought compensation only for their own injuries, rather than challenging discriminatory practices themselves. During their trials, they shaped their testimony to meet the legal basis of personal injury, emphasizing their own caution at the time of the accident, their chronic pain and weakness from the injury, and the loss of income they suffered. As in fraud cases, their claims of weakness and vulnerability reinforced white judges' and jury members' ideas about racial inequality.

Finally, Chapter 8 traces African Americans' continuing civil litigation in southern courts from 1921 to 1950. During these decades, the vast majority of cases still involved seemingly prosaic claims of personal injury, property, and insurance. But beginning in the 1920s, African Americans began to litigate a wider range of civil cases against whites in southern state supreme courts. They were no longer forced to rely so heavily on stereotypes and claims of ignorance and vulnerability to win cases. Moreover, during this period, black litigants' seemingly ordinary appellate civil cases increasingly protested intimidation and violence against African Americans or made claims for larger groups beyond just the individuals litigating the suit. A few cases even directly challenged discriminatory racial regimes, employing the techniques they had used to win other kinds of civil cases over the past decades. Although some of these cases were orchestrated by racial justice organizations like the NAACP, many others were brought by individuals. The chapter concludes by linking these cases with the NAACP's legal victories. Just like the civil litigation during the century preceding it, the civil rights movement's legal action affirmed some African Americans' hope in the courts as a path to justice while remaining limited in many ways.

Prologue

Many freedpeople's road to using the courts began decades earlier, under slavery. In the antebellum South, every level of the southern judicial system was deeply complicit in upholding and normalizing the system of slavery and racial difference. Local court officials, such as sheriffs, played a key role in the domestic slave trade by auctioning off slaves in probate and debt proceedings. In the four decades before the Civil War, for instance, roughly half of the sales of slaves in South Carolina were conducted by court officials and agents of law.[1] Judges and lawyers in local courts were just as complicit in legitimizing the bondage of human beings. As the southern economy depended upon slavery, civil proceedings involving human bondage formed a large proportion of southern courts' caseloads. A study of a local Mississippi court found that about half of the trials "involved the commercial law of slavery."[2] These court-sanctioned transactions and suits decided the fate of thousands of slaves across the antebellum South every year.

Despite the very real consequences of legal action for the lives of enslaved men and women, the vast majority of slavery-related civil cases involved only white litigants.[3] Enslaved men and women themselves had limited opportunities to formally access the courts. White southerners recognized that the strict, procedure-bound nature of the courts could not effectively regulate slaves' behavior. If masters had to go to court over minor crimes committed by slaves, they would lose power over their human chattel—as well as valuable time—as the case wound through the court system. Likewise, if slaves were allowed widespread access to courts throughout the South to sue for their freedom, the authority of their masters would lessen. The courts' dependence on precedent and formal procedures could also lead to decisions unfavorable to white masters. As a result, slaveholders handled most petty crime privately, on their plantations, and in much of the South, it remained difficult for slaves to petition for their freedom.[4]

At times, though, enslaved people's alleged crimes affected those beyond the slaves' own plantation, making it necessary for crimes to be arbitrated by people other than the slave's master. For this purpose, in some areas of the antebellum

South, white southerners set up special courts solely to hear crimes involving enslaved and free black people. In such courts, legal procedure was very different than due process for whites accused of crimes. Often, these tribunals were decided by slaveholders and justices of the peace who had little or no formal legal training. Slaves' guilt was often presumed, and, when appeals were possible, slaveholders, rather than slaves, made the appeal.[5] Increasingly, however, as their legal systems became more professionalized, southern states allowed slaves accused of capital crimes some access to the system of courts used by whites. Giving such slaves a full trial protected white southerners' property rights, for if convicted, the slave would die. Although some courts reimbursed whites for a portion of the value of slaves convicted of death, they were often not given the full value of the slave. White southerners also argued that including African Americans within the system of law would portray slavery as a just institution to its detractors and reduce the threat of northern intervention. In 1848, one South Carolina judge explained: "With well regulated and mercifully applied slave laws, we have nothing to fear for negro slavery .... Let me, however, assure my countrymen, and fellow slave-holders, that unjust laws, or unmerciful management of slaves, fall upon us, and our institutions, with more withering effect than anything else."[6]

In the antebellum South, then, when slaves committed more serious and violent crimes, their cases could sometimes be heard or appealed to circuit and superior courts, which decided cases involving white as well as black southerners. Such courts provided slaves with legal protections far greater than they received on plantations or in magistrates' courts, giving slaves' cases more consideration and employing judges familiar with the body of the law.[7] The protections offered to slaves in these courts generally increased over time, as the court system became more professionalized and developed. Thus as the regard for trials by jury grew among white Americans at the end of the eighteenth century, jury trials began to be extended to slaves.[8] Increasingly, slaves gained the right to appeal to many—although not all—of the state supreme courts in the South.[9] By the early nineteenth century, every southern state also made sure that slaves were provided lawyers if their master did not hire one on their behalf—even though white men often did not receive a similar guarantee.[10] African Americans' ability to testify in southern courtrooms, however, was purposefully very limited. Throughout the South, slaves could not testify in cases in which a white person served as a litigant.[11] Allowing slave testimony in cases involving white litigants would have given slaves far too much power over white southerners. By hearing only white testimony in such cases, the courts gave whites freedom to commit crimes against slaves with little fear of repercussion.[12]

In the antebellum South, criminal cases at least acknowledged enslaved people's humanity—if only to show they had committed a criminal act. Civil cases, on the other hand, ordinarily treated slaves only as property to be bought, sold, inherited, mortgaged, stolen, or refunded. In case after case, they are listed on inventories merely as another item of property alongside cattle, farming implements, and household goods.[13] If an administrator chose not to carry out a will affecting them, they often had little possibility of fighting his action. In one Tennessee case, a master directed his executor to free his slaves and send them to Liberia, if they desired. When questioned, the slaves "all expressed and declared the most unequivocal willingness and desire to be emancipated and sent to Liberia," the court clerk later recalled. But the administrator of the will realized that the enslaved men and women had limited legal power to enforce the will, and decided not to carry it out. It was not until the former slaves received their freedom from the Civil War that they were able to bring a legal challenge to the administrator's action.[14]

But even as the vast majority of slaves played no role in civil suits, the legal system's respect for property occasionally allowed a small number of slaves limited rights and protections in civil actions.[15] By appealing to southern courts' respect for the rights of white testators, slaves whose masters had left wills emancipating them sometimes succeeded in litigating suits for their freedom.[16] Slaves could also occasionally capitalize on the courts' dependence upon rules and procedures. In border states, in particular, some slaves sued their owners for their freedom by claiming to have been emancipated through travel to or residence in a free state.[17] Other enslaved men and women took advantage of white southerners' ideas about race to bring suits for their freedom. Slaves with light hair and fair skin who could pass undetected as whites threatened the very foundation of slavery. Therefore, when slaves like blonde-haired, blue-eyed Alexina Morrison brought suits for their freedom, claiming to be white, juries of local whites sometimes decided that they were indeed white, despite evidence in their heritage to the contrary.[18]

Free people of color also litigated certain kinds of civil cases in local and state courts in the antebellum South.[19] But because free men and women of color were deeply problematic for most white southerners, southern states generally sought to limit their population numbers. As a result, in 1860, free people of color composed only about 12.8 percent of black people in the Upper South and 1.5 percent of black people in the Lower South. To further minimize the threat free black people posed, antebellum laws sought to control their movement, activities, marriages, and occupations.[20] At a time when they had few other options to confront whites, free people of color in the South used the courts to assert their rights and challenge limitations placed on them, such as requirements to register and pay special taxes. To aid their litigation, they at times hired white lawyers, drew on relationships with powerful whites, and shaped the ways in which their reputations were presented to the court.[21]

Despite the limited role of some free and enslaved black southerners in legal actions, most black men and women never entered a courtroom in the antebellum South. But in the half-century before the Civil War, white Americans experienced the law as an integral part of their daily lives. Ordinary men and women played important roles in reporting and investigating crime scenes. When people had disputes, they frequently litigated court cases against each other. Others gave information to local magistrates about civil disputes or testified about their neighbors or family in court. Even when they were not personally taking part in a case, men and women paid close attention to the legal proceedings around them. Throughout the antebellum United States, members of the community witnessed the proceedings of justices of the peace as they occurred in local shops, fields, and homes, and attended the rotating circuit courts when they were in session. Those unable to attend discussed the latest court news with their friends and neighbors. After observing American society for 9 months in 1831 and 1832, the French observer Alexis de Tocqueville wrote, "In the United States, everyone is personally interested in the law."[22]

Undoubtedly, enslaved and free black men and women did not experience the law in the same way as whites in this law-obsessed society. As probably only about 5 to 10 percent of slaves knew how to read, bondpeople often did not know the exact laws governing their experience as human chattel.[23] Nonetheless, enslaved men and women were frequently all too aware of their legal status as property. Many slaves undoubtedly gained this knowledge through violent and abusive interactions with their owners.[24] Slaves often understood, too, the authority the law gave to their masters to sell them at any time.[25] In addition, some slaves knew that they could not testify against whites—and the consequences this testimony ban had for them. After her uncle was imprisoned in the South where she remained enslaved, Harriet Jacobs recalled feeling "anxious." "I was well aware," she explained, "that in court his word would not be taken against any white man's."[26]

At times, slaves and free people of color had more specialized legal knowledge. Slaves sometimes had knowledge of instructions in their master's wills about who would receive them on their master's death.[27] In addition, slaves occasionally learned about contracts and transactions as they participated in the market economy, with and without their masters' approval.[28] Certain slaves also seem to have been aware of some criminal procedure. Like other antebellum Americans, they occasionally played a role in investigating crimes and reporting them to local authorities.[29] A few slaves even gained knowledge about civil procedures. One enslaved woman, Lucile Tucker, learned about the legal process as she negotiated her own emancipation. Tucker had a letter written to her master R. C. Ballard, a former slave trader and wealthy plantation owner, in 1847. "I wish you could have emancipated me when you was last in New Orleans" the letter said, "and if you could do it without putting me to the expense of return-ing to New Orleans I should much prefer it for life you know is very uncertain and you might die before I can see you. But if you can send me a power of attor-ney directed to RJ Hanson I will make him do it as soon as he gets back from Mexico and save you any further trouble about it and myself the expensive trip to New Orleans. Write to me at your earliest convenience and enclose the power of attorney in your letter."[30] As she worked to gain her freedom, Lucile Tucker became familiar with the legal process necessary to obtain emancipation.

Most of all, living in a law-infatuated society in which their own lives were ruled and shaped by the law, many slaves and free people of color undoubtedly knew that the law had power.[31] When possible, they sought to access that power. Upon escaping to the North, a number of runaway slaves studied the southern states' laws as they sought to bring down the institution of slavery. As a result, the law pervades fugitive slaves' published narratives and public speeches.[32] To gain sympathy for the abolitionist cause, fugitive slaves noted the law's prohi-bitions against slaves meeting for religious instruction and learning to read the Bible.[33] They described, too, the violent and cruel punishments that the law proscribed for slaves.[34] Some pointed out, as well, how the law making black people into property allowed slaves to be sold at their master's will, and families cruelly separated.[35] Frederick Douglass explained: "I think no better exposure of slavery can be made than is made by the laws of the states in which slavery exists. I prefer reading the laws to making any statement in confirmation of what I have said myself; for the slave holders cannot object to this testimony, since it is the calm, the cool, the deliberate enactment of their wisest heads, of their most clear-sighted, their own constituted representatives."[36]

Clearly, then, free and enslaved people of color had many limitations in their legal action before the Civil War. In a society focused on the law and legal action, however, they often already recognized the power of the law. Some also realized ways they could use the law to their advantage, beginning important patterns that would persist in their litigation for almost a century. Their cases capitalizing on white southerners' property rights would continue after the war, as would their ability to take advantage of the southern legal system's dedication to prec-edent and procedures. Just as slaves like the blonde-haired Alexina Morrison had done in freedom suits, black southerners would use their savvy understanding of white racial attitudes to gain the upper hand in some postwar courtrooms. Faced with limited forums for protest as free blacks had been before the war, African Americans would turn to the courts to challenge unjust treatment. There they would continue to draw on their relationships with powerful local whites and work to shape how they were perceived in the courtroom. The legal system's complicity in upholding white supremacy, however, would also continue after the war.

PART I

CIVIL CASES BETWEEN BLACK AND WHITE SOUTHERNERS, 1861–1899

1

A Revolution in the Courts

Two months before the end of the Civil War, in March 1865, General Sherman's Union forces entered Cumberland County, North Carolina, where the enslaved Henry Buie lived. The Confederacy had a large arsenal in the county seat of Fayetteville, and Sherman planned to destroy it to cut off an important source of arms to the Confederacy. As Union troops advanced on the plantation where Henry Buie lived, his owner John Buie hurriedly departed, rather unchivalrously leaving his wife behind. As the master left, he told his slaves that "they could go to the Yankees or stay at home, as they pleased." Henry Buie chose to stay.[1]

Union troops soon set up camp in the town of Fayetteville. They searched for food from house to house, and when they encountered enslaved men and women, a former slave later recalled, they "told us we were all free." Smoke rose from the town day and night as the Union soldiers blew up the arsenal and set fire to foundries, cotton factories, and newspaper offices. After a few days, with their objective achieved, the Union forces moved on.[2]

Henry Buie soon discovered a bay-colored mule that the northern army had abandoned. Claiming the animal for himself, he named it Fau and put it in his absent former master's "horse lot." When his former mistress "expressed a wish for the mule," he refused to give it to her, telling her that he wanted the mule to farm for himself.[3]

After the end of the war, John Buie returned. Henry Buie remained on his former master's plantation and by the end of 1865, John Buie was paying him as a hired laborer. At first, whites in the area sought to re-create many of the strictures of slavery in black people's lives. One local black barber told a reporter in October 1865 that when Sherman's soldiers first left Fayetteville, "and the town was put in the hands of its citizens, they showed a disposition to revive the slave code, and to enforce certain city ordinances that were full of the old spirit." John Buie seems to have been no different. Despite Henry Buie's continued insistence that the mule was his, the white landowner argued that the mule belonged to him. When Buie wanted to move Fau off his former master's plantation at the end of 1865, the white man refused to let him to do so.[4]

In 1867, as Congressional Reconstruction began, a federal military garrison was stationed in town. In a radical turn of events, the North Carolina governor appointed three black men to the Fayetteville town board. And in the summer of 1867, 1,439 African Americans registered as new voters in Cumberland County.[5] Sometime between the end of 1865 and the beginning of 1868, as power in the county was rapidly shifting, John Buie took possession of the mule.

Henry Buie's attempts to gain the animal's return would transform his relationship with his former master. By the spring of 1868, the freedman no longer worked for his former master and had turned to the local branch of the Freedmen's Bureau to regain his mule. The Bureau, an agency set up by the federal government to help institute free labor in the South, responded by mobilizing the northern army to return the mule to the former slave.[6]

The freedman had only had the mule back for a month when John Buie filed a civil suit before the county court to regain the mule. In contrast to the Freedmen's Bureau, southern courts seemed much more likely to side with white southerners. For generations, they had upheld the institution of slavery and worked to sustain the power of white elites. Even though some of the judges in the postwar South belonged to the Republican Party, most judges and jurors were still white southerners. Somehow, the former slave managed to hire a local white attorney, 29-year-old James C. MacRae, to fight in court for the return of the mule. In a bold move, MacRae also requested "one hundred dollars damages for taking and withholding" the mule from his client.[7]

A long, hard-fought battle over black southerners' legal rights took place during and in the wake of the Civil War. Individual African Americans, like Henry Buie, who fought for their rights in the face of incursions by their former masters and other whites, were at the front lines of this battle. By appealing to federal agencies like the Freedmen's Bureau, hiring lawyers, and testifying in courtrooms throughout the South, they boldly claimed their new rights as citizens and, at times, shifted their relationships with former masters and employers. The enormous turmoil locally and nationally played a part in opening the courts to black southerners as well. During the Civil War, black soldiers in the Union Army gained experience with the law as they protested unjust treatment, carried out military regulations, and testified in military courts. The Freedmen's Bureau and the northern military occupying the South also worked to open southern courts to African Americans during the early years of Reconstruction. Additionally, Congressional Republicans' takeover of Reconstruction helped give some black southerners federal support to exercise the rights they claimed.

Despite these changes, African Americans continued to face immense limitations in southern courts after the Civil War. But the fact that during Reconstruction the 4.1 million black people in the South gained the right to testify in civil suits, litigate a variety of cases against whites, and serve on juries remained an extraordinary development.[8] Here is the story of how black southerners gained legal rights during Reconstruction and held onto them for decades after Reconstruction ended.

The contest over black southerners' legal rights that began in the antebellum South gained momentum during the Civil War.[9] In the months after Abraham Lincoln's election in November 1860, seven southern states seceded from the United States. By the spring of 1861, four more states—including Henry Buie's native North Carolina—had seceded and a war raged between the newly formed Confederacy and the states remaining in the Union. White men joined the Confederate Army in massive numbers, leaving slaves to work with far less supervision than before.[10]

Throughout the South, many courts conducted only infrequent business during the war, while some closed completely. In other places where the Union Army had seized control—like New Orleans—the US Army opened its own courts or reopened southern courts with newly installed Republican justices.[11] But in Confederate-controlled areas of the South, many of the cases over slavery that did reach state supreme courts remained much the same as before the war. The vast majority of civil cases involving slavery still involved only white litigants. As the future of their slave society was fought over on the battlefield, white southerners took each other to court over how slaves should be passed on after a slaveholder's death, contested individual slaves' ownership, and initiated warranty suits claiming that slaves they had bought were not in the condition promised.[12]

Other cases involving slavery revealed white southerners' new reality. Women widowed during the war litigated suits without husbands at their side. Particularly in the final years of the war, as the last remaining white men were called up for service, men brought cases seeking exemptions from military service because they were needed as owners or overseers of large plantations. If they left, they claimed, white women and children would be left with no protection or ability to control the slaves. Although the court sometimes granted exemptions, in many cases those who claimed to be the last white man on a plantation were not exempted.[13] White southerners also protested having their slaves taken by the Confederate Army for manual labor. One such Georgia slaveholder filed a suit against an army commandant after one of his slaves was claimed for service in a local army hospital.[14]

On the surface, criminal cases against slaves and free people of color also remained much the same during the war. But when put into the context of the war, cases in which a black person killed or attempted to kill a white person or stole from the plantation house gained new meaning.[15] Unsurprisingly, it seems to have become even more difficult for free black people and slaves to appear as litigants in wartime civil suits. In the Supreme Court of Georgia, no civil suits were found during the Civil War in which free people of color or slaves served as litigants.[16]

In January 1863, President Abraham Lincoln issued the Emancipation Proclamation, declaring slaves within the Confederate-controlled areas of the South to be free. Despite white southerners' attempts to prevent their slaves from hearing of Lincoln's bold measure, the news spread quickly among slaves. Some slaves sought to leverage the declaration to make new demands of their masters.[17] Other slaves conducted campaigns of everyday resistance, working more slowly than usual or refusing to obey orders. Still others ran away from their masters and crossed over to enemy lines. In time, about 98,500 former slaves from the Confederate states (about 13 percent of adult male slaves) joined the US Army.[18]

Within the military, newly free black men learned valuable lessons about rights and law. Army officers offered black soldiers instruction on American government and the system of army regulations that governed their daily lives. Black soldiers also received daily practice in carrying out military law and regulations. One commander of a black regiment testified that his soldiers "have a sense of law, and I think that the credit of it is partly due to the admirable training which military life gives of recognizing and administering law."[19]

In military courts, black soldiers gained experience testifying and making appeals. If accused of disobeying military regulations, they could be court-martialed. Unlike during slavery, though, they could testify in their own defense. Upon being charged with a disturbance after a religious meeting, one black Maryland soldier testified at the court-martial that he "was at that time carried away by the Power of the Almighty."[20] Other black soldiers invoked the rights laid out in army regulations in their appeals. William Mayo, a Louisiana sergeant who was sentenced to hard labor for disobeying orders and mutinous conduct, wrote to Abraham Lincoln that the court-martial had mistakenly limited his witnesses to only two even though the copy of the army regulations "that I bought and paid for with my own money" said that he could have more. Mayo received no aid from the president, but such experiences in the army gave black soldiers valuable training in bringing complaints and testifying against whites.[21]

In at least one Union-controlled area of the South, ordinary black southerners could participate in the military courts that the Union Army had put in place of civil courts. After the Union forces took control of New Orleans in the spring of 1862, a provost court was established by Union Major General Benjamin Butler to hear nonfelony criminal cases involving the local population, as well as a limited number of civil cases. In contrast to the previous practice in Louisiana courts, this court allowed African Americans to testify against whites. According to James Parton's 1864 account of the occupation, this development began shortly after the provost court was established. Parton explained: "A negro was called to the witness-stand. 'I object,' said the counsel for the prisoner; 'by the laws of Louisiana a negro can not testify against a white man.' 'Has Louisiana gone out of the Union?' asked Major Bell . . . . 'Yes,' said the lawyer. 'Well, then,' said the judge, 'she took her laws with her. LET THE MAN BE SWORN!' "[22]

Even as Union Armies brought greater justice to the occupied South, northerners remained divided about the legal rights that should be given to African Americans within their own states. Slavery was still part of the North's recent past. By 1804, all northern states had agreed to eventually end the institution of slavery within their borders.[23] But as most northern states had chosen to end slavery slowly to protect slaveholders' interests, in the first decades of the nineteenth century slavery remained a significant presence in the North.[24] Even after emancipation had largely taken effect around the North, black northerners at times received harsher sentences than whites for the same crime and were imprisoned in northern jails in disproportionate numbers. The legal rights African Americans could exercise varied widely across the North—not only across states, but also across localities and throughout different periods of time. Gradually, though, some progress was made in the North. By 1860, African Americans could testify in court against whites in every state in the North and Northwest except Indiana, Illinois, California, and Oregon. In some northern states, black northerners could serve on juries, but in other states they could not.[25]

With a population deeply divided over African Americans' legal rights, it comes as no surprise that the fight over legal rights also took place within the federal government during the Civil War. During the second year of the war, US Senator Charles Sumner, an ardent abolitionist, proposed legislation that prohibited discrimination against African American witnesses in federal courts. According to legal scholar Randall Kennedy's account, Sumner argued "that this reform would allow loyal blacks to testify against disloyal whites for purposes of identifying those who had participated in rebellion against the Union." Sumner's proposal failed to pass in 1862. Two years later, though, in 1864, the US Congress passed a law that allowed African Americans to testify to the same degree as whites in federal courts.[26]

The Union Army declared victory in April 1865.[27] That spring, the millions of African Americans who remained enslaved at last gained their freedom. Then, in December 1865, the 13th Amendment to the US Constitution was ratified, formally ending the practice of slavery within the United States and prohibiting involuntary servitude unless a crime had been committed.[28] In many ways, though, the conflict over power had only just begun. After the firing ended, the

US government turned its attention to rebuilding the shattered South and creating a system of free labor in the wake of slavery. White southerners, though, wanted to choose the shape of their own labor arrangements and government—preferably by keeping them as similar as possible to what had existed in the antebellum South.

As they watched the institution of slavery crumble around them, white southerners sought to limit African Americans' freedom as much as possible. Some claimed it was for black southerners' own good, arguing that African Americans could not handle freedom and would become extinct as a race if they were not controlled by whites. Many white people also openly worried that free black men and women would refuse to work unless coerced. The limitations on black people's freedom also grew out of fear. With the antebellum system of controlling African Americans upended, white southerners dreaded crime and violence by former slaves. Sensationalist news reporting played a part in convincing many white southerners that a black crime wave had followed the wake of war.[29]

Even as they largely agreed on the need to control black men and women, white southern elites disagreed on the means with which to do it. Some advocated turning to the law. In Mississippi, the chairman of the Joint Select Committee on Freedmen, Senator J. J. Hooker, argued that law should be used to restore order. "In view of the crimes, lawlessness, and demoralization, now prevalent in most localities throughout this State," Hooker declared, "order and good morals can alone be restored . . . by a speedy and rigid enforcement of the criminal laws."[30] Other white elites advocated violence as a more effective tool to control free African Americans. Many of these white leaders—including a number of southern Democrats—thought it was "too radical" to allow black southerners to be disciplined primarily through the courts. They worried that disciplining former slaves in the courts would make the law accessible to African Americans in dangerous ways.[31]

In the end, both violence and the law would be used to try to control free black southerners. When African Americans asserted their freedom and sought fair wages and labor contracts, white southerners responded with whippings and even murder. Refusals to treat whites with the same deference that had been expected on antebellum plantations led to widespread acts of terror.[32] Field reports from the Freedmen's Bureau between 1865 and 1869 relayed accounts of the rising violence. The reasons given for violent acts against freedpeople varied from "Not wanting to cut timber in the rain as per contract" and disputes over shares of the harvest to "Killed because he did not take off his hat to Murphy" and "Not giving way to a buggy."[33] White-led riots spread around the South, causing the deaths of forty-six African Americans in Memphis, Tennessee, in May of 1866 and thirty-four African Americans and three white Republicans 12 weeks later in New Orleans. The leading scholar of Reconstruction, Eric Foner, concludes that during the early years of this era, "in its pervasive impact . . . the wave of counterrevolutionary terror that swept over large parts of the South lacks a counterpart either in the American experience or in that of the other Western Hemisphere societies that abolished slavery in the nineteenth century."[34]

State legislatures throughout the South also passed a series of "black codes"— a set of laws applying only to African Americans. Many northerners viewed these codes as an attempt to replicate as much as possible the laws of slavery. But white southerners frequently viewed them as using the law—rather than merely violence—to control black men and women. In many southern states, the codes required that African Americans have written evidence of employment at all times and allowed any white person to arrest them if they left prior to the end of their employment contracts. As punishment for not having employment, black southerners were to be hired out on chain gangs, put in stocks, and left in solitary confinement with only bread and water. To deter black crime, the 1865 Mississippi legislature declared that thieves could be hanged from their thumbs and black people unable to pay fines would have their labor hired out to the highest bidder. Black southerners also still could not serve on juries.[35]

At the same time, black codes granted former slaves some legal rights that they had not had as slaves. In much of the South, African Americans had the right to litigate civil cases themselves. The December 1865 Alabama Code declared that all free people "shall have the right to sue and be sued . . . in all the different and various courts of this State, to the same extent that white persons now have by law." In a sharp departure from the laws of slavery, many codes proclaimed that black people could be "competent witnesses" against white people in civil and criminal cases in which they played a part. Throughout the South, former slaves gained the right to legally marry other people of color.[36]

To enforce black codes, some southern legislatures created new courts to hear cases involving black defendants. In Mississippi, these courts also heard cases involving whites, but they targeted freedpeople and resembled the magistrates' courts under slavery. They met monthly, often did not require a grand jury to take defendants to trial, and focused on controlling crime rather than allowing defendants all of the rights of due process.[37] As these courts began handing out sentences, southern prisons that had been largely white before emancipation filled with black prisoners. One freedman explained the shift: "In slavery times, jails was all built for the white folks. There warn't never nobody of my color put in none of them. No time . . . to stay in jail; they had to work; when they done wrong they was whipped and let go." Now, during Reconstruction, a Charleston attorney explained, "Most of the equity and civil business . . . in our courts is supplied by the whites. But the bulk of the criminal business is supplied by the blacks. A white is rarely seen in a Southern court for any crime other than murder or assault and battery. Whenever larceny, burglary, arson, and similar crimes

are committed in the South, no one is suspected of the crime save negroes. Out
of three hundred and fifty-five prisoners now in our state penitentiary, three hundred and twenty-five are colored!"[38]

Even as southern prisons overflowed with freedpeople, the law could be an
unwieldy vehicle to control free African Americans.[39] Former slaves imprisoned
for crimes could file habeas corpus petitions challenging their incarceration.
Judges concerned about their professional reputations did not always execute
discriminatory laws, instead allowing black defendants elements of due process
that no slave defendants had received. Juries frequently followed the same process with black defendants as they did with white defendants. Moreover, whites
found that manipulating legal processes had consequences for white citizens,
which could threaten their very system of law.[40] A Mississippi court designed to
circumvent the system of grand juries to easily prosecute black crime and control black labor was largely used by white people charging other whites of crimes.
Even worse, the juries in this Mississippi court convicted 64 percent of white
defendants and only 49 percent of black defendants.[41] Clearly, the courts were
not the solution to the problem of emancipation that white southerners sought.

Even as white southerners sought to limit the rights of African Americans, black
southerners turned to the power of government to shore up many of the rights
they believed should come with freedom. Historian Hasan Jeffries explains
that they sought rights set out in the US Constitution and state constitutions,
including the rights of "freedom of speech, religion, and assembly, and the right
to due process, [to] keep and bear arms, and [to] vote," as well as "the right to
own property, choose employment, enjoy economic security, marry and start
a family, move without restriction, and receive an education."[42] In the months
before and after the end of the Civil War, African Americans held mass meetings
around the South to draft petitions and make appeals, often insisting on equal
treatment before the law to prevent the unfair use of power against them. Many
black southerners recognized that suffrage was necessary to gain just treatment
from the government. "It behooves us, and is demanded of us . . . to speak and
act as freemen," a group of black Virginians proclaimed, "and as such to claim
and insist upon equality before the law, and equal rights of suffrage at the 'ballot
box.'"[43]

In Nashville, a petition written by a group of African Americans to the Union
Convention in January 1865 demanded more specific legal rights: "At present
we can have only partial protection from the courts. The testimony of twenty
of the most intelligent, honorable, colored loyalists cannot convict a white trai-
tor of a treasonable action. A white rebel might sell powder and lead to a rebel
soldier in the presence of twenty colored soldiers, and yet their evidence would
be worthless so far as the courts are concerned, and the rebel would escape.

A colored man may have served for years faithfully in the army, and yet his testimony in court would be rejected, while that of a white man who had served in the rebel army would be received. If this order of things continue, our people are destined to a malignant persecution at the hands of rebels and their former rebellious masters." The petition concluded with sixty-two signatures.[44] Even before the end of the war, black southerners already saw legal rights as a crucial part of achieving freedom.

In the months after the war ended, black-operated newspapers lobbied whites to allow African Americans full rights to testify. With a savvy understanding of whites' racial attitudes, *The Colored Tennessean* pointed out in October 1865 that white jury members could decide how they used black people's testimony: "In Ohio negro testimony is taken upon the same conditions as that of the whites, and the jury is left to determine what degree of credibility is to be given it." The same newspaper also invoked a permanent northern occupation of the South to apply pressure to whites to admit such testimony. If the people of Mississippi did not allow African Americans to testify in all legal matters, the article intoned, "the Freedmen's Bureau, which the News stigmatizes as 'an inquisition' and 'an oppression,' will assume a more permanent character than will be agreeable to the proslavery editor of the News."[45]

Indeed, as the Freedmen's Bureau was the most visible federal organization besides the army on the ground in the South in the wake of the war, black men and women often turned to the Bureau to achieve the rights they desired. The US government created the Freedmen's Bureau in 1865 to institute a system of free labor in the South.[46] Manned largely by Union Army officers and operating in southern states primarily between 1865 and 1869, the Bureau set up hospitals and distributed food, mediated disputes over labor contracts and apprenticeships, and, at times, intervened in the courts.[47] Bureau agents worked to educate black southerners about their new rights, reading to them the Declaration of Independence and giving speeches about the tradition of democracy in the United States. "The freedmen," said a December 1865 Bureau circular, "are not to be restrained in the exercise of their liberty by any rules or customs of the country that do not apply equally to white men."[48]

Newly free men and women often turned to the Freedmen's Bureau during disputes with their former masters and other white southerners, at times receiving death threats for doing so.[49] Frequently, they sought the Bureau's help in inducing white people to no longer treat them as slaves and to pay them a fair share of the crop. Others protested violence against them. "My office is so crowded . . . with freedmen coming to complain of not being settled with [by their employers]," one agent wrote in early 1867, "that it takes four of us from 9 o'clock in the morning to 5 o'clock in the evening doing scarcely anything but trying to adjust cases of cheating and stealing."[50] Bureau agents noted an intense interest in their rights in the black people who came to their offices. "The black man feels that he has certain rights and is anxious to know what they are and how to procure, protect, and maintain the same," a Virginia Bureau official wrote in 1867, "there is an inflexible will manifested that no white man shall trample with impunity on their own."[51]

When faced with disputes between white and black southerners such as this, the Freedmen's Bureau initially held temporary courts to decide the matter in areas where they believed that the local courts would not adequately guard the interests of African Americans.[52] As a federal institution frequently operated by Union Army officers, the Bureau often—although not always—took newly freed black southerners' sides in labor and property disputes. When Henry Buie approached them in early 1868, Bureau official Richard Dillon did not immediately take action. Instead, in May, Dillon wrote to the Bureau's North Carolina headquarters, informing his superiors that Henry Buie had made a complaint to the Bureau that "his former master John Bowie holds a mule of his that he picked up in the war of Genl Shermans Army and now refuses to give it up." In reply, Dillon received a command to help the freedman regain the animal. Following orders, Dillon wrote a letter to John Buie demanding that he turn over the mule. When the former slaveholder failed to respond, the northern military occupying the area ordered the county sheriff to return the mule to Henry Buie. In July 1868, the former slave regained possession of the animal.[53]

In other disputes, the Freedmen's Bureau advised African Americans to take their claims to local courts.[54] Viewing itself as temporary, the Bureau increasingly focused on helping black southerners gain justice within the existing legal system. In certain southern states, the Freedmen's Bureau successfully pushed courts to allow black testimony in all cases involving whites, agreeing to close the Bureau and provost courts if they did so. In a series of letters in April 1866 between Assistant Commissioner for the Freedmen's Bureau in North Carolina E. Whittlesey and the superior court judge in Raleigh, North Carolina, the judge complained bitterly about the Bureau and army holding their own legal proceedings to decide some cases involving both white and black Carolinians. In reply, the Bureau official asked the judge if the courts in the state could "receive the testimony of colored witnesses against white men accused of . . . crimes." If "no distinction will . . . be made on account of race or color," he wrote, "the chief difficulty in the way of 'yielding the exclusive jurisdiction' is in my judgement removed."[55]

The threat of keeping Freedmen's Bureau courts open worked. Although the judge's answer revealed that African Americans still did not have full legal rights in April 1866, by July 1866, a state convention had changed the laws regarding testimony in North Carolina. The Freedmen's Bureau was notified that "there now exists, under the laws of this State, no discrimination in the administration of justice to the prejudice of free persons." In response, historian Roberta Alexander writes, the assistant commissioner for the Bureau in North Carolina "issued General Order No.3 [on July 13, 1866], proclaiming that all cases, except claims for wages where the contracts had been witnessed by the Freedmen's Bureau, were to be tried in civil courts." Similarly, the South Carolina legislature passed a bill in October 1866 granting African Americans legal equality and the ability to testify in all types of cases. As a result, the Bureau and provost courts also closed in South Carolina.[56]

After closing most of its own courts in the first years of Reconstruction, the Freedmen's Bureau continued to monitor local and state court decisions involving freedpeople and retained the right to intervene in state courts if necessary. In an effort to improve the justice received by black litigants in state courts, Bureau officials attended civil courts in their districts and advised black men and women on their criminal and civil cases.[57] Bureau agents also retained lawyers for freedpeople who did not have representation or served as attorneys for black litigants who could not obtain other counsel.[58] When state courts failed to mete out equal justice, Bureau officials sometimes intervened on behalf of black litigants. A letter sent to the Bureau from the Advocate General's office noted this policy: "If the [state] courts fail in the performance of their duties the military authorities may then properly interfere." Upon finding discrimination in state courts, Bureau agents handed over cases to military authorities, facilitated appeals to federal courts, or sought clemency from governors.[59]

As they aided black southerners in the courts, Bureau agents met opposition from whites on all sides. Some courts refused to give black people equal treatment. In 1868, one Bureau agent assisted "numerous" freedmen in pursuing court cases demanding equitable division of proceeds from the "joint crops" they had grown on white people's land. He found it "impossible to procure anything like justice to the freedman . . . their cases have generally been dismissed by the courts."[60] All too often, white southerners responded to the Freedmen's Bureau interventions in southern labor relations with threats and violence. When the Alabama Freedmen's Bureau ruled in favor of a former slave in a dispute between the black man and his former master, the former master put a gun to the freedman's head and threatened to kill him if he did not go against the ruling. Similarly, one Georgia Bureau agent reported in 1868, "Nearly all freedmen who report cases of assault to me evince an utter unwillingness to return to the place they have left and invariably because they have been threatened with death in case they 'report to the Bureau,' and for the same reason it is extremely difficult to obtain witnesses to attest the truth of the complaints of freedmen."[61] Bureau agents also sometimes met opposition from other Bureau officials and Union Army officers as they sought to aid former slaves in the courts.[62] Nevertheless, some Bureau officials reported seeing progress in the courts in 1866 and 1867.[63]

The occupying Union Army—whose personnel overlapped with the Freedmen's Bureau—played a critical role in African Americans' ability to participate in southern courts, too. In the first years of Reconstruction, provost courts manned by Union Army officers—like the New Orleans provost court that had operated during the war—dispensed justice for black and white southerners. The army's power was further bolstered in the spring of 1867 when the Reconstruction Act was enacted, dividing the South (except Tennessee) into five military districts and making an army commander the supreme authority in each district. Drawing on the power given to them from this act, during 1867, US Army generals overseeing districts containing Texas, North and South Carolina, Georgia, Alabama, and Florida ordered southern courts to allow African Americans on their juries. Major General John Pope, who commanded the Third Military District, which included Georgia, Alabama and Florida, ordered on August 19, 1867, that African Americans in his district should be allowed on juries "without discrimination."[64] Legal scholar Christopher Waldrep notes that another Union commander, who oversaw the district that included Mississippi, "moved aggressively to dismiss sheriffs, mayors, justices of the peace, and other civil officers, replacing them with his appointees. In Vicksburg, he made a Union army veteran sheriff and appointed the first black justice of the peace in the state's history."[65]

These legal interventions by the Bureau and US military were widespread during the first years of Reconstruction. A Mississippi appellate judge's 1873 opinion remarked that from 1865 to 1870 there were "tens of thousands" of instances of "military interference in civil causes."[66] By providing arenas for justice during the first years of Reconstruction and by working to increase black litigants' chances of gaining equal treatment in state courts, the Bureau and the US Army served as crucial stepping stones in African Americans' quest for justice in southern courts.[67]

As black and white southerners both sought to access the power of the courts in the postwar South, national developments began to swing the balance of power in black people's favor. Before the Civil War, the citizenship of free black people had been questioned. Slaves had been denied citizenship all together. In a radical reversal, 1 year after the Civil War the US Congress passed the Civil Rights Act of 1866, granting citizenship to all native-born Americans, including former slaves, with the exception of Native Americans under tribal authority. To make this change permanent, Congressional Republicans proposed a new amendment to the US Constitution. Many white southerners responded in shock and disbelief, refusing to recognize black people's citizenship or approve an amendment. President Andrew Johnson, a southerner himself, did little to lessen white southerners' resistance. In 1867, that all changed. Believing that

President Johnson was not going far enough in forcing change on the former Confederacy, Republicans in Congress took control of the Reconstruction process. Each former Confederate state not already restored to the Union was required to ratify the 14th Amendment, which made citizenship colorblind, before regaining representation in Congress. The 15th Amendment to the US Constitution, ratified in 1870, further solidified African American men's right to vote. By law, all native-born black men gained the right to go to polling places and cast their ballots.[68]

Congressional Reconstruction upended the political system in the South. Before the war, the Democratic and Whig Parties had vied to be the most radical in protecting southern rights.[69] Now, after its conclusion, black men embraced their newfound suffrage, turning out in much higher numbers than whites and voting almost exclusively for the Republican Party. Voting was not without risks. Black men met physical violence going to and from voting places. Black political leaders experienced threats, violence, and assassination as they worked to gain votes for the Republican Party and held office.[70] Still, it was not uncommon for 90 percent of adult black men in a community to cast their votes. In some states, such as Mississippi, they made up the majority of eligible voters in the state. A minority of white southerners joined with black voters to vote Republican governors, legislators, and—if popularly elected—judges into power throughout the South. Republicans soon governed every former Confederate state.[71]

The new Republican leadership was composed primarily of native white southerners. They were often not political novices; a number of them had held office before the war. Even though some had spoken out against secession, many had fought for the Confederacy. But with the war over, they wanted to work with the North to begin rebuilding the nation. Some Republican leaders in the South also came from the North, motivated by ideological reasons or political gain.[72] Furthermore, in a radical change, black men filled local, state, and federal political offices that had been held only a few years earlier by slave-owners.

These Republican leaders reshaped the law and courts throughout the South. In a revolutionary act, they repealed the remaining black codes. Under their direction, courts no longer automatically took the employers' side in labor disputes. They largely halted, too, the practice of forcing black southerners arrested for vagrancy into coercive labor contracts. Even more important, during their tenure most southern states that had not yet granted African Americans full legal rights passed laws giving black men and women the same rights to litigate cases and testify and granting black men the right to sit on juries.[73] Each of these legal rights had important implications for black plaintiffs and defendants entering a court of law. The presence of black faces in the jury box gave black men a voice in deciding the cases of other African Americans. Juries that included black men were also less likely to rely solely on white testimony accusing black people of crimes, providing African Americans an important new protection before the law.[74] African Americans' greater freedom to testify allowed black litigants to better defend themselves against civil and criminal actions and to marshal black neighbors, acquaintances, and family members to testify on their behalf.

Republican governors and Republican-dominated state legislatures placed northern and Republican-leaning justices on southern state courts alongside justices who had served throughout the Civil War.[75] In Mississippi, fifty-five of the eighty-six judges on the "three courts of record" during the Reconstruction era were native southerners who belonged to the Republican Party and sixteen more judges were Republicans from the North. Thirteen judges in Mississippi during this period opposed Reconstruction.[76] In North Carolina, where Henry Buie lived, the chief justice of the state supreme court stayed on after the war, but four new white justices sympathetic to the Republican Party were added to the state's highest court.[77] One of these new justices, Republican Thomas Settle, argued in 1867 for "a general breaking up of the old ideas." "If we are to have any prosperity," he explained, "we must make up our minds to look at several things in a very different light from that in which we have been in the habit of viewing them." The Republican Party would help the South do just that, he argued, by working "to elevate mankind of all races and colors, and to develop the country."[78]

Black southerners played an important role in shaping this postwar legal system. Black-operated newspapers continued to lobby for legal rights.[79] Newly enfranchised black men also exercised their political power to influence the judicial system. In addition to sweeping the Republican Party to power, in certain states, such as Virginia, black men served in constitutional conventions that drafted new articles for the judiciary and voted to ratify state constitutions. Black voters helped choose judges in states where judges were popularly elected, and black state legislators participated in choosing judges in other states.[80] A few black men even served as justices of the peace and judges. The Mississippi governor appointed one former slave, John Roy Lynch, as justice of the peace in April 1869. "In consequence of my youth and inexperience," he later wrote, "I had, at first, serious doubts of my own ability to discharge the duties of the office creditably and acceptably, but I accepted the position with a determination to fill it, if possible, with credit to myself and satisfaction to the public. With that end in view, I took advantage of every spare moment to read and study, not only the manual, but the codes and statutes defining the duties of justice of the peace." [81] One year later, in 1870, Jonathan Jasper Wright was elected justice of the Supreme Court of South Carolina, becoming the first black person to sit on any US state supreme court. Then, in 1872, the South Carolina legislature elected George Lee as a judge of the superior court, making him the first black superior court judge in the South.[82] Although black legal officials remained rare throughout the South, it was a revolutionary turn of events for former slaves and other African Americans to hold legal office at all.

Many whites throughout the country were shocked and horrified by the changes. In October 1867, one Tennessee newspaper called the exclusion of some white men from jury lists and the "forcing upon juries of ignorant negroes" a "measure of infamy" without "precedent . . . on the blackest pages of human history." The article continued: "The negroes are too ignorant to decide a case on its merits, and too degraded in the social scale to feel any of those restraining influences. A man might as well stake his suit on the tossing of a copper as on the verdict of a negro jury." Some Northern newspapers struck a similar tone. The *New York Republic* described African American lawyers and juries in South Carolina "composed entirely of blacks," concluding, "They are having queer times down in South Carolina . . . the way the laws are administrated from day to day, is so extraordinary that a white man in South Carolina Courts might wonder whether he had emigrated to Liberia, or was a citizen of a mongrel Republic."[83] Similarly, the Louisiana correspondent for the *New York Times* lamented the "antebellum days, when cotton was king, law was a luxury and lawyers such as Slidell, Benjamin, Soule . . . and others like them who held distinguished positions at the Bar, amassed princely fortunes." Now, the correspondent wrote, in Reconstruction-era Louisiana "their places are filled on the bench and at the bar by men formerly slaves and lawyers of mediocre talent, who encourage litigation that they may thrive upon the disputes among a naturally passionate people, unaccustomed to legal restraint."[84] Clearly, the inclusion of black southerners in the workings of southern courts was not a welcome change for many white Americans.

But even as these whites bemoaned African Americans' new access to the courts, other white people saw African Americans' increased legal rights as relatively benign. In the fall of 1867, a Kentucky newspaper commented, "There can be no danger in permitting negro testimony to go to juries for they will weigh it and decide upon its value. The character of the witness for truth can always be investigated and his testimony be accepted or not accepted. His statements are by no means necessarily received as true, and intelligent jurors will usually be able to judge of the weight which should be given to the testimony." Clearly, the author of this article saw white jury members as more than capable of using their own ideas about race to interpret black testimony.[85]

Some even saw benefits for whites in giving black southerners more legal rights. The same Kentucky newspaper contended that not giving African Americans the right to testify in cases between whites could have detrimental effects on white litigants. "Suppose, for illustration," the newspaper said, "that a white man in company with a negro encounter a white highwayman who robs, perhaps wounds the negro's companion. The testimony of the negro would be important, and if the wounded man died justice would be defeated if the negro was not allowed to testify." Similarly, the article continued, "A negro may make a contract with a white man in the presence of another negro who is the only witness. He then seeks to evade the contract, and the fact of the contract can only be established by the testimony of the negro witness. If he is not allowed to testify, a white man and not a negro is wronged." The writer concluded that giving black southerners full rights to testify in all kinds of cases would not just "benefit the negro" but "the white man has a large interest also."[86]

Still other whites viewed African Americans' access to the courts as instrumental to maintaining order in the South. In an 1866 letter to a local judge, one South Carolina magistrate explained: "It is well known to me that serious disturbances in the country have been prevented by my course in assuring the freedmen that the law was amply sufficient and that they should have the benefit of the usual remedies which it provides."[87] When the legal system did not function for African Americans, this element of social control was lost, leading to crime and social disturbances. A Georgia Freedmen's Bureau agent noted such consequences in an 1868 letter. As a result of white southerners' practice of employing freedpeople for 9 or 10 months and then driving them away without paying for their months of work, the agent wrote, a "spirit of lawlessness" was developing among freedpeople. The freedman "becomes discouraged, disheartened and to a certain extent desperate; he has no tribunal to which he may appeal for justice, and his only resort, to prevent actual starvation, is to steal and to kill the stock of the planter who defrauds him."[88] To these observers, the law prevented social unrest by holding out the promise of justice. If it failed to function, they believed, it left crime and chaos in its wake.

Black southerners had a very different reaction to the changes during Reconstruction. Ordinary black men and women joyfully noted their new legal rights and the political shift in their favor, and sought to exercise their new rights. Contemporary observers recorded that black southerners displayed an intense desire to bring disputes to court. Black Justice of the Peace John Hope Franklin noted in his autobiography that participating in the courts "was entirely new" to many African Americans in his community and they were eager to take advantage of this opportunity. Similarly, in 1874, a *New York Times* reporter investigating a surge in racial discrimination suits in Louisiana observed: "There is no class of people here that are fonder of the pleasures of court proceedings, and of becoming parties to controversies in them, than the newly-enfranchised citizens. For every trivial matter wherein they believe their rights assailed or threatened, a rush is made to some court or other for redress. They think it is a glorious privilege to make an appearance in a law-suit, and will spend the last cent they can get to obtain what they consider and believe to be 'justice.'"[89] Despite this reporter's disdain, his words capture the eagerness of newly freed Americans to seize their new legal rights.

Beginning in the months immediately following the war's end—even before formally gaining citizenship or sweeping the Republican Party into power throughout the South—black men and women began to litigate civil cases against the masters who had previously held almost absolute power over them and against white employers, lenders, and neighbors. Hundreds of these civil suits involving black litigants seem to have been heard only by local courts. A limited number of disputes also originated in federal courts.[90] But at least 132 civil cases litigated by African Americans made it to eight southern state supreme courts during Reconstruction.

About 18 percent of these appellate cases took place between two or more black litigants. In the other 82 percent of suits between 1865 and 1877, when a black southerner's case made it to a southern state appellate court, it involved a dispute with a white person.[91] These disputes were often very personal. During Reconstruction, two-thirds of these appellate civil cases between white and black southerners involved litigants who had been connected during slavery, either as master and slave or as the heirs of former masters and their former slaves.[92] Despite their lack of experience with the law, black southerners frequently brought cases against whites, in addition to having cases brought against them.[93] White litigants often sought to use the courts to regain their control over the labor, property, and persons of their former slaves, while African Americans attempted to use litigation to free themselves from this control and gain economic independence.

Certain kinds of civil cases litigated by black southerners against whites had more traction in appellate courts during Reconstruction. The vast majority of litigants initiated cases on their own, without backing from larger organizations. Almost all of the civil cases between black and white southerners involved economic claims that would primarily impact only their own families. In just under half of the cases between white and black litigants during Reconstruction (46 percent), African Americans sought to gain bequests left to them in white men's wills and thus achieve a measure of financial independence. Frequently, their lawyers' petitions appealed to the courts' continuing respect for property rights and the law's concern that the will of the testator be carried out.[94] Almost one-third of civil cases between white and black southerners during Reconstruction (29 percent) show African Americans seeking to exercise the same economic rights as their white counterparts and meeting resistance from white employers, merchants, and neighbors. In these suits, too, they appealed to general laws of property and contracts as they made their claims.[95] Finally, in about one-sixth of such suits (17 percent), former slaves contested the apprenticeship of their children.[96] Here, newly free men and women fought for control over their families, as white southerners attempted to recreate the conditions of slavery in black children's lives.

Clearly the civil cases black southerners litigated in these eight state supreme courts remained limited. But these suits could make actual differences in individual litigants' lives. Black men and women had emerged from slavery with few resources to establish farms and work for themselves.[97] What many former slaves wanted more than almost anything else was economic independence—not to have to continue working for the same white men and women for whom they had toiled for so many years. At times, these civil cases allowed them to gain land, money, or livestock. Such resources might help them to finally achieve their goal of working independently. On occasion, court battles between former slaves and former masters could also shift their relations with each other, in small or large ways.

In May of 1868, when the Freedmen's Bureau decided in his favor regarding the contested mule, Henry Buie still bore his former master's last name. If referred to by a surname at all, slaves were customarily called by the last name of their masters, indicating their status as someone's property. But as he became embroiled in a civil suit with his former master, Henry discarded his family name and adopted the last name of Parker. In November 1868, in the answer to the suit filed against the freedman for the mule, his lawyer James C. MacRae referred to his client as "defendant Henry Parker, then called Henry Buie." If his former master John Buie was going to turn to the legal realm to try to take his property, Henry was not going to conduct the battle using the white man's name.[98]

With his new identity, Henry Parker turned to the business of defending his right to the mule in the courts. He labored under many disadvantages within the southern legal system. He does not seem to have been able to read or write. What was likely his main property was the item under dispute, undoubtedly leaving him with few other resources to conduct a suit. Nevertheless, his actions suggest that he felt he had a chance to win the case. Perhaps he knew that the rising power of the Republican Party had led to the appointment or election of southern judges much more favorable to African Americans. He may have known other former slaves who had litigated suits in the county court since the war and gained favorable outcomes. Some way or another, he engaged a local lawyer, James C. MacRae, who in November 1868 petitioned the court for the return of the mule or the reimbursement of the animal's value and "one hundred dollars damages." Parker himself did not testify before the court. John Buie, though, gave his side of the dispute in a deposition.

To John Buie's likely surprise, the judge of the Cumberland County trial court decided in the former slave's favor. The ruling ordered the white man to return the mule to the freedman or pay him the mule's value of $150 and to pay $12 in damages "for taking and withholding the same." Although John Buie appealed to the Supreme Court of North Carolina, in January 1869 the state's highest court affirmed the lower-court's ruling for the former slave. Their decision cited an 1862 Act of the US Congress, which declared that slaves of Confederates who "deserted" their slaves "shall be forever free of their servitude." Because the Union Army had won, the justice writing the opinion reasoned, this Act of Congress stood as law. This meant that as Parker's master had left him, Parker had been free when he found the mule, so the mule was his. In effect, the southern state's highest court was using the US government's actions to combat the Confederacy to decide in favor of a former slave.[99] As a result, Henry Parker got his mule Fau back.[100] Such an animal could aid him in planting and harvesting far more crops than he could do on his own. To make extra money, he could hire out the mule for 50 cents a day. Perhaps just as important, seemingly as a result of their confrontation in the courts, Parker no longer bore his former master's name. Instead, the highest court in the state had reaffirmed Parker's legal rights and citizenship in the face of his former master's claims. Throughout the South, in other cases, other black litigants also claimed their new rights as citizens and shifted—in some small way—the terms of their relationship with their former masters and other whites.

Even as black southerners like Henry Parker succeeded at times in litigating cases over their own economic welfare, it was difficult for them to bring cases challenging racial discrimination to most southern state appeals courts. Only one case directly confronted racial injustice during Reconstruction in the eight state supreme courts examined.[101] The lack of cases challenging racial discrimination in state courts was not for want of trying to make such claims. When there seemed to be opportunities for success in such litigation during Reconstruction, African Americans repeatedly brought such cases in local and federal courts.

At times, when state laws supported their litigation, African Americans brought cases over racial justice to state courts during Reconstruction. Five southern states passed laws about discrimination in public places during Reconstruction: Louisiana, Florida, South Carolina, Arkansas, and Mississippi.[102] In 1869, for instance, Louisiana passed a law prohibiting discrimination in "places of public resort." Drawing on this law, from 1869 to 1875 a wave of litigation to combat racial discrimination in saloons, railroads, steamboats, theaters, opera houses, and soda shops took place in local and state courts.[103] This litigation—together with threatened suits, boycotts, and investigations by the legislature—led to some progress in African Americans' obtaining equal treatment in public places in Louisiana during Reconstruction. In writing about one suit in 1875, the *Louisianian* newspaper reported, "Suits of this kind prosecuted under our State laws have proved very beneficial in causing the abandonment of the absurd conduct practiced so largely by these and similar places."

Even this progress was limited, however, and in two other states with similar leg-islation, Arkansas and Mississippi, such litigation does not seem to have made it to the states' highest court during these years.[104]

Federal courts must have seemed a more promising forum, particularly in the wake of the 1875 Civil Rights Act. The federal legislation guaranteed "all per-sons within the jurisdiction of the United States the full and equal enjoyment of the accommodations, advantages, facilities, and privileges of inns, public conveyances on land or water, theaters, and other places of public amusement." According to the law, all cases over violations of this Act should be brought in federal courts. If a federal court found someone guilty of such discrimination, the offending party should pay "five hundred dollars to the person aggrieved thereby."[105] After this Civil Rights Act, African Americans around the country—including many in the South—eagerly turned to federal courts to enforce their new rights. In general, though, such suits met with little support from federal officials in Washington, DC, and the outcomes of the cases frequently failed to enforce true equality. In deciding such suits, lower federal courts often ruled for black litigants if no separate facilities had been provided, but were unwilling to mandate real integration. After Reconstruction ended in 1877, the numbers of such cases in federal courts also fell.[106]

The US Supreme Court was even more disappointing for the struggle for racial justice. Despite a number of cases appealed from lower federal courts asking the Supreme Court to rule on the legitimacy of the 1875 Civil Rights Act, the Court refused to do so until 1883. The Supreme Court's lack of support played a significant role in the weak enforcement of the legislation.[107] When the country's highest court did issue decisions during Reconstruction, it limited the rights that African Americans could exercise, making it more difficult for them to litigate suits against individuals who had discriminated against them and cur-tailing their right to the vote.[108]

African Americans' experiences with criminal cases during Reconstruction were worse still. At times, they received relatively fair trials in appellate criminal cases. In the state supreme courts of Alabama and Georgia, black defendants won approximately 55 percent of their criminal appeals during Reconstruction, gaining a favorable outcome only slightly less often than in civil appeals cases against whites, which they won 65 percent of the time during this period.[109] But at the local level, the scales of justice were heavily weighted against black defendants. Local law enforcement and lower courts had powerful financial motivations to find defendants guilty due to the convict leasing system, in which counties leased their prisoners to private companies for profit. The more pris-oners who were hired out, the more profits county sheriffs, southern counties and states, and the companies leasing the prisoners received. Alabama and Texas began convict leasing in 1866, Arkansas in 1867, Georgia in 1868, Tennessee in

1871, and North Carolina in 1872. By Reconstruction's end in 1877, historian Douglas Blackmon explains, "every formerly Confederate state except Virginia had adopted the practice of leasing black prisoners into commercial hands." In the counties leasing out prisoners, Blackmon notes, "arrests surged and fell, not as acts of crime increased or receded, but in tandem to the varying needs of the buyers of labor." While black men formed the vast majority of convict leases, black women were also leased out.[110] Even during Reconstruction, then, black southerners were heavily constrained in suits over racial justice and criminal prosecutions.

The political revolution in the South proved short-lived. Gradually, the Republican Party largely lost control of southern state governments. The Democratic Party, which opposed many of the new rights and freedoms given to black southerners, regained power in Virginia in 1869, North Carolina in 1870, Georgia in 1871, Alabama and Arkansas in 1874, and South Carolina and Mississippi in 1876. In 1877, Reconstruction came to a close in a backroom deal. In return for Democrats conceding the contested presidential election to the Republican candidate Rutherford B. Hayes, Republicans withdrew federal troops from the three southern states where they remained.[111] With Democrats in power throughout much of the South, southern white men regained control over most of the southern political system.

Yet during the next two decades, the political structure put in place during Reconstruction remained. The Republican Party stayed in the South and continued to put forth candidates for many elections. Although it did not happen as often, Republicans, Independents, and Populists continued to win office in the South during the two decades after Reconstruction. Certain counties and districts elected non-Democrats to local, state and national offices. On a few occasions, non-Democrats even gained power in statewide elections. In Tennessee, Republicans carried the governorship in 1880. In Virginia, another opposition party—the Readjuster Party—gained control of the state legislature in 1879 and of the governorship in 1881. Until they lost power in 1883, the Readjuster coalition of black and white Virginians, historian Jane Dailey noted, worked to support "black suffrage, officeholding, and jury service." In other areas, Democrats were forced to ally with their opponents to gain support and win elections. As a result, the Democrats never felt quite secure.[112]

In particular, Democrats worried that black voters would unite with working-class white voters to return the Republican Party to power or to support the newly formed Populist Party. Indeed, some black men continued to serve in elected positions in the South and several largely black districts elected black representatives to the US Congress during the 1880s. Despite recurring efforts to prevent African Americans from voting in the two decades after Reconstruction, many black men in the South continued to exercise their right to vote. J. Morgan Kousser notes that "even in the 1890s, after several states had restricted the suffrage, nearly half of [African American men] are estimated to have voted in key gubernatorial contests."[113]

In each election, a number of fraudulent measures were used to lessen the impact of black men's vote. Local Democratic leaders destroyed their ballots or counted the ballots for another candidate. Ballot-box stuffing also occurred when extra, fraudulent ballots were added to the tally for a Democratic candidate.[114] In addition, as black men continued to exercise many of their political rights in the two decades after Reconstruction, homegrown terrorism contributed to an atmosphere of fear and violence around the South. The murders of black men by white mobs became public spectacles, attracting crowds of thousands. In 1892, at the peak of violence, 161 lynchings of African Americans were recorded in the United States, the vast majority of them in the South.[115]

Meanwhile, as Reconstruction ended in state after state, some of the people in power in the courts changed. Often, judges nominated by Republican governments were not reelected or reappointed at the end of their terms. Instead, Democrats appointed judges loyal to the Democratic Party. In some cases, though, judges stayed on after the party in power had changed.[116] Even if they did not, the legal structure put in place during Republican control continued. In appellate courts, many of the basic legal rights gained by African Americans during Reconstruction continued to be respected in civil—and at times in criminal—suits. Although it gradually became less common during this period, in some counties juries continued to include black, as well as white, members.[117]

Unlike black voting, African Americans' continuing access to the courts seemed harmless to many white southerners. With white, overwhelmingly Democratic judges and largely white juries making the decisions in southern courts, white residents felt the courts' decisions would generally be in their favor.[118] There was no chance for a widespread working-class uprising in the courts as they feared in politics. Most of the civil cases that the courts allowed black southerners to litigate also seemed relatively benign to many white southerners. Just like during Reconstruction, the civil cases black litigants managed to litigate before appellate courts in the 1880s and 1890s usually involved issues of property, contracts, and bequests that would impact only their own families. Many of their suits appealed to firmly established legal principles, such as property rights, in which judges largely agreed on the legal doctrines involved.

Between 1878 and 1899, however, there were some shifts in the civil cases African Americans litigated in state appellate courts. A smaller proportion of the cases took place between former masters and their former slaves, or the descendants of former masters and their former slaves. While about two-thirds of appellate civil cases between black and white litigants during Reconstruction had involved litigants who had been each other's masters and slaves or were the heirs of such masters and slaves, between 1878 and 1899, 35 percent of cases involved litigants who had been tied together by the relationship of bondage. Other cases involved employers and employees, white and black property owners in the same communities, or business owners and their customers. When African Americans were able to litigate cases over transactions, the economic dealings in their disputes were much more likely to have taken place after the Civil War, rather than during slavery. [119]

Some types of civil cases also occurred less frequently than during Reconstruction. While eighteen cases over apprenticeship and child custody were litigated between white and black southerners in the appellate courts examined during Reconstruction, no such cases appeared in these courts between 1878 and 1899. As the ties between former slaves and former masters weakened, fewer cases between white and black litigants over wills and estates were tried. And as the political climate became less favorable for African Americans, a smaller number of cases between white and black southerners over transactions and contracts took place. [120] In contrast, the number of personal injury cases brought by African Americans against whites or white-owned companies skyrocketed during the two decades after Reconstruction. Only four such suits occurred between 1865 and 1877, but thirty-one personal injury cases between black and white litigants took place in the courts examined between 1878 and 1899. This shift toward personal injury litigation partly reflected nationwide litigation trends. [121]

In general, though, the tone of these cases between 1878 and 1899 remained similar to that of Reconstruction-era cases. Even though the control of state governments was largely out of their hands, black men's continuing access to the vote played a part in allowing African Americans to conduct themselves in civil cases just as they had when Republicans had been in control of their states. Thus black litigants were intensely aware of racial mores and local whites' ideas about race as they testified. At the same time, they still frequently presented themselves to the courts as equal parties to whites and demanded that courts enforce their rights. [122]

Unlike most seemingly harmless civil cases, litigation that asserted rights for African Americans as a group continued to unsettle some white Americans in the two decades following Reconstruction. Indeed, the US Supreme Court finally ruled on the 1875 Civil Rights Act in 1883, only to declare the Act, upon which many of the racial justice suits in federal courts had been based, to be unconstitutional. [123] With one of their main avenues of litigating racial discrimination cases in federal courts blocked, a few African Americans protested unequal treatment on the basis of race in state supreme courts. Although such cases still remained rare in the eight state supreme courts examined, such cases jumped from one case in the eight state supreme courts between 1865 to 1877 to twelve cases between 1878 and 1899—eleven of which took place after the Supreme Court's 1883 decision. During the two decades after Reconstruction, racial justice cases made up 12 percent of the total civil suits between black and white southerners in these courts.[124]

Ida B. Wells was one of the black litigants who brought a suit over racial discrimination in state court in the wake of the US Supreme Court's 1883 decision. When a railroad conductor threw her off a whites-only railroad car in 1884, Wells challenged segregation on trains. In a local court in Tennessee, she recalled, "Judge Pierce, who was an ex-union soldier from Minnesota, awarded me damages of five hundred dollars." When the railroad appealed to the Tennessee Supreme Court, though, the higher court reversed the earlier decision. As a result of her loss in the appeals court, Wells wrote, she had to "pay out over two hundred dollars in court costs."[125]

Undoubtedly such cases over racial equality challenged white southerners in a way cases over property or contracts never could. Moreover, the law remained relatively unsettled on the issue of equal rights. Southern judges could often find legal justification for or against such cases.[126] Still, black litigants continued to win about half of these cases in southern appellate courts, a slightly lower rate than they won civil cases in general.[127] The outcome of each case was no doubt due to multiple factors, but key among them must have been the assumption that their outcomes were unlikely to bring real change.

In contrast, black defendants in criminal cases between 1878 and 1899 clearly continued to appear dangerous to many white southerners. Cases over murders, rapes, and thefts brought out all the worries that white men and women harbored about the darker-skinned people living alongside them.[128] White self-interest persisted in playing a large part in criminal proceedings as well. With Reconstruction over, whites were freer to use criminal law to try to control black southerners' labor and behavior. It became more and more common in the post–Reconstruction South, for instance, for white landowners to swear out criminal warrants against black tenants who had fallen behind on their debts. To avoid going to jail, black laborers would "confess judgement" and sign a contract to work without pay until they had paid the amount back. Furthermore, southern states and individual whites were making more and more money from black convicts whom they hired out for profit.[129]

The result was vastly uneven criminal sentencing based on race in the post–Reconstruction South.[130] One 1882 study of Georgia convicts found that black defendants had been given sentences twice as long as whites for burglary and five times longer than whites for larceny.[131] Unlike during Reconstruction, even in criminal cases appealed to the Georgia and Alabama appellate courts, black litigants now lost more cases than they won, gaining a favorable decision on appeal in only 41 percent of suits.[132]

At a time of great discrimination in the courts, African Americans' ability to consistently gain favorable decisions in seemingly ordinary kinds of civil suits in the post–Reconstruction South was the exception. As the law on such matters was already well established, deciding against precedent could have had implications for cases involving only white participants. More important, white southerners saw most civil cases litigated by individual black men and women over property and contracts as having little impact on their own lives. In contrast, white southerners saw criminal cases as playing a crucial role in controlling African Americans and upholding white power. But because black people's suits over property and contracts seemed innocuous and appeared to ward off even greater unrest, they continued to be considered, to some extent, on the merits of the case.

❦

In conclusion, African Americans made great progress in their access to the courts in the wake of the Civil War, but continued to contend with many of the problems they had experienced with the law in antebellum times. As a result of the intervention of the Union Army and Freedmen's Bureau, the revolutionary actions of Republicans in Congress and state governments and the bold assertions of rights by African Americans themselves, black southerners gained far more legal rights in civil cases than they had in the antebellum period. They could litigate a variety of civil cases against whites, testify against former masters and other whites, and at times serve on juries or even as justices of the peace and judges. A former slave like Henry Parker could take on his former owner in a state court and win. White southerners' ideas about race, however, continued to affect African Americans' experiences in the justice system. Criminal law—which had been used to control them during slavery—was once again put to the same use after the Civil War. In addition, the civil cases that they could litigate against whites still remained limited in many ways. As long as black men held on to the vote though, these limitations would fail to impede some black southerners from boldly taking on whites in their communities and asserting their rights in the process.

How to Litigate a Case Against a White Southerner

Abner Lattimore's dispute with Thomas Dixon began when Lattimore was still a slave. Before the war, Lattimore was known around the small town of Shelby, North Carolina, for his frequent livestock trades with local white men. Later, he would claim to have saved over a thousand dollars as a slave.[1] The law allowed slaves to trade, however, only with their masters' agreement. While many informal trades still occurred without slaveholders' permission, slaves like Lattimore who conducted extensive trading could find themselves in trouble with the law at any time.

The law finally caught up with Lattimore a few years before the Civil War began, when a local court indicted him for "free dealing as a slave." He sought to protect himself from further legal trouble by arranging for his own sale in 1858 to a local slave-owner named Thomas Dixon. Lattimore's conversations with Dixon convinced him that he would be given explicit written permission to continue trading. Just as important, Dixon promised to help Lattimore protect the approximately $1,100 in promissory notes that he had earned through livestock trading and money lending.[2] But Lattimore's status as a slave and lack of legal avenues to defend his property made it only too easy for Dixon to take advantage of him. In 1860, when Lattimore asked Dixon to return his notes, Dixon refused. The next morning, Lattimore discovered that his master had submitted an advertisement to sell him.

In response, Lattimore ran away, leaving Dixon's team of horses abandoned on the side of the road. For 8 months he hid in the nearby woods. But he could not give up on the notes he had entrusted to Dixon. In May 1861, Lattimore turned himself in to the town authorities and was put in the Shelby jail. From there, he attempted to obtain the return of his notes. He asked Dixon's business partner "to write to Mr. Dixon that I . . . was very sorry for running away & that I would git a man to buy me & would pay him for my lost time if he would pay me back the notes & interest on them." Dixon refused, and Lattimore remained in jail for 11 months, until another white southerner bought him.[3]

When Abner Lattimore was released from jail in 1862, a war raged between the newly formed Confederacy and the states remaining in the Union. Over 2,000 white men in surrounding Cleveland County had joined the Confederate Army, leaving primarily slaves, white women, and children behind. Schools around the county were closed, and industry had come to a grinding halt.[4] Although Abner Lattimore could not access the courts and remained enslaved, he used the events of the war to continue to try to regain his money. Nine months after his release, in January 1863, President Abraham Lincoln issued the Emancipation Proclamation, declaring slaves within the Confederate-controlled areas of the South to be free. Upon hearing the news, Lattimore used the proclamation as leverage to again demand his money from his former master, Thomas Dixon. Once again, the white slaveholder refused to return the notes.[5]

After the conclusion of the war, Abner Lattimore continued his attempts to regain his notes by appealing to the Freedmen's Bureau. Around 1866, he told agents at the Freedmen's Bureau in Shelby that his former master, Thomas Dixon, owed him money. One agent asked Lattimore how he could prove this, so the former slave went in search of proof. He approached one local white man out feeding his hogs and asked him to testify about his notes before the Freedmen's Bureau. "I will not come unless I am bound to come," the man replied, and "the Bureau will have nothing to do with the matter." Lattimore continued searching, finally returning to the Bureau office with a list of notes "amounting to some thirteen hundred dollars" and two white men. Upon questioning, one of these men "said he knew nothing about the notes on that list," but the other "stated that Mr Dixon did get some notes from Ab."[6]

Convinced that Abner Lattimore's claim had some merit, the Bureau held two trials on the matter. In at least one, Thomas Dixon appeared and testified. The agent overseeing the proceedings, however, decided that the Bureau did not have jurisdiction in the matter. The Bureau advised the freedman that he might have more success in the county court. So, after exhausting his other avenues, in early 1868, the former slave brought the long-running dispute to the courts.[7]

Black litigants—like Lattimore—who turned to the courts in the three and a half decades after the Civil War often had little formal preparation for such an endeavor. Even those who eventually succeeded in gaining a hearing of their cases before a state's highest court usually had very little formal education; most signed their names on court documents with a solitary "X." Many had lived part of their lives as slaves or were the children of former slaves. A large number of their cases were against the very whites who had enslaved them.[8] Moreover, almost half of these black litigants were women. Between 1865 and 1899, black women formed approximately 48 percent of African American litigants in civil cases between black and white litigants in the eight appellate courts examined.[9] Black women were more likely to litigate certain kinds of cases: During the three and a half decades after the Civil War, more than two-thirds of wills and estates cases between white and black litigants included at least one black female litigant. Black women also made up almost half of the litigants in cases over child custody and personal injury between 1865 and 1899.[10]

If these black litigants appeared exceptional in any way, it was in their ability to draw on long-term ties with local whites to gain the support of white lawyers and witnesses. Yet even the whites most sympathetic to a black litigant's cause frequently did not consider them equals; other whites wished they had never been freed and sought to re-create the conditions of slavery in the postwar South. Despite the obvious disadvantages they faced in the courtroom, black southerners seized their new legal rights. More often than not, they initiated the civil cases that later reached appellate courts. Indeed, as black southerners' other rights eroded, the percentage of these cases instigated by African Americans in lower courts increased.[11]

Black southerners had different reasons for turning to the courts.[12] In many cases, their experiences in the antebellum South shaped their view of the legal system. After years of legally sanctioned oppression with little chance for redress through the courts, black southerners knew that the law had power. As a result, once black southerners gained legal rights after the Civil War, they were eager to use them. They knew all too well the consequences of not having this access to the courts. One former slave noted during Reconstruction that many black people in his community took "advantage of the smallest and most unimportant offense to 'come to law'" as "they were anxious to avail themselves of such a glorious privilege."[13]

Potential black litigants also drew on knowledge of their new rights as citizens. In the first decades after the Civil War, their cases sometimes specifically appealed to these rights. One group of former slaves in Mississippi claimed in their 1872 suit that recent acts of the state and federal governments and amendments to the US Constitution had freed them, made them citizens, and given them the ability to inherit property.[14] Whether they specifically referred to their new rights or not, the very act of bringing a case demonstrated knowledge of their rights to own property, inherit, and serve as litigants.

The changes African Americans saw around them further convinced many of them that the law could be a legitimate avenue of justice.[15] Some former slaves must have seen other black men and women in their communities litigating cases in the postwar South and, at times, winning. After the Civil War ended, courthouses throughout the South reportedly filled with black witnesses and spectators. A South Carolina lawyer wrote in 1869 that, upon a recent visit to court, the courtroom was "*crowded* as thick as negroes could sit or stand; scarce a white man in the room." He continued, "The negroes have certainly taken possession of our courthouses, and of the area around the courthouses where the courts are sitting. They take the greatest delight in judicial proceedings—like to be witnesses, so as to get to attend court."[16]

Even if they did not personally attend court or know anyone who had litigated cases, African Americans may have read or listened to news about suits involving black litigants in the press. Both white- and black-owned newspapers covered cases involving black litigants.[17] At times, black newspapers were surprisingly hopeful about African Americans' chances of creating real change through victories in the courts. The *Richmond Planet* noted in 1895 that "much interest is being manifested in the case" of John Gibson and Charley Smith against the state of Mississippi "as it involves the question of colored men serving on juries in the south." Leaders of "the colored race," they wrote, "are hoping and believing that [their lawyer] Mr. Jones will be sustained." They concluded optimistically, "If the [US Supreme] court should sustain Mr. Jones it will revolutionize the present system of jury service in many states of the south."[18]

Yet African Americans were generally aware of the difficulties that people of color experienced in civil and criminal cases. The Freedmen's Bureau received letter after letter complaining about southern courts' treatment of African Americans and requesting the Bureau's aid. One committee of freedpeople writing the Freedmen's Bureau in 1867 complained: "as the Civil Courts are now managed in this County Freedmen can obtain very little justice."[19] Black newspapers also decried black litigants' losses in civil and criminal cases. In discussing lawsuits over Jim Crow laws in 1898, the *Richmond Planet* declared that "The judicial department is tainted from bottom to top with race prejudice."[20] Additionally, some court cases themselves protested African Americans' treatment in the suit at hand or in earlier suits.[21]

Indeed, the obstacles black litigants faced to litigate a civil case must have sometimes seemed insurmountable. Many black southerners lacked sufficient funds to pay court fees. One white magistrate explained, "The costs are required of the plaintiff in advance—$2.00 to the Clerk and the same to the Sheriff, before the case is docketed. A freedman may have $100 due him and be unable to sue for the want of the $4.00 thus required."[22] At times, courts allowed litigants to plead poverty and waive these court fees; at other times, they did not. Abner Lattimore, for instance, did not have to give "security" to the court because of his poverty.[23]

Many black southerners also found it difficult to gain legal counsel. In cases that did not offer the prospect of a significant award, the lawyers' fees could be impossible to pay.[24] Black sharecroppers who had been arbitrarily discharged before the end of their contracts without any pay, for instance, often did not have the resources to hire a lawyer. One Bureau agent explained, "In cases of arbitrary discharges, the most frequent cause of complaint of the freedmen, he has very nearly no remedy. His wages or his share in the crop almost invariably amount to more than one hundred Dollars and he therefore must in the majority of instances sue in the Superior Court. Before he can obtain the services of a lawyer he must pay a fee of from $25.00 to $50.00 or must secure the payment of it by giving a lien on his share of the crop, when in a majority of instances the same man who thus seeks to obtain payment for his labor after having worked perhaps nearly the whole year is driven off often with a family without one cent of money, or one mouthful of provisions."[25]

At first, white lawyers were condemned for representing black clients. Magistrate Julius J. Fleming wrote in November 1866, "I have represented both races as counsel and in every case where I have appeared for freedmen, I have been fully sensible of the fact that the popular current was against my client, although the law and evidence forced a decision in his favor (in the Provost Court). And planters have told me frankly that they did not believe that any lawyer should act as counsel for a negro . . . any lawyer must expect abuse if he gives a freedman the benefit of his services."[26]

Black litigants and jurors also faced potential violence or repercussions in their communities from whites who did not like being challenged. While before the war most mob violence had been targeted at other whites, after the war extralegal violence was often directed at African Americans to enforce white southerners' ideas of racial superiority. Throughout the South, the Ku Klux Klan attacked African Americans who served on juries and testified against whites.[27] Violence occasionally broke out in the courtroom, too. Tensions between black and white townspeople came to a head in Meridian, Mississippi, in 1871 during a trial of three black defendants charged with arson. "Almost everyone came to the courtroom well armed, as Mississippians had been doing for years," historian David Oshinsky explains. "This time shots rang out, killing the white Republican judge and several black spectators. The crowd surged forward, chasing down one defendant, whose body they riddled with bullets, and hurling another from the roof." The killing continued for three more days, leaving more than twenty-five black people dead, including most of the town's black leaders.[28]

The long time frame of cases proved problematic as well for newly freed African Americans who had transitory lives. One Bureau agent explained, "When suit is commenced six or twelve months will elapse until trial term, twelve or eighteen months until judgement term, the colored plaintiff has since had to change homes once or twice his patience in waiting for his money is nearly worn out & he has given up all hope of getting it."[29] It was also sometimes difficult for freedpeople to attend court without losing their jobs; at other times, freedpeople were not informed when court hearings were scheduled. Black witnesses were often just as transitory as the litigants, making it difficult to obtain their appearance to testify.[30]

African Americans had to have the right kind of case to have their cause heard by county trial courts, where the full machinery of justice—including a judge and at times a jury—would be in place.[31] Some disputes first had to be heard by inferior courts or by local justices of the peace. Other cases could be heard first by either a justice of the peace or by a trial court.[32] Unlike judges, justices of the peace were not required to have any legal training. Any man with the right to vote and no criminal record could normally be elected a justice of the peace. Although the vast majority of justices of the peace in the South were white, in a few heavily black communities African American men held these roles through the end of the nineteenth century. In many cases, the decisions of justices of the peace could be appealed to county trial courts if one of the parties disagreed with the decision.[33]

Despite these obstacles, some black southerners succeeded in hiring lawyers to represent them in legal action in county trial courts. Only a very small number of lawyers in postbellum southern states were African American. The

TRIAL OF A WHITE WOMAN BY A NEGRO JUSTICE OF THE PEACE AT NEWBERN.

Scene of the Trial in a Negro Barber Shop After the Case Had Been Transferred by "Justice" Douglass.

Fig 2.1 Image of a white woman being tried by black magistrates from *The Gold Leaf* newspaper, North Carolina, 1898. "Newbern's Awful Plight: The Negro Magistrates are Running Mad," *The Gold Leaf* (Henderson, NC), Sept. 29, 1898, Supplement, image 7, http://chroniclingamerica.loc.gov. Original held by The Wilson Library, University of North Carolina at Chapel Hill.

1900 census lists 266 black lawyers in the eight states examined, fewer than 2 percent of these states' total number of lawyers.[34] Some of these black lawyers were northerners who had moved south after the war. Many others were southern born and had trained with a practicing lawyer or attended law schools such as Howard University, Atlanta University, the University of Chicago, or the University of South Carolina.[35]

When these black lawyers represented African American clients, it was often in criminal trials—particularly in the lower courts. Even there, black lawyers' ability to make their clients' cases could be hampered by white southerners' racist attitudes. A notice in *The Emmanuel Magazine*, a monthly African American publication in North Carolina, explained: "The profession of law is the most difficult one a colored man can follow in the South, because he must deal with white judges, white jurors, white lawyers, and sometimes, white witnesses, and a public sentiment which is created by the whites."[36] One exception to black lawyers' general lack of participation in African Americans' civil cases was in Louisiana, where black lawyers played an important role in civil litigation. An 1874 newspaper article noted that during the recent wave of litigation over racial discrimination, "the plaintiffs have for the most part been represented by a colored lawyer, who is a candidate for member of Congress in the coming election for the district now represented by Hon. L. A. Sheldon." By 1891, though, black attorney Louis A. Martinet described local black attorneys in New Orleans, with the exception of himself, as "practice[ing] almost exclusively in the police courts."[37]

When litigating civil cases against whites, African Americans usually sought the services of white lawyers. Not only were many more white lawyers available, but potential black clients likely believed that they would gain more sympathetic hearings before white judges and juries and thus achieve more favorable outcomes. In civil cases that reached the appellate courts examined, black litigants' lawyers were almost always white, and often well-respected members of their communities.[38] Caroline Deberry's 1874 suit against her former master is one of the few civil cases found in which a black lawyer was involved. Even though both a white lawyer and a black lawyer had represented Caroline Deberry in the local trial of her suit, only the white lawyer represented Deberry during the appeal to the Tennessee Supreme Court.[39]

Over time, the practice of taking black clients in civil cases became widespread, rather than limited to a handful of specialized lawyers. While it was not uncommon for a white lawyer to represent black litigants in two or three appellate civil cases, such lawyers rarely represented black clients in their states' highest court more than three times. More often, a white lawyer represented only one black litigant in an appellate civil case during his entire career.[40] Prominent southern lawyers even applauded the legal profession's representation of former slaves. Georgia jurist John Reed noted in 1885, "When the courts of Middle Georgia in which we practiced were reopened after the late war, it was useless to submit the case of a negro to a jury of the whites . . . . But the [legal] profession stood by their clients faithfully . . . . The leading members of the bar spoke out unanimously on all fit occasions advising a better course. At last this persistence began to tell. The tide turned perceptibly in 1870, and after a while it was no wonder to see a negro obtain his due from a jury of his former masters."[41]

This willingness to take on black clients was limited to certain kinds of suits. In criminal matters—particularly when black defendants were accused of raping or murdering a white person—it could be difficult to gain adequate representation. White lawyers who vigorously defended such defendants could face the loss of business or ostracism from the white community.[42] Even when they received conscientious court-appointed lawyers in criminal cases, black litigants often had only a few minutes with their attorneys shortly before they argued their case before the court, leaving lawyers with almost no time to prepare.[43]

In contrast, white lawyers were especially willing to take on black clients in civil suits because, unlike criminal trials, these could prove exceptionally lucrative. Often, white lawyers took on black clients when their suits promised to yield a large reward from a corporation or estate. In such cases, lawyers frequently agreed to operate on contingency, requiring no fees up front. Instead, they agreed with their clients to take a portion (up to half) of whatever the litigant won.[44] The type of case influenced lawyers' decisions, too. Lawyers relied on their knowledge of similar cases involving black litigants, concluding that if these had been successful, the case at hand might be too. Attorneys' political leanings could affect their decision to represent black clients as well. Some white lawyers were also influenced by paternalism, viewing themselves as members of an elite class of whites who would protect vulnerable African Americans. Others acted partially out of a sense of professionalism and respect for the law. Occasionally, white lawyers seem to have genuinely sympathized with the causes of their black clients.[45]

Whatever their reasons, white lawyers' actions in civil cases were crucial to black access to state courts. A lawyer's commitment to his client, skill, and knowledge of the law often meant the difference between a successful or unsuccessful case. In civil cases that reached southern appellate courts, white lawyers generally represented their black clients well, crafting well-reasoned legal strategies and coaching their black clients on what to say in their testimony.[46] As they assisted black litigants in bringing claims against white southerners, lawyers aligned themselves—even if temporarily and solely for monetary reasons—with African Americans' quest for full citizenship. Nevertheless, black southerners' dependence on white lawyers limited their legal action. Black men and women could usually litigate only the cases that white lawyers were willing to take on. Less lucrative cases and suits over racial equality probably came before courts less frequently because they did not have the support of white lawyers. Moreover, because white lawyers decided on the legal strategies in these cases, their legal arguments often worked to uphold the system of the law and the property rights of white elites, rather than making larger claims for black rights and equality.

Realizing that he needed a lawyer, in 1867 or early 1868 Abner Lattimore approached a local white lawyer, 47-year-old William Preston Bynum, and asked him to take his case. A member of a wealthy North Carolina family, Bynum had belonged to the Whig Party before the Civil War. In the year leading up to the war, Bynum had publicly spoken out against secession, telling a North Carolina political meeting in 1860 that "peace, union & obedience to the laws" were "the only hope for the South." But like many other southern dissenters, Bynum had served in the Confederate Army. Now, with the fighting ceased, he was an elected solicitor, litigating cases on behalf of the state of North Carolina.[47]

Bynum left behind no papers explaining why he agreed to represent Lattimore, but there are tell-tale clues. During Reconstruction, Bynum supported the North Carolina Republican Party. At times, he sought to minimize these ties, presenting himself as outside of politics and allowing himself to be put forward as the candidate for solicitor in 1868 by both the Republican and Democratic Parties. In a draft of a speech from the fall of 1868, he wrote, "I do not appear before you as the Champion of any party or the accuser of any party. I see much in the Radical [Republican] party to condemn & . . . much that I do not approve; I see in the leaders of the Democratic party, those who . . . brought us to our present misery & I cannot now look for salvation to the authors of our ruin." Clearly, though, Bynum supported the Reconstruction government. He continued, in the same address, to wholeheartedly urge fellow North Carolinians to support the measures that had been required for the state to rejoin the Union. They were fortunate, he wrote, as "no vanquished race of people, after a war of such fury & duration, ever received more favorable terms from the victors." While some refused to accept the Republican-dominated Reconstruction government, he counseled his fellow North Carolinians to accept them as their valid representatives. Moreover, in the upcoming presidential election he would support Republican candidate Ulysses S. Grant, he explained, "because I believe the election of Grant will give us peace & Because he stands upon the laws."[48] Undoubtedly, Bynum's sympathies with the Republican Party played a role in his representation of Lattimore.

Bynum also seems to have been motivated by his desire to uphold the law. Again and again in his public writings he expressed his belief that the law of the land should be sustained, even if individual citizens did not agree with it.

Fig 2.2 William Preston Bynum. From Samuel A. Ashe, *Biographical History of North Carolina from Colonial Times to the Present*, vol. 2 (Greensboro, NC: Charles L. Van Noppen, Publisher, 1905). Courtesy of the Wilson Library, University of North Carolina at Chapel Hill.

Although he had opposed black suffrage in 1865, in the 1868 speech he encouraged other white southerners to accept it because it "is now part of the organic law of the land."[49] This strong desire to follow the law no doubt influenced Bynum's decision to help Lattimore exercise the legal rights guaranteed him by the US Constitution.

Money may have been a consideration as well. Lattimore had paid no money up front because of "poverty," but the former slave stood to win over $1,000 if he made his case successfully. As Lattimore's attorney, Bynum would receive a portion of this.[50] Or perhaps Bynum took the case as part of his position as a government solicitor. Although neither he nor Lattimore ever indicated that this played a part, Bynum held this elected position at the time he litigated the case.

Perhaps Bynum also sympathized to some extent with the cause of the freed slaves. Publicly, he mourned the end of the Old South, when "we lived in wealth; with our broad acres & countless slaves; our barns filled with plenty, & our tables groaning under the abundance of food." He firmly denied wanting social equality and denounced Republican radicals. His petition on behalf of Lattimore, however, made the claim that certain freedpeople should be reimbursed for their transactions and work as slaves in the antebellum South.[51] This claim went well beyond the normal claims white lawyers made for former slaves.

In addition, Lattimore may have helped to persuade Bynum to take his case. In their first meeting with a lawyer, clients often named likely supporting witnesses, mentioned where relevant documents were located, and explained the background of cases.[52] During his first meeting with Dixon, Lattimore may have mentioned some of the white witnesses who would testify in his favor in the coming trial. He could also have impressed the lawyer with his recall of the amounts of the notes, just as he would later do in the courtroom.

As in most civil cases, the next step in Lattimore's case was for the lawyer to file the suit. Southern counties had a range of different trial courts where litigants could bring their disputes. Depending on the county and the period, black litigants' trials took place in chancery courts, superior courts, circuit courts, courts of equity, and city courts. In March 1868, Bynum initiated Lattimore's case against his former master by submitting a bill of complaint to a court of equity, a local court in which the principles of "equity" and fairness were supposed to take priority. In the bill, Bynum demanded an account of the notes and

Fig 2.3 The law office of A. C. Wheeler, Gainesville, Georgia, around 1910. Mr. Wheeler, seated at the desk, is meeting with two clients. Courtesy of the Georgia Archives, Vanishing Georgia Collection, hal184.

requested a subpoena "commanding [Dixon] to be & appear before your Honor, at the Court House in Shelby, Cleveland County, at the next term of this Court." Embedded in this was the radical assertion that black men and women could force whites to appear in court to answer their claims. Dixon initially thought that his former slave's suit could be easily set aside and hired a local law firm to ask for the case to be dismissed. The local judge, however, did not dismiss the suit and instead scheduled the case for the court's next session.

Some southern trial courts, such as superior and circuit courts, met only a few weeks a year during much of the nineteenth century, whereas other city and county courts met for larger portions of the year. At times, then, litigants had lengthy waits before their cases were heard.[53] In Lattimore's case, the trial began in August, 5 months after the first filing, in his hometown of Shelby. Shelby was still a rural backwater, but in the midst of Congressional Reconstruction, it was occupied by Union soldiers. The county courthouse, an imposing two-story brick building erected two decades earlier, stood at the town's center.[54]

All over the South, courthouses like the one in Shelby often formed both the geographic and social heart of county seats in the nineteenth century. In many cases, they were the most imposing building in the town, built on a central square. Frequently, law offices and local businesses radiated out from the courthouse square. The proceedings inside courthouses also played a central role in southern communities. After observing trials, citizens not directly involved in cases often discussed them with their neighbors on the courthouse green and all over town. For those unable to attend, local newspapers gave detailed accounts of lawyers' arguments and evaluated their performances in the courtroom.[55] The public interest in court cases ensured that the ensuing cases between black and white southerners would work to influence not only the individuals involved, but other black and white members of the community.

Lattimore and Dixon would have climbed the imposing courthouse stairs and passed through a columned portico to reach the second-floor courtroom. They probably saw a wooden railing about one-third of the way back from the front of the room, separating the participants in the court case from the public audience. Most likely the spectators—as in most southern courtrooms—were separated by race. As a "matter of custom," one contemporaneous scholar, Gilbert Stephenson, explained, black men and women "[occupy] seats on one side of the room and white people on the other." When the time for their case arrived, the litigants walked down the center aisle and took seats inside the railing. In front of them was a raised judge's bench and the arbiter who would hear their case. To the right of the judge's seat would have been a witness box, where the litigants and witnesses sat as they testified.[56] The court was called to order, and the case began.

In similar courtrooms across the South, members of the community con-
vened to play different roles, which shaped their words and actions accordingly.
As the parties to the suit, the black and white litigants had the most to gain or
lose. For many of the white litigants in such trials, however, litigating a suit with
a black person probably played just as important a role in the trial as what was
at stake. They often shared a long history with the black litigants they faced. In
approximately half of the appellate cases between 1865 and 1899, the white litigants or their relatives had owned the black litigants during slavery.[57] In many
other cases, the white litigants had employed the black litigants after the Civil
War. For years, they had been accustomed to being in a position of power. To
have these black men and women then bring a suit against them in a court of
law must have been galling beyond words. To have to bring a suit against a black
person to gain their ends must have been just as maddening.

Yet the money and property that they stood to win was critical to some white
southerners' financial futures. Although many of them had been prosperous
slaveholders, much of their wealth disappeared with emancipation. Often, they
had put large portions of their money into Confederate currency, which became
worthless at the end of the war. Their land, too, lost part of its monetary value
during the war, and their debts piled up. Other white litigants had owned no
slaves and less property before the war, but also faced financial ruin.[58] White

Fig 2.4 Interior of Gordon County Courthouse, Georgia, 1889. Courtesy of the Georgia
Archives, Vanishing Georgia Collection, gor114.

southerners, then, sometimes needed to win these suits to maintain their financial stability.

As they participated in legal actions, white litigants increasingly recognized that there was a chance that black litigants could win civil cases against them. As a result, white litigants typically marshalled all their resources to win. A justice of the Supreme Court of Georgia observed of one such suit in 1879, "This contest, though opening as a mere skirmish at one of the outposts of equity, has drawn into it all the forces of both combatants, and proved a general engagement."[59]

White privilege was one of the key resources on which white litigants could draw. Because of their race, white plaintiffs and defendants likely had more experience and more knowledge of the law than the black men and women they litigated cases against. Often, they also appealed to the common racial interests of white judges and jury members. In several cases, white litigants testified that black men and women had been disloyal or rude to their former masters and employers. Nancy Burdine, for instance, brought a case in 1897 to obtain bank stock and property that she had contracted with her employer to receive if she served him faithfully until his death. In response, the white heirs claimed she was not entitled to the property because "she was disrespectful to Mr. and Mrs. Burdine . . . she kept a disorderly house, and . . . she refused to nurse and wait upon Mrs. Burdine, an invalid." Rather than being a "faithful" servant, their lawyer's answer stated, she was "unruly, vicious, aggravating, disobedient."[60]

White litigants also drew on stereotypes about black immorality and their long-term knowledge of the black litigants to attack their characters. They particularly assailed the character of black women, often making allegations about their sexual histories. The white heirs' lawyer, for instance, wrote that Nancy Burdine "converted the cabin house wherein she lived . . . into a veritable bawdy-house, and became so unchaste that she became pregnant, and from time to time gave birth to bastard children to the number of five or six . . . in fact, her conduct became so notoriously bad, that the said N. E. Burdine was compelled to move her away from his premises two or three miles to blot out and remove the disgrace and shame that so nearly approached his mansion house."[61]

Occasionally white litigants engaged in actual fraud to win their cases; others exercised more subtle influence over the proceedings. Outright witness tampering appears to have taken place in an 1866 Georgia suit. As he questioned witnesses, the black litigants' lawyer hinted that the opposing white litigants made an arrangement to release a witness from debt if the witness managed to overturn the will; further, he suggested that the white litigants offered a large sum of money "for testimony to break the will."[62] At other times, white litigants worked to block the trial from coming to court or arranged for the black litigants' witnesses not to show up at all. In one North Carolina case, an uncommon number of legal impediments appeared in the black plaintiff's path as she brought a case against the county commissioners. After moving her trial to a neighboring county because of the enormous influence of the opposing parties in her local county, the plaintiff Mary Ray had difficulty obtaining a trial, despite repeated attempts to do so. When she finally obtained a court date, her witnesses did not appear. At her trial in Orange County in August 1891, Ray brought these problems to the judge's attention, stating that during the last three terms of court she had not been able to get a trial "for causes beyond her control" and noting that the witnesses' "absences were by no procurement of her own."[63]

Sometimes white litigants flat-out lied. Thomas Dixon likely perjured himself as he denied Abner Lattimore's claims that he had been holding the notes on the former slave's behalf. He told the court that he had done Lattimore a great service in buying him, and all of the notes given to him by Lattimore had been used—at Lattimore's request—to buy the slave. He submitted to the court evidence the former slave could not hope to match: a small notebook, in which he had supposedly kept track of the notes Lattimore claimed. As he testified, he referred to the notations in the book. After years of battling over these notes with his former slave, Thomas Dixon was no doubt determined to win the case.[64]

Black men and women had even more compelling reasons to want to win these cases. A number of black litigants undoubtedly had been brutally whipped by the whites they faced in court, forced to work for decades without pay, or had their children or parents sold away from them, never to see them again. After gaining their freedom, their lack of land and money prevented them from leaving the employment of their former masters and other whites who still treated them in many ways as slaves. If they won these court cases, they might finally be able to gain a measure of financial independence and establish lives of their own. Through their litigation, black southerners also sought to exercise their new rights as citizens and show their former masters that they could appeal to a higher arbiter in their disputes.

As a result, black litigants often did everything in their power to overcome their lack of courtroom experience and win their suits. Case files hint that they gained some knowledge of the law from coaching and conversations with their lawyers. They also learned from participating in legal actions.[65] Emily Thomas went to court over a bequest from her former master (and father) in 1886. The state supreme court eventually decided the case in her favor, but her lawyer had persuaded her to sign an unfavorable contract in which he would receive $5,000 from the principal of the settlement as well as all of the interest from the settlement. Realizing her mistake, Thomas employed a new lawyer to represent her in a case against her former attorney.[66] Thomas's initial experiences in court helped her gain the knowledge of the law that led her to bring the second case.

In a number of cases, African Americans combatted the claims of white southerners by telling their own side of the story in the local trial. Such testimony appeared unthreatening to many whites because, as one white observer explained in a newspaper article in 1865, "With white judges, intelligent white jurors, a proper estimate will always be placed upon negro testimony."[67] Despite such statements, the trial transcripts reveal a respect for black people's words often missing from other areas of southern life. Lawyers' decisions to call black witnesses to the stand make clear that they believed black testimony would help their cases. At times, juries decided verdicts based on black testimony, even when such testimony contradicted that of white witnesses.[68]

Before giving their testimony, black litigants were often coached by their lawyers. They also decided what to say based on their knowledge of race relations in their communities and their understanding of relevant law and the facts of the case. In a number of cases, African Americans worked with their lawyers to appeal to the racial biases of white judges and juries. During the decades after the Civil War, black people's suits often appealed to long-term relationships with members of the white elite, including their former masters. In the rural South, in particular, personal relationships played a crucial part in the outcome of cases, as the participants had often known one another from birth.[69] A few former slaves, for instance, emphasized their loyalty and obedience to their former masters in their testimony.[70] In one 1881 Kentucky case, the elderly black litigant, Minta Simmons, testified that she remained with her former master "from the time she was freed to his death and performed her duties faithfully." She added: "they were a good and affectionate master and mistress to her and always treated her well and kindly and she can never think or speak of them but with the love and respect which their behavior to her demands." Similarly, although Nancy Burdine did not testify in her suit to obtain property for faithful service, her lawyer's bill stated that "she performed her duty faithfully, and, as she believes, to the satisfaction of those with whom she was required to live. For many years she had complete control and charge of the household affairs placed in her hands by an invalid mistress."[71]

Even as they appealed to white southerners' racial biases, in the three and a half decades after the Civil War, black southerners frequently presented themselves to the courts as equal parties to the white men and women participating in these civil suits. Such statements were not antithetical to their negotiation of racial biases. The same case could include declarations of the black litigants' faithfulness to their former masters as well as bold assertions of their rights. After proclaiming her faithfulness to her former master and mistress after the war, Minta Simmons testified that her former employer was "indebted to her for three years services at $120 per year, subject to a credit of about $50.00 per year for clothing + sundries furnished her by her said master and mistress." Her lawyer's petition asked the court to pay over this money and other funds owed her.[72]

Other black litigants' cases demonstrated a growing knowledge of what they needed to say in their testimony to win their legal cases. Abner Lattimore, for one, sought to use his testimony to shed doubt on his former master's case and strengthen the legal basis of his own claims. At his lawyer's urging, he recalled a long list of specific financial transactions he had conducted as a slave, including the sums, people involved, and in several cases the time span until the debt came due. "I had one note on Eli Williamson for $100 payable to H Noulin," he testified, "one note on H Noulin + David Bram payable to Dan'l Lattimore for $120 or $125 . . . . I had a forty dollar note one William Jenks payable to Abner Spangler for a horse sold to William Jenks. I had a note on Samuel Patterson + E McBrayer Secuity payable to H Noulin for $70 or $75 for a horse I sold to Mr Patterson." Despite Lattimore's admission to the court that he could not read or write, he presented himself as a competent businessman with an excellent memory. Yet his own inability to keep written records made it difficult for him to prove his claims. He did not know the dates that all the debts came due and when asked if he had "written authority to act for yourself & appropriate the profits while in the service of Dixon," he replied, "Did have but have not got it now. I lost it."[73] Clearly, Lattimore was giving the best legal testimony he could provide, considering the barriers of illiteracy and the lack of legal records.

Trials were often intensely personal for the witnesses, as well as for the litigants. The vast majority of people in the South in the nineteenth century lived in rural areas or small towns.[74] In these areas, many members of the community knew one another well and had long histories of social engagements, marriages, feuds, and transactions together. Witnesses often knew not only the litigants, but at times also the judges, lawyers, and jury members. Their testimony about the litigants' characters and the disputed action could thus carry tremendous weight.

In civil suits during the first three and a half decades after the Civil War, white southerners testified both for and against black people. Frequently they were local storeowners, planters, or relatives of black litigants' former owners who had known the freedpeople for years. The willingness of white witnesses to testify on behalf of a black litigant undoubtedly affected the success of suits, giving certain cases an edge and preventing cases without such witnesses from receiving full consideration. Indeed, almost all civil cases between white and black litigants that reached southern state supreme courts between 1865 and 1899 included white witnesses testifying on behalf of black litigants.

These white witnesses provided evidence for black litigants for a variety of reasons. Some testified because of their own economic interests. At times, they stood to benefit from a will being upheld; in other cases they profited from land being sold. Others testified as part of a family or community feud. They had bitter feelings toward the white party in the suit and wanted to prevent them from winning. Most often, though, whites had long-term connections with the black litigants. Some witnesses had lived on neighboring plantations, interacted with black litigants at their former masters' homes, or had given them medical care for years. In a number of cases, white witnesses even had blood ties to the black litigants. Victoria Monroe, the daughter of a slave and a slaveholder, litigated appellate suits in 1879 and 1880 over a trust left to her in her white father's will. During the two trials, Monroe's white half-brother as well as a number of white neighbors testified on her behalf.[75] In such cases, long-term relations between white and black southerners could supplant ingrained patterns of discrimination.[76]

Lattimore's trial had fourteen white witnesses, including many prominent members of the community. A number of these white men testified on Lattimore's behalf. Many of them seem to have been influenced by their long-term interactions with the former slave. Several explained that they had traded horses with Lattimore before the war or even borrowed money from him. Others testified that they had assisted him in protecting or counting his notes. A man to whom he had been hired out told the court that Lattimore "had some $700 or more in notes principal which he placed in my hands for safe keeping while he was living with me." Men whom Lattimore had encountered in his quest to gain the return of his notes also came before the court. The local jailor told the court about Lattimore's months in jail after he ran away. A Freedmen's Bureau official testified that Lattimore had submitted the dispute to the Bureau.[77]

During the examination of witnesses, lawyers sought not only to establish the facts of the case, but also the characters of those providing testimony.[78] Lawyers thus frequently asked white witnesses about the characters of the litigants. In Lattimore's case, the local sheriff, a Baptist minister, the county jailor, and a former official in the local Freedmen's Bureau all stated that they had known Dixon for decades and that his reputation was good. The jailor vouching for Dixon, for example, told the court that he had known Dixon "from his childhood over 40 years" and his character for "truth honesty—and piety" was "good." White witnesses gave similar recommendations of Lattimore's character. A white man who had hired Lattimore as a slave said he had known the black litigant since he was "a boy, never heard anything against him." Another white witness told the court: "I am acquainted with the general character of Ab Lattimore have known him ever since he was 14 years old, he is a shrewd, keen, industrious man. I do not know anything against his character as to honesty or truth."[79] Such testimony from local white men went a long way in aiding the case of a black litigant in the South.

Black witnesses often played an important role as well in testifying for (and occasionally against) black litigants. Many of these witnesses were family members; others were friends, acquaintances, and co-workers. They, too, experienced the legal process as citizens as they testified in the courtroom. Like black litigants, they sometimes drew on an understanding of the legal matter in dispute. In their testimony for Lattimore, two black witnesses attempted to provide evidence of Lattimore's notes. Andrew Dickson told the court that he had been a slave of Thomas Dixon and "hardly grown" when Lattimore and his master called him in to the parlor to witness Lattimore handing over "about $900 in notes to Dixon." Harry Collins testified that right before Lattimore ran away, he had talked with him. "Abb seemed to be a great deal troubled, I asked him what was the matter, he said his master owed him some money. I asked him how much, he said about $1100—I told him to cheer up his master would pay him." Lattimore had been unconvinced, Collins testified, as shortly after, "I found the team and waggon on the side of the Road and Abb was gone."[80]

Other black witnesses provided even more important testimony for black litigants' cases. In an 1892 Virginia case, an elderly white man's verbal gift of personal property to his daughter by his former slave depended on the testimony of Fanny Coles, the daughter's black companion and the only disinterested witness to the father's verbal gift. Coles's deposition fills sixty pages and includes, according to the opposing lawyer's account, "a surprising minutiae of detail." Under cross examination, Coles testified that the white father told his daughter that this property was "to be hers in case of his death" and "that he was then in his right mind, but that he was apprehensive that he would then shortly die." Her phrasing in this matter was crucial, as a verbal will was valid only if accompanied by the assertion that the person giving the gift expected shortly to die.[81] Although her testimony contradicted that of a number of white witnesses, her extended deposition led to victory for her friend in the Supreme Court of Virginia. The *Times*, a white Richmond newspaper, reported that Coles "was on the witness stand for six hours and it was through her evidence which the finest legal talent in Virginia could not successfully assail, that the case was won." The paper further described Coles's words in court as "the most convincing and consistent testimony" in the trial.[82]

Such testimony by black witnesses worked not only to help African Americans win cases, but supported black southerners' claims for full citizenship. By acting as competent witnesses in courts of law, black southerners showed themselves able to carry out the duties of citizens. Black witnesses learned about the legal process, too, as they participated in court cases. As they saw other black people in their communities battling in court with local whites and sometimes winning, they undoubtedly saw the possibilities—as well as the limits—of using the courts to uphold their own rights.

After a civil case's initial trial, a jury or a lower-court judge decided the outcome. Certain kinds of cases, such as probate and apprenticeship cases, were more likely to be decided in the lower courts by a judge. In contrast, juries often decided personal injury and fraud cases. While not representative of cases as a whole, from 1865 to 1877, about two-thirds of the appellate civil cases involving black and white litigants examined had been originally heard by a lower-court judge and about one-third of these cases were originally tried by a jury. Between 1878 and 1899, the percentage of such cases decided by a jury increased, with about half of these cases decided by a jury and about half by a judge.[83]

The trial court judges who heard these cases were almost exclusively white and usually came from wealthy families.[84] They had often risen to prominence as lawyers in their communities before becoming judges. During Reconstruction, many aligned themselves with the Republican Party; in the two decades following, most belonged to the Democratic Party.[85] Undoubtedly, the ideas of their time and the communities in which they lived influenced their rulings, as well as personal experiences and beliefs about race. Sometimes their elite position in southern society led them to try to protect especially vulnerable African Americans from lower classes of whites. Doing so demonstrated their own character and upheld the image of a white elite who sought to act in the best interests of black men and women.[86] Judges' political loyalties and view of the law also shaped their rulings. Additionally, the very nature of the legal system played a key part in judges' decisions. Judicial elections in many southern states were often not genuinely competitive, making it unnecessary for judges to take popular opinion into account.[87] Moreover, under the system of common law, judges relied heavily on precedent, including the earlier decisions of judges in the North and other parts of the South. To diverge from well-established law in a civil case involving a black litigant could have consequences for the many other similar cases involving only white litigants.[88] Finally, judges took pride in their knowledge and execution of the law, and deciding against precedent could undermine this professionalism.[89]

Unlike judges, jury members usually had no formal knowledge of the law.[90] Most southern jurors were working-class white men—farmers, carpenters, factory workers, and laborers. Between 1865 and 1890, a limited number of black jury members also served alongside whites in a number of counties, at times evoking surprise and outrage from white people attending court. In 1889, a Tennessee newspaper commented, "Another negro jury in Charleston released another murderer. Charleston appears to be a very good place to commit murder in. Also a good place to observe the practical workings of negro juries." After 1890, however, black men served on southern juries to a much lesser extent.[91]

Even as judges' politics changed and juries became whiter, black southerners continued to win civil cases in the lower courts against whites. From 1865 to 1899, African Americans litigating civil suits against whites in eight southern state supreme courts had won 50 percent of the time in the initial trial. Although not representative of all lower-court trials involving African Americans, these findings reveal that black litigants succeeded in gaining favorable decisions from members of their communities sitting on juries and from elite white judges in trial courts.[92] Indeed, in Lattimore's case, the judge of the lower court ruled that the clerk of the superior court should undertake a "discovery" to determine if—and how much—Dixon owed his former slave.

If black and white southerners did not win a lower-court trial, they had to decide whether to accept the decision or to appeal to a higher court (or, less often, to try to gain a new trial without appealing). Undoubtedly, the vast majority of cases went unappealed. In many cases black litigants lacked the financial and legal resources or a compelling basis to continue to litigate their cases. Other African Americans continued litigation after opposing parties appealed verdicts in the black litigant's favor. But some black litigants and their lawyers did decide to appeal to higher courts. Between 1865 and 1899, black litigants were the sole party appealing in 44 percent of cases, while white litigants were the sole party appealing in 50 percent of cases. The slightly higher percentage of civil cases appealed by white litigants to appellate courts during this time likely resulted in part from the greater resources whites had to appeal cases.[93]

Choosing to appeal a case demonstrated a belief by white lawyers and their black clients that they had a valid point of law to appeal and a real chance to win their cases before the appellate court.[94] Money undoubtedly also played a large part in the decision. An appeal required paying both court fees and a lawyer. On the other hand, if they won their cases at the next level, some black litigants could receive disputed property, a large sum of money from a will, or damages for a death or injury. The losing party in a case generally had to pay the costs of the case, including the lawyer's fees, so if a decision was overturned, a black litigant might not have to pay such costs.[95] Although most black litigants seem to have been primarily concerned about the economic implications of their cases, a few potential black appellants may have seen a decision to challenge lower courts as exercising their right to appeal to a higher governmental entity. The willingness of white lawyers to take part in these challenges made their appeals even more significant.

At different periods in time, some states had intermediate courts that losing parties could appeal to before appealing to the state's highest court. In the vast majority of appellate civil cases examined, though, black and white litigants appealed from county trial courts directly to the state supreme court. After a decision by the lower court to initiate a discovery to determine if and how much he might owe his former slave, for instance, Thomas Dixon appealed to the Supreme Court of North Carolina. State supreme courts were charged with reviewing decisions of the lower courts in their state, and when they found errors in the lower courts' handling of a case, they were to reverse the decisions. In addition, if two lower courts produced conflicting decisions, the state supreme court was charged with interpreting which decision reflected the law of the state.[96]

During the second half of the nineteenth century, the cases appealed to appellate courts throughout the nation often dealt with property and debt, reflecting the continuing importance of land in Americans' financial holdings and the still largely undeveloped state of the US credit system. A study of the case loads of sixteen representative state supreme courts between 1870 and 1900 found that approximately 26 percent of the cases sampled dealt with debt collection, 21 percent of cases dealt with property (not including estates), 11 percent of suits were appeals from criminal cases, 10 percent of cases claimed personal injury, and 6 percent of cases were suits over wills and estates.[97]

Black litigants brought certain kinds of cases to southern appellate courts much more often than such cases occurred in the general litigation of such courts. Often the cases that black southerners were especially able to litigate did not threaten the status quo or actually upheld whites' interests. Between the end of the Civil War and the turn of the century, for instance, slightly over one-third of cases (36 percent) litigated between black and white southerners in the appellate courts examined involved inheritance and bequests—far higher than the 6 percent nationwide figure for such cases. In most of these cases, black litigants claimed property from the wills of former slaveholders, thus appealing to the right of white southerners to leave their property to whomever they chose. Another quarter of suits litigated by African Americans against whites between 1865 and 1899 (25 percent) were over transactions, contracts, or property disputes unrelated to wills or fraud (see Table 2.1). At times, such suits claimed black men's and women's rights in bold terms. Yet the relatively small number of these suits and black southerners' continuing political power in many parts of the South made them acceptable to southern courts.[98] In these different kinds of appellate civil suits between black and white litigants, the amount of money involved varied, from cases involving only small amounts of money to suits over tens of thousands of dollars.

State supreme courts had varying policies about what constituted grounds for an appeal, which changed over time. Generally, throughout much of the nineteenth century, they had little discretion in deciding whether to hear the cases appealed to them. This varied across states, however, and laws within the same state repeatedly changed.[99] At certain times in certain states, appeals courts were obligated to hear every case that was appealed. Before the year of Dixon's appeal, the Supreme Court of North Carolina would have automatically taken his case. At different periods, certain states allowed only specific kinds of "errors" to be grounds for an appeal. The North Carolina State Constitution of 1868, for instance, now limited appeals to "matters of law or legal inference."[100] As Dixon's

Table 2.1 **Types of Civil Cases Between Black and White Southerners in the Eight State Supreme Courts Examined, 1865–1899**

Subject of Cases	1865–1877	1878–1899	Total, 1865–1899	Total Percentage of Cases, 1865–1899
Apprenticeship	18	0	18	8%
Racial justice	1	12	13	6%
Fraud	3	13	16	8%
Inheritance/bequests	50	27	77	36%
Personal injury	4	31	35	17%
Property dispute	11	12	23	11%
Transactions/contracts	20	9	29	14%
Grand total of all cases (including some not listed here)	108	104	212	

lawyer successfully argued that this case had a legitimate appeal on a matter of law, the appeals court agreed to hear the suit.

In much of the US South during the decades after the Civil War, state supreme courts like North Carolina's consisted of panels of three to six justices whom the state's citizens had elected to terms of about eight years. At times, state legislatures elected appellate court justices or governors appointed them to their posts.[101] During the higher-court proceedings, new testimony was rarely introduced. Occasionally, the lawyers appeared before the state supreme court to present their briefs or answer questions. In large part, though, the judges relied on the transcript from the lower court to decide the case.[102]

In 1869, when the Supreme Court of North Carolina heard Dixon's appeal, five justices sat on the court. The chief justice had been on the court for 21 years, whereas the other four justices had all been elected in the 4 years since the Union Army had occupied the South and sympathized with the Republican Party. Despite the court's Republican leanings, all of the justices had been born in North Carolina and had practiced law there for decades.[103]

Both lawyers drew heavily on precedent in presenting their arguments to the court of appeals. Dixon's attorney cited five previous North Carolina appeals court cases to show that the "contract" in which Dixon agreed to protect the notes was "void." According to the attorney, as "the defendant as master, in law" owned Lattimore when the slave gave him the notes, he also owned the notes.

Bynum went back to Roman law, explaining that Lattimore's earnings as a slave were similar to the slave's *peculium* under Roman law, "a specified and limited amount of property he was allowed to hold for the comfort and convenience of his family." Bynum then reframed antebellum southern law to aid his case, writing that in that period courts "lean as far as possible to the support of the slave." He cited several antebellum and wartime precedents in which southern courts had ruled in favor of slaves' right to property and one post-emancipation case much like Lattimore's. "The cases show," he wrote, "that the Court has never held that property of a slave, acquired by consent of the owner, belongs to the master." Finally, he attacked the antebellum laws that had forbidden slaves from making contracts or suing over economic matters: "The disability to make a contract or sue was incidental and collateral to the state of slavery, of arbitrary policy, not of natural right."[104] Through his brief, Bynum rewrote the history of slavery to favor his client and challenged what many white southerners viewed as the natural state of things.

After hearing a case, higher-court judges issued their decision.[105] From 1865 to 1877, African Americans received favorable rulings in 64 percent of the cases involving white and black litigants in southern state supreme courts, reflecting their revolutionary access and leadership in county, state, and federal government during much of this time. Yet from 1878 to 1899, black litigants continued to win, achieving a favorable ruling in 54 percent of their appellate suits (see Table 2.2). In almost two-thirds of these favorable rulings between 1865 and 1899, the higher court was upholding a decision of the trial court; in approximately one-third they were reversing a decision of the lower court.[106] Perhaps even more significant, state supreme courts were more likely to reverse decisions against African Americans and uphold decisions for African Americans than they were to do so for the white litigants in these suits.[107] By the numbers, the likelihood of overturning a lower-court decision in these cases was similar to the chances in other cases throughout America; the rate of reversal in appellate civil cases between black and white southerners from 1865 to 1899 paralleled those in state supreme courts nationally during this time.[108] Moreover, despite variation among different states, these patterns held throughout the South. African Americans lost more civil cases against whites than they won in only two of the eight state supreme courts during the three and a half decades after the Civil War.[109]

Indeed, in 1869, the Supreme Court of North Carolina issued its decision in the case of *Lattimore v. Dixon*, unanimously upholding the lower court ruling that the clerk of the superior court should undertake a "discovery" of how much Dixon owed his former slave. Justice Edwin Godwin Reade, who wrote the opinion, had opposed secession but had served in the Confederate States Congress

Table 2.2 **Appellate Civil Cases Between White and Black Litigants Won by Black Litigants in the Eight Southern State Supreme Courts Examined, 1865–1899**

Period	Cases Won by Black Litigants	Total Cases	Percentage of Cases Won by Black Litigants
1865–1877	69	108	64%
1878–1899	56	104	54%
Total, 1865–1899	125	212	59%

and then as a North Carolina superior court judge during the war. His opinion decidedly favored the former slave. "The simple story in the plaintiff's bill strongly moves the conscience of the Judge to give the relief which he seeks," he wrote. "We are clearly of the opinion that all the [promissory notes] . . . which the defendant had received for and on account of the plaintiff, at any time, even when he was a slave . . . were held in trust for the plaintiff." [110]

The matter then rested upon the shoulders of the superior court clerk. After taking evidence from a number of the parties involved, the clerk concluded that Dixon owed Lattimore $365.95.[111] This conclusion satisfied no one. Both Dixon and Lattimore again filed suit. This time, the county court decided that Dixon owed his former slave considerably more than the clerk had allotted. Dixon appealed, and in 1871, two years after the original suit, the state supreme court once again heard the case. There, the justices decided that the evidence was too unclear to go against the clerk's conclusions, and conceded only an extra $15 to Lattimore. Several newspapers around the state briefly noted the suit in long lists of the cases heard by the North Carolina supreme court that week, but made no mention of Lattimore's race. In the end, Lattimore received only a portion of what he thought Dixon owed him. Dixon, however, had to pay his own costs for litigating the case as well as almost $400 to his former slave.[112]

Abner Lattimore's attempts to regain his money were finally over. It had been a long journey spanning over a decade. He had first tried nonlegal means. While jailed during the Civil War, he had convinced his former owner's business partner to write a letter on his behalf asking for the return of the notes. After the Emancipation Proclamation was issued, he had tried to use it as leverage. When new laws granted him citizenship, he had appealed to these new rights in his communications with Dixon. Two years earlier, in 1866, he had appealed to the Freedmen's Bureau. Finally, after all these avenues had failed, he had decided to turn to the courts. But the lower-court trial had brought an unsatisfying conclusion. Only after two separate hearings by the state's highest court had he finally received a definitive outcome.

Throughout the South, other African Americans—many of them only recently free—successfully negotiated the complicated procedure of the courts. The reliance of courts on precedent helped black litigants to win suits against whites over well-established areas of the law such as property and contracts. Black litigants also successfully brought appeals of their cases over issues of procedure. But the tradition-bound nature of the legal system made the courts a difficult channel to use to change the direction of their society. Despite their success in certain types of civil suits claiming their own individual economic rights, black southerners found it challenging to bring suits seeking rights for all African Americans.

Undoubtedly, black litigants like Lattimore could not have used the courts without the support of white lawyers, witnesses, judges, and juries. But working with whites had consequences. White lawyers limited the kinds of cases black southerners could litigate and shaped the arguments they could make. The important role of white witnesses gave preference to suits in which whites agreed to testify. And to gain favorable outcomes, black litigants tailored their testimony to white juries and judges, presenting themselves as more loyal or ignorant or humble than they really were.

Despite African Americans' surprising success litigating civil cases in southern courts, there is no question that they were most successful litigating and winning certain kinds of cases. Analyzing the kinds of cases they most frequently litigated in appellate courts reveals important clues about why they were able to continue to participate in the courts during this time. The next chapters tell the stories of the black men and women who managed to bring the right kind of cases to southern courts, hire the right lawyers, and give the right kind of testimony in court. In short, these were the legal successes of the postwar South, even though they did not always win their suits. Examining these cases reveals the opportunities within the courts for black southerners as well as the all-too-present limitations in the types of cases that black litigants could litigate and win.

3

Challenging Whites' Bequests

In May 1859, 17-year-old William Walker set off for Liberia on the ship *M. C. Stephens*. His father, Francis Walker, had been one of the wealthiest slave-owners in Burke County, Georgia. His mother had been one of his father's slaves. Three years earlier, Francis Walker had died, leaving behind an estate worth around $30,000, including 2,000 or 3,000 acres of land. As he had never married and had no legitimate children, his brother and many nephews and nieces no doubt expected to inherit much of his property. To the great chagrin of his white relatives, Francis Walker's will emancipated his seven enslaved children and their four mothers and directed all of his property to be used to settle them in the African country of Liberia. A court sustained the will, allowing the emigration to move forward.[1]

After a long journey by sea, Walker and his family arrived in Liberia, where they became farmers and began new lives. When the American Civil War broke out 2 years after their arrival, Walker and his family probably followed the news with intense interest. They no doubt heard about the emancipation of southern slaves and, later, the revolutionary reforms of Reconstruction. They had a personal stake in these events as their former master's brother, Moses Walker, had failed to disburse the majority of the funds left for them to use in Liberia. The court sustaining the will had ordered them to be regularly paid interest from the estate and to be given their share of the estate when they came of age. Instead, their former master's white relatives seemed to have kept the money for themselves. Taking note of the new rights of black Americans, William Walker and his family decided to sue their white relatives for the remaining portion of the estate in US court.[2]

Francis Walker had not been alone in trying to leave property to people he enslaved. In the antebellum South, slaveholders occasionally used their wills to emancipate their own children or especially favored slaves. At times, such manumissions may have been to resolve doubts or guilt slave-owners harbored about the institution of slavery. Allowing slaves the opportunity to gain their freedom through hard work and loyal service was also used to motivate them. But the existence of free black men and women posed a fundamental challenge to the institution of slavery. A system built upon the relation of blackness to bondage could not stand if large numbers of free black people resided in the South. Many white southerners worried, too, that free people of color could incite slaves to violence, provide them with weapons, or help them to escape.[3]

To limit the numbers of free blacks, then, slave states passed laws controlling and limiting the emancipation of slaves. Over time, these state manumission laws repeatedly changed. Generally, in the early American Republic, southern slave-holders could choose where to emancipate their slaves. As a result, newly freed black people frequently remained in the state where they had been enslaved.[4] By the middle of the nineteenth century, state laws often required slavehold-ers to gain special permission from the courts or the legislature to emancipate slaves. If they did allow manumission, states commonly required that slaves be emancipated to a free state or to Africa.[5] Southern states also frequently required slaveholders to pay for their former slaves' relocation and to provide funds for their former slaves to settle in their new homes.[6] This was not out of charity or kindness; state legislators wanted to make sure that free black men and women left the South and did not come back.

As the laws changed, many slaveholders desiring to free their slaves revised the language of their wills in accordance with the law, requiring their slaves to move north or to Africa to gain their freedom.[7] To comply with the law, their wills left significant bequests to those emancipated, which former slaves would receive once they arrived at their destination. Once black Americans gained their freedom during the Civil War, former slaves who had been sent to Liberia or were scheduled to emigrate litigated suits to try to gain the funds that had been left for their emigration. In postwar courts, their suits appealing to white men's last testaments often fared well with judges and juries of white southern-ers, who sought to uphold the right of white Americans to do what they wished with their property upon their death.

The idea to relocate free black people to Africa had originated in colonial America. Wrestling with the contradictions between the new nation's claims of freedom and his own and other Americans' status as slaveholders, Thomas Jefferson argued as early as 1776 for the colonization of black Americans. Later, as president, Jefferson continued to discuss colonization with other leaders, and in 1811 he supported the United States' establishing a colony of black Americans in Africa. Black Americans also made their own proposals for relocation. As early as 1773, three slaves requested that the Massachusetts colonial assem-bly emancipate them so they could move to Africa. In 1815, a black ship cap-tain named Paul Cuffe transported a group of thirty-eight African Americans to Sierra Leone, and black Americans also expressed interest in immigrating to Haiti at the beginning of the nineteenth century.[8]

During the nineteenth century, one organization, the American Colonization Society (ACS), dominated the emigration movement. The members of the ACS worked to send black Americans out of the country for different reasons. Southern slaveholders belonging to the ACS worried that a free black presence undermined the system of slavery. In contrast, the mostly white antislavery leaders belonging to the ACS during the organization's early years generally viewed an African colony as a refuge where black Americans could be equal citizens. Yet both saw a bleak future for free black people who remained in the United States. As a result, free people of color largely united against the ACS's promotion of emigration to Liberia during the antebellum period. Most of the black people sent to Liberia by the ACS before the Civil War were slaves emancipated on condition of their emigration.[9]

In 1820, the ACS led its first group of black Americans to the western coast of Africa and, with the support of President James Monroe, bullied the local African government into ceding them land, which they named Liberia. Despite settlers' high rates of dissatisfaction and many deaths because of the inhospitable location, the ACS continued to bring settlers to the colony for the next 25 years. Liberia became an independent republic in July 1847, governed by a president and congress of black American settlers. Largely through the efforts of the ACS, nearly 13,000 black American settlers had relocated to Liberia by the early 1860s.[10]

Black southerners—if they had any choice in the matter at all—often faced extraordinarily hard decisions about migration. For the more fortunate, slaveholders' wills gave them a choice between finding freedom in the North or emigrating. Even going to the North required them to leave their families and friends and everything they knew. But many other final directives would emancipate slaves only if they moved to Liberia. Potential emigrants had often discussed Liberia with their masters or emigration agents and had sometimes heard from people who lived in the African country or had returned from there. What they learned about Liberia's high rates of disease, lack of adequate food, and harsh farming conditions made at least some question whether freedom was really worth the cost.

In many cases, slaves had little choice in the matter. For one thing, a will had to be declared valid by a probate court for it to be carried out. If the will was invalidated, the slaves would not be emancipated. Even if the court sustained a last testament, the executor or administrator of the will had to carry it out. Such men were generally close friends or relatives of the testator who had been judged trustworthy to carry out his last wishes. At times, executors followed wills and transported slaves to their new home; at other times, they did not.

If the executor did carry out the terms of a will directing slaves to be eman-cipated and sent to Liberia, slaves were typically sent on ships operated by the ACS. Upon arrival, many slaves were surprised at the rough physical conditions. Despite the negative reports many had heard before their voyage, they were often unprepared for dense forests filled with leopards. The lack of animals to pull plows or wagons also made farming more labor intensive than immigrants expected. The high death rates of new American immigrants to the colony came as a shock as well. In the early years, the ACS reported that 20 to 25 percent of the colonists regularly died of "acclimating fever" and other tropical diseases during their first years in Liberia.[11]

Some new Liberian settlers managed to maintain contact with their former circles in the South. William Walker's party continued to exchange letters with their former master's brother and executor, Moses Walker. One year after arriv-ing in Liberia, one of them wrote to Moses, expressing unhappiness with his new country. The white executor noted in a message to the ACS, "I have just recd a letter from Green Walker informing me of the death of Six of the Walker peo-ple . . . those that are there are not Satisfied." The executor did not mention that his own refusal to remit the rest of the Liberian settlers' trust probably played a part in their dissatisfaction. These discouraging communications from Liberia influenced the opinions of both Moses Walker and his slaves about the African republic. Moses Walker also had enslaved children, whom he considered send-ing to Liberia upon his death. In his 1859 letter to the ACS, though, he explained that he had decided against emancipating them to Liberia: "I have declined sending my people to Liberia in consequence of the sickness of that country." Furthermore, his slaves reportedly refused to go, after having heard discouraging news from Francis Walker's former slaves.[12]

Other former slaves managed to use their continuing ties with the US South to gain valuable supplies for their new lives in Liberia. In another case that would end up in a southern courtroom, Kentucky slaveholder F. W. Urey sent twelve former slaves to Liberia in 1858. Before their departure, Urey appointed his favored slave, 47-year-old Daniel Urey, as head of the settlement party. He would make the journey along with his 33-year-old wife, Phereby, and their children.[13] A few months after the emigrants arrived, F. W. Urey received word of Daniel's Urey death. He sent a letter to the ACS that same day, explaining his reaction to the news, "His family were great favorites with us. His Wife is a very delicate woman with five small children and we cannot bear the idea of her struggling with them and are determined to bring them back and Educate the children here and send them back when they grow up and get their Education. I am by this Mail writing to them via England to come back."[14] He sent regular letters to the ACS about the family's situation, writing a week later that he wanted to send Phereby Urey and her children back home "in the cabin of whatever Ship. They come in and well cared for and I will pay all expenses. . . . Mrs. Urey is extremely anxious to get them here."[15] Former slaves took advantage of this continued communication, while at times asserting their independence. Emancipated, and living on a different continent from her former master, newly widowed Phereby Urey chose not to return to the United States. F. W. Urey explained in a letter that she "thinks she can . . . get along" in Liberia. At the same time, Phereby Urey used this relationship with her former owner to gain a number of expensive supplies. In the letters they exchanged over the next several years, she asked for (and received) supplies to set up a shop, material to build a house, and paint for a local church, as well as garden seeds and provisions. F. W. Urey's wife Perucey also made Phereby and her family clothing and sent it to Liberia with the other supplies. Nonetheless, F. W. Urey did not trust Phereby Urey implicitly, and, on at least one occasion, asked the ACS about the necessity of the items she requested.[16]

Even if a will provided for emancipation to Liberia, many black southerners never received their freedom. At times, courts did not sustain the testator's will. Despite southern courts' interest in protecting property rights, they also had an interest in upholding the system of slavery. Emancipating slaves and providing them with property could weaken this institution. Therefore, if proof could be provided that some of the will's provisions went against established law or the testator had been of unsound mind or unduly influenced when he wrote it, the will might be invalidated. Wills could fail, too, if they had not been properly signed or, in the case of verbal directives, if no witnesses could be produced. In other instances, executors failed to execute wills benefiting slaves.[17] White heirs might keep the money set aside for emigration for themselves, realizing that slaves had little leverage to enforce the will's provisions. The Civil War also emancipated some slaves before the will could be carried out.[18] Less frequently, slaves refused to accept their freedom, preferring to remain enslaved at home rather than experience an often short and difficult life in an unknown country.[19]

Few slaves could gain access to southern courts to contest a will. Even though slaves had the right to bring suits over their freedom in certain instances, many of the litigants who contested wills emancipating slaves before the Civil War were white. In one Kentucky case, a female slave-owner directed in her will that her slaves be emancipated and sent to Liberia or a free state. In 1846, after her death, her white brothers and her executor contested the will. The court affirmed their challenge, and the African Americans remained enslaved. But in 1860, the slaves mentioned in the will attempted to become parties to the case, hiring a white lawyer who submitted their petition to the court. Despite their efforts, the court refused to allow them to take part in the case.[20]

In a few exceptional cases, emancipated slaves litigated cases in antebellum courts to prevent their relocation to Liberia. In Tennessee, several emancipated slaves took advantage of a law passed in 1854 stating that emancipated slaves "who from age or disease were unable to go with safety" to Africa would not be required to emigrate. One such litigant, 59-year-old Harry Turk, petitioned a local Tennessee court in 1857 to allow him to remain in the state as "at his advanced age a removal to Liberia or any portion of Africa would be tantamount to a sentence of speedy death from the effect of the climate." Turk produced multiple witnesses who testified as to his character and the negative effect of the Liberian climate. The county court ultimately ruled that because of Turk's age "it would be dangerous and hazardous for him to be removed to the western coast of Africa." In 1859, another Tennessee slave brought a petition for an exception to the migration requirement for emancipated slaves. He convinced the local court that he was "much attached" to his family, who remained enslaved, and wanted to continue living with them.[21] Such cases remain the exception. Most slaves had little legal recourse to facilitate or prevent their immigration to Liberia.

After the Civil War, black southerners could no longer be sent to another country against their will. Instead, former slaves turned to the courts to gain bequests they had been left in white men's wills. Southern courts heard a disproportionate number of African Americans' suits over white men's wills between 1865 and 1899 compared to such suits' incidence in court caseloads. While suits over wills made up about 6 percent of state supreme court caseloads around the nation during this time, approximately 36 percent of appellate cases between black and white litigants in the courts examined (77 cases) involved disputes over the bequests white southerners left African Americans in wills or trusts.[22] Slightly over one-third of these cases involved bequests of money and property left to black southerners by white employers or former masters in the years after emancipation. Almost two-thirds of these suits over white men's wills involved bequests that had been left to emancipate slaves.[23]

Because of the often rigid laws over emancipation in the antebellum South, a number of these suits involved bequests left for emancipation to Liberia. Between 1865 and 1899, of the forty-seven southern state supreme court cases between white and black litigants over wills manumitting slaves, seventeen suits involve wills emancipating slaves to Liberia. After the Civil War, the emigration directed in slaveholders' wills became an avenue for free men and women to gain property from the heirs of the masters for whom they had worked for so many years without pay.

Undoubtedly, cases like these over white southerners' wills formed a significant proportion of African Americans' postwar appellate cases because they rested upon the established law about how property should be distributed after a testator's death. A long history of precedents supported carrying out valid wills and fulfilling the testator's intentions. Perhaps even more important, these cases appealed to the rights of white men to leave their property as they pleased, just as

much as they dealt with the right of black litigants to gain property.[24] By bringing such cases, black litigants sought to turn a legal system that had long protected white men's property to their own advantage.[25]

In two of these cases, former slaves who had settled in Liberia crossed the ocean
again after the war to claim funds left in slaveholders' wills.[26] As citizens of a
black republic, Liberians had gained experience exercising their rights in the
legal and political realms. They felt empowered to stand up to their former masters, as Phereby Urey demonstrated in her refusal to return to the United States
after her husband's death, despite her former master's requests for her to do so.[27]
Their experiences in Liberia may have also emboldened Liberian residents to
claim their bequests in southern courts.

In 1878, one such Liberian, William Walker, borrowed several hundred
dollars to sail to the United States. After landing in Philadelphia, he took a
train to Georgia. There, he managed to hire several white lawyers to represent
him and the other legatees in a suit to regain the outstanding portion of the
bequest Francis Walker had left them in his will. One of his lawyers, 37-year-
old Michael P. Carroll, practiced general law in Burke County, Georgia. Unlike
some lawyers, Carroll does not seem to have been wealthy. Born in Maryland
and having served in a Virginia company of the Confederate Army, he did not
have long-established ties to other planters in the area.[28] The prospect of gaining a large portion of Francis Walker's estate seems to have been enough to
persuade him to take on a case against one of the region's most established
white families.

Walker's lawyers filed a suit against twenty-four local white men and
women, the heirs and relatives of Francis Walker's executors. The petition
explained that Francis Walker's will directed all of the testator's estate to be
used to settle his former slaves in Liberia. The document then alleged that the
executors had failed to give the black legatees the estate they were entitled
to and had instead "wasted and mismanaged said Estate and appropriated a
greater portion thereof to their own use." Walker's attorneys asked for the heirs
of the estate's executors to "answer and account to Complainant for the assets
and property of said estates which have come into their hands and possession
or control."

The case came to trial over a year after William Walker arrived in Georgia.
William Walker's lawyers argued that Francis Walker's will had not been properly carried out. As proof, they introduced a copy of the will into evidence and
called to the stand several white witnesses to back up their claims. William
Walker took the stand as well to assert his own right to the estate. He began by
affirming his identity as a son of Francis Walker and a legatee under the will. He

next explained the executors' failure to carry out the will, testifying that none of the black plaintiffs "ever received any interest money from Francis Walker's Estate. . . . Nothing was ever paid me when I got of age."

But even as he made these assertions about money owed by the white defendants, his testimony evidenced familiarity and associations with them. While the familial relationships among southerners across the color line were often spoken about only in whispers, Walker—perhaps as a result of his time away from the South—boldly referred to the white defendants in his testimony as "The defendants, my cousins." He added, "I know pretty well all of Defts" and then mentioned information he had learned from the defendants since his arrival about how they had inherited the land in dispute and how much it was worth. Additionally, he testified that the defendants had "carried me from Augusta" when he had arrived there by train. Extraordinarily, his white cousins were willing to provide him details about the contested land and transport him to their county after his arrival from abroad, even as they fought with him over the thousands of dollars at stake.

William Walker's testimony hints, too, of the rough life he and his fellow legatees experienced in Liberia, noting that at least five of the other legatees had died in Liberia. At the same time, he demonstrated a measure of pride in his country, saying that while he was a farmer in Liberia, "All of us are not farmers there." Perhaps sensing that he might appear less threatening if he had no plans to stay in the area, William Walker also told the court that he had come to Georgia only to regain the value of his father's property and planned to return to Liberia.

The white defendants denied all of the charges, arguing that the more than $16,000 remaining in the estate had been invested in Confederate currency during the Civil War. When the South was defeated and Confederate money lost all value, they claimed that all the money in the estate was lost. John Jones, a lawyer who had advised the executors, testified that Moses Walker had been hesitant to take Confederate money and had taken it only after an act had been passed authorizing executors to do so. Jones concluded: "I knew Moses Walker well. He was as honest as the days are long. If ever a man did attempt to faithfully and honestly discharge a trust—he did." The defense's claims thus directly contradicted the arguments of William Walker and his legal counsel.[29]

Many more trials involved former slaves who had been directed to emigrate to Liberia but never made it there. Despite a will ordering their emancipation, they had remained enslaved in the South until the Civil War. Emancipation and the changes wrought during Reconstruction now allowed black southerners to make their own decisions about whether to leave the United States. Unsurprisingly, every former slave in a postwar court case who had been directed by a master to go to Liberia chose not to relocate to Liberia after the Civil War. For many of them, Liberia remained a place where they had been ordered to be sent against their will. In the cases that took place during Congressional Reconstruction, many black people also undoubtedly hoped that real change had come to the South.[30]

Instead, these former slaves sought to gain the bequests set aside for their emigration without moving to the African country. They used the wills directing their emigration to reopen or begin cases claiming the property designated to fund their settlement.[31] They and their lawyers would have to convince the court that the funds were not irrevocably tied to their status as slaves and planned emigration. To do so, their cases frequently appealed to the law of bequests, southern courts' respect for property rights, white southerners' ideas about race, and their own new legal rights.

A range of these strategies made an appearance in the suit of one group of freedpeople in DeSoto County, Mississippi, who brought a suit against the executor of their former master's estate. In 1850, Abner Cowan had written a will directing that after his death "all and every of my Negroes slaves male and female with their increase shall be sent to Africa under the direction, and Superintendance of the American Colonization Society then to become and remain a free people." To pay for their travel, Cowan ordered his executors to collect his debts and sell all his property. They were then to give the resulting funds to his former slaves for their "use and benefit" upon "their arrival on that Continent." [32]

Abner Cowan did not die until 1864. At the time of his death, the area of Mississippi in which he lived was a no-man's-land between the lines of the Union and Confederate forces. Eight miles to the North, federal troops amassed, occasionally sending scouts and raiding parties down. Fifteen or twenty miles in the other direction, the Confederate forces gathered. The Cowans' land was at times too dangerous for the local sheriff and tax collector to visit. Although the county probate court continued to hold sessions, its records were "scattered," the court clerk later explained, "Some at TB Jones and Some at Dockeys about Eight miles west. They were put there for preservation from the depredations of the Federal Soldery."[33] In the chaos of the war, Abner Cowan's last wishes were not carried out. Instead of gaining their freedom through emancipation to Liberia, his slaves found freedom from the war.

Three years after the war ended, in May 1868, Cowan's executor filed a petition with the DeSoto County Probate Court to sell land from the former slaveholder's estate. The executor planned to give the funds from the sale to the former slaveholder's surviving white relatives. But the white slaveholder's will had not directed any of his estate to be given to his white relatives; instead the entirety had been left to his slaves for their emancipation. Realizing this, the former slaves listed in the will and their children—thirty-five black litigants in all—hired a lawyer, L. V. Dixon. Dixon then filed a petition in June 1868 requesting that the court allow them to become parties to the suit. The petition was granted.[34]

To appeal to the law, black litigants' petitions for bequests often highlighted the testator's intention, one of the most important legal considerations in deciding how a will should be carried out. Like many other cases, the Cowan suit sought to show that it was the testator's intention for them to have the funds, and thus they should receive them even if circumstances had changed. The lawyer for the former Cowan slaves began his petition with this argument: "It was the manifest intention and prevailing desire of the testator that Respondents who had faithfully served him during his life time as his slave and who had contributed to his comfort care and happiness . . . should enjoy after his death the bounty thus bestowed upon them by his said will." The emigration provision had been included in the will only to comply with state law, the petition asserted, and "the intention of the testator may be fully carried out without this requirement."[35] As well as seeking to put intention on their side, such claims spoke to white southerners' deep reverence for the property rights of the testator. Perhaps just as important, by aligning their cases with wealthy (but deceased) local white men, this legal strategy appealed to whites' sympathies for one of their own.

Black litigants and their lawyers further sought to gain the support of those deciding on their cases by presenting the images of people of color that white southerners desired. Frequently, their suits sought to gain the sympathy of white judges and jurors by emphasizing their loyalty and faithfulness as slaves. Even though the US Army was fighting in the area where the slaveholder had lived, the former Cowan slaves' petition stated, "your respondents adhearing to their ancient duty and love for the said testator who had ever been kind and considerate toward them they remained with him—laboring for him and sustaining him in all his orders and directions as dutifully as at any time during their bondage and so continued until the period of the death of their said master in April 1864." After their master's death, the petition continued, "they have remained upon the homestead plantation of said testator doing the best they could under the direction the said Stamps and other friends of the said Cowan decd to the present time."[36] Not only did the case portray the Cowans as faithful slaves before the war, but it said they had stayed loyal even with Union troops nearby and after receiving their freedom. During the first years of Reconstruction when this trial took place, such sentiments must have been reassuring to whites who longed for the antebellum way of life and hoped to re-create it as much as possible in the postwar South.

Even as they appealed to whites' racial attitudes, former slaves' petitions often asserted their new rights as citizens as well. The former Cowan slaves' lawyer cited the 1865 Constitution of the State of Mississippi, the 1866 national Civil Rights Bill, and acts of the Mississippi legislature to show that his clients were now citizens of the United States and "capable of buying selling holding having and inheriting property as other citizens of the United States might or could do." Almost all black litigants and their lawyers in such cases also argued that these new rights allowed black litigants to receive property from wills without immigrating to Liberia. According to their lawyer's petition, the former Cowan slaves now had the right to "inherit and take the estate so bequested to them by the Said Testator A. B. Cowan freed from any and all conditions of departing from the State of Mississippi and residing in the said Continent of Africa." The black litigants' petition then requested that all of the remaining land in the estate be "delivered over to them as tenants in common."[37] After years of being denied rights in the civil courts, these black litigants drew on their new legal rights to gain property within this very system.

White heirs and executors took these cases very seriously. The location of the Cowan case—DeSoto County, Mississippi—had been especially hard hit by the Civil War. Continually raided during the war, by the war's end the county's fields were empty and a number of its businesses had been burned. In December 1867, a local history notes, "a county meeting was called to discuss the prevention of famine in the months ahead."[38] The white Cowan relatives, then, had good reason to fight the black litigants' claims to money set aside for their settlement in Liberia. Their lawyer filed a petition for them to become parties to the case, which the court granted. Then, like other whites who had such suits brought against them, they argued that wartime emancipation nullified black litigants' claims to the money set aside for Liberia. According to the documents their lawyer submitted to the court, "by the laws of Mississippi at the time of Cowans death the said Will was absolutely null & void & the estate descended to the heirs at law." Moreover, their attorney asserted, none of the new laws referred to by the black litigants "give to said negroes any rights under said Will."[39]

White witnesses played an important role in such suits. Although some undermined former slaves' claims, others testified in favor of black litigants. Often all of these witnesses had known the black litigants for many years. In the Cowan case, a local white man who had served as the probate court clerk during the war testified against the black litigants, saying that the area in which the former slaves had lived had still been under Confederate power at the time of their master's death and so the will was void. [40] In contrast, a white doctor in an 1874 case over an antebellum will testified for the black plaintiffs, noting that he had known several of them "since I came to the County 36 years ago." He attested to the character of the black litigants, telling the court, "I know nothing against the character of the Slaves for the want of Industry or obedience." When he was attending their master in his final illness, he continued, "his negro man Perry waited on him, & I have never witnessed a more faithful attention than he gave his master up to the time of his death."[41] The participation of local white people like this court clerk and doctor played an important part in litigants' success or failure in their suits.

More often than not, between 1865 and 1899, black litigants gained favorable rulings from appeals courts in their civil suits against white heirs and executors over bequests. Out of seventy-seven such cases, forty-four resulted in favorable rulings for the black litigants. In cases specifically over bequests tied to emigration to Liberia, black litigants won 61 percent of their southern state supreme court cases.[42] But southern courts also disagreed over these cases.

Indeed, the local and higher courts decided differently in Walker's case. In 1879, the Burke County, Georgia, Superior Court, presided over by a former Confederate Army officer, heard the case.[43] In the end, the jury decided in favor of the former slaves, finding the executor of their former master's estate "guilty of moral fraud or corruption" and declaring that he used the trust funds for his own use. The jury found that the former slaves were entitled to recover almost $40,000 from the property of the defendants.[44] When the white heirs appealed the verdict to the Supreme Court of Georgia in 1880, however, the higher court overturned the earlier decision, and ruled in favor of the white litigants. The court declared that the executor had been justified in investing the funds from the estate in Confederate bonds and was not guilty of fraud in disposing of the money. William Walker returned to Liberia empty-handed.[45]

The Cowan case had a different outcome. The local Mississippi probate court had directed that the testator's property be sold, without giving the former slaves who had been left the property in the will the opportunity to keep it. When the former slaves appealed to the Supreme Court of Mississippi in 1872, the appeals court reversed the decree of sale, instead sustaining the will and discharging the formerly enslaved men and women from the necessity of moving to Africa to benefit from the will. The court declared that the black litigants could keep the land for themselves, although the estate would still remain subject to the testator's debts.[46]

Many factors went into these different courts' decisions. Undoubtedly, a state's political dynamics played a role. In 1880, at the time of William Walker's case, Georgia was solidly Democratic. In contrast, when the Supreme Court of Mississippi issued a decision in the Cowan suit in 1872, Republicans still held power in Mississippi. But some African American litigants lost such cases under Republican-controlled governments and others won after Democrats took back power in their states. Clearly, other factors played a part in decisions.

Arguably, the interests of whites were mixed in such cases. On the one hand, judges and juries took into consideration the interests of wealthy white men— a group the judges were likely a part of and jury members aspired to join. By upholding the will, they would reaffirm the white elite's property rights and their ability to leave their property to whomever they chose. In cases in which the black litigants were the children of the white testators, a ruling in their favor would also uphold the privilege of white men to continue to have sexual relations with black women and provide financially for the children they had with these women.[47] On the other hand, by leaving money and property to their black children or other African Americans, white testators disrupted the southern social order. Judges and jury members may have been concerned that ruling in favor of the illegitimate black children of a white southerner would normalize interracial sexual relationships. More personal, local factors played a part in weighing this as well: judges' and juries' views of the impact of such a bequest on the white community, their opinion of the testator himself, and their understanding of his relationship with the people to whom he left bequests.[48]

With whites' interests in such cases not completely clear, the ability of black litigants and their lawyers to craft their cases to appeal to the law undoubtedly played a part in the outcome. Judges considered how their petitions fit with established legal understandings about wills and property and with how past cases had ruled on these questions.[49] In particular, many judges concurred that the intent of the testator was central to legal understandings of how to interpret a will. Thus, a Tennessee judge wrote, "It is said that the great rule in the construction of wills is, that the intention of the testator . . . is to prevail and have effect."[50] The importance of intention in such cases led a number of judges to decide that if a testator wanted his slaves to receive his property and had mandated emigration to Liberia only to comply with existing law, the freedpeople could obtain the bequest without relocating. Following this logic, the judge deciding the Cowan case wrote, "When it can be ascertained, effect will be given to the intention of the testator . . . . It is apparent upon the face of the will under consideration, that there were in the mind of the testator two paramount purposes, to which he gave clear and decisive expression, viz.: the freedom of his slaves, and their pecuniary benefit." The judge then concluded that these two purposes could be carried out by allowing the freedpeople to receive the bequest without relocating.[51] To support their discussions of the law of bequests, the courts cited precedents from antebellum case law and English common law. In the Cowan suit, the higher court cited precedents relating to the ability of emancipated slaves to receive legacies in the antebellum South and Catholics' ability to inherit property in England. The judge also noted earlier inheritance cases involving only white southerners.[52]

Judges' and jury members' understandings of property rights undoubtedly played a role as well. For centuries in America, property ownership had been viewed as inextricably related to personal liberty and economic growth. In the antebellum period, the most prominent jurists agreed that the government's protection of property rights was necessary for freedom and economic progress. After the Civil War, courts throughout the nation continued to give special respect to the protection of property rights.[53] Judges in southern state supreme courts were no exception. In 1872, one Kentucky Appeals Court judge explained his ruling in favor of a group of former slaves by writing that "property will not be confiscated by the state except for some violation of law; and to hold that these appellants can not recover this fund would in effect to declare it forfeited to the commonwealth."[54] Other decisions in favor of black southerners' receiving bequests from white testators' wills also frequently cited the primacy of the right of property.

At times, then, a desire to uphold the interests of white elites, together with a strong commitment to guard the law of property and follow the intention of a testator—aided by the petitions and testimony of black litigants and their lawyers—were enough to overcome the personal reservations of white judges and juries toward black litigants seeking funds or property set aside for their emigration. Although many of these judges likely did not like the idea of black southerners gaining large amounts of property, weakening the rights of white testators to prevent black litigants from gaining this property was often too high a price to pay. In the larger picture, deciding against the individual white litigants in these cases upheld rights for other whites around the South.

In the end, the large number of postwar cases involving white slaveholders' wills underscores both the opportunities and the limits that African Americans encountered in southern courts. Even as black litigants' reliance on white testators' wills opened doors for them in southern courts, other legal claims often remained more difficult to pursue. Undoubtedly these cases enjoyed special favor from southern judges because they appealed to white testators' right to leave their property to whomever they chose and were firmly based in laws of property and inheritance. Moreover, they continued the cases brought by slaves petitioning for their freedom in antebellum courts by appealing to white southerners' wills. In many ways, therefore, these suits were rooted in tradition. Yet they also expose the radical changes in freedpeople's lives as they seized their new legal rights and faced the families of their former masters in the courtroom. After years of servitude, enforced expatriation, and blocked wills, African Americans could—at times—finally gain the bequests for which they had waited so long.

The Law of Contracts and Property

In 1870, black sharecropper Moses Summerlin's wife died. The grief-stricken widower failed to tend his cotton and corn crops for several weeks, but soon returned to the fields to harvest his crops in rural Coweta County, Georgia. But when he asked William Smith, the white owner of the land, to aid him in hauling the cotton and corn he had harvested, Smith refused. Instead, he accused the sharecropper of producing only half of the crop he would have produced had he worked more diligently. As a result, the landowner said, he was laying claim to the entire crop, instead of splitting it, as they had previously agreed.

Under slavery, an accusation of laziness would most likely have led to a beating for the accused slave. But in 1870, Coweta County was occupied by the Union Army. Soon after Summerlin picked his crop, the county elected a black man to represent them in the Georgia Legislature.[1] And as a result of the changes that had occurred during Reconstruction, freedpeople could defend their actions in a court of law. In response to the landowner's accusations, Summerlin hired a lawyer to bring a civil case against Smith. During the ensuing trial, the black sharecropper explained in his testimony that Smith refused to pay him his portion of the crop, as outlined in the contract. "He cultivated Said land in a farm like manner except about three weeks," the freedman told the court, "where it fell back a little owing to the fact of the death of plaintiffs wife." Moreover, the freedman claimed that Smith himself had caused damage to the crop by not erecting an adequate barrier between his pasture and the crops, thus allowing mules and horses to trample the fields for 2 months. Summerlin also appealed to the terms of the contract, testifying that although the white landowner was obligated to help him cart the crop in the contract, "he asked Defendant three times for a wagon to haul cotton and defendant refused and that he asked several times for a wagon to haul corn and was refused."[2]

～～

Five years later, in 1875, Mary Gracie sat in a courtroom in Selma, Alabama, answering a series of invasive and humiliating questions regarding her relations with her former master, James Johnston. Johnston had repeatedly had sexual relations with her while she was his slave. It is unclear whether he had used physical force to gain his ends, but whether he did so or not such relations were exploitative and coercive. As a slave, she had had no legal protections from sexual advances by her master. Under antebellum law, enslaved women did not have possession of their bodies and so their bodies could not be used against their will; they were presumed to be "always willing."[3] With the law essentially condoning sexual violence against them and under the control of the master committing the sexual coercion, female slaves' options in cases of sexual advances were extremely limited.[4] Sometime shortly before or during the war, Gracie gave birth to a son as a result of her master's actions.

For the first 2 years after emancipation, Gracie worked as a housekeeper and seamstress on Johnston's plantation, 4 miles outside of Selma. The balance of power in majority-black Dallas County was beginning to shift though. In the years immediately after the war, Selma served as the base for the Freedmen's Bureau and Union Army in the region. Then, in 1867, when Congressional Reconstruction set in, the army appointed a Republican mayor in Selma. Local whites' worst fears were realized when the town's new Republican leadership installed a black police officer and began to register black voters. Before long a former slave was elected to represent Selma in the Alabama House of Representatives, and another black man took over as clerk—and then briefly as judge—of the criminal court.[5]

As these changes occurred, in fall 1867, Mary Gracie left Johnston's plantation and moved to Selma to work as a seamstress. She continued to sew for Johnston for the next 6 years, however, and occasionally took the train to his plantation. When she wanted to buy a house 4 years later in East Selma and found that the owners did not want to sell to "coloreds," she turned to Johnston for assistance. Johnston agreed, and sometime in 1871, he used her earnings to buy the house and lot on her behalf. An economic depression hit the area soon after, though, causing Johnston's farming and sawmill venture to flounder. When he died in 1873, Johnston was about $1,500 in debt. To recoup the money owed them, his creditors claimed the house in which Gracie lived, claiming Johnston had given the lot to her for her services as a "mistress," rather than as part of a legitimate business deal.[6]

In the ensuing civil case, Mary Gracie sought to prove the home had been purchased with her own earnings so she could maintain her ownership. Her prewar sexual relations with her former master followed her into the courtroom, though, as his creditors painted her reputation as poor because of her antebellum liaison. This poor character, according to the creditors, was evidence that the lot had been given to her for sexual favors, and so the creditors had a claim on the land. Mary Gracie in turn, tried to separate herself from allegations of a continuing sexual relationship with Johnston after the war and claimed the property as her own.[7]

From Reconstruction to the end of the nineteenth century, African Americans throughout the South asserted their right to participate in the postwar economy on an independent, equal basis as they litigated some of the same types of civil cases that white litigants brought against one another. Between 1865 and 1899, 25 percent of civil cases between black and white litigants (fifty-two cases) in the eight southern appellate courts examined took place over contracts, trans-actions, or property disputes unrelated to wills or fraud. Forty-two percent of these cases involved black and white participants who had known one another as master and slave. Some black litigants, like Summerlin, demanded fair payment for work they had completed, fighting white landowners' efforts to cheat them out of their portion of the crop. Others, like Gracie, disputed transactions of land or livestock they had conducted with white southerners.[8]

These cases first entered the courts during the era of Reconstruction, as southern politics were upended. A number of these suits involved economic dis-putes between blacks and whites that had begun during the period of slavery; other suits took place over economic disagreements ensuing after the Civil War. Throughout Reconstruction, black southerners were often successful in these types of suits, winning the majority of their appeals between 1865 and 1877 in the eight appellate courts examined.[9]

The end of Reconstruction did not halt these cases. After the Reconstruction period concluded, black and white southerners continued to bring cases over contracts, transactions, and property against one another.[10] Like earlier cases, these civil suits between 1878 and 1899 frequently involved black and white southerners who had known one another since slavery. The economic dealings they highlighted, however, were less likely to have taken place before or during the Civil War and often involved economic disputes that originated after the war. Despite the largely Democratic control of southern states during this period, black litigants continued to obtain favorable decisions from appeals courts in the majority of these kinds of suits.[11] Only at the dawn of the twentieth century, as black men were largely disfranchised in the South, did these kinds of cases in which black litigants presented themselves as economic equals of whites largely disappear from southern courts.

In many ways, these were the most radical civil cases that black southerners were able to bring to appellate courts in significant numbers after the Civil War. Other cases, in which black litigants appealed to white men's wills to gain prop-erty, echoed slaves' suits for freedom in the antebellum South and appealed to white people's property rights. In contrast, in the cases examined here African Americans fought for their own right to fair economic transactions and labor contracts, claiming the same rights claimed by whites. But these cases were too few in number to significantly change the trajectory of labor relations in the South. Even as a few black litigants won cases over labor contracts or property disputes in the courts, millions more worked under coercive labor contracts or were cheated out of their property without the opportunity for legal redress. Nevertheless, these cases had the power to change individual black and white people's economic dealings and gave black southerners an opportunity to present their own visions for the postwar economic landscape.

In the wake of the Civil War, different groups put forward very different ideas about black southerners' place in the southern economy. A number of white northern leaders argued that the key to black southerners' new freedom would be to replicate the northern system of free labor. Black southerners, they said, should have the right to freely enter into contracts in which they agreed to labor and the employer agreed to pay them. In December 1865, for instance, radical Republican Congressman Charles Sumner told the US Senate that the key difference between freedom and slavery was the ability to make contracts. Following this, the Civil Rights Act of 1866 declared that the right of contract and the right of property were rights of citizenship.[12] According to northern leaders, the courts would play a key role in regulating this system of contract. As President of the American Anti-Slavery Society Wendell Phillips explained, "A man here makes a contract, and, if he does not keep it there's a court. If he does keep it and is not paid, there is a jury.... That is liberty."[13]

White southerners put forward contrasting aims for the new economic regime. Most of all, most white people in the South did not want black southerners to gain their own land. They had seen—in Haiti and then in the British Caribbean—that when land was available to former slaves, they quickly left behind plantations and became small, independent farmers. Only on a few islands like Barbados, where white elites retained possession of all of the land, did plantation agriculture profitably continue. As a result, in public meetings and in letters in 1865, white southern planters agreed not to allow freedmen to obtain land. Instead, they contended, black southerners needed to continue to work whites' land.[14] Many white southerners also insisted that former slaves would not work without coercion. Because of their race, planters argued, African Americans did not have the self-discipline or ability to respond rationally to market forces necessary to participate freely in the southern economy.[15]

Black southerners had their own conceptions about what labor should look like under freedom. After a lifetime of enslavement, what many newly free black men and women wanted most of all was the ability to control their own labor. Women wanted the option to remain at home with their children or to coordinate outside work with family caregiving. Men wanted the ability to choose what they planted, when they worked, and how they spent their free time. In a still largely agricultural economy, many black southerners believed that the best way to achieve this independence would be to have their own land.[16]

As these divergent visions of the South's economic future collided, conflict was inevitable. During the first years of Reconstruction, white southerners sought to force African Americans into oppressive labor contracts that mimicked the system of slavery as much as practically possible. If black southerners did not enter into these contracts, they were arrested and jailed for vagrancy. Often these contracts required laborers to obey their employers' every command, even outside of working hours.[17] Many contracts during the first years of Reconstruction sought to control former slaves' behavior as well, requiring them to be honest, not to quarrel or swear, and sometimes even to cook communally. Frequently, these contracts also mandated that black workers would be paid only if they completed a full year of labor; thus if an employer terminated a contract early, laborers would not be paid for any of their work throughout the year.[18]

Some black southerners responded by engaging in strikes and collective action. In 1866, a group of "colored washerwomen" in Jackson, Mississippi, put together a price code for their work and conducted a strike.[19] Other black men and women initially refused to enter into coercive contracts with white planters. In South Carolina, rice planters reported after the war's end that African Americans would not contract for the upcoming season.[20] Many freedpeople also resisted gang labor, choosing instead to work independently as sharecroppers and tenant farmers. Although most black southerners did not have the funds or legal access to bring their economic grievances to court, some were able to seek redress before the Freedmen's Bureau and the courts.

In the midst of this conflict over the direction of the southern economy, white northerners forced a number of compromises into place. As Republicans in Congress took over control of Reconstruction, many of the most coercive aspects of labor laws and contracts in the South were abandoned. At the same time, white northerners gave up many of their ideals of a system of free contract in the South, focusing instead on getting black laborers to work. During Reconstruction, the federal government also never gave black southerners the land that they desired. This left freedpeople dependent upon whites to earn a living, just as white southerners had desired. Bureau officials often noted freedpeople's desire for economic independence with a measure of consternation. One Bureau agent noted in 1867 that in many of the complaints brought to his office the freedmen claims "that being a partner in the concern he ought to be allowed to exercise his own judgment in the management of the plantation, that he ought to be permitted to loose time . . . that he ought to have a voice in the manner of gathering and dividing the corn and cotton and in the ginning, packing and selling of the latter product." The agent added, "The freedman . . . often claims an independence and freedom of action, which is justly incompatible with the faithful performance of his duties as a laborer and servant."[21]

The northern occupation of the South gradually ended state by state, ceasing entirely by 1877. But even as white southerners rewrote coercive labor laws into state statutes, black southerners' resistance to gang labor had earned them a measure of independence. Instead of working directly under the supervision of their employers like northern factory workers, more and more black southerners worked the land of whites as sharecroppers and tenants, receiving in return a portion of the crop at the end of the year. Often their share of the crop paid only for their food and clothing or caused them to fall more deeply into debt. But under this arrangement, they were able to control their own time, maintain gardens, undertake other household production to make extra income, and arrange work and family needs.[22] Similarly, as they came before the courts to seek redress for financial grievances or contest whites' claims against them, black southerners sought to assert principles of fairness and independence in their financial dealings with whites.

As African Americans turned to the Bureau and state courts to litigate economic grievances, they were no doubt influenced by their experiences with the market during slavery. Many slaves had experienced being hired out; others had traded horses, cattle, or baked goods either with their masters' permission or secretly. Mary Gracie, for one, had experience conducting dealings in the free market during slavery. Shortly after gaining her freedom, in 1866, she had almost $400 in savings—a sum so large her former master borrowed money from her.[23] During slavery, some slaveholders had also asserted the idea that slaves and masters had reciprocal duties to each other. In the postwar South, some freedpeople transferred this concept into their new lives as they made contracts with former masters and brought claims against them when the contracts were not fulfilled.[24]

In bringing civil suits, freedmen and freedwomen were likely influenced as well by Bureau agents' ideas about the freedom of contract and by the economic views of black southerners who had been free before the Civil War. One mass meeting of free people of color in New Orleans passed a resolution in March 1865, declaring, "There is no practical liberty for the laborers, without the right of contracting freely, and voluntarily, on the terms of labor." This ability to enter into a contract for their labor of their own free will, they continued, "is the unquestionable attribute of every freeman." African Americans also formed opinions about the law of contract as they took part in labor disputes with white landowners in the wake of the war.[25]

At the same time, black litigants were all too aware of the dangers they faced by bringing such cases against whites. Challenging white landowners and employers risked violent retaliation.[26] At times, such cases undoubtedly made it more difficult for the black litigants to obtain work afterward. As a result of a case, litigants might also have to move.

Despite these dangers, Moses Summerlin clearly saw the courts as a viable path to justice. When his employer would not give him his portion of the crop, he hired two white lawyers to bring a case against the landowner. As a defendant in her case, Gracie did not have a choice about going to court, but she worked hard to present her side of the story. She hired three local white lawyers, including former Confederate officer and independent Democrat Sumpter Lea, to represent her. Lea had formerly worked for Johnston's creditors in their attempt to regain their debts, but having become convinced of the merit of Gracie's case, he switched sides to represent her and testified on her behalf. Lea had considerable clout around town, having recently stepped in to help manage city government while the Republican mayor experienced health problems.[27]

These cases were taken on by white lawyers and allowed to enter southern courtrooms in part because they drew on well-established areas of the law. Frequently, these suits cited decisions from suits litigated by white southerners or drew on the opinions of noted legal authorities about these topics.[28] Such cases were easier for white lawyers to take on, as they could gauge the strength of the litigants' legal claims based on outcomes in similar cases. They were less threatening than suits over racial justice, as litigants focused only on their own claims. Judging by the disappearance of these kinds of cases when black men lost the vote at the beginning of the twentieth century, black political power played a role in these cases being heard as well. Allowing some of these cases into court also helped white southerners portray their legal system as fair and just, even as the suits inconvenienced the few white litigants involved.

But these suits could be far more subversive than they seemed at first glance. In their testimony, some black southerners presented to their communities a reality in which African Americans exercised economic independence even before emancipation. In a number of cases after the Civil War, former slaves testified about their experiences in the free market during slavery. Some black litigants' suits in the postwar South debated sums of money slaves had gained through trading during the antebellum era.[29] A freedman named Bedford Nelson testified that, while enslaved, he officially worked as a blacksmith, but he also "kept a bakery and sold cakes on public days and placed cakes in several groceries for sale in Crab Orchard." He kept a share of the profits that he made as a blacksmith and pocketed all of the profits from his side business.[30] Another former slave, Bristow Bugg, asserted in a civil suit against his former master that he had saved $75 in gold as a slave and had given money to his master to buy land on his behalf.[31] Such testimony refuted claims that African Americans did not have the ability to negotiate the workings of a capitalist economy on their own.

As they confronted white people in the courtroom over economic dealings, black litigants also presented themselves as able to function competently and independently in the postwar economic realm. Moses Summerlin, for one, testified that he had employed "five or six hands" to work for him in cultivating the 75 or 80 acres of land owned by the defendant. He showed business competence in discussing the crop yield, saying that "upon said land he produced eight 8 Bales of Cotton weighing from four hundred and fifty to five hundred pounds and one hundred and forty Barrels of Corn and twenty three hundred Bundles of fodder weighing from one and a quarter to one & a half pounds each." Similarly, another black litigant in a civil litigation case testified that, upon taking possession of a lot he had bought, he had "continued making other and more substantial improvements," including building and operating an "ice Cream saloon with all the necessary and suitable conveniences" on the property.[32]

Black women, too, asserted their economic competency and ability to negotiate the free market in their cases. When making a loan of $348 to her former master, Mary Gracie testified that she "asked him to pay me compound interest." Furthermore, she told the court about her improvements to the property: "I bought an out house from Lizzie Taylor for which I paid her twenty five dollars and had it moved on the said lot. I paid about Twenty five dollars for having this outhouse moved and put up. I paid Lundee nine dollars for painting paid Henry Graves fifteen dollars for painting paid Jim Pinkney fifteen dollars for brick and for fixing the front yard. I paid fifty-two dollars for lightening rods on the house. I gave Mr Semple one hundred ninety or Two hundred Dollars to pay Mr Noland for building the house." According to her testimony, she also paid $14 to put up a "hen house," $92 for window blinds, and $215 to put up fences around the lot.[33] She clearly kept detailed financial records to be able to testify to the court with such specificity.

In their civil cases, many black litigants also argued for contracts to be equitable and fairly enforced. Since the end of the civil war, the system of coercive labor contracts had played a large role in limiting the economic options of black southerners.[34] Yet in these cases, black southerners at times used the very contracts that so often limited them to assert their economic rights. In a number of cases that reached southern appellate courts, black litigants' lawyers drew on the established law of contract to gain legal justification for their clients' claims. Summerlin's lawyer, for one, alleged that the white landowner had broken his contract with his client and introduced the contract itself into evidence.

In their testimony, many former slaves employed the language of contracts to aid their cases. Moses Summerlin testified that, although the white landowner was obligated to help him cart the crop in the contract, "he asked Defendant three times for a wagon to haul cotton and defendant refused and that he asked several times for a wagon to haul corn and was refused."[35] Because of the landowner's refusal to carry out the terms of the contract, Summerlin implied, the black sharecropper could not be blamed for the lower crop yields. Mary Gracie also used the language of contract to support her case. To show the court how she earned the money to pay for the property, she testified, "In January 1866 Mr Johnson contracted with me to work for him and keep house for fifteen dollars per month." Other black litigants used similar language. One freedman told the court that he had brought the cotton he had grown "up to Mr. Barges gin house according to the contract between me and Mr. Barge" and had demanded the share of the crop the contract promised him.[36]

Black litigants further asserted that white southerners should deal honestly with them in property transactions. In 1878, Primus Cooper brought a suit against his former master T. P. Pease, alleging that Pease refused to give him the title of land he had purchased. Cooper explained that, in 1866, he approached his former master about buying a lot of land. Pease supposedly agreed to sell him the land, but refused to name the exact price, saying only that "his price would be the same or a little more than the price" of other lots in the area, which were being sold for $40 or $50. The newly free man agreed to the sale, took possession of the lot, and built a house there. During the next decade, Cooper testified, he continued to pay his former master for the land and each time Pease told him, "a little more money Primus and you will get your title." By 1878, the freedman claimed to have paid his former master $390. Pease responded that the lot's purchase price of $250 remained largely unpaid, stating that most of the money the former slave had paid had gone for supplies, leaving only $50 paid on the lot. Frustrated by having paid almost eight times the real value of the lot and still not having received the title, in 1878 Cooper brought a suit against his former master. In his testimony, the freedman claimed that he did not owe Pease any money and everything he had paid was meant to go toward the purchase price of the lot.[37]

Black litigants also worked to shift the basis of economic relations with whites from violence and coercion to the rule of law. At times, black sharecroppers risked their lives by revealing to the courtroom the brutality that laced their economic dealings with former masters and other whites. Summerlin saved his most explosive allegation for the end of the day of testimony. He told the court that when he had asked the white landowner to give him his portion of the crop, Smith ordered him out of the yard and told him "if he came back he would kill him." In making such allegations against a white man, Summerlin must have known that he was putting his own life and livelihood at risk. But as he made these claims, he put forth a vision in which black people would be fairly rewarded for their labor, and law would prevail over force. Similarly, one witness for Mary Gracie, a freedwoman named Agnes Pinkney, testified that Gracie's former master Johnston had repeatedly tried to coerce Mary Gracie into loaning him much of the approximately $400 she had saved. Mary Gracie told her, she said, that "Mr. Johnston had kept after her until she had loaned all of that money to him at last." Upon finally obtaining the money, Pinkney said, Johnston told her, "hell agnes I have got that money out of Mary at last." Pinckney clearly painted this loan as coercive, a bold claim for a black woman to make in a courtroom.[38]

As they recounted the ways they had been wronged and asserted their own economic vision, black litigants, along with their witnesses, often worked to shape their testimony and suits so white juries and judges would rule in their favor. Some framed their testimony to support the legal arguments that their lawyers were making. Gracie's case sought to prove that the property in question had been bought with her own money, rather than being given to her for sexual favors. As a result, Gracie sought to stress her independence from her former master throughout her testimony. In particular, Gracie emphasized how her relations with her former master shifted after the Civil War, testifying: "In January 1866 Mr Johnston contracted with me to work for him and keep house for fifteen dollars per month." Additionally, she elided the paternity of her son, stressing that Willie was "my son" and never acknowledging that he was Johnston's as well. Her friend Agnes Pinkney further supported her legal claims by characterizing Mary Gracie as "a very industrious girl she worked both in and out of her own home, she saved a great deal."[39]

As they worked to support their cases, black litigants had to contend with the weight of the past. In many instances, they brought cases against whites in communities where they had lived for decades and in some cases had been enslaved. Judges and juries often determined how much they could trust litigants' and witnesses' versions of events based on testimony about their character and reputation. Although whites had not recognized slaves as legally accountable for their morality and reputations, they judged freedpeople's reputations as important elements of their cases.[40] Often, events that occurred before the Civil War influenced testimony about black people's reputations. Prewar liaisons with white masters, though coerced, made the reputations of black women especially vulnerable.[41]

Mary Gracie's reputation in the neighborhood, in which her prewar sexual experiences figured largely, played an important part in the assertions of one of the white creditors that she had received the property in return for sexual favors. Although he did not have personal knowledge of postwar sexual relations between Mary Gracie and her former master, he told the court "She is reported to be a kept mistress." The white creditor also attempted to tarnish Gracie's reputation by testifying that two black men, a butcher and a tailor, "appear to be warm friends of Mary Gracie and say that they visit her frequently both in the day time and at night."[42]

Yet even as white southerners drew on black women's pasts to discredit them, freedwomen testified in their own defense—a marked shift from the era of slavery when the law had not recognized them as having a reputation to defend. In the face of accusations during the trial that Johnston had bought the lot for her

as his mistress, Gracie expressed innocence, saying "When a woman of easy virtue says she has 'a friend' among men I don't know what she means." Judging by
her efforts to refute this charge against herself, however, she knew very well the
nature of the accusation.[43]

As white southerners faced off against their former slaves and other African
Americans in the courtroom over contracts, transactions, and property disputes, they put forward their own plans for the postwar southern economy. At
the same time, the adversarial nature of the legal process and the long-standing
ties between many of the litigants could force whites to admit that certain black
southerners were able to negotiate the free market on their own—and had been
doing so even before emancipation.

In some postwar cases against former slaves, white witnesses and litigants
acknowledged the transactions and trades they had made in the antebellum
period with those very slaves. In Abner Lattimore's case, his lawyer and the
opposing counsel interviewed a number of men with whom Lattimore had conducted a variety of business dealings as a slave, including selling horses and making loans. Despite the extralegal nature of some of Lattimore's actions, the white
witnesses confirmed his trades and their participation in them in a matter-of-
fact manner. Abner Spangler, a white man to whom Lattimore was hired out in
1858, told the court that Lattimore "had some $700. or more in notes principal
which he placed in my hands for safe keeping." Other white witnesses testified
that they had borrowed money from Lattimore while he was still a slave. One
man explained: "I borrowed $100 from Abb Lattimore gave him my note & held
it till I confessed judgment to him for the same it was $120 or $125 when I paid
it."[44] In recognizing slaves' involvement with the market, white southerners inad-
vertently revealed that some black people had been managing their own labor
and finances long before emancipation.

Even as they manifested a general belief about the economic incompetency of
black southerners, the shared history of past transactions with former slaves they
were meeting in court could lead white litigants to recognize economic ability in
that individual. Before emancipation, one such litigant, Ann Nelson, had worked
closely with her slave, Bedford Nelson, as he operated a shop offering his blacksmith services to the community. When she came before a court after the war
to testify in a dispute over some of Bedford's earnings as a slave, Ann Nelson
said of her former slave: "he is shrewd and sharp and very watchful of his own
interests."[45] Such sentiments undermined attempts to gain control over the labor
of black southerners.

White witnesses who testified on behalf of black litigants also often spoke
to their economic competence. The local sheriff himself testified for Moses
Summerlin, stating that when he went to deliver legal documents to him, the

black sharecropper had shown him the corn he had raised. "Some of the corn seemed to have been bitten," the sheriff told the court, supporting Summerlin's claim that Smith had allowed his animals to destroy parts of the crop. Despite the existence of some rotten corn, the sheriff continued, "some of the corn was as fine as witness ever saw." A local white farmer testified for another black litigant in his suit against a white landowner. "I saw the darkies crop," the white witness told the court, "the part of the crop next to the house was very good—I will say it was fine for that year . . . I am sorry to state it but the negro made more cotton than I did or as much."[46]

While black litigants brought many of these suits over economic dealings against whites, whites also brought some of these suits against African Americans.[47] The fact that such disputes could not be settled through coercion or violence forced white litigants to confront black southerners' new power. For instance, Bristow Bugg reportedly bought a piece of property from his former owner, Walter Towner, while still a slave. After the war, Towner stated that he "demanded the place of Bugg" but "Bugg refused to yield the possession." Towner then filed an ejectment action against his former slave and won in the lower court. Unwilling to give up possession of the land, the freedman appealed to the Supreme Court of Georgia, which ruled in his favor.[48] Other white southerners brought similar cases against African Americans over contracts and transactions.[49]

Whether they served as plaintiffs or defendants, white southerners took such cases seriously. William Smith, the white landowner against whom Summerlin brought a suit, defended his treatment of the black sharecropper, telling the court that "he never refused to let Plff [plaintiff] have a wagon to haul up corn, that plaintiff applied for wagon on one occasion to haul cotton and defendants wagon was engaged and he told him he could get it next day." Moreover, he said, he "never told Plaintiff to leave his yard, and that if he came back he would kill him." In addition, Smith testified about his attempts to gain the best possible price for the cotton: "had the cotton ginned some time in January 1871 and tried two markets Sharpsburg and Newnan and the most he could get offered for it was eight cents per pound." Like Summerlin, Smith appealed to the law of contract, stating that he had "entirely fulfilled his part of the contract" and was "greatly damaged by Plaintiff by reason of the non performance of his contract." Other whites similarly defended their legal claims in the courtroom. T. P. Pease, whose former slave brought a suit against him after paying for land many times over without receiving the title, claimed most of the payments had gone toward goods the black buyer had bought from him over the years. "At the request of said Primus," Pease testified, "[I] furnished him with provisions and wearing apparel and with the distinct understanding that his account should be one and the same." All the payments the black buyer had made, the white man claimed, were "placed to his credit."[50]

In some ways, these cases may not have seemed much of a threat to the fabric of society. Only a few of the countless economic disputes between white and black southerners went to court. When black litigants gained a hearing in a courtroom, their cases often seemed to have little impact beyond the individuals involved in the suit. Whites no doubt realized that African Americans' access to the courts did little to halt the return to coercive labor laws as the North ended its occupation of the defeated Confederacy.

At times, too, these cases could be used to support white elites' ideas about the place of black southerners in the postwar South. In one Virginia case, a black man who had been free before the war claimed that in 1864 he had been whipped by a group of local white men and driven from the county. As a result, he was forced to sell his land for Confederate notes to a white man not involved in his persecution. In a later lawsuit between the buyer and a representative of the black landowner, the higher-court judge opined that "there is no proof the land was not sold for its full value" and ordered that the bankrupt black man pay all of the costs of the lawsuit.[51]

When they did decide in favor of black litigants, white jury members and judges could show the supposed justice of southern courts—eliding widespread unfairness in the labor system and property transactions. Elite judges could also manifest their paternalism, a belief that elite whites would protect African Americans who were unable to look after themselves. One Alabama appellate judge wrote in his decision for a black litigant, that the court had "consider[ed] the circumstances and the representations made by" two white "men of considerable property and standing" that led to the black litigant "reluctantly" being forced to allow his horse to be taken and a broken down mule left in its place.[52]

In other ways, though, these cases were potentially radical and threatening to whites.[53] Despite their seemingly prosaic subject matter, they showed black southerners exercising competence and financial savvy as they participated in the market independently. Many cases also presented black men and women's ideas about economic fairness and justice. Perhaps most disturbingly, these cases gave black southerners a forum to challenge their white employers during a period in which whites were doing everything possible to reestablish their dominance over the black workforce.

The way decisions were made in these cases was another possible cause for concern for white southerners. Although judges were clearly swayed by personal opinions, politics, and other factors, appellate judges also took rules of property and contracts into consideration in deciding these suits.[54] Frequently, judicial opinions mentioned the race of black litigants only in passing and largely resembled judgments on similar matters brought by white plaintiffs against other whites. By regarding African Americans as parties to whom the general laws of property and contracts applied, judges and juries performed a potentially radical action. In an 1899 Kentucky suit, for instance, the black heirs of an elderly African American disputed a transaction the deceased woman had supposedly entered into before her death. The state supreme court justice wrote in ruling for the black heirs, "It has been repeatedly held by this court that the object of the state . . . was to place the decedent and his live antagonist upon a perfect equality, and inasmuch as the decedent could not speak or testify of the transaction," the other party could not either.[55] At times, judges defended their opinions by listing previous suits over property and contracts that had pitted white litigants against one another. In the 1899 Kentucky opinion, the judge cited numerous precedents from other cases in which the transaction in question had been between a living person and a person since deceased. These precedents were not confined to the state of Kentucky, or even to the South, but included cases from the New York Court of Appeals, the Supreme Court of Texas, and the Supreme Court of Florida.[56] Of course, judges' reliance on the established body of law did not always benefit black litigants. But the fact that this was an important factor in the decision posed a threat.

As a result of these many factors, largely white juries and judges reached a range of decisions on these cases. During the Reconstruction era, African Americans won rulings in their favor in 65 percent of cases that dealt with property disputes or transactions (not involving wills).[57] During the 22 years after Reconstruction, black litigants obtained favorable rulings from the higher court in 57 percent of their suits.[58] Even a favorable decision, though, often resulted in black litigants receiving only a portion of the property or funds that they sought.

Summerlin's boldness and economic vision was rewarded, at least in part, by the courts, as a jury in the Coweta County Superior Court ordered the white landowner to pay $113.18 and legal costs to Summerlin. When the white landowner sought a new trial in an appeal to the Supreme Court of Georgia, the appeals court refused his request. In his 1873 opinion, Justice Robert Trippe—a former US congressman from Georgia and a member of the Confederate Congress—explained, "Nor was the verdict so unsupported by evidence as to call for the interference of this Court." This was not a complete victory for the black sharecropper, who had claimed in his suit that the white landowner owed him $508.75 for his labor and crop.[59] But by taking this economic contest out of the realm of threats and intimidation and into the realm of the law, Summerlin shifted the terms upon which he and Smith operated.

Primus Cooper, the ex-slave whose former master had made him pay almost eight times the value of a lot and then claimed it was still not fully paid for, also received a favorable decision. A jury in the local superior court found for the black litigant, and the court ordered the former master to "execute and deliver" a deed for the lot within 10 days and pay for the court costs or be brought before the court on a charge of contempt. Upon losing in the superior court, Cooper's former master appealed to the Supreme Court of Georgia. There, in 1878, the justices of the state appeals court affirmed the decision in favor of the former slave. Chief Justice Hiram Warner was a Massachusetts native who had served on the Georgia supreme court off and on since 1845. Although he had owned over a hundred slaves, Warner had opposed secession and had not fought in the Civil War. His opinion in Cooper's favor reeks of paternalism, stating that "the complainant was the former slave of the defendant, and, as is usually the case, reposed entire confidence in him."[60]

Other black litigants' suits proved less successful. When Mary Gracie's case came before the Dallas County Chancery Court in 1875, Democrats had taken back control of the Alabama state government the previous year. The local court, however, still ruled in Mary Gracie's favor. The chancery court judge wrote that he believed Gracie's claims of financial independence, stating in his ruling, "The evidence clearly shows that by far the largest share of the money paid for the lot and the improvements thereon was paid by the defendant [Gracie], and it is not shown that the same was not her money or that any of it came from Johnston." Although the judge acknowledged that "the reputation of some of the witnesses and of the defendant Mary Gracie and her relations with the deceased are calculated to cast some suspicion upon her claims," he wrote that "they may all be wanting in many of the virtues which adorn civilized and refined society and yet not wanting in truthfulness." When the creditors appealed the case to the Supreme Court of Alabama, a different interpretation of Gracie's postwar relationship with her former master led the higher court to reverse the earlier ruling. In their opinion, one of the appellate judges wrote, "A conveyance to a mistress, or to her and her children . . . intended merely as a provision for maintenance, cannot be sustained against existing creditors."[61] Gracie eventually lost the property she had worked for years to obtain because the higher court believed she received the land as her former master's mistress, despite her attempts to prove otherwise.

In the decades after the Civil War, certain African Americans had opportunities for legal recourse in their economic dealings. Although previously largely unable to defend themselves in economic disputes, these black litigants now put white southerners on the defensive, forcing them publicly to justify their dealings with them. On an individual level, these cases had important implications in the lives of the parties involved. Black litigants gained or lost property, livestock, and significant sums of money based on the courts' decisions. Trials between white landowners and African Americans over economic matters showed whites that African Americans could turn to the courts in their disputes. Yet suits over property dealings and transactions had seemed the most revolutionary of any non–race-based civil suits litigated by African Americans in southern courts. In the end, these suits did not bring the far-reaching transformations that black southerners sought. The southern judicial system, tied as it was to the decisions of the past, failed to usher in broader societal changes. By the end of the nine-teenth century, as these particular kinds of suits came to court less frequently, it was southern society that altered African Americans' cases in state courts.

PART II

CIVIL CASES BETWEEN BLACK AND WHITE SOUTHERNERS, 1900–1950

5

The New South and the Law

In 1897, on a farm near Atlanta, black sharecropper W. H. Weems worked the land of A. W. Barge. The contract that he had signed earlier that year promised the sharecropper half of the crop, with the other half going to the white landowner. After a month of bringing loads of cotton to the cotton gin, Weems repeatedly asked the white landowner to pay him for his portion of the crop. "I said to Mr. Barge my people has to have something to wear, they are naked," the sharecropper later testified. "I held up my foot showing him the only shoes I had and they were not as good as these (showing his shoes to the jury) and I said these are the only shoes I have got in the world. I said I have gathered the crop as fast as I could gather it and I said I have got to have something to live upon." Despite these pleas, Barge refused to hand over the payment, telling the sharecropper, "I haven't got time to settle." Instead, he said he would pay Weems at the end of the harvesting season.[1]

Even as race relations in the South worsened at the end of the nineteenth century, W. H. Weems still viewed white lawyers as people he could turn to in a dispute and the civil courts as a legitimate arena in which to gain justice. After talking with Barge, he consulted "some lawyers in town as to whether I could sell one of the bales of cotton." According to his later testimony, "3 or 4 lawyers" calculated his account with the landowner and then "said you are out of debt and you have a perfect right to sell it." As a result, Weems recalled, "I goes back home and I gets a man to haul [the cotton] . . . to town and I sold it." Around the same time, in early December 1897, Weems initiated a civil suit against Barge to force a settlement of their accounts. When the white landowner expressed concern about the legal action, the sharecropper reassured Barge that "if we come to a settlement I can stop that trial right now."[2]

Instead, the white man took steps to prevent the case. Apparently believing that he could forestall the black sharecropper's civil claim by initiating a criminal case for the sale of the cotton, Barge had a warrant sworn out for Weem's arrest. The warrant claimed that Weems had sold the cotton without permission, appealing to a part of the Georgia penal code that said a sharecropper could not "sell or otherwise dispose of any part of the crop grown by him, without the consent of the landlord." Soon after, the black sharecropper was arrested. Although he lived in Fulton County, he was brought before a judge in nearby Campbell County. Taking advantage of the fact that Weems had no lawyer present, Barge asked the judge to set the bail at $200 and said that "he objected to any person going on the bond who was not worth two thousand dollars over and above the homestead." In response, Weems begged the judge to set the bond at $50, telling him that he had "ten men" who could go on his bond for such a sum. But although $200 was an unusually high bond for such a case, the judge set the bond at the amount the white landowner had suggested.[3]

With such a steep bond Weems was unable to leave jail on bail as he waited for his trial. Instead, Weems remained imprisoned from December 7 until the beginning of March. While in jail, he later testified, "I got sick two or three times . . . laying on the iron, I was not use to it." It got very cold at night, he explained, and "I was surrounded by iron, an iron cage, iron all over us, and we laid on iron." Finally, he gained his release when the Campbell county sheriff posted his bail. The criminal case was then tried, and a jury found the black sharecropper not guilty.[4]

Despite this experience with the southern judicial system, Weems had not lost hope in gaining payment for the crops through the civil courts. Upon his release from jail, he hired the local law firm of Hunt & Golightly. On behalf of their black client, the two white attorneys brought a civil suit against Barge in the City Court of Atlanta for "malicious prosecution." This time, the case would take place in a form chosen by the black sharecropper.[5]

By the end of the nineteenth century, promoters around the South heralded the rise of a "New South" that looked to the future rather than to the past. Managing editor of *The Atlanta Constitution* Henry Grady repeatedly informed listeners that this New South was more self-sufficient, more industrialized, and better able to keep up with the North.[6] "The South has been rebuilt by Southern brains and energy," Grady proclaimed in 1889. "The industrial growth of the South in the past ten years has been without precedent or parallel. It has been a great revolution, effected in peace."[7]

There was some truth to the words of New South promoters like Grady. In the last two decades of the nineteenth century, new factories, saw mills, and mines sprang up all over the South. As a result, in the 1890s, production of raw materials like cotton, tobacco, and coal soared.[8] Between 1880 and 1890 the construction of railroads in the South outpaced the rest of the nation.[9] More people throughout the South were leaving farms and plantations to take up jobs within cities.[10]

But the promoters' rosy accounts left out other inconvenient facts. The South's latecoming industrial development had put it at the bottom of an economy dominated by Northern and foreign capital and manufacturing. The vast majority of the new industry in the South involved producing raw materials such as iron, coal, and lumber that would be shipped to the North or elsewhere to be finished into completed products and sold. The jobs created in the South from industrialization were often poorly paid and involved manual labor.[11] And the rise in railroad transportation resulted in alarming numbers of injuries to passengers and employees and a frustrating dependence on the northern capitalists who largely funded the railroads. Eventually, enthusiastic promotion of railroad construction gave way to a public outcry against railroad companies.[12]

The South as a whole was also still vastly less urbanized than the North. The 1900 census found that only ten percent of southerners lived in cities of 25,000 or more people. The men and women who did leave farms for the city often did so because of the limitations of southern agriculture.[13] Those who remained behind on farms were frequently caught up in a cycle of poor soil, low cotton prices, and high debt. As tenant farmers increasingly planted cotton instead of other crops to try to get themselves out of debt, the condition of their land only worsened and the price of cotton decreased. When traveling through rural Georgia around the turn of the century, black scholar W. E. B. Du Bois encountered a despondent-looking black tenant farmer and inquired, "What rent do you pay here?" "All we make," the man answered. Du Bois mused, "Why should he strive? Every year finds him deeper in debt." The position of renters "has sunk to a dead level of practically unrewarded toil."[14]

Moreover, even the optimistic promoter Henry Grady saw "the race problem" as a "shadow that rests on the South."[15] The country's black population had doubled since the beginning of the Civil War, from about 4.5 million people classified as "free colored and slaves" in the 1860 census to almost 9 million people recorded as "negro" in 1900. At the turn of the century, the vast majority of African Americans—about 8 million people—still lived in the South. While white southerners still outnumbered black southerners by about two to one, in certain areas of the South, black people outnumbered whites.[16]

In some whites' view, African Americans had too much independence. Although most black southerners endured high rents as tenant farmers, approximately a quarter of black farmers throughout the South owned their own agricultural land by 1900.[17] Slightly over half of African Americans over the age of 10 were literate.[18] In addition, the new generation of black southerners—many of whom had never lived in slavery—were not as deferential as white people would have liked. White southerners mourn "the slow, steady disappearance of a certain type of Negro," W. E. B. Du Bois observed, "the faithful, courteous slave of other days, with his incorruptible honesty and dignified humility."[19]

In the eyes of many white members of the Democratic Party, black southerners also still had far too much political power. Despite sporadic violence and
frequent instances of voter fraud in states with especially large black populations,
African American men continued to vote throughout much of the South.[20] All
too often they used this vote to support opposition parties. They sometimes even
swayed elections. At the end of the nineteenth century, white and black farmers
joined forces against white elite interests in the short-lived Populist Party. Some
leaders of the Populist Party, like Thomas Watson of Georgia, openly urged poor
whites and blacks to unite in the name of shared economic self-interest. "You are
kept apart that you may be separately fleeced of your earnings," Watson insisted
in 1892. "You are made to hate each other because upon that hatred is rested
the keystone of the arch of financial despotism which enslaves you both."[21]
Poor white and black farmers belonging to the Populist and Republican parties displaced Democratic officeholders in North Carolina in 1894 and 1896.
In Alabama, Democrats managed to overcome a coalition of white and black
Populists in the 1892 election only through spectacular voter fraud. On the
precinct and county level, too, black voters had the potential to shift elections
throughout the South.[22]

Watching these developments, many white southerners feared that as long
as black men continued to exercise the right to vote, they could help an opposition party gain power. Committing violence and altering election results to
diminish the opposing vote also did not align with the new image of a modern
South in white Democrats' minds. Some worried, too, about the demoralizing
effect that throwing elections would have on white southerners themselves. One
Mississippi man declared, "The old men of the present generation can't afford to
die and leave the election to their children and grandchildren, with shot guns in
their hands, a lie in their mouths and perjury on their lips in order to defeat the
negroes."[23]

As the nineteenth century came to a close, white southern Democrats took
action to permanently strip black men of their voting power. Throughout the
South, they stirred up racial antagonism between poor white and black people.
One of their tactics was declaring there to be a widespread epidemic of black
men raping white women. While there was no evidence of an increase in these
incidents, these claims reignited longstanding fears of black male criminality and
the danger that black men posed to white women. Black men around the South
were lynched for having reportedly raped white women, often based on extraordinarily flimsy evidence.[24]

At the same time, members of the southern Democratic Party turned to the
law to wrest the vote away from black men for good. Some white elites also
hoped to disfranchise many of the poorer whites who supported opposition

parties. Their plan was this: Instead of disfranchising voters at each election through voter fraud and violence, they would prevent the people who would be most likely to vote against them from registering to vote. Southern Democrats faced a dilemma in enacting this more permanent method of disfranchisement. The 15th Amendment to the US Constitution, passed during Reconstruction, prohibited race-based disfranchisement of US citizens. Northern Republicans in Congress could cite this amendment to block any methods that specifically disfranchised African Americans. On the other hand, poor and illiterate white southerners were unlikely to vote for measures that would lead to their own disfranchisement.[25]

To solve this conundrum, between 1890 and 1910, Democratic leaders in the South systematically targeted black and other non-Democratic voters for disfranchisement, without explicitly mentioning race. Meanwhile, they pointed out that they had left loopholes for whites to continue to vote. Their methods evolved over time as they watched what worked in other states and adapted them to their local political environments. As African Americans and poor white southerners had higher illiteracy rates than white southern Democrats, a favored method was literacy requirements. Calculating that those they hoped to disfranchise were less likely to own property, some states inserted property requirements for voting. And knowing that few black tenant farmers had extra cash laying around near election day, every former Confederate state instituted poll taxes that had to be paid for citizens to vote.[26] In 1896, a Mississippi judge forthrightly explained how this worked. The disfranchising convention in his state had acted "within the field of permissible action under the limitations imposed by the federal constitution . . . to obstruct the exercise of the franchise by the negro race." Because they were "restrained by the federal constitution from discriminating against the negro race, the convention discriminated against its characteristics and the offenses to which its weaker members were prone."[27]

As these measures would disfranchise large numbers of poor white voters as well as most black voters, state conventions and legislatures often included "saving" clauses that would allow some poor and illiterate white men to register to vote. Most famous was the "grandfather clause," which allowed citizens to register to vote if they had been able to vote in 1867, before the Second Military Reconstruction Act enfranchised black southerners, or if they were descended from someone who could vote then, even if they didn't meet the literacy or property requirements themselves. Other states included "understanding clauses" that permitted men to vote if they were judged to "understand" a clause of the state constitution, or some other element of the political process, to the election official's satisfaction. These clauses enabled Democratic officials to gain the white support needed to push through more restrictive voting laws. At the same time, "understanding clauses" allowed white officials to refuse to register black men who met the other voting requirements on the grounds that they did not understand part of the political process.[28]

To give these changes the force of law, some states held constitutional conventions to carry out disfranchisement. Other states amended existing constitutions to prevent African American and undesirable white men from registering to vote. Still others passed new laws and taxes to carry out their purposes. As many whites would also be disfranchised, they did all this largely without popular approval.[29] The result was a southern turnout rate at elections in the first decade of the twentieth century of around 30 percent. While voting fell among all groups of southern men, members of opposition parties were significantly less likely to vote than members of the Democratic Party. Southern black men, in particular, found it extremely difficult to vote by 1901 and nearly impossible to gain political office. Poorer, more transient, and urban whites also found it difficult to meet the new voting requirements and were sometimes too humiliated to register under the "saving clauses." The Democratic Party had achieved its long-sought-after goal of effectively destroying its opposition in the South.[30]

As they disfranchised African Americans, white southerners also passed a wide range of new laws extending and formalizing the racial separation that had been occurring in an uneven manner throughout the South since the war.[31] These segregation laws, many whites claimed, brought race relations in line with the new, more modern South. By clearly delineating how people seen as belonging to different races should be separated, white southerners argued that they were managing race relations in ways beneficial for all races and removing confusion from social situations.[32] The move toward greater segregation began in earnest in the late 1880s and 1890s as ten southern state governments mandated segregation in railroad cars. Then, the same legislatures implicated in disfranchising black men passed new laws separating more and more of everyday life for black and white southerners. Soon, elevators, ticket lines, streetcars, drinking fountains, public parks, telephone booths, waiting rooms, and even cemeteries that were not already segregated were often divided by race.[33]

Even as white southerners dismantled the political system built during Reconstruction and legalized widespread segregation, they did not change the structure of the legal system. They viewed black southerners' involvement in the courts as far less dangerous than African Americans entering the polling booth. If enough people voted a certain way, an election could quickly go against them. But the outcome of court cases was controlled by white judges and jury members, who many felt could make the "right" choices.[34] In 1914, Sidney Fant Davis, a white Mississippi lawyer, explained how this worked: "From the letter of our statutes, a stranger might justifiably infer that they applied to all persons within this state, without regard to race, color, or previous condition of servitude, but nothing is farther from the truth." He continued, "The judges, lawyers and jurors all know that some of our laws are to be enforced against everybody, while others are to be enforced against the white people, and others are to be enforced only against the negroes, and they are enforced accordingly."[35]

To ensure that the legal system remained in white hands, black men were chosen less often to serve on juries—and in many southern counties not included at all. To confirm this, in 1900 a 16-year-old white Wake Forest University student named Gilbert Thomas Stephenson sent questionnaires to clerks in southern counties in which African Americans "constituted one-half or more of the population." He asked: "I wish to know to what extent Negroes actually serve on juries, how Negro jurors are regarded by the court and the people at large, whether the number of colored jurors has increased or decreased in late years, [and] what has been the experience of your county as to the satisfaction of colored jurors?" Sixty-five clerks wrote back. Of these, forty-five said that their county did not draw African American men for jury service, unless in error. One Alabama clerk wrote, "Negroes are not allowed to sit upon juries in this county. It sometimes happens that names of Negroes are placed in our jury-box by mistake on the part of the jury commissioners and are ... drawn to serve as jurors; this, however, is a very rare occurrence." The clerk then noted, "Once in the past four years, a Negro was drawn as a grand juror (by mistake) who appeared and insisted upon the court's impaneling him with other jurors, which was done in accordance with law, the court having no legal right to discharge or excuse him. My recollection is he served two days, when he was taken out at night and severely beaten, and was then discharged on his own petition by the court." Other clerks replied that they had used African American jurors until a few years earlier, when the practice had stopped.[36]

Twenty clerks reported that their county still allowed some African Americans to serve on juries. Their counties were spread throughout the South: one county in Florida, three parishes in Louisiana, five counties in Mississippi, one county in Missouri, three counties in North Carolina, one county in Oklahoma, two counties in South Carolina, two counties in Texas, and two counties in Virginia. But most of these clerks acknowledged that black men formed a very small part of their overall jury pool. A Louisiana clerk gave a typical response: "Negroes serve as jurors in this parish to a limited extent. The jury commissioners, when they know of an exceptionally good, honest, sober and industrious Negro, have no objections to placing his name in the jury-box. It is true, however, that the number is very limited .... Out of the 300 names in the jury-box from which we draw out juries, there are about a dozen Negroes." The counties and parishes where black jury service continued in 1900 also frequently noted a drop in recent years in the numbers of black men included on lists of potential jurors.[37]

A number of black men and women agreed with white southerners that the justice system—and particularly criminal courts—would usually rule in favor of whites. Articles and editorials in African American newspapers all over the South in the first two decades of the twentieth century noted discrimination in the courts. When the Supreme Court of Kentucky upheld railroad segregation at the turn of the century, the *Richmond Planet* observed, "The judicial department is tainted from bottom to top with race prejudice." Similarly, in 1910, *The Savannah Tribune* opined, "When the issue is as between a Negro and a white man, and the decision must finally rest with a jury made up of white men there is rarely ever any other result save that which favors the white man." Again, in 1919, the Georgia newspaper declared that trials in Arkansas of African Americans charged with murder "proved to be of the type of those which characterized the semi-civilization of the Middle Ages when the king would say 'Take the victim out and give him a trial, and then take him over and deliver him to the executioner.' "[38]

Prominent African Americans made similar observations. W. E. B. Du Bois remarked, "It was not then a question of crime, but rather one of color, that settled a man's conviction on almost any charge. Thus Negroes came to look upon courts as instruments of injustice and oppression, and upon those convicted in them as martyrs and victims."[39] Even savvy black lawyer Wilford Smith, who devoted years of his life to bringing racial justice litigation to the US Supreme Court, commented, "With the population of the South distinctly divided into two classes, not the rich and poor, not the educated and ignorant, not the moral and immoral, but simply whites and blacks, all negroes being generally regarded as inferior and not entitled to the same rights as any white person, it is bound to be a difficult matter to obtain fair and just results, when there is any sort of conflict between the races. The negro realizes this, and knows that he is at an immense disadvantage when he is forced to litigate with a white man in civil matters, and much more so when he is charged with a crime by a white person."[40]

Black southerners also expressed their disillusionment with the legal system through music. At the beginning of the twentieth century, African Americans in Auburn, Alabama, put their grievances to song: "If a white man kills a negro, they hardly carry it to court, If a negro kills a white man, they hang him like a goat." And in the wake of World War I, one Texas blues singer sang, "White folks and nigger in great Co't house Like Cat down Celler wit' no-hole mouse."[41]

Indeed, in criminal cases, the high conviction rate of black men and women in the South continued. Southern states' continuing practice of hiring out convict labor only compounded the problem, motivating states to convict black defendants to fill their own coffers.[42] Even in criminal appeals to the Alabama and Georgia state supreme courts during the first two decades of the twentieth century, black defendants lost almost two-thirds of the time.[43] Social scientists also noted the high percentage of people of color in prisons throughout the United States. In 1910, African Americans comprised 11 percent of the US population and 34 percent of the convicts.[44]

Nonetheless, during the height of Jim Crow, some black southerners held out hope that the courts—particularly federal courts—could be used to preserve their voting rights and halt the spread of segregation. The courts had sometimes played a part in protecting their property and citizenship during Reconstruction and in the two subsequent decades, and black southerners had not forgotten it. Black newspapers reported civil and criminal cases from around the country in which the courts upheld black rights. When a circuit court judge decided that a Kentucky railroad segregation law was unconstitutional in 1894, the *Richmond Planet* reported: "This is a great victory for the colored people, not only of that state but of the entire country, and it is indeed a source of gratification that one upright judge could be found who would fearlessly deliver an opinion in accordance with the law and the facts." Similarly, in 1920, the *St. Louis Clarion* applauded the outcome of a criminal trial over the Elaine riots by declaring: "The judges of Arkansas may not know it, but by their decision they have put heart in the Arkansas Negro, and said to the absent Negro, come on back home, things are going to get better." Some articles took a nuanced approach, criticizing some court decisions and praising others.[45]

Civil cases were one vehicle to challenge inequality. A limited number of black litigants continued to bring civil cases challenging unequal treatment to local and state courts. Between 1900 and 1920, appellate courts in the eight states examined heard approximately twenty-three civil cases that directly challenged racial discrimination or pursued racial justice. Often such cases were initiated by individuals and sometimes received financial support from others in the community and African Americans shaken by recent political events. At other times, national organizations such as the Afro-American Council or Niagara Movement were behind such suits. Despite their importance, these cases made up only about 10 percent of the total civil appellate cases litigated between black and white litigants in the eight state supreme courts examined.[46]

The individual African Americans and organizations bringing civil suits over racial discrimination often seem to have sought to set precedents that would bring more equality for all African Americans. A number of these cases protested the discrepancies in funding for schools for white children and schools for black children in the Jim Crow South. In 1909, for instance, a black father and tax-payer named Robert Goins sued the tax collector and treasurer of Jasper County, Mississippi. In his suit, Goins challenged the constitutionality of a tax that had been assessed on all citizens of the county, but would be used to benefit only the white high school.[47] Other civil suits challenged new residential segregation ordinances. In April 1911, the town of Ashland, Virginia, passed an ordinance prohibiting white people from moving onto streets where the majority of houses were occupied by African Americans and making it illegal for African Americans to move onto majority-white streets. Several months later, John Coleman purchased a house on Clay Street in Ashland. Although the previous tenant had been a black renter, Clay Street had more white residents than African American ones. Coleman was convicted of violating the ordinance and fined. In response, he sued the city, arguing that the ordinance violated the 14th Amendment.[48]

When such cases did receive a hearing, the outcomes were decidedly mixed. Between 1900 and 1920, black litigants won 43 percent of their racial justice suits.[49] In the South, where the Republican Party was only a shadow of its former self and black men had been almost entirely disfranchised, judges were often uninterested in changing the status quo.[50] Because the law was largely unsettled on the matter of equal rights, it was undoubtedly easier for judges to decide against African Americans in these suits than in cases over property or wills. Yet even in the South, when civil suits over unequal treatment were heard in appeals courts, the formal procedure of the courts led some black litigants to win their cases.

Indeed, in Goins's case over the tax to benefit the white school, the local and higher Mississippi courts both ruled in his favor. The Supreme Court of Mississippi opined: "When the act in question is read in the light of the fourteenth amendment to the Constitution of the United States, its violation of same is too plain for argument." In contrast, both the Circuit Court and the Supreme Court of Virginia ruled against Coleman in his suit challenging housing segregation. In a decision that bundled his case with a similar suit, Virginia's highest court praised the town for recognizing "the grave danger liable to ensue ... from too close association of the races."[51]

At times, civil cases over discrimination heard by southern state supreme courts were explicitly designed to receive unfavorable decisions so that they could be appealed to the US Supreme Court. After Alabama instituted disfranchisement through a new constitution in 1901, Jackson Giles, a former slave and a post office employee in his early 40s, was turned away when he sought to register to vote.[52] In response, Giles and other disfranchised black men organized the Colored Men's Suffrage Association of Alabama, with the purpose of raising money to fund litigation challenging disfranchisement. A circular sent out by the Association explained that "the people of Montgomery county," had organized "for the purpose of raising money to test in the United States district court or supreme court at Washington, D.C., the constitutionality of the Alabama constitution." They needed to raise "$2,000 with which to commence."[53]

Despite his accommodationist rhetoric, Booker T. Washington agreed that the courts were the place to do battle over disfranchisement. Washington secretly arranged and paid for an African American lawyer named Wilford Smith to take on Giles's case. Smith planned a course of litigation in which he would bring several cases in different venues that challenged the disfranchisement of black men in Alabama—three civil cases before state courts, a civil case in district court, and a criminal case in state court. He would craft the cases to lose over federal questions, and then appeal one or more of the cases to the US Supreme Court. In essence, he was throwing as many different kinds of darts as possible and hoping at least one would hit the bull's-eye of reaching the nation's highest court. Right on cue, the Supreme Court of Alabama refused his appeals.

In the end, in 1903 and 1904, Smith managed to appeal three of the cases to the US Supreme Court. But in its decisions the Court shrugged off any responsibility for making a decision on disfranchisement, opining in *Giles v. Harris* that "relief from a great political wrong, if done, as alleged, by the people of a state and the state itself, must be given by them or by the legislative and political department of the government of the United States." In the end, Smith achieved no victories in any of the civil cases over Giles's disfranchisement, although the criminal case heard by the US Supreme Court—which sought to tie disfranchisement to jury discrimination—was a limited success.[54] Other civil cases challenging discrimination before the US Supreme Court at the turn of the century mostly proved unsuccessful.[55]

African Americans also challenged the constitutionality of discriminatory laws through criminal cases in state and federal courts. In many cases, they purposely tried to be arrested as they defied segregation in order to litigate cases over racial discrimination. When the Louisiana legislature passed a law in 1890 requiring "equal, but separate" seating for white and black railway passengers, a broad, multinational base of New Orleans men and women supported a Citizens' Committee in challenging the legislation. They hoped to bring a case to the state supreme court, and, upon losing there, to appeal to the US Supreme Court. Initially, the Citizens' Committee planned to use the arrest of 21-year-old Daniel F. Desdunes for riding in a white car between New Orleans and Mobile, Alabama, to challenge the law. Soon after, though, the US Supreme Court ruled in *Louisville, New Orleans and Texas Railway Company v. Mississippi* that a Mississippi segregation law might not apply to interstate transportation. When it became clear that the Desdunes case would no longer be the right avenue to challenge the Louisiana law, the Citizens' Committee chose a 30-year-old shoemaker named Homer Plessy to initiate a case on an intrastate railway journey. In 1892, Plessy boarded a whites-only train car from New Orleans to Covington, Louisiana. He was arrested, and in the ensuing criminal case, his lawyers claimed that discrimination in railroad travel based on race violated his constitutional rights. As planned, the local Louisiana court and state supreme court ruled against him, declaring that segregation based on race was constitutional.[56]

Plessy then appealed to the US Supreme Court. Upon gaining a hearing in 1896, though, the Supreme Court ruled that state laws requiring racial segregation were constitutional. The Court's opinion reasoned that "If one race be inferior to the other socially, the Constitution of the United States cannot put them upon the same plane." This was only one in a long line of lower federal court decisions ruling that separate did not necessarily mean unequal. Even though the reasoning in the ruling was not new, this decision set a precedent for segregation to continue.[57] Other criminal cases over racial justice that reached the US Supreme Court ended in much the same way.[58]

Even as they often could not litigate or lost cases that focused on aiding all those classified as African American, black southerners continued to litigate hundreds of appellate civil cases that sought benefits only for the individuals involved. Yet these suits also reflected the increasing loss of rights and racial separation occurring in the South at the turn of the century. As white southerners gained more power, the types of civil cases that posed a possible threat to whites became much less frequent. From Reconstruction to the end of the nineteenth century, civil cases litigated between black and white people in southern state supreme courts had frequently dealt with disagreements over wills, property, transactions, or contracts.[59] In these cases, the black litigants had often presented themselves as equal parties to the whites who participated in the suits. As the antebellum ties between white and black people weakened, though, cases in which a white testator had left money to a black person in a will became less common. At the end of the nineteenth century, southern courts were also less likely to hear suits over white and black southerners' ordinary economic dealings.

W. H. Weems discovered this increased opposition to such suits when he was jailed in 1897 for trying to bring a civil case against a white man over his sharecropping contract. In the ensuing civil trial in the City Court of Atlanta, the white landowner A. W. Barge made no effort to hide his actions from the court. After the sharecropper had threatened to sue him, he testified, he swore out a warrant for the black man's arrest and requested the criminal court to "have the bond fixed big enough to put him in [jail]."[60] The white landowner thus openly acknowledged his use of the criminal courts to thwart Weems's civil action.

In the end, the jury ruled in the black sharecropper's favor, awarding him $433.33 in damages. When the white landowner appealed in January 1900, the state supreme court affirmed the city court's decision for Weems. Writing the opinion for the majority, Georgia Supreme Court Justice P. J. Lumpkin began by declaring, "It would be a mockery of justice to set aside the verdict now under review." The state justice then noted that "Barge was instrumental in having the bond fixed at the amount mentioned, and, but for his insistence, a smaller bond, and one which Weems would have been able to give, would have been

exacted. Barge's conduct plainly indicated his desire to have Weems imprisoned." Lumpkin agreed, too, with the sharecropper's claim that "the warrant was
sworn out to defeat the civil suit of Weems." It was the "more plausible" explanation for Barge's initiating the criminal action, he wrote, "and this, most probably,
is the exact truth of the matter." He concluded: "Barge's treatment of his humble
cropper was oppressive and wrong from the beginning, and the persecution
(called prosecution) which he instituted was totally indefensible. If there is anything wrong about the verdict, it is the amount. The jury might well have made
it larger."[61] Despite this opinion overwhelmingly in the black-litigant's favor,
increased opposition to African Americans' involvement in civil cases over ordinary economic dealings would largely prevent similar cases from being heard in
the coming years. Yet, as Weems's case makes clear, African Americans continued to maintain a measure of faith that they could still sometimes gain justice
through civil courts even during the darkest years of Jim Crow.

During the first two decades of the twentieth century, almost three-fourths of
all appellate civil cases that black southerners were able to litigate against whites
involved personal injury claims or particularly egregious cases of fraud in property dealings.[62] To a limited degree, this reflected larger trends. Personal injury
cases increased on the whole nationally during this time, while cases over property decreased. But just as in the decades past, the kinds of cases black litigants
were most often able to bring to southern state courts diverged markedly from
the range of cases most often litigated by the general population.[63]

Unlike black litigants' cases in the previous decades, these suits usually presented African Americans in especially vulnerable, unequal roles. A disproportionate number of the cases involved very young or very old black plaintiffs, and
almost half of the suits had black female litigants.[64] To meet the legal terms of
fraud or personal injury, the plaintiffs in such cases had a strong motivation to
emphasize their weakness and inferiority. According to the law, it was difficult
to bring a case of fraud if both parties in the transaction stood on an equal foot-
ing. Only if one of the parties had significantly less knowledge or mental capacity that impaired him from fully understanding the contract would the courts
become involved and rescind the contract.[65] Similarly, in personal injury cases,
litigants needed to demonstrate that they had suffered injuries that caused them
pain and loss of income. Courts also gave plaintiffs seen as less capable more lee-
way as they judged responsibility for accidents, not expecting them to have exercised the same amount of caution as the "common man." Cornelius Mitchell's
personal injury suit after a railroad accident, for instance, revolved in part around
the fact that he was largely deaf and, according to a witness, couldn't "hear anybody speak at all, but he can hear a whistle."[66] In these types of cases, African
Americans bolstered their legal claims by consciously presenting themselves in
unequal positions with individual whites.

Fig 5.1 Photograph of North Carolina Supreme Court in their chambers, 1919. Courtesy of Miscellaneous Subjects Image Collection (P0003), North Carolina Collection Photographic Archives, The Wilson Library, University of North Carolina at Chapel Hill.

Black litigants understood all too well that as they lost more and more rights in the South, appealing to white southerners' ideas about race would aid their cases. Almost all white southerners believed that people of color were inherently unequal. Moreover, at the end of the nineteenth century, as white southerners sought to consolidate their power over black people, a Lost Cause movement romanticizing the antebellum South spread a myth of a past in which childlike black people had loyally served their former masters and their benevolent white owners had in turn taken good care of them. By presenting themselves as unequal and dependent and asking for white aid, black litigants appealed to white judges' and juries' idealized memories of the Old South and beliefs of racial superiority. White judges and jury members, in turn, were often happy to spotlight black men and women in such positions.[67]

Black southerners' new position as the aggrieved party in most personal injury and fraud cases reinforced this image. During Reconstruction, black and white southerners had both brought cases against one another, a pattern that continued to a lesser extent through the rest of the nineteenth century.[68] By 1900, black southerners still brought cases against white people in their state's highest court, but few white southerners bothered to seek legal action in their disagreements with black people. As segregation and disfranchisement became institutional-ized and written into law, marginalizing black southerners' political power, white southerners could usually resolve disagreements across the color line in their own favor outside of court. Black men and women, on the other hand, often could not—leading more than four-fifths of civil suits between white and black southerners from 1900 to 1920 in the eight appellate courts examined to be ini-tiated by black plaintiffs. The types of suits they remained able to litigate also contributed to this shift. In fraud and personal injury cases, the person who had suffered financial or bodily harm generally brought the case. This preponderance of black plaintiffs and white defendants in civil suits only reinforced the image of black people as vulnerable and in need of protection.[69]

The rising segregation in the South and increasing distance from the war influenced courtroom proceedings as well. A notable shift in people's familiarity with one another can be seen in the testimony of black and white southerners. Whereas earlier white and black litigants often had long-standing ties, by 1900 litigants mentioned experiences before the war less frequently and were less likely to know one another well.[70]

White witnesses continued to testify for as well as against black litigants, but their testimony was commonly more impersonal. Some white witnesses in fraud cases testified only about the price of land and had no previous relationship with the black litigants. In one Arkansas fraud case, three white men in the real estate business testified about the value of a lot in Little Rock. They gave varying esti-mates, ranging from $3,500 to $4,000. Then, during the lawyer's questioning, the witnesses learned from the questions directed at them that half of the lot in question had been owned by a black woman. One witness, H. L. Remmel, then asked, "How old a woman was the negro woman?" With this new information about the lot's owner, all three white men immediately downgraded the value of the property. R. C. Butler, for one, responded to a lawyer's question, "Of course, being owned in that way by negroes, would be a detriment to the property," with a strong "Yes, sir."[71]

Other white witnesses still noted connections with black employees or co-workers, but the increasing separation of races in the South undoubtedly influenced these interactions. Several white co-workers at the local lumber mill testified for the black plaintiff in one 1918 North Carolina fraud case. "I know Jake Sutton; have been knowing him about 5 or 6 years," one millworker told the court, "I think I know his general character; it is good. I work out at the mill at which he works." Another white co-worker testified: "I know Jake Sutton . . . . I have never heard aught against him."[72] Even though it went unsaid in their testimony, the labor at southern lumber mills was highly segregated, with whites getting the best jobs and black laborers receiving the worst paid, most unskilled jobs. The interactions at work among these white witnesses and the black plaintiff would have taken place in a racially divided, unequal environment.[73]

Even as the kinds of civil cases that African Americans could litigate in appellate courts changed, the outcomes of these ordinary civil cases remained much the same. Black litigants continued to win before juries as well as judges at the local level during the first two decades of the twentieth century. Of the cases between white and black litigants that later reached the eight state supreme courts, black litigants had won 129 of 220 cases at the county court level (59 percent) between 1900 and 1920. In the local trials of the appellate cases examined during this period, over two-thirds of the decisions favorable to African American litigants had been made by juries and a little over a fourth of such decisions had been made by judges. Although these local trials of appellate cases are not representative of all local cases during this period, they nonetheless show that juries—as well as judges—could decide in favor of black litigants even in the midst of Jim Crow.[74] When African Americans succeeded in litigating a civil case against a white person before a southern state's highest court, they were more likely to win the case than not. The eight state supreme courts examined decided in favor of African Americans in 63 percent of civil suits between white and black southerners from 1900 to 1920.[75]

As before, the role of white lawyers and white witnesses in these suits helped aid black litigants' cases, even as they shaped the arguments African Americans could make. The nature of the legal system, too, continued to give preference to cases that followed precedent, no matter the race of the litigants. Yet the vast shifts in the kinds of cases black people could litigate indicates that new factors were at work in these victories. For one, the nature of these cases made them especially unthreatening to white juries and judges. At times, they seemed to explicitly uphold racial inequality. By primarily taking cases in appellate courts that presented black people in unequal situations, whites highlighted their supposed racial superiority (without consideration of the structural factors that had led black men and women to be so vulnerable in the first place). At the same time, as they continued to allow black southerners to make claims in the courts, whites presented the New South as a fair place, where African Americans—even if they did not have access to the ballot box—could gain justice in the courts. Doing so upheld the legitimacy of their own legal system. Perhaps they hoped as well that upholding some African Americans' property rights would keep black citizens content despite the loss of so many of their other rights.

Yet these decisions in favor of African Americans can also be understood as successful assertions of legal rights, masked to look as unthreatening as possible. Even as black southerners largely failed to use the courts to help themselves as a whole, they succeeded at times in using the courts to benefit themselves as individual citizens. They maintained their access to the courts, limited as it was, by purposely presenting their cases in ways that would elicit favorable responses from whites. While failing to create broader change and sometimes even reinforcing ideas of white supremacy, the resulting cases left African Americans with one foot in the courts at a time when they no longer had standing in any other government institutions in the South.

Confronting Fraud Through the Courts

Around 1902, 18-year-old Lurena Ellard inherited 80 acres of land in Jefferson County, Alabama, from her father. The rapidly growing county was a center for mining and steel production in the South.[1] The young black woman soon encountered a barrage of threats to her land. First, two neighbors and a white man in a neighboring town laid claims to different portions of the land. They had bought "tax titles" when Ellard's family did not pay the taxes on time. Ellard and her family fought back in court, hiring a lawyer and bringing three suits of eject-ment to recover clear title. They won two of the suits and regained control of 60 acres of the land. The local deputy sheriff enforced the court's ruling, evicting the whites who had claimed the land. Only the third suit, over a 20-acre section, remained pending. In the midst of the litigation, Lurena Ellard married Isham Roebuck, a driller at one of the local mines.[2]

One May morning in 1906, while her husband was at work, a white saloon owner named John Leonard came to her house and offered to buy the 20 acres still in dispute. "I told him I did not know what about it; that I did not want to sell it," Lurena Roebuck later said, "and he said that makes no difference he wanted to buy it." Leonard offered $10 to hold the sale, to which Roebuck replied "that I did not want to take that, and he told me to take it anyhow." Eventually, Leonard pressured Roebuck into taking $35 for what she believed was 20 acres. He presented her with a legal document to sign, and, unable to read well, she signed it. Even if she had read the paper, the document gave only the compass points of the land and did not list the number of acres being transferred.

In the days that followed, Roebuck remained unsatisfied with the sale. She consulted William K. Terry, the white lawyer whom her family had used in their previous suits, to ask about canceling the sale. Terry examined the deed, and—to her dismay—told her that the documents she had signed granted Leonard all 80 acres, property she later testified was worth $2,400. Upon learning this, Roebuck traveled 9 miles to Birmingham to confront Leonard at his saloon. She offered him $35 to return her land. If he refused, she told him, "I would try the law about it." In reply, Leonard reportedly told her "to tell [your] lawyer to pop his whip." "I told him all right," Roebuck said, and "Then I left."[3]

John Leonard did not seem worried about Roebuck's threat. After all, he did not believe that a black woman could successfully challenge him before the law. Roebuck, however, understood the law as a legitimate remedy to the situation. She had successfully pursued legal action against whites before and could do so again.

Unlike Roebuck, most black southerners did not own their own land. Upon gaining their freedom, African Americans had demanded land from the federal government, but found that government promises went largely unfulfilled. Meanwhile, white southerners worked hard to keep land out of the hands of black people, as ownership allowed whites to continue to control black labor. Soon, a sharecropping system developed. Landowners provided land, seed, and farming equipment and received half to two-thirds of the crop. Black sharecroppers provided their labor in return for the remaining third to half of the crop. But at the end of the year, after the landowner subtracted the cost of food and clothing from the laborer's share, some sharecroppers ended up with little or no profit or even in debt.

Even more black farmers leased land from white landowners, paying 20 to 30 percent of their crop in rent. Black tenants had greater independence than sharecroppers and had the opportunity to make a real profit if their crops did well. Yet, as the land deteriorated, cotton prices fell, and rents rose, tenants' proceeds from their crops often failed to cover their basic expenses. Even if they had a good crop, it could be difficult to get ahead. "If a tenant worked hard and raised a large crop," W. E. B. Du Bois explained, "his rent was raised the next year; if that year the crop failed, his corn was confiscated and his mule sold for debt."[4]

Black sharecroppers and tenants faced fraud from some white landowners. Whites took advantage of many black laborers' limited reading and math abilities, used weighted scales, and made threats to gain the upper hand on settlement day. In recourse, many black laborers moved from plantation to plantation, but rarely found a better situation. If they owed money, they often did not even have the option to leave. "If a sharecropper is in debt he cannot leave without the landowner's consent," anthropologist Hortense Powdermaker explained. "Sometimes even if he has a clear receipt after the settlement is made, he is not allowed to go."[5]

Although most black southerners remained property-less, some freedpeople like Roebuck's father obtained agricultural land in the decades after the Civil War. The black southerners who did gain land, like most others, had often made little or no financial profit as tenants or sharecroppers; instead these jobs served largely to put a roof over their head and provide basic clothing and provisions. But in addition to their work growing crops for white landowners, these black men, women, and children frequently used any free time they had to produce goods within their homes, raise chickens or hogs, or grow extra produce in their gardens, which they could then sell for income. With one cow, historian Sharon Holt notes, a family could obtain 30 to 50 pounds of butter to sell over the course of one year. A few chickens could generate dozens of eggs to offer for purchase. Such small-scale, household production rarely attracted the attention of local whites. As a result, the violence that sometimes accompanied economic prosperity for African Americans could generally be avoided.[6] In time, the profits from such household enterprises could add up to enough to purchase land for themselves.

Black people in the Upper South proved more successful in acquiring and keeping land than their counterparts in the Deep South, but in the decades after Reconstruction, black land ownership increased throughout the region. By 1900, approximately one-fourth of black farmers in the South owned their own agricultural land.[7] Many of these black-owned farms were comparatively small and the land relatively cheap. Holt found that between 1872 and 1898 in Granville County, North Carolina, the median farm owned by African Americans was never above 16 acres in size.[8] Although most black southerners could not afford large tracts of land, limiting the size of their farms was also a conscious strategy to avoid repercussions from whites.[9]

Owning land completely changed the lives of African Americans. Because they did not have to give a percentage of their crop to someone else, it was much easier to make a profit and stay out of debt. Landowners could not cheat them on settlement day, and they did not have to move constantly in search of a better situation. Their everyday quality of life was usually better, too. Although sharecroppers and tenants often planted only a cash crop and maybe a small garden, a contemporary observer noted in 1915 that black landowners in Virginia "cultivate for their own use corn, cabbage, snaps, onions, melons, and other vegetables," had fruit trees, and raised chickens and a few cows or pigs. This diversity of agriculture insulated landowners from some of the pressures of the market and significantly increased the quality of their food.[10]

Despite these advantages, black landowners like Roebuck faced threats from all directions. Frequently without any form of insurance or safety net, black southerners could lose the fruits of many years of hard work in a single catastrophe. All too often, the failure of 1 year's crop led the government to sell the amount of their taxes in a "tax sale." The landowner normally had to reimburse the person who had paid his or her taxes, plus interest, within a year, to retain the land. At other times, African Americans had to use their land as collateral to borrow money and lost it if they could not repay the debt. White land agents, neighbors, and speculators also constantly eyed their property, waiting for a moment of weakness. Speculators tried to force them to sell by telling them their land was on the verge of being auctioned off or sold for taxes. Other whites tried to convince them to sign fraudulent bills of sale by presenting them as mortgage documents, threatening them with violence, or lying about the value and size of the land they were buying.

Black southerners worked extremely hard to hold onto their land. Black women in landowning families were more likely to work at home, as their gardening and domestic labor could make the family more self-sufficient. After their land had been paid for, black landowning families usually did everything in their power to avoid mortgaging it.[11] Often, black landowners would mortgage anything else they could—from their household goods to their livestock—to avoid mortgaging their land. When agricultural depressions hit, this typically meant that landowning families got by with just a bare minimum of other possessions in order to keep their land. Some white observers noticed African Americans' desire to keep their land. One white real estate developer in Arkansas observed in 1907: "when colored people get a hold of property it is a very hard thing to dislodge them, especially if they happen to have a good location, I know from experience they will hardly sell for any price."[12]

If they had to mortgage or sell some of their land, court cases reveal, black landowners typically acted with caution and suspicion, repeatedly trying to ensure that they were not being cheated. Frequently they obtained multiple opinions before going ahead with transactions. Yet at times their illiteracy and limited financial knowledge—alongside the threat of violence—led them to be defrauded out of their land.

When this occurred, some black men and women—like Roebuck—turned to the courts. Despite any misgivings they might have had about the legal system, for many the economic stakes were too high not to try every possible method to regain their land. Most such cases undoubtedly were heard only in local courts. When they reached state appeals courts, however, they formed an unusually large proportion of appellate civil cases involving black and white litigants during the first two decades of the twentieth century. Of the 220 civil cases between black and white litigants in eight southern state supreme courts between 1900 and 1920, 63 cases (29 percent of suits) involved claims of fraud. In contrast, a study found that fraud cases formed only about 4 percent of overall state supreme court cases nationally between 1870 and 1970.[13]

There was a fine line between having made a bad business decision and having been defrauded. Judges throughout the United States generally agreed that for fraud to occur, the two parties could not have entered into a contract on equal terms. As a result of their inequality in understanding, one person had been unable to comprehend the contract or to find out what it meant. A person who was illiterate or unfamiliar with the language of property transactions, for instance, could argue that he had not understood the terms of an unfavorable property transaction. But if the two parties had met on equal terms, they were expected to both have exercised caution in dealing with each other. Unless one of them perpetrated a deception that a "man of prudence" could not see through, the law viewed an ill-advised contract as merely a poor financial move, rather than an instance of fraud.[14]

The fraud suits litigated by African Americans in appellate courts in the first two decades of the twentieth century bore out this rule. Such suits often involved particularly egregious instances of duplicity in a property transaction. People viewed as less capable, especially young, elderly, or female black litigants, were the aggrieved parties in many of these cases. Black women, for one, made up slightly more than half of the litigants in fraud suits between 1900 and 1920. Because of their age, gender, and race, these litigants made especially strong claims that they had entered into a contract on unequal terms and met the legal terms for having been defrauded.[15]

In many of these suits, black property owners argued that they did not mean to sell their land at all. Often, they believed that they were signing a loan agreement or a mortgage, or paying back taxes to redeem land that had been foreclosed. Only later did they discover that they had put their mark to a document deeding away their property. Of the fraud cases between 1900 and 1920, 43 percent involved black plaintiffs who did not mean to sell their property or had their property claimed by white people.[16]

A bad harvest left an opening for local whites to take African Americans' land in many of these cases. One black landowner, 46-year-old H. A. McLaurin, had inherited 148 acres in Flea Hill Township, North Carolina, from his grandfather 20 years earlier. In 1914, he did not pay taxes on the land because, he later recalled, "that was the year everything was down low." As a result, his taxes were sold at a tax sale in 1915 to a local white man, T. F. Williams. Not long after, McLaurin met with Williams to arrange to pay the taxes back. The white man told him, McLaurin testified, "that if I would sign this paper it would strengthen him and give him a better title to give me a deed. I signed the paper on that day." Unknowingly, though, McLaurin had signed over the title of his property. When McLaurin attempted to buy back his property, Williams claimed that he would return the land to him only if he paid $925. Instead, McLaurin brought a civil suit against Williams, alleging fraud.[17]

In other cases, white land agents or neighbors threatened black landowners with violence or other repercussions if they did not sell. One black plaintiff in Arkansas, Young Hobbs, claimed that a local white merchant, John Ward, said he would kill him if he did not deed his 160 acres of land to Ward's wife. The merchant's business was about to go under, and he hoped that by pressuring Hobbs to deed the property to his wife, he could preserve something from his creditors. Although Hobbs owed the merchant several hundred dollars, the property was worth much more. Hobbs testified, "I declined to [sign over the deed]. When I told John Ward that, he commenced to walk backward and forward on the gallery, and said, 'By God, you've got to give it up; you have it to do. I will kill you if you don't do it,' and then I did it, and went down to the store and acknowledged the deed." Thirteen years later, in 1904, Hobbs brought a case to regain title to his land.[18]

An additional 16 percent of fraud cases in appellate courts between 1900 and 1920 involved black plaintiffs like Lurena Roebuck, who sold their property for a sum they later claimed was too low. In these cases, white neighbors and moneylenders often pressured black property owners into selling their land at extremely low prices by telling them they were about to lose their land because of an imminent lawsuit. Other whites played on black landowners' fears that their land would be sold for taxes. At times, white buyers failed to mention lucrative mineral deposits that they had discovered on the land, about which the black owners were unaware.[19]

Lawsuits also originated because of the difficulties black southerners faced in borrowing money. In some cases, moneylenders could force black landowners to use their property as collateral. This frequently ended badly: Between 1900 and 1920, 11 percent of the appellate fraud cases examined involved white creditors. In some cases, whites claimed they held mortgages on black people's land even when the black litigants claimed no such mortgages existed. In other suits, the lenders holding black landowners' mortgages claimed the owners owed more principal or interest than they actually did, or charged exorbitant rates of interest on the mortgages. Black litigants also brought suits contending that they had thought they were signing a mortgage document but had been deceived into signing away their property.[20]

In one 1913 Mississippi case, 65-year-old Mary Lee had no insurance, and after a fire burned down her house, she needed to borrow money. She went to a pawnshop owned by a white man and asked to borrow $15. He asked what she could put up as collateral. She replied, "You know I haven't got anything but those lots, all I got is burnt up; won't you let me have it on that?" He agreed, and she promised, "I will return it to you as soon as possible." A day or two later Mary Lee returned and, according to her testimony, the pawnbroker had "this paper . . . stretched out on the counter and turned it round, showing me where to sign. I paused and said, I don't like to sign nothing I cant read." He reassured her that she had no reason to fear, and she signed the document. In fact, she had been deceived into signing a deed selling him her property for $15. In the ensuing court case, Lee claimed that she had not meant to sell her land and had previously turned down an offer of $500 for the property.[21]

While the majority of fraud cases litigated by black southerners accused only white people of deceit, eight cases that reached southern courts of appeal between 1900 and 1920 accused a black person of collaborating with a white litigant to deceive a black landowner.[22] In 1905, for example, 16-year-old Bettie Arnold and 18-year-old Mary Arnold litigated a suit against a white money-lender named Storthz. They claimed that Storthz had sent Scipio Jones, a prominent black lawyer, to tell them that they were about to lose their land and had frightened them into selling the property for much less than its value.[23] Although Jones told them that their land was practically worthless and "wouldn't sprout peas," his employer (and possibly Jones as well) had thoroughly investigated the land's lucrative mineral deposits.[24]

As black southerners engaged lawyers to regain their property, they found that a set of statutes in each state, as well as a series of precedents that constituted the common law, governed the law of fraud. In addition to inequality between the contracting parties, it bolstered a case to show that the plaintiff had acted with as much caution as possible. It helped a case, too, if the plaintiff had a relationship with the defendant that led him to have a level of trust in the defendant. In addition, if the defendant had conspired with a third party to perpetrate the fraud, the case against the defendant was significantly stronger. In most states, a lawyer did not need to prove that the defendant had purposely intended to deceive the plaintiff, merely that the information he had given the plaintiff had led the plaintiff to make a decision grievously to his or her financial detriment.[25]

In their petitions and appeals, lawyers in these cases sought to show that their suits did or did not meet the legal guidelines of fraud. They coached litigants and witnesses on what to say in their testimony to strengthen or weaken the case for fraud. At times, they played a part in fraud disputes even before the parties filed suit. Roebuck turned to a white lawyer, 36-year-old William Terry, to regain her land. Terry had worked as a "general practice" lawyer in the Birmingham area for 16 years. He worked alone, without law partners, and had no property or family of his own, instead living in a boarding house. Roebuck's uncle had consulted Terry on her behalf several years before, shortly after she first inherited the property from her father. As a result of his success in bringing suits of ejectment against the neighbors who laid claim to her property, Roebuck trusted him to help her with this new matter. Upon hearing her problem, Roebuck testified, Terry "told me he would do all he could for me."[26]

First, Terry wrote a letter for Roebuck to bring when she confronted Leonard. When that proved unsuccessful, Terry went to Leonard's saloon to ask him to rescind the contract. Upon his refusal, Terry filed a suit in the court of equity to set the deed aside. In the petition, he followed a template used by almost all of the white lawyers who litigated fraud suits on behalf of black litigants. The language in the template was calculated to help their clients meet all the terms of fraud and prove a claim of fraud before the law. The same formula was used in some white litigants' suits alleging fraud, although it was not as widespread.[27] Terry emphasized his client's ignorance and helplessness and her need for protection from the law. "Complainant avers that she is ignorant and unacquainted with business affairs," he wrote, "and that she did not read over said deed, and would not have understood it if she had read it over."[28]

In other fraud cases, white southern lawyers highlighted their black clients' age, weakness of mind, and lack of education. In a 1919 North Carolina case, the plaintiff's lawyers stressed that their elderly black client had not had "sufficient mental capacity" to sell her land, "being then very old, about 78 years of age, and greatly enfeebled in mind and body and very decrepit, and her mental faculties impaired by the infirmities of old age and by 'wretched physical health.' "[29] Elsewhere, a lawyer in a 1907 Alabama fraud case wrote that his black client was "only able to slowly read simple words when in print and to scrawl his own name" and was "ignorant of business methods and legal requirements."[30] Such claims worked to prove that clients had been incapable of fully understanding a contract and had not met the person with whom they made the contract as an equal.

As part of this template, lawyers frequently emphasized that black plaintiffs had trusted white members of the community, who then betrayed that trust. Although Roebuck had never met Leonard before signing over her property, Terry claimed in his petition that, when signing the deed, Roebuck "relied entirely upon the representation of defendant in the matter." Had the two parties known each other longer, this claim would have been even stronger. In the eyes of the law, a relationship of trust between two contracting parties bolstered a legal claim of fraud, as the contracting parties were not as careful to check each other's claims in these cases. As these lawyers no doubt realized, such claims also appealed to fellow white southerners' common belief that "helpless" African Americans should trust more capable whites. Thus, when a white neighbor presented a bill of sale to an elderly black woman as a mortgage document, the woman's lawyers claimed that she "relied upon him to protect her."[31]

Especially in their appeals to higher courts, lawyers drew upon precedents that supported their cases. Terry cited three precedents from Alabama appeals courts showing that if a person obtained a signature on a deed by misrepresenting the deed's contents, it did not matter if the person had had an opportunity to read the deed. Leonard's attorney, in turn, cited an Alabama appellate court ruling declaring that plaintiffs could not obtain relief for fraud if they could read and write and understood what they were doing.[32] By framing their litigants' cases within the larger body of cases on that subject, lawyers strengthened their clients' claims for relief.

With the aid of their lawyers, African Americans who litigated fraud cases in appellate courts often seem to have understood the necessary claims for a successful fraud case. When testifying, they gave carefully choreographed performances, calculated to strengthen the legal arguments of their cases. Again and again, they emphasized their diligence in attempting to understand the contract, their own vulnerability to deception, and their trust in the defendant. Black men and women were attuned to attitudes about race in their communities, and many likely realized that their efforts to prove their lack of financial understanding and trust of whites also appealed to white beliefs of racial superiority. The most perceptive lawyers and litigants may even have seen that the convergence between the legal claims the law required and the performances that race relations in the South necessitated vastly increased the appearance of such cases in southern courts.

Often, black litigants explained that they had exercised caution in dealing with whites, getting second opinions or having a contract carefully explained to them before they signed it. When they found themselves defrauded, black men and women testified that they had confronted white buyers or creditors to cancel a fraudulent deed. Indeed, Roebuck told the court that she had wanted to get a second opinion before making the sale. "I told him I didn't want to sell it," she testified, "unless I could see my uncle." Then, after learning that the white speculator John Leonard had taken all of her family's land, Roebuck said, she confronted Leonard, telling him that she was going to bring a lawsuit against him.[33]

In case after case, black litigants framed their suits to show a "cunning" white speculator defrauding an "ignorant" black landowner. By emphasizing their vulnerability and ignorance, they sought to prove that they had been on unequal terms with the defendant when they made their contract and thus had a legal claim of fraud. Men and women alike depicted themselves in these ways, but the high proportion of fraud suits litigated by black women shows they straddled the line between highlighting their ignorance and pursuing legal action especially effectively. Black women were litigants in thirty-three of the sixty-three higher-court fraud cases (52 percent of cases) between white and black litigants in the eight appellate courts examined between 1900 and 1920. Although black women were generally not afforded the protections given to white women, their court cases seem to have more easily been viewed as pleas for protection, rather than as challenges to white supremacy, than those of black men.

To demonstrate their lack of knowledge, black litigants frequently emphasized their inability to read or understand financial documents. Lurena Roebuck characterized her reading and writing abilities as "not much" and told the court, "I have never had any experience in business affairs. I know nothing about land numbers. I do not know how many acres of land there are in quarter sections . . . . This is the only transaction of land I have ever had." Her husband, too, emphasized his lack of education, testifying, "I never went to school .... The only writing I can do is to write my name."[34] Similarly, in a 1905 North Carolina case, the black litigant, Isham Hodge, testified that, even after a deed was read to him, "a heap of it I didn't understand." In other cases, even when black litigants could read or write, they testified that they did not understand legal language, such as the difference between a sale and a loan. In turn-of-the-century Alabama, 81-year-old Andrew Carpenter admitted that he could read and write but testified, "I do not know anything about the significance of deeds and mortgages, or legal papers."[35]

Black litigants also followed the legal template laid out by their lawyers as they told the court that they had trusted white members of the community, who then betrayed that trust. "I relied on what Mr. Leonard told me," Lurena Roebuck testified. "I sold it to him for 20 acres because he told me it was 20 acres." Despite Roebuck's claim, she had never met Leonard before the transaction and most likely did not trust him.[36] Other black southerners had long-standing relations with the people they claimed to have trusted, but seemed aware of the ramifications of claiming to have "trusted" the person with whom they made a contract.[37]

Black litigants often did have a number of disadvantages in property transactions, including illiteracy, unequal political power, and lack of business experience. Their consistent use of the same claims of ignorance in case after case, though, points to a conscious strategy to strengthen their claims of fraud and make their cases acceptable to white judges and juries. Indeed, even as spoke about their weakness, black litigants frequently demonstrated boldness in their actions and, at times, in their testimony.

Often, black litigants showed a willingness to stand up to whites by turning to the law in disputes. In a 1907 Alabama fraud case, the white defendant J. W. Abercrombie had defrauded the elderly black plaintiff, Andrew Carpenter, by telling him that he was signing a mortgage when he was actually deeding away his property. When Carpenter confronted the white man, Abercrombie offered to pay him a small fraction of the cost of the property. Carpenter testified, "I told him I would not take $100 but that before I took that I would die first." He continued, "I came on then to see if I could get any rights in court."[38] Likewise, Jim Woodward testified that he had told the white litigant that he would not pay rent on his own land after he had lost it because of the other man's deception: "I told him I would pay no rent, he said he would get the rent, I told him if he got it it would be by law."[39] Other black litigants assertively testified about the fraud. Roebuck confidently told the court that Leonard had pressured her into signing over the land and lied about how much he was buying. She did not hesitate in giving the true value of her land. "That land is worth $30.00 per acre," she concluded her testimony. "The 30th of May, 1906, it was worth $30.00 an acre."[40]

White litigants in turn had to shape their testimony to make the strongest legal defense. Often, they emphasized that the black litigants had engaged in the contract voluntarily. "Lurena Roebuck and another woman were going through the field when we drove up," Leonard testified, ". . . her mother-in-law called her back. We sat on the gallery and . . . I asked her if she wanted to sell it. She said that she would and she sold it to me . . . she told me that her uncle had a lawyer attending to it for her, and that he was no good, and that she was glad to get what she did out of it, and that it was more than she expected to get."[41]

White litigants also challenged black people's expressions of helplessness and ignorance. To counter the claim that they had entered into a contract with an unequal party who could not comprehend the transaction, white defendants stated that black litigants had the requisite financial understanding to conduct complicated business dealings. In case after case, white defendants testified that those they had allegedly cheated were of the "best sort" of black people. During the Roebuck trial, the white litigant's lawyer asked him in reference to the black plaintiffs, "Are they or not above the ordinary intelligence of their class in society?" Leonard answered, "They are."[42] Even as black litigants emphasized their unequal circumstances, white litigants testified that black people knew what they were doing in property transactions.

Less often, white litigants in the Jim Crow South had no qualms about admitting to defrauding black people. These whites admitted their fraud in insolent terms, suggesting that they expected no punishment for their dishonest actions. In one 1908 Arkansas case, a white speculator told the court that he had paid an older black woman to use her influence over the 22-year-old black plaintiff Rosa Williams to get Williams to sell the property for a very low price. The white man further acknowledged that he knew the property was worth $4,000 to $5,000, although he had convinced Williams that it was worth much less.[43] Not making the slightest effort to lie or explain away his actions, the white speculator demonstrated that he believed the judges would rule for him even if they knew he had been at fault. But such cases form the minority of fraud cases during this time. Most whites earnestly tried to make the strongest legal defense possible, demonstrating a concern that the court might find them at fault.

The black and white men and women who took the stand to testify for and against fraud claims played important roles in the outcomes. Reflecting the increasingly segregated interracial interactions in the early twentieth century, some of the five white witnesses who testified for Lurena Roebuck did not know her. Ben Davis, a local white lawyer who did not know either of the parties in the suit, testified, "I know the market value of lands in that neighborhood and or that land . . . . The land described in the Bill is worth from $20.00 to $30.00 per acre." Jack Brown, the deputy sheriff, also testified for Roebuck.

He explained that he had recently served papers on a white man who had been occupying some of Roebuck's land, after Roebuck got a writ of repossession from the court. When asked about the value of land, Brown said that he thought Roebuck's land was worth $20.00 an acre. Like Davis, Brown did not seem to know Roebuck personally.[44]

At times, whites who testified for black litigants had their own economic motivations for doing so. One of Roebuck's white neighbors, Mrs. A. J. Wideman, appeared on Roebuck's behalf. Wideman had bought the tax title to another section of Roebuck's land. Only if Roebuck won the case would Wideman have a chance of gaining part of Roebuck's land for herself. She bolstered her black neighbor's case by stating that the land was worth far more than Leonard had paid for it. "I know the nature of the Ellard tract," she told the court, "it is a sandy clay land; it is a good piece of farming land." Other whites who testified for black litigants had previously cheated them. John Carter, a white witness in a 1914 North Carolina case, testified: "I knew Isham Hodges, and wife, M. A. Hodges .... I took mortgages from him and traded him stock .... He would not have taken such stock as we gave him some of the time if he had had good judgment." Despite this admission, Carter supported the plaintiff's claim that Isham Hodges had not had the mental capacity to make a contract. "I do not think he had his right mind along about June 25th, 1910," Carter testified. "I saw the old man trying to get some gear on a horse and he had it all twisted and Mr. A. R. Wilson said to me, 'John put that gear on this horse for this old negro. He has not got sense enough to hitch him to a buggy.'"[45]

Prominent members of the white community often testified for the defendant. Indeed, four white men, most of them neighbors of Roebuck, testified in favor of Leonard. Each argued that Roebuck's land was not worth much. John Vary, the defendant's lawyer who owned land 4 miles away, testified that he thought Roebuck's land was worth only 25 cents an acre. Under cross examination, though, he admitted that he had turned down offers of $100 an acre for his own land and did not know of any land in the area selling for as little as $10.00 an acre.[46]

Occasionally, black members of the community also testified for the defendant. One black witness, 25-year-old Will Hayes, testified on Leonard's behalf. Hayes worked as Leonard's employee at a Birmingham saloon and had strong economic reasons to appear for his employer. "Mr. Terry came [to the saloon] with Lurena Roebuck and her husband," Hayes testified. "They told Mr. Leonard in the presence of myself that they were satisfied with the trade." The defendant's lawyer questioned: "Was or not the lawyer, Mr. Terry, stirring up this litigation?" "Yes Sir," replied Hayes. "If you had seen Lurena Roebuck and Isham Roebuck wronged in a transaction, would you have stopped the transaction?" the lawyer pressed. "Yes, I would," said Hayes. Despite Hayes's assertions, Roebuck's lawyer

Will Terry denied ever having gone to Leonard's saloon with Roebuck. Terry said he had gone by himself to the saloon and had not seen Hayes.[47]

Others not directly involved in fraud cases sometimes weighed in. Whites in the community at times condemned the fraud perpetrated on black southerners. A 1913 Mississippi newspaper article about black plaintiff Mary Lee's case reported that "The Supreme Court refuses to let the alleged loan shark 'get by' on his scheme to get the woman's property for an insignificant sum of money. . . . And so now Mary M. Lee will get the chance she wants to get her property back."[48] Even as white Mississippians watched and participated in violent lynchings and disproportionately imprisoned African Americans, they condemned a white "loan shark" for cheating an elderly black woman. Unlike the prospect of black men voting or the threatening specter of black crime, Mary Lee posed no threat. Instead, her case reinforced the image of helpless African Americans in need of white aid that white southerners wanted to convey. Her suit thus allowed white Mississippians to demonstrate their benevolence toward African Americans.

Both juries and judges were frequently sympathetic to black litigants' assertions of fraud in cases that reached the appellate level. Juries heard about 40 percent of the initial trials of fraud suits that would go on to be appealed before state supreme courts. More often than not (60 percent of the time), these juries found in favor of black litigants.[49] For jury members, as for white community members, such cases publicly reaffirmed that black men and women could not make it on their own without white aid. Their decisions also helped maintain order within their communities. If black people felt that whites could take their land from them without any consequences, it could lead to social unrest. Additionally, white jury members undoubtedly valued property rights—even, at times, those of African Americans.

Judges decided another 51 percent of the initial trials of the appellate fraud cases examined, ruling for the black litigants in about half of these suits (in the remaining cases, it was unclear who decided the case at the lower-court level).[50] On appeal, panels of state supreme court justices also usually ruled in favor of black litigants in fraud cases, taking their side in 78 percent of the suits examined.[51] For judges with years of legal training and practice, the strength of black plaintiffs' legal claims played a larger part in their decisions than it did for juries. And in these suits, the black plaintiffs usually had the law squarely on their side. By the time a case reached the higher courts, the black plaintiff's claims of fraud were often very strong and the fraud itself especially egregious. Less outrageous instances of fraud no doubt were never brought to the courts or were heard only at the local level. Judges also looked to precedent as they made their decisions. In Roebuck's case, the Jefferson Chancery Court judge cited a number of past

Alabama appellate court cases involving white litigants as precedents for the rule that when a person misrepresents a legal document to persuade someone else to sign it, "the party so defrauded can avoid the effect of his signature, because of the fraud practiced upon him, notwithstanding he may have neglected to read the instrument, or to have it read to him."[52]

At the same time, judges used their opinions in fraud suits to validate and proclaim their own ideas about race. Frequently, they emphasized the differences between black and white southerners as they ruled that fraud had taken place. Higher-court justices often described black litigants in fraud cases as "ignorant," using this supposed disparity of knowledge as their rationale for deciding in favor of black litigants. One Arkansas judge described a female black litigant as "young, inexperienced as to value of real estate and densely ignorant." A Tennessee judge compared an elderly black landowner, whom he described as an "ignorant negro of very infirm mental capacity," with the white defendant, "a man of intelligence."[53] An Alabama judge made the racial differences between the litigants even more central to his discussion of the black litigants' vulnerability, writing, "The purported grantee was a prominent, intelligent, and influential member of the dominant race. The purported grantor was an illiterate negro and in failing health."[54] In case after case, judges invoked these differences to rule that fraud had taken place. Although proofs of ignorance were important in proving fraud, these statements and the disproportionate number of fraud cases indicates that they also aligned with many whites' beliefs about race relations in the South.

For judges—who ordinarily came from the most elite sector of southern society—class played an important part in many of their decisions as well. After 1900, in particular, some judges presented themselves as above the unscrupulous white speculators who had been accused of cheating often illiterate and elderly black southerners out of their property. In their rulings, these judges portrayed themselves as protecting especially vulnerable African Americans from these nonelite whites.[55] In a 1913 Mississippi case, Judge J. Cook ruled in favor of the black plaintiff, writing "appellee, a white man, doing business under the euphonious pseudonym 'Standard Loan & Pawn Brokerage Company,' is what is commonly termed a 'loan shark.' Mary is illiterate, but not ignorant. She, like many of her class, fell into the maw of the 'shark,' and the net result of her adventure was the loss of two residence lots."[56] Even when judges did not portray the white defendants in a negative light, their rulings often denigrated these litigants' use of their supposed superiority to defraud black litigants. In 1914, a judge wrote in his opinion, "Complainant was weak-minded, ignorant, and in necessitous condition. The respondent occupied a position of great superiority; and we are convinced that he used his position as mortgagee, and acquired an undue advantage over the complainant, which must meet the disapproval and condemnation of

a court of conscience."[57] By condemning whites who had defrauded those supposedly weaker than them, judges demonstrated their own good character and
reinforced their status in society.[58]

Many of these factors no doubt came into play when the Jefferson Chancery
Court judge, Alfred H. Benners, ruled in favor of Roebuck and decreed "a cancellation of the deed." In his reasoning, though, Benners noted only that the
plaintiff's testimony supported her claim, while Leonard had failed to deny that
he had misrepresented the deed. In response, Leonard appealed to the Supreme
Court of Alabama. During the 40 years since Reconstruction had ended in
Alabama, all but two of the seven justices on the court had belonged to the
Democratic Party. Most were born in Alabama and had been educated at the
conservative University of Alabama. Almost all of the justices who had been old
enough had served in the Confederate Army. Upon hearing the appeal, however,
they upheld the lower court's decision in favor of the black landowner.[59]

Like other opinions in such cases, the ruling set out the disparities between
the two litigants: "We have, then, an unlettered, ignorant woman, 22 years old,
who owned 80 acres of land, who was sought out by a man experienced in
affairs, and a real estate dealer." The court also decided that the law supported
Roebuck's claim, citing the same precedents and legal rules laid out by her
lawyer. In addition, Roebuck's bold testimony about the fraud played an important part in the court's decision. The appellate ruling repeatedly cited her testimony that Leonard had misrepresented the document she signed as evidence to
support the decision in her favor. The sheer outrageousness of buying 80 acres
for such a low price influenced the decision as well. "The evidence is reasonably
satisfactory to the effect that $35 was a grossly inadequate price for the 80 acres
of land, or even for 20 acres of it," Justice J. Haralson wrote in the opinion, adding that "the land was really worth $20 per acre, or $1,600 for the whole tract."[60]

After winning the suit, Lurena Roebuck regained ownership of her land. The
Montgomery, Alabama, newspaper briefly noted her case alongside the appeal
court's other decisions, writing, "John F. Leonard vs. Lurena Roebuck et al.
appeal from Jefferson Chancery Court affirmed." The newspaper item, like the
press coverage of many other appellate civil cases involving African Americans,
made no mention of race.[61] Lurena Roebuck next appears in the historical
record 4 years later, in 1910, when the US census takers came through Jefferson
County, Alabama. Lurena and Isham Roebuck still owned their own home and
land. Isham worked in the mines, while Lurena stayed home with their new son.
Eight years later, in September 1918, Isham Roebuck registered for the draft.
Military service was one area of government participation—like the courts—
in which African Americans could still participate. But 2 months after he registered, World War I ended, saving him from the fight. When the census takers

once again returned to Jefferson County in 1920, Isham and Lurena still owned their own home and held no mortgage, but it is not clear if they continued to own the farmland. They then disappear from the historical record, until Isham Roebuck's death in 1947 at age 65.[62]

The fraud cases that reached southern appellate courts in the first two decades of the twentieth century reflect the many types of deception perpetrated against black southerners. Yet most fraud against black people in the Jim Crow South went unremarked upon—a fact of life so common that it had become part of the fabric of southerners' everyday lives. African Americans were able to disrupt this cycle of deception only by acting within the white-dominated legal system, making the arguments that the law and white southern society required. In doing so, black litigants deviated from the powerless role that white southerners wanted them to play. By representing themselves as lacking power, black litigants managed to maintain a small measure of it. Even as fraud continued to occur throughout the Jim Crow South, these cases demonstrated that black people's legal rights had not been completely wrested away.

7

The Law of Bodily Injury

In 1910, 48-year-old Rebecca Sallee held down five jobs. She served as a janitor at two churches, cleaned a doctor's office, and took in washing from two homes—including the family of the mayor of Harrodsburg, Kentucky, C. D. Thompson. Her husband, James, worked as a sharecropper. Together, they struggled to support their eleven children. Rebecca lived on the poorer side of the midsize town of Harrodsburg, along an unpaved street.[1]

One night, after a long day's work, she and her 12-year-old daughter set off for a Baptist prayer meeting along one of the town's main roads. The night was dark; no moon or street lights illuminated her path. Suddenly, she stumbled over a pile of dirt in the street and fell hard into a gaping hole.

Her daughter helped her up, and they stopped at the mayor's nearby home, where the cook tied up her bleeding hand. They then continued on to the prayer meeting. But in the subsequent days, the severity of Sallee's fall became clear. The accident had caused severe injury to her back and damaged her kidneys. She couldn't draw a breath without pain. The doctors' bills added up.

Despite her efforts, Sallee found herself unable to do any work for 3 months. She could not sweep the churches, and her back hurt too much for her to lean over a laundry board and scrub dirty clothes. After 3 months, she returned to cleaning one church and doing laundry for the mayor's family. She remained in pain though, and earned less than half her previous wages.[2]

African Americans met frequent dangers to their health and bodies at the beginning of the twentieth century. Men and women got injured on the job, fell off streetcars, and were run over by trains. They faced violence on trains or streetcars and grew ill after nights in unheated "colored" waiting rooms. At times, these injuries were accidental; at other times they were the direct result of racial discrimination.

Such injuries could be catastrophic to African Americans' physical, as well as financial, well-being. Formerly healthy men and women lost limbs, went blind, found themselves unable to stand up, incurred irreversible damage to their reproductive organs, and, at times, died. They ran up medical bills that they were unable to pay and found themselves unable to work for long periods following an accident. Most of the women, like Sallee, worked as laundresses or domestic workers. A few labored as sick nurses or as cooks. The men's occupations ranged from mail clerks to construction workers and railroad employees. Almost all depended on their physical well-being to make a living.

In the wake of their own or loved one's injuries, some individual African Americans turned to the courts to gain damages. There, in a time of segregation and racial injustice, black litigants found disproportionate success in the realm of tort litigation. During the first two decades of the twentieth century, ninety-seven appellate-level personal injury cases involving African American litigants took place across eight states, forming 44 percent of the appellate civil suits between black and white litigants found during this period.[3]

To a certain extent, the rise in personal injury suits brought by black southerners reflected larger litigation trends in the nation. Throughout the United States, personal injury litigation was increasing at the end of the nineteenth century. One study found that tort cases formed only 6 percent of overall state supreme court cases between 1870 and 1880, but made up 16 percent of suits litigated in state supreme courts throughout America between 1905 and 1935.[4] While 16 percent of overall cases was much lower than the proportion of such cases litigated between black and white southerners (44 percent) in the first two decades of the twentieth century, this was still a significant shift.

But the specific nature of these cases and how they were litigated also played a key role in why these cases formed an especially large proportion of black litigants' cases during a period in which African Americans had lost many other rights. Perhaps most important, the nature of personal injury cases and the legal claims needed to win them led black litigants to present themselves as particularly vulnerable and weak. Allowing African Americans to litigate such cases, then, could publicly portray black men and women as helpless and in need of white assistance. In addition, black litigants in the first two decades of the twentieth century almost always sought compensation only for their own injuries, rather than challenging the underlying discriminatory practices that caused them. Personal injury cases therefore seemed to pose little threat to continuing power imbalances in southern society. Moreover, in some, but certainly not all, personal injury cases, black litigants faced off against northern-owned railroad companies, which were increasingly unpopular in the South. White judges and jury members also occasionally had a personal stake in the outcome of torts suits as they highlighted dangers in southern communities that could affect whites.

Because black men and women made these suits palatable to white judges and juries, personal injury cases remained the one other main type of civil suit, in addition to fraud cases, that black southerners continued to regularly litigate and win in appellate courts in the first two decades of the twentieth century. Through such suits, African Americans kept one foot in the door of the courts and continued to assert their legal rights even during the period of Jim Crow. At the same time, their personal injury cases' acceptability to whites profoundly limited these suits.

At the end of the nineteenth century, railroads and streetcars in the United States were a particular hazard. One-third of overall state supreme court torts cases between 1870 and 1920 and two-thirds of black southerners' appellate personal injury suits between 1900 and 1920 involved injuries on these forms of trans-portation.[5] Unlike most European nations, which attempted to protect passengers to a much greater degree, the United States had allowed railroad companies to proceed virtually unhindered in building tracks during the first part of the nineteenth century. But during the last decades of the century, as the number of tracks around the country rapidly expanded and new technology enhanced the speed of trains, the number of railroad-related injuries increased. Railroad accidents became increasingly publicized, and citizens began to worry about the threat railroads posed to their personal safety. To many Americans, railroads came to epitomize the dangers posed by modernization.[6]

For southerners, railroads had also come to represent northern intrusion into their lives. Earlier in the nineteenth century, southern states had heavily subsidized railroads and a spirit of excitement had surrounded their expansion across the South. After a financial panic in 1873 and as a number of southern states ended the financial support they had previously offered railroads, many southern carriers faced mounting financial problems. By 1880, northern investors had gained control of a number of southern railroad lines. With this change in ownership and shift in the perceived danger of railroads, white popular opinion in the South changed. Lawmakers throughout the South called for increased regulation, and ordinary citizens expressed resentment of the railroads' power and influence over economic life.[7]

Although news reports often highlighted major accidents in which trains crashed or derailed, for African Americans, like other passengers, the greatest dangers were "little accidents." Such accidents occurred when a single person was injured at a station, boarding or disembarking from a train, or crossing the tracks.[8] Cases litigated by African Americans show that even before boarding the steel behemoths, potential passengers faced inclement weather and violence in railroad waiting rooms or on railroad platforms.[9] The boarding process presented new dangers—the train could move as one was boarding or one could trip and fall in moving from the platform to the train.[10] Once on the train, passengers faced potential violence or angry words from other passengers and occasionally from train employees. Passengers without valid tickets could be thrown off the train (sometimes literally).[11] When they reached their destination, further opportunities for injury arose. At times the train went past the platform, and when passengers attempted to alight, they were forced to jump to the ground below. At other times, the platform was not well lit or the train started up again before the passengers had fully descended.[12]

As hazardous as transportation was, at the beginning of the twentieth century, workplace accidents formed the single largest cause of death for manual laborers in America. Employees were injured on the job because of hazardous work conditions, inadequate industry safety measures, carelessness, or just plain bad luck. Railroad employees met accidents in especially large numbers because of the size of the industry, which employed over 1 million workers in 1900, and uneven enforcement of industry safety measures. At the turn of the century, historian Barbara Welke writes, one railroad employee was "killed for every 420 employed and one injured for every 27 employed."[13] Indeed, 21 percent of overall torts cases in state supreme courts between 1905 and 1935 and 28 percent of black litigants' personal injury suits from 1900 to 1920 involved work-related injuries.[14] Some suits concerned black employees severely injured or killed by trains that seemingly came out of nowhere to strike them violently in railyards. Black employees might try to jump onto moving trains, only to fall under the wheels. Still others met injury as they switched train cars or constructed new railroad or streetcar lines.[15] Black men employed in construction sites, sawmills, mines, or factories also met frequent injury.[16]

Even those Americans not riding on public transportation or working in a hazardous profession found their everyday environment dangerous. Many communities' close proximity to railroads and the lack of safety crossings or barriers led to accidents. African Americans brought suits after oncoming trains crushed family members walking along the tracks, when an electric line put up by the railroad electrocuted a child, and even when a train struck a pile of timber and sent pieces of wood flying into their path.[17] Like the railroad, the new technology of the telegraph could also lead to misfortune when messages were misplaced or delayed. After being injured in a mining accident, an African American worker named John Beal was left with almost no medical attention. He later sued the telegraph company, alleging that if his mother had received his telegram earlier she could have cared for him.[18]

The lack of adequate public works in cities led to other accidents. Huge holes pocked city streets, bridges collapsed and went unrepaired, and streets remained unlit at night. Roadwork and laying of pipes surrounding new, modern innovations like indoor plumbing created problems as well. The hole Rebecca Sallee had stumbled into contained a sewage pipe that was bringing indoor plumbing to a 75-year-old white man living along College Street. The residents of the street had taken up a collection to put in a sewage pipe along the road and now were arranging for their homes to be connected to the main sewer line. The holes created by laying these pipes were an all-too-common sight for pedestrians in Harrodsburg.[19]

Such accidents on public property at times prompted litigation. In 8 percent of the personal injury cases examined, black litigants sued cities for injury incurred on public property, such as sidewalks or bridges.[20] Indeed, upon meeting a white acquaintance on the street 4 days after her accident, Rebecca Sallee told him of her injury. She then asked "What do you think of these holes being left open around on the street?" When he said that he didn't know, Sallee responded that she "thought she would sue the town." In reply, the white man said, "Aunt Becky, you ought to get you a crutch or two crutches, and if I was you I would go home go to bed, and send for the Doctor." To this white man, suing the city did not seem like a viable plan for an injured black woman. Sallee, nonetheless, hired an attorney and in May 1910 accused the city of Harrodsburg of shirking its responsibility to protect its citizens, asking for $1,500 in damages for "great bodily pain and mental anguish."[21]

Even as they reflected threats all Americans faced, black southerners' cases contained subtle differences. The poorly paid, manual nature of most African Americans' work likely increased their rates of injury. As a result of low pay, black men and women often worked multiple jobs and labored for long hours, walking to and from jobs early in the morning and late at night along unlit or poorly lit roads. The African American men who litigated personal injury cases also frequently worked in hazardous professions, and the women performed backbreaking labor throughout their lives. Their limited choices of employment thus increased the risk of injury.

As a result of precarious finances, African Americans sometimes lacked the cash to buy tickets on the railroad and could be violently thrown off the train when they stole rides. They often had no savings to live on if they suffered serious injury and could not work, and were frequently unable to pay mounting medical bills. The increasing segregation in the Jim Crow South also heightened their chances of injury. As residential areas became more segregated, black communities were often located in less desirable parts of town. In a number of cases, black litigants lived or walked to work near railroad tracks, putting them at particular risk from passing trains.

Moreover, as railroad cars began to be divided by race, the "colored" coach was generally the first passenger coach on a train and the one most likely to incur injuries in case of a head-on collision. Even if no collision occurred, train conductors often drew the colored coach past the platform at stations, forcing African Americans to alight onto bare, uneven ground. One passenger, Francis Briggs, testified that her injury occurred because the train "ran past" the end of the platform and she was forced to get off "between the station and the mail crank." Black litigants also sought damages for injuries resulting from the lack of lights and guards that resulted from the placement of "colored" cars before the platform.[22] Diana Hobbs argued that the railroad company did not provide a light at the northern part of the station where she was forced to exit, leading her to stumble accidentally over the turntable in the dark and injure herself.[23]

African American men and women also encountered violence from railroad employees or passengers as a result of racial classification in trains and stations. Several passengers brought personal injury suits when they were forcibly ejected from first-class cars or seats designated as "white."[24] The lack of protection for black women on public transit because of inferior segregated traveling accommodations and discrimination led to lawsuits as well. Railroad trains often had a special ladies' car to protect women from the vulgarity and smoke-filled atmosphere of the other cars. At times black women were able to ride in these cars if they met a certain level of respectability, but as time passed, they were more likely to be ejected. In removing black women from this car, the railroads rejected the presumption that because of their gender, black women also needed to be protected.[25] In addition, black female plaintiffs claimed to have become sick from poor conditions in "colored" waiting rooms or to have encountered violence and profanity in "colored" cars.[26] Three such women sued the railroad in 1902, charging that they had been locked inside a "colored" waiting room by several white men. When they asked for the room to be unlocked, the men reportedly directed "profane and abusive language, and vile and insulting signs" toward them. Their requests to railroad employees to unlock the door and build a fire met with more refusals. When the youngest member of the group, 12-year-old Dilsia Wilson, became sick as a result of exposure to the cold, the women sued for $1,500 in damages.[27]

Even as racial discrimination influenced their cases, the personal injury suits that African Americans were able to litigate in state courts at the beginning of the twentieth century generally asked only to be reimbursed for their injuries and did not seek larger changes to the system of segregation. Wilson's suit, for instance, sought damages for her own illness, but did not challenge the segregation of waiting rooms.[28] Such suits thus had a limited impact on the lives of African Americans as a whole. By litigating a suit at all, however, African Americans brought the facts of their injuries on segregated transportation into the open, even if in a highly constrained manner.

As they litigated these cases, African Americans took part in the growth of tort law, a previously relatively undeveloped branch of law. In the mid-nineteenth century, American officials and judges had largely blamed train accidents on the injured individual, rather than on the railroad. Judges typically acted on the

principle that if the plaintiff was at all negligent, he had no right to any damages.[29] But as public fear of railroads grew during the second half of the nineteenth century, officials began to rethink their policies and started to penalize
railroads that did not sufficiently protect passengers. At the beginning of the
twentieth century, judges also began to shift to a new standard of judging personal injury law suits, in which a railroad or other entity could be held liable even
if the victim was partially to blame for the accident. As a result, more people
successfully sued railroads, and railroads began to give greater attention to passenger safety. In the turn-of-the-century South, in particular, personal injury
lawsuits against railroads increased and the success rate of railroad companies in
these suits declined. These shifts in tort law led to greater numbers of successful
personal injury lawsuits against people, cities, and other corporate entities.[30]

Moreover, cases involving women set important legal precedents in the
field of personal injury law, in time causing states to become more involved in
protecting citizens from injury. Although the courts expected men to be able
to assess risks and take responsibility for their judgments, they blamed women
less for their injuries because of their supposed vulnerability and protected status in society. Juries and judges also sometimes expected companies to exhibit
more care for women and children. As a result, cases of female injury led courts
to broaden the kinds of personal injury cases they considered and widen their
understandings of injury. In particular, women litigated the majority of cases
alleging accidental injury, a category previously often dismissed by the courts,
and nervous shock, a form of emotional injury, in appellate courts.[31]

Even though African Americans were likely more prone to injury because of
the segregation of southern society, their cases also fit into some of these general trends. Like other women, African American women made claims that their
male counterparts had difficulty making. Between 1900 and 1920, 41 percent
of the appellate personal injury suits examined involved black women as litigants.[32] In a number of these cases, women sought damages for exposure to the
cold and injury to their reproductive organs, and, occasionally, for emotional
injury incurred along with their physical injuries. In contrast, most of the male
litigants brought personal injury suits only for physical injuries that rendered
them unable to work or for injuries inflicted by violence.

To win their suits, black litigants and their lawyers would also have to meet
certain legal criteria that had been influenced by general shifts in tort litigation.
To make a personal injury claim, plaintiffs needed to show that the company
or city had a responsibility to protect them from injury. The company or city's
action also needed to have played an important causal role in the accident. In
addition, the injured parties needed to demonstrate that they had acted with
"ordinary care." If they had acted prudently, they could still gain damages even if
they had contributed to their own injury. If the court judged them to have taken

excessive risks, their claims for damages were much weaker. Finally, the plaintiffs had to provide proof that an actual injury had occurred and show the financial loss and physical pain that the injuries had caused.[33]

Even if black men's and women's accidents met all the qualifications for a personal injury case, they met opposition from railroads, cities, or private companies every step of the way. Railroad companies put in place a process to prevent personal injury cases from ever making it to court. Once they learned of an accident, the railroad sent their battery of agents, doctors, and lawyers to meet with the victims. The railroad agents and lawyers sought to convince the victims and their families to settle out of court. Louisa Smith, for instance, testified that the lawyer representing the railroad came to visit her after the incident, finding her "in the field, where I was plowing."[34] The railroad doctors also examined the victims, so that they would be prepared to testify in favor of the railroad if a court case could not be avoided.[35]

Many black men and women refused to give in to intimidation to settle their personal injury suits out of court. Although some of those injured could not obtain a lawyer, others succeeded in finding representation. Rebecca Sallee, for one, convinced two local white lawyers, Benjamin F. Roach and Robert Harding, to take her case against the city of Harrodsburg. Roach had served as a county judge in 1897, and Harding had been a county attorney and was the son of Aaron Harding, who represented Kentucky's fourth district in Congress from 1861 to 1867.[36]

Such lawyers often agreed to take on black clients if they believed there was a good chance they would win their case. In personal injury cases, lawyers frequently received significant percentages of the damages or had their costs paid by the defendant if their client won. They stood to be rewarded handsomely, then, if their clients triumphed over wealthy railroads or other corporations. Sallee's legal fees, for instance, would be paid by the town if she succeeded in her suit. The severely injured or widowed black clients who litigated personal injury cases also appealed to the paternalist leanings of white lawyers. At times, the white lawyers had known the black southerners they represented for many years, occasionally even as employees. One such litigant, Elizabeth Duncan, washed and ironed for a lawyer named J. C. Sims. When Duncan brought a case against the city for an injury she incurred on a public street, Sims served as her counsel. Sims and Duncan revealed their long-standing interactions in the informal manner of their questioning and answers. Sims began by asking Duncan, "How long have you been living in Bowling Green?" She responded, "Well, I don't know just exactly, Judge, you know I came here in the Spring after the cholera broke out." Later in the questioning, Sims asked her, "Did you do any work [before the injury]?" to which Duncan responded, "I washed and ironed for you."[37] Such a connection did not guarantee representation. In a 1918 Mississippi case brought by an inmate's mother against a telegraph company when she did not receive a telegram asking for money to give her son a proper burial, the mother washed and ironed for the family of a local lawyer named Thompson. When she litigated her case, however, Thompson did not represent her.[38]

In a few cases, black litigants' lawyers seem to have genuinely sympathized with the causes of their black clients. Sallee's lawyers, Benjamin Roach and Robert Harding, were no doubt motivated by the opportunity to obtain a percentage of their client's damages. The suit they filed sought $1,500 in damages and the litigation costs. However, Roach also showed some understanding of her economic circumstances. His appellate brief began with a quotation from Byron: "I stood at Venice on the palace of sighs A palace and a prison on either hand." Roach then emphasized the disparity between the lives of Sallee and her employer, the mayor: "College Street, Harrodsburg, Kentucky, exemplifies a rule in life that extremes lie in close propinquity to each other. At one end of this classic thoroughfare, reside the Mayor and Attorney for the City, whom the people delight to honor; at the other end, are the denizens of the Cornishville pike, hidden in darkness of color and obscurity 'To fame unknown . . . . ' The connecting link between the two extremes of this vicinity is Becky Sallee, Appellee, herein. For many years, she has hied her from the noise and aroma of her crowded cabin, to the quiet perfumed halls of the Mayor's mansion, there as a washerwoman, to contribute her measure of service to continue that 'cleanliness which is next to Godliness.' "[39]

In suits that reached the appellate level, black litigants usually had lawyers who argued their cases skillfully and fought hard to gain damages for their clients. To meet the qualifications for a legal claim of personal injury, the petitions penned by their lawyers usually stated the responsibility a city or corporation had to its citizens and consumers. Roach claimed that the city of Harrodsburg had a responsibility to maintain public roads free from danger to passersby. "By virtue of the laws under which it is incorporated," Roach wrote, Harrodsburg is "required to keep its side-walks and other public ways free from obstructions of every kind and in a reasonable safe condition, for the use of persons using and traveling thereon." Other suits by African American litigants against railroad or streetcar companies alleged that the transportation carriers were responsible for providing a safe environment for travel, including properly heated waiting rooms, an accident-free journey, and railroad cars free of violence. When cities or corporations violated this responsibility, lawyers claimed, they were liable for the injuries that occurred. Indeed, Roach argued that because the city had failed to keep public roads safe, they were liable for Rebecca Sallee's injuries and her subsequent loss of work.[40]

Lawyers also sought to prove that the defendants had been aware of the danger and could have rectified it. Roach asserted that a hole had been dug along College Street and "dirt, brick, and piping" piled up next to it. This "obstruction [was] known by the defendant, its officers and agents," he wrote, and "negligently suffered and permitted . . . to remain on said sidewalk for a considerable time." As he questioned the witnesses, Roach attempted to show that city officials had indeed had knowledge of the hole.[41]

Additionally, to strengthen their legal basis for damages, plaintiffs' lawyers tried to minimize their clients' responsibility for the accident and usually denied any negligence on their part. Roach put all of the responsibility for Sallee's accident firmly on the city, writing that it occurred "without fault on the part of the Plaintiff" and because of the "negligence of defendant." In response to such claims, defendants' lawyers denied negligence and sought to shift the blame on to the plaintiff. In one case, the 22-year-old black plaintiff's lawyer accused a train employee of having "negligently violently and with great and unnecessary force backed a locomotive engine against the caboose which plaintiff was occupying," breaking several of her ribs. The railroad's lawyers denied this and attempted to prove the passenger's own negligence. This was the first time the plaintiff had been on a freight train, they argued, and she had gotten aboard without adequate knowledge of the dangers and customs of such trains.[42]

Plaintiffs' lawyers attempted to prove the accident's long-term ill effects on the health and earnings of their clients, too. "By reason of said fall and consequent injury," Roach wrote, "plaintiff suffered great bodily pain and mental anguish, and has sustained loss of time and labor and was compelled to incur indebtedness for medical aid and attention, and her power to earn money has been permanently lessened." In cases involving women, lawyers could make additional claims for damage from "nervous shock" that were rarely made for male victims. Roach argued, for instance, that "by the shock to plaintiff's nerves her kidneys were caused thereby to be disturbed and diseased."[43]

Black litigants' lawyers also worked to poke holes in the stories of the opposing witnesses. As they did so, they revealed the pressure that the railroad and other companies could put on their employees to testify against plaintiffs—and at times to blatantly lie in court. In a 1917 Arkansas case, in which Elizabeth Franklin sued the railroad after becoming sick from a freezing "colored" waiting room, Franklin's lawyer cleverly highlighted the holes in a railroad employee's story. The employee, W. D. Sample, claimed that a fire had been built in the "colored" waiting room early in the day in question, before the plaintiff's arrival at the station, and then gave detailed testimony about his multiple trips to throw more coal on the stove during the afternoon and evening. In contrast, the black plaintiff, who was stranded at the Dustin, Arkansas, station with a small baby when her train broke down mid-journey, claimed that the "colored" waiting room had been freezing and no fire had been built there for weeks. The plaintiff's lawyer allowed Sample to state his version of the story, and then asked, "What kind of town is Dustin as to allowing colored people to live there?" Sample replied, "Well they don't let colored people live at all in the town." After a few more questions, the lawyer asked, "When had there been another colored passenger in that room waiting?" Sample responded, "I don't know." Upon being pressed, he admitted that it was "very seldom" for them to have a "colored passenger" in their waiting room. The lawyer then asked, "Do you mean to sit here and tell this jury that day after day and week after week without a colored passenger coming to that depot that you kept a fire in that waiting room?" At this point, the witness's story began to fall apart.[44]

The lawyer pressed on, asking a few minutes later, "There wasn't anything out of the ordinary about this womans conduct or appearance or anything else to attract your special attention?" Sample replied, "No, sir I didn't see anything out of the ordinary." The lawyer then asked, "In February more than a month after this woman was there you can remember back and can tell 7 times you went into the colored waiting room practically the exact hour you went in, and practically the number of lumps of coal you put in each time you went in?" When the witness objected to the question, the lawyer replied, "This is to show how impractical . . . [being able to remember such actions] would be."[45]

Another white lawyer exposed one of the defendant's witnesses in a 1908 Arkansas case, in which a black plaintiff claimed to have been injured as she alighted from a train. During the trial, the railroad's lawyer questioned Joe Hines, a black witness for the railroad company. Hines worked as a train porter for the company being sued and had charge of the "colored" coach. The railroad's lawyer asked Hines if he remembered anyone being hurt that night in Emmett, Arkansas. Hines replied, "No sir." He then asked Hines, "Was anything said that night about anybody getting hurt?" Hines replied, "Not that I heard." Finally, he asked, "Was there anything that night in the management of that train out of the usual way it was run?" Again, Hines responded "No sir." When the black litigant's lawyer got up to cross-examine the witness, he asked only one question of Hines: "Do you remember anything about that train that night except that you were on it?" Hines replied, "No sir; I don't." In this brief answer, Hines completely invalidated his previous testimony about the night in question.[46] Through one well-placed question, the black plaintiff's lawyer made a major hole in the railroad's case.

In most of the personal injury cases, the black plaintiffs took the stand to testify. Negotiating the minefield of questions from lawyers required an understanding of southern race relations and some grasp of the nature of personal injury claims.

Yet even as black litigants showed a keen awareness of who was deciding a case and the factors being used to decide it, they faced considerable invasions of their own privacy and attacks on their character and judgment.

As they faced off against powerful corporations, towns, and individuals, black litigants came under special scrutiny and were often blamed for the injuries they had received. The city's lawyer asked Sallee if she had noticed the construction work in that spot when she had passed it on previous days. She admitted that she had noted some construction, but adamantly insisted that she had not known there was a hole there. Other assertions of negligence attacked black women's character or the character of their families. Belle Boston responded to a question from the opposing lawyer: "I did not jump off [the streetcar] in a mad fit because I saw my husband with another woman."[47]

At times, lawyers attempted to prove negligence by claiming that black women had worn impractical clothing or shoes. In fact, women's bulky and unwieldy clothing frequently increased their rate of injury on public transportation. Recognizing this, the courts measured women by a different standard than men when determining whether they had been to blame for an accident.[48] Black women existed in an uncertain area in this regard—as women, they wore bulkier clothing than men but as African Americans they were often not seen as meriting the same protection as white women. These tensions are evident in a 1908 Arkansas case. During cross-examination, the railroad's lawyer asked the black plaintiff what kind of shoes she had on at the time of the accident. She replied, "Like I have got on now." The lawyer pressed further, "Isn't it a fact that you had on a shoe with a very low heel that night?" At this point the plaintiff's lawyer objected, saying "the railroad has no right to say what she can wear." The judge agreed, telling the court: "She has a right to wear a high or low, new or old shoe if she wants to." Despite the judge's decision to side with the plaintiff, the fact that the railroad's lawyer believed black women might be negligent if they wore impractical, feminine shoes highlights the uncertainty of black women's gender-based claims for protection.[49]

The physical nature of injury claims also led to the close examination of bodies in the courtroom. In particular, African American women's weight came under special scrutiny.[50] Ellen Bland, who sued the city of Mobile, Alabama, after falling through a footbridge, found her weight discussed by her doctor. "The plaintiff is a very heavy woman," the doctor testified, "and I consider that the injuries which she sustained to the ligaments of her ankle would be very apt to cause her permanent trouble." By giving his medical diagnosis in the same sentence in which he characterized her weight, the doctor implied that her injuries were particularly serious because of her weight.[51] Similarly, in another case, the city's lawyer began his brief by noting, "The appellee, Elizabeth Duncan is a colored woman of considerable size weighing about 200 pounds." By emphasizing her weight at the beginning of his brief, the city's lawyer sought to blame her weight, in part, for the plank slipping and causing her injury. During cross-examination, the city's lawyer also questioned Duncan about changes in her weight before and after the accident. Despite the invasiveness of such questioning, Duncan was unapologetic. When asked if she had "lost very much flesh" since her accident, she replied, "I haven't lost any . . . . Larger than I ever was in my life." The lawyer then asked her exact weight—231.5 pounds—and when she had last weighed herself. After a series of questions about her weight, the city's lawyer attempted to use her size to minimize her injury, asking, "Notwithstanding the severity of this injury you fatten all the time?" She turned this line of questioning on him, answering, "Well, I reckon I have fattened upon laying in room and suffering; I lay there and keep the limb up in a chair."[52] Despite Duncan's bold response, such questioning undermined black women's right to privacy and exposed their bodies in disturbing ways. Litigating a personal injury case put black women's bodies—as well as their claims—on trial.

Lawyers occasionally asked black female litigants invasive questions about their sexual relations with their husbands in cases in which they alleged damage to their reproductive organs. Such questioning came from their own lawyers, as well as from opposing counsel. By answering frankly, black women worked to prove their own injury claims—but such victories came at a cost. After Annie Young's reproductive organs were allegedly injured while getting onto a streetcar, the lawyer bringing the claim for her injury asked her, "whether you have been able or not since the time of the injury to have any relation with your husband?" Young replied candidly, "I have felt like it sometimes, not often. I don't really feel like it every time, of course, I have to bear it sometimes. I have pains attending it all of the time." During the trial, the same lawyer also asked a doctor testifying on Young's behalf whether Annie Young could engage in sexual relations with her husband. He replied, "I don't think she could without severe pain on her part from the fact that the womb being so low down and tender and inflame it would naturally be painful. In my opinion as a medical expert, she could not conceive in her present condition and have children." The plaintiff in the case, Annie Young's husband, won $300 in damages in both the lower and higher courts.[53] But by the end of the trial, everyone in the courtroom knew the most intimate details of Young's sexual life.

Even as they sought to fend off charges of negligence and submitted to examinations of their bodies, black litigants used their knowledge of the law and of racial mores to perform roles that they thought white judges and juries would view most favorably. In their testimony, they provided the proof of physical injury and loss of income necessary to gain legal damages.[54] At the same time, by emphasizing their weakness and work ethic to the court, they appealed to white southerners' ideas about racial inequality and how black people should act. This testimony against a barrage of lawyers, doctors, and other witnesses helped many of their suits end in a favorable verdict.

First, the plaintiffs had to provide proof that an actual injury had occurred. As they took the stand, black litigants gave detailed accounts of the events surrounding their accidents and the physical injuries they had incurred. Often the injuries that black litigants had received were so severe that they presented themselves as weak and helpless merely by stating their situation. One such plaintiff, Elizabeth Franklin, testified that after her injury, "I suffered severe pain, it would almost take my breath away."[55] Another litigant, Anna Dougherty, told the court, "that she was very weak in health and was not strong at all, and was in a great deal of bad feeling and trouble; that she was going to Atlanta in consequence of the death of her husband, who had died in Atlanta."[56]

Some litigants went further to dramatically prove their injuries. Sallee seems to have gestured to her injuries, as she testified that her back "hurts me when I drew a long breath, right through here." She continued, "it never has quit hurting me. I can't work with my hands good, and my back hurts me and is weak." Similarly, Belle Boston testified about her railroad accident: "I held to the guard rail with my right hand and careened over and around and fell and was dragged some distance while thus hanging to the car, and in such a way as to cause my left arm to be thrown under one of the wheels of the car, where it was badly mashed and bruised." Then, in the midst of her testimony, the court reporter inserted: "Here the witness ripped her sleeve and exposed her arm, showing to the jury the cuts and scars on both sides and over her elbow joints, which she said was caused by the car wheel running over her arm."[57] Belle Boston clearly recognized the role of performance in the courtroom.

Even as they emphasized the harm caused by their injuries, black men and women sought to meet another legal requirement to gain damages: demonstrating proof of their loss of income. Here, black female litigants were aided by the expectation of whites that they would make a living through manual labor. As these cases reveal, whites expected black women—whether married or unmarried, childless or mothers—to work throughout their lives. Black women were not asked by lawyers if they worked, but only what kind of work they performed. Under cross-examination, an opposing lawyer questioned Alberta Petties, "Where were you at work at?" She replied, "I was not at work at all." The lawyer responded, "Why were you not at work?" She replied simply, "I just didn't have any work to do." The lawyer pressed on, unable to believe that she had never worked at all, asking, "What kind of work had you been doing?" Petties then explained to the court that she had previously worked as a cook.[58]

If black women were all expected to work, they naturally would lose income if injured. Indeed, with a few exceptions, such as Petties, the vast majority of female litigants in personal injury suits testified that they held down several jobs at the time of their injuries. Rebecca Sallee stated that at the time of her accident, "I was janitor at two churches, cleaned up Dr Witherspoon's office and had two washings." Less regularly, she served as a nurse for women or worked in the cornfield. Similarly, Antoinette Whitehead told the court: "I worked at any kind of work any human being in the shape of a woman can do; house work, hoeing, picking cotton."[59] Other women worked as sick nurses, domestic employees, cooks, and farm workers.

In their testimony and petitions, black women and their lawyers emphasized the damage the injuries had caused them in loss of work and in future earnings. Sallee explained to the court that after her accident, "I had to give up one of the churches and all my work except Mrs Thompson's [the mayor's wife], from the 7th of October until some time in January." When the lawyer inquired why she didn't continue with all of her work, she replied, "I couldn't, and couldn't wash—it hurt my back, and hurts it yet." Belle Boston's petition stated, "your petitioner shows that she earns her living, and did at the time of said accident by doing manual labor, and that since said accident her earning capacity has been reduced fully one-half, and that she is thirty years of age, and supports herself and her child by the proceeds of her labor."[60] Often, lawyers asked women during the trial if they had tried to go back to work after their injury. Adamantly, they insisted that they were unable to work at their previous rate or were unable to work at all, despite attempts to return to work. Elizabeth Franklin replied to a lawyer's query by stating, "I remember once that I went out and tried to wash the dishes and standing on my feet I suppose hurt me I suppose the muscles in my legs. My left ovary was bad and hurt so I had to go home and lie down."[61]

At times, women emphasized their families' dependence on their earnings. Most of the women litigating personal injury suits were married. Still, some such as Delia Fitzhugh were the primary providers for their families. Fitzhugh testified, "I am the Plaintiff in this Cause; am twenty three years old and the mother of two children and provide for them and myself by my own labor . . . . I cannot now wash as I could before I was injured & can be of little service to my mother in aiding her . . . . My husband abandoned me two years ago and now gives me no assistance."[62] By explaining the way in which their injuries affected their ability to provide for their families, black women strengthened their claims for compensation.

Emphasizing their employment history and hardworking nature also made litigants seem less threatening to white jury members and judges. After explaining the injuries he received in a railroad accident, a black mail clerk named G. H. Bowen testified: "I am attending to my duties as Mail Clerk now; I suffer almost continually now, and I am weak, not as strong as I was before I was hurt; I do not lay up; I do not avoid exertion; I go about all I can."[63] By making it clear that they were continuing to work as much as they could, black litigants attempted to dispel any belief that white juries and judges may have had that they were just looking for a handout. Such assertions spoke to white southerners' recurring fear that black men and women would not work without coercion.

To further strengthen their cases, a number of black litigants and their lawyers shifted the focus of their suits from the litigants' race to their role as women or as citizens of a community. Black women, in particular, emphasized their special need for protection as women. In their testimony and petitions, they highlighted situations in which they had been placed in compromising or dangerous positions by companies or towns. Anna Dougherty, an elderly black woman traveling to Atlanta for her husband's funeral, testified that a railroad conductor ejected her from her train around midnight, claiming that her ticket was for a different destination. She found herself alone in an unknown part of the countryside, late at night, with almost no money. She explained in her testimony, "the conductor had said . . . that there was a colored man going to get off at that station and that he (the colored man) would make some provision for her." Dougherty insisted that such a situation was not safe for a woman traveling alone, telling the conductor "that she knew nothing about the man." When the local man "told her he would do the best he could for her, that he was sorry his wife was not at home," she told him that "she did not care to go to his house if his wife was not at home."[64]

In response, the local man took her to the house of an elderly man two and a half miles from the station and asked him to take her in. Dougherty emphasized the rough conditions, saying that she "walked across a plank over a creek" to "a log cabin with only one room, having a bunk in it." Upon reaching the cabin, "she sat up all night in a hard, rough, chair." As a result of her exposure to "the night air in her condition of health and having to walk the distance she did," she claimed to have contracted neuralgia, a condition of pain in the nerves, and to be in a delicate state, having "to be very careful and wrap up all the time." Dougherty repeatedly highlighted conditions that she felt were not safe for a respectable woman traveling alone. By drawing on ideas of respectability and gender norms as well as her status as a consumer, she appealed to the white men serving on juries and as judges for protection and strengthened her injury claim against the railroad.[65]

Black litigants also spoke to dangers in the community that whites recognized and sought to address. Although black litigants met many obstacles when they litigated race-based cases that sought larger policy changes for African Americans, when the changes they sought benefited white southerners, making a claim for the broader impact of their suits could aid their cause. Cases litigated by African Americans highlighting the way the railroad killed, maimed, and severely injured passengers, employees, and passersby spoke to societal fears. Likewise, cases litigated by African Americans against towns for holes in the sidewalk or open water cisterns highlighted situations that white citizens also sought to remedy.

Ellen Bland, for instance, litigated a suit against the city of Mobile, Alabama, in 1904, after falling through a footbridge leading from the street to the sidewalk.[66] The condition of the roads was a cause for outcry in the white community at the time. A newspaper article less than a year after her suit explained that many business people in the area "are up in arms because of the conditions existing in the asphalted paving in that territory. Holes of all sizes have appeared in many of the blocks in the district from time to time and the board of public works, which has absolute charge of the territory, is now the brunt of the blame." The condition of the roads had been brought up before the board of public works a number of times, the reporter said, with no results. He concluded, "The repair work is essentially necessary and the interested persons are much concerned thereat."[67] Bland's suit over a dangerous footbridge along the road thus had the potential to remedy a longstanding problem in the community.

Sometimes, black litigants and their lawyers emphasized the ways a threat affected other white and black citizens. Rebecca Sallee's lawyer, Benjamin Roach, asked a white witness for Sallee, "Is there a considerable prt [part] of the town out on the Cornishville pike—out that way, that are foot passengers?" The witness, a white election official, replied, "Yes, a great many of the people who live out there are foot travelers . . . . Most everybody from out that way has to walk." Roach then asked a white witness for the defense: "How far is the [white] Graded School from where this accident occurred?" He replied, "I don't know, 400 or 500 yards."[68] Another black plaintiff, Diana Hobbs, fell into an unmarked, recently excavated hole as she walked along a path near the railroad late at night. During the trial, her lawyer asked her how much other members of the community used the path. She testified, "There is at least 25 school children and sometimes more, regularly travel that," both white and "colored." The defense counsel for the railroad made repeated attempts to have this portion of Hobbs's testimony stricken from the record, an indication of the power of her assertions. The judge, however, overruled the objections and allowed her testimony.[69] As black litigants and their lawyers emphasized the way the threats in question affected white and black members of the community, they transformed their cases from suits over an individual person's injury to suits over a danger that threatened the community. In doing so, they made their claims relevant to the white members of their community who would decide their cases.

With deep coffers to draw from, the defense frequently put forward powerful experts and officials to testify in its favor. Railroads, in particular, developed relationships with doctors whom they could then call upon in personal injury cases.

In some cases, they regularly paid these doctors; in other instances, they retained the doctors on a case-by-case basis. The railroads provided other doctors with free travel. When accidents occurred, the railroads encouraged the injured passengers and employees to see these doctors. As they treated these patients, the doctors' loyalty to their employers usually remained paramount. They carefully noted any preexisting conditions or other factors that could lessen the railroad's culpability for the accident and any damaging admissions their patients made.[70] If cases went to trial, the doctors ordinarily testified in favor of the railroad.

Cities also put powerful officials on the stand to testify in their defense.[71] In a 1906 Kentucky case, a black woman who had fallen through a plank in the sidewalk brought an injury claim against the city of Bowling Green. During the trial, Mayor George T. Wilson testified that he did not know the plaintiff Elizabeth Duncan and claimed that he had never received any information about a defect in the sidewalk where Duncan was injured.[72] Rebecca Sallee's employer, the city's mayor, also testified against her, stating that he had noticed she had stopped working for his family for several months, but didn't know "how she got hurt." Despite his clear efforts to aid the city's defense, his testimony about the inner workings of the city's sewer construction helped Sallee's cause. He admitted under cross-examination that to connect an individual home to the sewer pipe running along the street, a resident had to pay a tax and get a license from the town. It was therefore impossible, he revealed, for the town not to have known about the hole, because they had to permit it to be dug.[73] As the testimony of these city officials shows, litigants like Sallee and Duncan made their communities take notice of the black citizens in their midst and showed local leaders that they could exercise a measure of power in the courts.

To counteract the powerful experts and officials testifying against them, black litigants who succeeded in litigating personal injury cases in their state's highest courts drew on white witnesses of their own. In a number of cases, they managed to find doctors to testify for them. One of Sallee's witnesses, Dr. Witherspoon, was employed by the city of Harrodsburg—the defendant—as the town doctor. As such, he seemed an unlikely witness for a plaintiff in a suit against the city. But Sallee cleaned Witherspoon's office and had been his patient for several years. After her accident, he visited her several times to provide medical attention. When Sallee sued the city after her injury, he told the court that the accident that had befallen Sallee led to an inflammation of the lining of the kidneys.[74] Like Witherspoon, other doctors—even some on railroad and city payrolls— testified on behalf of black litigants. Some, like Witherspoon, had long-term relations with the litigants.[75] Most had financial motivations to testify on behalf of their patients. Unless their patient won their case, these doctors knew they would not get paid for their medical treatment.[76] After testifying for Elizabeth Duncan, for instance, Dr. O. D. Porter was asked under cross-examination if the medical bill Duncan owed him had been paid; he answered "No, sir; it has not been paid."[77]

Other white members of the community—including many who did not know the plaintiffs personally—testified in favor of injured black litigants as well. Some testified out of concern for the threat that such holes posed to themselves or to their communities. Occasionally they had ties to the plaintiff's lawyer or to the black plaintiff. One such witness for Sallee, a local election official named Z. D. Bryant, did not seem to know her at all. He explained that he had been out late counting ballots for an election on Tuesday night when he first saw the hole along College Street. He saw the hole again the next night, he said, while walking with his son and niece, and cautioned the young people to "look out." His testimony established that the hole had existed at least two days before Sallee's accident—directly contradicting the city's contention that it had been dug only a few hours before Sallee fell. Likewise, R. W. Keenon, a member of the town street committee, testified in Sallee's favor. He explained that the city had made a contract with Mr. Adams, the town plumber, to install a sewer pipe along College Street. The hole Sallee had fallen into had resulted from Adams's connecting this main sewer pipe to one of the residences. Keenon thus demonstrated the town's responsibility for the gaping hole in the street.[78] Whatever the reason white witnesses like these testified, their statements to the court proved crucial in establishing these accidents as matters of concern for the entire community, rather than only for its black members.

Unlike other types of cases, such as disputes over wills, which were often decided by judges, juries decided nine-tenths of personal injury suits. Although composed almost exclusively of white men by the first decade of the twentieth century, these juries decided for African Americans, as well as against them. Of the eighty-eight appellate fraud cases between white and black litigants involving juries, black litigants had won sixty-nine cases (78 percent of suits) at the lower-court level.[79] Indeed, in Sallee's trial, the city of Harrodsburg did not trust these white men to rule in the city's favor. To increase the odds in the city's favor, the city's lawyer requested that the judge give a "peremptory instruction" supporting the city to the jury. Such an "instruction" would strongly influence the jury to decide for the defendant and against Sallee. The judge refused the defendant's request.[80] Judges played an important role in guiding juries even if they did not direct their verdicts. In Sallee's case, the judge told the jury that they should find for the plaintiff if they believed that the obstruction was one that would "cause persons walking and who were exercising reasonable watchfulness for their own safety, to stumble and fall," if they found that the hole had been in place "an unreasonable length of time" before the accident, if any officers of the city government knew about the hole or "by the exercise of reasonable diligence might have known it," and if they believed that the plaintiff "was reasonably watchful for her own safety." The amount of damages, the judge told the jury, should "be for such sum as will fairly compensate the plaintiff for any physical pain and suffering, caused by her injury, for any loss of time as a laboring woman, and for any permanent impairment of her power to labor . . . all of which must be shown by the evidence."[81]

The jury left to confer. The nine white men had all been born in Kentucky except Joseph Kellar, an immigrant from Germany. All but two of the men were farmers; the others worked as a miller and as a gardener. Their average age was 46. They represented in many ways ordinary, white working-class southerners. After conferring, they returned with a verdict. They found in favor of Sallee, awarding her $300 in damages and ordering the city to pay her approximately $200 in litigation costs.[82]

The city appealed the ruling to the state of Kentucky's highest court, saying that the lower-court judge should have sustained its motion for a peremptory instruction to the jury. To decide the case, the appeals court relied on precedents set by earlier personal injury cases in Kentucky, as well as in Michigan, Nebraska, and Indiana.[83] In the end, the court decided that although the defendant city insisted that the dirt pile had been there for only 4 hours at the time of the accident and the city had no time to learn of the problem, this was "clearly in error." "The evidence clearly shows," the opinion said, "that the hole was dug on Wednesday afternoon—the day before the accident . . . . The obstruction, therefore, had been upon the sidewalk for about thirty hours previous to the accident . . . . Moreover, there was evidence strongly tending to show that the hole was dug and the dirt piled upon the sidewalk under the direction of Farney, the city's superintendent of its water works." As a result, the opinion concluded, the lower court's instructions to the jury had been proper and the judgment in favor of Sallee was affirmed. Sallee received $300 in damages from the city, the equivalent of 1 year's pay, as well as an additional $202 to cover her legal costs and pay interest on the damages.[84]

Other black litigants in personal injury suits in the eight appellate courts examined had similar success. Between 1900 and 1920, the eight state supreme courts examined affirmed lower-court rulings in favor of black litigants in 45 percent of such suits and reversed 14 percent of lower-court rulings against African Americans in these suits.[85] The personal injury cases involving black litigants that made it to appeals courts, of course, often had especially strong legal claims, and the decisions made by higher courts were not representative of those made by local courts in personal injury cases. Moreover, these appellate courts frequently awarded black litigants only a part of the damages they sought. Nevertheless, it remains significant that black litigants in personal injury suits gained any damages at all in southern state courts.

The news of Sallee's legal victory spread quickly around the town of Harrodsburg. Almost every witness during the trial had heard about her fall within a few days of her injury. Seventy-five-year-old Jim McCann, a black witness who lived in the same section of town as Sallee, said that "a few days after she got hurt, I heard of it." More surprising, young white teenagers, like the election official's niece Mary Gore and his son Christopher Bryant, testified that they had heard about Rebecca Sallee's fall two or three days after it occurred. Her court case—and the state supreme court's judgment in her favor—would have been even bigger news. The newspaper in Lexington, Kentucky—over 30 miles away—printed a notice of her case, alongside other decisions recently made by the state supreme court.[86]

One year later, the city of Harrodsburg sued the man who had left the hole in the ground in order to recoup its expenses from Sallee's case. This time, the city lost at the county court level but won its case before the state supreme court. C. S. Vanarsdall had to reimburse the city for the damages it had paid out to Rebecca Sallee.[87] Sallee herself remained in Harrodsburg surrounded by her large family. During the 1920s, she worked as a private nurse for a local family.[88] By 1930, 20 years after her case, the census lists her profession as a nurse for a private patient, but noted that she was unemployed. Perhaps her injuries prevented her from working as hard as she once had. Work was also likely hard to come by in 1930, as the Great Depression settled over the nation. Or maybe, at age 68, she finally had taken a much needed rest.[89]

Then, in 1932, Sallee reappeared in court as a key witness for the plaintiffs in a court case over the estate of her former employer. Labeling her a "colored nurse," the court record states that she was present when an agreement over the employer's estate was reached with his heirs in the 1920s. Partly on the strength of her testimony, the Mercer Circuit Court and then the Kentucky Court of Appeals—where her own case had been heard—decided in the plaintiffs' favor.[90] Despite no special legal knowledge or training, Rebecca Sallee had played a role in three cases that reached Kentucky's highest court.

As white southerners surmised, personal injury suits were not radical challenges to the status quo. They did not seek overt policy changes or advocate for larger groups. Even though the injuries had sometimes been caused by discrimination, the ensuing cases did not pose an outright challenge to segregation. Instead, they dealt with the health and future earnings of a single individual or family. At a time of rising discrimination, they highlighted African Americans in particularly vulnerable, helpless positions.

Yet these cases had real consequences. The public outcry over railroad safety and increasingly large number of lawsuits against transportation carriers contributed to better industry safety standards.[91] Because of these suits, individual

African Americans at times received the funds they needed to recover after an injury or to feed their families. In addition, these cases showed companies and communities that black southerners would continue to fight for their rights as citizens and as consumers. Even though their cases appeared relatively harmless to white southerners, the fact that African Americans continued to participate in the civil courts posed a subtle—but important—counterbalance to the discrimination and segregation of the Jim Crow South.

Fighting for Rights in the Courts

In 1935, Mary Jackson had owned a 10-acre plot of land in Hinds County, Mississippi, for 32 years. Her partner, Enoch Jackson, had bought the land in 1903, and even when he left her after 7 years, she stayed on the land. She was still there when he returned 14 years later. They reconciled and married, only to divorce 2 years later, in 1926. Once again, she remained on the land after he left. Then in 1928 she fell behind on her taxes, and a white neighbor bought a claim to her property at a "tax sale" of unpaid taxes. She fought off the tax title claim in the local court and prevailed. But in 1934, a white woman named Mrs. J. W. Broome purchased this same "tax title" to her property. With this in hand, Broome claimed the elderly black woman's property for herself. When Jackson refused to give up her land, her lawyer reported, an anonymous group of white men came "during the darkest hours of the night" and brutally beat her. She was warned as they left "to vacate her property or she would be given another beating more severe."[1]

Mary Jackson left her property, and not long afterward her house mysteriously burned down. Instead of abandoning her claim, Jackson turned to the courts to regain her property. In 1941, a white lawyer filed a petition on her behalf in the Hinds County Chancery Court requesting that the court confirm her claim to the property and reject Broome's claim. The petition explained that she had left her land only after being brutally beaten by men representing the white woman's interests.[2]

Ethel New's husband was stationed at Camp Pickett, Virginia in the summer of 1944, as World War II began to near its end. She had just spent the past few months at the camp visiting him and was returning home to Kentucky 3 months pregnant. She boarded the first bus of her journey late on the night of June 11. The bus, which she planned to take from Blackstone, Virginia, to Appalachia, Virginia, was full of soldiers and sailors. There were no available seats in the back section of the bus normally reserved for African Americans so Ethel stood up for the first 81-mile leg of the journey, despite feeling tired and nauseated from her pregnancy. Finally, at the stop in Lynchburg, Virginia, many of the passengers on the bus got off and the exhausted woman gratefully sat down in a reclining seat in the second to last row.[3]

Ethel New had just drifted off to sleep when the bus driver shook her to wake her up, ordering her to move to the last row of the bus. A number of white passengers had just gotten on, and African American passengers, like New, were expected to make way for whites. Unlike New's current seat, though, the back bench of the bus was hard and did not recline. Its position—directly on top of the bus's motor and below a ventilator that drew in hot air from the rest of the bus—made it even more uncomfortable. The weary woman refused to move. Angered by her refusal, the bus driver left to call local police officers to the scene. Soon, two officers arrived and again asked her to move back. She replied that she had been visiting her husband "and that he was a soldier wearing the uniform of the United States, a representative of our country, and she has as much right to ride there as anybody else." In response, the officer told her, "Now you be a good soldier, as good a soldier as your husband, and come on and get back in the back seat." Unpersuaded, New told the officer: "it says in the Bible that you must love your neighbor as yourself." He replied that "the Bible did say that, but that had nothing to do with this situation," and she needed to "go ahead and move on back there." When she still did not move, the bus driver and an officer dragged her off by her shoulders and legs, as she screamed and cried in protest. The bus left without her, and she was forced to board the next bus 2 hours later.[4]

After reaching Kentucky, New's back and leg still ached from being pulled off the bus. One week after her return, she suffered a miscarriage, which she blamed on her treatment by the officers. Ethel New then hired a lawyer who filed a personal injury suit on her behalf in a Richmond, Virginia, court. The suit protested not only her own treatment and the loss of her unborn child, but also the segregation laws that required her to sit in the back of the bus.[5]

~~

For generations, black barbers in Atlanta, Georgia, had cut the hair of many of the city's white residents. During the first decades of the twentieth century, many operated out of black-owned barbershops downtown and, to preserve their white clientele, refused service to African Americans. The black men who owned the shops had commonly started as barbers themselves, eventually buying one or more barbershops of their own. While some barbershops undoubtedly struggled to get by, others catered to the white elite. Alonzo Herndon's well-known establishment at 66 Peachtree Street boasted in advertisements of its twenty-five nickel-plated barber chairs upholstered with "fine Spanish leather in a rich green shade," at which twenty-three barbers worked. The barbershop's enormous walls were lined with "French beveled mirrors," the ceilings covered in white pressed-tin, and the floors laid with white tile. Overhead, four crystal chandeliers lit the room. A steady stream of white judges, politicians, and wealthy businessmen came through its mahogany doors to be shaved, bathe, have their shoes shined and suits pressed, and, of course, get haircuts.[6]

Alonzo Herndon himself was one of the wealthiest black men in America by the mid-1920s. Almost seven decades earlier, in 1858, he had been born a slave in rural Social Circle, Georgia. His father—a white slave-owner—had several children with multiple enslaved women as well as a white family of his own. After gaining his freedom at the end of the Civil War, Herndon tried his hand at sharecropping. Then, at the age of 20, Herndon recalled, "I went to Jonesborough and hired myself to a barber for six dollars a month and learned the barbers trade." Soon, he had his own barbershop in Jonesboro. After 4 years, Herndon decided to move on, eventually ending up in Atlanta in 1882. The city had been rebuilt after the war and was quickly becoming the region's commercial hub. After partnerships with several established barbers, Herndon went into business for himself in 1890. By 1926, 68-year-old Herndon owned three barbershops, including the "Crystal Palace" on Peachtree Street, had extensive real estate holdings around Atlanta, and operated a large insurance association named Atlanta Mutual for African Americans.[7]

Then, in the mid-1920s, at the height of Prohibition, a few police reports began to come in of illicit sales of alcohol at black-owned Atlanta barbershops. Around the same time, an African American man was caught engaged in sex with a white woman, whom he had reportedly met in a black-operated barbershop. White barbers in Atlanta saw a chance to rid themselves of their competition. At the instigation of the white barbers' union, in February 1926 the General Council of the City of Atlanta pushed through a city ordinance prohibiting African Americans from cutting the hair of whites. This ordinance was too extreme for many white Atlantans, who relied on black barbers' services. In addition to the protests of black barbershop owners, letters poured in to the council, the mayor, and *The Atlanta Constitution* from white people outraged at the new law. T. J. Hightower, for one, wrote to the *Constitution*: "I have had a colored barber since I was old enough to receive that service, and am old-fashioned enough to want to continue it."[8]

As a result, two weeks later the city council revised the ordinance to only prohibit black barbers from cutting the hair of white women and children and from operating after 7 p.m. on weekdays and after 9 p.m. on Saturdays. This ordinance still cut into the business of the city's black barbershops, who did a steady business in the evening hours when men stopped by their shops after work. In response, a group of black barbershop owners—including Alonzo Herndon—filed a civil suit in the Fulton County Superior Court to overturn the

Fig. 8.1 Full-page newspaper advertisement for Alonzo Herndon's barbershops, 1914. *The Atlanta Constitution*, May 12, 1914, p. 12. Courtesy of The Herndon Foundation.

discriminatory city ordinance. Not only did the city council not have the power to pass such an ordinance, their suit claimed, but the ordinance deprived them of their property rights and violated the 14th Amendment of the US Constitution.[9]

Between 1921 and 1950, black southerners continued to participate in a steady stream of civil suits, litigating 548 civil cases against white litigants in eight southern state supreme courts. During these three decades, the kinds of cases that

Fig. 8.2 Inside of Tattnall County Courtroom, Georgia, 1930s. Courtesy of the Georgia Archives, Vanishing Georgia Collection, tat049.

African Americans could litigate in southern courts broadened and they began making stronger claims in their suits. Even seemingly ordinary types of civil cases over property, contracts, wills, and personal injury—like the case of Mary Jackson—began to sometimes make bolder claims and protest the violence experienced by black southerners. Other civil cases that initially appeared to be just about an individual's economic claims at times made larger assertions about African Americans' right to equal treatment. For instance, while personal injury cases during the first two decades of the twentieth century had shied away from making larger claims about the inequality often at the root of African Americans' injuries, some personal injury cases during the following three decades, like the one brought by Ethel New, challenged that very inequality on behalf of all African Americans. In addition, just as they had throughout the decades since the Civil War, a limited number of cases between 1921 and 1950—like Alonzo Herndon's case over the barbershop ordinance—challenged racial discrimination head-on. Many of these civil cases demanding racial justice in state courts seem to have originated with individuals, rather than having been orchestrated by national organizations; at times, though, such cases overlapped with the efforts of organizations.

Compared with those of the previous two decades, black litigants' civil cases were being heard by state courts in higher numbers. While their civil cases against both white and black litigants had made up 1 of every 193 appellate cases between 1900 and 1920, from 1921 to 1950, their cases made up 1 of every 119 civil and criminal appellate cases in the states examined. The volume increased in part during these decades as state populations grew and the number of cases heard by southern appellate courts increased across the board. But their cases more than doubled during a time when cases as a whole increased by a little over a third.[10] The rise in African Americans' case volumes and the boldness of many of their suits was likely due in large part, then, to changes in society that made such cases possible.

Like earlier civil cases between white and black southerners, these cases were a product of their times. The two world wars played a part in defining this period. In 1921, World War I had ended just three years previously. World War II would last from 1939 to 1945, bringing more than a million black soldiers to the front and other African Africans to the North and the West for jobs in the booming war industry. Black soldiers' experiences at war—as well as their families' experiences supporting them at home—undoubtedly influenced their ideas about rights.[11] Ethel New's husband was preparing to ship off to Europe when officers asked her to move to the back of the bus. Her response that her husband "was a soldier wearing the uniform of the United States, a representative of our county, and she has as much right to ride there as anybody else" drew a connection between her husband's service and her own right to equal treatment. Other black veterans and their family members called attention to their military service as they claimed rights in court. In the Atlanta barbershop case, one of the plaintiffs fighting the discriminatory ordinance pointed out that his son—one of the barbers in his shop—was a recent veteran of World War I.[12]

The Great Depression of the late 1920s and 1930s affected African Americans' civil cases as well. People all over the country struggled to pay mortgages and lost their jobs, but black southerners found themselves hit especially hard. It was during 1929—the year of the stock market crash—that Mary Broome failed to pay her taxes and had the tax title to her property sold, leading to her legal troubles.[13] Franklin Roosevelt's New Deal impacted suits too. Although many parts of the New Deal excluded African Americans, black southerners benefited from it on a limited basis. In 1935, for instance, the Social Security Act created a system of pensions for the elderly and unemployment compensation. In one 1943 Arkansas case resulting from this Act, a corporation battled in the courts over whether it was responsible for paying the unemployment compensation claim filed by a black laborer.[14]

The Great Migration, a decades-long movement of black and white southerners from the South to the North, was also already underway by the second decade of the twentieth century and would permanently reshape the country's demographics. While the vast majority of African Americans had lived in the South until this time, between 1915 and 1970, approximately 6 million black southern-ers moved north and west. In the North, black southerners found higher wages and could exercise some rights, like voting, that had become nearly impossible to wield in the South. Additionally, black southerners, like Ethel New, who spent time in the North, were undoubtedly affected by their experiences there. Upon being asked to move to the back of the bus, New told the officer that "she had been living in Chicago, and in Chicago where she had been . . . the white and col-ored folks got along very nicely, and down here we appeared that we didn't want to cooperate together." Even in the North, though, African Americans would encounter discrimination in housing and employment as well as race riots and discrimination in the courts.[15]

Back in the South, grassroots mobilization for rights continued. At the begin-ning of this period, black men and women found it difficult to vote throughout much of the South. American women had ostensibly received the vote nationally in 1920, but black women in the South found their voting rights highly curtailed. As more and more black southerners moved northward, the Great Migration began to change political calculuses in the North, making some politicians dependent on African American votes to win elections. When pushing through the New Deal, President Roosevelt created a new Democratic political coalition, of which African Americans were a part. In part because of African Americans' rising power in national politics, black southerners' efforts to exercise their vot-ing rights began to bear some fruit. In the mid-1940s, voting drives throughout the South led to increases in black voter registration. At times, new black voters had to pay decades of cumulative poll taxes. Others faced violence and threats. A number of black voters persevered, though, often voting for the Democratic Party. By 1947, an estimated 12 percent of African Americans had registered to vote in the South. As voter registration lists in southern counties were generally linked to jury rolls, African Americans also began to serve on southern juries in somewhat larger numbers.[16]

Despite some black southerners' ability to practice political rights, the vast edifice of institutional racism remained in place. Although public lynchings had begun to decrease, violence still played an integral role in southern life. Mary Jackson, for instance, had been brutally beaten to get her to abandon her land.[17] While it continued to be challenged, segregation remained integral to the opera-tion of southern race relations. A number of personal injury cases highlight the unequal conditions that led to injuries for African Americans. In one 1921 Tennessee suit, the white employees at a chemical factory were provided with hot water to wash up after the day's work while black employees at the factory had to use a reservoir outside to clean the chemicals off their bodies. When one of the African American employees drowned in the reservoir, his parents brought a personal injury suit against the factory. Segregation affected whites'

suits as well. One Kentucky coal mine provided water only to its white employees. After "colored" employees began to drink the water as well, a superintendent
electrified the metal drinking cup to prevent people of color from drinking from
it. When a white employee was electrocuted by the cup and lost the use of his
arm, he brought a suit against his employer for damages.[18]

Other national trends affected African Americans' cases, too. From 1920 to
1933, during Prohibition, the sale of alcohol was banned in the United States.
Instead of disappearing, alcohol sales and consumption went underground.
Several criminal cases involving African Americans accused the defendants
of buying or selling moonshine and other forms of illegal alcohol. While
Prohibition appeared less often in civil cases, the testimony of several police-
men about illicit alcohol sales in black barbershops during evening hours
would play an important role in the Atlanta barbershop trial of *Chaires v. City
of Atlanta* in 1926. One of the officers testifying in support of the city's case
reported three criminal cases in the last year in which a black barbershop
employee had been caught with alcohol. In one of these cases, the officer testified, a barber named Woodson Jackson "was caught in possession of nine gal-
lons of corn whiskey in cans at a barber shop at No.226 Houston Street"; in the
other two cases the same bootblack was caught with whiskey in two different
barbershops.[19]

In addition, new technologies such as automobiles and electric light became
a larger part of all Americans' lives during the 1920s, 1930s, and 1940s. As more
Americans gained access to these inventions, African Americans' personal injury
cases increasingly involved claims for injuries from automobile and electrical
accidents. Julia DeGraffenreid brought such a suit against the Nashville Railway
& Light Company in 1924, for instance, after she had been electrocuted while
attempting to turn on an overhead light in her home. Alleging faulty wiring, she
asked for $10,000 in damages from the electric company.[20]

Even as changes occurred in the world around them, many aspects of black litigants' suits remained the same. Between 1921 and 1950 most appellate civil
cases examined between black and white litigants involved economic matters
that would impact an individual black person's life, rather than make claims for
larger groups or for all those classified as African American. Limitations in the
kinds of civil cases that black southerners could litigate persisted. As whites continued to bring a broad range of cases against other whites, personal injury and
fraud suits remained the most common types of cases litigated between black
and white southerners. Together, they made up more than half of the civil suits
litigated by African Americans in eight state supreme courts. Between 1921 and
1950, 212 cases were litigated over personal injury (39 percent of suits) and 75
cases were litigated over cases of fraud (14 percent of suits).[21]

Just as they had in preceding decades, white lawyers and their black clients sometimes used racial stereotypes to advance their litigation. One such stereotype was that of the faithful black servant. In a 1940 Mississippi case, the black plaintiff, Walter Hickman, claimed to have a verbal agreement with an elderly white man whom he cared for during the last 5 years of the man's life. According to their agreement, Hickman would not be regularly paid during his service, but would be generously provided for after the man's death. But when the white man died, his will left nothing for Hickman. In response, Hickman brought a civil suit against the estate. Although the case transcript is missing, he and his lawyer were sufficiently convincing of his loyalty and faithfulness that the appellate court opinion in Hickman's favor described him as "faithful to the end." The plaintiff's side had shown, the opinion said, "that this old negro consented to sell his live stock, wagon, etc., which he had been using on his own ten-acre farm, and to forego making further crops, in order that he might thereafter give his time to the constant care of his friend and the neighbor in his great need."[22] Clearly, this stereotype still held power in influencing the decisions of southern courts.

Other stereotypes damaged both black litigants' cases and their characters. The continuing attempt in certain cases to portray black women as sexually aggressive and deviant was particularly pernicious. In Ethel New's case, the police officer who removed New from the bus noted at trial that the expectant black woman had on "a low neck dress" when he confronted her about moving seats. Such a detail had absolutely nothing to do with the case, except to impugn New's character. A few suits made such stereotypes central to the white litigants' claims. In a Mississippi suit, a white man wrote in his will that he desired the majority of his estate to go to his mixed-race son, Edward Provenza. When the testator died in 1943, 19-year-old Edward was serving in the US Army. But at the end of World War II, the testator's white relatives instigated a suit against Provenza, claiming that his mother Genie Rawls "had, by undue influence and persuasion, fraudulently induced the testator to erroneously believe that her son was his child." In fact, their petition asserted, Rawls was "a colored prostitute" and had "lived in prostitution with various men of both the colored and white races" throughout her life, making the paternity of her son unclear. As evidence, several white witnesses testified that they had seen Rawls in the rooms of another white man with whom they claimed she had an "intimate relationship." As before, though, black women defended their reputations in the courtroom. In her testimony, Genie Rawls firmly denied having a relationship with any other men at the time her son was conceived.[23]

Black litigants continued to face many challenges in taking part in civil cases. Just as before, the costs of mounting a civil case could be insurmountable. Litigants continued to face largely white juries and white judges and usually had to work with white lawyers.[24] In public, elite southern lawyers still at times asserted their fairness toward African American clients. In 1923, state supreme court justice J. B. Holden noted in an address to the Mississippi Bar Association, of which he was president, "We like to have the respect of the colored people, and every lawyer, in my experience, had stood for a square deal before the law for the colored race. And often, as we know, in the last ditch, the colored man has only one friend, and that is his lawyer."[25] Other white lawyers, though, took advantage of their black clients' lack of knowledge about the legal process. In 1940s Arkansas, a 60-year-old black woman testified that a local lawyer who had previously represented her husband told her that an upcoming case against her by a white litigant was "nothing" and that she had no need to go to court. As a result, she did not hire a lawyer or attend the hearing of a suit against her and lost the case.[26]

Even with these continuing limitations and challenges, black litigants continued to win civil cases in county courts and to obtain favorable decisions in the majority of their civil suits against whites in appeals courts. In the 548 civil cases examined that would later be heard by appellate courts, black litigants won the lower-court trial in 318 cases. Similarly, black litigants ultimately won 319 of the 548 civil suits they litigated against whites throughout this period, gaining a favorable decision in an appellate court in 58 percent of suits. More than two-thirds of these favorable decisions by state supreme courts upheld the lower-court decisions on the black litigant's behalf. The overall rate of reversal in their cases remained similar to cases nationally at the time.[27]

Some important differences emerged in black southerners' civil cases between 1921 and 1950. Despite the continuing limitations in the types of cases litigated by African Americans during this period, they litigated a somewhat broader range of cases than in the first two decades of the twentieth century. While 73 percent of civil cases between black and white litigants in eight state supreme courts from 1900 to 1920 had involved fraud and personal injury, between 1921 and 1950 only 52 percent of such suits were over these two matters. In addition to fraud and personal injury suits, seventy-one cases took place over insurance, sixty-five cases over property disputes, eighteen cases over wills and estates, seventeen cases over debt, fifteen cases over damages, twelve cases over contracts or transactions, and seven cases over education. A limited number of cases continued to directly involve issues of racial justice. Over the 30-year period, thirty-three civil cases explicitly involving issues of racial discrimination or inequality came before southern appellate courts in the eight states examined.[28]

Although the vast majority of suits continued to be fought by individuals over economic issues not explicitly tied to equal rights, even in these cases, there were important differences in the tone and claims of the suits, compared with suits earlier in the century. Despite the occasional use of stereotypes in cases involving black litigants during this time, the tactic of presenting themselves as ignorant and vulnerable was employed less often. In fraud cases, in which claims of ignorance and vulnerability had occurred in every appellate case examined involving black litigants between 1900 and 1920, black litigants did not always rely on assertions of their ignorance. In litigating a suit of fraud against a local white man over the mortgage on a piece of property, for instance, Ezzie Morris and his mother Mary Morris made no efforts to appear ignorant or vulnerable. Instead, when Ezzie Morris was asked "how much is seventy times twenty-five," he replied, "Seven hundred dollars, I figure it up." When asked if he could read, Morris did not dissemble at all, replying "Yes, sir." His octogenarian mother also replied adroitly to all the questions regarding the specifics of the mortgage payments in questions, telling the court exactly how much she had paid at different times. The Morrises' presentation of themselves as intelligent and able was not lost on the court. In ruling in favor of Ezzie and Mary Morris in 1949, the Supreme Court of Alabama noted that at the time of the supposed fraud Mary Morris was, "as her evidence goes to show, a woman of firmness of character, and intelligent, though she was not able to read and write." Nonetheless, the Alabama supreme court still ruled that she and her son had been the victims of fraudulent action by a white person. It had not been the ignorance of the black parties involved, according to the court, but the "collusive" and deceitful actions of the white parties that had led to the fraud.[29]

In contrast to civil suits between white and black litigants from 1900 to 1920, black litigants and their lawyers were more likely to make arguments in favor of legal equality and economic rights, similar to those they had made in some cases during Reconstruction. In his argument to the jury in a 1930 Alabama personal injury suit, for instance, the black plaintiff's lawyer argued: "The result in this case ought to be the same as if, instead of a negro man being killed by falling from a truck and being run over by a street car, a small white child had come suddenly out from behind an automobile and been killed by the street car."[30] Other suits—like cases over economic dealings with whites in the decades after the Civil War—argued that African Americans should be treated fairly in the marketplace. Willie Lee Walker implicitly highlighted the unfair and coercive treatment of black tenants in his suit against the Mississippi Cooperative Cotton Association. His wife, Lillie Walker, had grown over 5,000 pounds of cotton in 1935 on land she rented from C. C. Nelly, a local white landowner. After Walker picked the cotton, Nelly took it and had it ginned despite Lillie Walker's objections. The white landowner then sold it to the Mississippi Cooperative Cotton Association without Walker's knowledge. In protest, the black tenant's husband brought a suit against the Association to obtain the value of the cotton. Walker won the suit and, in doing so, continued the tradition of black litigants asserting their own vision of how economic dealings with whites should occur.[31]

Some cases over seemingly ordinary economic matters protested violence and intimidation against individual African American litigants. In some ways, Mary Jackson's civil case against Mrs. J. W. Broome over a property dispute was much like any other property case. To prove the claim, Mary Jackson's lawyer put forth a chain of title to the land that showed Jackson had been in possession of it continuously from 1903 to 1935. Her lawyer's petition further appealed to a previous decision of the same court, stating that when the court dismissed an earlier suit regarding the tax title, "that was a definite termination of the basis of any possible title that defendant Mrs. J. W. Broome can now establish."

But Mary Jackson's claim also sought to regain possession of her land after a group of white men brutally beat her and burned down her house to force her off the property. Her lawyer's complaint drew on this violence to make her claim, saying that "said 10 acre tract of Real Property is in no way the property of the defendant because complainant was forced by brutal beatings administered to her at the hands of parties unknown" to leave her property. As a result, the lawyer continued, "complainant did leave her property through the medium of fear and duress."[32]

Six years after she lost her property, in September 1941, the Hinds County, Mississippi, Chancery Court heard Mary Jackson's suit. The local court ruled in favor of the African American owner of the property, overruling Broome's demurrer to the suit.[33] In response, the white woman appealed to the Supreme Court of Mississippi. The appeals court took the case and, in 1942, Mississippi's highest court issued an opinion stating that Broome had no claim on the land but had merely "forced [Jackson] out of possession." The title of the land, the court opined, rightfully belonged to Mary Jackson.[34]

Other seemingly ordinary civil cases in southern courts protested violence and intimidation against African Americans in their workplaces.[35] In one such case, a black sharecropper in Kentucky named Ed Lee Allen brought a civil suit for damages against a white landowner. Allen claimed that the white man had assaulted him with a corn knife during a dispute over the sharecropper's tobacco crop, cutting off his right thumb and injuring his head. Although the landowner claimed that he acted in self-defense, the black sharecropper testified that, while they were arguing, he had made no move against the landowner, but the white man had "grabbed the corn knife and struck at me." Likewise, in North Carolina in 1929, a black restaurant owner brought a civil suit against one of his white customers for assaulting him with a catsup bottle when he thought that the price charged for oyster soup was too high.[36]

Others challenged violence done to them as consumers and passengers. In one 1949 Arkansas case, 11-year-old Thomas Dooley had gone to the local store, Sterling's, to purchase valentines with money his father had given him. Dooley was examining a fountain pen when a store employee accused him of stealing. According to the suit, the young boy was then taken to the back of the store where he was "pushed under the elevator." The opening of the elevator "was then closed with boards and the elevator lowered." Dooley was then reportedly "put on a table" and "struck with a baseball bat." The resulting suit brought by Thomas Dooley and his father asked for $22,000 in damages. Similarly, a 1944 Arkansas case brought by a black litigant against a bus company alleged that one of the company's bus drivers had hit him over the head because he had inadvertently boarded the bus before other passengers.[37]

At times, black litigants' civil suits protested white southerners' use of the criminal justice system against them. In North Carolina, a black minister named Jesse W. Jackson filed a civil suit against his landlord in 1935 when the white landowner took his entire crop without any compensation. In response, the landlord swore out a complaint charging Jackson with larceny. While the larceny suit was eventually dismissed as "malicious and frivolous," Jackson was confined in an insane asylum until it was resolved. Upon Jackson's release, he filed a new civil suit against his landlord for damages. Other civil suits challenged threats made against them to use the criminal courts for a white person's or white-owned company's ends.[38]

At least one personal injury suit during this time protested a black person's treatment while hired out as a convict laborer. In North Carolina in 1931, a former convict brought a personal injury suit against the granite company that had hired him during his prison term. His hand and arm were severely injured after becoming entangled in a machine for scooping stone at the company's granite works. Alleging that the company had not provided him with safe working conditions or taken proper care of their equipment, he asked for $15,000 in damages. His suit echoed the claims of earlier personal suits as he explained the loss of his future earnings due to the permanent injuries to his arm. At the same time, his case went a step further by exposing the dangerous working conditions that many African American convict laborers faced during the course of their sentences.[39]

Along with these shifts in the seemingly ordinary kinds of cases that made up the vast majority of black litigants' claims, some civil cases between black and white southerners made larger rights claims either implicitly or explicitly. On the surface, some of these cases over personal injury, property disputes, and fraud appear similar to earlier cases on these matters. Upon closer inspection, though, it becomes clear that these suits challenged segregation and inequality at their core. Other cases placed claims of racial discrimination and equality front and center and had the potential to significantly impact race relations in southern communities.

Perhaps for this very reason, in the portion of these appellate suits that directly involved racial justice, southern courts usually did not rule in favor of African Americans. While African Americans won 58 percent of their civil suits against whites as a whole during this period, they won only eight of their thirty-three racial justice suits in the eight state supreme courts examined, an average of 24 percent of such suits. Clearly, southern courts could allow some black men and women to assert greater rights and protest violence in their cases over personal injury, fraud, and property, but cases explicitly centered around claiming rights for all those classified as African American still often went too far. When they did win cases focused on racial discrimination and inequality, though, African Americans employed many of the same strategies they had been using for generations. They found success when they appealed to white people's property rights, convinced judges and juries that deciding in their favor would benefit whites, and aligned themselves with prominent white community members.

Many of these new cases were hidden in plain sight as seemingly ordinary cases. Personal injury cases, in particular, at times explicitly linked black men and women's injuries to larger issues of segregation.[40] Ethel New had stood up to segregation when she had refused to move to the back of the bus, even if she did so more because she was feeling ill than as a matter of principle. After New suffered a miscarriage, she hired the Richmond law firm of Hill, Martin & Robinson to file a suit against the bus carrier, asking for $10,000 in damages. Her lawyer Martin A. Martin's complaint in May of 1945 contained the usual claims in personal injury suits: that she had suffered significant injuries as well as "great loss of compensation and income . . . and will continue to suffer great loss from the permanent diminution of earning capacity." During her testimony, Ethel echoed these claims, telling the court that upon returning home to Kentucky, she had to stay in bed for three weeks as she "was getting worse all the time, couldn't hardly walk." She told the court, too, that the incident had led to the loss of her unborn child 1 week after she had been thrown off the bus.[41]

However, this case went much further than most earlier personal injury suits by stating that New's injuries had been a direct result of her race and by challenging the practice of segregation itself. While earlier generations of litigants had generally left the racial bias behind their injuries unsaid, New's lawyer made this one of the central arguments of the case. According to her lawyer's 1945 complaint, the bus driver had "willfully, wantonly, maliciously, and with gross neglect and indifference, and in reckless and utter disregard, to and of plaintiff's rights and of all considerations save that plaintiff was Negro, demanded and insisted in a loud, boisterous, disorderly and violent manner, that plaintiff remove from the seat which she then occupied." The case also revolved around a challenge to how segregation was carried out. According to her lawyer's petition, the back bus seat was not equal to the reclining seat in front of it, but was "inferior . . . in point of quality, comfort and convenience." As a result, the lawyer alleged, the bus had not been carrying out the "separate but equal" mandate for segregation.[42]

In addition to contesting the workings of segregation, the case challenged the validity of segregation on any railroad transportation in Virginia. National events aided litigants like Ethel New in making these stronger claims. A jury in the Court of the City of Richmond ruled against Ethel New on June 11, 1946. One week earlier, the US Supreme Court had made a ruling directly linked to Ethel New's case. In *Morgan v. Virginia*, a 27-year-old African American woman named Irene Morgan had refused to give up her seat on an interstate bus in Virginia to a white person. In response, she was thrown off the bus and charged with resisting arrest and violating the state segregation laws. She refused to plead guilty to the segregation charge and pay a $10 fine. Instead, she hired Spottswood W. Robinson III, of the same Richmond firm of Hill, Martin & Robinson that was representing Ethel New, to challenge her conviction. Thurgood Marshall and William Hastie, on behalf of the NAACP, also took up Morgan's case. The Supreme Court of Virginia ruled against Morgan in June 1945. Her legal team then appealed to the US Supreme Court, which ruled on June 3, 1946, that segregation on interstate buses in Virginia was invalid. The decision made no mention, however, of how or when desegregation on buses in Virginia and other states should take place.[43]

Recognizing the opportunity to use this new decision to appeal his client's case, New's attorney filed an appeal to the Supreme Court of Virginia, citing the *Morgan v. Virginia* decision. While Ethel New had been on an intrastate bus between two locations in Virginia, Martin claimed the recent decision of the US Supreme Court over interstate buses made segregation on all buses in Virginia invalid, regardless of whether the bus was traveling within the state or beyond it. He concluded: "there was no valid segregation law in Virginia at the present time affecting persons traveling in either intrastate or interstate commerce."[44]

Despite the US Supreme Court decision, the Supreme Court of Virginia ruled against Ethel New, explaining that it had been the intention of the Virginia legislature to "separate white and colored passengers" as much as possible when they passed a segregation statute, so, to uphold the statute, intrastate transportation could remain segregated, even if interstate transportation was not. The court contended too, that despite some differences in the back seat and the seat Ethel New had occupied, "It is impossible for the accommodations on the bus to be absolutely identical in all respects." Although the back bench lacked "an adjustable back," it had "the same kind of springs, padding, and covering as the aisle seat she occupied." They concluded: "A minor or trifling inconvenience or difference in seating is inevitable under the most favorable conditions, and minor disadvantages in travel do not necessarily indicate discrimination."[45]

Wills and estate cases could also make larger claims. In one 1948 suit, a white man left property in his will to fund the construction of a hospital for African

Americans in the town of Mt. Sterling, Kentucky. He directed the new hospital to be built on the grounds of an existing local hospital for whites. When the white hospital refused to take the funds from the property to build the hospital for the black community, several black citizens, including two ministers, a truck driver, and an undertaker, sued the hospital and the white man's heirs. In their suit, they demanded that the hospital for African Americans still be built, but asked for it to be located elsewhere in the community. Their lawyer's petition explained that their suit was on behalf of "themselves and all other members of their race within the hospitalization zone of Mt. Sterling."[46]

Even property cases at times dealt with issues of race-based discrimination. In a 1943 Kentucky case, African American property owners brought a suit over their right to use an alley south of their lots. The white defendants, in turn, contended that the original owner who had developed the land had wanted to exclude African Americans from the alley. As evidence they showed the document filed by the original owner that included a clause "prohibiting the sale, transfer, or leave of the property to persons of African descent." During the trial, the black plaintiffs asserted that they had been using the alley for years and should be able to continue to do so. While they did not explicitly claim that barring them from using the alley was racial discrimination, their suit and subsequent testimony defending their right to use the alley implied their right to use it regardless of their color.[47]

A limited number of civil cases in southern state supreme courts between 1921 and 1950 even more directly challenged discriminatory racial regimes by making claims in which discrimination itself was front and center. African Americans contested existing discrimination in these suits as well as new segregation laws. In many of these cases, African Americans explicitly acknowledged that they were litigating the cases not only for themselves, but also for others classified as African American. Through such cases, litigants sought to topple discriminatory practices in their own communities and throughout the South.

Some racial justice cases—like the many civil cases that preceded them— would directly affect the black litigants' finances—as well as those of many other African American families. In many cases, they fought discrimination that threatened both their rights and their occupations. The Atlanta barbers who brought a suit against the City of Atlanta in 1926 stood to lose large amounts of money—and even their barbershops—if the city ordinance limiting their customers and hours of work stood. Similarly, a railroad employee brought a suit in 1943 on behalf of "Negro locomotive firemen" alleging that the railroad and a white-only union had conspired to limit the employment of black firemen and firemen's "seniority rights." As a result of the union's and railroad's agreement, the worker had lost all of his seniority rights and had been moved to a less desirable job within the railroad. In 1950, four black law school graduates brought suit, claiming that the Alabama Board of Bar Commissioners put additional barriers to their admission to the state bar. If they were not allowed to earn their licenses, they would not be allowed to practice law in Alabama. These cases mattered economically to the men and women litigating them but also held the power to bring greater equality for black Americans.[48]

Other racial justice cases had no explicit link to the litigants' finances and instead sought rights for the community as a whole. One black editor brought a case in Kentucky in 1929 protesting a city ordinance barring African Americans from most public parks in Louisville. In Mississippi in 1925, the black trustees of a school for African American children challenged taxes that benefited only the county's white public school. Other black litigants brought suits claiming their right to register to vote and challenging the all-white primary.[49]

As individual African Americans brought these cases in southern state courts, racial justice organizations also pursued litigation. At times, these individuals overlapped with such organizations. They may have attended a civil rights meeting or have been local members of the NAACP. When these men and women litigated civil cases against whites over racial discrimination in southern state courts, however, they sometimes appear to have done so without the explicit backing of organizations.

In 1905, Alonzo Herndon and his son attended the founding meeting of the Niagara Movement, an early racial justice organization led by W. E. B. Du Bois. Herndon was never an especially active participant in the movement and may have been encouraged to attend by his wife. His presence at the Niagara Movement's founding, however, likely indicates his approval of the movement's plan to use litigation to overturn discriminatory practices against African Americans. In the coming years, the organization established a legal department and decided "to push test cases in courts until the matter of interstate travel was squarely brought before the Supreme Court." Its legal department took part in several racial justice cases, including bringing a case in Minnesota protesting segregated railroad cars in the South and aiding a South Carolina civil rights case.[50]

Years later, Alonzo Herndon was likely influenced by his involvement in the Niagara Movement when he served as a litigant in the 1926 suit of *Chaires v. City of Atlanta*. The suit was initiated by him and several other black barbers to overturn the discriminatory city ordinance that prohibited black barbers from cutting the hair of white women and children and mandated that they close at 7 p.m. on weeknights and 9 p.m. on Saturdays. Like earlier suits, their suit would advance the legal claims necessary to make their case as well as appeal to whites' racial attitudes.

The petition submitted by the barbers' lawyers boldly asserted their clients' constitutional rights, claiming that the segregation ordinance violated the 14th

Amendment. According to the petition, the ordinance "deprives petitioners, and each of them, of their liberty and property without due process of law." By tying their 14th Amendment rights to the right of property, these black litigants appealed to the same right that black litigants had been appealing to since slavery. The testimony of barbershop owners added to this legal argument. Three barbershop owners and managers laid out the expenditures that they already put into their businesses and listed the losses they would incur if the segregation ordinance was not overturned. One barbershop owner, R. E. Chaires, testified in an affidavit that he had a 5-year lease on his shop with a rental payment of $500 a month. He noted, too, "that the equipment in his shop consisting of barber chairs, mirrors, plumbing and fixtures, workstands for barbers, a cash-stand and cash-register, other chairs, sterilizers for barbers' tools . . ." cost more than $4,000. Moreover, he stated that when he bought this equipment and obtained the lease to his shop, the ordinance was not yet "pending before the City Council."[51]

Viola Herndon, the manager and cashier of Alonzo Herndon's flagship barbershop at 66 Peachtree Street, also testified about the losses that the Herndon establishments were incurring from the ordinance. She explained that it was her duty "to check up the receipts and disbursements" of Herndon's three Atlanta barbershops. On average, she testified, the shops had each taken in more than $11 a day on weekday evenings after 7 p.m. and the 66 Peachtree Street store had earned over $40 on Saturdays after 9 p.m. All this income would continue to be lost if the ordinance remained in place. Like Chaires, she laid out how much Alonzo Herndon had invested in his businesses before the ordinance was passed. The "fixtures in the shop at 66 Peachtree Street are worth at least $1200," she noted, and "the lease at No.66 Peachtree Street runs seven years from January 1, 1926."[52]

In addition to tying their constitutional rights to property rights, successful racial justice suits at times sought to align their cause with prominent whites and with whites' perceived interests. Chaires, for one, listed a number of members of the white elite who frequented his barbershops: "he himself has done Mr. J. C. Vaughn's barbering for a number of years . . . and affiant has done the barbering for a long time for Mr. J. B. Carr and his son, and his son's children . . . and affiant has done the barbering for a long time for Mr. W. H. Terry, and his son and his son's children." The barbershop owners also claimed that they needed to stay open later because their white customers were not able to go to a barbershop during general daytime hours. Chaires testified that he observed the hours he did "because the convenience of his white customers requires it . . . a number of business men in Atlanta and its vicinity cannot get to a shop until 7:00 o'clock PM or later, and . . . many of them . . . cannot get to barber shops to have their barbering done until after 9:00 o'clock on Saturday nights." Undoubtedly recognizing the complaints of whites in the wake of the first ordinance's passage,

the barbers' lawyers additionally made the ban on cutting the hair of white children appear to be restrictive to whites. The ordinance, they noted in the petition, "has no regard to the wishes of white people who would be perfectly free,
in the absence of such an ordinance, to employ, or to refuse to employ colored
barbers."[53]

The Superior Court of Fulton County, Georgia, heard the case in August 1926.
The judge issued a split decision. While invalidating the section of the ordinance
that prohibited black barbers from cutting the hair of white children, he upheld
the reduced evening hours for black barbershops. Both the plaintiffs and defendants then appealed to the Supreme Court of Georgia, which invalidated the
city ordinance altogether. "We can reach no other conclusion than that . . . the
ordinance is not based upon a lawful classification, and that it is discriminatory,"
the decision began. The opinion cited the violation of property rights, saying
that sections of the ordinance were in conflict with "the 14th amendment of the
constitution of the United States, and the similar provision in the constitution
of the State of Georgia, which forbids the enactment of a law which deprives any
person of life, liberty, or property without due process of law, or which denies
to any person the equal protection of the laws." It then directly tied these violations to racial discrimination, writing, "The right to carry on a lawful business is
here denied to one class of the citizens of the State, and the denial is based upon
a distinction which is not permissible under the constitution to make. It is the
distinction that is based upon the color of that class of citizens." Finally, the decision acknowledged the interests of whites in overturning the ordinance: "There
is ample evidence in the record to show that if the barber-shops are closed at 7
o'clock in the evening and not permitted to open until next morning, there will
be a large and numerous class of citizens, both white and colored, who can not
avail themselves of the service of barbers. It is shown that certain mercantile
establishments, having in their service numerous employees, require the attendance of those employees until a later hour than that at which the barber-shops
under this ordinance would be required to close."[54]

Undoubtedly, the Georgia supreme court justices decided in favor of the
Atlanta barbers for multiple reasons. But a central reason why African American
litigants won in this racial discrimination case—but not in many others—was
likely because in this case winning was in the interest of many whites. A number
of white men would be inconvenienced by black-operated barbershops closing
early. If such shops went out of business, it would inconvenience white men even
more. On the question of illegal alcohol during Prohibition, white Atlantans
were likely divided.[55]

In addition to grassroots suits initiated by individuals, racial justice organizations explicitly funded or backed a limited number of civil suits in southern state

courts challenging racist practices and discrimination. In 1909, an interracial group established the National Association for the Advancement of Colored People (NAACP) in an attempt to combat the increased racial discrimination and violence faced by African Americans in the United States. From its outset, the NAACP concentrated its efforts in the courts. Its favored legal strategy was the "test case." NAACP lawyers actively sought out potential litigants for cases that contested inequality and discrimination and worked to craft legal claims that would have the best chance of gaining favorable decisions. Recognizing the limitations of bringing racial justice cases in southern state courts, NAACP lawyers often sought to have cases reach federal courts, especially the US Supreme Court. To get there, though, they sometimes had to bring civil cases to southern state supreme courts, where their suits might stall.[56]

This decision to focus on the judicial system undoubtedly resulted in part from African Americans' previous decades of civil litigation in both state and federal courts. In the wake of the 1875 federal civil rights legislation guaranteeing all people in the United States "the full and equal enjoyment . . . of inns, public conveyances on land or water, theaters, and other places of public amusement," African Americans around the country had fought to enforce these rights in federal courts. Despite the limited outcomes of many of their suits, a number of federal judges ruled for black litigants if no separate facilities had been provided.[57] In battling education discrimination in the Midwest in the decades after the Civil War, African Americans found considerable success in state courts.[58] And of course, in the South, African Americans had still been able to litigate and win certain kinds of suits claiming their rights, even as other avenues closed to them. It made sense, then, that NAACP leaders saw the courts as the natural venue to carry out their fight for racial justice.

Indeed, when NAACP leaders explained why they turned to the courts, they emphasized the likelihood that they would win there and the impact of litigation even when they did not win. In a 1935 discussion of the possible methods to achieve racial progress, NAACP leader Charles Thompson concluded that African Americans "have no other reasonable, legitimate alternative than resort to the courts." Thompson explained that African Americans "*can* resort to the courts with a reasonable certainty of favorable decisions" and contended that even when African Americans lost, their legal action itself raised public awareness of racial inequities. To NAACP leaders, court cases also required a relatively small outlay for a potentially large impact. The organization's 1926 Annual Report explained that the courts—particularly federal courts—provided the best path available to reach the organization's goals because court cases were "clear-cut" and provided precedents to be "built upon," while their cost to the NAACP was "almost negligible."[59] Although other NAACP leaders argued that legal action was ineffective and jeopardized racial progress by antagonizing whites, the NAACP sector supporting litigation successfully shaped the organization's strategies for decades.[60]

As NAACP leaders led initiatives in racial justice litigation, individual black southerners gave crucial backing to these suits. Indeed, legal scholar Mark Tushnet asserts that the NAACP's legal actions were successful only when local communities threw their support behind the litigation. Although not all African Americans agreed with the NAACP's decision to focus on progress through the courts, evidence suggests that the majority of African Americans supported the legal campaign. Requests poured in from all around the country for the NAACP to take on legal cases. NAACP members volunteered to serve as litigants in test cases, provided financial support for litigants who lost their jobs as a result of legal action, collected data about their children's education, and attended trials to show their support. Despite numerous setbacks in the courts, many black southerners maintained hope that the American legal system provided an avenue for racial and economic equality.[61]

At times, NAACP litigation drew on some of the same tactics African Americans used in their seemingly more mundane civil cases. As residential segregation became an increasing issue around the nation, the NAACP decided to challenge municipal segregation ordinances through a test case in Louisville, Kentucky, involving William Warley, the president of the newly formed Louisville NAACP chapter and founder of the *Louisville News*. Warley had been crusading against encroaching segregation in the city for years, starting the black newspaper in 1912 to campaign against inequality and leading a boycott of the local theater in 1914 to protest segregated entrances and seating. With the assistance of a white real estate agent who opposed segregation, Warley and the NAACP put the pieces into action to initiate a test case. In November 1914 Warley bought a home in a largely white neighborhood, noting in the contract that he would pay the purchase price only if he was able to live in the home. When Warley withheld the full purchase price for the home because local residential segregation ordinances prohibited him from inhabiting it, the real estate agent, Charles Buchanan, initiated a suit against the black editor for the money. A prominent white Louisville lawyer associated with the NAACP represented Buchanan in his trial, and African Americans all over the city donated funds to support the NAACP's case. The county circuit court and the Court of Appeals of Kentucky, however, both upheld the segregation ordinance.[62]

In response, NAACP President and renowned white lawyer Moorfield Storey joined the real estate agent's legal team to appeal the case to the US Supreme Court. Storey argued for the right of a white person to sell his property to the buyer of his choice and to make contracts freely. His brief noted that "The ordinance under review . . . destroys, without due process of law, fundamental rights attached by the law to ownership of property." As in earlier cases, this emphasis on white people's property rights—rather than equal rights—proved successful. In the landmark 1917 decision of *Buchanan v. Warley*, the US Supreme Court ruled that the Louisville residential segregation ordinance was unconstitutional. This decision would overturn some residential segregation ordinances around the nation, although white communities quickly found other ways to maintain separate neighborhoods. Despite its limitations, *Buchanan* showed that African Americans could gain traction in the highest court in the land by appealing to whites' interests.[63]

In addition to continuing to draw on tactics used by African Americans in earlier cases, some NAACP litigation seems to have begun with local chapters, and even with individual members, continuing the tradition of individual-led civil litigation in state courts. In 1929, William Warley initiated another case challenging segregation—this time against the Board of Park Commissioners and City of Louisville. Informal segregation had existed for years in Louisville parks, but after a group of African American children visited a "white" park on a school picnic in 1924, the city formalized the segregation with a temporary resolution segregating Louisville's parks. In response, the local chapter of the NAACP helped form a citizen's committee to protest the segregated parks. Although Warley was no longer president of the Louisville NAACP, he was part of the committee. By the end of the 1924, though, the NAACP turned to other matters. In 1928, when the board made the segregation ordinance permanent, Warley filed a suit in Jefferson County Circuit Court challenging it. Warley later claimed that the NAACP gave him no support during this fight in the courts, although another black Louisville newspaper editor insisted that the local NAACP tried to support the continuing fight against park segregation.[64]

Either way, Warley spearheaded the legal efforts to battle racial discrimination against African Americans in Louisville parks. He saw his suit as benefiting the city's entire black population. In his petition, his lawyer noted that he brought his suit on behalf of the "many thousands" of "colored people and citizens and taxpayers of Louisville, Kentucky" who "have a common interest in the subject matter of this action and will all be affected alike in the result and the relief sought therein." The petition argued that the black citizens of Louisville had been paying taxes that went to fund all the city parks and thus they were "entitled to the common use and enjoyment" of all of the city's parks. Moreover, the petition claimed, the board did not have the power to segregate the city's parks.[65]

The circuit court dismissed Warley's petition. In response, the editor appealed to the Court of Appeals of Kentucky. Like *Buchanan v. Warley*, this appeal sought to show whites how actions against African Americans also potentially threatened their own rights. "If such excuses as these could furnish authority for dividing the park property between the colored and white people of the city of Louisville," the appellate brief argued, "then the board could also divide the park property between members of different political parties, between "native born" and "foreign born" citizens, or between "a group of religious people of one belief and another group of a different religious belief."[66]

Unlike the Atlanta barbershop case and *Buchanan v. Warley*, though, this suit challenged whites' actions more than it upheld whites' rights. At least in part because local whites stood to lose little from the case's dismissal, Warley lost once again before the Court of Appeals of Kentucky. The state's highest court upheld the lower court's dismissal of the case, declaring that separate parks did not violate the 14th Amendment and that there was no "proof of any discrimination in the furnishing of these things, or that equal facilities are not furnished each race." Without the support of the NAACP, Warley did not have the money to appeal to the US Supreme Court. As a result, the state supreme court's decision stood and the city's parks remained segregated.[67]

In contrast to this individual-led case loosely tied to the NAACP, other suits were in the model of *Buchanan v. Warley*—part of a carefully thought-out national NAACP plan to battle discrimination through the courts. From the 1920s to the 1940s, the NAACP brought suits against racial discrimination in education, including unequal pay for teachers and disparate funding for black and white schools. Rather than directly challenging the policy of segregation in these cases, the NAACP alleged that the doctrine of "separate but equal," instituted in the 1896 US Supreme Court decision of *Plessy v. Ferguson,* had not been carried out equitably.[68] The NAACP took on cases in which African Americans were accused of murder, too. They gained national attention in the early 1920s for defending a group of Arkansas farmers who had fired back as local whites shot and killed over a hundred African Americans in 1919.[69] During the 1940s, the white and black lawyers working for the NAACP also began to bring cases that sought economic equality for African Americans. In the first decades of its existence, the NAACP had largely ignored requests from black members and its more radical leaders to expand the organization's litigation to include cases over labor rights and unfair employment practices. Although they still largely ignored the concerns of agricultural workers, the NAACP litigated cases in the 1940s that sought fair employment and collective bargaining for workers in the industrial sector.[70]

Despite limitations in the NAACP's litigation, their strategy of orchestrating test cases to reach federal courts increasingly achieved legal victories. The NAACP attained a few legal successes in federal courts throughout the 1920s and 1930s and won a case protesting unequal funding for segregated graduate schools before Maryland's highest state court in 1936. Despite these victories, these cases had only a minor impact on the country's widespread racial discrimination.[71] During the 1940s and 1950s, though, a series of test cases orchestrated by the NAACP would receive favorable decisions from the US Supreme Court with far-reaching consequences. In 1944, the US Supreme Court ruled against the constitutionality of the whites-only primary in *Smith v. Allwright*.[72] Then, in 1946, in *Morgan v. Virginia*, the US Supreme Court declared that segregation on interstate buses in Virginia was invalid.[73] Two years later, in *Shelley v. Kraemer*, the nation's highest court struck a blow against restrictive covenants, which had become one of the methods to enforce residential segregation in the wake of *Buchanan v. Warley*. Then, in 1950, in *Sweatt v. Painter*, the Supreme Court decided that segregated law schools in Texas were not equal, weakening the legal justifications for segregation in graduate schools. Finally, in 1954, the US Supreme Court unanimously ruled in *Brown v. Board of Education of Topeka* that "separate educational facilities are inherently unequal," effectively declaring segregated schools at all levels to be unconstitutional.[74]

The Brown decision, in particular, deeply impacted the public's understanding of the courts, revealing the opportunities as well as the limitations within the law—something many African Americans had known all along. On the one hand, the decision brought heightened attention to the fight for civil rights, forcing many white Americans to take a side in the fight for integrated schools. The decision also had enormous symbolic significance to many African Americans and seemed to show that attacks on white supremacy could have real success in the halls of government. The massive white resistance that *Brown* engendered had indirect effects on the civil rights movement as well. By radicalizing southern politics and leading to the election of politicians adamantly opposed to segregation, *Brown* ensured that when the civil rights movement used direct action, violence would ensue. This violence—broadcast on television screens around the nation—would help the civil rights movement gain the sympathy of many white Americans. Moreover, the landmark decision gave impetus to other minority groups to use the courts to achieve social change. On the other hand, the decision led the white southern power structure to initiate a coordinated attack against the NAACP that devastated the organization's local branches in much of the South during the second half of the 1950s. In some areas, laws outlawed the NAACP from operating; in others, members experienced threats and violence or lost their jobs. The Court's opinion also lacked any real method of enforcement. The subsequent 1955 decision elaborating on *Brown* gave states a wide berth regarding the timeline for change. In the end, the enforcement of *Brown* dragged on throughout the next decades, and many American schools remained just as segregated as they had been before the decision.[75]

While the NAACP-led test cases received most of the attention between 1921 and 1950, black Americans were litigating a variety of civil suits in southern courts during these decades. As they regained a measure of political power they were once again able to assert their rights more forcefully in the courts and litigate a broader range of cases. More and more of their seemingly ordinary suits over personal injury, fraud, and property incorporated protests against violence and unequal treatment. Although NAACP litigation was often orchestrated by a select few, in many of the civil cases over racial justice brought in state courts individual African Americans initiated legal action when both their economic and constitutional rights were threatened. Some suits, like the Atlanta barbershop case, began with individuals who cared about their rights as well as about how discrimination would affect their own family's finances and occupations. Other suits—like William Warley's case over segregated parks—had only loose support from the NAACP and were spearheaded by individuals. Overall, these cases filed in state courts present a much more grass roots, individual-led image of legal action, alongside the NAACP legal machine.

The civil cases litigated by African Americans during this period had many limits. Individual African Americans' grassroots civil litigation continued to be constrained by the white lawyers who took their cases and the largely white juries and judges who decided them. The majority of their suits still focused only on the individuals involved in the litigation. As a racial justice strategy, litigation could accomplish only so much. Even if courts decided in favor of racial equality, their decisions were often difficult to enforce and white communities found ways to continue discrimination. Arguably, much of the progress of the mid-twentieth-century civil rights movement came from direct action such as sit-ins, boycotts, marches, freedom rides, and registration drives, rather than from court decisions.

In the end, though, as cases litigated by civil rights organizations began to overlap with the suits African Americans had been using for decades, their individual suits over economic matters—which had always been important to the individuals litigating them—took on broader significance in the fight for racial justice as a whole. In certain ways, legal actions in state courts about economic issues that mattered to everyday black Americans were just as radical and significant as cases focused on civil rights that gained the nation's attention. At a time of tremendous constraints, individual African Americans stood up to southern whites by demanding legal and economic rights. In doing so, they drew on their long experience of negotiating southern race relations. As their cases show, the courts were not just a battleground for the elite. Throughout the South's history—from Reconstruction to the darkest years of Jim Crow to the emerging civil rights movement—the courts were an important part of the grassroots struggle between ordinary black and white Americans.

Epilogue

African Americans' experiences in southern courts during the eight-and-a-half decades after the Civil War is part of a larger, global story of struggles for rights within the courts. White southerners' efforts to control people of color through the courts is also part of that wider, global history. The very structure of judicial systems often enabled them to serve as both a conservative and a progressive force. In many countries around the world, the courts have been used both to uphold elites' power and to challenge that same power.

On the one hand, courts are unique from other institutions in ways that can allow individuals to challenge those in power. Unlike other methods, court challenges can be mounted by an individual, often at fairly limited cost. Because of how cases are decided, disadvantaged groups at times have a chance of winning, even if the larger current of discrimination is against them. Moreover, they are not always easy for the powerful to completely control. Courts can be an unwieldy method of exercising power. Judges are all too often swayed by their own personal agendas and experiences, their ideas of professionalism and impartiality, and their concern about following precedent and procedure. When they decide cases, juries, too, can be fickle and unreliable. Many legal systems have some degree of remove from popular politics.

As a result, people shut out of other institutions of government can at times still operate within the legal system. African Americans in the US South could operate within the courts even after being disfranchised. At the beginning of the twentieth century, Russian peasants litigated economic disputes in local township courts despite their marginalization from many other parts of imperial governance. Similarly, during the period between the two world wars, disenfranchised Russian outcasts could successfully draw on the law to petition the Soviet regime for reinstatement as citizens.[1]

Disadvantaged groups have also used the courts, with varying degrees of success, to help change other parts of their society or government. African Americans' civil cases against whites in state courts generally impacted only their own families, but occasionally their cases may have encouraged other black southerners to litigate cases of their own or have played a part in the battle over legal and economic rights. Despite its limitations, the NAACP's litigation undoubtedly affected the progress of the twentieth-century civil rights movement. In Cuba, enslaved Cuban men and women markedly sped up the process of emancipation in the 1880s by appealing for their freedom to *juntas*, local bodies charged with carrying out the law. And in South Africa, black and white lawyers fought the institutionalized system of apartheid through the legal system of the very government that had mandated segregation while also facing barriers within that system.[2]

Even when the views of judges largely went against the interests of a disadvantaged group, the power of precedent and a deep respect for certain kinds of law could lead to litigants from that group winning their cases. African Americans found that civil cases appealing to the law of property and to white testators' wills were particularly successful in southern courts. Similarly, at the end of the nineteenth and beginning of the twentieth centuries, Chinese immigrants submitted habeas corpus petitions in federal courts in California, seeking to be admitted to the country despite recently passed legislation excluding them. These immigrants found federal judges ruled in their favor in many cases, not because judges personally sympathized with their cause but because of their respect for the law of habeas corpus and their desire to work within the bounds of the legal system.[3]

On the other hand, courts can be a powerful tool of social control, whether through the guise of impartiality or by handing down vastly unequal criminal sentences. In criminal cases, minority groups have all too often found the legal system's justice far different for them than for others. Throughout the post–Civil War US South, courts dealt out vastly uneven justice to black and white men and women, leading southern jails to overflow with black occupants. In addition, when the outcome of cases truly mattered to those in power, less powerful groups have frequently come up short in the courts. Even as African Americans succeeded in litigating and winning certain kinds of civil cases, they found it much more difficult to litigate cases that had the potential to improve the lot of all black southerners. Throughout southern history, they won criminal cases and racial justice cases that reached the eight appellate courts far less often than they won civil cases as a whole. While black litigants won 59 percent of overall civil cases against white southerners between 1865 and 1950, they won only 36 percent of civil suits directly challenging racial discrimination in the eight courts examined and only 38 percent of their criminal appeals in the Georgia and Alabama appellate courts.[4] Similarly, when the expansion of the US's western boundaries hung in the balance, many American courts proved willing to collaborate in taking Native Americans' land by providing politicians and settlers with legal justifications for violence and removal.[5]

At times, litigants have had to make significant concessions in the way they framed or fought their cases to win their suits. Particularly during the first two decades of the twentieth century, African Americans often found it necessary to present themselves as particularly vulnerable and ignorant to win personal injury and fraud suits against whites. Likewise, in mid-twentieth-century California, a group of Hispanic American parents gained a decision in their favor over segregated schools, but only by claiming to be "white," rather than challenging educational segregation head-on.[6]

In the twenty-first century, the courts have continued to be both a partner and a sharp thorn in the side of people of color in the United States. Even as the US Supreme Court upheld affirmative action in *Grutter v. Bollinger* and *Fisher v. University of Texas*, they overturned parts of the 1965 Voting Rights Act designed to prevent discrimination in the 2013 case of *Shelby County v. Holder*.[7] As the hugely disproportionate criminal sentencing and the Black Lives Matter Movement have shown all too clearly, the criminal justice system in the United States also continues to exhibit enormous biases.[8]

In the end, then, as the civil cases in this book show, the courts defy simple characterization. The US legal system—like many other systems of law around the globe—has proven to be an ally for both elites and those they sought to control. But the American legal system has never been as easy to use to change society as both groups often wished. As a result, from the Civil War to the civil rights movement, individual African Americans were at times able to work within the limitations of the US court system to gain decisions in their favor. Even then, the justice that they received remained only a limited, partial justice—forged within a system of white supremacy and often designed to benefit whites just as much as the African Americans litigating these suits.

Appendix A

NOTES ON METHODOLOGY,
SOURCES, AND FINDINGS

To find the appellate cases analyzed in this book, I searched LexisNexis by a number of key terms such as "slave," "Africa," "African," "freedman," "negro," "negress," "of color," "black," and "colored" between 1865 and 1950 in the online records of cases heard by the state supreme courts of eight states: Alabama, Arkansas, Georgia, Kentucky, Mississippi, North Carolina, Tennessee, and Virginia. Although Kentucky was a border state that sided with the Union in the Civil War, it was also a slave state, and so I included it to compare it with other states that remained part of the Confederacy. I decided not to examine the records of South Carolina because the state archives said that many of their nineteenth-century archival case files had been destroyed, and I omitted Louisiana and Florida because of the influence of French law on their legal systems. I also did not include slaveholding states such as Texas, Maryland, and West Virginia. After searching the eight state supreme court records by key terms, I then looked carefully at all of the cases that my search found between 1865 and 1950. Because of the nature of my search, I found only state supreme court cases in which black litigants' race was explicitly mentioned in the court record. More civil suits involving black litigants undoubtedly exist in which the litigants' race went unnoted in the official court summary and opinion.[1]

After conducting this online research, I turned to archives in each of the eight states, where I examined the surviving case files in their original manuscript form. Fortunately, the vast majority of the case files have survived and are available within the archives. As the case files generally include the full record of the initial trial—the testimony, petitions, court proceedings, jury instructions, and decisions—as well as later appeals, the case files often numbered 200 or 300 pages, or more.[2]

In addition to this analysis of civil cases involving African Americans between 1865 and 1950, I searched LexisNexis for cases involving slavery in the Supreme

Court of Georgia from 1846 to 1864. Between 1846 and 1861, I found 224 state supreme court civil cases relating to slavery with all white litigants and 8 state supreme court civil cases with at least one free black or slave litigant. I then examined the surviving case files at the Georgia Archives and online on the Adam Matthew Slavery, Abolition and Social Justice electronic database.[3] In addition, to compare the experience of black litigants in civil cases with their experiences and outcomes in criminal prosecutions, I conducted a thorough examination on LexisNexis, and then in the archives, of criminal cases in the state supreme courts of Alabama and Georgia between 1865 and 1950, finding 561 criminal cases involving black defendants in the two state supreme courts during this period.

The key to this story, though, lies in the civil cases appealed to southern appellate courts between 1865 and 1950. I read almost all of the surviving appellate civil case files (and the court reporter for cases in which the archival case file does not survive). Then I entered data for each case into a spreadsheet, noting the gender of the black and white litigants, the type of case, whether the black litigants had been the plaintiff or defendant, who appealed the case, whether the black litigants won at the lower and appellate levels, the name of the lawyer litigating the case on behalf of the black litigants, whether the suit was decided by a judge or jury at the trial court, and if the parties litigating the suit had been each other's slaves and masters or were heirs of former slaves and their former masters. With this database, I was able to generate tables analyzing a wide range of factors, which allowed me to discern patterns in this litigation across time and space.

I paid particular attention to change across time, tracing shifts in each of these factors during the period of Reconstruction (1865–1877), from 1878 to 1899, during the first two decades of the twentieth century, and then from 1921 to 1950. I chose these periods because of the political and societal shifts occurring in the South. The first period ends with the death of Reconstruction, the second closes as segregation and disfranchisement began to set in, and the final period begins in the wake of World War I and the first massive exodus from the South. Of course, Democrat rule ended much earlier than 1877 in many southern states, and massive disfranchisement set in both before and after 1900 in southern states. However, dividing these cases into specific time periods allows an analysis of change across time that otherwise would not have been possible.

I also looked for other elements in these case files that were impossible to quantify. I noted the difficulties that black litigants encountered in trying to hire a lawyer and litigate a case. To find patterns across cases, I analyzed the petitions of black and white litigants' lawyers, and the questions they asked witnesses. I studied who testified in civil cases between black and white litigants and what they said in their testimony. In particular, I noted the ways that black litigants shaped their own testimony and legal action and the ways in which whites sought to negotiate the legal system to their advantage. To better understand the outcome of these suits, I scrutinized what judges wrote in their opinions for and against African Americans and the instructions given to juries. I paid special attention to the role of gender in these suits and to the long histories that former slaves and former masters brought into the courtroom.

In addition, for key cases that would frame particular chapters, I gathered additional information about the participants from census data, birth and death certificates, and war service records. I also found information about these participants in newspapers, local histories, biographical dictionaries, and archival collections. To better understand these cases, I looked at the histories that the black and white litigants had with each other before entering the legal system and analyzed local histories to understand the communities in which the cases took place. Realizing the crucial role of lawyers, judges, and jury members in these suits, I examined the backgrounds of certain lawyers to better understand why they represented black clients and studied the lives of some of the jurors and judges. I searched for newspaper coverage of these cases and, in a few cases, examined local newspapers at the time of the suit to better understand central issues in the counties in which trials were held.

I also used a variety of other sources to add depth to my study. I searched the records of white-owned and black-owned newspapers throughout the South to determine what kinds of cases were covered in local papers and to learn more about attitudes toward the courts. I examined selected records of the Freedmen's Bureau to discover how the Bureau helped set the stage for African Americans' access to southern courts and traced several claims that were appealed to both the Bureau and state courts. Finally, I used contemporary legal manuals, texts, and memoirs to better understand the legal process of the time and gain insights into the decisions of southern judges.

Findings

Through this search of the records of eight southern state supreme courts between 1865 and 1950, I unearthed 1,377 civil appeals cases litigated by African Americans. These cases made up a small proportion of overall suits in southern appeals courts: about 1 of every 162 civil and criminal cases in the state supreme courts where they were litigated between 1865 and 1950 (1,377 of 223,331 total civil and criminal appellate cases in the state supreme courts examined). This ratio shifted over time. The proportion of civil cases involving black litigants decreased in the two decades after Reconstruction, only to begin to rise again at the beginning of the twentieth century. The proportion changed from 1 in every

163 cases between 1865 and 1877 to an average of 1 in every 303 cases from 1878 to 1899. The proportion then rose again to an average of 1 in every 193 cases between 1900 and 1920 and an average of 1 in every 120 cases between 1921 and 1950.[4] Certain states also had higher proportions of civil cases with black litigants in their appellate courts. Mississippi had almost triple the number of civil suits involving black litigants than Georgia. While 1 percent of all cases before Mississippi's highest court from 1865 to 1950 were civil suits involving black litigants, only 0.34 percent of cases, or 1 of every 295 cases, before the Supreme Court of Georgia were civil suits involving African American litigants.[5]

Civil Cases Between Black Litigants

Twenty-nine percent of these civil appeals cases involving African Americans (397 of 1,377) were litigated between two or more black litigants, with no white litigants participating.[6] By far the greatest number of appellate civil suits between black litigants were disputes over wills and estates. Over the period from 1865 to 1950, 40 percent of their suits (158 of 397) involved wills and estates. In addition, disputes over property formed 21 percent of these appellate civil cases between black litigants (84 of 397), reflecting the importance of property ownership to black southerners throughout much of this period and southern courts' continuing respect for property rights. Ten percent of suits also involved black churches (38 of 397) and 9 percent of suits (37 of 397) involved black fraternal organizations. Finally, 8 percent of their suits involved divorce or custody (30 of 397), 4 percent of suits involved insurance (15 of 397), 3.5 percent of suits involved fraud (14 of 397), 1 percent of suits involved debt, 1 percent involved transactions and contracts, and 1 percent involved personal injury.[7]

Civil Cases Between Black and White Litigants

The remaining 71 percent of civil cases involving black litigants in the state supreme courts (980 of 1,377) took place between white and black litigants. One hundred and eight of these suits took place during Reconstruction, 104 suits took place from 1878 to 1899, 220 cases occurred from 1900 to 1920, and 548 cases were litigated from 1921 to 1950.[8]

During Reconstruction, men and women who had previously been considered property sued the very people who had owned them or their former owners' heirs in 72 of 108 civil cases in the eight appellate courts examined (67 percent of cases). Between 1878 and 1899, 35 percent of these civil cases (36 of 104 such cases) continued to involve former slaves and their former masters or the heirs of former slaves and their former masters. By the first two decades of the twentieth century, only 9 cases (4 percent of suits) involved former slaves and their former masters or the heirs of such parties, and by the period of 1921 to 1950, no such civil cases appeared in the eight state supreme courts examined.[9]

Role of Black Women in Civil Suits

Between 1865 and 1950, at a time when white men dominated the courtroom, black women litigated 41 percent of these suits. During this period, black women were at least one of the litigants in 404 of 980 civil suits in the eight appellate courts examined. Black women's involvement in almost half of these civil suits is a stark contrast to criminal cases with black defendants during this period. Of 561 appellate criminal cases with black defendants in the Alabama and Georgia state supreme courts from 1865 to 1950, only 5 percent of cases (29 suits) included black female defendants and 95 percent of cases (532 suits) had black male defendants.[10]

When broken down by period, between 1865 and 1877, there were black female litigants in 53 of 108 appellate civil cases between white and black litigants in the eight states examined. Black women thus participated in 49 percent of such suits during Reconstruction. Between 1878 and 1899, I found black female litigants in 48 of 104 such cases (litigating 46 percent of suits). Between 1900 and 1920, there were black female litigants in 89 of 220 such cases (litigating 40 percent of suits). Finally, between 1921 and 1950, there were 214 cases involving black female litigants of 548 such cases (litigating 39 percent of suits).

Black women were more likely to serve as litigants in certain kinds of appellate civil cases. They were especially likely to serve as litigants in wills and estate cases, which often involved a group of several male and female black litigants bringing suit against a white testators' heirs, and in fraud cases, in which their gender allowed them to present themselves as especially weak and vulnerable. Although black women took part in almost as many suits as black men over property disputes and transactions during Reconstruction, in the two decades following Reconstruction, they litigated far fewer cases than their male counterparts over property and transactions. From 1865 to 1950, they were less likely to be litigants, too, in cases over racial justice. In the eight appellate courts examined, between 1865 and 1877 black women served as one of the litigants in 33 of 50 wills and estate cases (66 percent), 7 of 18 custody cases (39 percent), 12 of 31 property disputes, contracts or transaction cases (39 percent) and 1 of 1 racial justice cases (100 percent). Between 1878 and 1899, black women in these eight appellate courts served as litigants in 21 of 27 wills and estate cases (78 percent), 16 of 31 personal injury cases (52 percent), 5 of 13 fraud cases (38 percent), 2 of 12 racial justice cases (17 percent), and 4 of 21 property dispute, contracts, and transaction cases (19 percent). In the suits examined between 1900 and 1920, black women served as litigants in 33 of 63 fraud cases (52 percent), 4 of 9 wills and estate cases (44 percent), 40 of 97 personal injury cases (41 percent), 8 of 21 property dispute and transaction suits (38 percent), and 3 of 23 racial justice cases (13 percent). Finally, between 1921 and 1950, black women served as litigants in 35 of 71 insurance cases (49 percent), 36 of 75 fraud suits (48 percent), 76 of 212 personal injury suits (36 percent), 27 of 77 property dispute, contracts, and transactions cases (35 percent), and 4 of 33 racial justice suits (12 percent).[11]

Types of Cases Between Black and White Litigants

During Reconstruction, many cases centered around property left to newly free black men and women in a former master's will, appealing to white men's rights to leave their property to whom they wanted. Of the 108 suits between black and white litigants during Reconstruction, 46 percent of cases (50 suits), involved bequests and trusts left to African Americans in white men's wills. Thirteen of these cases involved emigration to Liberia. Other cases between black and white southerners between 1865 and 1877 took place over transactions, contracts, and property and asserted black litigants' ideas of economic equality and independence. Thirty-one percent of civil cases between white and black southerners during Reconstruction (33 of 108 cases) involved economic disputes over transactions, contracts, or property dealings.[12] Finally, in 17 percent of such suits (18 of 108 cases) during Reconstruction, African American parents contested the apprenticeship of their children.

During the two decades after Reconstruction, from 1878 to 1899, the 104 civil cases litigated by African Americans against white southerners in the eight state supreme courts examined remained relatively similar to cases litigated during Reconstruction. Some types of civil cases, however, occurred less frequently than during Reconstruction. As the ties between former slaves and former masters weakened, fewer cases between white and black litigants occurred over probate matters. There were 50 cases between black and white litigants over inheritance or bequests that reached the eight state supreme courts during Reconstruction, but only 27 cases over inheritance or bequests (26 percent of suits) from 1878 to 1899. And as the political climate became less favorable for African Americans, a slightly smaller number of cases between white and black southerners over transactions and contracts took place. Although there were 31 such civil cases over transactions, contracts, or property dealings during

Reconstruction (29 percent of suits), I found only 21 cases over such matters from 1878 to 1899 (20 percent of suits). Finally, while 18 cases over apprenticeship and child custody had been litigated between white and black southerners in the appellate courts examined during Reconstruction, no such cases seem to have appeared in these courts between 1878 and 1899. During this post–Reconstruction period, cases over personal injury also began to form a larger proportion of African Americans' suits. Although only 4 such suits occurred during Reconstruction, 31 personal injury cases between black and white litigants took place between 1878 and 1899, making up 30 percent of their cases during this period.[13]

In the first two decades of the twentieth century, the types of civil cases African Americans litigated in southern state supreme courts shifted again, becoming even more limited. The vast majority of cases now involved cases of personal injury or fraud in which black southerners had to emphasize their ignorance and vulnerability to gain white support for their cases. Of the 220 total cases between black and white litigants in eight southern states between 1900 and 1920, 63 cases involved fraud (29 percent of suits) and 97 cases involved personal injury (44 percent of suits). Cases involving fraud or personal injury therefore made up 160 of the 220 total cases, or a combined 73 percent of all cases involving black litigants between 1900 and 1920. Cases over property disputes, transactions, and contracts now made up only 10 percent of African Americans' cases (21 of 220 cases), and cases over inheritance and bequests made up an even smaller 4 percent of suits between black and white litigants (9 of 220 cases).[14]

Beginning in the 1920s, the types of cases that black southerners could litigate broadened once again. While 73 percent of civil cases between black and white litigants in eight state supreme courts from 1900 to 1920 involved fraud and personal injury, between 1921 and 1950 only 52 percent of such suits (287 of 548) were over these two matters. In addition to fraud and personal injury suits, 77 cases now took place over property disputes, contracts, or transactions (14 percent of suits), 71 cases over insurance disputes (13 percent of suits), 18 cases over inheritance and bequests (3 percent of suits), 17 cases over debt (3 percent of suits), 15 cases over damages (3 percent of suits), and 7 cases over education (1 percent of suits). Between 1921 and 1950, more and more everyday kinds of suits over personal injury, property, contracts, and wills began to include challenges to the racial status quo and to the violence perpetrated against African Americans. Unlike many earlier cases, some of these cases now made claims for all people classified as African American, rather than just for individual black men and women. A limited number of cases continued to directly involve issues of racial justice. Over the 30-year period, 33 civil cases explicitly involving issues of racial discrimination came before southern appellate courts in the eight states examined (6 percent of such suits).[15]

Trial Court Case Outcomes

Between 1865 and 1950, 47 percent of the initial trials of civil cases between black and white litigants that would later be heard by the eight appellate courts were decided by a jury and 46 percent were decided by a judge (the cases not accounted for had a split decision at the lower-court level or it could not be determined what body made the lower-court judgment). This proportion shifted over time. During Reconstruction, 66 percent of appellate civil cases involving black and white litigants were originally heard by a lower-court judge (71 of 108 suits), and 30 percent of these cases were originally tried by a jury (32 of 108 cases). In the following decades, the percentage of such cases decided by a jury increased to 53 percent of suits between 1878 and 1899 (55 of 104 cases) and 55 percent of suits between 1900 and 1920 (121 of 220 cases). Then, between 1921 and 1950, the number of cases decided by each body evened out, to 47 percent of these appellate civil suits between black and white litigants decided by judges (255 of 548 cases) and 47 percent decided by juries (257 of 548 cases).[16]

The changes over time in the proportion of cases heard by juries and judges were due, in part, to changes in the types of cases most likely to involve black litigants during different eras. Probate and apprenticeship cases, which made up many of the cases involving black litigants in the three-and-a-half decades after the Civil War, were more likely to be decided in the lower courts by a judge. In contrast, juries often decided personal injury and fraud cases, which made up most of the cases involving black litigants between 1900 and 1950. As the types of cases involving black litigants shifted, the likelihood of a judge or jury deciding the lower-court trial seems to have changed as well. It should be noted, though, that judges still influenced jury trials, sometimes even directing juries to decide for or against a black litigant.

Although the trial court outcomes of cases that reached appellate courts are not representative of trial court outcomes as a whole, I found that between 1865 and 1950, the lower court decided in favor of the black litigant in an average of 56 percent of civil cases between black and white litigants that reached one of the eight state supreme courts examined (in 552 of 980 cases). In such cases initially decided by a judge, the black litigants won 43 percent of the time in the local trial (192 of 451 suits), whereas in such cases initially decided by a jury, they won 71 percent of the time in the lower court (331 of 465 suits). In the remaining cases, it was unclear who had decided at the lower-court level or it was a split decision.[17]

Appealing and Appellate Court Outcomes

Between 1865 and 1950, African American litigants were the sole party appealing a civil case in the eight states examined in 41 percent of suits (400 of 980) and white litigants were the sole party appealing the case in 56 percent of suits (548 of 980). In the remaining 2 percent of suits, both white and black litigants appealed (18 of 980 suits).[18] It is likely that white litigants had the resources to appeal cases more often than black litigants, though black litigants may have been more motivated than white litigants to appeal a case when the outcome would affect their financial future while making only a dent in a white person's financial well-being. Whatever the case, without knowing the numbers of cases that were not appealed—and the race of the litigants in those cases—it is unclear whether most of the cases that white litigants lost to black litigants were being appealed but only a handful of the strongest cases lost by black litigants to white litigants were being appealed, or if the appeals were more evenly distributed across racial lines.

At the appellate court level, in all eight states examined, black litigants won more than 50 percent of their civil suits against whites in their state's highest appellate court when the outcomes of their cases are averaged across the period between 1865 and 1950. African Americans' civil suits against whites in state supreme courts were slightly more successful in certain states than others. Black litigants won most often in Georgia (68 of 104 cases, or 65 percent), North Carolina (79 of 124 cases, or 64 percent), Arkansas (60 of 96 cases, or 63 percent), and Virginia (46 of 74 cases, or 62 percent). Black litigants won slightly less often in Tennessee (39 of 66 cases, or 59 percent), Mississippi (80 of 135 cases, or 59 percent), Alabama (107 of 184 cases, or 58 percent) and Kentucky (103 of 197 cases, or 52 percent).[19]

When all eight states are averaged together, black litigants won more than 50 percent of their civil appellate cases against whites in each of the four periods examined. During Reconstruction (1865 to 1877), black litigants won 69 of 108 such cases (64 percent of suits). Their rate of success dropped slightly during the two decades after Reconstruction (1878 to 1899), when black litigants won 56 of 104 such cases (54 percent). Then, during the first two decades of the twentieth century, black litigants won 138 of 220 such cases (63 percent of suits). Finally, between 1921 and 1950, black litigants won 319 of 548 such cases (58 percent of suits).[20]

When the eight states are examined together, black litigants won 59 percent of their civil cases against whites in the eight southern appellate courts examined between 1865 and 1950 (in 582 of 980 cases). Of these 582 cases that black litigants won, in 376 suits the appellate court was upholding the decision of the trial court (65 percent of the time) and in 150 cases the trial court was reversing the lower-court decision (26 percent of the time).[21] The eight southern supreme courts upheld cases in favor of black litigants and reversed trial decisions against black litigants more often than they did for the white litigants. This may be due in part to whites' greater ability to appeal and to the fact that when black litigants appealed, they did so when they had a particularly strong legal claim. Between 1865 and 1950, the state supreme courts examined reversed 20 percent of cases to decide in favor of the black litigants (192 of 980 suits) while reversing only 15 percent of cases (150 of 980) to favor the white litigants. Similarly, between 1865 and 1950, the southern state supreme courts examined upheld 38 percent of cases to decide in favor of black litigants (376 of 980) while upholding only 19 percent of lower-court decisions to decide for white litigants (187 of 980).[22]

The overall reversal rates in civil appellate suits between black and white litigants were similar to appellate reversal rates throughout the nation. The authors of a study that examined a sampling of cases every 5 years in sixteen representative state supreme courts throughout the United States between 1870 and 1970 found that the courts affirmed approximately 61.5 percent of suits and reversed approximately 38.5 percent of suits.[23] As Table B.22 (tables that are prefaced with "B" are given in Appendix B) demonstrates, the suits between black and white southerners that I examined between 1865 and 1950 had a similar reversal rate of 35 percent (342 cases of 980 cases were reversed) and a similar 57 percent rate of lower-court decisions being upheld (563 cases of 980 suits were upheld).[24]

Findings in Criminal Cases

Through a LexisNexis search to find cases involving African American litigants and then by searching the records in state archives, I found 561 criminal cases involving black litigants in the Alabama and Georgia state supreme courts between 1865 and 1950. In comparison, I found 280 civil cases involving black litigants in the state supreme courts of Alabama and Georgia between 1865 and 1950, making a total of 841 civil and criminal appeals cases involving African Americans in these two courts during this period. Criminal cases thus made up 67 percent of appellate suits involving African Americans in these two state appellate courts while civil suits accounted for 33 percent of black litigants' appellate suits in Alabama and Georgia during this period.[25]

To put this in context, the proportion of appellate criminal cases involving African Americans in these two states was about five times higher than the proportion of criminal cases involving the general population in state supreme courts throughout the United States during this period. According to Robert Kagan et al., criminal cases made up approximately 13.6 percent of overall cases heard by the state supreme courts examined throughout the United States between 1870 and 1970. The authors found that criminal cases made up 10.7 percent of the cases examined between 1870 and 1900, 11.6 percent of cases examined between 1905 and 1935, and 18.2 percent of cases examined between 1940 and 1970.[26]

In Georgia and Alabama, black litigants won 64 percent of their civil cases against white litigants on appeal between 1865 and 1950. In contrast, of the 561 criminal cases involving black defendants in those two states during that period, black defendants received a decision in their favor from the appellate court in only 38 percent of their suits (in 211 of 561 cases). In many of the criminal cases in which the higher court overturned the sentence, their cases were sent back to the lower court for a retrial, where in many cases they may have still received a hefty sentence. When outcomes in these criminal cases are broken down by period, black litigants won 55 percent of their cases during Reconstruction (60 of 110 cases), 41 percent of their suits between 1878 and 1899 (63 of 152 cases), 38 percent of their suits from 1900 to 1920 (35 of 93 cases), and 26 percent of their suits from 1921 to 1950 (53 of 206 cases).[27]

For certain kinds of crimes, such as the rape of a white woman, the reversal rate for black defendants was even lower. The Alabama and Georgia supreme courts ruled in favor of the black defendants in only 24 percent of appeals cases in which the black defendant had been convicted of raping a white woman. In contrast, they were more likely to rule in favor of the black defendant in cases in which black defendants had been convicted of raping a black woman. Black defendants received an appellate court ruling in their favor in approximately 63 percent of the cases examined in the Georgia and Alabama supreme courts between 1865 and 1950 in which black defendants had been convicted of raping a black woman compared with 24 percent of cases in which they had been convicted by the lower court of raping a white woman. Surprisingly, though, in the Georgia and Alabama appellate courts between 1865 and 1950, black defendants were more likely to receive a higher-court decision in their favor in cases in which they had been convicted of murdering a white person than in cases in which they had been accused of murdering a black person. Black defendants won 35 percent of appellate suits in which the black defendant had been accused of murdering a white person compared with 27 percent of verdicts in which the black defendant had been accused of murdering a black person.[28]

Appendix B

TABLES

Tables comparing the proportion of civil cases between African Americans, civil cases between black and white litigants, and overall appellate court cases

Table B.1 **Proportion of civil cases with black litigants in the eight appellate courts examined by period, 1865–1950**

Year	Civil cases involving black litigants	Percentage of cases involving black litigants	Overall number of appellate court cases
1865–1877	132	0.6%	21,542
1878–1899	150	0.3%	45,501
1900–1920	340	0.5%	65,780
1921–1950	755	0.8%	90,508
Total, 1865–1950	1,377	0.6%	223,331

Table B.2 **Number of civil cases with black litigants in the eight appellate courts examined, divided by state, 1865–1950**

	AL	AR	GA	KY	MS	NC	TN	VA	TOTAL, 8 states
Number of civil cases between white and black litigants	96	184	104	197	135	124	66	74	980
Number of civil cases between two or more black litigants	49	80	31	79	58	45	22	33	397
Number of civil cases involving black litigants	145	264	135	276	193	169	88	107	1377
Percentage of cases involving black litigants	0.42%	0.95%	0.34%	0.57%	1.0%	0.56%	0.7%	0.93%	0.62%
Total number of appellate cases by state	34,569	27,902	39,825	48,165	18,406	30,350	12,585	11,529	223,331

Table B.3 **Proportion of civil cases between white and black litigants and civil cases between two or more black litigants in the eight appellate courts examined, 1865–1950**

Years	Civil cases between white and black litigants	Percentage of civil cases involving black litigants between white and black litigants	Civil cases between two or more black litigants	Percentage of civil cases involving black litigants between two or more black litigants	Total number of civil cases involving black litigants
1865–1877	108	82%	24	18%	132
1878–1899	104	69%	46	31%	150
1900–1920	220	65%	120	35%	340
1921–1950	548	73%	207	27%	755
Total, 1865–1950	980	71%	397	29%	1377

Tables analyzing civil cases between two or more black litigants

Table B.4 **Appellate civil cases between two or more black litigants in the eight appellate courts examined by state and period, 1865–1950**

	1865–1877	1878–1899	1900–1920	1921–1950	Total	*Percentage of cases between two black litigants out of total appellate cases in state*
Alabama	3	5	17	24	49	0.14%
Arkansas	1	4	19	56	80	0.29%
Georgia	5	7	9	10	31	0.08%
Kentucky	12	6	12	49	79	0.16%
Mississippi	2	2	27	27	58	0.32%
North Carolina	0	12	21	12	45	0.15%
Tennessee	1	6	9	6	22	0.17%
Virginia	0	4	6	23	33	0.29%
Total	24	46	120	207	397	0.18%

Table B.5 **Most common types of civil suits litigated between two or more black litigants in the eight appellate courts examined, 1865–1950**

Type of cases	Number of cases of that type	Percentage of cases of that type out of all civil cases between two or more black litigants in the appellate courts examined
Church dispute	38	9.6%
Debt	3	0.8%
Divorce/custody	30	7.6%
Fraternal organization dispute	37	9.3%
Fraud	14	3.5%
Insurance	15	3.8%
Personal injury	3	0.8%
Property dispute	84	21.2%
Transaction/contract	4	1.0%
Wills/estates	158	39.8%
Total number of civil cases between black litigants	397	

Tables analyzing kinds of civil cases between white and black litigants

Table B.6 **Most common kinds of appellate civil cases between white and black litigants in the eight southern state supreme courts examined, 1865–1950**

Subject of cases	1865–1877	1878–1899	1900–1920	1921–1950	Total
Apprenticeship	18	0	0	0	18
Racial justice	1	12	23	33	69
Education	0	0	1	7	8
Fraternal organizations	0	0	6	0	6
Fraud	3	13	63	75	154
Inheritance/bequests	50	27	9	18	104
Personal injury	4	31	97	212	344
Property dispute	11	12	13	65	101
Transactions/contracts	20	9	8	12	49
Grand total of all cases (including some cases not listed here)	108	104	220	548	980

Table B.7 **Most common types of civil cases litigated between black and white southerners in the eight appellate courts examined during Reconstruction, 1865–1877**

Types of cases	Number of cases	Percentage of all civil cases between black and white litigants in appellate courts examined, 1865–1877
Apprenticeship	18	17%
Racial justice	1	1%
Fraud	3	3%
Inheritance/bequests	50	46%
Personal injury	4	4%
Property dispute	11	10%
Transactions/contracts	20	19%
Topic undetermined	1	1%
Total	108	

Table B.8 **Most common types of civil cases litigated between black and white southerners in the eight appellate courts examined between 1878 and 1899**

Subject of case	Number of cases	Percentage of all civil cases between black and white litigants in appellate courts examined, 1878–1899
Racial justice	12	12%
Fraud	13	13%
Inheritance/bequests	27	26%
Personal injury	31	30%
Property dispute	12	12%
Transactions/contracts	9	9%
Total	104	

Table B.9 **Most common types of civil cases litigated between black and white southerners in the eight appellate courts examined between 1900 and 1920**

Subject of case	Number of cases	Percentage of all civil cases between black and white litigants in appellate courts examined, 1900–1920
Racial justice	23	10%
Fraud	63	29%
Inheritance/bequests	9	4%
Personal injury	97	44%
Property dispute	13	6%
Transactions/contracts	8	4%
Total	220	

Table B.10 **Most common types of civil cases litigated between black and white southerners in the eight appellate courts examined between 1921 and 1950**

Subject of case	Number of cases	Percentage of all civil cases between black and white litigants in appellate courts examined, 1921–1950
Racial justice	33	6%
Education	7	1.3%
Fraud	75	14%
Inheritance/bequests	18	3%
Insurance	71	13%
Personal injury	212	39%
Property dispute	65	12%
Transactions/contracts	12	2%
Damages	15	3%
Debt	17	3%
Total	548	

Attributes of black litigants in cases between black and white litigants

Table B.11 **Number of appellate civil cases between black and white litigants in which litigants or their heirs had been master and slave in the eight appellate courts examined, 1865–1950**

	Cases in which litigants or their heirs had been master and slave	Number of civil cases between black and white litigants in eight appellate courts examined	Percentage of appellate civil cases in which litigants or their heirs had been master and slave
1865–1877	72	108	67%
1878–1899	36	104	35%
1900–1920	9	220	4%
1921–1950	0	548	0%
Total	117	980	12%

Table B.12 **Appellate civil cases between black and white southerners involving black female litigants in the eight appellate courts examined by time period, 1865–1950**

Period	Number of appellate civil cases between white and black southerners with black female litigants in eight states examined	Number of appellate civil cases between black and white southerners in eight states examined	Percentage of appellate civil cases examined with black female litigants
1865–1877	53	108	49%
1878–1899	48	104	46%
1900–1920	89	220	40%
1921–1950	214	548	39%
Total, 1865–1950	404	980	41%

Appendix B

Table B.13 **Most common kinds of appellate civil cases between black and
white southerners litigated by black female litigants in the eight
southern state supreme courts examined, 1865–1950**

Subject of cases	Civil cases between black and white litigants with at least one black female litigant	Total civil cases between black and white litigants in appellate courts examined	Percentage of black female litigants in that type of civil case between black and white litigants
Apprenticeship	7	18	39%
Racial justice	10	69	14%
General damages	6	15	40%
Debt	3	17	18%
Education	5	8	63%
Fraternal orgs	1	6	17%
Fraud	74	154	48%
Inheritance/bequests	71	104	68%
Insurance	35	71	49%
Personal injury	132	344	38%
Property dispute	37	101	37%
Transactions	15	49	31%
Grand total	404	980	41%

Tables about lower-court trials of civil cases between black and white litigants that later reached appellate courts

Table B.14 **Percentage of civil cases between black and white litigants in which black litigants served as plaintiffs in suits later appealed to the eight appellate courts examined, 1865–1950**

Period	Number of appellate civil cases between white and black southerners with a black plaintiff in initial trial	Total number of appellate civil cases between black and white southerners in eight states examined	Percentage of appellate civil cases examined with black plaintiffs in initial trial
1865–1877	69	108	64%
1878–1899	76	104	73%
1900–1920	184	220	84%
1921–1950	461	548	84%
Total, 1865–1950	790	980	81%

Table B.15 **Percentage of the appellate civil cases between black and white litigants decided by a judge or jury in their initial trial, 1865–1950**

Period	Appellate cases between white and black litigants in which a judge decided the initial trial	Percentage of appellate cases between white and black litigants in which a judge decided the initial trial	Appellate cases between white and black litigants in which a jury decided the initial trial	Percentage of appellate cases between white and black litigants in which a judge decided the initial trial	Number of appellate civil cases between white and black litigants heard before the courts examined
1865–1877	71	66%	32	30%	108
1878–1899	45	43%	55	53%	104
1900–1920	80	36%	121	55%	220
1921–1950	255	47%	257	47%	548
Total, 1865–1950	451	46%	465	47%	980

Table B.16 How often black litigants in appellate civil cases between black and white litigants won and lost in their initial trials, 1865–1950

Period	Number of appellate cases in which the black litigants won the initial trial	Percentage of appellate cases in which the black litigants won the initial trial	Number of appellate cases in which the black litigants lost the initial trial	Percentage of appellate cases in which the black litigants lost the initial trial	Number of appellate cases in which the results of the initial trial were split or unclear	Percentage of appellate cases in which the results of the initial trial were split or unclear	Total number of appellate cases in the eight states examined
1865–1877	47	44%	52	48%	9	8%	108
1878–1899	58	56%	42	40%	4	4%	104
1900–1920	129	59%	81	37%	10	4%	220
1921–1950	318	58%	213	39%	14	3%	548
Total, 1865–1950	552	56%	388	40%	37	4%	980

Table B.17 How often black litigants in appellate civil cases between black and white litigants won and lost in their initial trials before a judge versus initial trials before a jury, 1865–1950

Period	Number of appellate cases initially decided by a judge	Number of appellate cases initially decided by a judge in which the black litigants won the initial trial	Number of appellate cases initially decided by a judge in which the black litigants lost the initial trial	Number of appellate cases initially decided by a jury	Number of appellate cases in which the black litigants won the initial trial through a jury's verdict	Number of appellate cases in which the black litigants lost the initial trial through a jury's verdict	Total number of appellate civil cases between black and white litigants in the eight states examined
1865–1877	71	29	36	32	16	15	108
1878–1899	45	19	24	55	36	17	104
1900–1920	80	32	45	121	90	26	220
1921–1950	255	112	135	257	189	62	548
Total 1865–1950	451	192	240	465	331	120	980

Analysis of appeals and outcome of appellate civil cases between white and black litigants in the state supreme courts examined

Table B.18 **Appellate civil cases between white and black litigants won by black litigants in the eight southern state supreme courts examined, 1865–1950**

Period	Appellate civil cases between black and white litigants won by black litigants	Total appellate civil cases between black and white litigants	Percentage of appellate civil cases between black and white litigants won by black litigants
1865–1877	69	108	64%
1878–1899	56	104	54%
1900–1920	138	220	63%
1921–1950	319	548	58%
Total, 1865–1950	582	980	59%

Table B.19 **How African American litigants in civil cases between white and black litigants appealed to state supreme courts fared in local and appellate courts in the eight southern state examined, 1865–1950**

Era	Lower court lost; higher court won	Lower court won; higher court won	Lower court won; higher court lost	Lower court lost; higher court lost	Lower court split or inconclusive; higher court won	Lower court split or inconclusive; higher court lost	Lower court won; higher court split or inconclusive	Lower court lost; higher court split or inconclusive	Lower court split or inconclusive; higher court split or inconclusive	Total civil cases between black and white litigants
1865–1877	32	33	14	20	4	0	0	0	5	108
1878–1899	21	35	23	21	0	0	0	0	4	104
1900–1920	45	89	40	35	4	4	0	1	2	220
1921–1950	94	219	73	111	6	0	26	8	11	548
Total, 1865–1950	192	376	150	187	14	4	26	9	22	980
Percentage of all cases, 1865–1950	20%	38%	15%	19%	1%	0.4%	3%	0.9%	2%	

Table B.20 **Number of appellate civil cases between white and black litigants won by black litigants by state in the eight states examined, 1865–1950**

State	Appellate civil cases between black and white litigants won by black litigants	Total appellate civil cases between black and white litigants	Percentage of appellate civil cases between black and white litigants won by black litigants
Arkansas	60	96	63%
Alabama	107	184	58%
Georgia	68	104	65%
Kentucky	103	197	52%
Mississippi	80	135	59%
North Carolina	79	124	64%
Tennessee	39	66	59%
Virginia	46	74	62%
Total	582	980	59%

Table B.21 **Who appealed civil cases between white and black litigants that reached the eight appellate courts examined, divided by race, 1865–1950***

Period	Number of cases black litigant appealing	Percentage of cases black litigant appealing	Number of cases white litigant appealing	Percentage of cases white litigant appealing	Number of cases both parties appealing	Percentage of cases both parties appealing	Total number of cases
1865–1877	52	48%	48	44%	3	3%	108
1878–1899	42	40%	57	55%	2	2%	104
1900–1920	87	40%	130	59%	2	1%	220
1921–1950	219	40%	313	57%	11	2%	548
1865–1950	400	41%	548	56%	18	2%	980

*In the remaining cases, it was unclear who was appealing the case.

Table B.22 **How often civil cases between white and black litigants appealed to the eight appellate courts examined were reversed by the appellate court, 1865–1950***

Period	Number of cases reversed	Percentage of cases reversed	Number of cases upheld	Percentage of cases upheld	Total number of appellate civil cases between black and white litigants
1865–1877	46	43%	53	49%	108
1878–1899	44	42%	56	54%	104
1900–1920	85	39%	124	56%	220
1921–1950	167	30%	330	60%	548
1865–1950	342	35%	563	57%	980

*In the remaining cases, the lower- and/or higher-court outcome was unclear.

Table B.23 How often civil cases between white and black litigants appealed to the eight appellate courts examined were reversed by the appellate court, divided by race, 1865–1950*

Period	Number of cases in which black litigant lost after appellate court reversed lower court	Percentage of cases in which black litigant lost after appellate court reversed lower court	Number of cases in which black litigant won after appellate court upheld lower court	Percentage of cases in which black litigant won after appellate court upheld lower court	Number of cases in which black litigant won after appellate court reversed lower court	Percentage of cases in which black litigant won after appellate court reversed lower court	Number of cases in which black litigant lost after appellate court upheld lower court	Percentage of cases in which black litigant lost after appellate court upheld lower court	Total appellate civil cases between black and white litigants
1865–1877	14	13%	33	31%	32	30%	20	19%	108
1878–1899	23	22%	35	34%	21	20%	21	20%	104
1900–1920	40	18%	89	40%	45	20%	35	16%	220
1921–1950	73	13%	219	40%	94	17%	111	20%	548
1865–1950	150	15%	376	38%	192	20%	187	19%	980

*In the remaining cases, the lower- and/or higher-court outcome was unclear.

Table B.24 **How often appellate courts changed the lower-court decision for and against black litigants in civil cases between white and black litigants appealed to the eight appellate courts examined, 1865–1950***

Period	Appellate court upheld lower-court decision and black litigant won in appellate court	Appellate court reversed lower-court decision and black litigant won in appellate court	Appellate court decided in favor of black litigant**	Total number of appellate civil cases between black and white litigants
1865–1877	33	14	69	108
1878–1899	35	23	56	104
1900–1920	89	40	138	220
1921–1950	219	73	319	548
1865–1950	376	150	582	980

*In the remaining suits, the lower- and/or higher-court outcome was unclear.

**These numbers include some suits not included in first two columns in which the trial court outcome was unclear or split.

Analysis of criminal cases in Alabama and Georgia state supreme courts and comparison with civil cases in Alabama and Georgia state supreme courts

Table B.25 **Criminal cases won by black litigants at the appellate court level in the Alabama and Georgia state supreme courts, 1865–1950**

Period	Appellate criminal cases won by black litigants	Total appellate criminal cases with black litigants	Percentage of appellate criminal cases won by black litigants
1865–1877	60	110	55%
1878–1899	63	152	41%
1900–1920	35	93	38%
1921–1950	53	206	26%
Total, 1865–1950	211	561	38%

Table B.26 **Number of civil and criminal cases involving black litigants in Alabama and Georgia state supreme courts, 1865–1950**

Cases	Civil cases between white and black litigants	Civil cases between black litigants	Total civil cases involving black litigants	Criminal cases involving black litigants	Total appellate cases involving black litigants	Total appellate cases involving all litigants
Number of cases	200	80	280	561	841	74,394
Percentage of appellate cases involving black litigants	24%	9.5%	33%	67%	100%	
Percentage of appellate cases involving all litigants	0.3%	0.1%	0.4%	0.8%	1.1%	100%

Table B.27 How often black litigants won in criminal versus civil appellate cases (against a white litigant) in Alabama and Georgia state supreme courts, 1865–1950

Period	Appellate criminal cases won by black litigants	Total appellate criminal cases	Percentage of criminal cases won by black litigants on appeal	Appellate civil cases won by black litigants against whites	Total number of appellate civil cases between black and white litigants	Percentage of civil cases won on appeal against whites	Criminal and civil appellate cases with black litigants in AL and GA*
1865–1877	60	110	55%	20	31	65%	141
1878–1899	63	152	41%	19	34	56%	186
1900–1920	35	93	38%	32	47	68%	140
1921–1950	53	206	26%	57	88	65%	294
Total, 1865–1950	211	561	38%	128	200	64%	761

*Table includes only civil cases between black and white litigants.

Table B.28 **Most common kinds of criminal cases in Alabama and Georgia appellate courts, 1865–1950**

Kinds of cases	Number of cases	Percentage of total cases
Adultery/miscegenation	12	2%
Arson/attempted arson	12	2%
Assault on black person	6	1%
Assault on white person (not with intent to rape)	14	2%
Assault on white person with intent to rape	10	2%
Murder of black person	137	24%
Murder of white person	136	24%
Murder of person, race unknown	32	6%
Rape of black woman	8	1%
Rape of white woman	55	10%
Robbery/burglary/larceny	68	12%
Total cases	561	100%

Table B.29 **Gender of black defendants in appellate criminal cases in Alabama and Georgia supreme courts, 1865–1950**

Gender of black defendant	Number of cases	Percentage of cases
Cases involving black male defendants	532	95%
Cases involving black female defendants	29	5%
Total cases	561	100%

Table B.30 **How often Appellate Criminal Cases with Black Defendants were Reversed in Georgia and Alabama, 1865-1950 (cases with unclear verdicts are only included in the total number)**

State	Lower court lost, higher court lost*	Lower court lost, higher court won	Lower court won, higher court won	Lower court won, higher court lost	Total
Number of cases in Alabama	164	112	0	1	278
Percentage of cases in Alabama	59%	40%	0%	0.36%	100%
Number of cases in Georgia	179	98	1	0	283
Percentage of cases in Georgia	63%	35%	0.35%	0%	100%
Number of cases in GA and AL	343	210	1	1	561
Percentage of cases in GA and AL	61%	37%	0.18%	0.18%	100%

*A lost case refers to a case that upheld a conviction of the black defendant. A case won refers to a case with a favorable decision for the black defendant (a new trial or an acquittal).

Table B.31 **Impact of race of victims in violent crimes on outcome of criminal cases with black litigants in Georgia and Alabama appellate courts, 1865–1950**

Crime	Number of cases won by black defendants	Total cases with black defendants accused of that crime	Percentage of appellate cases won by black defendants
Murder of black person	37	137	27%
Murder of white person	48	136	35%
Rape of black woman	5	8	63%
Rape of white woman	13	55	24%

Data on overall appellate cases in state supreme courts throughout the United States

Table B.32 **State supreme court cases by area of law from a study of sixteen representative state appellate courts, 1870–1970***

Area of law	1870–1900	1905–1935	1940–1970	All periods
Debt collection	25.8%	18.8%	7.5%	25.8%
Contracts	3.3%	4.8%	2.9%	3.6%
Real property	21.4%	15.4%	10.9%	15.8%
Torts	9.6%	16.4%	22.3%	16.2%
Criminal	10.7%	11.6%	18.2%	13.6%
Inheritance/Estates	6.3%	7.0%	6.4%	6.6%
Total Cases in Sample	1,872	2,016	2,016	5,904

*Data from Kagan, "The Business of State Supreme Courts, 1870–1970," 133–135.

Table B.33 **How Often Cases in Three Southern Appellate Courts were Reversed from a Study of 16 Representative State Appellate Courts, 1870–1970***

Period	Rate of reversal in Alabama	Rate of reversal in North Carolina	Rate of reversal in Tennessee	Average appellate reversal rate of three southern states
1870–1900	49.2	46.8	50.4	49%
1905–1935	39.2	35.2	42.7	39%
1940–1970	30.3	47.2	40.8	39%
Average Reversal Rate of All Kinds of Cases, 1870-1970	38.2	43.1	40.1	40%

*Data from "Courting Reversal: The Supervisory Role of State Supreme Courts," *The Yale Law Journal* 87, no.6 (May 1978): 1215.

NOTES

Introduction

1. Isham Hodge appears on the 1870, 1880, 1900, and 1910 censuses in Black River Township, Cumberland County, where he is listed as a "farmer." 1870 United States Federal Census; 1880 United States Federal Census; 1900 United States Federal Census; 1910 United States Federal Census, all published online by Ancestry, Provo, Utah. According to Roy Parker, "In 1884, 1,219 blacks and 1,794 whites [in Cumberland County] paid poll taxes." In contrast, he writes, "by 1916 only 631 whites and 205 blacks paid poll taxes." Roy Parker Jr., *Cumberland County: A Brief History* (Raleigh, NC: Division of Archives and History, 1990), 86–87. In 1898 and again in 1900, white Democratic politicians in North Carolina ran on campaigns of limiting political participation to whites. For more on political campaigns in Cumberland County and in North Carolina as a whole in 1898 and 1900, see also Parker, *Cumberland County*, 86–87; J. Morgan Kousser, *The Shaping of Southern Politics: Suffrage Restriction and the Establishment of the One-Party South, 1880–1910* (New Haven, CT: Yale University Press, 1974), 182–195, 239. See also James L. Hunt, "Disfranchisement," in William S. Powell, ed., *Encyclopedia of North Carolina* (Chapel Hill: University of North Carolina Press, 2006), http://ncpedia.org/disfranchisement.

2. According to a 1905 newspaper account of the superior court proceedings, William L. Hudson lived in Dunn, North Carolina, in Harnett County. Harnett County borders Cumberland County on the north. Hudson is listed on the 1900 US Census as a white, divorced, 52-year-old physician living in Harnett County. 1900 United States Federal Census, published online by Ancestry, Provo, Utah; *Hudson v. Hodge*, 139 N.C. 308 (1905); *Hodge v. Hudson*, 139 N.C. 358 (1905); "Superior Court Notes: Important Decisions by Judge Ferguson," *Fayetteville Weekly Observer* (Fayetteville, NC), April 6, 1905, 1. When I refer to cases in the notes in this book, I am referring to the case file in an archive as well as to the record of the case in the court reporter (with a few exceptions when the original case file was not available—in that case I am referring only to the published account in a court reporter). For reasons of space, I have not included the specific archives each of the cases is located in, but a list of the archives containing the state supreme court case files is included in the Bibliography under "Manuscripts." For more on my methodology and sources, see Appendix A: Notes on Methodology, Sources, and Findings.

3. *Hudson v. Hodge*, 139 N.C. 308 (1905); *Hodge v. Hudson*, 139 N.C. 358 (1905). For more on Hodge's lawyer, Neil Angus Sinclair, see R. D. W. Connor, *History of North Carolina*, vol. 6 (Chicago: Lewis Publishing Co., 1919), 70–72.

4. For instance, my research found that 36 percent of cases between white and black litigants in the eight southern supreme courts examined from 1865 to 1899 involved wills and estates— almost always over a bequest left by a white person to an African American man or woman (77 of 212 cases between black and white southerners in the eight southern appeals courts

examined). In contrast, cases over inheritance and estates comprised approximately 6 percent of appeals suits litigated by Americans between 1870 and 1900, according to a sampling of cases from sixteen state supreme courts throughout the continental United States. Through random sampling, the authors of a study analyzed almost 6,000 appellate cases in sixteen state supreme courts between 1870 and 1970 and found 118 cases involving wills and estates between 1870 and 1900 out of 1,872 cases (6 percent of cases) in the state supreme courts examined during this period. For the methodology of the study of the case load of the sixteen state supreme courts and an analysis of the kinds of cases litigated in the sixteen representative state supreme courts across the United States between 1870 and 1970, see Robert A. Kagan, Bliss Cartwright, Lawrence M. Friedman, and Stanton Wheeler, "The Business of State Supreme Courts, 1870–1970," *Stanford Law Review* 30, no.1 (1977): 121–156, particularly the tables broken down by type of case and period on pp.133–135. To compare other types of cases, see Tables B.6 and B.32 (tables that are prefaced with "B" are given in Appendix B).

5. When the eight states are examined together, black litigants won 59 percent of their civil cases against whites in the eight southern appellate courts examined between 1865 and 1950 (582 of 980 cases). Despite variations across the eight states and shifts as society changed, this pattern held true in every state examined in the South between 1865 and 1950. When one averages the outcomes of appellate civil cases between white and black litigants in each state across the entire period from 1865 to 1950, black litigants won over 50 percent of the time in all eight southern states examined. African Americans' civil suits against whites in state supreme courts were slightly more successful in certain states than others. Between 1865 and 1950, black litigants won most often in Georgia (68 of 104 cases or 65 percent of the time), North Carolina (79 of 124 cases or 64 percent), Arkansas (60 of 96 cases or 63 percent), and Virginia (46 of 74 cases or 62 percent). Black litigants won slightly less often in Tennessee (39 of 66 cases or 59 percent), Mississippi (80 of 135 cases or 59 percent), Alabama (107 of 184 cases or 58 percent) and Kentucky (103 of 197 cases or 52 percent). See Table B.20. To view this in another way, of these 582 cases, in 376 suits the appellate court was upholding the decision of the trial court (65 percent of the time), and in 150 cases the trial court was reversing the lower court (26 percent of the time). When all eight states are averaged together, black litigants also won more than 50 percent of their civil appellate cases against whites in each of the four periods examined. During Reconstruction (1865 to 1877), black litigants won 69 of 108 such cases (64 percent of suits). Their rate of success then dropped slightly during the two decades after Reconstruction (1878 to 1899), when black litigants won 56 of 104 such cases (54 percent of suits). Then, during the first two decades of the twentieth century (1900 to 1920), black litigants won 138 of 220 such cases (63 percent of suits). Finally, between 1921 and 1950, black litigants won 319 of 548 such cases (58 percent of suits). For more on this data, see Tables B.16, B.18, B.19, B.20, B.22, and B.23. The data on these cases are based on a thorough examination of the appellate cases between black and white litigants in the state supreme courts of the following eight states: Alabama, Arkansas, Kentucky, Georgia, Mississippi, North Carolina, Tennessee, and Virginia. After finding the cases on LexisNexis, I then examined all of the surviving original transcripts of the suits. For more on my sources and method, see Appendix A: Notes on Methodology, Sources, and Findings.

6. Between 1865 and 1950 in the civil suits examined, state supreme courts reversed 20 percent of cases to decide in favor of the black litigants, whereas they reversed only 15 percent of cases to favor the white litigants. Similarly, in upholding lower-court decisions, the southern state supreme courts examined were more likely to uphold cases in which the lower court had decided in favor of black litigants (in 38 percent of suits) than to uphold lower court decisions that favored white litigants (in 19 percent of suits). See Table B.23. As for how representative these suits were of overall reversal rates in the nation, the authors of a study that examined a sampling of cases every five years in sixteen representative state supreme courts throughout the United States between 1870 and 1970 found that the courts affirmed approximately 61.5 percent of suits and reversed approximately 38.5 percent of suits. See "Courting Reversal: The Supervisory Role of State Supreme Courts," *The Yale Law Journal* 87, no.6 (1978): 1198 and Table B.33. As Table B.22 demonstrates, the suits between black and white southerners that I examined in eight southern appellate courts between 1865 and 1950 had a similar reversal rate of 35 percent (342 of 980 cases were reversed) and a similar 57 percent

rate of lower-court decisions being upheld (563 of 980 suits were upheld). For more on these data, see Tables B.16, B.18, B.19, B.20, B.22, and B.23.

7. Throughout this period of 1865 to 1950, in an average of 56 percent of civil cases between black and white litigants that reached a state supreme court, the lower court had decided in favor of the black litigant (552 of 980 cases). They lost their initial trials in 40 percent of civil cases between black and white litigants that reached a state supreme court between 1865 and 1950 (388 of 980 cases). In the remaining cases, the results of the initial trial were split or unclear. See Table B.16.

8. In this book, I seek to examine the lives of black and white southerners together, instead of separately. In part, I was inspired by Nell Irvin Painter's call to do this in *Southern History Across the Color Line*. See Nell Irvin Painter, *Southern History Across the Color Line* (Chapel Hill: University of North Carolina Press, 2002), 1–4. Similarly, Howard Rabinowitz and Fitzhugh Brundage have called for historians to examine "the fluidity" in the interactions between black and white southerners during the Jim Crow era. See W. Fitzhugh Brundage, *Lynching in the New South: Georgia and Virginia, 1880–1930* (Urbana: University of Illinois Press, 1993), 13; Howard N. Rabinowitz, "More than the Woodward Thesis: Assessing the Strange Career of Jim Crow," *Journal of American History* 75 (Dec. 1988): 848. For examples of other historians also examining the lives of black and white southerners together, see Peggy G. Hargis, "For the Love of Place: Paternalism and Patronage in the Georgia Lowcountry, 1865–1898," *The Journal of Southern History* 70, no.4 (2004): 825–864; Erskine Clarke, *Dwelling Place: A Plantation Epic* (New Haven, CT: Yale University Press, 2005).

9. See, for instance, David Oshinsky, *"Worse Than Slavery": Parchman Farm and the Ordeal of Jim Crow Justice* (New York: Simon & Schuster, 1996); Christopher Waldrep, *Roots of Disorder: Race and Criminal Justice in the American South* (Urbana: University of Illinois Press, 1998); Christopher Waldrep and Donald G. Nieman, eds., *Local Matters: Race, Crime, and Justice in the Nineteenth-Century South* (Athens: University of Georgia Press, 2001); Randall Kennedy, *Race, Crime, and the Law* (New York: Vintage Books, 1997); Edward L. Ayers, *Vengeance & Justice: Crime and Punishment in the 19th-Century American South* (New York: Oxford University Press, 1984); Douglas A. Blackmon, *Slavery By Another Name* (New York: Doubleday, 2008); Neil R. McMillen, *Dark Journey: Black Mississippians in the Age of Jim Crow* (Urbana: University of Illinois Press, 1989); Talitha A. LeFlouria, *Chained in Silence: Black Women and Convict Labor in the New South* (Chapel Hill: University of North Carolina Press, 2015); Sarah Haley, *No Mercy Here: Gender, Punishment, and the Making of Jim Crow Modernity* (Chapel Hill: University of North Carolina Press, 2016); and Martha A. Myers, *Race, Labor & Punishment in the New South* (Columbus: Ohio State University Press, 1998).

10. No other historians have conducted an in-depth, thorough examination of all kinds of civil cases involving African American litigants in multiple postwar southern state supreme courts during this period. For examples of studies that include an examination of civil cases in the postwar South in which race was in the forefront, see Martha Hodes, *White Women, Black Men: Illicit Sex in the Nineteenth-Century South* (New Haven, CT: Yale University Press, 1997); Peggy Pascoe, *What Comes Naturally: Miscegenation Law and the Making of Race in America* (New York: Oxford University Press, 2009); Michael A. Elliott, "Telling the Difference: Nineteenth-Century Legal Narratives of Racial Taxonomy," *Law & Social Inquiry* 24, no.3 (1999): 611–636; Ariela J. Gross, *What Blood Won't Tell: A History of Race on Trial in America* (Cambridge, MA: Harvard University Press, 2008); Julie Novkov, *Racial Union: Law, Intimacy, and the White State in Alabama, 1865–1954* (Ann Arbor: University of Michigan Press, 2008); J. Morgan Kousser, *Dead End: The Development of Nineteenth-Century Litigation on Racial Discrimination in Schools: An Inaugural Lecture Delivered Before the University of Oxford on 28 February 1985* (Oxford: Clarendon, 1986); Mark V. Tushnet, *The NAACP's Legal Strategy Against Segregated Education, 1925–1950* (Chapel Hill: University of North Carolina Press, 1987); Barbara Welke, "When All the Women Were White, and All the Blacks Were Men: Gender, Class, Race, and the Road to Plessy, 1855–1914," *Law and History Review* 13 (1995): 261–316; Susan D. Carle, *Defining the Struggle: National Organizing for Racial Justice, 1880–1915* (Oxford: Oxford University Press, 2013); and Shawn Leigh Alexander, *An Army of Lions: The Civil Rights Struggle Before the NAACP* (Philadelphia: University of

Pennsylvania Press, 2012). Other legal scholars have studied black men's and women's participation in all kinds of civil cases during this period, but their analysis has generally not been systematic across multiple states, and it has often been limited to judicial opinions or a small sample of local cases. For example, Samuel Pincus also emphasizes the importance of looking at all kinds of civil cases, rather than only ones focusing on race, but focuses only on judicial opinions in Virginia. See Samuel N. Pincus, *The Virginia Supreme Court, Blacks, and the Law, 1870–1902* (New York: Garland, 1990), xxii–xxiii, xxix. Similarly, Laura Edwards focuses on Reconstruction-era cases in Granville County, North Carolina, in *Gendered Strife and Confusion: The Political Culture of Reconstruction* (Urbana: University of Illinois Press, 1997). Dylan C. Penningroth is currently researching black people's encounter with the law and the making of African American legal cultures from the 1830s to the 1960s. See, for instance, his examination of local civil cases between black litigants over divorce in Virginia and Washington DC: Dylan C. Penningroth, "African American Divorce in Virginia and Washington DC, 1865–1930," *Journal of Family History* 33, no. 1 (2008): 21–35.

11. In his seminal article, "On Agency," Walter Johnson cautions against focusing too much on resistance, as it can lead historians to fail to notice other aspects of their subjects' lives. See Walter Johnson, "On Agency," *Journal of Social History* 37, no.1 (2003): 113–124. However, even these suits not overtly focused on resisting and challenging the system of white supremacy are not in complete compliance with white southerners. James C. Scott recognizes that "Most of the political life of subordinate groups is to be found neither in the overt collective defiance of powerholders nor in complete hegemonic compliance, but in the vast territory between these two polar opposites." See James C. Scott, *Weapons of the Weak: Everyday Forms of Resistance* (New Haven, CT, and London: Yale University Press 1985), 136.

12. These conclusions are based on my examination of a sampling of the superior court records of Troup County, Georgia, and Liberty County, Georgia, between 1860 and 1940. See Superior Court Minute Books, Superior Court Records. Troup County, Georgia, 1827–1937, Troup County Archives, LaGrange, Georgia, and Superior Court Minutes, Liberty County, Georgia, 1859–1935, RH 774–778, Microfilm drawer 30, boxes 48–52, Georgia Archives, Morrow, Georgia.

13. For more on this process of locating cases involving black litigants through LexisNexis, see Appendix A: Notes on Methodology, Sources, and Findings.

14. In Kentucky, for instance, the microfilm index for cases from the 1930s and 1940s was missing and the cases could not be found without it; an archivist noted that no one else seemed to have noticed or requested it since the indexes were first made several decades ago. The original transcripts of the state supreme court cases are generally held in the state archives of each state or in a law library in the state capitol. For a description of where the archival case files for these suits can be found, see the manuscript section of the Bibliography. For more on my research process, see Appendix A: Notes on Methodology, Sources, and Findings.

15. Cases that were appealed seem to be more likely to involve large amounts of money, more likely to involve white lawyers and white witnesses, and the legal basis of the cases was likely especially strong. In certain states, at different times, appeals courts were more likely to hear appeals of cases involving certain types of law. Unsuccessful white litigants probably had the resources to appeal cases more often than black litigants, further skewing the results. For examinations of the factors that could lead certain parties to appeal more often than others and skew the representativeness of appeals, see "Courting Reversal," *The Yale Law Journal*, 1199, and Marc Galanter, "Why the 'Haves' Come Out Ahead: Speculations on the Limits of Legal Change," *Law & Society Review* 9, no.1 (1974): 97–104. Another article points out that in many states certain types of appeals "are preferred by law. Some states provide for direct SSC [state supreme court] review of all capital cases; others provide for direct appeal to the SSC for workmen's compensation cases; in still another, disputes over taxation received direct review for most of the period" from 1870 to 1970. See Kagan et al., "The Business of State Supreme Courts, 1870–1970," 154.

16. For a discussion and examples of state supreme court civil cases involving black litigants in which the case record did not mention that one of the litigants was black, see Barbara Welke, *Recasting American Liberty: Gender, Race, Law, and the Railroad Revolution, 1865–1920* (Cambridge: Cambridge University Press, 2001), 296. In two of the cases included in my

dataset the court report did not include the litigants' race. Instead, I verified through other means that one of the litigants was African American. See *Hannon v. Grizzard*, 96 N.C. 293 (1887) and *O'Hara v. Powell*, 80 N.C. 103 (1879). In both cases, a black politician challenged election fraud in their county.

17. For more on racial classifications in the courtroom, see Hodes, *White Women, Black Men*, 96–122; Ariela Gross, *What Blood Won't Tell*; and Walter Johnson, "The Slave Trader, the White Slave, and the Politics of Racial Determination in the 1850s," *The Journal of American History* 87, no.1 (2000): 13–38.

18. Different state supreme courts had varying policies about what constituted grounds for an appeal, which changed over time. At certain times in certain states, appeals courts heard every case that was appealed. Other states, at certain times, allowed only certain errors, such as an error of "law," to be grounds for an appeal. Generally, though, throughout much of the nineteenth century, US state supreme courts had little choice in the cases that were heard before them. Only when case volumes increased exponentially as state populations grew at the beginning of the twentieth century, did many states in the United States begin to allow their highest courts more discretion in what cases to take. For an examination of how much discretion state supreme courts had in the United States between 1870 and 1970 and the change in this over time, see Kagan, "The Business of State Supreme Courts," 128–132. The Mississippi Code of 1880, for instance, states that "writs of error as heretofore used are abolished, and all cases, civil and criminal, at law and in chancery, shall be taken to the supreme court by appeal . . . and shall be dealt with by said court without regard to the manner of removing said cases to such court." An 1890 legal manual notes that appeals could be made to the Tennessee Supreme Court, "In all cases in which the jurisdiction of the county court is concurrent with the circuit or chancery courts, or in which both parties consent." For more on appeals to the state supreme courts of Mississippi and Tennessee, see James R. Chalmers, *The Probate Law and Practice in the Courts of Mississippi and Tennessee* (Rochester, NY: The Lawyers' Co-Operative Publishing Company, 1890), 401, 407–408. In North Carolina, the state supreme court accepted all cases that were appealed to it from 1810 to 1868. After 1868, the jurisdiction of the Supreme Court of North Carolina was limited to "appeals on matters of law or legal inference." Cecil J. Hill, *When the North Carolina Supreme Court Sat In The Capitol* (West Publishing Company, 1984), 10 (quote is from p.10); Kemp P. Battle, "An Address on the History of the Supreme Court Delivered in the Hall of the House of Representatives, February 4th, 1889, At the Request of the members of the Court and Of the Bar, In Commemoration of the First Occupancy By the Court of the New Supreme Court Building, March 5th 1888" (Raleigh, NC: Edwards & Broughton, Printers, 1889), 50–51, compiled in Clark Battle, *Supreme Court of North Carolina* (Chapel Hill: University of North Carolina, North Carolina Collection). For more on individual state appellate court's policies about which cases to take at different times, see also John B. Harris, ed., *A History of the Supreme Court of Georgia* (Macon, Ga.: J. W. Burke:1948), 56; Abram Whitenack Cozart, *Georgia Practice Rules as Laid Down by the Supreme Court and Court of Appeals of Georgia* (Atlanta, GA: Harrison Company, 1918), 87–94; and Judith Kelleher Schafer, *Slavery, the Civil Law, and the Supreme Court of Louisiana* (Baton Rouge: Louisiana State University Press, 1994), xi–xii.

19. Walter Johnson famously described court cases as "sworn lies given in support of high-stakes legal action" in *Soul by Soul: Life Inside the Antebellum Slave Market* (Cambridge, MA: Harvard University Press, 1999), 12–13. In addition, in the article, "Inconsistency, Contradiction, and Complete Confusion: The Everyday Life of the Law of Slavery," Walter Johnson notes: "Laws and legal decisions are documents that erase the trace of ongoing contests with the languages of precedent, resolution, and progress: as guides to the reality they purport to represent, they are unreliable." See Walter Johnson, "Inconsistency, Contradiction, and Complete Confusion: The Everyday Life of the Law of Slavery," *Law and Social Inquiry* 22, no.2 (1997): 430. For a brilliant analysis of the factors in judges' decisions and the legitimacy that such decisions give to that side of the dispute, see Pierre Bourdieu, "The Force of Law: Toward a Sociology of the Juridical Field," trans. Richard Terdiman, *Hastings Law Journal* 38 (July 1987): 827–828, 830–833.

20. For more on my research process to find these cases, see Appendix A: Notes on Methodology, Sources, and Findings.

21. The 1,377 civil appellate cases in which the case record notes that one of the litigants was black formed approximately 0.62 percent of the total criminal and civil appellate cases in the eight states examined between 1865 and 1950 (1,377 of 223,331 total civil and criminal appellate cases in the state supreme courts examined, or approximately 1 of every 162 cases). This ratio shifted over time. The proportion of appellate civil cases involving black litigants decreased in the two decades after Reconstruction, only to begin to rise again at the beginning of the twentieth century. The proportion changed from 1 in every 163 cases between 1865 and 1877 to an average of 1 in every 303 cases from 1878 to 1899. The proportion then rose again to an average of 1 in every 193 cases between 1900 and 1920, and an average of 1 in every 120 cases between 1921 and 1950. See Table B.1. Certain states also had higher proportions of civil cases with black litigants in their appellate courts. Mississippi had almost triple the number of civil suits involving black litigants than Georgia. While 1 percent of all cases before Mississippi's highest court from 1865 to 1950 were civil suits involving black litigants, only 0.34 percent of cases, or 1 of every 295 cases, before the Supreme Court of Georgia were civil suits involving African American litigants (see Table B.2). Although the number of appellate civil suits between black and white litigants remained less than 1 percent of all civil and criminal cases in each of the courts examined in the 85 years after the Civil War, the number of appellate cases involving only black litigants was much lower still. Between 1865 and 1950, the number of appellate civil suits between black litigants averaged approximately 0.18 percent, or 1 of every 562 civil and criminal appellate cases in the appeals courts examined. The number of these suits in the eight appellate courts examined grew somewhat over time, from an average of two such suits a year (out of all eight courts) during the period of Reconstruction, to an average of approximately seven such cases a year during the period between 1921 and 1950.

22. One study of US state supreme courts analyzed 5,904 cases across sixteen representative states between 1870 and 1970 and found that civil cases made up 86 percent of overall appellate court business, whereas criminal cases made up 14 percent of court business. See Table B.32 and Kagan, "The Business of State Supreme Courts, 1870–1970," 133–135. While African Americans litigated more criminal appellate cases than civil appellate cases in the two states where I examined criminal cases, they were still vastly outnumbered by whites' civil suits. In the state supreme courts of Alabama and Georgia between 1865 and 1950, criminal cases made up 67 percent of suits involving African Americans whereas civil suits accounted for 33 percent of black litigants' suits. See Table B.26.

23. Twenty-nine percent of these civil appeals cases involving African American litigants (397 of 1,377 suits) were litigated between two or more black litigants, with no white litigants participating. For data on the proportion of civil appellate cases between black litigants versus the proportion of civil appellate cases between black and white litigants, see Table B.3. For data on the number of appellate civil cases between two or more black litigants by state and period, see Table B.4.

24. By far the greatest number of appellate civil suits between black litigants were disputes over wills and estates. Over the period from 1865 to 1950, 40 percent of their suits (158 of 397) involved wills and estates. In addition, disputes over property formed 21 percent of these appellate civil cases between black litigants (84 of 397), reflecting the importance of property ownership to black southerners throughout much of this period and southern courts' continuing respect for property rights. Ten percent of suits also involved black churches (38 of 397), and 9 percent of suits (37 of 397) involved black fraternal organizations. Finally, 8 percent of their suits involved divorce or custody (30 of 397), 4 percent of suits involved insurance (15 of 397), 3.5 percent of suits involved fraud (14 of 397), 1 percent of suits involved debt, 1 percent involved transactions and contracts, and 1 percent involved personal injury. For more data on the types of civil suits between black litigants that reached the state supreme courts examined, see Table B.5. For an examination of cases between black litigants over divorce in Virginia and Washington, DC, between 1865 and 1930, see Penningroth, "African American Divorce in Virginia and Washington D.C., 1865–1930," 21–35.

25. According to the 1860 US Census, 437,404 "colored" people lived in Mississippi out of a total state population of 791,305. Joseph C. G. Kennedy, *Population of The United States in 1860, Compiled from the Original Returns of The Eighth Census* (Washington, DC: Government Printing Office, 1864), iv, xiii. According to the 1900 census, there were 907,630 people classified as "Negro" in Mississippi and 641,200 people classified as "white" in Mississippi in 1900. The 1900 census also reported several states in which the black population came near to the population of "white" men and women, including Alabama, (1,001,152 "white" residents and 827,307 "Negro" residents) and Georgia (1,181,294 "white" residents and 1,034,813 "Negro" residents). States in which whites vastly outnumbered African Americans in the 1900 census included Arkansas (944,580 "white" residents and 366,856 "Negro" residents) and Kentucky (1,862,309 "white" residents and 284,756 "Negro" residents). For a population breakdown by state and race in 1900, see "Table 41: Population Classified by Sex and Race: 1900," *Abstract of The Twelfth Census of the United States 1900* (Washington, DC: US Government Printing Office, 1902), 43.

26. Georgia instituted a cumulative poll tax in 1877 that disfranchised many African American voters (as well as many white voters). For more on disfranchisement in Georgia and North Carolina, see Kousser, *The Shaping of Southern Politics*, 65–68, 182–195, 239.

27. Seventy-two of 108 civil cases in the eight appellate courts examined between 1865 and 1877 involved former slaves and their former masters or their former masters' heirs (67 percent). Thirty-six of 104 such cases between 1878 and 1899 involved former slaves and their former masters or their former masters' heirs (35 percent). For more data on how many of these cases involved former masters and their former slaves or the heirs of former masters and former slaves and how this changed over time, see Table B.11.

28. Between 1865 and 1950, black women were at least one of the litigants in 404 of 980 civil suits in the eight appellate courts examined (41 percent of suits). For a breakdown of the proportion of female litigants in these civil suits by period, see Table B.12. Black women's involvement in almost half of these suits is a stark contrast to their involvement in criminal cases with black defendants during this period. Of 561 appellate criminal cases with black defendants in Alabama and Georgia supreme courts from 1865 to 1950, only 29 cases (5 percent of suits) included black female defendants and 95 percent of cases (532 cases) had black male defendants. For data on the gender of black defendants in criminal cases in these two appellate courts, see Table B.29.

29. *Sweeney v. City of Louisville*, 309 Ky. 465 (1949).

30. *Hudson v. Hodge*, 139 N.C. 308 (1905); *Hodge v. Hudson*, 139 N.C. 358 (1905).

31. Black litigants had more success bringing cases over discrimination before state courts in the Midwest, where the Republican Party still needed black votes to win elections. For an examination of African Americans' success in school integration cases in the nineteenth century, see J. Morgan Kousser, "Why Were There So Many Legal Cases on School Integration in Nineteenth-Century America?," unpublished paper prepared for delivery at the Social Science History Association Convention, Washington DC, October 1997, and Kousser, *Dead End*, 5–12, 59.

32. A limited number of cases between 1921 and 1950 also continued to directly demand equal rights. Despite the slightly lower percentage of cases focusing on racial discrimination from 1921 to 1950, compared with the period between 1878 and 1920, a larger actual number of cases directly involving racial injustice were heard by southern appeals courts during the period of 1921–1950, and many other cases not explicitly revolving around issues of equal rights began to bring issues of racial equality into the courtroom. This latter phenomenon was also occurring in criminal cases between 1921 and 1950. Although none of the criminal appeals cases in the Alabama or Georgia state supreme courts during this time explicitly centered around arrests for challenges to equal rights, 24 of the 206 other kinds of criminal cases (12 percent of cases) included challenges to the racial status quo, including alleging jury discrimination or unjust treatment in the legal system because of their race. For data on the numbers of civil cases explicitly demanding racial justice in these state supreme courts during different periods, see Tables B.7, B.8, B.9, and B.10.

33. 1910 United States Federal Census, published online by Ancestry, Provo, UT; Connor, *History of North Carolina*, vol. 6 (1919), 70–72.

34. Similarly, in a later, 1914 case over Isham Hodge's land, too, Jim Woodward testified that in his last years, Isham Hodge's "mind would come and go" and "His wife acted sorter queer to me. She did not act like a bright woman." *Hudson v. Hodge*, 139 N.C. 308 (1905); *Hodge v. Hudson*, 139 N.C. 358 (1905); *Hodges v. Wilson*, 165 N.C. 323 (1914).

35. See Tables B.1 and B.2.

36. *Hodge v. Hudson*, 139 N.C. 358 (1905).

37. See, for instance, "Letter to Bv't Maj. O. H. Howard from Georgia Freedmen's Bureau Agent G. Ballou, October 1868," in LaWanda Cox and John H. Cox, eds., *Reconstruction, the Negro, and the New South* (New York: Harper & Row, 1973), 275–278.

38. See note 21 of this chapter.

39. Cases directly challenging racial discrimination, for instance, made up approximately 7 percent of civil appellate cases between black and white litigants between 1865 and 1950. I found 69 civil appellate cases centering around issues of racial discrimination between 1865 and 1950, of a total of 980 cases. Between 1865 and 1877, 1 percent of cases involved such issues; between 1878 and 1899, 12 percent of cases involved such issues; between 1900 and 1920, 10 percent of cases involved such issues; and between 1921 and 1950, 6 percent of cases centered around racial discrimination. Despite the slightly lower percentage of cases focused on racial discrimination from 1921 to 1950, a larger number of cases centering on other issues, such as personal injury, brought issues of racial equality into the courtroom during these three decades than in the preceding decades. For an analysis of these data and how the number of cases focused on discrimination varied over time, see Tables B.6–B.10. Moreover, while black litigants won 59 percent of their civil cases on appeal between 1865 and 1950 in the eight states examined, in civil appellate cases directly challenging racial discrimination between 1865 and 1950, African Americans won only 36 percent of the cases examined (twenty-five of sixty-nine). Black litigants were often more successful in bringing and winning discrimination cases in nonsouthern state courts—particularly in the Midwest—during the three and a half decades after the Civil War. See Kousser, *Dead End*, 5–12, 59, and Kousser, "Why Were There So Many Legal Cases on School Integration in Nineteenth-Century America?," 1–28. For more on African Americans' national fight for rights in the courts at the end of the nineteenth and beginning of the twentieth centuries, see Carle, *Defining the Struggle*, and Alexander, *An Army of Lions*. For a discussion of the issues with putting cases on racial discrimination and racial justice during the Jim Crow era under the umbrella of "civil rights," see Christopher Schmidt, "Legal History and the Problem of the Long Civil Rights Movement," *Law & Social Inquiry* 41 (2016): 1081–1103.

40. In the state supreme courts of Alabama and Georgia between 1865 and 1950, criminal cases made up 67 percent of suits involving African Americans whereas civil suits accounted for only 33 percent of black litigants' suits. More specifically, between 1865 and 1950, I found 280 civil cases involving black litigants in the state supreme courts of Alabama and Georgia, of a total of 841 civil and criminal appeals cases involving African Americans. During this same period, I found 561 criminal cases involving black defendants in the Alabama and Georgia State Supreme Courts. See Table B.26.

41. One study of state supreme courts throughout the country between 1870 and 1970 found that civil cases made up 86 percent of overall appellate court business, whereas criminal cases made up only 14 percent of court business. The study authors found that criminal cases made up 10.7 percent of the cases examined between 1870 and 1900, 11.6 percent of cases examined between 1905 and 1935, and 18.2 percent of cases examined between 1940 and 1970. The proportion of appellate criminal cases involving African Americans was thus about five times higher than the proportion of criminal cases involving the general population in state supreme courts throughout the United States during this period. See Table B.32 and Kagan, "The Business of State Supreme Courts," 135, 145–146.

42. In Georgia and Alabama, black litigants won 64 percent of their civil cases on appeal between 1865 and 1950. Similarly, in the eight states examined black litigants won 59 percent of their civil cases on appeal between 1865 and 1950. In contrast, of the 561 criminal cases involving black defendants that I found in the state supreme courts of Georgia and Alabama during that period, black defendants received a decision in their favor from the appellate court in only 38 percent of their suits (in 211 cases). See Tables B.18, B.27, and B.30.

43. The Alabama and Georgia supreme courts, for example, ruled in favor of the black defendants in only 24 percent of appeals cases in which the black defendants had been convicted of raping a white woman. In contrast, they were more likely to rule in favor of the black defendant in cases in which black defendants had been convicted of raping a black woman. Black defendants received an appellate court ruling in their favor in approximately 63 percent of the cases examined in the Georgia and Alabama supreme courts between 1865 and 1950 in which black defendants had been convicted of raping a black woman compared with 24 percent of cases in which they had been convicted by the lower court of raping a white woman. Surprisingly, though, in the Georgia and Alabama appellate courts between 1865 and 1950, black defendants were more likely to receive a higher-court decision in their favor in cases in which they had been convicted of murdering a white person than in cases in which they had been accused of murdering a black person. Black defendants won 35 percent of appellate suits in which the black defendant had been accused of murdering a white person compared to 27 percent of verdicts in which the black defendant had been accused of murdering a black person. For more data on the impact of the race of victims on the outcome of criminal cases in the Georgia and Alabama appeals courts, see Table B.31. For more on the types of criminal cases involving black defendants in the state supreme courts of Georgia and Alabama between 1865 and 1950, see Table B.28.

44. Oshinsky, *"Worse Than Slavery,"* 32–33.

45. For instance, David Oshinsky writes that one 1882 study of Georgia convicts found that "coloreds" had been given sentences "twice as long as whites for burglary and five times as long for larceny." Oshinsky, *"Worse Than Slavery,"* 60, 63 (quote is on p.63). See also the graph showing the increase in the black prison population in four states in the South from 1865 to 1900 in Ayers, *Vengeance & Justice,* 170, and Blackmon, *Slavery By Another Name,* 56–112.

46. For another analysis of cases in which the structure of the legal system and ideas of professionalism played an important role in allowing a disadvantaged group access to the courts, see Lucy E. Salyer, *Laws Harsh as Tigers: Chinese Immigrants and the Shaping of Modern Immigration Law* (Chapel Hill: University of North Carolina Press, 1995).

47. For more on the Cumberland County courthouse that was used in 1905, see Roy Parker, "Old Courthouse Lives On," *The Fayetteville Observer,* June 27, 1993, and Parker, *Cumberland County,* 88–89. See also *Hudson v. Hodge,* 139 N.C. 308 (1905); *Hodge v. Hudson,* 139 N.C. 358 (1905).

48. Whites formed a slight majority in Cumberland County—but only just barely. Roy Parker writes that "In 1880 black citizens comprised 47 percent of the county population of 23,836" and "By 1910, the total population of Cumberland had reached 32,284, of which 43 percent were black." Parker, *Cumberland County,* 80. For more on segregation in southern courtrooms, see Gilbert Thomas Stephenson, *Race Distinctions in American Law* (New York: Appleton and Company, 1910), 237–238. The quote from the North Carolina court clerk is from Stephenson, *Race Distinctions in American Law,* 266. In 1900, Gilbert Thomas Stephenson wrote to the court clerk in all the counties in the South that had majority-black populations to inquire about black jury service. Of the sixty-five court clerks who replied, twenty reported that a very limited number of black men still served on their juries. All of these twenty also reported, though, that jury service by black men had decreased in their county in the past few years. For the reports from North Carolina clerks, see Stephenson, *Race Distinctions in American Law,* 265–267.

49. *Hudson v. Hodge,* 139 N.C. 308 (1905); *Hodge v. Hudson,* 139 N.C. 358 (1905); "Superior Court Notes: Important Decisions by Judge Ferguson," *Fayetteville Weekly Observer,* April 6, 1905, 1.

50. For more on the Supreme Court of North Carolina and the building where it was housed at this time, see Hill, *When the North Carolina Supreme Court Sat In The Capitol,* 10–16; Walter Clark, *History of the Supreme Court of North Carolina* (Raleigh, NC: Reprinted from the N.C. Booklet, 1919), 26–28.

51. *Hudson v. Hodge,* 139 N.C. 308 (1905); *Hodge v. Hudson,* 139 N.C. 358 (1905). *The Fayetteville Weekly Observer* (Fayetteville, NC), *The Wilmington Messenger* (Wilmington, NC), and *The Morning Post* (Raleigh, NC) all very briefly noted the state supreme court decisions in the *Hodge v. Hudson* and *Hudson v. Hodge* suits. See "Cumberland Supreme Court Decisions,"

Fayetteville Weekly Observer, Oct. 19, 1905, 2; "Supreme Court Opinions," *The Wilmington Messenger*, Oct. 20, 1905, 6; "Digest Supreme Court Decisions," *The Morning Post*, Oct. 29, 1905, 10.

52. For the later case involving Hodge's land (litigated by his heirs after his death), see *Hodges v. Wilson*, 165 N.C. 323 (1914). The higher court's decision in this suit upheld the lower court's cancellation of the deed.

53. See, for instance, Judith Kilpatrick, "(Extra) Ordinary Men: African American Lawyers and Civil Rights in Arkansas Before 1950," *Arkansas Law Review* 53 (2000): 299–399; Michael J. Klarman, *From Jim Crow to Civil Rights: The Supreme Court and the Struggle for Racial Equality* (Oxford: Oxford University Press, 2004); Gary M. Lavergne, *Before Brown: Heman Marion Sweatt, Thurgood Marshall, and the Long Road to Justice* (Austin: University of Texas Press, 2010); and Kenneth W. Mack, *Representing the Race: The Creation of the Civil Rights Lawyer* (Cambridge, MA: Harvard University Press, 2012).

54. Instead, a number of scholars have focused on white southerners' hostility and violence toward African Americans during the century after the Civil War. If they have looked at government institutions, they have generally portrayed them as oppressive and largely impenetrable to African Americans by the end of the nineteenth century. Other scholars show African Americans resisting white domination, but still portray black southerners as almost entirely separated from white institutions by the period of Jim Crow. The "political" action and resistance that they portray during this time largely lies in labor unions, all-black organizations, emigration movements, and black churches. Leon Litwack and Joel Williamson, for instance, see white attitudes toward African Americans as largely forming a hostile consensus. See Leon F. Litwack, *Been in the Storm So Long: The Aftermath of Slavery* (New York: Knopf, 1980), and Joel Williamson, *The Crucible of Race: Black-White Relations in the American South Since Emancipation* (New York: Oxford University Press, 1984). More recently, scholars such as Mary Louise Wood, Grace Elizabeth Hale, and Fitzhugh Brundage have examined lynching during the Jim Crow period. Other scholars, such as Darlene Clark Hine, Hannah Rosen, and Crystal Feimster have highlighted sexual violence against black women. In addition, scholars such as David Oshinsky, Randall Kennedy, Douglass Blackmon, Sarah Haley, and Talitha LeFlouria have highlighted the violence and inequality within the criminal justice system. On the other hand, scholars such as Steven Hahn, Evelyn Higginbotham, and Tera Hunter have done important work on how African Americans themselves resisted in the post–Civil War decades, but have largely looked at resistance outside of white institutions during the Jim Crow years. In *A Nation Under Our Feet*, for instance, Steven Hahn examines African Americans' largely separate political mobilization from whites at the end of the nineteenth and beginning of the twentieth century. Glenda Gilmore's *Gender & Jim Crow: Women and the Politics of White Supremacy in North Carolina, 1896–1920* is an exception to this general trend. Gilmore examines the role of middle-class African American women in North Carolina local political action. Sarah Haley's *No Mercy Here: Gender, Punishment, and the Making of Jim Crow Modernity* also shows black women's sabotage and deliberate self-presentation within the realm of the criminal justice system. See Steven Hahn, *A Nation Under Our Feet, Black Political Struggles in the Rural South From Slavery to the Great Migration* (Cambridge, MA: Harvard University Press, 2003); Glenda Gilmore, *Gender & Jim Crow: Women and the Politics of White Supremacy in North Carolina, 1896–1920* (Chapel Hill: University of North Carolina Press, 1996); Haley, *No Mercy Here*.

55. By focusing on individual's assertions of their rights in the courts, this book thus connects studies of African Americans' struggles for their rights during Reconstruction to the scholarship of the long twentieth-century civil rights movement. Scholarship that examines African Americans' struggle for rights until the end of the nineteenth century includes W. E. B. Du Bois, *Black Reconstruction: An Essay Toward a History of the Part Which Black Folk Played in the Attempt to Reconstruct Democracy in America, 1860–1880* (New York: Russell & Russell, 1935); Elsa Barkley Brown, "To Catch a Vision of Freedom: Reconstructing Southern Black Women's Political History, 1865–1880," in Ann Gordon et al., eds., *African American Women and the Vote, 1837–1960* (Amherst: University of Massachusetts Press, 1997), 66–99; Hahn, *A Nation Under Our Feet*; Tera Hunter, *To 'Joy My Freedom: Southern Black Women's Lives and Labors After the Civil War* (Cambridge, MA: Harvard University Press, 1997); and R. Volney

Riser, *Defying Disfranchisement: Black Voting Rights Activism in the Jim Crow South, 1890–1908* (Baton Rouge: Louisiana State University Press, 2010). More and more studies are beginning to show groups mobilizing for economic, legal, and political rights in the 1920s, 1930s, and 1940s, decades before the traditional civil rights narrative usually begins. In a path-breaking 2005 article, Jacquelyn Dowd Hall called for scholars to reframe the civil rights movement as beginning decades earlier than it has previously been framed and to study the participation of ordinary men and women, rather than focusing on the largely male black leadership of the 1950s and 1960s. See Jacquelyn Dowd Hall, "The Long Civil Rights Movement and the Political Uses of the Past," *The Journal of American History* 91, no.4 (2005): 1233–1263. Even before the publication of Hall's article, scholars like Charles Payne, Adam Fairclough, and Robin D. G. Kelley were examining the grassroots mobilization of ordinary black southerners in the 1920s and 1930s. See Charles M. Payne, *I've Got the Light of Freedom: The Organizing Tradition and the Mississippi Freedom Struggle* (Berkeley: University of California Press, 1995); Adam Fairclough, *Race & Democracy: The Civil Rights Struggle in Louisiana, 1915–1972* (Athens: University of Georgia Press, 1995); Robin D. G. Kelley, *Hammer and Hoe: Alabama Communists During the Great Depression* (Chapel Hill: University of North Carolina Press, 1990). Since Hall's article, a number of scholars have analyzed the civil rights movement's early twentieth-century roots further, often locating the movement's roots in the 1920s, 1930s, and 1940s. See Glenda Gilmore, *Defying Dixie: The Radical Roots of Civil Rights, 1919–1950* (New York: Norton, 2008); Tomiko Brown-Nagin, *Courage to Dissent: Atlanta and the Long History of the Civil Rights Movement* (Oxford: Oxford University Press, 2011); Risa L. Goluboff, *The Lost Promise of Civil Rights* (Cambridge, MA: Harvard University Press, 2007); Danielle L. McGuire, *At the Dark End of the Street: Black Women, Rape, and Resistance—A New History of the Civil Rights Movement From Rosa Parks to the Rise of Black Power* (New York: Knopf, 2010); Patricia Sullivan, *Lift Every Voice: The NAACP and the Making of the Civil Rights Movement* (New York: New Press, 2009). Other scholars, however, have questioned and problematized the helpfulness of the long civil rights framework for legal and historical scholarship. See Schmidt, "Legal History and the Problem of the Long Civil Rights Movement," and Eric Arnesen, "Reconsidering the Long Civil Rights Movement," *Historically Speaking* 10, no.2 (2009): 31–34.

56. Historians and scholars who have recently examined African Americans' challenges to the southern status quo at the end of the nineteenth century and in the first two decades of the twentieth century include Blair Kelley, *Right to Ride: Streetcar Boycotts and African American Citizenship in the Era of Plessy v. Ferguson* (Chapel Hill: University of North Carolina Press, 2010); Greta de Jong, *A Different Day: African American Struggles for Justice in Rural Louisiana, 1900–1970* (Chapel Hill: University of North Carolina Press, 2002); Gilmore, *Gender & Jim Crow*; Carle, *Defining the Struggle*; Alexander, *An Army of Lions*; Sullivan, *Lift Every Voice*.

57. In *Bloody Lowndes*, Hasan Jeffries, for one, notes that "at the moment of emancipation, [freedpeople] reflected on their enslavement and identified their freedom rights, or those civil and human rights that slaveholders denied them." In the decades after emancipation, he writes, black southerners' "primary focus remained the guarantee of freedom rights." But at any given moment, Jeffries writes, black southerners did not fight for all of these freedom rights "with equal vigor. Instead, they carefully assessed the risks and rewards associated with each." Similarly, in "To Catch a Vision of Freedom," Elsa Barkley Brown argues that African Americans had their own unique vision of what freedom looked like. In the years after emancipation, she writes, they placed special value on their economic independence, choosing to move from job to job in many cases to preserve it. Likewise, Robin D. G. Kelley's book *Freedom Dreams* shows how African Americans' visions of freedom informed individuals' participation in and support for various social movements such as the Back to Africa Movement, Communism, and Black Feminism. See Brown, "To Catch a Vision of Freedom," in *Unequal Sisters*, 3rd ed., 127; Hasan Kwame Jeffries, *Bloody Lowndes: Civil Rights and Black Power in Alabama's Black Belt* (New York: New York University Press, 2009), 7–37; Robin D. G. Kelley, *Freedom Dreams: The Black Radical Imagination* (Boston: Beacon Press, 2002). See also Eric Foner, "Rights and the Constitution in Black Life During the Civil War and Reconstruction," *The Journal of American History* 74, no.3 (1987): 863–883.

58. For more on the use of litigation by national organizations fighting racial injustice at the end of the nineteenth and beginning of the twentieth centuries, see Carle, *Defining the Struggle*, and Alexander, *An Army of Lions*. For more on the NAACP's rationale for turning to the courts, see NAACP Annual Report for 1926, 3. This report is quoted in Tushnet, *The NAACP's Legal Strategy Against Segregated Education*, 1–2.

59. For a discussion of the results of examining black and white southerners' history in concert, see Painter, *Southern History Across the Color Line*, 1–4. For an analysis of the dynamism of white supremacy and the variation in how it was carried out, see "Introduction," in Jane Dailey, Glenda Elizabeth Gilmore, and Bryant Simon, eds., *Jumpin' Jim Crow: Southern Politics From Civil War to Civil Rights* (Princeton, NJ: Princeton University Press, 2000), 3–4.

60. See, for instance, Mark Tushnet, *The American Law of Slavery, 1810–1860: Considerations of Humanity and Interest* (Princeton, NJ: Princeton University Press, 1981); Thomas D. Morris, *Southern Slavery and the Law, 1619–1860* (Chapel Hill: The University of North Carolina Press, 1996). In addition, see the scholarship of legal scholar A. Leon Higginbotham.

61. Hendrik Hartog set out important ideas about law-in-action with his path-breaking article "Pigs and Positivism," *Wisconsin Law Review* 4 (1985): 899–935. Walter Johnson also played an important role in this shift through his critique of the focus on appellate judges' opinions in his review of Thomas Morris's *Southern Slavery and the Law* (1996). Johnson argues that Morris's approach ignores the actions of African Americans in contesting the law and elides the confusion and contradiction that occurred in trials in local courtrooms around the South as judges sought to justify and deal with cases involving slavery. See Johnson, "Inconsistency, Contradiction, and Complete Confusion: The Everyday Life of the Law of Slavery," 405–433. Laura Edwards also forcefully argues for recognizing the difference between the laws written in statutes and opinions and how the law was experienced by ordinary people in local areas. Edwards also demonstrates how slaves and other individuals could affect and influence legal processes at the local level in her articles "Status without Rights" and "Enslaved Women and the Law" and her book *The People and their Peace*. Ariela Gross pioneered the new field of cultural legal history in her article "Beyond Black and White: Cultural Approaches to Race and Slavery," *Columbia Law Review* 101 (April 2001): 640–690. For examples of this new legal history, see Ariela Gross, *Double Character: Slavery and Mastery in the Antebellum Southern Courtroom* (Princeton, NJ: Princeton University Press, 2000); Laura Edwards, "Status Without Rights: African Americans and the Tangled History of Law and Governance in the Nineteenth-Century U.S. South," *The American Historical Review* 112, no.2 (2007): 365–393; Laura Edwards, "Enslaved Women and the Law: The Paradoxes of Subordination in the Post-Revolutionary Carolinas," *Slavery & Abolition* 26 (August 2005): 305–323; Laura Edwards, *The People and Their Peace: Legal Culture and the Transformation of Inequality in the Post-Revolutionary South* (Chapel Hill: University of North Carolina Press, 2009); Dylan Penningroth, *The Claims of Kinfolk: African American Property and Community in the Nineteenth-Century South* (Chapel Hill: University of North Carolina Press, 2003); Rebecca J. Scott, *Degrees of Freedom: Louisiana and Cuba after Slavery* (Cambridge, MA: Belknap Press of Harvard University Press, 2005); Brown-Nagin, *Courage to Dissent*. For a discussion of the use of theories of text in the context of legal history, see Steven Wilf, "Law/Text/Past," *UC Irvine Law Review* 1, no.3 (2011): 543–564. For a thought experiment on law and performance, see Barbara Welke, "Owning Hazard, A Tragedy," *UC Irvine Law Review* 1, no.3 (2011): 693–762. For a discussion of how this new legal history has played out in examinations of the civil rights movement, see Risa Goluboff, "Lawyers, Law, and the New Civil Rights History," *Harvard Law Review* 126, no.8 (2013): 2312–2335.

62. For examples of new legal histories that focus on one case or a small number of cases and examine the cases in context, see Kevin Boyle, *Arc of Justice: A Saga of Race, Civil Rights, and Murder in the Jazz Age* (New York: Holt, 2004); Michael A. Ross, *The Great New Orleans Kidnapping Case: Race, Law, and Justice in the Reconstruction Era* (New York: Oxford University Press, 2015); Michael Grossberg, *A Judgment for Solomon: The D'Hauteville Case and Legal Experience in Antebellum America* (Cambridge: Cambridge University Press, 1996); Hodes, *White Women, Black Men*. On the other hand, Ariela Gross's book *Double Character*, examining hundreds of cases involving slavery in one Mississippi county, and Walter Johnson's examination of the domestic slave trade, *Soul by Soul*, both draw on ideas of the new cultural–legal

history while still examining many trial court cases in a systematic manner. Similarly, Kali Gross's *Colored Amazons: Crime, Violence, and Black Women in The City of Brotherly Love, 1880–1910* (Durham, NC: Duke University Press, 2006) examines the criminal records of black women in Philadelphia between 1880 and 1910 using techniques of social and cultural history.

63. In addition, I use nonlegal sources to better understand the context of these suits, to discern the meaning of witnesses' and litigants' testimony, and to follow the participants in particular suits before and after their trials. In placing law firmly within the social world, rather than discussing "law and society," I have been influenced by Robert Gordon's foundational "Critical Legal Histories," as well as the work of scholars responding to his work at a 2002 Law & Social Inquiry Symposium. See Robert W. Gordon, "Critical Legal Histories," *Stanford Law Review* 36 (Jan. 1984): 57–125; Hendrik Hartog, "Introduction to Symposium on 'Critical Legal Histories,'" *Law & Social Inquiry* 37 (Winter 2012): 147–154; Laura F. Edwards, "The History in 'Critical Legal Histories,'" *Law & Social Inquiry* 37 (Winter 2012): 187–197; Susanna L. Blumenthal, "Of Mandarins, Legal Consciousness, and the Cultural Turn in U.S. Legal History," *Law & Social Inquiry* 37 (Winter 2012): 167–183. I have also been influenced by the conception of "Law as . . ." discussed in the *UC Irvine Law Review* Symposium Issue in September 2011. See, for instance, Catherine L. Fisk and Robert W. Gordon, "'Law As . . .': Theory and Method in Legal History," *UC Irvine Law Review* 1, no. 3 (2011): 519–541.

Prologue

1. Thomas D. Russell, "Slave Auctions on the Courthouse Steps: Court Sales of Slaves in Antebellum South Carolina," in Paul Finkelman, ed., *Slavery & The Law* (Lanham, MD: Rowman & Littlefield, 1997), 349–350.

2. Gross, *Double Character*, 23. A different study by Judith Kelleher Schafer found 1,118 cases involving slavery before the Supreme Court of Louisiana out of a total of 13,528 cases between 1809 and 1862 (thus 8 percent of Louisiana supreme court cases during this time involved slaves). However, the Supreme Court of Louisiana could not hear criminal appeals involving slaves until 1846. See Schafer, *Slavery, the Civil Law, and the Supreme Court of Louisiana*, 31, 14–15.

3. My examination of slavery cases heard by the Supreme Court of Georgia between 1846 and 1861, for instance, found 224 civil cases relating to slavery with all white litigants but only 8 civil cases with at least one free black or slave litigant. I conducted a thorough examination of slavery cases in the Georgia supreme court between 1846 and 1861 on the legal database LexisNexis, online at www.lexisnexis.com, and the Adam Matthew Slavery, Abolition and Social Justice electronic database, online at http://www.amdigital.co.uk/m-collections/collection/slavery-abolition-and-social-justice/.

4. In certain states, such as Missouri, Louisiana, and Kentucky, black litigants were able to bring many more freedom suits. For instance, 301 legal petitions for freedom in the St. Louis Circuit Court between 1814 and 1860 are listed on the following website: St. Louis Circuit Court Historical Records Project, Washington University in St. Louis, http://www.stlcourtrecords.wustl.edu/about-freedom-suits-series.php. For more on freedom suits in the antebellum South, see Kelly M. Kennington, *In the Shadow of Dred Scott: St. Louis Freedom Suits and the Legal Culture of Slavery in Antebellum America* (Athens: University of Georgia Press, 2017); Loren Schweninger, *Appealing for Liberty: Freedom Suits in the South* (Oxford: Oxford University Press, 2017); David Thomas Konig, "The Long Road to Dred Scott: Personhood and the Rule of Law in the Trial Court Records of St. Louis Slave Freedom Suits," *University of Missouri-Kansas City Law Review* 75 (Fall 2006): 53–79; Jason A. Gillmer, "Suing for Freedom: Interracial Sex, Slave Law, and Racial Identity in the Post-Revolutionary and Antebellum South," *North Carolina Law Review* 82, no. 2 (2004): 535–619; Paul Finkelman, *An Imperfect Union: Slavery, Federalism, and Comity* (Chapel Hill: University of North Carolina Press, 1981). See also Thomas D. Morris, "Slaves and the Rules of Evidence in Criminal Trials," in, Paul Finkelman, ed., *Slavery & the Law* (Madison, WI: Madison House, 1997), 210; Christopher Waldrep, "Substituting Law for the Lash: Emancipation and Legal Formalism in a Mississippi Court," *The Journal of American History* 82, no. 4 (1996): 1428–1433.

5. A committee of two justices of the peace and five local slaveholders, for example, decided many of the cases of slaves and free people of color in 1850s Mississippi. After examining the witnesses and the evidence, they made their decision. If they found the slave guilty of a noncapital crime, they decided on a "corporeal punishment to be inflicted upon the accused (not extending to the taking away of life or member)." *The Revised Code of the Statute Laws of the State of Mississippi* (Jackson, MS: E. Barksdale, state printer, 1857), 250–251; Waldrep, "Substituting Law for the Lash," 1428–1433; Daniel J. Flanigan, "Criminal Procedure in Slave Trials in the Antebellum South," *The Journal of Southern History* 40, no. 4 (1974): 539–546. The 1857 Mississippi Code allowed slaveholders to make appeals on behalf of their slaves from the justice of the peace to circuit courts. See *The Revised Code of the Statute Laws of the State of Mississippi* (1857), 252. These tribunals came under harsh criticism from reformers and even some jurists. See Flanigan, "Criminal Procedure," 542–543. For a history of the involvement of magistrates in the punishment of slaves beginning in the seventeenth century, see Morris, *Southern Slavery and the Law*, 210–215.

6. John Belton O'Neall, *The Negro Law of South Carolina* (Columbia, SC: printed by John G. Bowman, 1848), 12. See also Waldrep, "Substituting Law for the Lash," 1430–1433; Ayers, *Vengeance & Justice*, 11; Flanigan, "Criminal Procedure," 546–548. Judith Kelleher Schafer notes that "By the beginning of the Civil War, all southern states except South Carolina, Virginia, and Louisiana had abolished special slave tribunals and tried slaves in the same courts as whites." See Schafer, *Slavery, the Civil Law, and the Supreme Court of Louisiana*, 65. Thomas Morris contends that the increasing application of the same legal procedures used for whites to trials involving slaves was largely a result of changes in the court system. See Morris, *Southern Slavery and the Law*, 224–225. Mark Tushnet, on the other hand, writes that jurists "may have wished to relax various technicalities in slave cases, but they ran the risk that elimination of concern for technicality in slave cases would reflect back onto cases involving whites." See Tushnet, *The American Law of Slavery*, 121–122.

7. See, for instance, Return J. Meigs and William F. Cooper, *The Code of Tennessee Enacted by the General Assembly of 1857-'8* (Nashville, TN: Eastman and Company, State Printers, 1858), 510. Even in the circuit and appeal courts, though, a sensational crime or slave insurrection could lead courts to ignore the common law. The appellate court in Mississippi for example, appointed counsel for slaves who did not have lawyers representing them and would not admit slave confessions into evidence if they had been coerced. Waldrep, "Substituting Law for the Lash," 1430–1433; *The Revised Code of the Statute Laws of the State of Mississippi* (1857), 249–250. Waldrep found that "few slaves reached circuit court." He wrote that "In Warren County [Mississippi]—where 70 percent of the population was slave—97 percent of circuit court defendants were white. Only Blacks accused of the most violent crimes made it to circuit court, and they made up just 8 percent of defendants charged with such crimes." He calculated this from a series of intact bundles of Warren County Circuit Court case files, 1850–1854, Warren County Circuit Court Papers. See also *The Revised Code of the Statute Laws of the State of Mississippi*, which states: "Upon examination and investigation aforesaid, if it shall appear to said justices and slaveholders assembled for the trial of any slave as aforesaid, and a majority of them shall be of the opinion that the slave so tried by them is guilty of any crime punishable with death by the laws of the State, it shall be the duty of the said justices, or one of them, to commit said slave to prison, to be tried by the circuit court of the proper county, and immediately after such commitment of any such slave for trial in the circuit court as aforesaid, said justices or one of them, shall send up and file in the circuit court clerk's office of the proper county, among the papers of the State cases for trial therein, all the evidence taken down by them on the trial of such slave aforesaid, and shall also recognize the witness or witnesses brought before them on such trial, to appear at the proper time before said circuit court." *The Revised Code of the Statute Laws of the State of Mississippi* (1857), 251.

8. For more about the history of jury trials being extended to slaves and the effect of juries on the trials for slaves, see Morris, *Southern Slavery and the Law*, 215–218; Flanigan, "Criminal Procedure," 548–549, 553.

9. Daniel Flanigan explains that in South Carolina, slaves were not allowed to appeal to the state's highest court until 1833 and then did so very rarely. Moreover, according to Flanigan, in Virginia slaves didn't successfully appeal to the state supreme court until 1865 and no

slave defendants appealed to the highest courts in Delaware and Maryland "in the antebellum period." Flanigan, "Criminal Procedure," 540–546; Morris, *Southern Slavery and the Law*,
226–227; Schafer, *Slavery, the Civil Law, and the Supreme Court of Louisiana*, 65; A.E. Keir
Nash, "Fairness and Formalism in the Trials of Blacks in the State Supreme Courts of the Old
South," *Virginia Law Review* 56, no.1 (1970): 73–74.

10. See, for instance, *The Code of Tennessee* (1858), 511. According to Daniel J. Flanigan, in
the nineteenth century, "every southern state . . . [ensured] that slaves would have counsel in capital cases no matter what crime they were accused of committing. One method
was to force the owner to hire a lawyer. If the master refused to employ counsel, the court
appointed an attorney to defend the slave and charged the costs to the master. In other
states the government assumed the responsibility and the costs of providing counsel for
slaves whose owners refused to defend them." Flanigan, "Criminal Procedure," 553–554.
Flanigan writes that one exception to states generally not ensuring counsel for white
men was Kentucky's provision of counsel in civil but not criminal cases and Alabama,
Missouri, and Georgia's provision of counsel to "indigent persons." Flanigan, "Criminal
Procedure," 554.

11. For instance, *The Negro Law of South Carolina* (1848) says "A slave cannot testify, except as
against another slave, free negro, mulatto, or mestizo, and that without oath." See O'Neall, *The
Negro Law of South Carolina* (1848), 23. *The Code of Tennessee* (1858) says "A negro, mulatto,
Indian, or person of mixed blood, descended from negro or Indian ancestors, to the third
generation inclusive . . . is incapable of being a witness in any cause, civil or criminal, except
for or against each other." Meigs, *The Code of Tennessee Enacted by the General Assembly of
1857–'8* (1858), 687. However, in breach of warranty cases, in which slave owners claimed
that a slave was not in the condition promised when they had bought him, the courts allowed
white witnesses to refer to hearsay from slaves. For more about the use of hearsay by slaves in
the testimony of warranty suits, see Ariela Gross, "Pandora's Box: Slave Character on Trial in
the Antebellum Deep South," in *Slavery & The Law*, 316–319. Thomas Morris examines some
of the other exceptions to the rule against slave testimony, including cases involving slave-
insurrection conspiracies, confessions to a crime, and criminal cases against free black people
and Indians. See Morris, "Slaves and the Rules of Evidence in Criminal Trials," in *Slavery &
The Law*, 209, 220.

12. Even when they could not testify themselves, however, enslaved men's and women's words
could come through to the court through the testimony of others. In some cases, "information" that enslaved people had collected or noticed about a crime scene was passed on to the
magistrate during the initial phase of the investigation. At times, slaves' version of events was
repeated in the testimony of whites, occasionally even leading to a white person being put on
trial for a crime against a slave. See Edwards, "Status Without Rights," 377–379, and Edwards,
"Enslaved Women and the Law," 312–314.

13. The antebellum documents in the *Armstrong v. Pearre* case file, for instance, list the testator's
slaves by age and value, noting the appreciation of their worth over time. Eureline was valued at $700 and Mary at $850. John was worth $1,000. *Armstrong v. Pearre*, 47 Tenn. 171
(1869). See also Saidiya V. Hartman, *Scenes of Subjection: Terror, Slavery, and Self-Making in
Nineteenth-Century America* (New York: Oxford University Press, 1997), 93–95; Tushnet,
The American Law of Slavery, 142–147.

14. *Armstrong v. Pearre*, 47 Tenn. 171 (1869).

15. For a discussion of the role of the idea of property in slavery, see James Oakes, *Slavery and
Freedom: An Interpretation of the Old South* (New York: Vintage Books, 1990), 71–73.

16. For more about cases brought by slaves claiming their freedom in courts during the antebellum period, see Kennington, *In the Shadow of* Dred Scott; Schweninger, *Appealing for Liberty*;
Konig, "The Long Road to Dred Scott"; Gillmer, "Suing for Freedom," 535–619; Finkelman,
An Imperfect Union; Arthur F. Howington, *What Sayeth The Law: The Treatment of Slaves and
Free Blacks in the State and Local Courts of Tennessee* (New York: Garland,1986), 13–21. For a
contemporary account of the laws regarding freedom suits, see Abraham Caruthers, *History
of a Lawsuit in the Circuit Court of Tennessee on the Basis of The Code* (Nashville, TN: A.A.
Stitt, 1860), 382–384. Important work has also been done on slaves' claims-making in South
and Central America. For a discussion of slaves' freedom suits in Cuba, see Alejandro de la

Fuente, "Slave Law and Claims-Making in Cuba: The Tannenbaum Debate Revisited," *Law and History Review* 22, no. 2 (2004): 339–369.

17. For more on freedom suits over travel or residence beyond state boundaries, see Finkelman, *An Imperfect Union*, 181–235.

18. See *Morrison v. White*, Louisiana Supreme Court case 442, 16 La. Ann. 100 (1861); Gross, *What Blood Won't Tell*, 1–15, 48–72. For more on freedom suits over racial determination, see Walter Johnson, "The Slave Trader, the White Slave, and the Politics of Racial Determination in the 1850s," 13–38; Gillmer, "Suing For Freedom," 535–619; Howington, *What Sayeth The Law*, 13–21. For a contemporaneous account of the laws regarding freedom suits and the process of making such a suit, see Caruthers, *History of a Lawsuit* (1860), 382–384.

19. Kimberly Welch's forthcoming book examining the antebellum trial records of four counties in Louisiana and Mississippi found approximately 1,000 cases in which free people of color and slaves litigated suits. See also Kimberly Welch, "Black Litigiousness and White Accountability: Free Blacks and the Rhetoric of Reputation in the Antebellum Natchez District," *Journal of the Civil War Era* 5, no. 3 (2015): 372–398. In addition, Martha Jones examines the litigation of free people of color in her forthcoming book. Jones explains in an article on the *Hughes v. Jackson* case that "even before Dred Scott, free African Americans rarely sought out federal courts as a venue . . . . The story of race and rights before the Civil War played out, not in federal courts, but in state and local venues." Martha S. Jones, "Hughes v. Jackson: Race and Rights Beyond Dred Scott," *North Carolina Law Review* 91 (June 2013): 1762. Ted Maris-Wolf also found free people of color litigating civil cases and hiring white lawyers to represent them in antebellum Virginia. See Ted Maris-Wolf, *Family Bonds: Free Blacks and Re-Enslavement Law in Antebellum Virginia* (Chapel Hill: University of North Carolina Press, 2015).

20. At different times and to different degrees, southern states sought to limit the number of free people of color in their state through laws limiting manumission and laws preventing free people of color from relocating to their state. Not all southern states limited manumission to the same degree, and state laws changed over time so the free black population grew differently in various states during the antebellum period. For more on the law of manumission in America as compared with that of other parts of the American hemisphere, see Robert Cottrol, *The Long, Lingering Shadow: Slavery, Race, and Law in the American Hemisphere* (Athens: University of Georgia Press, 2013), 6–11. These figures on the percentages of free people of color in the upper and lower South come from Ira Berlin, *Slaves Without Masters: The Free Negro in the Antebellum South* (New York: Vintage Books, 1976), 136–137. For more on free people of color during this time in the South and the law, see also Berlin, *Slaves Without Masters*, 138–157; John Hope Franklin, *The Free Negro in North Carolina, 1790–1860* (1943; reprinted New York: Russell & Russell, 1969), 85–86, 94–101, 151–156; Gross, *What Blood Won't Tell*, 29–30. According to Steven Mintz, around 1790, "six states (Maryland, Massachusetts, New York, North Carolina, Pennsylvania, and Vermont) permitted free African Americans to vote." Steven Mintz, "Winning the Vote: A History of Voting Rights," *History Now: The Journal of the Gilder Lehrman Institute*, http://www.gilderlehrman. org/history-by-era/government-and-civics/essays/winning-vote-history-voting-rights. In North Carolina, for instance, free blacks could vote before 1835. See Parker, *Cumberland County*, 43.

21. According to the Code of South Carolina, free black people could make contracts, purchase and transfer real estate, sue and be sued, and invoke the writ of habeas corpus. O'Neall, *The Negro Law of South Carolina* (1848), 12–13. For more on how free people of color used relationships with powerful whites to aid their cases and tried to shape the court's conceptions of their reputations, see Welch, "Black Litigiousness and White Accountability," 372–398. See also Martha S. Jones, "Leave of Court: African-American Legal Claims Making In the Era of *Dred Scott v. Sandford*," in Manisha Sinha and Penny Von Eschen, eds., *Contested Democracy: Politics, Ideology and Race in American History* (New York: Columbia University Press, 2007), 56–68; Jones, "Hughes v. Jackson," 1757–1783; Maris-Wolf, *Family Bonds*. In Georgia, several cases brought by free black people protested their imprisonment after they had been unable to pay heavy fines and taxes levied on free people of color. See *Yancy v. Harris*,

9 Ga. 535 (1851); *Cooper and Worsham v. The Mayor and Aldermen of Savannah,* 4 Ga. 68 (1848); *Hargrove v. Webb and Allen,* 27 Ga. 172 (1859).

22. Alexis de Tocqueville, *Democracy in America,* vol. I (New York: Knopf, 1945), 257, 290. See also Nan Goodman's discussion of Tocqueville and of the popular interest in the law in Nan Goodman, "Law in Popular Culture, 1790–1920," in Michael Grossberg and Christopher Tomlins, eds., *The Cambridge History of Law in America,* vol. II (Cambridge: Cambridge University Press, 2008), 387–394; Laura Edward's discussion of the primacy of law in every-day people's lives in the late eighteenth and nineteenth centuries in Edwards, "Enslaved Women and the Law," 309, and Edwards, "Status Without Rights," 377–381, and Gross, *Double Character,* 22–46.

23. After escaping slavery, for instance, Henry Bibb wrote in a narrative of his life that he had not known of laws that allowed slaves to be branded, have their arms cut off, or be killed and quartered: "at the time I joined my wife in holy wedlock . . . I knew not that I was propogating victims for this kind of torture and cruelty." Henry Bibb, *Narrative of the Life and Adventures of Henry Bibb: An American Slave* (1849; reprinted New York: Dover, 2005), 15. During the antebellum era, a little fewer than half of southern states had laws prohibiting slaves from learning to read, but such laws were not always understood or enforced. Christopher Hager estimates that "If literate individuals composed at least 5 percent and perhaps upwards of 10 percent of the entire slave population, then at least 200,000 and possibly almost half a million people achieved literacy while they were enslaved." For more on antiliteracy laws and slave literacy, see Christopher Hager, *Word by Word: Emancipation and the Act of Writing* (Cambridge, MA: Harvard University Press, 2013), 40–46 (quote is from p.46).

24. Harriet Jacobs, for instance, wrote of her master, "He told me I was his property; that I must be subject to his will in all things," Harriet Jacobs, "Incidents in the Life of a Slave Girl," in Yuval Taylor, ed., vol. 2 of *I Was Born A Slave: An Anthology of Classic Slave Narratives, 1849–1866* (Chicago: Lawrence Hill, 1999), 559. Harriet Jacobs also wrote to her read-ers: "You never knew what it is to be a slave; to be entirely unprotected by law or custom; to have the laws reduce you to the condition of a chattel, entirely subject to the will of another." Jacobs, "Incidents in the Life of a Slave Girl" in *I Was Born a Slave,* 578–579. See also Jacobs, "Incidents in the Life of a Slave Girl," in *I Was Born A Slave,* 547; Douglass, *The Frederick Douglass Papers,* 476.

25. "Sometimes, when my master found that I still refused to accept what he called his kind offers, he would threaten to sell my child," Harriet Jacobs wrote, "his threat lacerated my heart. I knew the law gave him the power to fulfill it." Jacobs, "Incidents in the Life of a Slave Girl," in *I Was Born a Slave,* 593.

26. Harriet Jacobs, "Incidents in the Life of a Slave Girl," in *I Was Born a Slave,* 615; Gross, *Double Character,* 42. In addition, Solomon Northup notes the testimony ban in his later narrative, although it is unclear if he knew of it at the time he was enslaved. See Solomon Northup, "Twelve Years a Slave: Narrative of Solomon Northup" in Yuval Taylor, ed., *I Was Born a Slave: An Anthology of Classic Slave Narratives, 1849–1866* (Chicago: Lawrence Hill, 1999), 2:219. Former slave Frederick Douglass also noted the testimony ban in *The Frederick Douglass Papers,* 476.

27. At times, slaveholders made sales, bequests, or freedom conditional on the black beneficia-ries' behavior. In his 1855 will, one such slaveholder, William Cox of Kentucky, wrote that "if any of the negroes belonging to my estate will not obey their mistres she has the rite to sell said negroes." "Will of William Cox," Trigg County Court Records, KDLA, quoted in Yvonne M. Pitts, "'I Desire to Give My Black Family Their Freedom': Manumissions, Inheritance, and Visions of Family in Antebellum Kentucky" in Angela Boswell and Judith N. McArthur, eds., *Women Shaping the South: Creating and Confronting Change* (Columbia: University of Mississippi Press, 2006), 55–57. Slave narratives and court cases frequently recount prom-ises that masters gave to slaves to free them in their wills—many of which went unfulfilled. See Jacobs, "Incidents in the Life of a Slave Girl," in *I Was Born a Slave,* 546; Bibb, *Narrative of the Life and Adventures of Henry Bibb,* 18; Pitts, "I Desire to Give My Black Family Their Freedom," 57–58.

28. Slaves obtained experience with the market by providing authorized and unauthorized paid services to the larger community, servicing plantations beyond their own as carpenters

and blacksmiths, selling goods or livestock, or plying their trade rowing clients across rivers. Jonathan D. Martin, *Divided Mastery: Slave Hiring in the American South* (Cambridge, MA: Harvard University Press, 2004), 2–5, 138–140, 159–160; Ira Berlin, *Generations of Captivity: A History of African-American Slaves* (Cambridge, MA: Belknap Press of Harvard University Press, 2003), 90–92, 221–224. For examples of hiring slaves in court cases, see *Jameson v. McCoy*, 52 Tenn. 108 (1871); *Lattimore v. Dixon*, 63 N.C. 356 (1869); *Lattimore v. Dixon*, 65 N.C. 664 (1871). State supreme courts across the South consistently supported the position that slaves could trade if they had the permission of their masters. Some southern legislatures, however, put restrictions on slaves' rights to use and dispose of property, even with the consent of their masters. Penningroth, *The Claims of Kinfolk*, 45, 208, notes 2–5; Morris, *Southern Slavery and the Law*, 348–350. The law also put penalties on trading with slaves without the permission of the slaves' master. By 1824, in Georgia, for instance, slaves "would receive thirty-nine lashes for selling any amount of cotton, tobacco, wheat, rye, oats, corn, rice, or poultry without a ticket." Many jurisdictions also fined white people dealing with slaves without the master's permission. Morris, *Southern Slavery and the Law*, 251–253. For laws regarding trading with slaves, see Thomas Cooper and McCord, compilers, *The Statutes at Large of South Carolina* (Columbia, SC: printed by A.S. Johnston, 1836–1841), 7:454; Henry A. Bullard and Thomas Curry, *New Digest of the Statute Laws of Louisiana* (New Orleans, LA: E. Johns & Co., 1842), 55–56, and *The Revised Code of the Statute Laws of the State of Mississippi* (1857), 244. The line separating the official, legal economy and the informal, sometimes underground, economy was not always clear. Some states, for instance, made it illegal for masters to hire out their slaves. Berlin, *Generations of Captivity*, 116–117, 132–133, 220–225. For an examination of the informal economy, see also Penningroth, *The Claims of Kinfolk*; Berlin, *Generations of Captivity*, 79–80; Sophie White, "Wearing Three or Four Handkerchiefs Around His Collar, and Elsewhere About Him: Slaves' Constructions of Masculinity and Ethnicity in French Colonial New Orleans," in Sandra Gunning, Tera W. Hunter, and Michele Mitchell, eds., *Dialogues of Dispersal: Gender, Sexuality and African Diasporas* (Oxford: Blackwell, 2004), 136–137.

29. Historian Laura Edwards recounts how Joe, an enslaved man in South Carolina, reported at an inquest that he deliberately did not touch the dead body of another slave when he came upon it in the field. Instead, Joe said he gave "information"—a legal term for a report about an offense or facts about the offense—to a Mr. Gordon about the possible crime. Edwards, "Status Without Rights," 377–378.

30. Lucile Tucker, June 25, 1847, subseries 1.3, Folder 113 in the Rice C. Ballard Papers #4850, Southern Historical Collection, Wilson Library, University of North Carolina at Chapel Hill. Kim Welch's forthcoming book also includes an examination of a number of civil cases litigated by slaves.

31. In her study of peasants' use of local courts in early twentieth-century Russia, Jane Burbank also deals with the issue of how much legal knowledge her subjects had. She suggests shifting the discussion on such matters from "expertise to process, away from knowing laws to accepting, employing and respecting legal institutions." She concludes: "Rural people knew that the law could be used; they knew many of its protections and rules; the precise language of statutes was a matter for clerks and judges to engage." See Jane Burbank, *Russian Peasants Go to Court: Legal Culture in the Countryside, 1905–1917* (Bloomington: Indiana University Press, 2004), 7.

32. Jon-Christian Suggs, *Whispered Consolations: Law and Narrative in African American Life* (Ann Arbor: University of Michigan Press, 2000), 28–30; Gross, *Double Character*, 42.

33. Bibb, *Narrative of the Life and Adventures of Henry Bibb*, 13; Harriet Jacobs, "Incidents in the Life of a Slave Girl," in *I Was Born a Slave*, 590–591.

34. Bibb, *Narrative of the Life and Adventures of Henry Bibb*, 15.

35. William Craft noted, for example, that according to Article 35 of the Civil Code of Louisiana, "A slave is one who is in the power of a master to whom he belongs. The master may sell him, dispose of his person, his industry, and his labour; he can do nothing, possess nothing, nor acquire anything but what must belong to his master." William and Ellen Craft, *Running a Thousand Miles for Freedom* (electronic resource, Charlottesville: University of Virginia Library, 1999), 13–15.

36. Douglass, *The Frederick Douglass Papers*, 141, 279. Another former slave, William Craft, explained that he quoted extensively from the southern statutes and sections of state constitutions regulating slavery "to give some idea of the legal as well as the social tyranny from which we fled." Craft, *Running a Thousand Miles for Freedom*, 13–15. See also Bibb, *Narrative of the Life and Adventures of Henry Bibb*, 3, 13, 15–18.

Chapter 1

1. *Buie v. Parker*, 63 N.C. 131 (1869). See also Parker, *Cumberland County*, 67–75.
2. The account of the former slave is from Parker, *Cumberland County*, 67–68. Parker writes, "When it happened in the first days of March, 1865, Sarah Louise Augustus was a slave child. Sixty years later she could recall the events clearly: 'The Yankees came through Fayetteville wearing large blue coats with capes on them. Lots of them were mounted, and there were thousands of foot soldiers. The southern soldiers retreated, and then in a few hours the Yankees covered the town. They busted into the smokehouse on Marster's, took the meat, meal, and other provisions . . . . They took all they wanted. They told us we were all free. The Negroes began visiting each other in the cabins and became so excited they began to shout and pray.'" For more on the destruction of the arsenal and the Union occupation of Fayetteville, see Parker, *Cumberland County*, 67–75.
3. *Buie v. Parker*, 63 N.C. 131 (1869).
4. The quote from black barber Isham Sweatt is from Parker, *Cumberland County*, 81–83. See also *Buie v. Parker*, 63 N.C. 131 (1869).
5. Parker, *Cumberland County*, 81–83.
6. Records of the Assistant Commissioner of North Carolina, Bureau of Refugees, Freedmen and Abandoned Lands, 1865–1870, roll 12, record group 105, microfilm publication 843, National Archives; *Buie v. Parker*, 63 N.C. 131 (1869).
7. James C. MacRae was born about 1839 in North Carolina and is listed in the 1880 US census as a white lawyer in Cumberland County. 1880 United States Federal Census, published online by Ancestry, Provo, Utah. See also Records of the Assistant Commissioner of North Carolina, Bureau of Refugees, Freedmen and Abandoned Lands, 1865–1870, roll 12, record group 105, microfilm publication 843, National Archives; *Buie v. Parker*, 63 N.C. 131 (1869).
8. The 1860 census lists 4,119,671 African Americans in the South (slave and free together). It also lists in the United States at this time, 488,070 free black people and 3,953,760 slaves. When the number of slaves in the United States at this time is subtracted from the number of African Americans in the South in 1860 (as even with gradual manumissions there was virtually no slavery left in the North by 1860), the number remaining is approximately 165,911 free black people in the South in 1860. "Proportion of the different classes to each other and to the white and aggregate population. Census of 1860" and "The colored population and its proportions–1860," Joseph C. G. Kennedy, *Population of The United States in 1860; Compiled From the Original Returns of The Eighth Census* (Washington, DC: US Government Printing Office, 1864), xii, xiii.
9. See, for instance, the cases of *Lattimore v. Dixon*, 63 N.C. 356 (1869); *Lattimore v. Dixon*, 65 N.C. 664 (1871).
10. Cumberland County, where Buie lived, contributed eight companies of troops to the war effort. Roy Parker Jr. writes that Cumberland County "provided eight initial companies of Confederate troops. Scores of other volunteers and conscripts were added as the war went on." Parker, *Cumberland County*, 74–75.
11. Thomas W. Helis, "Of Generals and Jurists: The Judicial System of New Orleans Under Union Occupation, May, 1862–April, 1865," *Louisiana History* XXIX (Spring 1988): 143–162; James Parton, *General Butler in New Orleans* (Boston: Farwell & Co., 1864), 114. For a contemporary account of southern courts closing during the war, see John Hallum, *The Diary of an Old Lawyer or Scenes Behind the Curtain* (Nashville, TN: Southwestern Publishing House, 1895), 112.
12. Cases in the Supreme Court of Georgia during the Civil War over how slaves should be passed on after a slaveholder's death included *Alderman v. Chester*, 34 Ga. 152 (1865); *Allen v. Whitaker*, 34 Ga. 6 (1864); *Bullard v. Farrar*, 33 Ga. 620 (1863); *Mason v. Mason*, 33 Ga.

435 (1863); and *Duncan v. Taylor*, 33 Ga. 312 (1862). Georgia supreme court suits during the Civil War that contested individual slaves' ownership included *Mourning v. Hodges*, 33 Ga. Supp. 104 (1864); *Cornett v. Fain*, 33 Ga. 219 (1862); *Rich v. Mobley*, 33 Ga. 85 (1861). Warranty suits in the Supreme Court of Georgia during the war included *McCurdy v. Terry*, 33 Ga. 49 (1861); *Watkins v. Defoor*, 33 Ga. 494 (1863); and *Gaulden v. Lawrence*, 33 Ga. 159 (1862). For more on the operation of courts in the Confederacy, see Laura F. Edwards, *A Legal History of the Civil War and Reconstruction* (Cambridge: Cambridge University Press, 2015), 47–49, 55, 58.

13. For example, after Jesse Hooks was summoned to report to Macon, Georgia, for military service in the Confederate Army, he filed a plea of habeas corpus, claiming exemption on the grounds that he was the owner of a plantation of 1,200 acres on which he worked 25 slaves. He stated that he was the only white man on the farm, that his wife was an invalid, and that he was growing grain and other necessary provisions. Both the lower court and, on appeal, the Supreme Court of Georgia denied his plea, claiming that he did meet the grounds for exemption. *Hooks v. Harris*, 33 Ga. Supp. 81 (1864). For examples of cases in which exemptions were granted, see *Andrews v. Strong*, 33 Ga. Supp. 166 (1864), and *Gates v. McManus*, 33 Ga. Supp. 67. For examples of cases in which exemptions were not granted, see *Barber v. Irwin*, 34 Ga. 27 (1864); *Camfield v. Patterson*, 33 Ga. 561 (1863).

14. *Tyson v. Rogers*, 33 Ga. 473 (1863). The commandant argued that it was necessary for him to take 60 slaves from local slaveholders for service within the local army hospitals because of a shortage of army personnel to perform certain tasks. The superior court held that a case of extreme necessity had not been shown to justify the impressment. The court affirmed. For more on the Confederacy's attempts at slave impressment during the Civil War, see Stephanie McCurry, *Confederate Reckoning: Power and Politics in the Civil War South* (Cambridge, MA: Harvard University Press, 2010), 223–226, 241–247, 263–288.

15. Supreme Court of Georgia cases during the Civil War in which a black person was accused of killing or attempting to kill a white person include *Monday (a slave) v. State*, 32 Ga. 672 (1861). Supreme Court of Georgia cases during the Civil War in which a black person was accused of stealing from the plantation house include *Davis v. Georgia*, 33 Ga. 98 (1861).

16. In the Supreme Court of Georgia, one suit was brought by a white administrator, Hugh Walton, on behalf of a free black person, Joseph Nunez. See *Bryan v. Walton*, 33 Ga. Supp. 11 (1864).

17. Upon hearing the news, one slave, Abner Lattimore, used the statement of emancipation as leverage to demand his money from his former master, Thomas Dixon. The white slaveholder refused to return the notes. *Lattimore v. Dickson*, 63 N.C. 356 (1869); *Lattimore v. Dixon*, 65 N.C. 664 (1871).

18. During the Civil War, there were an estimated 950,000 male slaves in the United States. Approximately 180,000 black soldiers served in the Union Army or Navy, where they made up approximately 10 percent of the Union Army. See McCurry, *Confederate Reckoning*, 318–319.

19. His black soldiers knew the regulations, he explained, such as the law that "a guard was only to take orders from the officer of the guard or the commanding officer of the post." As a result, "You cannot get a soldier in this regiment to take an order from anyone else." "Testimony by the Commander of a South Carolina Black Regiment before the American Freedmen's Inquiry Commission" [Beaufort, S.C. 1863], in Ira Berlin et al., eds., *Freedom: A Documentary History of Emancipation, 1861–1867*, Series II. The Black Military Experience (Cambridge: Cambridge University Press, 1982), 58–60; Donald G. Nieman, "The Language of Liberation: African Americans and Equalitarian Constitutionalism, 1830–1950," in Donald G. Nieman, ed., *Black Southerners and the Law, 1865-1900* (New York: Garland, 1994), 73.

20. "Excerpts from the proceedings of a general court-martial in the cases of Private William H. Thomas," 7th USCI, 24 Oct. 1865, MM-3244, Court-Martial Case Files, ser.15, RG 153 [H-34], in Berlin, *Freedom: A Documentary History of Emancipation*, Series II, 606–610.

21. Berlin, *Freedom: A Documentary History of Emancipation*, Series II, 253–254, 452–453.

22. Parton, *General Butler in New Orleans* (1864), 114; Helis, "Of Generals and Jurists," 148–149. Parton does not cite his sources for Major Bell's decision to allow black witnesses to testify. He also recounts, though, that in the same provost court, "Henry Dominque, a free man of

color, was arrested for not having free papers. The prisoner could only protest that he was a free man. The court decided, that every man must be presumed to be free until the contrary was shown. Dominique was discharged." See Parton, *General Butler in New Orleans*, 114.

23. Despite this 1883 decision of the Massachusetts Supreme Judicial Court, full emancipation in Massachusetts would take several more years. Evelyn Brooks Higginbotham writes that by the 1890 census, though, there is no record of any more slaves in Massachusetts. Evelyn Brooks Higginbotham, "Foreword," in Anne Farrow, Joel Lang, and Jenifer Frank, eds., *Complicity: How the North Promoted, Prolonged, and Profited from Slavery* (New York: Ballantine Books, Reprint ed., 2006), xii–xiv. See also Ira Berlin, *Many Thousands Gone: The First Two Centuries of Slavery in North America* (Cambridge, MA: Harvard University Press, 1998), 228–238; Peter Kolchin, *American Slavery, 1619–1877* (New York: Hill and Wang, 2003), 63–85; Joanne Pope Melish, *Disowning Slavery: Gradual Emancipation and "Race" in New England, 1780–1860* (Ithaca, NY: Cornell University Press, 1998), 1–29, 50–79 (for more on where slaves were clustered in the North, see pp.15–16); Farrow, *Complicity*; Leslie M. Harris, *In the Shadow of Slavery: African Americans in New York City, 1626–1863* (Chicago: University of Chicago Press, 2003).

24. According to historian Ira Berlin, 27,000 men and women remained enslaved in the North in 1810. Berlin, *Many Thousands Gone*, 228–238. See also Melish, *Disowning Slavery*, 64–79; Higginbotham, "Foreword," in Farrow, *Complicity*, xiii–xiv.

25. I take Paul Finkelman's definitions of which states constituted the "antebellum North." See Paul Finkelman, "Prelude to the Fourteenth Amendment: Black Legal Rights in the Antebellum North," *Rutgers Law Journal* 17 (1986): 417–450. See also Leon F. Litwack, *North of Slavery: The Negro in the Free States, 1790–1860* (Chicago: University of Chicago Press, 1961), 91–97. Finkelman contests many of Litwack's statements regarding the lack of rights for black northerners in the decades before the Civil War. According to Finkelman, in 1860 African Americans could vote in the northern states of Maine, New Hampshire, Vermont, Massachusetts, Rhode Island, and to a more limited extent, in New York, Ohio, and Michigan. They could not vote in 1860 in the states of Connecticut, New Jersey, Pennsylvania, Indiana, Illinois, Iowa, Wisconsin, Minnesota, California, and Oregon. For a state-by-state analysis of black northerners' rights in 1860, see the table outlining "Rights of Free Blacks in North in 1860" in Finkelman, "Prelude to the Fourteenth Amendment," 425. For a contemporary account of what states blacks could testify against whites in, see the letters of Indiana Governor Oliver P. Morton to a number of "free" states in December 1864 to inquire about their laws regarding black testimony. The states that replied back that African Americans could not testify against whites were Maryland, West Virginia, Tennessee, Illinois, Missouri, and Indiana. Excerpts of the exchanges are reprinted in "Negro Testimony," *Brownlow's Knoxville Whig, and Rebel Ventilator* (Feb. 15, 1865), 1.

26. Kennedy, *Race, Crime, and the Law*, 38; U.S. Congress Senate Committee on Slavery and the Treatment of Freedman. Equality Before the Law in the Courts of the United States. S. Rep. No.25, 38th Cong., 1st Sess. At 10 (1864), quoted in Kennedy, *Race, Crime and the Law*, 38.

27. For more on the US Civil War and the Confederacy's loss, see James McPherson, *Battle Cry of Freedom: The Civil War Era* (New York: Ballantine Books, 1988); Bruce Levine, *The Fall of the House of Dixie: The Civil War and the Social Revolution That Transformed the South* (New York: Random House, 2013); McCurry, *Confederate Reckoning*.

28. The 13th Amendment did not apply to the territories controlled by Indian nations that were viewed as legally outside of US jurisdictions. Instead, treaties, such as those with the Cherokee nation and the Seminoles, formally ended slavery in Indian territories. See Vine Deloria Jr. and David E. Wilkins, *Tribes, Treaties, and Constitutional Tribulations* (Austin: University of Texas Press, 1999), 140.

29. Oshinsky, *"Worse Than Slavery,"* 19; Waldrep, "Substituting Law for the Lash," 1433; Carole Emberton, *Beyond Redemption: Race, Violence, and the American South after the Civil War* (Chicago: University of Chicago Press, 2013), 26–35.

30. *Journal of the Senate of the State of Mississippi*, 1866, 121, quoted in Waldrep, "Substituting Law for the Lash," 1436.

31. Waldrep, "Substituting Law for the Lash, 1436–1437; Dan Carter, *When the War Was Over: The Failure of Self-Reconstruction in the South, 1865–1867* (Baton Rouge: Louisiana State University Press, 1985), 221–223.
32. Brundage, *Lynching in the New South*, 6.
33. Philip Dray, *At the Hands of Persons Unknown: The Lynching of Black America* (New York: Random House, 2002), 37. Dray seems to be citing Record Group 105, Assistant Commissioners' Reports, Bureau of Refugees, Freedmen and Abandoned Lands (1865–1869), National Archives, Washington, DC.
34. Eric Foner, *Reconstruction: America's Unfinished Revolution, 1863–1877* (New York: Harper & Row, 1988), 261–263, 425; Kennedy, *Race, Crime, and the Law*, 39–40.
35. *Laws of the State of Mississippi Passed at a Regular Session of the Mississippi Legislature Held in the City of Jackson, October, November and December 1865* (Jackson, MS: J.J. Shannon & Co., State Printers, 1866), 68, 71, 82–86; *Acts of the Session of 1865–6 of the General Assembly of Alabama Held in the City of Montgomery Commencing on the 3rd Monday of November, 1865* (Montgomery, AL: Reid & Screws, 1866), 111–112, 119–121; *Acts of the State of Tennessee Passed at the Second Session of the Thirty-Fourth General Assembly for the Years 1865–66* (Nashville, TN.: S.C. Mercer, 1866), 65; *Acts of the General Assembly of the State of Virginia Passed in 1865–66, in the Eighty-Ninth Year of the Commonwealth* (Richmond, VA: Allegre & Goode, Printers, 1866), 91–93; State Black Code Laws, Reprinted in 39th Congress, 2nd Session, Senate Executive Document No.6, Laws in Relation to Freedmen (1867), in Christian Samito, ed., *Changes in Law and Society During the Civil War and Reconstruction: A Legal History Documentary Reader* (Carbondale: Southern Illinois University Press, 2009), 189–196.
36. *Acts of the Session of 1865–6 of the General Assembly of Alabama Held in the City of Montgomery Commencing on the 3rd Monday of November, 1865* (1866), 98; *Laws of the State of Mississippi Passed at a Regular Session of the Mississippi Legislature Held in the City of Jackson, October, November and December 1865* (1866), 83; *Acts of the State of Tennessee Passed at the Second Session of the Thirty-Fourth General Assembly For the Years 1865–66* (1866), 65, 80; *Acts of the General Assembly of the State of Virginia Passed in 1865–66, in the Eighty-Ninth Year of the Commonwealth* (1866), 85–86, 89–90; State Black Code Laws, Reprinted in 39th Congress, 2nd Session, Senate Executive Document No.6, Laws in Relation to Freedmen (1867), in Samito, ed., *Changes in Law and Society During the Civil War and Reconstruction*, 189–196.
37. Waldrep, "Substituting Law for the Lash," 1436–1437.
38. The quote from the freedman is from Oshinsky, "Worse Than Slavery," 34. The quote from the Charleston attorney is from A South Carolinian, "South Carolina Morals," *The Atlantic Monthly*, April 1877, 474. Backing up such quotes, historian David Oshinsky found that by 1866, "the Natchez city jail held sixty-seven black prisoners and just eleven whites. In Grenada, to the north, there were seventeen blacks and one white. In Columbus, to the east, there were fifty-three blacks and no whites." Oshinsky, *"Worse Than Slavery,"* 33–34. See also Ayers, *Vengeance & Justice*, 176–77.
39. According to Christopher Waldrep, "Evidence from Mississippi's Presidential Reconstruction experience demonstrates that a legal culture existed in trial courts that did not respond well to elite manipulation. Inertia and legal formalism at the grass-roots level of jurisprudence not only hamstrung would-be tyrants but opened up new avenues for oppressed people." Waldrep, "Substituting Law for the Lash," 1451.
40. Waldrep, "Substituting Law for the Lash," 1427–1428, 1441–1442, 1444–1445, 1448–1449.
41. According to Waldrep, "The Warren County Court never became an instrument to control Blacks' labor. Legislators had designed the county courts for easy access, and in theory anyone could persuade the prosecuting attorney or court clerk to write an information . . . . It was almost always whites who provided the information necessary to prosecute county court cases. But they usually charged other whites. Of individuals identified as victims in extant informations, 80 percent were white. Crime control concerns dominated the county court. Not only did the courts allow victims to prosecute whites, but their juries seemed as willing to convict whites as Blacks. Of whites accused by county court information, only 15.6 percent won a 'not guilty' verdict; juries and judges convicted 64.2 percent. But 31.4 percent of Black defendants won acquittals; juries and judges convicted only 49 percent." Waldrep, "Substituting Law for the Lash," 1439–1440.

42. Jeffries, *Bloody Lowndes*, 8. See also Foner, "Rights and the Constitution in Black Life During the Civil War and Reconstruction," 863–883.

43. Nieman, "The Language of Liberation," 72, 77–79.

44. "Nashville Blacks to the Union Convention of Tennessee, Nashville, January 9, 1865," unidentified newspaper clipping of Andrew Tait et al. to the Union Convention of Tennessee, 9 Jan. 1865, enclosed in Col. R.D. Mussey to Capt. C.P. Brown, 23 Jan. 1865, Letter Received, ser. 925, Dept. of the Cumberland, RG 393 Pt.1 [C-12]) in Berlin, *Freedom: A Documentary History of Emancipation,* Series II, 811–816. Black people in Kentucky also participated in conventions advocating for the right to testify in court against whites. Victor B. Howard, "The Black Testimony Controversy in Kentucky, 1866–1872," in Donald G. Nieman, ed., *Black Southerners and the Law, 1865-1900* (New York: Garland, 1994), 154–157.

45. "The Contest in Mississippi About Negro Testimony," *The Colored Tennessean* (Nashville, TN), Oct. 14, 1865.

46. The bulk of the Bureau's work took place between 1865 and 1869. After 1869, the Bureau's activities were much more limited. Much of the relief provided by the Bureau benefited white southerners in addition to black southerners. The hospitals set up by the Freedmen's Bureau treated white as well as black southerners, for instance, and much of the food relief efforts went to poor white southerners, in addition to former slaves. For more about the organizational history of the Bureau and the legislation that provided for its existence, see Paul Skeels Peirce, *The Freedmen's Bureau: A Chapter in the History of Reconstruction* (Iowa City: State University of Iowa Press, 1901), 68–104. For more about the relief efforts and establishment of schools and hospitals, see Martin Abbott, *The Freedmen's Bureau in South Carolina, 1865–1872* (Chapel Hill: University of North Carolina Press, 1967), 37–51, 82–98.

47. Records of the Bureau of Refugees, Freedmen, and Abandoned Lands, 1865–1872, Record Group 105; Joseph A. Ranney, *In the Wake of Slavery: Civil War, Civil Rights, and the Reconstruction of Southern Law* (Westport, CN: Praeger, 2006), 56–57; Foner, *Reconstruction,* 142–170; Donald Nieman, *The Freedmen's Bureau and Black Freedom* (New York: Garland,1994); Peirce, *The Freedmen's Bureau,* 129–171; Abbott, *The Freedmen's Bureau in South Carolina,* 66–81.

48. Circular 35, Dec. 12, 1865, Circulars and Orders, 1865–1868, Assistant Commissioner, Louisiana, Bureau of Refugees, Freedmen and Abandoned Lands, R.G. 105, National Archives, quoted in Nieman, "Language of Liberation," 75–76.

49. One Bureau official wrote: "Nearly all freedmen who report cases of assault to me evince an utter unwillingness to return to the place they have left and invariably because they have been threatened with death in case they "report to the Bureau," and for the same reason it is extremely difficult to obtain witnesses to attest the truth of the complaints of freedmen, and if these witnesses are compelled to give evidence in a case between a white man & a freedman, they will in nearly all cases sustain the white man." "Letter to Bv't Maj. O.H. Howard from Georgia Freedmen's Bureau Agent G. Ballou, October 1868," in Cox and Cox, eds., *Reconstruction, the Negro, and the New South,* 275–278. In documenting disputes between freedpeople and their employers, many Bureau records do not specify if the parties involved had previous ties during slavery. A few cases, however, mention that the disputants were formerly master and slave. Thos F. Forbes to?, May 4, 1866, Records of the Assistant Commissioner of Georgia, Bureau of Refugees, Freedmen and Abandoned Lands, 1865–1869, Roll 13, R.G. 105, National Archives, Southeast Region; Atlanta, Georgia; Affidavit of Marion Green, Daniel L. Lain to Major General Meade, Jan. 28, 1868, Records of the Assistant Commissioner of Georgia, Bureau of Refugees, Freedmen and Abandoned Lands, 1865–1869, Roll 20, R.G. 105, microfilm publication 798, National Archives.

50. Captain H. Sweeney to General John Sprague, Jan. 5, 1867, Assistant Commissioner, Arkansas, Letters Received, Bureau of Refugees, Freedmen and Abandoned Lands, R.G. 105, National Archives, quoted in Nieman, "Language of Liberation," 76. See also Foner, *Reconstruction,* 150.

51. E. M. Webber to Lieutenant Garrick Mallery, July 24, 1867, Letters Received, Assistant Commissioner, Virginia, Bureau of Refugees, Freedmen and Abandoned Lands, R.G. 105, National Archives, quoted in Nieman, "Language of Liberation," 77.

52. At times, these Bureau courts consisted of only the local Bureau official. At other times, a Bureau agent and two local civilians, one appointed by the white disputant and one by the black disputant, made up the Bureau court. Elsewhere, Bureau agents mediated disagreements over custody, pay, and property ownership without the formal procedure of a court. Peirce, *The Freedmen's Bureau*, 143–144. For an example of black southerners' interest in protecting their rights at this time, see E. M. Webber to Lieutenant Garrick Mallery, July 24, 1867, Letters Received, Assistant Commissioner, Virginia, Bureau of Refugees, Freedmen and Abandoned Lands, R.G. 105, National Archives, quoted in Nieman, "Language of Liberation," 77.

53. In the trial transcript of a later case, a judge's statement credits the US military for the mule's return, noting that army officials ordered the county sheriff to take the mule from Buie, whereas Parker's lawyer credits the Freedmen's Bureau. As the Bureau official Richard Dillon was also a US Army captain, he may have been viewed as a member of the military by the judge and as a Bureau official by Parker. Or perhaps Dillon used the overlapping nature of the military and Freedmen's Bureau to enforce his superior's order. Records of the Assistant Commissioner of North Carolina, Bureau of Refugees, Freedmen and Abandoned Lands, 1865–1870, roll 12, R.G. 105, microfilm publication 843, National Archives; *Buie v. Parker*, 63 N.C. 131 (1869).

54. See, for instance, *Lattimore v. Dickson*, 63 N.C. 356 (1869); *Lattimore v. Dixon*, 65 N.C. 664 (1871).

55. Based on the judge's reply, African Americans still could not testify against whites in North Carolina in cases in which they had no personal interest in April of 1866. Superior Court Judge Daniel G. Fowle responded to the Bureau official's query about whether black witnesses could now testify against whites in North Carolina with the following reply: "if the chief difficulty in the way of yielding the exclusive jurisdiction in criminal matters to our Courts, consists in the apprehension that any unjust discrimination against the negro race would be made in regard to the right to testify, such apprehension ought to be removed by the recent act to which you refer, in-as-much as by sec.9th it is declared, that whenever matters relating to freedmen shall be fully committed to the Courts of this State, 'That persons of color, not otherwise incompetent, shall be capable of bearing evidence in all controversies at law and in equity, where the rights of persons or property of persons of color shall be put in issue … and also in please of the State where the violence, fraud, or injury alleged shall be charged to have been done by or to persons of color. In all other civil or criminal cases such evidence shall be deemed inadmissible unless by consent of the parties to the record.'" Their letters are printed in *The Weekly North Carolina Standard*, April 25, 1866, 4. See also Abbott, *The Freedmen's Bureau in South Carolina*, 103–105; Peirce, *The Freedmen's Bureau*, 143–149; Ranney, *In the Wake of Slavery*, 56; Litwack, *Been in the Storm So Long*, 283–284; Foner, *Reconstruction*, 148–149.

56. For more on the July 1866 order to close the Freedmen's Bureau courts in North Carolina, see Order of July 13, 1866, Report of Howard, November 1, 1866, 734, quoted in Roberta Sue Alexander, "North Carolina Faces the Freedmen: Race Relations During Presidential Reconstruction, 1865–1867," vol. 2 (PhD dissertation, University of Chicago, 1974), 570. For more on the courts closing in South Carolina, see Abbott, *The Freedmen's Bureau in South Carolina*, 103–105.

57. In some cases, Bureau agents also acted as black litigants' representatives or "next friend." See, for instance, *Hunt v. Wing*, 57 Tenn. 139 (1872). In this suit, which originated in 1867, a Bureau agent served as the next friend of a group of former slaves as they attempted to become parties to a case involving the proceeds of a cotton crop.

58. One Georgia Bureau official attempted to make such arrangements in an 1867 letter, requesting the Bureau to appoint "some legal gentleman to represent and counsel the Freedmen both in and out of Court whenever they were in difficulty." Mr. Miller to?, Jan. 12, 1867, Records of the Assistant Commissioner of Georgia, Bureau of Refugees, Freedmen and Abandoned Lands, 1865–1869, Roll 30, R.G. 105, microfilm publication 798, National Archives.

59. Office of Judge Advocate to?, April 30, 1868, Records of the Assistant Commissioner of Georgia, Bureau of Refugees, Freedmen and Abandoned Lands, 1865–1869, Roll 21, R.G. 105, microfilm publication 798, National Archives; Peirce, *The Freedmen's Bureau*, 145–146.

60. H. F. Young to Captain H. Frank Gallagher, Oct. 16, 1868, Records of the Assistant Commissioner of Georgia, Bureau of Refugees, Freedmen and Abandoned Lands, 1865–1869, Roll 23, R.G. 105, microfilm publication 798, National Archives.

61. The master apparently later said, "A nigger has no use for a horse like that. I just put my Spencer to Sip's head, and told him if he pestered me any more about that horse, I'd kill him. He knew I was a man of my word, and he never pestered me any more." Quoted in Litwack, *Been in the Storm So Long*, 276. The excerpt from a Georgia Bureau agent's letter is from "Letter to Bv't Maj. O.H. Howard from Georgia Freedmen's Bureau Agent G. Ballou, October 1868," in Cox and Cox, eds., *Reconstruction, the Negro, and the New South*, 275–278.

62. In several cases, superiors questioned or reprimanded Bureau subordinates after white southerners complained about these agents' interventions. One Georgia Bureau agent wrote to a superior, defending his actions in the courtroom: "I certainly did not intend to convey the idea to the Court that I was ever clothed with any military authority as I did not wear my insignia of my rank. I took my seat in the Court room by the side of the counsel for the accused and, occasionally, made a suggestion to the counsel in the cross examination of the witnesses against the accused." Despite the apparent reprimand, this Bureau agent appeared unrepentant, concluding, "I certainly informed the Judge privately, that the prisoner was innocent as he had not been proven guilty and that he must not be punished, and he certainly ought not to have been." Letter to Col. C.C. Sibley, June 29, 1867, Records of the Assistant Commissioner of Georgia, Bureau of Refugees, Freedmen and Abandoned Lands, 1865–1869, Roll 30, R.G. 105, microfilm publication 798, National Archives.

63. After examining the Bureau records for North Carolina, for instance, Roberta Alexander wrote: "In September, 1866, John R. Edie, Superintendent of the Western District, observed that 'there are at present but few complaints of injustice towards Freedmen by the Whites.' Noting that all cases, except violations of labor contracts witnessed by Freedmen's Bureau officers, had been turned over to the civil courts, he maintained that he was 'satisfied' that the civil authorities were disposing of these cases 'with impartiality.' [quoting Semi-monthly Report by John R. Edie, September 30, 1866, Semi-monthly Reports] In the same month, Stephen Moore, Superintendent of the Eastern District, also reported that cases tried in the civil courts 'have generally favorably [sic] to the negro.' [Semi-monthly Report by Stephen Moore, September 13, 1866, Semi-monthly Reports]." She continued, writing that "H.H. Foster, Assistant Superintendent of Duplin, Onslow, and Sampson Counties, after attending 'all the courts,' noted that there 'seemed to be an earnest idea of the Court and the Bar that the Freedmen should have all the protection of the Law.' [H.H. Foster to Allan Rutherford, October 30, 1866, Letters Received by the Superintendent of the Southern District]." See Alexander, "North Carolina Faces the Freedmen," 570–571.

64. Christopher Waldrep, *Jury Discrimination: The Supreme Court, Public Opinion, and a Grassroots Fight for Racial Equality in Mississippi* (Athens: University of Georgia Press, 2010), 105–107. Waldrep states that by the end of 1867, a new commanding general had been put in charge of Texas and "he backed away from [the previous commander] Griffin's order [to open juries to African Americans], saying that civil authorities ought not be 'embarrassed' by military interference with jury selection." For more on military courts and the military's involvement in civilian courts during the first years of Reconstruction, see Gregory P. Downs, *After Appomattox: Military Occupation and the Ends of War* (Cambridge, MA: Harvard University Press, 2015), 72–78.

65. No doubt partly as a result of these personnel changes, by 1870, Waldrep writes, "blacks made up nearly half of Vicksburg's grand jurors." Waldrep, *Jury Discrimination*, 107.

66. *Welborn v. Mayrant*, 48 Miss. 652 (1873).

67. Alexander, "North Carolina Faces the Freedmen," 570–571.

68. Randall Kennedy contends that the racially motivated violence of Reconstruction played an important role in leading to the 14th and 15th Amendments. See Kennedy, *Race, Crime, and the Law*, 40.

69. See Michael F. Holt, *The Fate of their Country: Politicians, Slavery Extension, and the Coming of the Civil War* (New York: Hill and Wang, 2004), 9–18, 50–91.

70. Edward L. Ayers, *The Promise of the New South: Life After Reconstruction* (New York: Oxford University Press, 1992), 155–163; Foner, *Reconstruction*, 425–427; Justin Behrend,

Reconstructing Democracy: Grassroots Black Politics in the Deep South After the Civil War (Athens: University of Georgia Press, 2015), 77–116.

71. David Oshinsky writes that after the passage of the Reconstruction Act in the winter of 1867, in Mississippi "more than 80,000 black voters were registered by federal officials, as opposed to fewer than 60,000 whites." Oshinsky, *"Worse Than Slavery,"* 22; Nieman, "Language of Liberation," 78–79; Foner, *Reconstruction,* 279–307.

72. Carl Degler, *The Other South: Southern Dissenters in the Nineteenth Century* (New York: Harper & Row, 1974), 191–229; David Gaffney Sansing, "The Role of the Scalawag in Mississippi Reconstruction" (PhD dissertation, University of Southern Mississippi, 1969); Sara Van Woolfok, "The Role of the Scalawag in Alabama Reconstruction" (PhD dissertation, Louisiana State University, 1965).

73. One exception was in Kentucky, where in 1867, the Court of Appeals of Kentucky upheld the law prohibiting a black person from testifying against a white person. See Laws of Ky., 1865–66, 38–39, cited in Stephenson, *Race Distinctions in American Law,* 243. For a discussion of the laws of different states allowing African Americans legal rights during Reconstruction, see Stephenson, *Race Distinctions in American Law,* 241–249.

74. Nieman, "Language of Liberation," 79–80.

75. Braswell D. Deen, Jr. and William Scott Henwood, *Georgia's Appellate Judiciary: Profile and History* (Norcross, GA: Harrison Company, 1987); Warren Grice, *The Georgia Bench and Bar: The Development of Georgia's Judicial System,* vol. 1 (Macon, GA: J.W. Burke Company, 1931), 338–347; R. Ben Brown, "The Tennessee Supreme Court During Reconstruction and Redemption," in *A History of the Tennessee Supreme Court,* 100–131; Ranney, *In the Wake of Slavery,* 18–28, 126–128, 154–156; Timothy S. Huebner, *The Southern Judicial Tradition: State Judges and Sectional Distinctiveness, 1790–1890* (Athens: University of Georgia Press, 1999), 1–4, 8–9, 186–191. For an example of a "carpetbagger" judge from the North, see Mark Elliott, *Color-Blind Justice: Albion Tourgee and the Quest for Legal Equality from the Civil War to Plessy v. Ferguson* (New York: Oxford University Press, 2006).

76. Sansing, "The Role of the Scalawag in Mississippi Reconstruction," 156–166; Degler, *The Other South,* 199.

77. In 1869, when the first appeal of this case was heard before the Supreme Court of North Carolina, the justices were Richmond Mumford Pearson, Chief Justice (first elected to the court in 1848); Edwin Godwin Reade (first elected in 1866); William Blount Rodman (first elected in 1868); Robert Paine Dick (first elected in 1868); and Thomas Settle (first elected in 1868). During the 1871 appeal, Justice Nathaniel Boyden (appointed 1871) had replaced Justice Thomas Settle. Although Pearson had been serving on the court since 1848, he was nominated by both the Republican and Democratic Parties in the election after the Civil War. Reade was a native of North Carolina, had run as a Whig for the state legislature, and for one term beginning in 1855 served as a congressman in the US Congress for the Whig party and had opposed secession. William Blount Rodman, another Republican justice, had roots in the North; his father was from New York state although Rodman himself had been born and raised in North Carolina. Justice Robert Dick was a member of the Democratic Party before the Civil War, but became a Republican after the war and in 1867 was part of the political convention that organized the Republican Party in North Carolina. Justice Thomas Settle was a Democrat before the war, but became a Republican after the war. Boyden was born in Massachusetts and attended college in New York. He came to North Carolina after college in 1822 and practiced law there. In 1868 he was elected as a Republican to the Fortieth Congress. Kemp Battle, *History of the Supreme Court,* North Carolina Collection, 66–73; Walter Clark, *The Supreme Court of North Carolina,* North Carolina Collection, UNC-Chapel Hill, 536, 569–577; Jerome Dowd, *Sketches of Prominent Living North Carolinians* (Raleigh, NC: Edwards & Broughton, Printers, 1888), 92–97, 109–115.

78. Speech of March, 1867, in Thomas Settle Papers, Folder 4, Southern Historical Collection, Chapel Hill, NC.

79. See, for instance, "Highly Creditable," *New Orleans Tribune* (New Orleans, LA), Jan. 27, 1869, 4; "Courage and Cowardice," *The Weekly Louisianian* (New Orleans, LA), May 18, 1871, 2; "Speech of Hon. F.T. Frelinghuysen on the Civil Rights Bill," *The Weekly Louisianian,* May 16,

1874, 1; "An Important Decision. Colored Citizens Entitled to the Same Accommodations Given to the White," *The Weekly Louisianian*, April 11, 1874, 2.

80. For instance, in Virginia, where the Virginia General Assembly elected the states' judges, the black representatives in the General Assembly from 1869 to 1890 helped to choose these judges. Pincus, *The Virginia Supreme Court*, 6. During the period of 1865 to 1920, most of the eight states examined here had popular elections for judges.

81. John Hope Franklin, ed., *John Roy Lynch: Reminiscences of an Active Life: The Autobiography of John Roy Lynch* (Chicago: University of Chicago Press, 1970), 55–60. At least four black men still held the office of justice of the peace in New Bern, North Carolina, in 1898, according to newspaper accounts of white men and women arrested and sentenced by these men. See "White Men and Women Read This Affidavit," *Fisherman & Farmer* (Edenton, NC), September 30, 1898, 1; "Newbern's Awful Plight: The Negro Magistrates Are Running Mad," *The Gold Leaf* (Henderson, NC), Sept. 29, 1898, Supplement. [Note: While the town referred to is now known as New Bern, NC, it seems to have often been spelled as Newbern in 19th century and early 20th century sources, including this edition of *The Gold Leaf* newspaper.]

82. See Richard Gergel and Belinda Gergel, " 'To Vindicate the Cause of the Downtrodden,': Associate Justice Jonathan Jasper Wright and Reconstruction in South Carolina," in James Lowell Underwood and W. Lewis Burke, eds., *At Freedom's Door: African American Founding Fathers and Lawyers in Reconstruction South Carolina* (Columbia: University of South Carolina Press, 2000), 36–71; From Slavery to the Supreme Court Online Exhibit, Just The Beginning Foundation, http://www.jtbf.org/index.php?su bmenu=Slavery&src=gendocs&link=FromSlaverytotheSupremeCourtOnlineExhibit&cat egory=Main. For an example of a black criminal court judge in Alabama from 1874 to 1875 (R. B. Thomas of Selma, AL), see Alston Fitts III, *Selma: Queen City of the Blackbelt* (Selma, AL: Clairmont Press, 1989), 79.

83. "Motives of Faction," *Memphis Daily Appeal*, Oct. 25, 1867 (some of this quote may have been reprinted in the *Daily Appeal* from The New York *Herald*—the start and end of what the editorial is reprinting from the *Herald* is unclear); "Negro Lawyers," *The Atlanta Constitution*, Oct. 31, 1869. The "Negro Lawyers" article was reprinted from the *New York Republic* newspaper. The "Negro Lawyers" article also included a letter from Edgefield, South Carolina, that noted the writer's observations of the Circuit Court there: "Tuesday was occupied in organizing the juries. The grand jury consisted of eight whites and eleven blacks; petit jury, No.1 was composed entirely of blacks, and No.2, had a sprinkling. Several negro constables were employed about the Court House."

84. "The State of Louisiana: A Deplorable Condition of Affairs," *New York Times*, June 2, 1874, 1. See also "South Carolina Letter," *The Atlanta Constitution*, Aug. 4, 1869, 1; "Editorial Correspondence," *The Daily Telegraph* (Macon, Georgia), Oct. 25, 1865, 2.

85. "Negro Testimony," *The Louisville Daily Courier*, Aug. 27, 1867, 1.

86. "Negro Testimony," *The Louisville Daily Courier*, Aug. 27, 1867, 1.

87. Excerpts from the letter of Julius J. Fleming to Judge Aldrich, November 1866, included in the letter, "Julius J. Fleming to General R. K. Scott, South Carolina, February 8, 1867" in Cox and Cox, eds., *Reconstruction, the Negro, and the New South*, 6–9 (quote is from p.7).

88. "Letter to Bv't Maj. O.H. Howard from Georgia Freedmen's Bureau Agent G. Ballou, October 1868," in Cox and Cox, eds., *Reconstruction, the Negro, and the New South*, 275–278.

89. Franklin, ed., *John Roy Lynch: Reminiscences of an Active Life*, 61; "The State of Louisiana: A Deplorable Condition of Affairs," *New York Times*, June 2, 1874, 1. For more on black southerners' interest in their rights during Reconstruction, see Foner, "Rights and the Constitution in Black Life During the Civil War and Reconstruction," 863–883.

90. See, for instance, Superior Court Minute Books, Troup County Georgia, 1862–1940, *Troup County Archives*, LaGrange, Georgia. Stephen J. Riegel writes that "The official legal reporters contain over forty cases arising in the lower federal courts under civil rights amendments and laws from 1865 to 1896. Many other cases were reported in newspapers." See Stephen J. Riegel, "The Persistent Career of Jim Crow: Lower Federal Courts and the 'Separate but Equal' Doctrine, 1865–1896," *American Journal of Legal History* 28, no. 1 (1984): 21.

91. Out of a total of 132 civil suits involving black litigants between 1865 and 1877 in the eight appellate courts examined, I found 108 cases between black and white litigants and 24 cases

between two or more black litigants. See Table B.3 (tables that are prefaced with "B" are given in Appendix B).

92. Between 1865 and 1877, 67 percent of the appellate civil cases between white and black southerners in the eight state supreme courts examined involved former slaves and former masters or the former master's heirs (72 of 108 cases). See Table B.11.

93. In about two-thirds of cases that reached higher state courts during Reconstruction, African Americans had initiated the lower-court cases (69 of 108 civil cases between black and white litigants between 1865 and 1877); in the other one-third, whites had filed suit. These data are not representative of all lower-court cases. Of the 108 civil cases between black and white litigants in the eight state supreme courts examined between 1865 and 1877, 52 cases involved black appellants and 48 cases involved white appellants (both parties appealed the case in 3 cases and the race of the appellant was unclear in 5 cases). See Tables B.14 and B.21.

94. In southern state supreme courts between 1865 and 1877, there were fifty wills and trusts cases (46 percent of cases between white and black southerners during this period). Thirteen of these cases involved emigration from the United States to Liberia. See Table B.7.

95. Thirty-one of 108 court cases (29 percent) between white and black southerners during Reconstruction involved economic disputes over transactions or property dealings. Included in this number are cases over property disputes and cases over transactions and contracts. This does not include cases over fraud. See Table B.7.

96. There were eighteen apprenticeship and custody cases between white and black litigants in southern state supreme courts during Reconstruction (17 percent of cases between white and black southerners during this period). See Table B.7.

97. As Dylan Penningroth shows, at times slaves gained livestock and other possessions in the antebellum South, often through legal or illegal trading or through cultivating small plots of land or raising animals. Some of these possessions, however, were taken or destroyed during the Civil War. See Penningroth, *The Claims of Kinfolk.*

98. In the answer to the suit filed against the freedman for the mule, Henry Parker's lawyer James C. MacRae wrote in November 1868: "The Defendant Henry Parker by James C. MacRae, his attorney, answering the Complaint herein . . . For a second defense alleges That on the 28th day of May 1868 in an action brought before the 'Bureau of Freedmen, Refugees and Abandoned Lands' by the defendant against the plaintiff, for the possession of the mule named in the Complaint, the defendant Henry Parker, then called Henry Buie, recovered judgement duly give on the merits thereof, against the said John Buie." *Buie v. Parker,* 63 N.C. 131 (1869).

99. *Buie v. Parker,* 63 N.C. 131 (1869). The Act of Congress cited in the state supreme court's opinion is Act of Congress, 17 July, ch.195, sec.9.

100. There is no record of how long Henry Parker was able to keep the mule or if John Buie later tried to take it from him by extralegal means.

101. *Anthony v. Stephens,* 46 Ga. 241 (1872).

102. Stetson Kennedy, *Jim Crow Guide to the U.S.A.: The Laws, Customs and Etiquette Governing the Conduct of Nonwhites and Other Minorities as Second-Class Citizens* (1959; reprinted Tuscaloosa: University of Alabama Press, 2011), 191. Also available at http://site.ebrary.com/id/10527743?ppg=191.

103. The *New York Times'* New Orleans correspondent reported in 1874: "these people have been rushing to the courts of this city for the recovery of damages to which they consider themselves entitled for a denial of equal privileges with the Caucasian race in the entertainments, at saloons, and other public places . . . There have been about fifty of these suits brought in one of the principal District Courts of this city by parties who allege themselves aggrieved and injured in the infringement of their so-called civil rights. Among those tried, and judgments rendered, the defendants have been the Captain of a steam-boat, several keepers of saloons, and the proprietor of a public place of amusement. The sums for which judgement has been rendered in these cases have varied from $250 to $1000." See "The State of Louisiana: A Deplorable Condition of Affairs," *New York Times,* June 2, 1874, 1; John W. Blassingame, *Black New Orleans, 1860–1880* (Chicago: University of Chicago Press, 1973), 183–193. Blassingame lists a number of newspaper articles that discuss cases over racial discrimination heard by courts in Louisiana during Reconstruction in note 31 in

Blassingame, *Black New Orleans*, 271. Another case heard by a local court and then by the Supreme Court of Louisiana, *Josephine Decuir v. John G. Benson* (1874) is mentioned in "An Important Decision, Colored Citizens Entitled to the Same Accommodations Given to the White," *The Weekly Louisianian* (New Orleans, LA), April 11, 1874.

104. The newspaper quote is from the New Orleans *Louisianian*, April 3, 1875, cited in Blassingame, *Black New Orleans*, 186. See also Blassingame, *Black New Orleans*, 183–193; Charles A. Lofgren, *The Plessy Case: A Legal-Historical Interpretation* (New York: Oxford University Press, 1987), 17. The conclusions about Arkansas and Mississippi are from my own examination of state supreme court cases there.

105. 18 Stat. 335 (1 March 1875); John Hope Franklin, "The Enforcement of the Civil Rights Act of 1875" in *Race and History: Selected Essays 1938–1968* (Baton Rouge: Louisiana State University Press, 1989), 116–117.

106. Legal scholar Stephen Riegel notes that lower federal courts in the South and North heard cases over "lynchings, arrests for miscegenation, exclusion of blacks from juries, child servitude . . . conspiracies to prevent blacks from voting or assembling" and the "rights of blacks to have access to accommodations in public conveyances, inns, theatres, and schools." Riegel, "The Persistent Career of Jim Crow," 17–40 (quote is from p. 21); Franklin, "The Enforcement of the Civil Rights Act of 1875" in *Race and History: Selected Essays*, 118–131.

107. Franklin, "The Enforcement of the Civil Rights Act of 1875" in *Race and History: Selected Essays*, 128–131.

108. In *United States v. Cruikshank*, 92 U.S. 542 (1875), the US Supreme Court ruled that the 14th Amendment's prohibition of "a State from depriving any person of life, liberty, or property without due process of law, and from denying to any person within its jurisdiction the equal protection of the laws . . . adds nothing to the rights of one citizen as against another. It simply furnishes an additional guaranty against any encroachment by the States upon the fundamental rights which belong to every citizen as a member of society. The duty of protecting all its citizens in the enjoyment of an equality of rights was originally assumed by the States, and it still remains there. The only obligation resting upon the United States is to see that the States do not deny the right. This the Amendment guarantees, but no more. The power of the National Government is limited to the enforcement of this guaranty." In *United States v. Reese*, 92 U.S. 214 (1876), the US Supreme Court held that "The Fifteenth Amendment to the Constitution does not confer the right of suffrage; but it invests citizens of the United States with the right of exemption from discrimination in the exercise of the elective franchise on account of their race, color, or previous condition of servitude, and empowers Congress to enforce that right by 'appropriate legislation.' "

109. According to my analysis of criminal cases involving black defendants in the state supreme courts of Alabama and Georgia between 1865 and 1877, black defendants won a favorable decision from the appellate court in 60 of 110 cases. In some of these cases, however, their suits were sent back to the lower court for a retrial, where they may have been resentenced. In civil cases against whites that reached the appellate courts examined between 1865 and 1877, black litigants won twenty of thirty-one suits (65 percent). For more on the outcomes of black litigants' civil and criminal cases during Reconstruction and the change over time in the outcome of their civil and criminal appellate suits, see Table B.27. For an extended analysis of a criminal case that the African American defendants won during Reconstruction, see Ross, *The Great New Orleans Kidnapping Case*.

110. Blackmon, *Slavery By Another Name*, 54–57, 64–66 (quotes are from p. 56 and pp. 65–66). According to Talitha L. LeFlouria, black women generally formed between 2 and 4 percent of all leased southern convicts between 1873 and 1899. Sarah Haley explains that black female convicts in Georgia were often undercounted in official numbers because they served their sentences in city and county misdemeanor camps that kept poor records. For more on black female convicts in the postbellum South, see LeFlouria, *Chained in Silence*, 1–171 (table with percentage of black female convicts is on p. 11 of *Chained in Silence*); Haley, *No Mercy Here* (discussion of the number of black female convicts on pp. 29–31).

111. Ayers, *The Promise of the New South*, 8–9.

112. Kousser, *The Shaping of Southern Politics*, 11–29, 43; Michael Perman, *Struggle for Mastery: Disfranchisement in the South 1888–1908* (Chapel Hill: University of North

Carolina Press, 2001), 9–36; Ayers, *The Promise of the New South*, 8–9, 37–39, 146–49; Ranney, *In the Wake of Slavery*, 135–142, 145–146. For more on the Readjusters gaining and losing power in post–Reconstruction Virginia, see Walter T. Calhoun, "The Danville Riot and Its Repercussions on the Virginia Election of 1883," in *Studies in the History of the South, 1875–1922* (Greenville, NC: East Carolina College Press, 1966), 25–51, and Jane Dailey, "The Limits of Liberalism in the New South: The Politics of Race, Sex, and Patronage in Virginia, 1879–1883," in *Jumpin' Jim Crow*, 88–114 (quote is from p. 89). For more on Republican Alvin Hawkins winning the governorship in Tennessee in 1880, see "The New Republican Governor of Tennessee," *Chicago Tribune*, Dec. 27, 1880, 3.

113. Kousser, *The Shaping of Southern Politics*, 11–29, 43; Ayers, *The Promise of the New South*, 37–39, 146–149; Dailey, "The Limits of Liberalism in the New South," in *Jumpin' Jim Crow*, 88–114; J. Morgan Kousser, *Colorblind Injustice: Minority Voting Rights and the Undoing of the Second Reconstruction* (Chapel Hill: University of North Carolina Press, 1999), 20–22 [quote is from p. 20].

114. To combat the black and non-Democrat vote, southern states increasingly passed laws to restrict suffrage during the late 1880s and 1890s. Some states adopted poll taxes; others adopted new voter registration laws or literacy and property requirements. In addition to disfranchising many black voters, these measures disfranchised large numbers of white voters. For more on the strength of opposition parties in the post–Reconstruction South and tactics to reduce the non-Democrat vote in the 1880s and 1890s, see Kousser, *The Shaping of Southern Politics*, 11–62; Kousser, *Colorblind Injustice*, 20–36; Perman, *Struggle for Mastery*, 14–15.

115. One scholar of lynching, Amy Louise Wood, writes that "we can ascertain that, between 1880 and 1940, white mobs in the South killed at least 3,200 black men." Many more lynchings undoubtedly went unreported and unrecorded. Amy Louise Wood, *Lynching and Spectacle: Witnessing Racial Violence in America, 1890–1940* (Chapel Hill: University of North Carolina Press, 2009), 3; *Thirty Years of Lynching in the United States, 1889–1918* (New York: NAACP, 1919; reprint, Clark, NJ: The Lawbook Exchange, 2012); Dray, *At the Hands of Persons Unknown*, x (Dray and the NAACP report are the sources for the list of infractions that led to lynching); Perman, *Struggle for Mastery*, 268–269. It has not been clearly established how often lynchings were directly related to politics. They may have been the results of Republicans and Populists losing power, thus making it safer for whites to engage in lynching. It is also difficult to calculate the exact number of lynchings because many lynchings went unrecorded and organizations tracking this violence used different kinds of data. For one set of lynching statistics by year and state, however, see "Lynchings: By Year and Race," University of Missouri Kansas City Law School, http://law2.umkc.edu/faculty/projects/ftrials/shipp/lynchingyear.html and http://law2.umkc.edu/faculty/projects/ftrials/shipp/lynchingsstate.html. Statistics provided by the Tuskegee Institute Archives. Randall Kennedy writes that the states with the most reported instances of lynching between 1882 and 1968 were "Mississippi (539 black victims), Georgia (492 black victims), Texas (352 black victims), Louisiana (335 black victims) and Alabama (299 black victims)." Kennedy, *Race, Crime, and the Law*, 42. For more on lynching and violence toward African Americans in the post–Reconstruction period, see Kennedy, *Race, Crime, and the Law*, 42–45; Dray, *At the Hands of Persons Unknown*; Brundage, *Lynching in the New South*; Wood, *Lynching and Spectacle*, Hodes, *White Women, Black Men*, 176–208.

116. In some states, such as Tennessee, judges favoring the Unionist cause were ousted as early as 1870. However, in other states, such as Florida, Reconstruction judges continued in their positions on the Florida Supreme Court until 1885. In Georgia, for instance, Reconstruction judges were replaced at different times, with two judges resigning in 1870 and 1875 and the third remaining on the court until he died in 1881. R. Ben Brown, "The Tennessee Supreme Court During Reconstruction and Redemption," in *A History of the Tennessee Supreme Court*, 100–131; Ranney, *In the Wake of Slavery*, 18–28, 126–128, 154–156; Huebner, *The Southern Judicial Tradition*, 1–4, 8–9, 186–191. For an example of a "carpetbagger" judge from the North, see Elliott, *Color-Blind Justice*.

117. Stephenson, *Race Distinctions in American Law*, 258–272; Ranney, *In the Wake of Slavery*, 135–142, 145–146; Klarman, *From Jim Crow to Civil Rights*, 39–40.

118. For an example of white newspapers not considering black participation in the courts dangerous, see for instance, "Negro Testimony," *The Louisville Daily Courier*, Aug. 27, 1867, 1. Occasionally, through at least the end of the nineteenth century, black justices of the peace still served in heavily black communities in the South. At least two black men still held the office of justice of the peace in New Bern, North Carolina, in 1898, according to a newspaper account of a white woman arrested and sentenced by these men. See "White Men and Women Read This Affidavit," *Fisherman & Farmer* (Edenton, NC), Sept. 30, 1898, 1.

119. Between 1865 and 1877, 72 civil cases between black and white litigants that reached the eight state supreme courts of 108 such cases took place between former slaves and their former masters or the heirs of former slaves and former masters (67 percent of cases). Between 1878 and 1899, 36 such cases of a total of 104 cases took places between former slaves and their former masters or the heirs of former slaves and former masters (35 percent of cases). See Table B.11. Between 1878 and 1899, thirty-two appellate cases between white and black litigants involving postwar transactions or property disputes took place and two cases involving transactions that took place during slavery occurred. Cases over transactions during slavery included *Wilson v. James*, 79 N.C. 349 (1878); *Heyer v. Beatty*, 83 N.C. 285 (1880). Cases over postwar transactions or property disputes included *Cunningham's Administrator v. Speagle*, 106 Ky. 278 (1899); *Priebatsch v. Baptist Church*, 66 Miss. 345 (1899); *Pease v. Cooper*, 61 Ga. 626 (1878); *Reynolds v. Reynolds' Ex'r*, 88 Va. 149 (1891); *Sweetser v. Shorter*, 123 Ala. 518 (1898); *Waller v. Johnson*, 82 Va. 966 (1887); *Yon v. Blanchard*, 75 Ga. 519 (1885); *Barge v. Weems*, 109 Ga. 685 (1900); *Capehart v. Stewart*, 80 N.C. 101 (1879). For a comparison of the kinds of cases heard by the state supreme courts examined during Reconstruction and between 1878 and 1899, see Tables B.7 and B.8.

120. There were fifty cases between black and white litigants over inheritance or bequests that reached the eight state supreme courts during Reconstruction (1865–1877), but only twenty-seven from 1878 to 1899. In addition, there were twenty such civil cases over transactions and contracts during Reconstruction, but only nine cases over transactions and contracts from 1878 to 1899. See Tables B.7 and B.8.

121. See Tables B.7 and B.8. For more on general trends in state supreme courts regarding personal injury at this time, see Kagan, "The Business of State Supreme Courts," 134–135, 142–143. From an extensive analysis of state supreme court cases in sixteen representative US states, the article's authors found that tort cases rose from "5.7 percent of SSC [state supreme court] cases in 1870–1880 to 16.4 percent in the 1905–1935 period." The most common type of tort suit heard by state supreme courts during this time, the article further explains, were personal injury suits involving railroad and streetcar accidents. "From 1885 to 1920, one-third of all tort suits on SSC dockets, and 4 percent of all SSC cases, were lawsuits arising out of railroad and streetcar accidents" (quotes from Kagan, pp.142–143).

122. See, for instance, *Simmons v. Fannie Hessey. Hessey's Exr. v. Simmons*, 11 Ky. Op. 40 (1881); *Helm's Ex'r v. Rogers*, 81 Ky. 568 (1884).

123. *Civil Rights Cases*, 109 U.S. 3 (1883). The decision's syllabus states: "1. The 1st and 2d sections of the Civil Rights Act . . . are unconstitutional enactments as applied to the several States, not being authorized either by the XIIIth or XIVth Amendments of the Constitution. 2. The XIVth Amendment is prohibitory upon the States only, and the legislation authorized to be adopted by Congress for enforcing it is not direct legislation on the matters respecting which the States are prohibited from making or enforcing certain laws, or doing certain acts, but is corrective legislation such as may be necessary or proper for counteracting and redressing the effect of such laws or acts. 3. The XIIIth Amendment relates only to slavery and involuntary servitude (which it abolishes), and, although, by its reflex action, it establishes universal freedom in the United States, and Congress may probably pass laws directly enforcing its provisions, yet such legislative power extends only to the subject of slavery and its incidents, and the denial of equal accommodations in inns, public conveyances, and places of public amusement (which is forbidden by the sections in question), imposes no badge of slavery or involuntary servitude upon the party but at most, infringes rights which are protected from State aggression by the XIVth Amendment." See also Franklin, "The Enforcement of the Civil Rights Act of 1875," in *Race and History: Selected Essays*, 129–131; Riegel, "The Persistent Career of Jim Crow," 17–40; Klarman, *From Jim Crow to Civil Rights*,

49–50; Lawrence Goldstone, *Inherently Inequal: The Betrayal of Equal Rights By the Supreme Court, 1865–1903* (New York: Walker, 2011), 118–129.

124. See Table B.8. Racial justice court cases that were heard before state supreme courts in the eight states examined between 1878 and 1899 included *Chesapeake vs. Wells*, 85 Tenn. 613 (1887); *Board of Education v. Cumming*, 103 Ga. 641 (1898); *Duke v. Brown*, 96 N.C. 127 (1887); *Markham v. Manning and The Durham Graded School*, 96 N.C. 132 (1887); *Puitt v. Commissioners of Gaston County*, 94 N.C. 709 (1886); *Brown v. Owen*, 75 Miss. 319 (1897); *Maddox v. Neal*, 45 Ark. 121 (1885); *Harrodsburg Educational Dist. v. Trustees of Colored School Dist.*, 105 Ky. 675 (1899); *Leeds v. Shaw's Adm'r*, 82 Ky. 79 (1884); and *Chrisman v. Mayor, etc., of Brookhaven*, 70 Miss. 477 (1892).

125. See Ida B. Wells, *Crusade for Justice: The Autobiography of Ida B. Wells* (Chicago: University of Chicago Press, 1970), 19–20; *Chesapeake vs. Wells*, 85 Tenn. 613 (1887); "A Darky Damsel Obtains a Verdict for Damages Against the Chesapeake and Ohio Railroad," *Memphis Appeal-Avalanche*, Dec. 25, 1884.

126. Michael Klarman writes of civil rights cases: "When the law is clear, judges will generally follow it, unless they have very strong personal preferences to the contrary. When the law is indeterminate, judges have little choice but to make decisions based on political factors." Klarman, *From Jim Crow to Civil Rights*, 5–6. Black litigants had more success bringing cases over discrimination before state courts in the Midwest, where the Republican Party still needed black votes to win elections. For an examination of African Americans' success in school integration cases in the nineteenth century in the Midwest, see Kousser, "Why Were There So Many Legal Cases on School Integration in Nineteenth-Century America?" and Kousser, *Dead End*, 5–12, 59.

127. Of the twelve civil cases between black and white litigants over racial discrimination that occurred between 1878 and 1899 in the eight appellate courts examined, black litigants won six cases and lost six cases at the appellate level. Of the six cases that they won, in five the lower court had ruled against the black litigants and the higher court reversed the lower court's ruling. In one, both the lower and higher courts ruled in favor of the black litigant. Of the six cases that they lost, in three cases the lower court ruled in black litigants' favor and the higher court ruled against them and in 3 cases black litigants lost in both the higher and lower courts. See Table B.8.

128. Oshinsky, *"Worse Than Slavery,"* 32.

129. Blackmon, *Slavery by Another Name*, 61–154 (the explanation of the system of confessing judgement is on pp.66–68); Oshinsky, "Worse Than Slavery," 40–84.

130. See, for instance, Sidney Fant Davis, *Mississippi Negro Lore* (Jackson, TN: McCowat Mercer, 1914), 21–22.

131. Hugh C. Bailey refers to the Georgia sentencing study in *Liberalism in the New South*, 158–159. For more about the increase in the black prison population in the South after Reconstruction, see Ayers, *Vengeance & Justice*, 169–171, note 57, 321.

132. My analysis of criminal cases with black defendants in the state supreme courts of Georgia and Alabama between 1878 and 1899 found that black defendants won 63 of 152 criminal appeals, or 41 percent of their criminal appeals. See Table B.27.

Chapter 2

1. *Lattimore v. Dixon*, 63 N.C. 356 (1869); *Lattimore v. Dixon*, 65 N.C. 664 (1871). For more on Cleveland County and Shelby, North Carolina, see "History of Shelby," National Park Service, https://www.nps.gov/nr/travel/shelby/history.htm.

2. In contrast, Dixon claimed the amount to be only $355.95 when he bought Lattimore. According to Thomas Dixon's court testimony, page 6 of Dixon's account book "contains a list of notes that I got from Abner Lattimore, the Plff, in this case, the entry in the memorandum was made at the time I got them. It is a full list of all I received and the figures represent the full amount of principal and interest at that time the entry was made shortly after the sale Samuel Latimore—deceased in the Fall of 1858." Page 6 of the account book says "A. Spanglers Note $25.25 L.L. Flake 47.70 H. Knoland 107.50 W. Williamson 100.50 S. Patterson 75.00

Total: $355.95." See also *Lattimore v. Dixon*, 63 N.C. 356 (1869); *Lattimore v. Dixon*, 65 N.C. 664 (1871).

3. *Lattimore v. Dixon*, 63 N.C. 356 (1869); *Lattimore v. Dixon*, 65 N.C. 664 (1871).
4. *Cleveland County Heritage, North Carolina*, vol. 2 (Shelby, NC: Broad River Genealogical Society, 2004), 2–3.
5. *Lattimore v. Dickson*, 63 N.C. 356 (1869); *Lattimore v. Dixon*, 65 N.C. 664 (1871).
6. *Lattimore v. Dixon*, 63 N.C. 356 (1869); *Lattimore v. Dixon*, 65 N.C. 664 (1871).
7. *Lattimore v. Dickson*, 63 N.C. 356 (1869); *Lattimore v. Dixon*, 65 N.C. 664 (1871).
8. During Reconstruction (between 1865 and 1877), 67 percent of civil cases between white and black southerners in the eight appellate courts examined took place between former slaves and their former masters or their former masters' heirs (72 of 108 cases). In the two decades after Reconstruction (1878 to 1899), 35 percent of these cases involved former slaves and their former masters (36 of 102 cases). Between 1865 and 1899, therefore, 108 of 210 cases (51 percent) involved former slaves and their former masters.
9. From 1865 to 1899, black women were one of the litigants in 101 of 212 suits between black and white southerners that reached the eight state supreme courts (litigating 48 percent of suits). Between 1865 and 1877, there were approximately 53 female litigants out of 108 appellate cases between white and black litigants in the eight states examined (litigating 49 percent of suits). Between 1878 and 1899, there were approximately 48 female litigants out of 104 such cases (litigating 46 percent of suits). Between 1900 and 1920, there were approximately 89 female litigants out of 220 such cases (litigating 40 percent of suits). Between 1921 and 1950, there were 214 cases involving female litigants out of 548 such cases (litigating 39 percent of suits). See Table B.12 (tables that are prefaced with "B" are given in Appendix B).
10. Between 1865 and 1899, black women were at least one of the litigants in fifty-four of seventy-seven wills and estate cases (probate cases often had multiple parties as litigants). In addition, black women served as litigants in sixteen of the thirty-five personal injury suits during this period and seven of the eighteen apprenticeship or custody suits. When this period is broken up into the period during Reconstruction and the period after Reconstruction, other patterns emerge. While black women took part in almost as many suits as black men over property disputes and transactions during Reconstruction, in the two decades following Reconstruction, they litigated far fewer cases than their male counterparts over property and transactions. They were much less likely to be litigants, too, in cases directly confronting racial discrimination. In the eight appellate courts examined, between 1865 and 1877 black women served as litigants in seven of eighteen custody cases (39 percent), thirty-three of fifty wills and estate cases (66 percent), and twelve of thirty-one property disputes or transaction cases (39 percent). Between 1878 and 1899, black women in these eight appellate courts served as litigants in two of twelve cases over racial injustice (17 percent), five of thirteen fraud cases (38 percent), sixteen of thirty-one personal injury cases (52 percent), and four of twenty-one property dispute and transaction cases (19 percent). See also Table B.13.
11. Between 1865 and 1877, black litigants served as plaintiffs in 68 of 108 civil cases in state supreme courts (63 percent). Between 1878 and 1899, they served as plaintiffs in 74 of 102 cases (73 percent). Between 1900 and 1920, they were plaintiffs in 182 of 218 cases (83 percent). From 1921 to 1950, black litigants served as the plaintiffs in 462 of 551 cases (84 percent). Overall, they served as plaintiffs in 786 of 980 cases (80 percent).
12. For an examination of black men's and women's attitudes toward the law, as seen in African American writing, see Suggs, *Whispered Consolations*. For an examination of African Americans' concern for law and equal rights, see Nieman, "The Language of Liberation," 72–87; Foner, "Rights and the Constitution in Black Life During the Civil War and Reconstruction."
13. Franklin, ed., *John Roy Lynch: Reminiscences of an Active Life*, 61.
14. *Cowan v. Stamps*, 46 Miss. 435 (1872). Similarly, in Georgia, the mixed-race daughter of a white man took legal action in 1872, according to her lawyer, "for the purpose of recovering her just rights" to funds from her father's estate "through the medium of the Courts." *Duncan v. Pope*, 47 Ga. 445 (1872). See also *Cochreham v. Kirkpatrick*, 48 Tenn. 327 (1870).
15. African Americans had played an important role in sweeping Republicans into power and voting in new judges and state constitutions. In Virginia, for instance, where the Virginia

General Assembly elected the states' judges, the black representatives in the General Assembly from 1869 to 1890 helped to choose these judges. Pincus, *The Virginia Supreme Court*, 6. During the period of 1865 to 1920, most of the eight states examined here had popular elections for judges. Victor B. Howard, "The Black Testimony Controversy in Kentucky, 1866–1872," in *Black Southerners and the Law,* 154–157.

16. "South Carolina Letter," *The Atlanta Constitution,* Aug. 4, 1869. Similarly a social scientist named Alrutheus Taylor noted at the beginning of the twentieth century: "During the days of slavery they could not frequent the county court house or the city tribunals to witness the presentation of persons charged with crimes. Such a thing was the prerogative of the master class. As soon as the Negroes became free, however, they crowded these 'palaces of justice.'" Alrutheus A. Taylor, *The Negro in the Reconstruction of Virginia* (Washington DC: Association for the Study of Negro Life and History, 1926), 45.

17. For examples of articles about appellate civil cases between white and black southerners that appeared in white-owned newspapers, see "Decisions of the Supreme Court of Georgia," *The Atlanta Constitution,* July 20, 1870, 2; "Current News and Comment," *Shenandoah Herald* (Woodstock, VA), Oct. 10, 1890; *Augusta County Argus,* Jan. 13, 1891; "Bettie Thomas-Lewis," *The Times* (Richmond, VA), June 19, 1892; "Bettie Thomas Lewis Case," *The Times* (Richmond, VA), July 21, 1892; "Bettie Will Be Rich," *Richmond Dispatch,* July 24, 1892; "Bettie Thomas Lewis Case," *The Times* (Richmond, VA), Nov. 17, 1892. For examples of black newspaper coverage of suits involving African Americans, see the coverage of the *Atlanta Independent* and the *Richmond Planet.* Articles in these newspapers also included accounts of celebrated criminal cases involving African Americans, at least some of which black litigants won, including, "Simon Walker Saved!" *Richmond Planet,* Nov. 16, 1889, 1; "New Trial Granted," *Richmond Planet,* Nov. 30, 1895, 1; "The Day Set. Another Chapter in the Lunenburg Case," *Richmond Planet,* Feb. 22, 1896, 1; "Judge Emory Speer's Opinion. The Fourteenth Amendment. A Colored Man Released," *Richmond Planet,* July 23, 1904, 1; "A White Man The Victim. U.S. Supreme Court and the Caleb Powers Case," *Richmond Planet,* March 17, 1906, 1. Articles in these black newspapers about local cases involving African Americans include, "A Sunday Murder!" *Richmond Planet,* March 1, 1890, 1; "Sued the Editor and Lost," *Richmond Planet,* Nov. 17, 1900, 1; "In the recorder's court ..." *Atlanta Independent,* Feb. 13, 1904.

18. "Lawyer Jones Plea: Color Line in Juries," *Richmond Planet,* Dec. 21, 1895. Their hope was not born out in the decisions of the US Supreme Court in these suits, which did not rule in favor of the black litigants. See *Gibson v. Mississippi,* 162 U.S. 565 (1896); *Smith v. Mississippi,* 162 U.S. 592 (1896). See also "The Negro's Right to Sit on Grand Juries Vindicated By the United States Supreme Court," *Rising Son* (Kansas City, MO), Feb. 12, 1904.

19. Freedmen's Committee to Maj. Genl John Pope, July 7, 1867, Records of the Assistant Commissioner of Georgia, Bureau of Refugees, Freedmen and Abandoned Lands, 1865–1869, Roll 18, R.G. 105, microfilm publication 798, National Archives. See also "Introduction," in *Black Southerners and the Law,* vii–xii.

20. "A Court's Decision," *Richmond Planet,* Oct. 15, 1898, 4. See also "A White Man The Victim: U.S. Supreme Court and the Caleb Powers Case: Remands the Prisoner to the Custody of Kentucky Authorities," *Richmond Planet,* March 17, 1906, 1; "Peonage and the Peon Elaborately Discussed on the Bench by Judge Speer," *Atlanta Independent,* Apr. 1, 1905, 4.

21. See, for instance, *Cobb v. Battle,* 34 Ga. 450 (1866); *Ray v. The Commissioners of Durham County,* 110 N.C. 169 (1892); *Cochran v. Henry,* 107 Miss. 233 (1914); *Jackson v. State,* 176 Ga. 148 (1932); *Barringer v. Whitson,* 205 Ark. 260 (1943).

22. Excerpts from the letter of Julius J. Fleming to Judge Aldrich, November 1866, included in the letter, "Julius J. Fleming to General R.K. Scott, South Carolina, February 8, 1867" in Cox and Cox, eds., *Reconstruction, the Negro, and the New South,* 6–9.

23. *Lattimore v. Dickson,* 63 N.C. 356 (1869).

24. In 1867, for instance, a committee of freedpeople explained the difficulty of paying for legal counsel, writing that "the Freedmen are too poor to employ Lawyers to present their claims." Freedmen's Committee to Maj. Genl John Pope, July 7, 1867, Records of the Assistant Commissioner of Georgia, Bureau of Refugees, Freedmen and Abandoned Lands,

1865–1869, Roll 18, R.G. 105, microfilm publication 798, National Archives. See also Mr. Miller to?, Jan. 12, 1867, Records of the Assistant Commissioner of Georgia, Bureau of Refugees, Freedmen and Abandoned Lands, 1865–1869, Roll 30, R.G. 105, microfilm publication 798, National Archives. According to one contemporary account, lawyers generally charged most clients between 8 and 10 percent of what they won in the years after the Civil War. Garnett Andrews, *Reminiscences of an Old Georgia Lawyer* (Atlanta, GA: Franklin Steam Printing House, 1870), 102–103.

25. Letter of Georgia Bureau agent Charles Raushenberg to Brvt Major O. H. Howard, November 1868, in Cox and Cox, eds., *Reconstruction, the Negro, and the New South*, 348–351.

26. Excerpts from the letter of Julius J. Fleming to Judge Aldrich, November 1866, included in the letter, "Julius J. Fleming to General R. K. Scott, South Carolina, February 8, 1867" in Cox and Cox, eds., *Reconstruction, the Negro, and the New South*, 6–9.

27. Oshinsky, *"Worse Than Slavery,"* 26; Brundage, *Lynching in the New South*, 5–8.

28. Oshinsky, *"Worse Than Slavery,"* 27–28.

29. Letter of Georgia Bureau agent Charles Raushenberg to Brvt Major O. H. Howard, November 1868, in Cox and Cox, eds., *Reconstruction, the Negro, and the New South*, 348–351.

30. A letter to Bv't Maj. O. H. Howard from Georgia Freedmen's Bureau agent G. Ballou, October 1868, stated, "great difficulty is experienced by me in securing the attendance of freedmen at the time they are most needed to testify, as they often come many miles to report a case to me and after a warrant is issued for the arrest of the offending parties, they (the freedmen) are compelled to return to their work, as a matter of course no day can be fixed for the trial of the case, as the time of arrest is uncertain, consequently when the arrest is finally made, the guilty party is discharged for want of any prosecution, and this evil I am unable to obviate as I have no means of securing the attendance of either witness or prosecutor." Cox and Cox, eds., *Reconstruction, the Negro, and the New South*, 275–278.

31. Southern counties had a wide range of county and city trial courts, which shifted over time and changed names. The trial courts in which black litigants' cases arose from included chancery courts, superior courts, circuit courts, courts of equity, city courts, and probate courts. Some circuit courts covered only one county while other circuit courts seem to have covered two or three or even more counties.

32. There was variation across states regarding what kinds of cases should first be heard by a justice of the peace, which cases could be heard first by either legal body, and which cases should originate in county trial courts. Despite differences on jurisdiction across different states, the southern states examined all had some kind of monetary limitation—often ranging from $100 to $150—for cases that should be heard first by justices of peace. In Alabama, for instance, justices of the peace had original jurisdiction on all disputes dealing with contracts, actions for damages for wrong or injuries, and for actions brought to recover specific property as long as the value that the party sought to recover was not more than $100. A. Leo Oberdorfer, *Oberdorfer's Alabama Justices' Practice* (Charlottesville, VA: Michie Company, Publishers, 1905), 16–17. In Arkansas, justices of the peace first heard civil disagreements over matters of contract "where the amount in controversy does not exceed the sum of one hundred dollars." Either the justice of the peace or the circuit court could first hear contract disputes over sums between $100 and $300 and actions for recovery of damages to personal property worth up to $100. Justices of the peace had no jurisdiction in Arkansas over disputes in which the title of land was at stake. J. S. Duffie and W. F. Hill, *The Arkansas Justice: A Treatise on the Powers and Duties of Justices of the Peace, Embraced in their Civil and Criminal Jurisdiction in the State of Arkansas* (St. Louis, MO: Gilbert Book Co., 1888), 19–26. In Mississippi, justices of the peace had jurisdiction "of all actions for the recovery of debts and damages, or personal property, where the principal of the debt, the amount of the demand, or the value of the property . . . shall not exceed one hundred and fifty dollars." L. O. Bridewell, *The Mississippi Justice of the Peace: A Manual of the Laws Relating to the Courts of Justices of the Peace, and the Practice Therein, in the State of Mississippi* (Jackson, MS: Clarion Steam Printing Establishment, 1877). In Georgia, "A justice's court has jurisdiction of suits, when not more than $100 principal is claimed, for damages arising through physical injuries to personal property." See Cozart, *Georgia Practice Rules as Laid Down by The Supreme Court and Court of Appeals of Georgia*

(1918), 5. In Louisiana, "the jurisdiction of Justices of the Peace shall not exceed, in civil cases, the sum of one hundred dollars, exclusive of interest, subject to an appeal to the Parish Court in all cases when the amount in dispute exceeds ten dollars, exclusive of interest." Julien A. Seghers and Patrice Leonard, *The Louisiana Magistrate and Parish Officer's Guide Containing Copious Forms and Instructions*, 2nd ed. (Parish of Plaquemines, LA: Office of the Empire Parish Register, 1870), 16–17.

33. John Roy Lynch, however, served as a justice of the peace in a mixed-race area during Reconstruction. See Franklin, ed., *John Roy Lynch: Reminiscences of an Active Life*, 55–60. At least four black men still held the office of justice of the peace in the "negro settlement" of New Bern, North Carolina, in 1898, according to newspaper accounts of white men and women being arrested and sentenced by these men. See "White Men and Women Read This Affidavit," *Fisherman & Farmer* (Edenton, NC), Sept. 30, 1898, 1; "Newbern's Awful Plight: The Negro Magistrates Are Running Mad," *The Gold Leaf* (Henderson, NC), Sept. 29, 1898, Supplement.

34. The 1900 census found 266 "Negro" lawyers in the eight states examined: 6 in Alabama, 27 in Arkansas, 33 in Georgia, 25 in Kentucky, 24 in Mississippi, 25 in North Carolina, 73 in Tennessee, and 53 in Virginia. Black lawyers formed only a very small part of the overall bar in such states (approximately 1.7 percent); the 1900 census identified 15,242 white male lawyers in these eight states. From *The Twelfth Census, Special Reports, Occupations Available* (1904) at 220–420. I used the data from this document provided in a table in J. Clay Smith, *Emancipation: The Making of the Black Lawyer, 1844–1944* (Philadelphia: University of Pennsylvania Press, 1993), 624–625.

35. For more on black lawyers during this period in the US South, see Smith, *Emancipation: The Making of the Black Lawyer*, 1–20, 191–343, 624–625; Pincus, *The Virginia Supreme Court*, 39–43; Paul Finkelman, "Not Only the Judges' Robes Were Black: African American Lawyers as Social Engineers," *Stanford Law Review* 47, no. 1 (1994): 161–209; Kilpatrick, "(Extra) Ordinary Men: African American Lawyers and Civil Rights in Arkansas Before 1950," 299–399; W. Lewis Burke Jr., "The Radical Law School: The University of South Carolina School of Law and Its African American Graduates, 1873–1877," in James Lowell Underwood and W. Lewis Burke Jr., eds., *At Freedom's Door: African American Founding Fathers and Lawyers in Reconstruction South Carolina* (Columbia: University of South Carolina Press, 2000), 90–115; John Oldfield, "The African American Bar in South Carolina," in James Lowell Underwood and W. Lewis Burke Jr., eds., *At Freedom's Door: African American Founding Fathers and Lawyers in Reconstruction South Carolina* (Columbia: University of South Carolina Press, 2000), 116–29.

36. *The Emmanuel Magazine*, July 3, 1909, quoted in Stephenson, *Race Distinctions in American Law*, 240–241. Neil McMillen also notes the barriers before black lawyers in arguing before white juries in *Dark Journey*, 215.

37. "The State of Louisiana: A Deplorable Condition of Affairs," *New York Times*, June 2, 1874, 1; Martinet to Tourgée, Oct. 25 and 28, 1891, Dec. 7 and 28, 1891, quoted in Lofgren, *The Plessy Case*, 30–31. It is unclear exactly which black lawyer the 1874 *New York Times* article is referencing. The district represented by Lionel Allen Sheldon from 1869 to 1875 was Louisiana's 2nd Congressional District. In 1875, however, a Democratic candidate won the election for this district. Two black lawyers who were practicing in Louisiana in 1874 were Louis A. Bell and Thomas Morris Chester. For more on Louis Martinet and other black lawyers practicing in Louisiana from 1871 to the mid-twentieth century, see Smith, *Emancipation: The Making of the Black Lawyer*, 282–288.

38. A notable exception to the general lack of black lawyers in appellate civil cases in southern courts was the appearance of prominent black lawyer Scipio Jones in the Arkansas case of *Cook v. Ziff Colored Masonic Lodge*, 80 Ark. 31 (1906). Jones also testified in favor of the white litigant and against the black litigants in the cases of *Storthz v. Arnold, Arnold v. Storthz*, 74 Ark. 68 (1905). In addition, Jones appeared in at least two appellate cases in which both litigants were black. See *Grand Camp of Colored Woodmen v. Johnson*, 109 Ark. 527 (1913); *Grand Camp Colored Woodman v. Ware*, 107 Ark. 102 (1913).

39. The court record lists Caroline Deberry's solicitors in the lower court trial as "Caruthers & Talbot, Sols," and then later refers to Ned Caruthers "(col'd)." The only Ned Caruthers listed in the 1870 census for Madison County, Tennessee, is a 50-year-old black man, described

as a laborer. In 1880, this Ned Caruthers is listed as having the occupation of farming. It is possible that despite this Ned Caruther's occupation as a farmer, he may also be the lawyer described in this case. It was difficult for black lawyers in the post–Civil War South to work as full-time lawyers because of the poverty of their generally black clientele. 1870 United States Federal Census and 1880 United States Federal Census, published online by Ancestry, Provo, Utah; Oldfield, "The African American Bar in South Carolina," 119–120; *Deberry v. Hurt*, 66 Tenn. 390 (1874).

40. To determine this, I noted on an excel spreadsheet the name of the lawyer for each case I examined. I then analyzed how often each lawyer's name appeared on the spreadsheet. There were a few exceptions to this rule, such as Kentucky lawyer Aubrey Hester and North Carolina lawyer W. P. Bynum, who each represented black litigants in appellate cases at least four times.

41. John C. Reed, *Conduct of Lawsuits Out Of and In Court* (Boston: Little, Brown, 1885), 66–67. For a later example of lawyers' assertions of their fairness toward African American clients, see the reported remarks of Supreme Court of Mississippi Justice J. B. Holden in 1923 in Michael de L. Landon, *The Honor and Dignity of the Profession: A History of the Mississippi State Bar, 1906–1976* (Jackson: University Press of Mississippi, 1980), 56. For further discussion of white Mississippi lawyers representing themselves as paternalistic and fair in the twentieth century, see McMillen, *Dark Journey*, 216–217.

42. McMillen, *Dark Journey*, 214–215.

43. McMillen, *Dark Journey*, 215–216.

44. The higher courts also heard some cases, though, that did not involve large amounts of money. For an example of a higher-court case not involving a significant sum of money, see the case of *Andrews v. Page*, in which the black female litigant litigated as a pauper. *Andrews v. Page*, 49 Tenn. 634 (1871).

45. Gross, *Double Character*, 27–30; John W. Wertheimer, *Law and Society in the South: A History of North Carolina Court Cases* (Lexington: University Press of Kentucky, 2009), 5.

46. Although black litigants' lawyers usually represented them well in higher-court cases, at times lawyers did not act in the best interests of their clients. For instance, in an 1869 Georgia case, a group of former slaves attempted to claim part of their former master's land, which he had left them in his will. In their petition, the black litigants charged that in January 1869, a white man named Abner Underwood told them that a white heir "would probably claim the inheritance left to your Orators." Underwood then stated that he was a lawyer and offered to defend their claim in court. Despite his promises, the lawyer was working against their interests, for the white heirs. In this case, the black litigants demonstrated their developing legal understanding as they recognized the fraud, hired a new lawyer, and claimed in court that Underwood had attempted to defraud them. In the end, the appeals court dismissed the black litigants' case. *Briley v. Underwood*, 41 Ga. 9 (1869). Even some black lawyers did not deal honestly with black litigants. See *Storthz v. Arnold; Arnold v. Storthz*, 74 Ark. 68 (1905); *Johnson v. Hall*, 87 Miss. 667 (1905).

47. William Preston Bynum (June 10, 1820–Dec. 30, 1909) rose to the position of colonel in the Confederate Army before resigning in 1863, when the North Carolina legislature elected him solicitor of the Seventh Judicial District. He continued in the position of an elected solicitor, litigating cases on behalf of the government, for nine years after the war. More information about Bynum can be found in "William Preston Bynum" in Samuel A. Ashe, ed., *Biographical History of North Carolina From Colonial Times to the Present*, vol.2 (Greensboro, NC: Charles L. Van Noppen, Pub., 1905), 33–41; "William Preston Bynum," *Charlotte Daily Observer*, Jan. 17, 1910; John L. Bell, Jr., "Bynum, William Preston," in William S. Powell, ed., *Dictionary of North Carolina Biography* (Chapel Hill: University of North Carolina Press, c.1980-1996), http://ncpedia.org/biography/bynum-william-preston.

48. Bynum did not initially give public speeches during his run for solicitor, he wrote, because "I was not running for a political office, & I could not well see what my opinions about the Constitution or reconstruction, had to do with my qualifications for solicitor." Far from being alone in this stance, he explained, "all the Judicial officers in the State, adopted this view, & wisely, as I think, abstained from politics." "Correspondence and Legal Papers,"

William Preston Bynum Papers, Southern Historical Collection, Manuscripts Department, Chapel Hill, NC; "William Preston Bynum," *Charlotte Daily Observer,* Jan. 17, 1910.

49. In the 1868 speech, Bynum also urged his fellow white southerners to support Reconstruction because they followed the law and upheld the US Constitution. "If every man has a right to judge whether a law is constitutional & obey or disobey, accordingly," he observed, "it at once dissolves all government & leaves every one free to follow his own unbridled will." Bynum said in this speech as well, that supporting black men's right to vote would "forever get rid of a vexed political problem" and would lead to very little real change. "Correspondence and Legal Papers," William Preston Bynum Papers, Southern Historical Collection, Manuscripts Department, Chapel Hill, NC. His desire to uphold the law seems to have influenced his decision to take other African Americans' suits as well. Although white lawyers generally represented a black litigant in an appellate case only once or maybe twice during their careers, Bynum served as the legal counsel for a black litigant in at least four North Carolina state supreme court cases. Only a few years after representing Lattimore, in 1873, Bynum would be appointed a justice of the Supreme Court of North Carolina. He remained on North Carolina's highest court until 1879. During his time on the state's highest court, he wrote approximately 346 opinions, including dissents. See "William Preston Bynum" in *Biographical History of North Carolina,* 32–41.

50. Lattimore did not have to give "security" to the court because of his poverty. Bynum was described as "a man of means." See Clark, *The Supreme Court of North Carolina,* 577.

51. In the same speech, Bynum opined that "Negro suffrage has been in force for two elections & they have done their best & probably their worst & what is the result of this alarming negro democratization over the white man? Out of 170 members of the Convention . . . he has been able to elect 15 members & those 15 confessedly no discredit to any legislative body." "Correspondence and Legal Papers," William Preston Bynum Papers. See also *Lattimore v. Dickson,* 63 N.C. 356 (1869); *Lattimore v. Dixon,* 65 N.C. 664 (1871). Another case, *Nelson v. Nelson,* 7 Ky. Op. 384 (1873), also made a similar claim.

52. Reed, *Conduct of Lawsuits* (1885), 39–41.

53. Generally, circuit courts and superior courts seem to have met in each county less often than some other local courts, such as city courts. In discussing superior courts in the nineteenth century, for instance, Erwin Surrency notes that "The session of the Superior Court or the 'Big Court' as it was known, was limited to a week or two at the most, but much business had to be completed." Erwin C. Surrency, *The Creation of a Judicial System: The History of Georgia Courts, 1733 to Present* (Holmes Beach, FL: Gaunt, 2001), 266. In contrast, some city courts seem to have met almost year-round. In Jefferson County, Alabama, for instance, an 1887 account said that when the "circuit court docket was getting sadly overcrowded," in 1886 "the city court of Birmingham, with common law and equity jurisdiction, was established. This court is in session the year round, with the exception of June and December." According to the 1887 account, the city court "has taken long strides toward relieving the circuit court, and it has almost absorbed the civil business of the county." See John Witherspoon DuBose, *Jefferson County and Birmingham Alabama: Historical and Biographical* (Birmingham, AL: Caldwell Printing Works, 1887), 83. For more on how often local courts met in the antebellum South, see Gross, *Double Character,* 24–25.

54. According to Cleveland County Heritage, after the Civil War, "Union soldiers took possession of the courthouse and court square and tried to control county elections and appoint county officers. Some of them remained as long as 1872." *Cleveland County Heritage,* 2–3. For more on Shelby, North Carolina, see "History of Shelby," National Park Service, https://www.nps.gov/nr/travel/shelby/history.htm. For more on the Cleveland County Courthouse in Shelby, NC, see "Courthouses in North Carolina," National Register of Historic Places Inventory–Nomination Form, http://www.hpo.ncdcr.gov/nr/CL0001.pdf; "Old Cleveland County Courthouse," North Carolina Historic Structures Short Data Sheet, https://www.webgis.net/linkedfiles/nc/cleveland/historical/CL001.pdf and *Our Heritage: A History of Cleveland County* (Shelby, NC: Shelby Daily Star, 1974), 23–30.

55. In addition, "court week"—when the superior or circuit court was in session—was an important social event in southern communities. Some of the action took place outside of the courtroom. Local merchants brought their wares to town for the week. Farmers

came to conduct legal business and sell their goods. Men and women planned yearly social events to coincide with the court's session. Edwin Surrency gives a detailed analysis of court week in southern counties in the nineteenth century, based on newspaper coverage at the time, in Surrency, *The Creation of a Judicial System,* 263–270. See also the description of antebellum court weeks in Gross, *Double Character,* 24–25. For more on the central role of courthouses in southern counties, see "Courthouses in North Carolina," National Register of Historic Places Inventory–Nomination Form, http://www.hpo.ncdcr.gov/nr/CL0001.pdf and Edward T. Price, "The Central Courthouse Square in the American County Seat," *Geographical Review* 58, no. 1 (1968): 29–60. See also the descriptions and photographs of southern courthouses in Surrency, *The Creation of a Judicial System,* 269–271; Robert H. Jordan, *Courthouses in Georgia* (Norcross, GA: Harrison Company, 1984); Wilber W. Caldwell, *The Courthouse and the Depot: The Architecture of Hope in an Age of Despair: A Narrative Guide to Railroad Expansion and Its Impact on Public Architecture in Georgia, 1833–1910* (Macon, GA: Mercer University Press, 2001).

56. A photograph of the second Cleveland County courthouse, built in 1845, is in *Our Heritage: A History of Cleveland County,* 25. For descriptions of the interior of southern courthouses in the nineteenth century and how their design shifted over time, see "Courthouses in North Carolina," National Register of Historic Places Inventory–Nomination Form, http://www.hpo.ncdcr.gov/nr/CL0001.pdf and Surrency, *The Creation of a Judicial System,* 269–271. For more on segregation in southern courtrooms, see Stephenson, *Race Distinctions in American Law,* 237–238.

57. During Reconstruction (between 1865 and 1877), 67 percent of civil cases between white and black southerners in the eight appellate courts examined took place between former slaves and their former masters or their former masters' heirs (72 of 108 cases). In the two decades after Reconstruction (1878 to 1899), 35 percent of these cases involved former slaves and their former masters (36 of 104 cases). Between 1865 and 1899, therefore, 108 of 212 cases (51 percent) involved former slaves and their former masters. See Table B.11.

58. Bankruptcy scholar Elizabeth Lee Thompson explains that "the war resulted in the destruction of two-thirds of the value of southerners' assessed property." Elizabeth Lee Thompson, *The Reconstruction of Southern Debtors: Bankruptcy After the Civil War* (Athens: University of Georgia Press, 2004), 1, 15–16 (quote is from p.15).

59. *Arnold v. Arnold* or *Arnold v. Thomson,* 62 Ga. 627 (1879).

60. According to Nancy Burdine's petition, she brought the suit "to require specific performance of a contract, dated April 6th, 1883, whereby the said N. E. Burdine agreed with your petitioner and her mother, that if they would 'live and remain' with his wife and himself during their natural lives; that he would 'make or cause to be made a good will,' devising to your petitioner and her said mother a certain valuable farm in Russell county, Virginia, then owned by him, and that in addition to the farm, he would also give to the said parties bank stock, and other personal property." N. E. Burdine never made a will, and at his death, his widow refused to convey the property and bank stock to Nancy Burdine. *Burdine v. Burdine's Ex'or,* 98 Va. 515 (1900). See also *Simmons v. Hessey. Hessey's Exr. v. Simmons,* 11 Ky. Op. 40 (1881).

61. *Burdine v. Burdine's Ex'or,* 98 Va. 515 (1900). Similarly, the suits of *Dush v. Fitzhugh,* 70 Tenn. 307 (1879) and *Potter & Son v. Gracie,* 58 Ala. 303 (1877), contain allegations of sexual misconduct on the part of black female plaintiff made by the white defendants.

62. *Cobb v. Battle,* 34 Ga. 450 (1866).

63. *Ray v. Commissioners of Durham County,* 110 N.C. 169 (1892).

64. *Lattimore v. Dickson,* 63 N.C. 356 (1869).

65. Examples of black southerners gaining knowledge through consulting with lawyers include *Lattimore v. Dixon,* 65 N.C. 664 (1871). Examples of black southerners gradually gaining knowledge during the legal process include *Briley v. Underwood,* 41 Ga. 9 (1869); *Thomas v. Turner's Adm'r,* 87 Va. 1 (1890). African Americans could also gain knowledge of the law by being present when their former masters or mistresses dictated or signed a will or deed benefiting them. See, for instance, *Briley v. Underwood,* 41 Ga. 9 (1869) and *Davis v. Strange's Ex'r,* 86 Va. 793 (1890).

66. *Thomas v. Turner's Adm'r,* 87 Va. 1 (1890).

67. "Editorial Correspondence," *The Daily Telegraph* (Macon, GA), Oct. 25, 1865. See also Pincus, *The Virginia Supreme Court*, 27–29; Charles S. Mangum Jr., *The Legal Status of The Negro* (Chapel Hill: University of North Carolina Press, 1940), 350–355.

68. In an 1895 Virginia case, for instance, the jury and higher-court rulings both accepted the testimony of a black witness to a man being run over by a train and did not believe the testimony of the train's white engineer. See *Seaboard & R.R.R. v. Joyner's Adm'r*, 92 Va. 354 (1895). Black witnesses were important enough for litigants to sometimes try to influence black witnesses to fabricate their testimony. See, for instance, the case of *Davis v. Franke*, 74 Va. 413 (1880). For more on black witnesses' importance in cases involving both black and white litigants, see Pincus, *The Virginia Supreme Court*, 31–33; Mangum, *The Legal Status of the Negro*, 355.

69. Kent Leslie also argues that personal relations played an important part in a black litigant's postwar case. See Kent Anderson Leslie, *Woman of Color, Daughter of Privilege: Amanda America Dickson, 1849–1893* (Athens: University of Georgia Press, 1995). For more about the long-term connections between white and black southerners that began during slavery and continued after emancipation, see Clarke, *Dwelling Place*, which traces the black and white residents of one household from slavery to Reconstruction, and Elizabeth Fox-Genovese, *Within the Plantation Household: Black and White Women of the Old South* (Chapel Hill: The University of North Carolina Press, 1988).

70. *Ray v. The Commissioners of Durham County*, 110 N.C. 169 (1892); *Briley v. Underwood*, 41 Ga. 9 (1869); *Cowan v. Stamps*, 46 Miss. 435 (1872); *Simmons v. Hessey. Hessey's Exr. v. Simmons*, 11 Ky. Op. 40 (1881).

71. *Simmons v. Hessey. Hessey's Exr. v. Simmons*, 11 Ky. Op. 40 (1881); *Burdine v. Burdine's Ex'or*, 98 Va. 515 (1900). Minta Simmons added further that "neither she nor her said mistress never once thought about the eight hundred dollars or the probability that nay one would claim that she had forfeited it by separating from each other. She says that she believes that her said mistress had this defendants good at heart when parting with her as much as she did her own interest, inasmuch as this defendant had children living in Louisville, whom her said mistress knew she desired to see and be with and the morning of the separation said to her that now she could get along without her, she (meaning the deft) could go and be with her children."

72. *Simmons v. Hessey. Hessey's Exr. v. Simmons*, 11 Ky. Op. 40 (1881). See also *Helm's Ex'r v. Rogers*, 81 Ky. 568 (1884).

73. *Lattimore v. Dixon*, 65 N.C. 664 (1871).

74. According to the 1900 US census, only 2,488,553 people out of 24,523,527 people in the South Atlantic and South Central divisions of the continental United States lived in cities of more than 25,000 people. The states included in this statistic are Delaware, Maryland, District of Columbia, Virginia, West Virginia, North Carolina, South Carolina, Georgia, Florida, Kentucky, Tennessee, Alabama, Mississippi, Louisiana, Arkansas, Indian Territory, Oklahoma, and Texas. "Table 37: Population Living in Cities Within Specified Limits of Size and In Country Districts: 1900" in *Abstract of the Twelfth Census of the United States 1900* (Washington, DC: US Government Printing Office, 1902), 37. See also C. Vann Woodward, *Origins of the New South, 1877–1913* (Baton Rouge: Louisiana State University Press, 1971), 139; Ayers, *The Promise of the New South*, 24–25; Philip Alexander Bruce, "Social and Economic Revolution in the Southern States," *Contemporary Review* 78 (1900): 67.

75. *Munroe v. Phillips*, 64 Ga. 32 (1879); *Munroe v. Phillips*, 65 Ga. 390 (1880). Black litigants also used long-term ties with local white people to find out information for their cases. The plaintiff in one case, William Walker, noted conversations with the white defendants (his cousins) regarding how they obtained the property he claimed and about the lands' value, concluding, "I know pretty well all of Defts [Defendants]." *Walker v. Walker*, 66 Ga. 253 (1880). See also *Urey's Adm'r v. Urey's Ex'r*, 86 Ky. 354 (1887).

76. For more on long-standing personal relations between black and white southerners before and after the Civil War, see Ayers, *The Promise of the New South*, 134–136; Clarke, *Dwelling Place*; Hargis, "For the Love of Place," 825–864. For examples of white witnesses testifying on behalf of black litigants because of personal ties, see *Munroe v. Phillips*, 64 Ga. 32 (1879); *Munroe v. Phillips*, 65 Ga. 390 (1880).

77. *Lattimore v. Dickson*, 63 N.C. 356 (1869); *Lattimore v. Dixon*, 65 N.C. 664 (1871)

78. Reed, *Conduct of Lawsuits* (1885), 247, 279.

79. *Lattimore v. Dickson*, 63 N.C. 356 (1869); *Lattimore v. Dixon*, 65 N.C. 664 (1871).
80. *Lattimore v. Dickson*, 63 N.C. 356 (1869); *Lattimore v. Dixon*, 65 N.C. 664 (1871).
81. For more on nuncupative wills, in which a testator orally declares his will before witnesses while on his deathbed, see Abraham Caruthers, *History of a Lawsuit*, revised by Andrew B. Martin, 4th ed. (Cincinnati, OH: W. H. Anderson Company, 1903), 559–561. This contemporary manual for lawyers states that such a will "must be made in his last sickness. It must be in apprehension of speedy dissolution. If he recovers, the will is not valid."
82. *Thomas' Adm'r v. Lewis*, 89 Va. 1 (1892). Because of the extraordinarily large amount of money at stake in this Virginia case—over $200,000—details of the trial appeared in at least six newspaper articles in at least four different newspapers throughout Virginia. As a result of her legal victory, Bettie Thomas Lewis received the bulk of her father's estate, which was estimated at over $200,000. Several newspapers surmised that this made Bettie Thomas Lewis the wealthiest black person in Virginia. For newspaper coverage of this case, see "Current News and Comment," *Shenandoah Herald* (Woodstock, VA), Oct. 10, 1890; *Augusta County Argus*, Jan. 13, 1891; "Bettie Thomas-Lewis," *The Times* (Richmond, VA), June 19, 1892; "Bettie Thomas Lewis Case," *The Times* (Richmond, VA), July 21, 1892; "Bettie Will Be Rich," *Richmond Dispatch*, July 24, 1892; "Bettie Thomas Lewis Case," *The Times* (Richmond, VA), Nov. 17, 1892. For more on how celebrated cases could provoke widespread interest and public debate, see Grossberg, *A Judgment for Solomon*.
83. Clearly, the cases that eventually were heard by state supreme courts do not form a representative sample of lower-court cases. Analysis of the lower-court trials of these suits shows, though, that the percentage of such cases decided by a jury increased, from 30 percent during Reconstruction to 53 percent between 1878 and 1899 and 55 percent between 1900 and 1920. Then, between 1921 and 1950, the number of cases decided by each body evened out, to 47 percent, of these appellate civil suits between black and white litigants decided by judges and 47 percent decided by juries. In contrast, during Reconstruction judges decided 66 percent of the initial cases while between 1878 and 1899 judges decided 43 percent of such cases. In a certain number of cases, it could not be determined who decided the case. At times cases were decided by more than one lower court before they reached the state's highest court—in this case, I used the lowest court they were heard in and then the highest court they were heard in for purposes of calculation. In at least four cases involving black litigants, suits were decided in one lower court by a judge and in another lower court by a jury. The changes over time appear to be due, in large part, to changes in the types of cases involving black litigants during these different eras. Probate and apprenticeship cases, which made up many of the cases involving black litigants in the three-and-a-half decades after the Civil War, were more likely to be decided in the lower courts by a judge. In contrast, juries often decided personal injury and fraud cases, which made up most of the cases involving black litigants between 1900 and 1920. As the types of cases involving black litigants shifted, the likelihood of a judge or jury deciding the lower-court trial seems to have changed as well. See Table B.15.
84. Historian Kermit Hall found that approximately 67.2 percent of southern judges between 1832 and 1920 were from the upper-middle class ("sons of successful professionals, planters, merchants and bankers"), 15 percent were from elite families, and 17.7 percent came from modest origins. Kermit L. Hall, "The 'Route to Hell' Retraced: The Impact of Popular Election on the Southern Appellate Judiciary, 1832–1920," in David J. Bodenhamer and James W. Ely, Jr., eds., *Ambivalent Legacy: A Legal History of the South* (Jackson: University Press of Mississippi, 1984), 245–247. A few exceptions to this included Jonathan Jasper Wright, who was elected justice of the Supreme Court of South Carolina in 1870, becoming the first black to sit on any state supreme court. In addition, in 1872 the South Carolina legislature elected George Lee as a judge of the Supreme Court, making him the first black superior court judge in the South. See Richard Gergel and Belinda Gergel, " 'To Vindicate the Cause of the Downtrodden,': Associate Justice Jonathan Jasper Wright and Reconstruction in South Carolina," in *At Freedom's Door*, 36–71; From Slavery to the Supreme Court Online Exhibit, Just The Beginning Foundation, http://www.jtbf.org/index.php?submenu=Slavery&src=gendocs&link=FromSlaverytotheSupremeCourtOnlineExhibit&category=Main.
85. In Georgia, for instance, Joseph Emerson Brown (1868–1870) and Henry Kent McCay (1868–1875) both seem to have broken from the Democratic Party during Reconstruction.

Another Reconstruction-era justice, Osborne Augustus Lochrane (1871–1872), had migrated to Georgia from Ireland as a young man and cooperated with the Republican Party after the Civil War, and yet another, Robert P. Trippe (1873–1875), had been a Whig before the Civil War. For more about the political sympathies of Supreme Court of Georgia and superior court judges during Reconstruction, see Deen, *Georgia's Appellate Judiciary*; Grice, *The Georgia Bench and Bar*, vol. 1 (1931), 338–347.

86. Ayers, *The Promise of the New South*, 134.

87. Kermit Hall contrasts the lack of competitiveness in most southern judicial elections, with judicial elections in the Midwest during this time, which were much more competitive and partisan. The lack of more than one competitive political party in the South during much of this time was an important factor in this difference. Hall, "The 'Route to Hell' Retraced," 238–243. Jed Shugerman writes that there were surprisingly competitive judicial elections in Tennessee and Texas during this time, however. See Jed Handelsman Shugerman, *The People's Courts: Pursuing Judicial Independence in America* (Cambridge, MA: Harvard University Press, 2012), 145.

88. Reed, *Conduct of Lawsuits* (1885), 104, 112; Peter Karsten, *Heart versus Head: Judge-Made Law in Nineteenth-Century America* (Chapel Hill: University of North Carolina Press, 1997), 26–128. Similarly, Christopher Waldrep argues that slaves could not achieve fair hearings in local courts in the antebellum period, but were able to achieve a surprising level of justice in appellate courts during Reconstruction because of the legal system's adherence to precedent. See Waldrep, "Substituting Law for the Lash," 1432–1433.

89. Pincus, *The Virginia Supreme Court*, xxvii; Waldrep, "Substituting Law for the Lash," 1444–1449.

90. Pincus, *The Virginia Supreme Court*, 18.

91. For examples of shock and outrage about black jury members at the beginning of Reconstruction, see "Negro Lawyers," *The Atlanta Constitution*, Oct. 31, 1869, 1; "South Carolina Letter," *The Atlanta Constitution*, Aug. 4, 1869. For the Tennessee comment about black jury members in Charleston, see *The Tennessean* (Nashville, TN), July 3, 1889, 4. My analysis of black jury service continuing after 1890 to a lesser extent in the South is based on a study by Gilbert Thomas Stephenson. In 1900, Stephenson wrote to the court clerk in all the counties in North Carolina that had majority-black populations to inquire about black jury service. Of the sixty-five North Carolina court clerks that replied, twenty reported that a very limited number of black men still served on their juries. All of these twenty also reported, though, that jury service by black men had decreased in their county in the past few years. See Stephenson, *Race Distinctions in American Law*, 258–272. Even at the end of the nineteenth century and beginning of the twentieth century, a small number of African Americans were able to serve on southern juries in certain counties. See for instance, the service of Pinkard C. Dowans in Mississippi in 1907. Waldrep, *Jury Discrimination*, 1–3; Stephenson, *Race Distinctions in American Law*, 258–272.

92. As this book examines only lower-court cases that were accepted by a higher court on appeal, there is not a representative sample to judge how often black litigants won their cases in lower courts. Of the lower-court cases appealed to the higher court, black litigants won 47 of 108 cases at the lower-court level (44 percent) between 1865 and 1877 and in 58 out of 104 cases at the lower-court level (56 percent) between 1878 and 1899. Overall they won in the lower-court trial of the appellate suits they brought against whites in the courts examined in 105 out of 212 cases between 1865 and 1899 (50 percent of suits). When all lower-court trials between 1865 and 1950 are examined, black litigants won in 552 out of 980 of the initial trials (56 percent of suits). See Table B.16. Juries decided 41 percent of the initial trials between 1865 and 1899 (87 of 212 cases), and judges decided 55 percent of these trials (116 of 212 cases). In the remaining cases, it was unclear who decided the initial trial. For data on how often these initial trials between 1865 and 1899 were decided by a jury or a judge, see Table B.15.

93. African American litigants were the sole party appealing the case in 52 out of 108 cases (48 percent) between 1865 and 1877 and 42 out of 104 cases (40 percent) between 1878 and 1899. Between 1865 and 1899, then, black litigants were the sole party appealing the case in 94 of 212 cases (44 percent of suits). White litigants were the sole party appealing

the case in 48 of 108 cases (44 percent) between 1865 and 1877 and 57 of 104 cases (55 percent) between 1878 and 1899. Between 1865 and 1899, then, white litigants were the sole party appealing the case in 105 of 212 cases (50 percent of suits). Overall, between 1865 and 1950, African Americans were the sole party appealing in 400 cases (41 percent of suits), and whites were the sole party appealing in 548 cases (56 percent of suits). These numbers do not include the instances in which both parties appealed the case. See Table B.21.

94. In his 1885 manual for lawyers, Reed, a contemporary Georgia jurist, advised other attorneys that lawyers should discourage their clients from appealing "unless you see that the verdict is really wrong." Reed, *Conduct of Lawsuits* (1885), 402. For more on clients and their lawyers deciding to appeal to state supreme courts based on the perceived strength of their case during this time, see also "Courting Reversal," *The Yale Law Journal*, 1199, and note 33, 1199.

95. Caruthers, *History of a Lawsuit* (1860), 278.

96. *Lattimore v. Dixon*, 63 N.C. 356 (1869); "Courting Reversal," *The Yale Law Journal*, 1191–1196.

97. Kagan, "The Business of State Supreme Courts," 132–140.

98. There were 77 suits over inheritance and bequests between black and white litigants in the eight appellate courts from 1865 to 1899 out of 212 total such suits (36 percent of suits). In addition, there were 52 suits over property disputes, transactions, and contracts between black and white litigants in the eight appellate courts from 1865 to 1899 of 212 total such suits (25 percent of suits). See Tables B.7 and B.8.

99. For an examination of how much discretion state supreme courts had to choose cases in the United States between 1870 and 1970 and the change in this over time, see Kagan, "The Business of State Supreme Courts," 128–132. For more on individual state appellate court's policies about which appeals to take at different times, see Chalmers, *The Probate Law and Practice in the Courts of Mississippi and Tennessee* (1890), 401–422; Harris, *A History of the Supreme Court of Georgia*, 56; Cozart, *Georgia Practice Rules as Laid Down by the Supreme Court and Court of Appeals of Georgia* (1918), 87–94; Schafer, *Slavery, the Civil Law, and the Supreme Court of Louisiana*, xi-xii; Battle, "An Address on the History of the Supreme Court," in Battle, *Supreme Court of North Carolina.*

100. From 1810 to 1868, the Supreme Court of North Carolina had accepted all cases that were appealed to its court. To appeal to their state's highest court, the counsel of the appealing party sent a bill of exceptions to the higher court, laying out the alleged errors of the lower court. According to Kemp P. Battle, "By act of 1799 the Court therein organized had jurisdiction of questions of law and equity which any judge on the circuit was unwilling to decide, or on which there was a disagreement between the judges. By act of 1810, any party dissatisfied with the ruling of the Superior Court had a right to remove it to the Supreme Court. By the act of 1818 the judges were to have all the powers of the Superior Court Judges, except that of holding a Superior Court. Any party could appeal from the final judgment, sentence or decree of the Superior Court on giving security to abide the judgment or decree of the Supreme Court, which was authorized to give such judgment as should appear to them right in law, to be rendered on inspection of the whole record. Equity cases could be removed to the Supreme Court for hearing, upon sufficient cause appearing, by affidavit or otherwise, showing that such removal was required for purposes of justice, but no parol evidence was received before the court, or any jury impaneled to try issues, except witnesses to prove exhibits or other documents. Under this provision it became customary to remove all important equity causes, so that the Superior Court Judge escaped the responsibility of giving any opinion in the matter. The Constitution of 1868 and that of 1876 put a stop to these proceedings by confining the jurisdiction of the Supreme Court to appeals on matters of law or legal inference .... The provision of the Constitution giving to the Court original jurisdiction to hear claims against the State, and to report their decisions to the General Assembly, has been construed by the Court to embrace only cases involving questions of law." Battle, "An Address on the History of the Supreme Court," in Battle, *Supreme Court of North Carolina.* See also Hill, *When the North Carolina Supreme Court Sat in the Capitol*, 10. Similarly, the Mississippi Code of 1880 states that "writs of error as heretofore used are abolished, and all cases, civil and criminal, at law and in chancery, shall be taken to the supreme court by appeal ... and shall be dealt with by said court without regard to the manner of

removing said cases to such court." However, an 1890 legal manual notes that appeals could be made to the Tennessee Supreme Court only in "cases in which the jurisdiction of the county court is concurrent with the circuit or chancery courts, or in which both parties consent." For more on appeals to the state supreme courts of Mississippi and Tennessee, see Chalmers, *The Probate Law and Practice in the Courts of Mississippi and Tennessee* (1890), 401, 407–408.

101. In Georgia and Virginia, the legislature elected appellate judges for most or all of this time, and in Mississippi the governor appointed appellate judges for much of this period. In Virginia, the legislature elected appellate judges throughout the period of 1865 to 1920. In Georgia, appellate judges were elected by the legislature until 1896, when the state adopted the method of popular election. Mississippi had a system of popular election until 1868, when it changed to having appellate judges appointed by the governor. Mississippi changed back to the system of popular election in 1914. In Tennessee, North Carolina, Alabama, Kentucky, and Arkansas, appellate judges were elected by popular vote during this period (in North Carolina they were elected for terms of eight years beginning in 1868). In many of these states, governors could appoint judges to the court if vacancies occurred between elections. Jed Shugerman explains that many of these changes in the term limits of judges and in whether they were appointed or elected were politically moti- vated. For instance, during Reconstruction some Republican southern state governments lengthened term limits for judges to try to keep the judges they had appointed in office after Republicans lost power in the South. See Shugerman, *The People's Courts*, 148–149; James W. Ely, Jr., ed., *A History of the Tennessee Supreme Court* (Knoxville: University of Tennessee Press, 2002), 84–89, 101–105; Harris, *A History of the Supreme Court of Georgia*, 54–55, 171–174; Clark, *History of the Supreme Court of North Carolina*, 5–8; Hill, *When The North Carolina Supreme Court Sat In The Capitol*, 3; Pincus, *The Virginia Supreme Court*, 4; J. E. Livingston, "A History of the Alabama Judicial System," http://judicial.alabama.gov/docs/judicial_history.pdf; Third Constitution of Kentucky (1850); Present Constitution of the Commonwealth of Kentucky (1891); Constitution of the State of Arkansas of 1874; Mississippi Constitution of 1868; Mississippi Constitution of 1890; Hall, "The 'Route to Hell' Retraced," 229–255.

102. In Georgia, however, lawyers from each side appeared before the state supreme court to read a brief to the judges. Other parts of the record of the lower-court proceedings could also be read. Caruthers, *History of a Lawsuit* (1860), 271–272, 532.

103. In 1869, when the first appeal of this case was heard before the Supreme Court of North Carolina, the justices were Richmond Mumford Pearson, Chief Justice (first elected to the court in 1848); Edwin Godwin Reade (first elected in 1866); William Blount Rodman (first elected in 1868); Robert Paine Dick (first elected in 1868); and Thomas Settle (first elected in 1868). During the 1871 appeal, Justice Nathaniel Boyden (appointed 1871) had replaced Justice Thomas Settle. Although Pearson had been serving on the court since 1848, he was nominated by both the Republican and Democratic Parties in the election after the Civil War. Reade was a native of North Carolina, had run as a Whig for the state legislature, and for one term beginning in 1855 served as a congressman in the US Congress for the Whig Party and had opposed secession. William Blount Rodman, another Republican justice, had roots in the North; his father was from New York State although Rodman himself had been born and raised in North Carolina. Justice Robert Dick was a member of the Democratic Party before the Civil War, but became a Republican after the war and in 1867 was part of the political convention that organized the Republican Party in North Carolina. Justice Thomas Settle was a Democrat before the war, but became a Republican after the war. Boyden was born in Massachusetts, attended college in New York. He came to North Carolina after col- lege in 1822 and practiced law there. In 1868 he was elected as a Republican to the Fortieth Congress. Hill, *When the North Carolina Supreme Court Sat in the Capitol*, 11, 16; Clark, *History of the Supreme Court of North Carolina*, 26.

104. *Lattimore v. Dickson*, 63 N.C. 356 (1869).

105. Although often unanimous, at times individual judges dissented from the court's decision. For examples of dissenting opinions by judges who did not agree with a decision against a black litigant, see *Welborn v. Mayrant*, 48 Miss. 652 (1873); *Paxton v. Meyer*, 58 Miss. 445 (1880); *Arnold v. Storthz*, 74 Ark. 68 (1905); *St. Louis & San Francisco Railroad Company*

v. Petties, 99 Ark. 415 (1911); *Yazoo & M. V. R. Co. v. Walls,* 110 Miss. 256 (1915); *Louisville, N. & G. S. R.R. Co. v. Fleming,* 82 Tenn. 128 (1884); *Hopkins v. City of Richmond, and Coleman v. Town of Ashland,* 117 Va. 692 (1915); *Harden v. City of Atlanta,* 147 Ga. 248 (1917); *Cowart vs. Singletary,* 140 Ga. 435 (1913); *Ashe v. Camp Manufacturing Company,* 154 N.C. 241 (1911); *Greenhow v. James' Ex'r,* 80 Va. 636 (1885). For examples in which a judge dissented with a decision in favor of a black litigant, see *Maddox v. Neal,* 45 Ark. 121 (1885); *The Georgia Railroad & Banking Co. v. Dougherty,* 86 Ga. 744 (1890); *Slade v. Sherrod,* 175 N.C. 346 (1918); *Lawrence v. Western Union Telegraph Company,* 171 N.C. 240 (1916); *Railway Companies v. Foster,* 88 Tenn. 671 (1890); *Boutten v. Wellington & P. R. Co,* 128 N.C. 337 (1901); *Empire Improv. Co. v. Lynch,* 181 Ala. 473 (1913); *Henderson Tobacco Extracts Works v. Wheeler,* 116 Ky. 322 (1903); *Hayley v. Hayley,* 62 N.C. 180 (1867); *Thomas v. Turner's Adm'r,* 87 Va. 1 (1890); *Young v. Cavitt,* 54 Tenn. 18 (1871); *Thomas' Adm'r v. Lewis,* 89 Va. 1 (1892); *Davis v. Strange's Executor,* 86 Va. 793 (1890); *Berry v. Meir,* 70 Ark. 129 (1902).

106. Black litigants won 69 of 108 civil cases against white southerners in the eight state supreme courts between 1865 and 1877 out of a total of 108 cases (64 percent). Black litigants won 56 out of 104 civil cases against white southerners in the eight state supreme courts between 1878 and 1899 out of a total of 104 cases (54 percent). Together then, between 1865 and 1899, black litigants won 125 out of 212 such civil appellate suits (59 percent of their suits) See Table B.18. Of these cases they had won between 1865 and 1899, there were 108 cases in which the lower-court decision went clearly one way or the other (in the other cases the lower-court decision was split or unclear). In 68 of these 108 cases, the appellate court upheld a ruling in favor of the black litigant (63 percent of the time) and in 37 out of 108 cases (34 percent of suits) they reversed a lower court decision that had been in favor of the white litigant. See Table B.24. For a more in-depth analysis of how often African Americans won these cases compared with cases involving all litigants appealing cases, see Appendix A: Notes on Methodology, Sources, and Findings.

107. Of these reversals, the state supreme courts were more likely to reverse a decision that had been against a black litigant than to reverse a decision that had been against a white litigant. Throughout this period of 1865 to 1899, the eight southern supreme courts examined reversed 53 of 212 suits (25 percent of cases) to decide in favor of the black litigants while reversing only 37 of 212 suits (17 percent of cases) to favor the white litigants. Similarly, in upholding lower-court decisions, the southern state supreme courts examined were more likely to uphold cases in which the lower court had decided in favor of black litigants (in 68 of 212 cases, or 38 percent of suits) than to uphold lower-court decisions that favored white litigants (in 41 out 212 cases, of 19 percent of suits). This may be due in part to whites' undoubtedly greater ability to appeal; perhaps when black litigants did appeal, they did so when they had a particularly strong legal claim. Nevertheless, it is striking that at this time in history black litigants fared so well in appellate civil cases against whites. See Tables B.23 and B.24.

108. As for how representative these suits were of overall reversal rates in the nation, the authors of a study that examined a sampling of cases every 5 years in sixteen representative state supreme courts throughout the United States between 1870 and 1970 found that the courts affirmed approximately 61.5 percent of suits and reversed approximately 38.5 percent of suits. See "Courting Reversal," *The Yale Law Journal,* 1198 and Table B.33. As Table B.22 demonstrates, the suits between black and white southerners that I examined in eight southern appellate courts between 1865 and 1899 had a reversal rate of 42 percent (90 cases of 212 cases were reversed) and a 51 percent rate of lower-court decisions being upheld (109 cases of 212 suits were upheld).

109. From 1865 to 1899, black litigants won in 8 of 14 civil cases in Alabama (57 percent), 2 of 7 cases in Arkansas (12 percent), 31 of 51 cases in Georgia (61 percent), 17 of 33 cases in Kentucky (52 percent), 13 of 23 cases in Mississippi (57 percent), 28 of 41 cases in North Carolina (68 percent), 20 of 28 cases in Tennessee (71 percent), and 6 of 15 cases in Virginia (40 percent). When one averages the outcomes of appellate civil cases between white and black litigants in each state across the entire period from 1865 to 1950, though, black litigants won over 50 percent of the time in all eight southern states examined. African Americans'

civil suits against whites in state supreme courts were slightly more successful in certain states than others. Between 1865 and 1950, black litigants won most often in Georgia (68 of 104 cases, or 65 percent of the time), North Carolina (79 of 124 cases, or 64 percent), Arkansas (60 of 96 cases, or 63 percent), and Virginia (46 of 74 cases, or 62 percent). Black litigants won slightly less often in Tennessee (39 of 66 cases, or 59 percent), Mississippi (80 of 135 cases, or 59 percent), Alabama (107 of 184 cases, or 58 percent) and Kentucky (103 of 197 cases, or 52 percent). See Table B.20.

110. Edwin Godwin Reade had been a member of the North Carolina Whig Party before the war. In the months after the war ended, he had attracted widespread attention when, after being elected president of the North Carolina State Convention of 1865, he gave an address beginning "We are going home," implying that rejoining the Union was a return to the state's rightful place. The next year, in 1866, the North Carolina General Assembly elected him to the state supreme court, a position he would hold until 1879. Clark, *The Supreme Court of North Carolina*, 569–572; Dowd, *Sketches of Prominent Living North Carolinians* (1888), 92–97. For the full decision, see *Lattimore v. Dickson*, 63 N.C. 356 (1869).

111. Elsewhere, in the prior history of the case, it says that the clerk decided that Dixon owed Lattimore $170. In the 1871 opinion of the case, however, the judge says that the clerk decided that he owed $365.95. I have decided to use the figure from that opinion. *Lattimore v. Dixon*, 65 N.C. 664 (1871).

112. *Lattimore v. Dixon*, 65 N.C. 664 (1871). Judge Nathaniel Boyden, a recent, Massachusetts-born addition to the court, wrote in the 1871 opinion, "There was much testimony taken in this cause, some forty pages closely written, and much time spent thereon; and, upon examining this mass of testimony, it leaves many of the charges on the part of the plaintiff and defendant in much doubt and perplexity." Boyden was born in Massachusetts and attended college in New York. He came to North Carolina after college in 1822 and practiced law there. He served in the state senate and was elected a member of the US Congress. In 1868 he was elected as a Republican to the Fortieth Congress. When appointed by the governor in 1871 to the Supreme Court, he was 75 years old. He died 2.5 years later. See Kemp Battle, *History of the Supreme Court*, 66; Clark, *The Supreme Court of North Carolina*, 576–577. Newspapers reporting on the hearing of the case included "Proceedings in Supreme Court," *Raleigh Daily Telegram*, July 1, 1871, 3; "Opinions Were Delivered by the Court on Monday as Follows," *Carolina Watchman*, July 28, 1871, 1; "Opinions Were Delivered by the Court on Yesterday as Follows," *Raleigh Daily Telegram*, July 18, 1871, 3; "N.C. Supreme Court," *The Charlotte Democrat*, July 25, 1871, 2; "Opinions Were Delivered by the Supreme Court, on Monday Last, as Follows," *Tri-Weekly Era*, July 20, 1871, 3.

Chapter 3

1. William Walker, one of the children Francis Walker freed, was accompanied on the voyage across the Atlantic by his 34-year-old mother, Louisa, his brother, Green, and his sister, Elizabeth. William's mother Louisa was approximately 16 when she gave birth to him and only 14 when she gave birth to his older brother, Green, age 20. Robert T. Brown, *Immigrants to Liberia, 1843 to 1865, an Alphabetical Listing* (Philadelphia: Institute for Liberian Studies, 1980), 60; *Walker v. Walker*, 66 Ga. 253 (1880).

2. *Walker v. Walker*, 66 Ga. 253 (1880).

3. For more on free people of color during this time in the South, see Berlin, *Slaves Without Masters*; Franklin, *The Free Negro in North Carolina*; Cottrol, *The Long, Lingering Shadow*, 6–11.

4. In Tennessee, for instance, the General Assembly passed a law in 1831 prohibiting the manumission of slaves unless the newly freed black people left the state. As fears of slave revolts lessened in the early 1840s, Tennessee lawmakers softened the 1831 law by permitting county courts to make exceptions to this prohibition and allow certain emancipated slaves to remain in Tennessee. Yet, only a few years later, as events on the national scene split the country along slavery lines, Tennessee again changed its manumission laws, reverting to the earlier prohibition on emancipated slaves staying in the slave South. Then, in 1854, Tennessee lawmakers passed a new law stating that all emancipated slaves had to emigrate to Liberia, forbidding them from moving to a free state, as they had allowed earlier. Huebner, "Judicial Independence

in an Age of Democracy, Sectionalism, and War, 1835–1865," in *A History of the Tennessee Supreme Court*, 90–93. For more on manumission and the law in the antebellum South, see also Paul Finkelman, *The Law of Freedom and Bondage: A Casebook* (New York: Oceana Publications, 1986), 95–189; Howington, *What Sayeth the Law*, 23–25; Ranney, *In the Wake of Slavery*, 152; Caruthers, *History of a Lawsuit* (1860), 385.

5. For example, Kentucky passed a constitution in 1850, stating that emancipated slaves must leave the state. For more on manumission laws, see Berlin, *Slaves Without Masters*, 138–157; Ranney, *In the Wake of Slavery*, 152; Bernie D. Jones, *Fathers of Conscience: Mixed-Race Inheritance in the Antebellum South* (Athens: University of Georgia Press, 2009), 53–57, 92–93.

6. Bartholomew F. Moore and Asa Biggs, *Revised Code of North Carolina* (Boston: Little, Brown, 1855), 573; *The Revised Code of the Statute Laws of the State of Mississippi* (1857), 236.

7. Slave-owners usually emancipated their slaves to northern states (such as Ohio) or Liberia. In one case, the testator directed removal to Mexico. See *Robinson v. McIver*, 63 N.C. 645 (1869).

8. Claude A. Clegg, *The Price of Liberty: African Americans and the Making of Liberia* (Chapel Hill: University of North Carolina Press, 2004), 20–27; Tom W. Shick, *Behold the Promised Land: A History of Afro-American Settlers in Nineteenth-Century Liberia* (Baltimore: Johns Hopkins University Press, 1980), 3–6.

9. The different purposes of ACS members caused tension within the movement during its early years, and in the 1830s, most white abolitionists turned against the society. For more on different group's attitudes toward migration to Liberia and early settlement in Liberia, see James Sidbury, "Becoming American in Liberia and in the United States, 1820–1830," in *Becoming African in America: Race and Nation in the Early Black Atlantic, 1760–1830* (Oxford: Oxford University Press, 2007), 181–202; Eric Burin, *Slavery and the Peculiar Solution: A History of the American Colonization Society* (Gainesville: University Press of Florida, 2005), 34–56; Kenneth C. Barnes, *Journey of Hope: The Back-to-Africa Movement in Arkansas in the Late 1800s* (Chapel Hill: University of North Carolina Press, 2004), 3–4; Clegg, *The Price of Liberty*, 4; Allen E. Yarema, *The American Colonization Society: An Avenue to Freedom?* (Lanham, MD: University Press of America, 2006); C. Abayomi Cassell, *Liberia: History of the First African Republic* (New York: Fountainhead, 1970), 17–64; John Stauffer, *The Black Hearts of Men: Radical Abolitionists and the Transformation of Race* (Cambridge, MA: Harvard University Press, 2002), 94; Michele Mitchell, *Righteous Propagation: African Americans and the Politics of Racial Destiny After Reconstruction* (Chapel Hill: University of North Carolina Press, 2004), 21–24; Bruce Dorsey, "A Gendered History of African Colonization in the Antebellum United States," *Journal of Social History* 34, no.1 (2000): 77–103.

10. Barnes, *Journey of Hope*, 4–5; Mitchell, *Righteous Propagation*, 21–24.

11. Eric Burin, "Envisioning Africa: American Slaves' Ideas About Liberia," *Liberian Studies Journal* 47, no. 2 (2002): 1–17; Burin, *Slavery and the Peculiar Solution*, 57–78. For an example of a letter from Liberia settlers influencing US slaves' decisions about migration, see *The American Colonization Society Records* (hereinafter referred to as *ACS Records*), Series 1A, Vol. 158, Part 1, Reel 88, p. 494.

12. *ACS Records*, Series 1A, Vol. 158, Part 1, Reel 88, p. 494; *The African Repository* 35, no.7 (Washington, DC, July 1859): 223.

13. Brown, *Immigrants to Liberia*, 46, 59. The case that would result from this manumission was *Urey's Adm'r v. Urey's Ex'r*, 86 Ky. 354 (1887).

14. "Letter from F. W. Urey to Rev. McLain," *ACS Records*, Series 1A, Vol. 190, Reel 101, p. 445 and *ACS Records*, Series 1A, Vol. 153, Reel 85, p. 263.

15. Even 2 years after their former slaves arrived in Liberia, the Ureys continued to take a hands-on approach to their former slaves' welfare. When the Ureys received word in October 1860 that two of Phereby's sons had fallen sick, they immediately wrote the ACS requesting that the boys be sent back to the United States on the next ship, adding that they would pay for a cabin berth for the boys. "Letter from F.W. Urey to Rev. McLain," *ACS Records*, Series 1A, Vol. 154, Reel 85, p. 17; Letter from F.W. Urey to Rev. McLain," *ACS Records*, Series 1A, Vol. 161, Reel 90, p. 12; Letter from F.W. Urey to Rev. McLain," *ACS Records*, Series 1A, Vol. 161, Reel 90, p. 73.

16. "Letter from F.W. Urey to Rev. McLain," *ACS Records*, Series 1A, Vol. 155, Part 1, Reel 86, p. 197, p. 265; Vol. 156, Reel 87, p. 244. For another example of letters between a white former

master's family and the family of slaves he emancipated, see Randall M. Miller, ed., *Dear Master: Letters of a Slave Family* (Ithaca, NY: Cornell University Press, 1978).

17. For more on when wills could be contested in the nineteenth century, see William L. Smith, *The Practice in Proceedings in the Probate Courts* (Boston: Little, Brown, 1868), 25–36; Chalmers, *The Probate Law and Practice in the Courts of Mississippi and Tennessee* (1890), 81–104. For more on the considerations of southern judges in deciding on wills benefiting people of color and the parties that could oppose testator's wishes, see Jones, *Fathers of Conscience*, 16–17, 21–67, 81.

18. Cases in which wills were not enforced included *Berry v. Hamilton*, 64 Ky. 361 (1866); *Jones's Adm'r v. Jones's Adm'r*, 92 Va. 590 (1896); *Estill v. Deckerd*, 63 Tenn. 497 (1874); *Armstrong v. Pearre*, 47 Tenn. 171 (1869); *Milly v. Harrison*, 47 Tenn. 191 (1869); *Whedbee v. Shannonhouse*, 62 N.C. 283 (1868); *Shannonhouse v. Whedbee*, Ib. 283 (1867). Cases in which the Civil War emancipated slaves before they could emigrate included *Kelly's v. Pettus*, 145 Ky. 250 (1911); *Neely v. Merritt*, 72 Ky. 346 (1872); *Strong v. Middleton*, 51 Ga. 462 (1874); *Thweatt v. Redd*, 50 Ga. 181 (1873); *Lynch v. Burts*, 48 Tenn. 600 (1870); *Cowan v. Stamps*, 46 Miss. 435 (1872); *Todd v. Trott*, 64 N.C. 280 (1870).

19. Eric Burin, "Envisioning Africa," 13–14.

20. The former slaves again brought a case attempting to become parties to the suit in 1866, only to be denied from becoming parties to the suit by the local court. They appealed to the Court of Appeals of Kentucky, which affirmed their right to appeal and serve as parties to the case but denied their claim to a bequest from their former mistress. *Berry v. Hamilton*, 64 Ky. 361 (1866).

21. In addition, Joseph Jones, a 67-year-old man who had "purchased his freedom," requested the county court in 1855 to allow him to stay in Tennessee, arguing that "from his age he could not go to Liberia with safety." The county court granted his petition. Davidson County, County Court, *Minutes*, October 1855, 498; Knox County, County Court, *Minutes*, August 1857, 108; Knox County, County Court, *Minutes*, August 1857, 103–105, 108–109; Circuit Court, *Minutes*, October 1857, 77. These cases are cited in Howington, *What Sayeth the Law*, 52–53.

22. A study of the case loads of sixteen representative state supreme courts between 1870 and 1900 found that approximately 6.3 percent of cases were suits over inheritance and estates. Kagan, "The Business of State Supreme Courts," 135, 150–151. Of the 212 appellate cases between white and black litigants in the eight higher courts examined, 77 cases (36 percent of suits) involved wills or trusts. Of these cases, 47 took place over antebellum wills in which slaveholders had left funds for the emancipation of their slaves. During Reconstruction, 39 bequest cases involving antebellum manumission took place, including *Hayley v. Hayley*, 62 N.C. 180 (1867); *Hoover v. Brem*, 43 Miss. 603 (1870); *Nelson v. Nelson*, 7 Ky. Op. 384 (1873); *Bedford v. Williams*, 45 Tenn. 202 (1867); *Deberry v. Hurt*, 66 Tenn. 390 (1874); *Berry v. Alsop*, 45 Miss. 1 (1871); *Cobb v. Battle*, 34 Ga. 450 (1866); *Green v. Anderson*, 38 Ga. 655 (1869); *Jacks v. Adair*, 31 Ark. 616 (1876); *Anderson v. Green*, 46 Ga. 361 (1872); *Johns v. Scott*, 64 Va. 704 (1873); *Klair v. Asby*, 8 Ky. Op. 894 (1875); *Ashburn v. Battle* (1875); *Monohon v. Caroline (of color)*, 65 Ky. 410 (1867); *Parish v. Hill*, 63 Ky. 396 (1866); *Bennett v. Williams*, 46 Ga. 399 (1872); *Bramlett's Ex'r v. Bramlette*, 6 Ky. Op. 718 (1873); *Raines v. Raines's Ex'rs*, 51 Ala. 237 (1874); *Robinson v. McIver*, 63 N.C. 645 (1869); *Robinson v. Johnson*, 67 Ky. 433 (1868); *Cochreham v. Kirkpatrick*, 48 Tenn. 327 (1870); *Redding v. Alsop*, 5 Ky. Op. 413 (1870); *Simmerman v. Songer*, 70 Va. 9 (1877); *Walters v. Ratliff*, 68 Ky. 575 (1869); *Young v. Cavitt*, 54 Tenn. 18 (1871). Manumission cases that involved Liberia between 1865 and 1877 included *Lynch v. Burts*, 48 Tenn. 600 (1870); *Berry v. Hamilton*, 64 Ky. 361 (1866); *Cowan. v. Stamps*, 46 Miss. 435 (1872); *Armstrong v. Pearre*, 47 Tenn. 171 (1869); *Hargroves v. Redd*, 43 Ga. 142 (1871); *Estill v. Deckerd*, 63 Tenn. 497 (1874); *Whedbee v. Shannonhouse*, 62 N.C. 283 (1868); *Todd v. Trott*, 64 N.C. 280 (1870); *Milly v. Harrison*, 47 Tenn. 191 (1869); *Neely v. Merritt*, 72 Ky. 346 (1872); *Redd v. Hargroves*, 40 Ga. 18 (1869); *Shannonhouse v. Whedbee* (1867); *Strong v. Middleton*, 51 Ga. 462 (1874); *Thweatt v. Redd*, 50 Ga. 181 (1873). Manumission cases that were litigated in the post–Reconstruction South included *Allen v. Patton*, 83 Va. 255 (1887); *Garrison v. Garrison*, 10 Ky. Op. 43 (1878); *Hargraves v. Lott*, 67 Ga. 133 (1881); *Holmes v. Holmes*, 86 N.C. 205 (1882); *Webster v. Diamond*, 36 Ark. 532 (1880). Post–Reconstruction

cases involving Liberia included *Jones's Administrator v. Jones's Administrator,* 92 Va. 590 (1896); *Urey's Adm'r v. Urey's Ex'x,* 86 Ky. 354 (1887); *Walker v. Walker,* 66 Ga. 253 (1880).

23. Of the seventy-seven southern state supreme court cases between white and black litigants over bequests left to black southerners between 1865 and 1899, thirty cases involved wills that left bequests to black southerners after the Civil War, and forty-seven cases involved wills written in the antebellum South that emancipated slaves and provided property for their new lives.

24. For analyses of the contemporary law surrounding wills and trusts, see Chalmers, *The Probate Law and Practice in the Courts of Mississippi and Tennessee* (1890); Lewis N. Dembitz, *Kentucky Jurisprudence in Four Books,* book 2 (Louisville, KY: Morton & Company, 1890), 152–388.

25. For instance, the higher-court opinions in the following cases related to Liberia cite precedents involving white litigants and inheritance law/testamentary freedom: *Cowan v. Stamps,* 46 Miss. 435 (1872); *Lynch v. Burts,* 48 Tenn. 600 (1870); *Kelly's Ex'r v. Pettus,* 145 Ky. 250 (1911); *Thweatt v. Redd,* 50 Ga. 181 (1873). Although the vast majority of white testators in such cases were men, occasionally white women also left wills emancipating their slaves. For an example of such a case involving a white female testatrix, see *Berry v. Hamilton,* 64 Ky. 361 (1866).

26. See *Urey's Adm'r v. Urey's Ex'r,* 86 Ky. 354 (1887); *Walker v. Walker,* 66 Ga. 253 (1880). In the case of *Frierson v. Presbyterian Church,* 54 Tenn. 683 (1872), the slaves made it to Liberia, but they were not involved in the later case contesting the will. In the case of *Urey's Adm'r v. Urey's Ex'r,* a group of Liberian residents, the family of Daniel and Phereby Urey, litigated a suit in southern court over a will directing their migration to Liberia. While all of Phereby's children except Esther seem to have lived out their lives in Carysburg, Liberia, they seem to have maintained their contact with the United States. Although Esther Urey had returned to the United States by 1868, she desired to return to Liberia, writing twice to the head of the ACS, William Coppinger, at the end of 1868, and again at the beginning of 1869, asking for a berth on an ACS ship. Esther never seems to have made it back to Liberia, being last known to be living in Memphis, Tennessee. In 1887, almost 30 years after they emigrated to Liberia, their former mistress Perucey Urey brought a court case against these former slaves to gain clear title to land she wanted to sell. In turn, her former slaves in Liberia claimed between $12,000 and $15,000 that their former master left to help maintain them in Liberia, claiming that their former mistress had "failed to send or pay" what was owed them. "Letter from Esther V. Urey to William H. Coppinger," *ACS Records,* Series 1A, Vol. 191, Reel 102, p. 244; "Letter from Esther V. Urey to William H. Coppinger," *ACS Records,* Series 1A, Vol. 194, Reel 103, p. 103; *Urey's Adm'r v. Urey's Ex'r,* 86 Ky. 354 (1887).

27. "Letter from F.W. Urey to Rev. McLain," *ACS Records,* Series 1A, Vol. 190, Reel 101, p. 445.

28. Michael P. Carroll (1841–1920), the son of Henry Carroll, was a white, general practice lawyer born in Maryland who practiced in Burke County, Georgia, and Richmond County, Georgia. He was married to Georgia V. Carroll, a native Georgian woman. He owned no real estate in 1910. He served in the 21st Virginia Company of the Confederate Army, enlisting as a captain. See 1867 Georgia Returns of Qualified Voters; U.S. Civil War Soldier Records and Profiles; Georgia Confederate Pension Applications; Georgia Property Tax Digests; 1910 United States Federal Census, published online by Ancestry, Provo, Utah; Georgia, Deaths Index, 1914–1927. The other lawyers representing William Walker are identified only as "Hook & Webb."

29. *Walker v. Walker,* 66 Ga. 253 (1880).

30. Eric Foner notes that African Americans were generally less interested in emigration to Liberia during Congressional Reconstruction, but interest increased again after Democrats gradually took part control of southern state governments. See Foner, "Rights and the Constitution During the Civil War and Reconstruction," 876.

31. For instance, in the case of *Berry v. Hamilton,* 64 Ky. 361 (1866), the slaves had been denied from becoming parties to the suit in 1860. The case was reopened in 1866 and tried before the Court of Appeals of Kentucky, which ruled in the former slaves' favor. Similarly, the 1868 North Carolina case of *Whedbee v. Shannonhouse,* 62 N.C. 283 (1868) began in 1857 and continued after the war. After its first hearing in 1857, the case was entered into the court records every year thereafter until a jury decision in June 1861. In 1868, the case was

brought again—this time with forty former slaves also becoming litigants to the case. See also *Kelly's Ex'r v. Pettus*, 145 Ky. 250 (1911); *Neely. v. Merritt*, 72 Ky. 346 (1872); *Jones's Administrator v. Jones's Administrator*, 92 Va. 590 (1896); *Estill v. Deckerd*, 63 Tenn. 497 (1874); *Cowan v. Stamps, Exr.*, 46 Miss. 435 (1872); *Todd v. Trott*, 64 N.C. 280 (1870); *Whedbee, Ex'r., v. Shannonhouse*, 62 N.C. 283 (1868). Other African Americans were less successful in becoming parties to such suits. One group of former slaves was not able to take part in the first two trials (in 1869 and 1871) over funds set aside for their settlement in Liberia, although their claims played a central role in the cases. Nevertheless, in these two trials the local and higher courts sided with the black heirs, despite their inability to participate in the court proceedings. Perhaps bolstered by the rulings in their favor, during the third trial in 1873, the surviving twenty-six former slaves mentioned in the will, along with their descendants, contested the white executor's authority to bring the case to court and asserted their own right to serve as parties in the case. Through their lawyer, the former slaves submitted a signed document to the court, declaring that "they, at their own expense imployed counsel" and thus "there was no necessity for the said Executor to employ other counsel." In the end, the former slaves failed to become defendants in the third (and final) trial of the case, but the lower and higher courts again interpreted the will in favor of the newly free black men and women, ruling that the estate should be divided among them. *Redd v. Hargroves*, 40 Ga. 18 (1869); *Hargroves v. Redd*, 43 Ga. 142 (1871); *Thweatt v. Redd*, 50 Ga. 181 (1873).

32. *Cowan v. Stamps*, 46 Miss. 435 (1872).
33. Although the probate court remained in session, the county courthouse in Hernando had been destroyed a year earlier by Union troops. The testimony of Andrew W. Smith, the probate clerk court during the Civil War, is from the trial transcript of *Cowan v. Stamps*, 46 Miss. 435 (1872). In addition to discussing the probate court records, he also stated, "There was times when the Shff [sheriff] and Tax collector were afraid to go to the neighborhood of Cowans and they generally avoided going there owing to Federal raids at other times they could go with Safety." For more on DeSoto County during the Civil War, see "A Brief History of DeSoto County Mississippi," DeSoto County Genealogical Society, 4, http://www.desotocountyms.gov/DocumentCenter/View/56.
34. *Cowan v. Stamps*, 46 Miss. 435 (1872).
35. *Cowan v. Stamps*, 46 Miss. 435 (1872).
36. *Cowan v. Stamps*, 46 Miss. 435 (1872).
37. *Cowan v. Stamps*, 46 Miss. 435 (1872).
38. "A Brief History of DeSoto County Mississippi," 4–5.
39. *Cowan v. Stamps*, 46 Miss. 435 (1872).
40. *Cowan v. Stamps*, 46 Miss. 435 (1872).
41. *Estill v. Deckerd*, 63 Tenn. 497 (1874).
42. Between 1865 and 1899, black litigants received favorable rulings at the appellate level in cases over bequests (against white litigants) in forty-four of seventy-seven cases (57 percent of cases). They gained favorable rulings in thirty-one of fifty cases between 1865 and 1877 (62 percent of suits) and in thirteen of twenty-seven cases between 1878 and 1899 (48 percent of suits). In cases specifically regarding bequests tied to emigration to Liberia, black litigants won eleven of eighteen cases between 1865 and 1899 (61 percent of cases).
43. The white superior court judge was Claiborne Snead (1836–?). He was born in Georgia and enlisted in the Confederate Army as a first lieutenant in April 1861. He served in the 3rd Infantry Regiment Georgia, ending his time in the army as a full lieutenant colonel. As part of this company, he was present at the Confederate surrender at Appomattox on April 9, 1865. He is listed on the 1870 census as a "lawyer" living in Richmond County. In 1880, Snead was 44 years old and listed on the census as an inhabitant of Richmond County and "Judge Supr Court." American Civil War Soldiers, http://www.ancestry.com; 1870 United States Federal Census and 1880 United States Federal Census, published online by Ancestry, Provo, Utah.
44. The only member of the jury whose name is in the court record, the foreman, 50-year-old Amos P. Lambeth, was a white native of Georgia who is listed as a magistrate on the 1880 U.S. Census. 1880 United States Federal Census, published online by Ancestry, Provo, Utah; *Walker v. Walker*, 66 Ga. 253 (1880).

45. There is no opinion in the court report for this case, but the opinion appears in a newspaper article covering the case. See "The Supreme Court," *The Atlanta Constitution*, Dec. 11, 1880, 4; *Walker v. Walker*, 66 Ga. 253 (1880).

46. *Cowan v. Stamps*, 46 Miss. 435 (1872).

47. Mary Frances Berry, *The Pig Farmer's Daughter and Other Tales of American Justice: Episodes of Racism and Sexism in the Courts from 1865 to the Present* (New York: Knopf, 1999), 80–81, 83–84, 87–88; Jonathan Bryant, "Race, Class, and Law in Bourbon Georgia: The Case of David Dickson's Will," *Georgia Historical Quarterly* 71 (Summer 1987): 226–242; Susanna L. Blumenthal, "The Deviance of the Will: Policing the Bounds of Testamentary Freedom in Nineteenth-Century America," *Harvard Law Review* 119, no. 4 (2006): 959–1034; Jones, *Fathers of Conscience*, 2–15, 21–42; Pitts, "I Desire to Give My Black Family Their Freedom," 50–73.

48. Berry, *The Pig Farmer's Daughter*, 80–81, 83–84, 87–88; Bryant, "Race, Class, and Law in Bourbon Georgia," 226–242; Blumenthal, "The Deviance of the Will," 959–1034; Jones, *Fathers of Conscience*, 2–15, 21–42; Pitts, "I Desire to Give My Black Family Their Freedom," 50–73.

49. See, for example, *Urey's Adm'r v. Urey's Ex'r*, 86 Ky. 354 (1887).

50. *Lynch v. Burts*, 48 Tenn. 600 (1870). Other state supreme court judges also expressed similar opinions about the importance of a testator's intention in deciding cases litigated by former slaves who desired bequests without migrating to Liberia in the cases of *Milly v. Harrison*, 47 Tenn. 191 (1869) and *Urey's Adm'r v. Urey's Ex'r*, 86 Ky. 354 (1887).

51. *Cowan v. Stamps*, 46 Miss. 435 (1872).

52. *Cowan v. Stamps*, 46 Miss. 435 (1872).

53. James W. Ely, *The Guardian of Every Other Right: The Constitutional History of Property Rights* (New York: Oxford University Press, 1992), 3, 48, 80–100.

54. *Neely v. Merritt*, 72 Ky. 346 (1872).

Chapter 4

1. Union troops remained in Coweta County until 1872. African American legislator Sam Smith was elected to the Georgia Legislature in the fall of 1870. See *A History of Coweta County, Georgia* (compiled and written by The Newnan-Coweta Historical Society), 17; W.C. Anderson, *A History of Coweta County from 1825 to 1880* (publication date unknown), 63, https://archive.org/details/historyofcowetac00ande.

2. *Smith v. Summerlin*, 48 Ga. 425 (1873).

3. Although a slave had no protection against rape by her own master, very occasionally a slave might have limited legal protection from rape by others. Peter W. Bardaglio explains that "The Bondwomen's status as property meant that the law treated the rape of one man's slave by another white man as a trespass against the slave woman's master rather than a crime against the woman herself." He adds that "The lack of legal protection for African American women in bondage surfaced as an issue in the courtroom only when the assailant was black." For example, it was made a crime in Mississippi for "a black man to rape or attempt to rape a black girl younger than twelve years old." In one exception to this, in 1861, a law against raping a woman, "whether slave or free" was put on the Georgia statute books. Bardaglio, "Rape and the Law in the Old South," 756–760. Other historians have also found that occasionally free black women could bring charges against slaves or other free people of color for rape. Thomas Morris points out cases in Virginia, for instance, in which a slave was hanged for the rape of a free black woman. Victoria Bynum also notes that free black women brought charges of rape in a handful of instances. Morris, *Southern Slavery and the Law*, 305–307; Victoria Bynum, *Unruly Women: The Politics of Social & Sexual Control in the Old South* (Chapel Hill: University of North Carolina Press, 1992), 81–82. For more on sexual violence against slave women and the law, see Gross, *Double Character*, 47–48; Gross, "Pandora's Box," 296–304; Hartman, *Scenes of Subjection*, 79–112; Joshua D. Rothman, *Notorious in the Neighborhood: Sex and Families Across the Color Line in Virginia, 1787–1861* (Chapel Hill: University of North Carolina Press, 2003), 133–163; Melton A. McLaurin, *Celia, A Slave* (Athens: University of Georgia Press, 1991); Hugh P. Williamson, "Document: The State Against Celia, a Slave,"

Midwest Journal 8 (1957): 408–420. For an examination of southern lawyer Thomas R. R. Cobb's thoughts regarding the rape of slaves and the law, see Paul Finkelman, "Thomas R. R. Cobb and the Law of Slavery," *Roger Williams University Law Review* 5, no. 1 (1999): 104–105.

4. A limited number of black women in such situations attempted to defend themselves with violence, but, as the slave Celia discovered, were often executed as a result. See McLaurin, *Celia, A Slave* and Williamson, "Document: The State Against Celia, a Slave." Harriet Jacobs also succeeded in rebuffing her master's advances but only by marrying another white man and then hiding for years in her grandmother's attic. Harriet Jacobs, "Incidents in the Life of a Slave Girl." For more on the consequences of such sexual violence toward the black women involved, see Painter, *Southern History Across the Color Line*, 15–39.

5. The black court clerk and judge in Selma, Alabama, was R. B. Thomas. According to Alston Fitts, Thomas "was born free in Tennessee around 1848, and moved to Selma with his mother after the war. His opponents said Thomas was 'highly educated,' but did not tell where he got his education . . . . Thomas was elected clerk of the criminal court of Dallas County in 1869, and Selma city councilman in 1873. The following year he was nominated for judge of the criminal court and elected without opposition." His term as judge ended in February 1875, when the Democrats won control of the legislature and passed a bill abolishing the criminal court of Selma and then creating a new "criminal court of Selma, whose judge was to be chosen, not by the people of Selma, but by the governor. The new judge was a white Democrat." See Fitts, *Selma*, 79. For more on the history of Selma, Alabama, during the Civil War and Reconstruction see Fitts, *Selma*, 33–83; John Hardy, *Selma: Her Institutions and Her Men* (Selma, AL: Times Book and Job Office, 1879), 53–57. See also the trial transcript of *Potter & Son v. Gracie*, 58 Ala. 303 (1877).

6. *Potter & Son v. Gracie*, 58 Ala. 303 (1877).

7. *Potter & Son v. Gracie*, 58 Ala. 303 (1877).

8. Out of 212 civil appellate cases between white and black litigants in eight appellate courts between 1865 and 1899, 52 suits involved property dealings or transactions unrelated to wills or allegations of fraud. Thirty-one out of 108 civil cases (29 percent) between white and black southerners during Reconstruction involved economic disputes over transactions or property dealings and 21 out of 104 civil cases (20 percent) between white and black southerners during the post–Reconstruction period (1878 to 1899) involved economic disputes over transactions or property dealings. Of these 52 cases, 22 cases (42 percent) involved black and white litigants who had been tied together as masters and slaves and heirs of masters and slaves in the antebellum South. Thirteen cases involving former slaves and former masters took place during Reconstruction (1865–1877) and nine cases took place in the post–Reconstruction period (1878–1899).

9. Between 1865 and 1877, thirty-one cases occurred between white and black litigants in appellate courts that involved disputes over property, transactions or contracts unrelated to wills or allegations of fraud. Of these suits, at least nine cases occurred involving transactions that took place during slavery. Of the thirty-one appellate civil cases between white and black litigants between 1865 and 1877 involving property disputes or transactions (not involving wills or fraud), black litigants won favorable rulings from the higher court in twenty cases (65 percent). Reconstruction-era (1865–1877) cases over postwar transactions or property disputes included *Allen v. Paul*, 65 Va. 332 (1874); *Allum v. Stockbridge*, 67 Tenn. 356 (1875); *Berry v. Berry's Ex'r*, 69 Ky. 594 (1869); *Bugg v. Towner*, 41 Ga. 315 (1870); *Haden v. Ivy*, 51 Ala. 381 (1874); *Godfrey v. Walker*, 42 Ga. 562 (1871); *Buie v. Parker*, 63 N.C. 131 (1869); *Buie v. Carver*, 75 N.C. 559 (1876); *Newman v. Proctor*, 73 Ky. 318 (1874); *Perry v. Tupper*, 74 N.C. 722 (1876); *Boram v. Thweatt*, 45 Ga. 94 (1872); *Dudley v. Abner*, 52 Ala. 572 (1875); *Moore v. Fitzpatrick*, 66 Tenn. 350 (1874); *Hays v. Callaway*, 58 Ga. 288 (1877); *Johnson v. Perkins, Adm'r*, 60 Tenn. 367 (1872); *Thrasher v. Dicken*, 58 Ga. 360 (1877); *Potter v. Gracie* 58 Ala. 303 (1877); *Talley v. Robinson's Assignee*, 63 Va. 888 (1872); *Hunt v. Wing*, 57 Tenn. 139 (1872); *White v. Millbourne*, 31 Ark. 486 (1876); *Smith v. Summerlin*, 48 Ga. 425 (1873); *Jones v. N.C.R. Co.*, 70 N.C. 626 (1874).

10. For more on the changing labor and property laws in the South in the post–Reconstruction period, see Foner, *Reconstruction*, 593–594; Klarman, *From Jim Crow to Civil Rights*, 71–72.

11. Between 1878 and 1899, twenty-one appellate cases between white and black litigants involving property disputes, transactions, and contracts occurred (not involving wills). Not included in this number are property and contract disputes involving allegations of fraud during this period (those are listed under fraud). Of these kinds of suits not involving wills or fraud, nineteen cases were over postwar transactions or property disputes and two cases involved transactions that took place during slavery. Out of twenty-one appellate civil cases between white and black litigants between 1878 and 1899 involving property disputes or transactions (not involving wills), black litigants won favorable rulings from the higher court in twelve cases (57 percent). The cases over transactions during slavery were *Wilson v. James*, 79 N.C. 349 (1878); *Heyer v. Beatty*, 83 N.C. 285 (1880). Cases over postwar transactions or property disputes included *Cunningham's Administrator v. Speagle*, 106 Ky. 278 (1899); *Priebatsch v. Baptist Church*, 66 Miss. 345 (1899); *Pease v. Cooper*, 61 Ga. 626 (1878); *Reynolds v. Reynolds' Ex'r*, 88 Va. 149 (1891); *Sweetser v. Shorter*, 123 Ala. 518 (1898); *Waller v. Johnson*, 82 Va. 966 (1887); *Yon v. Blanchard*, 75 Ga. 519 (1885); *Barge v. Weems*, 109 Ga. 685 (1900); *Capehart v. Stewart*, 80 N.C. 101 (1879); *Davis v. Cross* (1885); *Dowd v. Hurley*, 78 Ky. 260 (1880); *DuBose v. Ball*, 78 Ga. 413 (1887); *Fitzgerald v. Allman*, 82 N.C. 492 (1880); *Kelly v. Carter*, 55 Ark. 112 (1891); *Kilpatrick v. Strozier*, 67 Ga. 247 (1881); *Swann v. Kidd*, 78 Ala. 173 (1884); *Wetter v. Campbell*, 60 Ga. 266 (1878); *Georgia Railroad v. Cox*, 64 Ga. 619 (1880). See Table B.8.

12. *Congressional Globe*, 39 Cong., 1 sess., Dec. 20, 1865, 91, quoted in Amy Dru Stanley, "Conjugal Bonds and Wage Labor: Rights of Contract in the Age of Emancipation," *The Journal of American History* 75, no. 2 (1988): 471. See also Stanley, "Conjugal Bonds and Wage Labor," 474–475.

13. *National Anti-Slavery Standard*, Feb. 24, 1866, quoted in Stanley, "Conjugal Bonds and Wage Labor," 475.

14. Large-scale plantation agriculture, in particular, had historically required an enslaved labor force or laborers without other employment options. See Foner, *Reconstruction*, 128–129, 133–134.

15. For more on white southerners' attitudes toward black labor after the Civil War, see Amy Dru Stanley, *From Bondage to Contract: Wage Labor, Marriage, and the Market in the Age of Slave Emancipation* (Cambridge: Cambridge University Press, 1998), 41–42; Foner, *Reconstruction*, 131–132, 153–175; Litwack, *Been in the Storm So Long*, 336–396, Jacqueline Jones, *Labor of Love, Labor of Sorrow: Black Women, Work, and the Family From Slavery to the Present* (New York: Basic Books, 1985), 45, 52.

16. Jones, *Labor of Love*, 46; Foner, "Rights and the Constitution in Black Life During the Civil War and Reconstruction," 870–871.

17. For instance, one Georgia Freedmen's Bureau agent wrote in November 1867 that in many of the complaints lodged in his office the employer claims that he "must have the sole and exclusive management of the plantation and that the freedman must obey his orders and do all work required." Report of Charles Raushenberg, a Georgia Freedmen's Bureau agent, in November 1867, in Cox and Cox, eds., *Reconstruction, the Negro, and the New South*, 339–347.

18. Foner, *Reconstruction*, 134–135; Stanley, *From Bondage to Contract*, 41–42.

19. Jones, *Labor of Love*, 56.

20. Leslie A. Schwalm, *A Hard Fight For We: Women's Transition From Slavery to Freedom in South Carolina* (Urbana: University of Illinois Press, 1997), 194.

21. Report of Charles Raushenberg, a Georgia Freedmen's Bureau agent, in November 1867, in Cox and Cox, eds., *Reconstruction, the Negro, and the New South*, 339–347. See also Foner, *Reconstruction*, 164–165.

22. Jones, *Labor of Love*, 46, 52; Sharon Ann Holt, *Making Freedom Pay: North Carolina Freedpeople Working for Themselves, 1865–1900* (Athens: University of Georgia Press, 2003), 2–3, 6.

23. *Potter & Son v. Gracie*, 58 Ala. 303 (1877). For more on slave hiring in the antebellum South, see Martin, *Divided Mastery*. For reference to slave hiring in postbellum court cases, see *Jameson v. McCoy*, 52 Tenn. 108 (1871); *Lattimore v. Dixon*, 63 N.C. 356 (1869); *Lattimore v. Dixon*, 65 N.C. 664 (1871).

24. Stanley, *From Bondage to Contract*, 42–43.

25. Stanley, *From Bondage to Contract*, 42–44. Quotes from the free people of New Orleans are from "New Orleans Free People of Color to the Commander of the Department of the Gulf, and the Latter's Reply," in Ira Berlin et al., eds., *Freedom: A Documentary History of Emancipation, 1861–1867* (Cambridge: Cambridge University Press, 1990), series 1, vol. 3, 594–595.
26. Oshinsky, *Worse Than Slavery*, 26–28.
27. Mary Gracie was represented by Sumpter (sometimes spelled Sumter) Lea and Reid & May. Lea's testimony on her behalf, despite having represented the creditors at the time he was testifying about, was one of the issues that the creditors appealed. As an independent Democrat, Sumpter Lea seems to have had ties to both local Republicans and local Democrats. When a Republican took over as mayor from 1873 to 1875, he turned over city government to Sumpter Lea at one point because he was experiencing "serious eye problems." In addition, when voting on convention delegates to write the new state constitution in 1875, the local Republican Party urged Republicans to vote for "independent Democrats" instead of mainstream Democrats. Sumpter Lea was one of the "independent Democrat" delegates from Selma at the constitutional convention that Republicans helped vote in. See Fitt, *Selma*, 82–83; 1870 United States Federal Census, published online by Ancestry, Provo, Utah; *Potter & Son v. Gracie*, 58 Ala. 303 (1877).
28. For examples of cases that cite property or contract suits involving white litigants as precedents, see the state supreme court judges' opinions in *Dudley v. Abner*, 52 Ala. 572 (1875); *Sweetser v. Shorter*, 123 Ala. 518 (1898); *Cunningham's Adm'r v. Speagle*, 106 Ky. 278 (1899). Other judges' opinions did not cite specific precedents, but drew on the opinions of noted legal authorities or established law about these topics. See, for instance, *Yon v. Blanchard*, 75 Ga. 519 (1885).
29. Out the sixty-eight cases between white and black litigants involving economic transactions or property disputes between 1865 and 1899, eleven cases (16 percent) involved economic dealings that took place before or during the Civil War. Reconstruction-era cases over transactions during slavery include *Lattimore v. Dickson*, 63 N.C. 356 (1869); *Lattimore v. Dixon*, 65 N.C. 664 (1871); *Caldwell v. Watson*, 74 N.C. 296 (1876); *Chandler v. Holland*, 61 N.C. 598 (1868); *Noland's Ex'r v. Golden*, 66 Ky. 84 (1867); *Porter v. Blakemore*, 42 Tenn. 556 (1865); *Shelby v. Offutt*, 51 Miss. 128 (1875); *Washington v. Barnes*, 41 Ga. 307 (1870); *Andrews v. Page*, 50 Tenn. 653 (1871).
30. *Nelson v. Nelson*, 7 Ky. Op. 384 (1873).
31. Bristow Bugg testified that he had paid this $75 to a local white man named Walter Towner, with the agreement that Towner would use the money to purchase him, and upon buying him let him earn money to pay off the rest of his purchase price and gain his freedom. *Bugg v. Towner*, 41 Ga. 315 (1870). See also *Wilson v. James*, 79 N.C. 349 (1878).
32. *Smith v. Summerlin*, 48 Ga. 425 (1873); *Pease v. Cooper*, 61 Ga. 626 (1878).
33. In her testimony, Gracie stated that she also agreed to loan Johnston half of the wages he would have paid her to keep house for him in return for interest on this money. *Potter & Son v. Gracie*, 58 Ala. 303 (1877).
34. In many cases, the contracts between white and black southerners were verbal, thus making it more difficult for black laborers to enforce their rights. Goluboff, *The Lost Promise of Civil Rights*, 59. For more about coercive contracts, see also Schwalm, *A Hard Fight For We*, 199–200.
35. *Smith v. Summerlin*, 48 Ga. 425 (1873). See also Stanley, *From Bondage to Contract*, 42–43.
36. *Potter & Son v. Gracie*, 58 Ala. 303 (1877); *Barge v. Weems*, 109 Ga. 685 (1900). See also the case of *Pease v. Cooper*, 61 Ga. 626 (1878), in which a Georgia freedman testified that he had thought his former master intended to "carry out faithfully and comply with his said Contract" to give him a deed to property he had bought "but your Orator has found out that the said [former master] does not."
37. *Pease v. Cooper*, 61 Ga. 626 (1878).
38. *Smith v. Summerlin*, 48 Ga. 425 (1873); *Potter & Son v. Gracie*, 58 Ala. 303 (1877).
39. *Potter & Son v. Gracie*, 58 Ala. 303 (1877).
40. Gross, "Pandora's Box," in *Slavery & The Law*, 316–318; Morris, "Slaves and the Rules of Evidence in Criminal Trials," in *Slavery & The Law*, 209–229.

41. Allegations of sex across the color line often harmed black women more than they did former slaveholders, as a result of their gender and status. This method of attacking black women's reputations remained imbued with white assumptions about black guilt for interracial liaisons. See Gross, *Double Character*, 51, 61; Kirsten Fischer, *Suspect Relations: Sex, Race, and Resistance in Colonial North Carolina* (Ithaca, NY: Cornell University Press, 2002), 134, 141.

42. *Potter & Son v. Gracie*, 58 Ala. 303 (1877). In addition, a black female servant who received money in a will from her white employer found her morality and reputation questioned in a 1903 Virginia case, *Johnston v. Colley and Others*, 101 Va. 414 (1903). Although the black female litigant in the case does not seem to have been a slave for her white employer before the war, as a single woman with two illegitimate children her reputation also came into question. See also the questioning of the morality of the child of a liaison between a former slave and a former slaveholder in *Burdine v. Burdine's Ex'r*, 98 Va. 515 (1900).

43. *Potter & Son v. Gracie*, 58 Ala. 303 (1877). For a more in-depth examination of Gracie's attempts to defend her reputation in this case and a discussion of the way in which her continuing interactions with her former master after the war complicated her attempts to defend herself, see Chapter 5 of Melissa Milewski "From Slave to Litigant: African Americans in Court in the Post-War South, 1865–1920" (PhD dissertation, New York University, 2011).

44. *Lattimore v. Dickson*, 63 N.C. 356 (1869); *Lattimore v. Dixon*, 65 N.C. 664 (1871).

45. *Nelson v. Nelson*, 7 Ky. Op. 384 (1873).

46. *Smith v. Summerlin*, 48 Ga. 425 (1873); *Barge v. Weems*, 109 Ga. 685 (1900).

47. The appellate cases examined do not form a representative sample of how often white and black southerners initiated such cases. However, they do show that whites served as plaintiffs in some of these cases. Of the appellate cases from 1865 to 1877 between black and white southerners over contracts, property, and transactions (not related to wills) examined in this chapter, white southerners served as plaintiffs in 41 percent of cases (fourteen of thirty-four cases) and black southerners served as plaintiffs in 59 percent of cases (twenty of thirty-four cases). Of the appellate cases from 1878 to 1899 examined in this chapter, white southerners served as plaintiffs in 50 percent of the cases (seventeen of thirty-four cases) and black southerners served as plaintiffs in 50 percent of the cases (seventeen of thirty-four cases).

48. *Bugg v. Towner*, 41 Ga. 315 (1870); "Decisions of the Supreme Court of Georgia," *The Atlanta Constitution*, July 20, 1870.

49. These types of cases brought by white plaintiffs include *Sweetser v. Shorter*, 123 Ala. 518 (1898); *Talley v. Robinson's Assignee*, 63 Va. 888 (1872); *Priebatsch v. Baptist Church*, 66 Miss. 345 (1899); *Allen v. Paul*, 65 Va. 332 (1874); *Buie v. Carver*, 75 N.C. 559 (1876); *Kelly v. Carter*, 55 Ark. 112 (1891).

50. *Smith v. Summerlin*, 48 Ga. 425 (1873); *Pease v. Cooper*, 61 Ga. 626 (1878).

51. *Talley v. Robinson's Assignee*, 63 Va. 888 (1872).

52. *Dudley v. Abner*, 52 Ala. 572 (1875). The idea of paternalism, put forward by Eugene Genovese in *Roll, Jordan, Roll*, is now regarded as an ideology that the slave-owning class used to justify and defend slavery. After the Civil War, appeals to this paternalist ideology continued to be found in some whites' attitudes toward African Americans in the courtroom. See Eugene Genovese, *Roll, Jordan, Roll: The World the Slaves Made* (1974; reprinted New York: Vintage Books, 1976); James D. Anderson, "Aunt Jemima in Dialectics: Genovese on Slave Culture," *The Journal of Negro History* 61, no. 1 (1976): 99–114.

53. I infer this also from the way such cases became much less common in southern state supreme courts around the turn of the century, as white southerners gained more power in the US South. After 1900, black southerners could generally bring such cases only if they involved allegations of fraud or if they portrayed themselves as especially ignorant or vulnerable.

54. For a discussion of the different factors used by judges in deciding cases, including the role of personal sentiment, see Karsten, *Heart versus Head*.

55. *Cunningham's Adm'r v. Speagle*, 106 Ky. 278 (1899). See also *Yon v. Blanchard*, 75 Ga. 519 (1885).

56. *Cunningham's Adm'r v. Speagle*, 106 Ky. 278 (1899). For more examples of cases in which judges cited precedents involving white litigants in their opinions, see *Dudley v. Abner*, 52 Ala.

572 (1875); *Sweetser v. Shorter*, 123 Ala. 518 (1898); *Talley v. Robinson's Assignee*, 63 Va. 888 (1872).

57. Of the thirty-one appellate civil cases between white and black litigants between 1865 and 1877 involving property disputes or transactions (not involving fraud or wills), black litigants won favorable rulings from the higher court in twenty cases (65 percent of suits). In thirteen of these cases, the higher court affirmed the lower court's decision in favor of the black litigants, and in seven cases, the higher court overturned the lower court's decision against the black litigants.

58. Out of twenty-one appellate civil cases between white and black litigants between 1878 and 1899 involving property disputes or transactions (not involving fraud or wills), black litigants won favorable rulings from the higher court in twelve cases (57 percent of suits). In ten of these cases, the higher court affirmed the lower court's decision in favor of the black litigants, and in two cases, the higher court overturned the lower court's decision against the black litigants.

59. *Smith v. Summerlin*, 48 Ga. 425 (1873). The case outcome was noted in *The Atlanta Constitution*. See "Decisions of the Supreme Court of Georgia," *The Atlanta Constitution*, April 9, 1873, 2. For more on Judge Robert P. Trippe, see "Appendix," in 112 Ga. Reports, 953–957; *Georgia Biographical Dictionary* (New York: Somerset, 1994), 460.

60. *Pease v. Cooper*, 61 Ga. 626 (1878). For more on Hiram Warner, see Kenneth Coleman and Charles Stephen Gurr, eds., *Dictionary of Georgia Biography*, vol. 2 (Athens: University of Georgia Press, 1983), 1037–1038; "Appendix" in 68 Ga. Reports, 845–855.

61. *Potter v. Gracie*, 58 Ala. 303 (1877). Democrats regained control of the Alabama governorship and legislature in the November 1874 election. See Fitts, *Selma*, 82.

Chapter 5

1. *Barge v. Weems*, 109 Ga. 685 (1900).
2. *Barge v. Weems*, 109 Ga. 685 (1900).
3. *Barge v. Weems*, 109 Ga. 685 (1900).
4. *Barge v. Weems*, 109 Ga. 685 (1900).
5. The City Court of Atlanta was in Fulton County, Georgia. According to the court records, Barge was a "citizen of Fulton County" – as a result it is probable that the land Weems farmed was also in Fulton County. *Barge v. Weems*, 109 Ga. 685 (1900).
6. Woodward, *Origins of the New South*, ix; Henry Grady, *The New South: Writings and Speeches of Henry Grady* (Savannah, GA: Beehive Press, 1971). See also Paul M. Gaston, *The New South Creed: A Study in Southern Mythmaking* (New York: Knopf, 1970).
7. "Articles from the New York *Ledger*, November–December, 1889," in Grady, *The New South*, 120, 123.
8. Woodward, *Origins of the New South*, 126, 132; Ayers, *The Promise of the New South*, 21–22.
9. C. Vann Woodward states that between 1880 and 1890, railroads in the South "increased from 16,605 miles in 1880 to 39,108 in 1890, or 135.5 per cent as compared with the national expansion of 86.5 per cent." From Eleventh Census, 1890, Transportation by Land, Pt. I, 4, 6, cited in Woodward, *Origins of the New South*, 120. "By 1890," Edward Ayers found, "nine of every ten Southerners" now had a railroad running through their county, connecting them with economic centers, consumer goods, and factories. See Ayers, *The Promise of the New South*, 9–13.
10. Ayers, *The Promise of the New South*, 10, 24, 55–56. C. Vann Woodward, however, states that despite this urbanization, the South's urbanization still remained far less than that of the North. See Woodward, *Origins of the New South*, 139.
11. Woodward, *Origins of the New South*, 302–318; Ayers, *The Promise of the New South*, 22.
12. Ayers, *The Promise of the New South*, 9–10; Woodward, *Origins of the New South*, 380–381.
13. This statistic is for the South Atlantic and South Central divisions of the continental United States according to the 1900 US census. The states included in this statistic are Delaware, Maryland, District of Columbia, Virginia, West Virginia, North Carolina, South Carolina, Georgia, Florida, Kentucky, Tennessee, Alabama, Mississippi, Louisiana, Arkansas, Indian Territory, Oklahoma, and Texas. According to the 1900 US census, 2,488,553 people

out of 24,523,527 people in these two divisions lived in cities of more than 25,000 people. "Table 37: Population Living in Cities Within Specified Limits of Size and In Country Districts: 1900" in *Abstract of the Twelfth Census of the United States 1900* (Washington, DC: US Government Printing Office, 1902), 37. See also Woodward, *Origins of the New South*, 139; Ayers, *The Promise of the New South*, 24–25; Philip Alexander Bruce, "Social and Economic Revolution in the Southern States," *Contemporary Review* 78 (1900): 67.

14. W. E. B. Du Bois, *The Souls of Black Folk* (1903; reprinted New York: Dover, 1994), 79, 95–96; Woodward, *Origins of the New South*, 185.

15. "Articles from the New York *Ledger*, November–December, 1889," in Grady, *The New South*, 136.

16. Joseph C. G. Kennedy, *Population of The United States in 1860; Compiled from the Original Returns of the Eighth Census* (Washington, DC: US Government Printing Office, 1864), ix–x; "Table 41: Population Classified By Sex and Race: 1900," in *Abstract of the Twelfth Census of the United States 1900* (Washington: US Government Printing Office, 1902), 43. According to the 1900 US census, there were approximately 16,521,970 white people in the Southern Atlantic and Southern Central divisions, and approximately 7,922,969 "negro" people in these two divisions.

17. Ayers, *The Promise of the New South*, 208–210, 513–514. See also Leon F. Litwack, *Trouble in Mind: Black Southerners in the Age of Jim Crow*, 1st ed. (New York: Knopf, 1998), 120–122.

18. "Table 57: Illiterate Population At Least 10 Years of Age Classified By Sex, And By Race and Nativity: 1900," in *Abstract of the Twelfth Census of the United States 1900* (Washington, DC: US Government Printing Office, 1902), 75.

19. Du Bois, *The Souls of Black Folk*, 50. For two other contemporary accounts of this, see A South Carolinian, "South Carolina Morals," *The Atlantic Monthly*, April 1877, 470; Ray Stannard Baker, *Following the Color Line: An Account of Negro Citizenship in the American Democracy* (New York: Doubleday, Page & Company, 1908), 44, http://www.gutenberg.org/files/34847/34847-h/34847-h.htm. See also Ayers, *The Promise of the New South*, 427; Howard Rabinowitz, *Race Relations in the Urban South, 1865–1890* (Urbana: University of Illinois Press, 1980), 333–339.

20. Fraud was especially prevalent in states such as Louisiana, South Carolina, and Mississippi, but also occurred in a more uneven manner throughout the US South during this time. See Kousser, *The Shaping of Southern Politics*, 14, 45–47; J. Morgan Kousser, *Colorblind Injustice: Minority Voting Rights and the Undoing of the Second Reconstruction* (Chapel Hill: University of North Carolina Press, 1999), 23–25. Representative George White blamed the desire for white political power for disfranchisement. He said, "There never has been, nor ever will be, any negro domination in [North Carolina], and no one knows it any better than the Democratic party. It is a convenient howl, however, often resorted to in order to consummate a diabolical purpose by scaring the weak and gullible whites into support of measures and men suitable to the demagogue and the ambitious office seeker, whose craving for office overshadows and puts to flight all other considerations, fair or unfair." See "Representative George White of North Carolina Delivers His Final Speech on the Floor of Congress, 1901," in Thomas C. Holt and Elsa Barkley Brown, eds., *Major Problems in African-American History: Documents and Essays*, vol. 2 (Boston: Houghton Mifflin, 2000), 97–98. White's speech is excerpted from *Congressional Record*, 56th Cong., 2nd sess., pt. 2, Jan. 29, 1901, 1635–1636, 1638.

21. Thomas E. Watson, "The Negro Question in the South," in *Arena*, VI (1892), 548. See also Woodward, *Origins of the New South*, 255–258; C. Vann Woodward, *Thomas Watson: Agrarian Rebel* (1938; reprinted New York: Oxford University Press, 1987); Perman, *Struggle for Mastery*, 24–28.

22. Samuel L. Webb, "The Populist Revolt in Alabama: Prelude to Disfranchisement," in Bailey Thompson, ed., *A Century of Controversy: Constitutional Reform in Alabama* (Tuscaloosa: University of Alabama Press, 2002), 1–14; Ayers, *The Promise of the New South*, 266–269.

23. Ayers, *The Promise of the New South*, 147, quoting William Charles Sallis, "The Color Line in Mississippi Politics, 1865–1915" (PhD dissertation, University of Kentucky, 1967), 281–282. See also "Richmond Times," *Richmond Planet*, Dec. 10, 1898, quoted in Perman, *Struggle for*

Mastery, 15; Woodward, *Origins of the New South*, 326–327; Kousser, *The Shaping of Southern Politics*, 46–47.

24. For more on politicians' use of rape for political ends at this time, see Jane Dailey, *The Age of Jim Crow: A Norton Casebook in History* (New York: Norton, 2009), xxii–xxiv; Glenda Gilmore, *Gender and Jim Crow: Women and the Politics of White Supremacy in North Carolina, 1896–1920* (Chapel Hill: University of North Carolina Press, 1996), 82–88; Hodes, *White Women, Black Men*, 176–208. For a statistical analysis of the most common charges against those who were lynched between 1882 and 1930, separated by race and gender, see Amy Kate Bailey and Stewart E. Tolnay, *Lynched: The Victims of Southern Mob Violence* (Chapel Hill: University of North Carolina Press, 2015), 190–192. Bailey and Tolnay found that the most common reason for rape during this period was charges of violence; the second most common reason was charges of sexual violence. For more on lynching during this period, see also Brundage, *Lynching in the New South*, 68; Griffin, *Women Lynched*, 202, no.21; *Thirty Years of Lynching in the United States*; Wood, *Lynching and Spectacle*, 5–8; Crystal N. Feimster, *Southern Horrors: Women and the Politics of Rape and Lynching* (Cambridge, MA: Harvard University Press, 2009); W. E. B. Du Bois, "Rape," *The Crisis: A Record of the Darker Races* 18 (May 1919): 12. For lynching statistics by year and state, see "Lynchings: By Year and Race," University of Missouri Kansas City Law School, http://law2.umkc.edu/faculty/projects/ftrials/shipp/lynchingyear.html and http://law2.umkc.edu/faculty/projects/ftrials/shipp/lynchingsstate.html. Statistics are provided by the Tuskegee Institute Archives.

25. In addition, the 14th Amendment to the US Constitution ordered a reduction in a state's representation in Congress if the right to vote was denied to any male citizens in a state "except for participation in rebellion, or other crime." U.S. Const. amend. XIV; U.S. Const. amend. XV; Kousser, *The Shaping of Southern Politics*, 45; Woodward, *Origins of the New South*, 330–331.

26. J. Morgan Kousser found that seven ex–Confederate states put literacy requirements into place (in all but two states, an illiterate person could still qualify to vote, however, if they owned enough property). Kousser, *The Shaping of Southern Politics*, 67–58. Edward Ayers explains that by 1908, "every state of the former Confederacy had instituted a poll tax." Ayers, *The Promise of the New South*, 309. Some states required those registering to also pay the poll taxes that they owed from two or more previous elections to be able to vote. C. Vann Woodward states that the poll tax "was cumulative for the entire period of liability in two states, for three years in one, and two in another." Woodward, *Origins of the New South*, 321–331, 334–336 (quote is from p. 336). J. Morgan Kousser examines more disfranchising methods in Kousser, *The Shaping of Southern Politics*, 47–81.

27. *Ratliff v. Beale*, 74 Miss. 247 (1896).

28. Many of the loopholes were temporary and allowed whites not meeting the voting requirements to register only during a finite period of time. Kousser, *The Shaping of Southern Politics*, 59–60; Woodward, *Origins of the New South*, 335. For an example of a grandfather clause, see "Constitution of the State of Louisiana, Adopted May 12, 1898," in Walter L. Fleming, ed., *Documentary History of Reconstruction*, vol. 2 (Cleveland, OH: Arthur H. Clark Company, 1906), 451–453.

29. C. Vann Woodward notes that "all southern states that made new constitutions except Alabama avoided ratification by popular vote." Woodward, *Origins of the New South*, 321–323, 341 (quote is from p. 341); Kousser, *The Shaping of Southern Politics*, 57–58.

30. J. Morgan Kousser calculates that "in the early twentieth century, there was a decrease of 47 percent in the average percentage of adult males for the Democrats, but a 62 percent drop in the already lower opposition totals." Kousser, *The Shaping of Southern Politics*, 59–62, 224–226 (quote is from p. 224); Blackmon, *Slavery By Another Name*, 121; Suggs, *Whispered Consolations*, 252; Ayers, *The Promise of the New South*, 410. For an in-depth examination of how disfranchisement took place in Alabama, see Harvey H. Jackson III, "White Supremacy Triumphant: Democracy Undone," in Bailey Thompson, ed., *A Century of Controversy: Constitutional Reform in Alabama* (Tuscaloosa: University of Alabama Press, 2002), 17–33, and Wayne Flint, "A Tragic Century: The Aftermath of the 1901 Constitution," in Bailey Thompson, ed., *A Century of Controversy: Constitutional Reform in Alabama* (Tuscaloosa: University of Alabama Press, 2002), 34–49.

31. The exact extent of segregation before the end of the nineteenth century and how formalized it was in the law has been debated by many historians, most notably by C. Vann Woodward in *The Strange Career of Jim Crow* (New York: Oxford University Press, 1955; commemorative edition 2002), 22–109. For an examination of the history and current state of this debate, see J. Morgan Kousser, "Strange Career and the Need for a Second Reconstruction of the History of Race Relations," in Raymond Arsenault and Orville Vernon Burton, eds., *Dixie Redux: Essays in Honor of Sheldon Hackney* (Montgomery, AL: NewSouth Books, 2013), 398–416. For a contemporary account of the school and transportation segregation laws put into place before 1890 in the South, see Stephenson, *Race Distinctions in American Law*, 170–188, 207–221.

32. Ayers, *The Promise of the New South*, 145.

33. Tennessee led the way in separating railroad passengers in 1881. For more on increasing segregation during this time, see Woodward, *Strange Career*, 97–109; Ayers, *The Promise of the New South*, 136–49; Perman, *Struggle for Mastery*, 245–269; Kelley, *Right to Ride*; Jerrold M. Packard, *American Nightmare: The History of Jim Crow* (New York: St. Martin's, 2002), 88–94; Dailey, *The Age of Jim Crow*, xiii-xiv. For a contemporary examination of segregation at the beginning of the twentieth century, and the laws governing it, see Stephenson, *Race Distinctions in American Law*, 170–199, 217–233 (a listing of the years that states passed laws separating passengers on railroads is on p. 216). Stephenson notes that although the laws requiring segregation of streetcars generally came at the beginning of the twentieth century, Georgia passed such a law along with its railroad segregation legislation in 1891 (Stephenson, *Race Distinctions in American Law*, 227–228).

34. For earlier versions of this sentiment, see "Editorial Correspondence," *The Daily Telegraph* (Macon, GA), Oct. 25, 1865; "Negro Testimony," *The Louisville Daily Courier*, Aug. 27, 1867, 1.

35. Davis, *Mississippi Negro Lore* (1914), 21–22.

36. Stephenson, *Race Distinctions in American Law*, 253–272 (quote is from pp. 253–254); Kennedy, *Race, Crime, and the Law*, 172–173. For more on Gilbert Stephenson, see "Gilbert Thomas Stephenson, 1884–1972," Documenting the American South, http://docsouth.unc.edu/wwi/stephenson/bio.html.

37. Stephenson, *Race Distinctions in American Law*, 258–272 (quotes from p. 258); Kennedy, *Race, Crime, and the Law*, 172–173.

38. "A Court's Decision," *Richmond Planet*, Oct. 15, 1898; "The Negro Before the Law," *The Savannah Tribune*, Nov. 20, 1920, 4; "Speedy Trials and Justice," *The Savannah Tribune*, Nov. 29, 1919, 4. A search for articles with negative opinions about the courts in black newspapers in the South between 1900 and 1920 yields many articles. A few others include "Three Men Killed in Court," *Richmond Planet*, Jan. 13, 1900, 8; "Columbia, S.C., Jan. 10," *The National Pilot* (Petersburg, VA), Feb. 1, 1900, 4; "Washington News," *The Savannah Tribune*, June 4, 1910, 1; "Negroes Barred From School, the Color Line is Drawn By Court in Washington," *The Savannah Tribune*, Dec. 31, 1910, 6; "The Negro in Court," *The Savannah Tribune*, Dec. 7, 1918, 4; "The Recorder," *The Savannah Tribune*, Feb. 1, 1919, 4.

39. Du Bois, *The Souls of Black Folk*, 108. See also W. E. B. Du Bois, "Race Relations in the United States, 1917–1947," *Phylon* 9, no. 3 (1948): 237.

40. Wilford H. Smith, "The Negro and the Law," in Booker T. Washington, ed., *The Negro Problem: A Series of Articles by Representative American Negroes of To-day* (New York: James Pott, 1903), 144.

41. White, *American Negro Folk-Songs*, 382, and Russell Ames, "Protest and Irony in Negro Folksong," *Science and Society* 14 (1950): 210, both quoted in Lawrence W. Levine, *Black Culture and Black Consciousness: Afro-American Folk Thought From Slavery to Freedom* (New York: Oxford University Press, 1977), 251. See also Sarah Haley's discussion of black women's use of blues music as "sonic sabotage" to protest their treatment in the criminal justice system. Haley, *No Mercy Here*, 212–246.

42. For more on black convict labor in the "New South," see Blackmon, *Slavery By Another Name*; McMillen, *Dark Journey*; LeFlouria, *Chained in Silence*, 61–139; Ayers, *The Promise of the New South*, 154; Oshinsky, *"Worse Than Slavery,"* 60.

43. Black litigants won thirty-five of ninety-three appeals (38 percent of appeals) in criminal cases appealed to the Alabama and Georgia State Supreme Courts between 1900 and 1920. See Table B.25 (tables that are prefaced with "B" are given in Appendix B).

44. Oshinsky, *"Worse Than Slavery,"* 60–63, 95. See also the graph showing the increase in the black prison population in four states in the South from 1865 to 1900 in Ayers, *Vengeance & Justice,* 170.

45. "The Kentucky Jim Crow Law," *Richmond Planet,* June 9, 1894; "Governor and Judges," *St. Louis Clarion,* Dec. 18, 1920, 2. One article that both praised the courts in general and condemned a particular decision was "Savannah Justice," *The Savannah Tribune,* Nov. 2, 1918, 4. A search for such articles in black newspapers in the South between 1900 and 1920 yields many articles. A few others include "A New Dawning," *The Savannah Tribune,* April 28, 1900, 2; "A Ray of Light in the Blackness of Our Night," *The Savannah Tribune,* Feb. 24, 1900, 2; "The Negro's Right to Sit on Grand Juries Vindicated By the United States Supreme Court," *Rising Son* (Kansas City, MO), Feb. 12, 1904; "Law Knows No Color," *The Savannah Tribune,* April 9, 1910, 4; "N.A.A.C.P Announces Victory Supreme Court of Arkansas Reverses Decision of Lower Court," *The Savannah Tribune,* Dec. 18, 1920, 1.

46. The 23 civil cases explicitly over racial justice between black and white litigants in the eight state supreme courts examined between 1900 and 1920 were 10 percent of the total of 220 such civil cases heard by these courts during this time. See Table B.9. For examples of such cases over racial justice, see, for instance, *Lowery v. Board of Graded School Trustees,* 140 N.C. 33 (1905); *McFarland v. Goins,* 96 Miss. 67 (1909); *Glover v. City of Atlanta,* 148 Ga. 285 (1918); *Harden v. City of Atlanta,* 147 Ga. 248 (1917); *Carey v. City of Atlanta,* 143 Ga. 192 (1915); *Hopkins and Others v. City of Richmond,* and *Coleman v. Town of Ashland,* 117 Va. 692 (1915); *Board of Trustees of the Graded Free Colored Common Schools of Mayfield, Ky. v. Board of Trustees of the Graded Free White Common Schools of Mayfield,* 181 Ky. 810 (1918); *Board of Trustees of the Graded Free Colored Common School of Mayfield, Kentucky v. Board of Trustees of the Graded White Common School of Mayfield, Kentucky,* 181 Ky. 303 (1918); *Trustees of Graded Free Colored Common Schools of the City of Mayfield, Kentucky v. Trustees of the Graded Free White Common Schools of the City of Mayfield, Kentucky,* 180 Ky. 574 (1918); *Harris v. City of Louisville. Buchanan v. Warley,* 165 Ky. 559 (1915); *Thornton v. White,* 162 Ky. 796 (1915); *Peoples Pleasure Park Co. v. Rohleder,* 109 Va. 439 (1909); *Peoples Pleasure Park Co. v. Rohleder,* 109 Va. 439 (1908); *Hooker v. Greenville,* 130 N.C. 472 (1902); *Hickman College v. Trustees Colored Common School Dist,* 111 Ky. 944 (1901); *Crosby v. Mayfield,* 133 Ky. 215 (1909); *Board of Education v. Earlington Graded School,* 171 Ky. 125 (1916); *Moss v. Mayfield,* 186 Ky. 330 (1919); *Epps v. Thomas,* 131 Ga. 64 (1908); *Illinois Central Railroad Company v. Samuel Dunnigan,* 95 Miss. 749 (1909). For examples of civil cases over racial justice backed by national organizations, see the 1901 to 1904 litigation in the Louisiana case of *Ryanes v. Gleason,* backed by the Afro-American Council, and the Virginia civil case brought by Barbara Pope in 1906 challenging her fine in a criminal case over transportation segregation that was backed by the Niagara Movement. See Carle, *Defining the Struggle,* 126–128, 205–206.

47. According to Goins's appeal, such a tax to pay for a school that "only children of the white race can attend" violated the 14th Amendment of the US Constitution and "[abridged] the privileges . . . of the negro citizens of Jasper county." *McFarland v. Goins,* 96 Miss. 67 (1909). Other racial discrimination cases that were heard before state supreme courts in the eight states examined between 1900 and 1920 that involved education included *Lowery v. Board of Graded School Trustees,* 140 N.C. 33 (1905); *Board of Trustees of the Graded Free Colored Common Schools of Mayfield, Ky. v. Board of Trustees of the Graded Free White Common Schools of Mayfield,* 181 Ky. 810 (1918); *Board of Trustees of the Graded Free Colored Common School of Mayfield, Kentucky v. Board of Trustees of the Graded White Common School of Mayfield, Kentucky,* 181 Ky. 303 (1918); *Trustees of Graded Free Colored Common Schools of the City of Mayfield, Kentucky v. Trustees of the Graded Free White Common Schools of the City of Mayfield, Kentucky,* 180 Ky. 574 (1918); *Hickman College v. Trustees Colored Common School Dist,* 111 Ky. 944 (1901); *Board of Education v. Earlington Graded School,* 171 Ky. 125 (1916).

48. John Coleman's suit also argued that the Ashland Town Council did not have the authority to pass such an ordinance. *Hopkins and Others v. City of Richmond,* and *Coleman v. Town of*

Ashland, 117 Va. 692 (1915). For other racial discrimination cases appealed to southern state appellate courts between 1900 and 1920 involving residential segregation, see *Glover v. City of Atlanta*, 148 Ga. 285 (1918); *Harden v. City of Atlanta*, 147 Ga. 248 (1917); *Carey v. City of Atlanta*, 143 Ga. 192 (1915); *Harris v. City of Louisville. Buchanan v. Warley*, 165 Ky. 559 (1915); *Peoples Pleasure Park Co. v. Rohleder*, 109 Va. 439 (1909); *Peoples Pleasure Park Co. v. Rohleder*, 109 Va. 439 (1908).

49. Of the twenty-three racial discrimination cases that occurred between 1900 and 1920 in the eight appellate courts examined, black litigants won ten cases at the appellate level (43 percent) and lost thirteen cases (57 percent) at the appellate level.

50. In general, black litigants had much more success challenging segregation in the Midwest, where Republicans still wielded political power and black men continued to exercise their right to vote. J. Morgan Kousser shows that of the 105 cases litigated over racial discrimination in schools between 1834 and 1916, 60 suits took place in the Midwest (IA, IL, IN, KS, MI, OH). During the same period, he found 12 such suits in the South (AR, GA, LA, MS, NC) and 14 such suits in border states (DC, KY, MO, OK, WV). Kousser also found that black litigants were most likely to win such suits in the Midwest: "In Iowa, Illinois, Indiana, Kansas, Michigan, and Ohio, African-Americans won 62 percent of the cases that they brought, while in every other section, they prevailed in at most 50 percent of the cases." See Kousser, "Why Were There So Many Legal Cases on School Integration in Nineteenth-Century America?," 13–20.

51. According to the Mississippi supreme court's *McFarland v. Goins* decision, the town "was acting clearly within its powers, when it undertook to preserve good order within its confines by the passage of this ordinance." *McFarland v. Goins*, 96 Miss. 67 (1909). In the *Hopkins* suit, on the question of the 14th Amendment, the opinion was extraordinarily confusing: "The Constitution forbids the abridging of the privileges of a citizen of the United States, but does not forbid the State from abridging the privileges of its own citizens." *Hopkins and Others v. City of Richmond*, and *Coleman v. Town of Ashland*, 117 Va. 692 (1915).

52. Historian R. Volney Riser explains that Giles "had kept his poll taxes current, and did not suffer from any of the character disqualifications prescribed by the 1901 constitution" but as an independent, black Republican, "he was also the type of man they most feared." For an in-depth discussion of antidisfranchisement litigation and the Giles cases, see R. Volney Riser, *Defying Disfranchisement*, 150–240 (the quote is from p. 150).

53. Riser explains that "no actual copy of the CMSAA's initial circular survives," but the text survives in the Montgomery Journal which "intercepted a copy and printed it verbatim, along with Giles' accompanying cover letter." Riser, *Defying Disfranchisement*, 151–152.

54. The state supreme court cases included *Ex parte Giles*, 133 Ala. 211 (1901); *Giles v. Teasley et al. Board of Registrars*, 136 Ala. 228 (1902); and *Giles v. Teasley et al., Board of Registrars*, 136 Ala. 164 (1902). The US Supreme Court decisions were *Giles v. Harris*, 189 U.S. 475 (1903); *Rogers v. Alabama*, 192 U.S. 226 (1904); and *Giles v. Teasley*, 193 U.S. 146 (1904). For a further discussion of this litigation and the US Supreme Court opinions, see Riser, *Defying Disfranchisement*, 150–240. Riser explains that the one disfranchisement case that Smith won at this time, the criminal case *Rogers v. Alabama*, "brought positive change to the state's juries." (Riser, *Defying Disfranchisement*, 247). Some African Americans heralded *Rogers v. Alabama* as a success: See, for instance, "The Negro's Right to Sit on Grand Juries Vindicated By the United States Supreme Court," *Rising Son* (Kansas City, MO), Feb. 12, 1904.

55. See, for instance, the US Supreme Court cases of *Cumming v. Richmond Board of Education*, 175 U.S. 528 (1899), and *Berea College v. Kentucky*, 211 U.S. 45 (1908). In *Cumming*, several black litigants brought a civil case protesting having to pay taxes to fund a Georgia county's school system after the county closed their only black public high school but left the county's white schools intact. The case was appealed from state courts to the nation's highest court, but ended in a US Supreme Court decision in 1899 that declared that the federal government did not have the authority to interfere in a state's schools, "except in the case of a clear and unmistakable disregard of rights secured by the supreme law of the land." According to the US Supreme Court, segregated and unequal education was not such a "disregard for rights." See *Cumming v. Richmond County Board of Education* (1899); J. Morgan Kousser, "*Cumming v. Richmond County*," in *Oxford Companion to the Supreme Court of the United States*

(New York: Oxford University Press, 1992). *Berea College v. Kentucky* challenged a Kentucky law requiring segregation at all private and public colleges: It resulted in a US Supreme Court decision in 1908 upholding segregation in education. The US Supreme Court decision of *Berea College v. Kentucky* was an appeal from the Supreme Court of Kentucky criminal case, *Berea College v. Commonwealth*, 123 Ky. 209 (1906). See also Klarman, *From Jim Crow to Civil Rights*, 23–28.

56. *Plessy v. Ferguson*, 163 U.S. 537 (1896); Lofgren, *The Plessy Case*, 28–60; Thomas J. Davis, "Race Identity, and the Law: Plessy v. Ferguson," in Annette Gordon-Reed, ed., *Race on Trial: Law and Justice in American History* (Oxford: Oxford University Press, 2002), 61–76; Elliott, *Color-Blind Justice*; Rebecca J. Scott, "The Atlantic World and the Road to 'Plessy v. Ferguson,' *The Journal of American History* 94, no. 3 (2007): 726–733; Keith Weldon Medley, *We as Freemen: Plessy v. Ferguson* (Gretna, LA: Pelican, 2003); Williamjames Hull Hoffer, *Plessy v. Ferguson: Race and Inequality in Jim Crow America* (Lawrence: University Press of Kansas, 2012).

57. *Plessy v. Ferguson*, 163 U.S. 537 (1896); Davis, "Race Identity and the Law," 72–74; Klarman, *From Jim Crow to Civil Rights*, 17–23, 48–52; Riegel, "The Persistent Career of Jim Crow," 17–40; Medley, *We as Freemen: Plessy v. Ferguson*; Lofgren, *The Plessy Case*, 148–195.

58. See, for instance, *Williams v. Mississippi*, 170 U.S. 213 (1898), which upheld disfranchisement in Mississippi.

59. Out of the 210 total civil cases between white and black litigants from 1865 to 1899, 108 involved former masters and former slaves (51 percent of suits).

60. *Barge v. Weems*, 109 Ga. 685 (1900).

61. *Barge v. Weems*, 109 Ga. 685 (1900).

62. Of 220 total cases between black and white litigants in eight southern states between 1900 and 1920, 63 cases involved fraud (29 percent of suits) and 97 involved personal injury (44 percent of suits). Cases involving fraud or personal injury therefore made up 160 of the 220 total cases, or a combined 73 percent of all cases involving black litigants between 1900 and 1920. See Table B.9.

63. As US society shifted, shifts would also occur in state supreme courts' overall caseloads. One study found that during the first half of the twentieth century, state supreme courts would begin to hear more cases not directly dealing with the market, including a greater proportion of suits involving public law, personal injury and criminal cases. The same study found that between 1905 and 1935, 19 percent of a sampling of cases from the sixteen state supreme courts involved debt collection, 16 percent of cases made claims of personal injury, 15 percent of cases took place over property, 12 percent were criminal cases, and 7 percent of cases involved inheritance and estates. These trends took place in appellate courts throughout the nation—in the northern, western, and southern state supreme courts sampled. Kagan, "The Business of State Supreme Courts," 132–143.

64. Out of a total of 160 fraud and personal injury cases between black and white litigants from 1900 to 1920 in the eight state supreme courts examined, 73 cases (46 percent of suits) involved black female litigants.

65. John W. Smith, *A Treatise on The Law of Frauds and The Statute of Frauds* (Indianapolis, IN: Bobbs-Merrill Company, 1907); Henry Campbell Black, *A Treatise on the Rescission of Contracts and Cancellation of Written Instruments*, vol. 1 (Kansas City, MO: Vernon Law Book Company, 1916); Causten Browne, *A Treatise on the Construction of the Statute of Frauds* (Boston: Little, Brown, and Company, 1895).

66. Mitchell is described in the Supreme Court of North Carolina's opinion as "a deaf and dumb negro man." Although the lower court ruled in favor of Mitchell's personal injury suit, the Supreme Court of North Carolina reversed the lower court's decision. *Mitchell v. Seaboard*, 153 N.C. 116 (1910). See also Archibald Robinson Watson, *A Treatise on the Law of Damages for Personal Injuries, Embracing a Consideration of the Principles Regulating the Primary Question of Liability, As Well as the Measure and Elements of Recovery After Liability Established* (Charlottesville, VA: Michie Company, 1901); John L. Hopkins, *The Law of Personal Injuries and Incidentally Damage to Property by Railway-Trains* (Atlanta, GA: Foote & Davies Company, 1902); John L. Hopkins, *The Law of Personal Injuries and Incidentally Damage to Property by Railway-Trains* (Atlanta, GA: Harrison Company, 1912). In addition, see statutes

on fraud during this time, such as "Statute of Frauds," in *Park's Annotated Code of The State of Georgia*, vol. 2 (Atlanta, GA: Harrison Company, 1918), 1617–1631.

67. For an examination of the projection of antebellum ideas about slaves on twentieth-century African Americans, see Micki McElya, *Clinging to Mammy: The Faithful Slave in Twentieth-Century America* (Cambridge, MA: Harvard University Press, 2007). For an analysis of the Lost Cause as expressed in a cult of memory and reunion with the North, see David Blight, *Race and Reunion: The Civil War in American Memory* (Cambridge, MA: Belknap Press of Harvard University Press, 2001); W. Fitzhugh Brundage, "White Women and the Politics of Historical Memory in the New South, 1880–1920," in *Jumpin' Jim Crow*, 115–139. For an examination of the impact of memory on Alabama supreme court judges in the Reconstruction and post–Reconstruction periods, see Glory McLaughlin, "A 'Mixture of Race and Reform': The Memory of the Civil War in the Alabama Legal Mind," *Alabama Law Review* 56 (Fall 2004): 285–309; Royal Dumas, "The Muddled Mettle of Jurisprudence: Race and Procedure in Alabama's Appellate Courts, 1901–1930," *Alabama Law Review* 58 (2006): 417–442. In her examination of black women in the Georgia criminal justice system, Sarah Haley also documents the advocates of black women presenting them as particularly ignorant in clemency petitions, which were then approved by white clemency boards. See Haley, *No Mercy Here*, 17–21.

68. Black litigants served as plaintiffs during Reconstruction (1865–1877) in 69 of 108 civil appellate cases (64 percent of suits). In the post–Reconstruction period (1878–1899), they were plaintiffs in 76 of 104 such cases (73 percent of suits). See Table B.14.

69. Between 1900 and 1920, black southerners were plaintiffs in 184 of 220 cases (84 percent of suits). See Table B.14. In civil appellate cases involving fraud and personal injury between 1900 and 1920, the black litigants were the plaintiffs in 143 of 160 cases (89 percent of suits).

70. Although 67 percent of suits took place between former slaves and their former masters or their heirs between 1865 and 1877 and 35 percent of suits took place between former slaves and their former masters or their heirs between 1878 and 1899, between 1900 and 1920, only 4 percent of suits took places between parties who had a relationship during slavery. See Table B.11.

71. In this suit, a young African American woman had inherited a piece of land in Little Rock. The owners' agent allegedly misrepresented the value of the land and she sold it for $300, although witnesses testified that the true value was between $900 and $2,500. When she discovered the land's true value, she filed an action to set the deed aside. *Storthz v. Williams*, 86 Ark. 460 (1908).

72. *Sutton v. Dunn*, 176 N.C. 202 (1918).

73. See Nan Elizabeth Woodruff, *American Congo: The African American Freedom Struggle in the Delta* (Cambridge, MA: Harvard University Press, 2003), 15–18.

74. As this article examines only lower-court cases that were accepted by a higher court on appeal, there is not a representative sample to judge how often black litigants won their cases in lower courts. Of the lower-court cases appealed to the higher court, black litigants won 129 of 220 cases at the lower-court level (59 percent of suits) between 1900 and 1920. In 23 percent of the cases they won at the local level (32 of 138 cases), a judge had made the ruling, and in 65 percent of the cases they won (90 of 138 cases), juries had made the decision. The cases not accounted for here were decided by both judges and juries at the lower-court level or it could not be determined what body made the lower-court judgment. Judges still influenced jury trials in a number of cases, even directing juries to decide for or against a black litigant. See Tables B.17 and B.18.

75. Of the 220 suits involving white and black litigants between 1900 and 1920, black litigants won 138 cases (63 percent of suits).

Chapter 6

1. Lurena Roebuck inherited the land sometime between June 1900 and 1905. Jackson Ellard, her father, was still living at the time of the June 1900 US census. William Terry, her lawyer, testified in 1906 that Roebuck had inherited the land several years earlier. The year of 1902, therefore, is my best guess of when she might have inherited it. See 1900 United States

Federal Census, published online by Ancestry, Provo, Utah; *Leonard v. Roebuck*, 152 Ala. 312 (1907). For more on Jefferson County during this period, see Jefferson County Commission, *Your County Commission Presents Important Facts and History of Jefferson County, Alabama* (Birmingham, AL: The Commission, 1966).

2. Legal scholar Lawrence Friedman explains that tax titles "came about when local government sold off property for delinquent taxes and issued a deed to the purchaser." According to Friedman, tax titles were "notoriously weak" and often looked upon with suspicion. However, they were a popular means that white people (and more rarely, other black people) used to deprive black landowners of their property. Lawrence M. Friedman, *A History of American Law* (New York: Simon & Schuster, 2005), 324; Raleigh Colston Minor, "Title Under Delinquent Tax Sales," in *The Law of Real Property* (Charlottesville, VA: Anderson Bros, Publishers, University of Virginia, 1908), 1515–1549; *Leonard v. Roebuck*, 152 Ala. 312 (1907); 1900 United States Federal Census and 1910 United States Federal Census, published online by Ancestry, Provo, Utah.

3. *Leonard v. Roebuck,* 152 Ala. 312 (1907).

4. Du Bois, *The Souls of Black Folk*, 95–96.

5. Powdermaker's remarks are based on her ethnographic research in Mississippi between 1932 and 1934. See Hortense Powdermaker, *After Freedom: A Cultural Study in the Deep South* (New York: Viking, 1939), 86–87; Oshinsky, "*Worse Than Slavery*," 118–120.

6. Holt, *Making Freedom Pay*, 1–4, 64. Holt states that the agricultural census provides evidence that "that a family could produce thirty to fifty pounds of butter in a year from one milk cow." See Holt, *Making Freedom Pay*, 64, citing 10th Census of Agriculture, 1880, Granville County, North Carolina.

7. James S. Fisher states that "by 1900 slightly more than twenty-five percent of all Negro farm operators were either full or part owners." For this quote and data to support this statement, see James S. Fisher, "Negro Farm Ownership in the South," *Annals of the Association of American Geographers* 63, no. 4 (1973): 478, 481–482 (quote is from p. 478; table is on p. 482). In 1910, 19 percent of black people owned farms in the Deep South and 44 percent owned farms in the Upper South. See Ayers, *The Promise of the New South*, 208–210; Litwack, *Trouble in Mind*, 120–122. In addition, Sharon Holt found that in Granville County, North Carolina, "approximately 2 percent of adult black males owned land in 1870, a proportion that grew to 5 percent in 1880, 15 percent in 1890, and 17 percent in 1900." She adds that in Granville County, "black landowning continued to grow toward its peak in 1915." Holt, *Making Freedom Pay*, 58. See also Manning Marable, "The Politics of Black Land Tenure: 1877–1915," *Agricultural History* 53, no. 1 (1980): 142.

8. Holt, *Making Freedom Pay*, 58–59.

9. Holt, *Making Freedom Pay*, 68–69.

10. The quote is from Samuel T. Bitting, *Rural Land Ownership Among the Negroes of Virginia* (Charlottesville: Publications of the University of Virginia Phelps-Stokes Fellowship Papers, 1915), 18, 38, and is quoted in Ayers, *The Promise of the New South*, 209. See also Ayers, *The Promise of the New South*, 203–204, 208–209.

11. Ayers, *The Promise of the New South*, 209–210.

12. Holt, *Making Freedom Pay*, 67, 73–75. Holt notes that this strategy seems to have been largely successful in Granville County during the agricultural depression of the 1890s as "the median value of black-owned land stayed exactly the same through the hardest years of the agricultural depression." The quote from the Arkansas real estate developer is from the 1907 trial transcript of *Storthz v. Williams*, 86 Ark. 460 (1908).

13. Of the sixty-three fraud cases between 1865 and 1920, twenty-seven cases (43 percent) involved black plaintiffs who did not want to or mean to sell their property or had their property claimed by white people. Ten cases (16 percent) involved black plaintiffs who sold their property for a sum they later claimed was too low. Seven cases (11 percent) involved white creditors who supposedly charged exorbitant rates of interest on mortgages or notes of credit. In contrast, Robert Kagan and his coauthors found that fraud and deceit cases amounted to "almost 4 percent" of state supreme court cases throughout the period that they examined (1870–1970). See Kagan, "The Business of State Supreme Courts," 145, note 58. For

a broader study of fraud in America during this period, see Edward J. Balleisen, *Fraud: An American History From Barnum to Madoff* (Princeton, NJ: Princeton University Press, 2017).

14. Smith, *A Treatise on The Law of Frauds and The Statute of Frauds* (1907); Black, *A Treatise on the Rescission of Contracts and Cancellation of Written Instruments*, vol. 1 (1916); Browne, *A Treatise on the Construction of the Statute of Frauds* (1895). For a list of the statutes relating to fraud in each of the eight states examined, and an explanation of the common law relating to these statutes, see Smith, *A Treatise on the Law of Frauds* (1907), 585–602 (Alabama), 605–609 (Arkansas), 650–668 (Georgia), 736–743 (Kentucky), 838–848 (Mississippi), 974–984 (North Carolina), 1041–1056 (Tennessee), 1086–1092 (Virginia).

15. Black women were litigants in thirty-three of the sixty-three higher-court fraud cases (52 percent) between 1900 and 1920.

16. Appellate cases between white and black litigants from 1900 to 1920 in which black landowners did not mean to or want to sell their property include *McKinnon v. Henderson*, 145 Ga. 373 (1916); *Dixon v. Green*, 178 N.C. 205 (1919); *Culberth v. Hall*, 159 N.C. 588 (1912); *Pearsall v. Hyde*, 189 Ala. 86 (1914); *Morton v. Davis*, 105 Ark. 44 (1912); *Grimsley v. Singletary*, 133 Ga. 56 (1909); *McLaurin v. Williams*, 175 N.C. 291 (1918); *Pritchard v. Smith*, 160 N.C. 79 (1912); *Lee v. Wilkinson*, 105 Miss. 358 (1913); *Kirby v. Arnold*, 191 Ala. 263 (1915); *Abercrombie v. Carpenter*, 150 Ala. 294 (1907); *Hays v. Emerson*, 75 Ark. 551 (1905); *Hudson v. Hodge*, 139 N.C. 358 (1905); *Hodge v. Hudson*, 139 N.C. 358 (1905); *Moring v. Privott*, 146 N.C. 558 (1908); *Culver v. Baker*, 155 Ala. 181 (1907); *Barden v. Grace*, 167 Ala. 453 (1910); *Reynolds v. Blanks*, 78 Ark. 527 (1906); *Bryan v. Hobbs*, 72 Ark. 635 (1904); *Pendergrass v. Butcher*, 158 Ky. 321 (1914); *Castillo v. McBeath*, 162 Ky. 382 (1915); *Jordan v. Cromwell*, 166 Ky. 397 (1915); *Brown v. Bonds*, 125 Ga. 833 (1906); *Reeves v. Callaway*, 140 Ga. 101 (1913); *Culp v. Wooten*, 79 Miss. 503 (1901); *Herring v. Sutton*, 86 Miss. 283 (1905); *Smith v. Hargraves*, 114 Miss. 687 (1917). In a small number of cases between black litigants, African Americans were accused of deceiving other African Americans. See *Sutton v. Dunn*, 176 N.C. 202 (1918); *Johnson. v. Hall*, 87 Miss. 667 (1905).

17. Both the lower and higher courts ruled in favor of the black litigant. *McLaurin v. Williams*, 175 N.C. 291 (1918).

18. Although the lower court ordered the land returned to him and canceled his debt, the Supreme Court of Arkansas disagreed with the debt cancellation, saying he still owed the merchant's wife several hundred dollars. If he could not pay her, the opinion stated, the land would be sold to reimburse the debt. *Bryan v. Hobbs*, 72 Ark. 635 (1904).

19. Cases that involved claims of fraud due to selling property for a price later claimed to be too low include *Storthz v. Williams*, 86 Ark. 460 (1908); *Storthz v. Arnold*, 74 Ark. 68 (1905); *Arnold v. Storthz*, 74 Ark. 68 (1905); *Broughton v. Walker*, 197 Ala. 284 (1916); *Cox v. Morton*, 193 Ala. 401 (1915); *Leonard v. Roebuck*, 152 Ala. 312 (1907); *Hodges v. Wilson*, 165 N.C. 323 (1914); *Miller v. Mateer*, 172 N.C. 401 (1916); *Danforth v. Burchfield*, 201 Ala. 550 (1918); *Carter v. Eastman-Gardner Co.*, 95 Miss. 651 (1909).

20. For examples of fraud cases involving white creditors, see *Johnson v. Smith*, 190 Ala. 521 (1914); *Cannon v. Gilmer*, 135 Ala. 302 (1902); *Kincaid v. Bull*, 159 Ky. 527 (1914); *Elks v. Hemby*, 160 N.C. 20 (1912); *Wimberly v. Scoggin*, 128 Ark. 67 (1917); *Lines v. Brandon*, 129 Ark. 27 (1917); *Scott v. Jenkins*, 155 Ky. 817 (1913).

21. The lower court decided in favor of her creditor, but the Supreme Court of Mississippi reversed the decision, ruling for Mary Lee. *Lee v. Wilkinson*, 105 Miss. 358 (1913).

22. In eight fraud cases, a black defendant was accused of acting alone in committing fraud against the black plaintiff—see *Sutton v. Dunn*, 176 N.C. 202 (1918); *Johnson v. Hall*, 87 Miss. 667 (1905); *Robinson v. Griffin*, 173 Ala. 372 (1911); *Strickland v. Smith*, 131 Ark. 350 (1917); *Gardner v. Duncan*, 104 Miss. 477 (1913); *Webb v. Webb*, 99 Miss. 234 (1911); *Norfleet v. Beall*, 82 Miss. 538 (1903); *Bacon v. Dabney*, 183 Ky. 193 (1919). In four fraud cases, African American plaintiffs accused other black southerners of collaborating with white defendants in defrauding them—see *Abercrombie v. Carpenter*, 150 Ala. 294 (1907); *Storthz v. Williams*, 86 Ark. 460 (1908); *Storthz v. Arnold*, 74 Ark. 68 (1905); *Arnold v. Storthz*, 74 Ark. 68 (1905).

23. Scipio Jones is best known for his later involvement in a high-profile race case, defending the black so-called "Elaine 12" for their role in the deadly racial conflict of 1919 in Elaine, Arkansas. In this conflict, five white people died and it is likely that hundreds of black

people were killed. Grif Stockley, *Blood in Their Eyes: The Elaine Race Massacres of 1919* (Fayetteville: University of Arkansas Press, 2001). See also Judith Kilpatrick, *Arkansas' Early African-American Lawyers: A Pictorial History* (Fayetteville: University of Arkansas School of Law, 2002), 13–14; Octavius Coke, ed., *The Scrapbook of Arkansas Literature* (American Caxton Society Press, 1939), 312–314; "Scipio Africanus Jones," in Nancy A. Williams, ed., *Arkansas Biography: A Collection of Notable Lives* (Fayetteville: University of Arkansas Press, 2000).

24. The younger sister, a minor at the time of the supposed fraud, won her case before the Arkansas lower and higher courts, but her older sister lost her case in the local court and on appeal. *Storthz v. Arnold*, 74 Ark. 68 (1905); *Arnold v. Storthz*, 74 Ark. 68 (1905). In a 1908 case against the same moneylender, Rosa Williams, a 22-year-old black woman, inherited land in a town in which she did not live. Storthz reportedly paid an older black woman whom Williams trusted, and who had administered the estate, to persuade Williams to sell the lot to Storthz. The older woman told Williams that the real estate agent "was a gentleman and would do what was right by me." Despite the older woman's promises, the white purchasers misrepresented the value of the lot, telling Williams that it was worth only $300. Upon discovering that her land was actually worth between $4,000 and $5,000, Rosa Williams brought a suit to have the deed canceled. Rosa Williams won in both the higher and lower courts. See *Storthz v. Williams*, 86 Ark. 460 (1908).

25. Smith, *A Treatise on the Law of Frauds and the Statute of Frauds* (1907); Black, *A Treatise on the Rescission of Contracts and Cancellation of Written Instruments*, vol. 1 (1916); Browne, *A Treatise on the Construction of the Statute of Frauds* (1895). For a list of the statutes relating to fraud in each of the eight states examined and an explanation of the common law relating to these statutes, see Smith, *A Treatise on the Law of Frauds* (1907), 585–602 (Alabama), 605–609 (Arkansas), 650–668 (Georgia), 736–743 (Kentucky), 838–848 (Mississippi), 974–984 (North Carolina), 1041–1056 (Tennessee), 1086–1092 (Virginia).

26. See 1880 United States Federal Census, 1900 United States Federal Census, 1910 United States Federal Census, and 1930 United States Federal Census, all published online by Ancestry, Provo, Utah; Alabama, Deaths and Burials Index, 1881–1974, online at www.ancestry.com; *Leonard v. Roebuck*, 152 Ala. 312 (1907).

27. *Leonard v. Roebuck*, 152 Ala. 312 (1907). See, for instance, the following cases involving white plaintiffs in which the formula showing the plaintiff's weakness and vulnerability was used: *Johnson v. Coleman*, 134 Ga. 696 (1910); *Basch v. Frankenstein*, 134 Ga. 518 (1910).

28. *Leonard v. Roebuck*, 152 Ala. 312 (1907).

29. *Dixon v. Green*, 178 N.C. 205 (1919).

30. *Abercrombie v. Carpenter*, 150 Ala. 294 (1907).

31. *Leonard v. Roebuck*, 152 Ala. 312 (1907); *Dixon v. Green*, 178 N.C. 205 (1919). In cases in which black people collaborated with white defendants to deceive black plaintiffs (or deceived them on their own), the plaintiffs also testified that they had relied on the black people involved. See *Storthz v. Williams*, 86 Ark. 460 (1908); *Sutton v. Dunn*, 176 N.C. 202 (1918).

32. In his appellate brief, Terry cited the cases of *Beck. v. Houppert*, 104 Ala. 503 (1894) and *Bank of Guntersville v. Webb*, 108 Ala. 132 (1895). John Vary, Leonard's attorney, cited the case of *Goetter, Weil & Co. v. Pickett*, 61 Ala 387 (1878).

33. *Leonard v. Roebuck*, 152 Ala. 312 (1907).

34. *Leonard v. Roebuck*, 152 Ala. 312 (1907).

35. *Hudson v. Hodge*, 139 N.C. 308 (1905); *Abercrombie v. Carpenter*, 150 Ala. 294 (1907). See also *Sutton v. Dunn*, 176 N.C. 202 (1918).

36. *Leonard v. Roebuck*, 152 Ala. 312 (1907).

37. For a discussion of honor and the system of slavery in the antebellum South, see Gross, *Double Character*, 47–48; Oakes, *Slavery and Freedom*, Chapter 1; Bertram Wyatt-Brown, *Southern Honor: Ethics and Behavior in the Old South* (New York: Oxford University Press, 1982).

38. *Abercrombie v. Carpenter*, 150 Ala. 294 (1907).

39. *Hudson v. Hodge*, 139 N.C. 308 (1905). Other cases give evidence of cases outside of the courtroom in which black southerners stood up to whites. See, for instance, the testimony of A. V. Hall, the son-in-law of the black plaintiff in the case of *Hall v. Holloman*,

136 N.C. 34 (1904). Hall testified about a dispute with the white defendant: "The fuss [illegible] Holloman and myself & for which he had me bound over to keep the peace occurred while he was walking around the yard of Emma Butler, my wife's mother. He was speaking of the farm as his and I said "I will show you whose farm this is" and then we had a difficulty."

40. *Leonard v. Roebuck*, 152 Ala. 312 (1907).
41. *Leonard v. Roebuck*, 152 Ala. 312 (1907).
42. *Leonard v. Roebuck*, 152 Ala. 312 (1907).
43. *Storthz v. Williams*, 86 Ark. 460 (1908). In this case, the black litigant Rosa Williams won in both the higher and lower courts.
44. The white witnesses testifying for Roebuck were Ben Davis, Mrs. A. J. Wideman, Jack Brown, J. A. Gaddis, and W. K. Terry. Lurena Roebuck and her husband Isham Roebuck also testified for their suit. *Leonard v. Roebuck*, 152 Ala. 312 (1907).
45. *Leonard v. Roebuck*, 152 Ala. 312 (1907); *Hodges v. Wilson*, 165 N.C. 323 (1914)
46. The four white witnesses testifying for Leonard were A. W. Fulghum, H. A. Kimball, B. F. Meyer, and John Vary. John Leonard also testified in favor of his own suit. *Leonard v. Roebuck*, 152 Ala. 312 (1907).
47. *Leonard v. Roebuck*, 152 Ala. 312 (1907).
48. "Takes Little Rap at Gulfport P.B.: Case Which Went Up From Gulfport to Supreme Court Results in Reversal," *The Daily Herald* (Biloxi, MS), June 18, 1913.
49. Appellate cases do not provide a representative sample of cases that reached the lower courts. However, of the appellate cases examined here, juries had decided twenty-five of the sixty-three fraud cases between black and white litigants at the lower-court level between 1900 and 1920 (40 percent). Of the twenty-five appellate fraud cases between white and black litigants involving juries, black litigants had won fifteen cases (60 percent) at the lower-court level. Judges still influenced jury trials, sometimes even directing juries to decide for or against a black litigant.
50. Appellate cases do not provide a representative sample of cases that reached the lower courts. However, in these suits judges had decided thirty-two of these cases at the lower-court level (51 percent). In the remaining cases, it was unclear who decided the personal injury cases at the lower-court level. Of the thirty-two appellate fraud cases between white and black litigants that were heard before a lower-court judge, sixteen cases were decided in favor of the black litigant (50 percent).
51. Higher-court judges ruled in favor of black litigants in forty-nine of sixty-three appellate-level fraud cases between 1900 and 1920 (78 percent of suits). In appellate-level fraud cases between white and black litigants from 1900 to 1920, higher-court judges upheld lower-court (usually jury) decisions in favor of black litigants in thirty-two cases and reversed lower-court decisions that had been against the black litigant in seventeen cases.
52. *Leonard v. Roebuck*, 152 Ala. 312 (1907). The precedents cited included *Beck v. Houppert*, 104 Ala. 503 (1894); *Bank of Guntersville v. Webb*, 108 Ala. 132 (1895); *Tillis v. Austin*, 117 Ala. 262 (1897). The case of *Beck v. Houppert* was first heard in the Circuit Court of Jefferson County, Alabama, the same county in which the *Leonard v. Roebuck* case originated.
53. See *Storthz v. Williams*, 86 Ark. 460 (1908); *Mann v. Russey*, 101 Tenn. 596 (1898).
54. See *Harrison v. Rodgers*, 162 Ala. 515 (1909), and the discussion of this case in Dumas, "The Muddled Mettle of Jurisprudence: Race and Procedure in Alabama's Appellate Courts," 440–441. See also *Broughton v. Walker*, 197 Ala. 284 (1916); *Morgan v. Gaiter*, 202 Ala. 492 (1919); *Hodges v. Wilson*, 165 N.C. 323 (1914).
55. An element of paternalism played a part in these judges' attitudes toward black litigants. At the turn of the century, as white southerners experienced a revival of the glorification of ante-bellum times and the "Lost Cause," appeals to a paternalist ideology with roots in slavery are found in a number of suits. For more on the concept of paternalism, see Genovese, *Roll, Jordan, Roll*; Anderson, "Aunt Jemima in Dialectics: Genovese on Slave Culture," 99–114.
56. *Lee v. Wilkinson*, 105 Miss. 358 (1913).
57. *Pearsall v. Hyde*, 189 Ala. 86 (1914). See also *Cannon v. Gilmer*, 135 Ala. 302 (1902).
58. Ayers, *The Promise of the New South*, 134. For more on southern judges during this time, see Ranney, *In the Wake of Slavery*, 13–14, 27–28; Huebner, *The Southern Judicial Tradition*.

59. *Leonard v. Roebuck*, 152 Ala. 312 (1907). The seven justices on the court had been nominated at a party convention or county primary and then elected by the states' citizens. Robert J. Norrell, "Law in a White Man's Democracy: A History of the Alabama State Judiciary," *Cumberland Law Review* 32 (2001): 135–143. The seven justices on the Supreme Court of Alabama in 1907 were Samuel D. Weakley (1906–1907); John R. Tyson (1898–1909); James R. Dowdell (1898–1909); R. T. Simpson (1904–1912); John C. Andersen (1904–1914); N. D. Denson (1904–1909); and Thomas C. McClellan (1906–1923). For more about the Supreme Court of Alabama during this time, see J. Ed Livingston, "A History of the Alabama Judicial System," http://judicial.alabama.gov/docs/judicial_history.pdf; Pat Boyd Rumore, *From Power to Service: The Story of Lawyers in Alabama* (published by The History and Archives Committee of the Alabama State Bar in conjunction with the Alabama Bench and Bar Historical Society, 2010), 121–122; 155–156; Dumas, "The Muddled Mettle of Jurisprudence: Race and Procedure in Alabama's Appellate Courts," 417–442; McLaughlin, "A 'Mixture of Race and Reform,'" 285–309.

60. *Leonard v. Roebuck*, 152 Ala. 312 (1907).

61. "John F. Leonard v. Lurena Roebuck," *The Montgomery Advertiser*, June 14, 1907.

62. 1910 United States Federal Census; World War I Draft Registration Cards, 1917–1918; 1920 United States Federal Census; Alabama, Deaths and Burials Index, 1881–1974. All published online by Ancestry, Provo, Utah.

Chapter 7

1. The 1910 US census lists Rebecca as having given birth to sixteen children and having nine surviving children. However, from the census records, it appears that she had eleven surviving children. 1880 United States Federal Census, 1900 United States Federal Census, and 1910 United States Federal Census, all published online by Ancestry, Provo, Utah; *City of Harrodsburg v. Sallee*, 142 Ky. 829 (1911). For more on Harrodsburg, Kentucky, during this period, see "Harrodsburg," in John E. Kleber, ed., *The Kentucky Encyclopedia* (Louisville: University Press of Kentucky, 2014), 414.

2. *City of Harrodsburg v. Sallee*, 142 Ky. 829 (1911).

3. Although personal injury cases had made up only 4 of 108 total appellate cases between white and black litigants (4 percent of suits) between 1865 and 1877, 31 such personal injury cases took place between 1878 and 1899 out of 102 total cases (30 percent of these suits between 1878 and 1899), and 97 of these personal injury cases occurred between 1900 and 1920 out of 220 total cases during this period. In this chapter, I am looking only at cases that alleged actual injury, whether physical or mental or both. Therefore, some lawsuits by African Americans during this period (especially involving the railroad) that allege only discrimination and do not claim damages for injuries are not included in this chapter. In contrast, Barbara Welke studies the broad spectrum of railroad suits in the United States that alleged discrimination in her book *Recasting American Liberty*.

4. Kagan and his coauthors found that between 1870 and 1880, torts cases made up 9.6 percent of all the criminal and civil state supreme court cases sampled whereas between 1903 and 1935, they made up 16.4 percent of state supreme court suits sampled. As criminal cases made up between 10 and 12 percent of state supreme court cases sampled between 1870 and 1935, the vast majority of the overall sample was civil cases. Kagan, "The Business of State Supreme Courts," 134–135, 142–143.

5. Between 1878 and 1899, twenty-four of the thirty-one appellate personal injury cases examined involved the railroad (77 percent) and four of the thirty-one such cases (13 percent) concerned streetcars. Between 1900 and 1920, sixty of the ninety-seven personal injury cases examined (62 percent) involved the railroad and four of the ninety-seven cases (4 percent) concerned streetcars. In turn, Kagan found that "From 1885 to 1920, one-third of all torts suits on SSC dockets, and 4 percent of all SSC cases, were lawsuits arising out of railroad and streetcar accidents." Kagan, "The Business of State Supreme Courts," 143.

6. Welke, *Recasting American Liberty*, 14–20; Mark Aldrich, *Death Rode the Rails: American Railroad Accidents and Safety, 1828–1965* (Baltimore: Johns Hopkins University Press, 2006), 182–184. For statistical data on the changes in injury rates during this period, see

"Tables with Passenger Fatality and Injury Rates per Billion Passenger Miles, Selected Causes, 1889–1965" in Aldrich, *Death Rode the Rails*, 323. For more on railroad expansion during the nineteenth century, see Richard White, *Railroaded: The Transcontinentals and the Making of Modern America* (New York: Norton, 2011); Christian Wolmar, *The Great Railroad Revolution: The History of Trains in America* (New York: PublicAffairs, 2012), 1–215.

7. James W. Ely, Jr., *Railroads and American Law* (Lawrence: University Press of Kansas, 2001), 68–69, 80–83.

8. Aldrich, *Death Rode the Rails*, 4. Aldrich explains that he borrowed the term "little accidents" from "Ralph Richards, dean of railroad safety workers."

9. See *Mills, Receiver Ft. Smith & Western Rd. Co., v. Franklin*, 130 Ark. 80 (1917); *St. Louis Southwestern Railway Company v. Green*, 99 Ark. 572 (1911); *St. Louis, Iron Mountain & Southern Railway Company v. Wilson*, 70 Ark. 136 (1902); *Ward v. Yazoo & M. V. R. Co.*, 79 Miss. 145 (1901); *Rose v. Louisville, N. O. & T. R. Co.*, 70 Miss. 725 (1893); *Neville v. Southern R. Co.*, 126 Tenn. 96 (1912).

10. See *St. Louis, Iron Mountain & Southern Railway Company v. Richardson*, 87 Ark. 101 (1908); *Georgia P. R. Co. v. Robinson*, 68 Miss. 643 (1891); *Dillahunty v. Chicago, R. I. & P. R. Co.*, 119 Ark. 392 (1915); *Louisville & I. R. Co. v. Hardin*, 157 Ky. 13 (1914); *Atlanta Rapid Transit Co. v. Young*, 117 Ga. 349 (1903).

11. See *The Georgia Railroad & Banking Co. v. Dougherty*, 86 Ga. 744 (1890); *Union Railway Company v. Carter*, 129 Tenn. 459 (1914); *Central of Georgia Railway Company v. Gross*, 192 Ala. 354 (1914); *Hale v. Chesapeake & Ohio Ry. Co.*, 142 Ky. 835 (1911); *Louisville & Nashville Railroad Company v. Bell. Same v. Jones*, 166 Ky. 400 (1915); *Wood, &c v. L. & N. R. R. Co.*, 101 Ky. 703 (1897); *Royston v. Illinois C. R. Co.*, 67 Miss. 376 (1889); *Southern R. Co. v. Hunter*, 74 Miss. 444 (1896); *Alabama & V. R. Co. v. Holmes*, 75 Miss. 371 (1897); *Mississippi Central Railroad Company v. Dacus*, 97 Miss. 768 (1910); *Jones v. Mobile & O. R. Co.*, 112 Miss. 283 (1916); *Alabama & V. R. Co. v. McAfee*, 71 Miss. 70 (1893); *Louisville, N. & G. S. R.R. Co. v. Fleming*, 82 Tenn. 128 (1884); *Lewis v. Norfolk & W. R. Co.*, 132 N.C. 382 (1903); *Sibley v. Smith*, 46 Ark. 275 (1885); *Louisville & N. R. Co. v. Scott*, 141 Ky. 538 (1911); *Gasway v. Atlanta & W. P. R. Co.*, 58 Ga. 216 (1877); *Richmond & D. R. Co. v. Jefferson*, 89 Ga. 554 (1892); *Hillman v. Georgia R. & B. Co.*, 126 Ga. 814 (1906). At times, this violence was clearly racially motivated and an attempt to enforce segregation—see, for instance, *Britton v. Atlanta & Charlotte Air-line Railway Company*, 88 N.C. 536 (1883); *Bowie v. Birmingham Railway & Electric Company*, 125 Ala. 397 (1899); *Ohio Valley v. Lander*, 104 Ky. 431 (1898); *Little Rock Railway & Electric Company v. Hampton*, 112 Ark. 194 (1914); *Chiles v. Chesapeake & O. R. Co.*, 125 Ky. 299 (1907).

12. See *Coast Line R.R. v. Boston*, 83 Ga. 387 (1889); *St. Louis, Iron Mountain & Southern Railway Company v. Briggs*, 87 Ark. 581 (1908); *Alabama & Vicksburg Ry. Co. v. Jones*, 86 Miss. 263 (1905); *Central of G. R. Co. v. McNab*, 150 Ala. 332 (1907).

13. Welke, *Recasting American Liberty*, 18–19; Aldrich, *Death Rode the Rails*, 2, 189; White, *Railroaded*, 282–286.

14. Twenty-seven suits between black and white litigants in the eight appellate courts examined of 97 total suits (28 percent of appellate-level personal injury suits with black litigants) involved work-related injuries. For comparison, a study sampling state supreme court suits as a whole around the United States found 20.5 percent of torts cases (68 of 331) involving workplace accidents between 1905 and 1935. See Kagan, "The Business of State Supreme Courts," 134, 144–145.

15. Although railroad employees were injured far more often than passengers, suits involving employees are a minority of the overall cases because legal rules made it more difficult for them to litigate and win such suits. Aldrich, *Death Rode the Rails*, 159. In approximately half of black southerners' appellate cases over workplace injury (thirteen of twenty-seven) between 1900 and 1920, railroad or streetcar employees or their heirs sued over injuries or deaths in the workplace. See *Yazoo & M. V. R. Co. v. Carroll*, 103 Miss. 830 (1912); *St. Louis & S. F. R. Co. v. Bowles*, 107 Miss. 97 (1914); *Alabama & V. R. Co. v. Jones*, 111 Miss. 196 (1916); *Kelly v. Howard*, 98 Miss. 543 (1910); *Louisiana & N. W. R. Co. v. Smith*, 74 Ark. 172 (1905); *Nashville, C. & S. L. R. Co. v. Hayes*, 117 Tenn. 680 (1906); *Bean v. Western N. C. R. Co.*, 107 N.C. 731 (1890); *Smith v. Atlanta & Charlotte Air Line Ry. Co.*, 147 N.C. 603 (1908); *St. Louis,*

I. M. & S. R. Co. v. Thurmond, 70 Ark. 411 (1902); *Bush v. Jenkins,* 128 Ark. 630 (1917); *Illinois C. R. Co. v. Mayes,* 142 Ky. 382 (1911); *Jones v. Southern R.,* 175 Ky. 455 (1917).

16. Fourteen of the ninety-seven personal injury cases examined in this study involved cases in which employees or their families sued over workplace injuries or deaths not relating to railroads or streetcars. These cases include *Black's Administrator v. Virginia Portland Cement Co.,* 104 Va. 450 (1905); *Black's Admr. v. Virginia Portland Cement Co,* 106 Va. 121 (1906); *Central Mfg. Co. v. Cotton,* 108 Tenn. 63 (1901); *Henderson Tobacco Extracts Works v. Wheeler,* 116 Ky. 322 (1903); *Hughes v. Louisville, H. & S. L. R. Co,* 174 Ky. 611 (1917); *Interstate Coal Co. v. Garrard,* 163 Ky. 235 (1915); *J. J. Newman Lumber Co. v. Dantzler,* 107 Miss. 31 (1914); *Lax-Fos Co. v. Rowlett,* 144 Ky. 690 (1911); *Morriss Bros. v. Bowers,* 105 Tenn. 59 (1900); *Nicholson Coal Mining Co. v. Moulden,* 143 Ky. 348 (1911); *Peele v. Bright,* 119 Va. 182 (1916); *Stewart Dry Goods Co. v. Boone,* 180 Ky. 199 (1918); *Whitehead v. Newton Oil & Mfg. Co,* 105 Miss. 711 (1913); *White's Adm'r v. Kentucky Public Elevator Co,* 186 Ky. 91 (1919).

17. Railroad cases not involving passengers or railroad employees include *Railway Companies v. Foster,* 88 Tenn. 671 (1890); *Norfolk & P. Traction Co. v. Daily's Adm'r,* 111 Va. 665 (1911); *Washington & O. D. R. Co. v. Jackson's Adm'r,* 117 Va. 636 (1915); *Jones v. Alabama & V. R. Co.,* 72 Miss. 22 (1894); *Alabama & V. R. Co. v. Jones,* 73 Miss. 110 (1895); *Southern R. Co. v. Free,* 95 Miss. 739 (1909); *Southern Railway Company v. Pittman,* 97 Miss. 416 (1910); *Yazoo & M. V. R. Co. v. Huff,* 111 Miss. 486 (1916); *Yazoo & M. V. R. Co. v. Washington,* 113 Miss. 105 (1916); *Boutten v. Wellington & P. R. Co.,* 128 N.C. 337 (1901); *Mitchell v. Seaboard A. L. R. Co.,* 153 N.C. 116 (1910); *Henderson v. Atlantic Coast Line R.R. Co.,* 171 N.C. 397 (1916); *Richmond & D. R. Co. v. Howard,* 79 Ga. 44 (1887). See also Aldrich, *Death Rode the Rails,* 117.

18. Eight of ninety-seven appellate civil suits involving black litigants (8 percent of suits) between 1900 and 1920 involved mistakes made by telegraph companies. For the case brought by John Beal, see *Postal Telegraph v. Beal,* 159 Ala. 249 (1909). For other personal injury suits against telegraph companies, see also *Forney v. Postal Tel. Cable Co,* 152 N.C. 494 (1910); *Forney v. Postal Telegraph-Cable Company,* 152 N.C. 496 (1910); *Western Union Tel. Co. v. Cross' Adm'r,* 116 Ky. 5 (1903); *Western Union Tel. Co. v. Fisher,* 107 Ky. 513 (1900); *Western Union Tel. Co. v. Teague,* 117 Miss. 401 (1918); *Western Union Telegraph Co. v. Spratley,* 84 Miss. 86 (1904); *Lawrence v. Western Union Telegraph Company,* 171 N.C. 240 (1916).

19. *City of Harrodsburg v. Sallee,* 142 Ky. 829 (1911); *City of Harrodsburg v. Vanarsdal,* 148 Ky. 507 (1912).

20. See *Mayor, etc., of Knoxville v. Cox,* 103 Tenn. 368 (1899); *Bland v. City of Mobile,* 142 Ala. 142 (1904); *City of Bowling Green v. Duncan,* 122 Ky. 244 (1906); *City of Harrodsburg v. Sallee,* 142 Ky. 829 (1911); *Idlett v. Atlanta,* 123 Ga. 821 (1905); *Jackson v. Laird,* 99 Miss. 476 (1911); *Owensboro v. Knox's Adm'r,* 116 Ky. 451 (1903); *Covington v. Bryant,* 70 Ky. 248 (1970).

21. *City of Harrodsburg v. Sallee,* 142 Ky. 829 (1911).

22. *St. Louis, Iron Mountain & Southern Railway Company v. Briggs,* 87 Ark. 581 (1908); Welke, *Recasting American Liberty,* 62.

23. *Louisville & Nashville Railroad Company v. Hobbs,* 155 Ky. 130 (1913).

24. Lawsuits in which violence was clearly racially motivated or an attempt to enforce segregation included *Britton v. Atlanta & Charlotte Air-line Railway Company,* 88 N.C. 536 (1883); *Bowie v. Birmingham Railway & Electric Company,* 125 Ala. 397 (1899); *Ohio Valley v. Lander,* 104 Ky. 431 (1898); *Little Rock Railway & Electric Company v. Hampton,* 112 Ark. 194 (1914); *Chiles v. Chesapeake & O. R. Co.,* 125 Ky. 299 (1907).

25. The renowned antilynching crusader Ida B. Wells famously tested this in the 1887 case of *Chesapeake, Ohio & Southwestern Railroad Company v. Wells,* 85 Tenn. 613 (1887). See also Welke, "When All the Women Were White."

26. *Mills, Receiver Ft. Smith & Western Rd. Co., v. Franklin,* 130 Ark. 80 (1917); *St. Louis, Iron Mountain & Southern Railway Company v. Wilson,* 70 Ark. 136 (1902); *St. Louis Southwestern Railway Company v. Green,* 99 Ark. 572 (1911).

27. *St. Louis, Iron Mountain & Southern Railway Company v. Wilson,* 70 Ark. 136 (1902).

28. *St. Louis, Iron Mountain & Southern Railway Company v. Wilson,* 70 Ark. 136 (1902).

29. Negligence was judged based on the vague standard of what the "reasonable man" might have done in such a situation. In practice, such legal principles led mid-nineteenth-century

American officials and companies to give preference to individual autonomy rather than to safety. Kermit L. Hall, *The Magic Mirror: Law in American History* (Oxford: Oxford University Press, 1989), 124–126; Friedman, *A History of American Law*, 350–253.

30. Hall, *The Magic Mirror*, 297, Friedman, *A History of American Law*, 519; Welke, *Recasting American Liberty*, 30–39; Aldrich, *Death Rode the Rails*, 183–184. For statistics on numbers of personal injury suits between 1905 and 1935, see Kagan, "The Business of State Supreme Courts," 134, 143.

31. Welke, *Recasting American Liberty*, xi–xii, 57; Aldrich, *Death Rode the Rails*, 26.

32. Between 1900 and 1920, 40 of the 97 appellate personal injury suits between black and white litigants involved black women as litigants (41 percent). Of all the different kinds of suits litigated by African American women in the eight appellate courts examined between 1865 and 1950, black women litigated more suits involving personal injury than any other single kind of suit (132 personal injury suits between 1865 and 1950 of a total of 404 cases involving black female litigants, or 44 percent of suits litigated by black female litigants). Sixteen of the 48 appellate-level suits involving black female litigants (33 percent) between 1878 and 1899 related to personal injury. Forty of 89 (45 percent) of these suits involving black female litigants between 1900 and 1920 related to personal injury. Seventy-six of 214 of these suits involving black female litigants between 1921 and 1950 (36 percent) related to personal injury. In contrast, in looking at lawsuits involving racial discrimination on public transit, Barbara Welke finds that in the period before 1887, black men brought most such cases. In the period from 1887 to the 1920s, she argues that African American men brought the most racial discrimination cases, although a significant number of cases also involved African American women. See Welke, *Recasting American Liberty*, 296–297; 300–301.

33. Watson, *A Treatise on the law of Damages for Personal Injuries* (1901); Hopkins, *The Law of Personal Injuries and Incidentally Damage to Property by Railway-Trains* (1902); Hopkins, *The Law of Personal Injuries and Incidentally Damage to Property by Railway-Trains* (1912).

34. Louisa Smith testified in the suit *St. Louis v. Wilson*, 70 Ark. 136 (1902). She had been traveling with her friend Dilsia Wilson, when Wilson had suffered injuries from the unequal conditions in a "colored" railroad waiting room. See also *St. Louis v. Briggs*, 87 Ark. 581 (1908).

35. Welke, *Recasting American Liberty*, 75–79.

36. Robert Harding's father Aaron Harding was initially elected to Congress as a Unionist and then later elected as a Democrat. Robert Harding became a county attorney in 1897, but it is unclear how long he remained a county attorney. H. Levin, ed., *The Lawyers and Lawmakers of Kentucky* (Chicago: Lewis Publishing Company, 1897, reprinted 1982), 501; 1920 United States Federal Census, published online by Ancestry, Provo, Utah; Death certificate for Benjamin Roach (July 7, 1923). Roach is listed on his death certificate as "Judge B. F. Roach."

37. *City of Bowling Green v. Duncan*, 122 Ky. 244 (1906).

38. *Western Union Tel. Co. v. Teague*, 117 Miss. 401 (1918).

39. *City of Harrodsburg v. Sallee*, 142 Ky. 829 (1911).

40. *City of Harrodsburg v. Sallee*, 142 Ky. 829 (1911).

41. *City of Harrodsburg v. Sallee*, 142 Ky. 829 (1911).

42. *City of Harrodsburg v. Sallee*, 142 Ky. 829 (1911); *St. Louis v. Richardson*, 87 Ark. 101 (1908).

43. *City of Harrodsburg v. Sallee*, 142 Ky. 829 (1911); Welke, *Recasting American Liberty*, 171–203.

44. *Mills, Receiver Ft. Smith & Western Rd. Co., v. Franklin*, 130 Ark. 80 (1917).

45. *Mills, Receiver Ft. Smith & Western Rd. Co., v. Franklin*, 130 Ark. 80 (1917).

46. *St. Louis, Iron Mountain & Southern Railway Company v. Briggs*, 87 Ark. 581 (1908).

47. *Coast Line R.R. v. Boston*, 83 Ga. 387 (1889).

48. Welke, *Recasting American Liberty*, 56–59.

49. *St. Louis, Iron Mountain & Southern Railway Company v. Briggs*, 87 Ark. 581 (1908). Barbara Welke examines African American women's quandary in this regard in Welke, "When All the Women Were White, and All the Blacks Were Men," 261–316.

50. White women's weight was also sometimes mentioned in the context of personal injury lawsuits. See, for instance, *Nashville, Chattanooga & St. Louis Ry. v. Akin*, 140 Tenn. 34 (1917).

51. *Bland v. City of Mobile*, 142 Ala. 142 (1904).

52. *City of Bowling Green v. Duncan*, 122 Ky. 244 (1906). See also the comments of Dr. W. J. Auten testifying about the plaintiff's health before the injury in the case of *Atlanta Rapid Transit Co.*

v. Young, 117 Ga. 349 (1903): "She appeared to be a stout young negro woman. I would have taken her to be a robust hearty woman, I never saw one more so."

53. *Atlanta Rapid Transit Co. v. Young*, 117 Ga. 349 (1903).

54. Watson, *A Treatise on the Law of Damages for Personal Injuries* (1901); Hopkins, *The Law of Personal Injuries and Incidentally Damage to Property by Railway-Trains* (1902); Hopkins, *The Law of Personal Injuries and Incidentally Damage to Property by Railway-Trains* (1912).

55. *Mills, Receiver Ft. Smith & Western Rd. Co., v. Franklin*, 130 Ark. 80 (1917).

56. *The Georgia Railroad & Banking Co. v. Dougherty*, 86 Ga. 744 (1890).

57. *City of Harrodsburg v. Sallee*, 142 Ky. 829 (1911); *Coast Line R.R. v. Boston*, 83 Ga. 387 (1889).

58. *St. Louis & San Francisco Railroad Company v. Petties*, 99 Ark. 415 (1911).

59. *City of Harrodsburg v. Sallee*, 142 Ky. 829 (1911); *Central Railroad v. Whitehead*, 74 Ga. 10 (1885).

60. *City of Harrodsburg v. Sallee*, 142 Ky. 829 (1911); *Coast Line R.R. v. Boston*, 83 Ga. 387 (1889).

61. *Mills, Receiver Ft. Smith & Western Rd. Co., v. Franklin*, 130 Ark. 80 (1917).

62. *Dush v. Fitzhugh*, 70 Tenn. 307 (1879).

63. *Atlantic and Birmingham Railway Co. v. Bowen*, 125 Ga. 460 (1906).

64. *The Georgia Railroad & Banking Co. v. Dougherty*, 86 Ga. 744 (1890).

65. *The Georgia Railroad & Banking Co. v. Dougherty*, 86 Ga. 744 (1890).

66. Bland sued the city of Mobile for $1,000, and when she lost in the lower court, appealed her case to the Supreme Court of Alabama. She lost the appeal. *Bland v. City of Mobile*, 142 Ala. 142 (1904).

67. "The News of Mobile," *The Montgomery Advertiser*, May 27, 1905, 5.

68. *City of Harrodsburg v. Sallee*, 142 Ky. 829 (1911).

69. *Louisville & Nashville Railroad Company v. Hobbs*, 155 Ky. 130 (1913).

70. Welke, *Recasting American Liberty*, 75–78.

71. In at least two cases, the mayor and white members of the board of public works testified in defense of a city. *City of Bowling Green v. Duncan*, 122 Ky. 244 (1906); *City of Harrodsburg v. Sallee*, 142 Ky. 829 (1911).

72. *City of Bowling Green v. Duncan*, 122 Ky. 244 (1906).

73. *City of Harrodsburg v. Sallee*, 142 Ky. 829 (1911).

74. Not every doctor felt comfortable taking on the city. The judge told Sallee that she should be examined by another doctor, a Dr. Robards. However, Dr. Robards reportedly felt hesitation about becoming involved in a suit against the city and did not examine her. Despite having only one doctor testify for her, Rebecca Sallee won in both the local and state supreme courts. *City of Harrodsburg v. Sallee*, 142 Ky. 829 (1911).

75. See *Atlanta Rapid Transit Co. v. Young*, 117 Ga. 349 (1903), in which the wife of the black plaintiff worked as a domestic employee for the doctor who testified on her behalf.

76. Welke, *Recasting American Liberty*, 75–78.

77. *City of Bowling Green v. Duncan*, 122 Ky. 244 (1906).

78. *City of Harrodsburg v. Sallee*, 142 Ky. 829 (1911).

79. Appellate-level cases do not provide a representative sample of lower-court cases. However, of the appellate cases examined here, almost exclusively white juries had decided eighty-eight of the ninety-seven personal injury cases between black and white litigants at the lower-court level between 1900 and 1920 (91 percent of suits). Judges had decided eight of these cases at the lower-court level, and it was unclear who decided one personal injury case. Black litigants won sixty-nine of the eighty-eight personal injury cases decided by juries in the trial court and four of the eight personal injury cases decided by judges in the trial court.

80. At least 23 of the 465 civil appellate cases between black and white litigants examined between 1865 and 1950 in which juries made the decision at the lower-court level involved peremptory instructions or directed verdicts.

81. *City of Harrodsburg v. Sallee*, 142 Ky. 829 (1911).

82. *City of Harrodsburg v. Sallee*, 142 Ky. 829 (1911). The jury members were Ed Gill (white, miller, born in Kentucky, 44 years old), Joseph Kellar (born in Germany, farmer, 44 years old), R. S. Bunton (white, farmer, born in Kentucky, 32 years old), W. C. Carr (farmer, born in Kentucky, 43 years old), Calvin N. Wilder (white, gardener, born in Kentucky, 44 years old), Tomas S. Cloyd (white, farmer, born in Kentucky, 54 years old), J. W. Jenkins (white, farmer,

born in Kentucky, 42 years old), J. T. Houchins (white, farmer, born in Kentucky, 52 years old), and H. C. Graham (white, farmer, born in Kentucky, 55 years old)

83. The higher-court opinion cites the following cases as precedent: *Canfield v. Newport*, 73 S.W. 888; *Bell v. Henderson*, 74 S.W. 206; *Breil v. Buffalo*, 144 N.Y. 163, 38 N.E. 977; *Reed v. Detroit*, 99 Mich. 204, 58 N.W. 44; *Davis v. Omaha*, 47 Neb. 836, 66 N.W. 859; *Warsaw v. Dunlap*, 112 Ind. 576, 11 N.E. 623; *City of Midway v. Lloyd*, 24 Ky. L. Rep. 2448, 74 S.W. 195; *City of Covington v. Asman*, 24 Ky. L. Rep. 415; *Canfield v. City of Newport*, 24 Ky. L. Rep. 2213, 73 S.W. 788.

84. In her testimony, Sallee explained that she made approximately $5 a week. *City of Harrodsburg v. Sallee*, 142 Ky. 829 (1911). The subsequent suit that the city brought against the owner of the property where she had fallen said that the city had paid $502.25 to Rebecca Sallee for "costs, interest and damages . . . as of May 1st 1911." *City of Harrodsburg v. Vanarsdal*, 148 Ky. 507 (1912).

85. Between 1878 and 1899, state supreme courts reversed 16 percent of lower-court rulings against African Americans in personal injury suits and affirmed lower-court rulings in favor of black litigants in 39 percent of suits. Between 1900 and 1920, black litigants lost in both the lower and higher courts in seven of the ninety-seven appellate-level personal injury cases examined. In eleven of the cases examined, black litigants lost in the lower court and won in the higher court (in three additional cases, the lower-court decision was split and they won in the higher court). In twenty-nine of these cases, they won in the lower court and lost in the higher court. In forty-four cases, they won in both the lower and higher courts. The rest of the cases had split verdicts.

86. *City of Harrodsburg v. Sallee*, 142 Ky. 829 (1911); "City of Harrodsburg v. Sallee," *The Lexington Herald*, April 11, 1911, 3.

87. *City of Harrodsburg v. Vanarsdal*, 148 Ky. 507 (1912).

88. *Brewer's Executor v. Smith*, 242 Ky. 175 (1932).

89. 1930 United States Federal Census, published online by Ancestry, Provo, Utah.

90. *Brewer's Executor v. Smith*, 242 Ky. 175 (1932).

91. Aldrich, *Death Rode the Rails*, 237–308; Wolmar, *The Great Railroad Revolution*, 259–288.

Chapter 8

1. *Broome v. Jackson*, 193 Miss. 66 (1942). Quotations are from the petition submitted to the Hinds County Chancery Court by Mary Broome's lawyer in July 1941. This petition can be found in the trial record of the case.

2. *Broome v. Jackson*, 193 Miss. 66 (1942).

3. *New v. Atlantic Greyhound Corporation*, 186 Va. 726 (1947).

4. *New v. Atlantic Greyhound Corporation*, 186 Va. 726 (1947).

5. Ethel New's case was tried in the Law and Equity Court in the city of Richmond, Virginia. *New v. Atlantic Greyhound Corporation*, 186 Va. 726 (1947).

6. For background on the black business community in Atlanta in the 1920s, see Herman "Skip" Mason, Jr., *Black Atlanta in the Roaring Twenties* (Charleston, SC: Arcadia Publishing, 1997), 8. For more on black barbershops that served only white patrons, see Quincy T. Mills, *Cutting Along the Color Line: Black Barbers and Barber Shops in America* (Philadelphia: University of Pennsylvania Press, 2013), 61–64. For more on Alonzo Herndon's barbershop, see "Herndon's Crystal Palace Barber Shop," *The Atlanta Constitution*, May 25, 1913, 6; "The Largest and Finest Barber Shop in the World," *The Atlanta Constitution*, May 7, 1916, 2; Carole Merritt, *The Herndons: An Atlanta Family* (Athens: University of Georgia Press, 2002), 156–159; Alexa Benson Henderson, "Alonzo Herndon (1858–1927)," *New Georgia Encyclopedia*, http://www.georgiaencyclopedia.org/articles/business-economy/alonzo-herndon-1858–1927. Mills states that "Based on barber Alonzo Herndon's 1902 account book, many of his customers visited the shop daily, most likely for shaves, but also for other services." Although the invention of the safety razor had somewhat decreased such visits by the 1920s, it is likely that a number of men still came regularly. See Alonzo Herndon, Barber Shop Ledger, 1902, Alonzo Herndon unprocessed collection, The Herndon Home, Atlanta, Georgia, cited in Mills, *Cutting Along the Color Line*, 68.

7. Quote is from Alonzo Herndon, Autobiographical Statement, in Herndon Family Papers, Herndon Home, Atlanta, Georgia, quoted in Merritt, *The Herndons*, 4. For more on Herndon's early career, see Merritt, 4, 32–39. For more on his involvement in Atlanta Mutual, see Merritt, *The Herndons*, 75–84; Mills, *Cutting Along the Color Line*, 100, 102.

8. *Chaires v. City of Atlanta,* 164 Ga. 755 (1927); Mills, *Cutting Along the Color Line*, 135–136. For accounts of whites against this initial city ordinance, see "Negro Barber Ban Will Be Enjoined By City Chamber," *The Atlanta Constitution*, Feb. 3, 1926, 1; "Reconsider It," *The Atlanta Constitution*, Feb. 3, 1926, 4; "Methodist Women Protest Barber Act," *The Atlanta Constitution*, Feb. 4, 1926; "Council To Act on Barber Ban," *The Atlanta Constitution*, Feb. 4, 1926, 1; M. Ashby Jones, D.D., "Text and Pretext: The Negro Barber Shop and Southern Tradition," *The Atlanta Constitution*, Feb. 21, 1926, 12. Quote from T. J. Hightower is part of a letter to the editor in "Citizens Protest Against Recent Barber Ordinance," *The Atlanta Constitution*, Feb. 5, 1926, 4.

9. *Chaires v. City of Atlanta,* 164 Ga. 755 (1927); "Compromise Seen on Barber Bill," *The Atlanta Constitution*, Feb. 12, 1926; "Negro Barber Ban Limited to White Women, Children," *The Atlanta Constitution*, Feb. 16, 1926, 1; "Atlanta Chamber Plans to Enjoin Barber Measure," *The Atlanta Constitution*, Feb. 19, 1926, 1; "Court Enjoins Barber Measure," *The Atlanta Constitution*, Feb. 24, 1926, 1.

10. Between 1900 and 1920, black southerners litigated 340 civil cases in appellate courts out of a total of 65,780 civil and criminal suits in the eight appellate courts examined during this period. Between 1921 and 1950, black southerners litigated 755 civil cases in appellate courts out of a total of 90,508 civil and criminal suits in the appellate courts examined during this period. See Table B.1 (tables that are prefaced with "B" are given in Appendix B).

11. I have taken the number of black soldiers who participated in World War II from William H. Chafe, *The Unfinished Journey: America Since World War II*, 8th ed. (Oxford: Oxford University Press, 2014), 80. For more on African Americans' experiences during World War I and World War II, see Jeffrey T. Sammons and John H. Morrow Jr., *Harlem's Rattlers and the Great War: The Undaunted 369th Regiment and the African American Quest for Equality* (Lawrence: University Press of Kansas, 2014); Neil A. Wynn, *The Afro-American and the Second World War*, rev. ed. (New York: Holmes & Meier, 1993). For recent historiography on the link between African Americans and claims of rights during and in response to World War II, see the introduction and essays in Kevin M. Kruse and Stephen Tuck, eds., *Fog of War: The Second World War and the Civil Rights Movement* (New York: Oxford University Press, 2012).

12. For examples of civil cases in which the litigants or their family members are currently serving in the army or are veterans, see *New v. Atlantic Greyhound Corporation*, 186 Va. 726 (1947); *Chaires v. City of Atlanta*, 164 Ga. 755 (1927); *Provenza v. Provenza*, 201 Miss. 836 (1947). Criminal appellate cases involving black veterans included *Handspike v. State*, 203 Ga. 115 (1947), and *Scott v. State*, 247 Ala. 62 (1945).

13. *Broome v. Jackson*, 193 Miss. 66 (1942).

14. *Southern Kraft Corporation v. McCain, Commissioner of Labor*, 205 Ark. 943 (1943). For more on African Americans during the New Deal era, see Patricia Sullivan, *Days of Hope: Race and Democracy in the New Deal Era* (Chapel Hill: University of North Carolina Press, 1996), and Kimberley Johnson, *Reforming Jim Crow: Southern Politics and State in the Age Before Brown* (Oxford: Oxford University Press, 2010), 72–84.

15. Quote from Ethel New is from the trial transcript of *New v. Atlantic Greyhound Corporation*, 186 Va. 726 (1947). For the number of African Americans who moved north and south during the Great Migration, I relied on Isabel Wilkerson, *The Warmth of Other Suns: The Epic Story of America's Great Migration* (New York: Random House, 2010), 9. For more on The Great Migration, see Wilkerson, *The Warmth of Other Suns*; James Gregory, *The Southern Diaspora: How the Great Migrations of Black and White Southerners Transformed America* (Chapel Hill: University of North Carolina Press, 2005); James R. Grossman, *Land of Hope: Chicago, Black Southerners, and the Great Migration* (Chicago: University of Chicago Press, 1989).

16. Sullivan, *Days of Hope*, 8–9, 171–220; Michael J. Klarman, *Brown v. Board of Education and the Civil Rights Movement* (Oxford: Oxford University Press, 2007), 153. I have taken the percentage of African Americans who succeeded in registering to vote in the South by 1947 from

Chafe, *The Unfinished Journey*, 80. Historians debate, as well, whether World War II played a part in setting the scene for African Americans' battle for their political rights. For a thoughtful discussion of this debate, see "Introduction," in Kruse and Tuck, eds., *Fog of War*, 3–14. For more on the scholarship of a long history of the civil rights movement in the South in the first half of the twentieth century, see Brown-Nagin, *Courage to Dissent*; Fairclough, *Race & Democracy*; de Jong, *A Different Day*; Françoise N. Hamlin, *Crossroads at Clarksdale: The Black Freedom Struggle in the Mississippi Delta after World War II* (Chapel Hill: University of North Carolina Press, 2012); Kruse and Tuck, eds., *Fog of War*; Hall, "The Long Civil Rights Movement and the Political Uses of the Past," 1233–1263.

17. *Broome v. Jackson*, 193 Miss. 66 (1942). Although statistics on lynchings are notoriously difficult to calculate and many lynchings went unrecorded, one set of data records fifty-three lynchings of African Americans in the United Stated in 1921 and one such lynching in 1950. See "Lynchings: By Year and Race," University of Missouri Kansas City Law School, http://law2.umkc.edu/faculty/projects/ftrials/shipp/lynchingyear.html and http://law2.umkc.edu/faculty/projects/ftrials/shipp/lynchingsstate.html. Statistics provided by the Tuskegee Institute Archives. See also "Table A.7.1: Distribution of Black Male, White Male, and Female Victims by State and Decade, 1882–1930" in Bailey, *Lynched*, 230.

18. *Tennessee Chemical Company v. Smith*, 145 Tenn. 532 (1921). The case brought by the white employee against the coal mine is *Thompson v. Wisconsin Steel*, 214 Ky. 221 (1926).

19. Criminal cases involving illegal alcohol during the period of Prohibition included *Austin v. State*, 160 Ga. 509 (1925) and *Robinson v. State*, 158 Ga. 47 (1924). See also *Chaires v. City of Atlanta*, 164 Ga. 755 (1927). According to the officer's testimony, the barber Woodson Jackson was "convicted by a jury and sentenced to pay a fine or go to the chain gang for twelve months and afterwards forfeited his bond." For more on the period of Prohibition, see Coffey M. Thomas, *Long Thirst: Prohibition in America, 1920–1933* (New York: Norton, 1975), and Daniel Okrent, *Last Call: The Rise and Fall of Prohibition* (New York: Scribner, 2010).

20. *DeGrafenreid v. Nashville Ry. & Light Co.*, 162 Tenn. 558 (1931). For other personal injury cases involving electrical accidents, see *Mississippi Power & Light Co. v. Goosby*, 187 Miss. 790 (1939). For personal injury cases involving car and truck accidents, see *Alabama Power Co. v. Elmore*, 222 Ala. 6 (1930); *Scott v. Birmingham Electric Co.*, 250 Ala. 61 (1948). For more on the process of electrification in 1920's and 1930's America, see Ernest Freeberg, *The Age of Edison: Electric Light and the Invention of Modern America* (New York: Penguin, 2013), 298–302.

21. Black southerners were litigants in 75 fraud suits (14 percent of suits) and 212 personal injury suits (39 percent of suits) out of a total of 548 civil suits between black and white litigants from 1921 to 1950 in the eight appellate courts examined. For more on the types of cases African American were able to litigate during this time, see Table B.10. For an examination of the kinds of cases heard by state supreme courts in general at this time, see Kagan, "The Business of State Supreme Courts," 133–135.

22. *Hickman v. Slough*, 187 Miss. 525 (1940). The case transcript is missing from the Mississippi Department of Archives and History. For more on the stereotype of the faithful slave during the first decades of the twentieth century, see McElya, *Clinging to Mammy*.

23. *New v. Atlantic Greyhound Corporation*, 186 Va. 726 (1947); *Provenza v. Provenza*, 201 Miss. 836 (1947). See for instance the 1945 petition to the Chancery Court of Washington County, Mississippi, in the case of *Provenza v. Provenza* and the trial testimony of Mr. Bob Callaway (white) and Mr. L. Freeman (White). It is unclear what dates Edward Provenza served in the U.S. Army during World War II, but in a November 1945 court document he is listed as "Edward Provenza, a resident of the City of Greenville, Washington County, Mississippi, but in the United States Army."

24. For more on the rise of black lawyers during this period, see Mack, *Representing the Race* and Smith, *Emancipation: The Making of the Black Lawyer*. Mack notes, however, that he found few black lawyers in the South during the first half of the twentieth century and found far more in other parts of the United States (Mack, *Representing the Race*, 9–10). Indeed, most black litigants' lawyers in civil cases against whites that reached the eight state supreme courts examined still seem to have been white. For a case illustrating the barriers to black lawyers

gaining their law licenses in southern states during this time, see *Ex Parte Banks,* 254 Ala. 117 (1950).

25. Landon, *The Honor and Dignity of the Profession,* 56. For further discussion of white Mississippi lawyers representing themselves as paternalistic and fair in the twentieth century, see McMillen, *Dark Journey,* 216–217.

26. When the sheriff attempted to seize her home to fulfill the judgment in the case, though, she appealed to overturn the decision. See *Barringer v. Whitson,* 205 Ark. 260 (1943).

27. In the 548 civil cases examined that would later be heard by appellate courts, black litigants won the lower-court trial in 58 percent of suits. Of the 319 cases in which black litigants gained a favorable decision from the appellate courts from 1921 to 1950, appellate courts were upholding a lower-court decision in favor of the black litigants in 219 suits (69 percent of suits). As for how representative these suits were of overall reversal rates in the nation, the authors of a study that examined a sampling of cases every 5 years in sixteen representative state supreme courts throughout the United States between 1870 and 1970 found that the courts affirmed approximately 61.5 percent of suits and reversed approximately 38.5 percent of suits. See "Courting Reversal," *The Yale Law Journal,* 1198. As Table B.22 demonstrates, the suits between black and white southerners that I examined in eight southern appellate courts between 1921 and 1950 had a reversal rate of 30 percent (167 cases of 548 cases were reversed) and a 60 percent rate of lower-court decisions being upheld (330 cases of 548 suits were upheld). See Tables B.16, B.18, B.19, B.22, and B.24.

28. Between 1900 and 1920, there were 63 civil cases between black and white litigants in the appellate courts examined over fraud and 97 such cases over personal injury out of 220 total appellate civil suits between black and white litigants in the courts examined. Between 1921 and 1950, there were 75 civil cases between black and white litigants in the appellate courts examined over fraud and 212 such cases over personal injury out of 548 total appellate civil suits between black and white litigants in the courts examined. For the numbers and percentages of different kinds of civil cases between black and white litigants from 1900 to 1920 and from 1921 to 1950 in the eight state supreme courts examined, see Tables B.9 and B.10.

29. For examples of fraud cases between 1921 and 1950 in which black litigants continued to present themselves as ignorant and/or vulnerable, see *Carpenter v. Ingram,* 152 Va. 27 (1929); *Barner v. Handy,* 207 Ark. 833 (1944). For fraud cases in which black litigants were presented as intelligent, see *Jackson v. Stephens,* 251 Ala. 559 (1949).

30. *Alabama Power v. Elmore,* 222 Ala. 6 (1930).

31. *Mississippi Cooperative Cotton Ass'n v. Walker,* 186 Miss. 870 (1939).

32. Broome's lawyer also requested that his client receive any profits from the property that had accrued over the past six years. See case file of *Broome v. Jackson,* 193 Miss. 66 (1942).

33. *Broome v. Jackson,* 193 Miss. 66 (1942).

34. *Broome v. Jackson,* 193 Miss. 66 (1942).

35. For examples of cases protesting violence and intimidation against individual African American litigants, see *Melton v. Allen,* 212 Ky. 310 (1925); *Dooley v. Sterling Stores,* 214 Ark. 895 (1949); *Hough v. Leech,* 187 Ark. 719 (1933); *Tri-State Transit v. Westbrook,* 207 Ark. 270 (1944); *Hayes v. Lancaster,* 200 N.C. 293 (1931); *Montgomery v. Wallace,* 216 Ark. 525 (1950).

36. *Melton v. Allen,* 212 Ky. 310 (1925); *Hayes v. Lancaster,* 200 N.C. 293 (1931).

37. *Dooley v. Sterling Stores,* 214 Ark. 895 (1949); *Tri-State Transit v. Westbrook,* 207 Ark. 270 (1944).

38. *Jackson v. Parks,* 216 N.C. 329 (1939). For an example of a suit protesting using threats to put the black litigant in jail, see *Union Life Insurance Company v. Johnson,* 199 Ark. 241 (1939).

39. *Smith v. Raleigh Granite Company,* 202 N.C. 305 (1932). See also the suit of *McLaughlin v. R.W. Fagan-Peel Co.,* 125 Miss. 116 (1921), which protested dangerous labor conditions for an African American minor that led to the amputation of a teenager's arm.

40. See, for instance, *New v. Atlantic Greyhound Corporation,* 186 Va. 726 (1947); *Hardrick v. Southeastern Greyhound Lines,* 306 Ky. 579 (1947).

41. *New v. Atlantic Greyhound Corporation,* 186 Va. 726 (1947).

42. *New v. Atlantic Greyhound Corporation,* 186 Va. 726 (1947).

43. See *Morgan v. Commonwealth of Virginia*, 328 U.S. 373 (1946); Sullivan, *Lift Every Voice*, 316–317; "Morgan v. Virginia (1946)," Encyclopedia Virginia, http://www.encyclopediavirginia.org/morgan_v_virginia#start_entry.

44. *New v. Atlantic Greyhound Corporation*, 186 Va. 726 (1947).

45. *New v. Atlantic Greyhound Corporation*, 186 Va. 726 (1947).

46. *Hampton v. O'Rear*, 309 Ky. 1 (1948). Although this case did not directly confront racial discrimination (and so is thus not calculated as a racial discrimination case), it did bring a claim for a larger group beyond just the individuals involved.

47. The African American plaintiffs also asked for $500 in damages for being blocked from using the alley. See *Johnson v. Cooper*, 294 Ky. 295 (1943). For another property case that includes issues of segregation, see *Foos v. Engle*, 295 Ky. 114 (1943).

48. The Atlanta barbershop case is *Chaires v. City of Atlanta*. The case over labor discrimination in the railroad industry is *Steele v. Louisville & N.R. Co.*, 245 Ala.113 (1943). The case petitioning to practice law is *Ex parte Banks*, 254 Ala. 117 (1950). Another case with an economic impact on the litigants was a suit seeking to recoup the costs of transporting the plaintiff's children to a segregated school: *Warren v. Knox County Board of Education*, 258 Ky. 212 (1935).

49. The 1929 case challenging the segregation of public parks in Louisville, Kentucky, is *Warley v. Board of Park Commissioners*, 233 Ky. 688 (1930). Another similar case was also heard by the Supreme Court of Kentucky almost two decades later: *Sweeney v. City of Louisville*, 309 Ky. 465 (1949). The case over school taxes was *Bryant v. Barnes*, 144 Miss. 732 (1925). The case over voting registration was *Boswell v. Bethea*, 242 Ala. 292 (1942). The case challenging the all-white primary was *Robinson v. Holman*, 181 Ark. 428 (1930).

50. Lacking funds, the Niagara Movement dispersed in 1909. For more on Alonzo Herndon's role in the Niagara Movement, see Merritt, *The Herndons*, 72–73; Mills, *Cutting Along the Color Line*, 102; David Levering Lewis, *W. E. B. Du Bois: Biography of a Race* (New York: Holt, 1993), 316–320. For more on the Niagara Movement's legal strategy, see "Third Annual Meeting of the Niagara Movement," in Herbert Aptheker, ed., *Pamphlets and Leaflets by W. E. B. Du Bois* (White Plains, NY: Kraus-Thomson Organization, 1986), 74; Leaflet written by W. E. B. Du Bois (March 14, 1908), in *Pamphlets and Leaflets by W. E. B. Du Bois*, 77; Leaflet written by W. E. B. Du Bois (1909), in *Pamphlets and Leaflets by W. E. B. Du Bois*, 79. Other meeting minutes, abstracts, and pamphlets published by the Niagara Movement are contained in Aptheker, ed., *Pamphlets and Leaflets by W. E. B. Du Bois*, 59–81. See also Susan D. Carle, "Race, Class, and Legal Ethics in the Early NAACP (1910–1920)" in Susan D. Carle, ed., *Lawyers' Ethics and the Pursuit of Social Justice* (New York: New York University Press, 2005), 114–116; Carle, *Defining the Struggle*, 174–220.

51. *Chaires v. City of Atlanta*, 164 Ga. 755 (1927).

52. *Chaires v. City of Atlanta*, 164 Ga. 755 (1927).

53. *Chaires v. City of Atlanta*, 164 Ga. 755 (1927).

54. *Chaires v. City of Atlanta*, 164 Ga. 755 (1927).

55. This aligns with the interest–convergence theory put forward by Derrick A. Bell in "*Brown v. Board of Education* and the Interest-Convergence Dilemma," *Harvard Law Review* 93 (1979–1980): 518–533.

56. Although a bare-bones version of the organization was founded in 1909, the organization was given the name, the "National Association for the Advancement of Colored People" in May 1910. For more on the beginnings of the NAACP and their early focus on the courts, see Sullivan, *Lift Every Voice*, 1–19, 47; Carle, "Race, Class, and Legal Ethics in the Early NAACP," 114–119.

57. 18 Stat. 335 (1 March 1875); Riegel, "The Persistent Career of Jim Crow," 17–40; Franklin, "The Enforcement of the Civil Rights Act of 1875," in *Race and History: Selected Essays*, 118–131.

58. For an examination of African Americans' success in cases over education discrimination around the United States in the decades after the Civil War, see Kousser, *Dead End*, 5–12, 59, and Kousser, "Why Were There So Many Legal Cases on School Integration in Nineteenth-Century America?," 1–28.

59. NAACP Annual Report for 1926, 3. This report is quoted in Tushnet, *The NAACP's Legal Strategy Against Segregated Education*, 1–2.

60. Charles Thompson, "Court Action the Only Reasonable Alternative to Remedy Immediate Abuses of the Negro Separate School," *Journal of Negro Education*, 4, no. 3 (July 1935): 419–426. Other NAACP leaders, such as W. T. B. Williams and Ralph Bunche, disagreed with Thompson, arguing that favorable court decisions would not be enforced and that the NAACP should focus on uniting with white laborers to pursue economic progress. W. T. B. Williams, "Court Action by Negroes to Improve Their Schools a Doubtful Remedy," *Journal of Negro Education*, 4, no. 3 (July 1935): 435–441; Ralph J. Bunche, "A Critical Analysis of the Tactics and Programs of Minority Groups," *Journal of Negro Education* 4, no. 3 (July 1935): 308–320. For a discussion of this debate, see Tushnet, *The NAACP's Legal Strategy Against Segregated Education,* 11–12.

61. Sullivan, *Lift Every Voice,* 46–47; Tushnet, *The NAACP's Legal Strategy Against Segregated Education,* 147–153; Nieman, "The Language of Liberation," 85–87.

62. William Warley was born on January 6, 1884. He founded the *Louisville News* in 1912 and used it to crusade for black rights. George Wright explains that in 1914, "Warley led a black boycott against the National Theater's policy of restricting blacks to the gallery and back entrance." The boycott led to a partial victory. See George C. Wright, *Life Behind a Veil: Blacks in Louisville, Kentucky, 1865–1930* (Baton Rouge: Louisiana State University Press, 1985), 200–202; *Buchanan v. Warley,* 245 U.S. 60 (1917); R. Wigginton, "But He Did What He Could: William Warley Leads Louisville's Fight for Justice, 1902–1946," *Filson History Quarterly* 76, no. 4 (2002): 427–439; Sullivan, *Lift Every Voice,* 46–47.

63. *Buchanan v. Warley,* 245 U.S. 60 (1917); Sullivan, *Lift Every Voice,* 47, 72–73; Wigginton, "But He Did What He Could," 428, 439.

64. *Warley v. Board of Park Commissioners,* 233 Ky. 688 (1930); Wright, *Life Behind a Veil,* 274–278; "He Can't Quit," *Chicago Defender,* May 11, 1929, A2; Wigginton, "But He Did What He Could," 446–449. The two points of view on the NAACP's involvement in the case are presented in the *Chicago Defender* article and in Wigginton, "But He Did What He Could," p. 278, note 35.

65. *Warley v. Board of Park Commissioners,* 233 Ky. 688 (1930); Wigginton, "But He Did What He Could," 449.

66. *Warley v. Board of Park Commissioners,* 233 Ky. 688 (1930).

67. *Warley v. Board of Park Commissioners,* 233 Ky. 688 (1930); Wright, *Life Behind a Veil,* 278.

68. Using analysis of school budgets, NAACP cases showed that black separate schools received fewer funds and had fewer resources than white schools. Other suits pointed to disparities in the education offered to black and white students at the graduate and professional levels, claiming, for instance, that no comparable black law schools existed in certain states. Lawyers within the NAACP—including future US Supreme Court Justice Thurgood Marshall—took on such cases individually and at the branch level until 1935, when the NAACP established a permanent legal department. Tushnet, *The NAACP's Legal Strategy Against Segregated Education,* 21–81; Sullivan, *Lift Every Voice,* 101–144; Gilbert Jonas, *Freedom's Sword: The NAACP and the Struggle Against Racism in America, 1909–1969* (New York: Routledge, 2005), 32–47; Minnie Finch, *The NAACP: Its Fight For Justice* (Metuchen, NJ: Scarecrow Press, 1981), 84–100.

69. Similarly, in 1925, the NAACP arranged legal defense for black Detroit doctor Ossian Sweet, who had encountered a mob of whites throwing rocks at his newly purchased home in a white neighborhood and was accused, along with several associates, with shooting into the mob and killing a man. Sullivan, *Lift Every Voice,* 101–144; Jonas, *Freedom's Sword,* 32–47; Finch, *The NAACP: Its Fight for Justice,* 84–100. For an extended examination of the NAACP's involvement in the legal case of Ossian Sweet, see Boyle, *Arc of Justice.*

70. Indeed, legal scholar Risa Goluboff contends that although civil rights advances eventually came in the form of suits over constitutional equality, issues of labor equality were equally at issue during this time, and the civil rights movement could have taken a very different turn if economic equality had continued to be pursued through the courts. Goluboff, *The Lost Promise of Civil Rights,* 174–216.

71. Cases won by the NAACP between 1920 and 1940 before the US Supreme Court included *Moore et al. v. Dempsey,* 261 U.S. 86 (1923); *Missouri ex. rel. Gaines v. Canada,* 305 U.S. 337

(1938). The case won before the Maryland Court of Appeals was *Pearson v. Murray*, 182 A. 590 (1936). See Jonas, *Freedom's Sword*, 32–45; Sullivan, *Days of Hope*, 5.

72. *Smith v. Allwright*, 321 U.S. 649 (1944); Patricia Sullivan, "Movement Building During the World War II Era: The NAACP's Legal Insurgency in the South," in *Fog of War: The Second World War and the Civil Rights Movement*, 71.

73. See *Morgan v. Commonwealth of Virginia*, 328 U.S. 373 (1946); "Morgan v. Virginia (1946)," Encyclopedia Virginia, http://www.encyclopediavirginia.org/morgan_v_virginia#start_ entry.

74. *Shelley v. Kraemer*, 334 U.S. 1 (1948); *Sweatt v. Painter*, 339 U.S. 629 (1950); Lavergne, *Before Brown*; *Brown v. Board of Education of Topeka*, 347 U.S. 483 (1954).

75. *Brown v. Board of Education of Topeka*, 347 U.S. 483 (1954); *Brown v. Board of Education of Topeka*, 349 U.S. 294 (1955). For more on the *Brown* decision and its impact on the civil rights movement and understandings of the role of the courts, see Richard Kluger, *Simple Justice: The History of Brown v. Board of Education and Black America's Struggle for Equality* (1975; reprinted New York: Knopf, 1976); Klarman, *Brown v. Board of Education and the Civil Rights Movement*; Tushnet, *The NAACP's Legal Strategy Against Segregated Education*, 167–185; Klarman, *From Jim Crow to Civil Rights*, 385–442; Mark Tushnet, "Brown v. Board of Education," in Annette Gordon-Reed, ed., *Race on Trial: Law and Justice in American History* (Oxford: Oxford University Press, 2002), 160–176; Bell, "*Brown v. Board of Education* and the Interest-Convergence Dilemma," 492–494; Peter Irons, *Jim Crow's Children: The Broken Promise of the Brown Decision* (New York: Penguin, 2002); Michael W. McCann, "Reform Litigation on Trial," *Law and Social Inquiry* 17 (1992): 735–742; Aldon Morris, *The Origins of the Civil Rights Movement* (New York: Free Press, 1984), 26–39.

Epilogue

1. See Burbank, *Russian Peasants Go to Court*; Golfo Alexopolous, *Stalin's Outcasts: Aliens, Citizens, and the Soviet State, 1926–1936* (Ithaca, NY: Cornell University Press, 2003).

2. For more on the use of the law by enslaved men and women in Cuba, see Rebecca J. Scott, *Slave Emancipation in Cuba: The Transition to Free Labor, 1860–1899* (Princeton, NJ: Princeton University Press, 1985). For examples from South Africa, see Joel Joffe, *The State vs. Nelson Mandela: The Trial that Changed South Africa* (Oxford: Oneworld Publications, 2007); Kenneth S. Broun, *Black Lawyers, White Courts: The Soul of South African Law* (Athens: Ohio University Press, 2000). The question of how and whether litigation can lead to social reform has been widely debated in legal and political science scholarship, with the case of *Brown v. Board of Education* often used as a point of debate. See, for instance, Gerald N. Rosenberg, *The Hollow Hope: Can Courts Bring About Social Change?* (Chicago: University of Chicago Press, 1991), and Michael W. McCann's critical response to Rosenberg, "Reform Litigation on Trial," 715–743.

3. For an analysis of the habeas corpus petitions of Chinese immigrants, see Salyer, *Laws Harsh as Tigers*. Recognizing the courts' limits in the task of keeping "undesirable" immigrants out of the United States, at the beginning of the twentieth century a Bureau of Immigration was established, and according to Salyer, "By 1905, policy makers had achieved their goal: The jurisdiction of the courts to hear Chinese and other immigration cases was sharply curtailed" (Salyer, xvi–xvii).

4. In Georgia and Alabama, black litigants won 64 percent of their civil cases on appeal between 1865 and 1950. Similarly, in the eight state supreme courts examined, black litigants won 59 percent of their civil cases on appeal between 1865 and 1950. In contrast, of the 561 criminal cases involving black defendants that I found in the state supreme courts of Georgia and Alabama during that period, black defendants received a decision in their favor from the appellate court in only 38 percent of their suits (in 211 cases). See Table B.27 and Table B.18 (tables that are prefaced with "B" are given in Appendix B). In addition, in civil appellate cases directly challenging racial discrimination between 1865 and 1950, African Americans won only 36 percent of the cases examined (25 of 69).

5. For more on the role of the courts in Indian removal and the seizure of Indian land, see Walter R. Echo-Hawk, *In the Courts of the Conqueror: The 10 Worst Indian Law Cases Ever Decided*

(Golden, CO: Fulcrum, 2010); Stuart Banner, *How the Indians Lost Their Land: Law and Power on the Frontier* (Cambridge, MA: Harvard University Press, 2005).

6. *Mendez v. Westminster School District of Orange County*, 64 F. Supp. 544 (1946); *Westminster School District of Orange County v. Mendez*, 161 F.2d 774 (1947). For an examination of Mexican Americans' experiences in US courts in the *Mendez* cases, see Philippa Strum, *Mendez v. Westminster: School Desegregation and Mexican-American Rights* (Lawrence: University Press of Kansas, 2010).

7. *Grutter v. Bollinger*, 539 U.S. 306 (2003); *Fisher v. University of Texas*, 570 U.S. _____ (2013); *Fisher v. University of Texas*, 579 U.S. _____ (2016); *Shelby County v. Holder*, 570 U.S. _____ (2013).

8. For more on mass incarceration in the late twentieth and twenty-first centuries, see Michele Alexander, *The New Jim Crow: Mass Incarceration in the Age of Colorblindness* (New York: New Press, 2010); Elizabeth Hinton, *From the War on Poverty to the War on Crime: The Making of Mass Incarceration in America* (Cambridge, MA: Harvard University Press, 2016). For more on the Black Lives Matter Movement, see Keeanga-Yamahtta Taylor, *From #BlackLivesMatter to Black Liberation* (Chicago: Haymarket Books, 2016); Black Lives Matter Network, http://blacklivesmatter.com/.

Appendix A

1. For a discussion and examples of state supreme court civil cases involving black litigants in which the case record did not mention that one of the litigants was black, see Welke, *Recasting American Liberty*, 296.

2. The original transcripts of the state supreme court cases are held in the state archives of each state or in a law library in the state capitol. Although most of the original case files survive, some of the files can no longer be located. For a list of where the case files for each state can be located, see the Manuscripts section of the Bibliography.

3. Slavery, Abolition and Social Justice Database, Adam Matthew Digital, http://www.amdigital.co.uk/m-collections/collection/slavery-abolition-and-social-justice/.

4. See Table B.1 (tables that are prefaced with "B" are given in Appendix B).

5. See Table B.12.

6. To see the percentages of appellate civil suits between black litigants and appellate civil suits between black and white litigants broken down by period, see Table B.3. For data on the number of appellate civil cases between two or more black litigants by state and period, see Table B.4.

7. For data on the types of civil suits between black litigants that reached the state supreme courts examined, see Table B.5.

8. See Table B.3.

9. For more data on how many of these cases involved former masters and their former slaves or the heirs of former masters and former slaves and how this changed over time, see Table B.11.

10. For a breakdown of the proportion of female litigants in civil appellate suits by time period, see Table B.12. For an analysis of how often black women appeared as defendants in criminal appellate cases in the Alabama and Georgia state supreme courts between 1865 and 1950, see Table B.29.

11. See Tables B.12 and B.13.

12. Included in the number of cases involving economic disputes are cases over fraud, cases over property disputes, and cases over transactions and contracts. See Table B.7.

13. See Tables B.7 and B.8. This shift toward personal injury litigation partly reflected nationwide litigation trends, including a vast increase in tort suits against railroad companies at the end of the nineteenth century. For more on general trends in state supreme courts regarding personal injury at this time, see Kagan, "The Business of State Supreme Courts," 134–135, 142–143.

14. See Table B.9.

15. For the numbers and percentages of different kinds of civil cases between black and white litigants from 1900 to 1920 and from 1921 to 1950 in the eight state supreme courts examined, see Tables B.9 and B.10.

16. See Table B.15. In a certain number of cases, it could not be determined whether a jury or judge decided the case. In addition, at times cases were decided by more than one lower court before they reached the state's highest court—in this case, I used the lowest court they were heard in and then the highest court they were heard in for purposes of calculation. In at least four cases involving black litigants, suits were decided in one lower court by a judge and by another lower court by a jury.
17. See Table B.17.
18. See Table B.21.
19. See Table B.20.
20. See Table B.18.
21. See Tables B.18 and B.23.
22. See Table B.23.
23. See "Courting Reversal," *The Yale Law Journal*, 1198.
24. For more on these data, see Tables B.16, B.18, B.19, B.20, B.22, and B.23.
25. See Table B.26.
26. See Table B.32, and Kagan, "The Business of State Supreme Courts," 135, 145–146.
27. See Table B.27.
28. For more data on the impact of the race of victims on the outcome of criminal cases in the Georgia and Alabama appeals courts, see Table B.31.

BIBLIOGRAPHY

Manuscripts

Note: For reasons of space, I have not included in my citations the specific archives in which the case files for the court cases cited in this book are located. However, when I have cited a case I am referring to both the archival case file and the record of the case in the court reporter except for a few exceptions when the original case file was missing from the archives. The list of archives containing the case files I consulted is subsequently given.

ALABAMA CASE FILES

Alabama Department of Archives & History, Montgomery, Alabama
Alabama Court of Appeals, 1910–1969, Record Group SX-519-5
Supreme Court of Alabama Record of cases, 1824–1974

ARKANSAS CASE FILES

University of Arkansas at Little Rock, Pulaski Law Library, Little Rock, Arkansas
Arkansas Supreme Court Briefs and Records, 1836–1926. Series I, II, and III

GEORGIA CASE FILES

Georgia Archives, Morrow, Georgia
Georgia Supreme Court Case Files, 1846–1917. Record Group 92-1-1
Georgia Supreme Court Case Files, 1917–1990. Record Group 92-1-3
Superior Court Minutes, Liberty County Georgia, 1859–1935, RH 774-778. Microfilm drawer 30, boxes 48–52
Troup County Archives, LaGrange, Georgia
Superior Court Minute Books, Superior Court Records. Troup County Georgia, 1827–1937

KENTUCKY CASE FILES

Kentucky Department for Libraries and Archives, Frankfort, Kentucky
Case Files, 1854–1976. Kentucky Court of Appeals. Record Group 0126

MISSISSIPPI CASE FILES

Mississippi Department of Archives & History, Jackson, Mississippi
Mississippi High Court of Errors and Appeals, Case Files, 1832–1870, Series 208
Mississippi Supreme Court Case Files, Series 6

NORTH CAROLINA CASE FILES AND RECORDS

The State Archives of North Carolina, Raleigh, North Carolina
Estate Records, Orange County, North Carolina
North Carolina Supreme Court Records, Record Group 69
Walter Clark (1846–1924) Papers, Record Group 517
Wilson Library, University of North Carolina, Chapel Hill, Chapel Hill, North Carolina
Clark Battle. *Supreme Court of North Carolina.* North Carolina Collection
North Carolina County Collection
Rice C. Ballard Papers, Southern Historical Collection
Thomas Settle Papers, Southern Historical Collection
William Preston Bynum Papers, Southern Historical Collection

TENNESSEE CASE FILES

Tennessee State Library and Archives, Nashville, Tennessee
State Supreme Court Case Files, Trial Cases, 1796–1955, Record Group 170

VIRGINIA CASE FILES

The Library of Virginia, Richmond, Virginia
Records and briefs of the Virginia Supreme Court, 1865–1950. State government records
    collection
Virginia State Law Library, Richmond, Virginia
Supreme Court of Appeals of Virginia, Records and Briefs for Published Cases, 1849–Present
William Taylor Muse Law Library, University of Richmond, Richmond, Virginia
Virginia Supreme Court Records & Briefs, 1871–Present

OTHER DOCUMENTARY SOURCES

National Archives, Washington, DC
American Colonization Society. *The African Repository,* 1826–1892 (Washington, DC)
Records of the American Colonization Society. Domestic Letters, 1823–1912, I-298
    (Microfilm Publication, Series 1, Vol. 153–191).
National Archives, Southeast Region, Morrow, Georgia
Records of the Assistant Commissioner for Alabama (National Archives Microfilm Publications
    M1900), Records of the Bureau of Refugees, Freedmen, and Abandoned Lands, 1865–1872,
    Record Group 105
Records of the Assistant Commissioner for the State of Georgia (National Archives Microfilm
    Publications M798), Records of the Bureau of Refugees, Freedmen and Abandoned Lands,
    Record Group 105
Records of the Assistant Commissioner for Kentucky (National Archives Microfilm Publications
    M1904), Records of the Bureau of Refugees, Freedmen, and Abandoned Land, Virginia,
    Record Group 105
Records of the Assistant Commissioner for the State of North Carolina (National Archives
    Microfilm Publications M1909), Records of the Bureau of Refugees, Freedmen and
    Abandoned Lands, Record Group 105
Records of the Assistant Commissioner for Tennessee (National Archives Microfilm
    Publications M1911), Records of the Bureau of Refugees, Freedmen, and Abandoned Land,
    Virginia, Record Group 105
Records of the Assistant Commissioner for Virginia (National Archives Microfilm Publications
    M1913), Records of the Bureau of Refugees, Freedmen, and Abandoned Land, Virginia,
    Record Group 105
United States District Court, Civil, Criminal, Admiralty Case Files 1867–1878, Record
    Group 21

Published Federal Census Records

Abstract of The Twelfth Census of the United States 1900. Washington, DC: US Government Printing Office, 1902

Kennedy, Joseph C. G. *Population of The United States in 1860, Compiled From the Original Returns of The Eighth Census.* Washington, DC: US Government Printing Office, 1864

State Supreme Court Reports

State Supreme Court Reports. 1835–1865.
Alabama and Georgia.
State Supreme Court Reports. 1865–1950.
Alabama, Arkansas, Florida, Georgia, Kentucky, Louisiana, Mississippi, North Carolina, Tennessee, Texas, and Virginia.

Newspapers

The Atlanta Constitution (Atlanta, GA)
Atlanta Independent (Atlanta, GA)
The Atlanta Journal (Atlanta, GA)
Augusta County Argus (Staunton, VA)
Birmingham Age-Herald (Birmingham, AL)
Brownlow's Knoxville Whig, and Rebel Ventilator (Knoxville, TN)
Carolina Watchman (Salisbury, NC)
Charlotte Daily Observer (Charlotte, NC)
The Charlotte Democrat (Charlotte, NC)
Chicago Tribune (Chicago, IL)
The Colored Tennessean (Nashville, TN)
The Daily Constitution (Atlanta, GA)
The Daily Herald (Biloxi, MS)
The Daily Telegraph (Macon, GA)
The Fayetteville Observer (Fayetteville, NC)
Fayetteville Weekly Observer (Fayetteville, NC)
Fisherman & Farmer (Edenton, NC)
Georgia Weekly Telegraph (Macon, GA)
The Gold Leaf (Henderson, NC)
The Lexington Herald (Lexington, KY)
The Louisville Daily Courier (Louisville, KY)
Memphis Daily Appeal (Memphis, TN)
The Montgomery Advertiser (Montgomery, AL)
The Morning Post (Raleigh, NC)
The National Pilot (Petersburg, VA)
New Orleans Tribune (New Orleans, LA)
New York Times
Raleigh Daily Telegram (Raleigh, NC)
Richmond Dispatch (Richmond, VA)
Richmond Planet (Richmond, VA)
The Savannah Tribune (Savannah, GA)
Shenandoah Herald (Woodstock, VA)
The Tennessean (Nashville, TN)
The Times (Richmond, VA)
Tri-Weekly Era (Raleigh, NC)
The Weekly Louisianian (New Orleans, LA)

The Weekly North Carolina Standard (Raleigh, NC)
The Wilmington Messenger (Wilmington, NC)

Digital Collections and Sources

American Civil War Soldiers. http://www.ancestry.com.

Ancestry. http://www.ancestry.com.

Chronicling America Database. Library of Congress. http://chroniclingamerica.loc.gov/.

Confederate States Field Officers. http://www.ancestry.com.

Documenting the American South. http://docsouth.unc.edu.

Encyclopedia Virginia. http://www.encyclopediavirginia.org.

Encyclopedia of North Carolina. Edited by William S. Powell. University of North Carolina Press, 2006. http://ncpedia.org.

From Slavery to the Supreme Court. Online Exhibit. Just The Beginning Foundation. http://www.jtbf.org/index.php?submenu=Slavery&src=gendocs&link=FromSlaverytotheSupremeCourtOnlineExhibit&category=Main.

Livingston, J. Ed. "A History of the Alabama Judicial System." http://judicial.alabama.gov/docs/judicial_history.pdf.

LexisNexus. http://www.lexis.com.

"Lynchings: By Year and Race." University of Missouri Kansas City Law School. http://law2.umkc.edu/faculty/projects/ftrials/shipp/lynchingyear.html and

http://law2.umkc.edu/faculty/projects/ftrials/shipp/lynchingsstate.html. Statistics provided by the Tuskegee Institute Archives.

The Making of Modern Law: Primary Sources, 1620–1926. http://www.gale.com/moml-primary-sources-part-i/.

The New Georgia Encyclopedia. The Georgia Humanities Council and the University of Georgia Press. http://www.georgiaencyclopedia.org.

Newspapers.com. Ancestry. https://www.newspapers.com.

Slavery, Abolition and Social Justice Database. Adam Matthew Digital. http://www.amdigital.co.uk/m-collections/collection/slavery-abolition-and-social-justice/

St. Louis Circuit Court Historical Records Project. Washington University in St. Louis. http://www.stlcourtrecords.wustl.edu/about-freedom-suits-series.php.

Vanishing Georgia Photographic Collection. Georgia Archives. http://cdm.sos.state.ga.us/cdm4/vanishing.php.

Published Primary Sources

Acts of the General Assembly of the State of Virginia Passed in 1865–66, in the Eighty-Ninth Year of the Commonwealth. Richmond, VA: Allegre & Goode, Printers, 1866.

Acts of the Session of 1865–6 of the General Assembly of Alabama Held in the City of Montgomery Commencing on the 3rd Monday of November, 1865. Montgomery, AL: Reid & Screws, 1866.

Acts of the State of Tennessee Passed at the Second Session of the Thirty-Fourth General Assembly For the Years 1865–66. Nashville, TN: S.C. Mercer, 1866.

Andrews, Garnett. *Reminiscences of An Old Georgia Lawyer*. Atlanta, GA: Franklin Steam Printing House, 1870.

Aptheker, Herbert, ed. *Pamphlets and Leaflets by W. E. B. Du Bois*. White Plains, NY: Kraus-Thomson Organization, 1986.

Berlin, Ira, Thavolia Glymph, Steven F. Miller, Joseph P. Reidy, Leslie S. Rowland, and Julie Saville, eds. *Freedom: A Documentary History of Emancipation, 1861–1867*. Series 1, Vol. 3, The Wartime Genesis of Free Labor: The Lower South. Cambridge: Cambridge University Press, 1990.

Berlin, Ira, Joseph P. Reidy, and Leslie S. Rowland, eds. *Freedom: A Documentary History of Emancipation, 1861–1867*. Series 2, The Black Military Experience. Cambridge: Cambridge University Press, 1982.

Bibb, Henry. *Narrative of the Life and Adventures of Henry Bibb: An American Slave*. 1849; Reprinted New York: Dover, 2005.

Black, Henry Campbell. *A Treatise on the Rescission of Contracts and Cancellation of Written Instruments*. Kansas City, MO: Vernon Law Book Company, 1916.

Bridewell, L. O. *The Mississippi Justice of the Peace: A Manual of the Laws Relating to the Courts of Justices of the Peace, and the Practice Therein, in the State of Mississippi*. Jackson, MS: Clarion Steam Printing Establishment, 1877.

Browne, Causten. *A Treatise on the Construction of the Statute of Frauds*. Boston: Little, Brown, 1895.

Bullard, Henry A. and Thomas Curry. *New Digest of the Statute Laws of Louisiana*. New Orleans, LA: E. Johns & Co., 1842.

Bunche, Ralph J. "A Critical Analysis of the Tactics and Programs of Minority Groups." *Journal of Negro Education* 4, no. 3 (July 1935): 308–320.

Candler, Allen D., ed. *The Confederate Records of the State*. Atlanta, GA: Chas P. Byrd, 1911.

Caruthers, Abraham. *History of a Lawsuit in The Circuit Court of Tennessee On the Basis of The Code*. Nashville, TN: A.A. Stitt, 1860.

Caruthers, Abraham. *History of a Lawsuit*, 4th ed. Cincinnati, OH: W. H. Anderson Company, 1903.

Chalmers, James R. *The Probate Law and Practice in the Courts of Mississippi and Tennessee*. Rochester, NY: Lawyers' Co-Operative Publishing Company, 1890.

Clark, R. H., T. R. R. Cobb, and D. Irwin, Preparers. *The Code of the State of Georgia*. Atlanta, GA: John H. Seals, 1861.

Clark, R. H., T. R. R. Cobb, and D. Irwin, Preparers. *The Code of the State of Georgia*. Atlanta, GA: Franklin Steam Printing House, 1867.

Clark, R. H., T. R. R. Cobb, and D. Irwin, Preparers. *The Code of the State of Georgia*, 2nd ed. Macon, GA: J.W. Burke & Co., 1873.

Clark, Walter. *History of the Supreme Court of North Carolina*. Raleigh, NC: Reprinted from the N.C. Booklet, 1919.

Cobb, Howell. *A Compilation of the General and Public Statutes of the State of Georgia*. New York: Edward O. Jenkins, 1859.

Connor, R. D. W. *History of North Carolina*, Vol. 6. Chicago: Lewis Publishing Co., 1919.

Constitution, Ordinances, and Resolutions of the Georgia Convention Held in the City of Atlanta in 1867 and 1868. Atlanta, GA: New Era Job Office, 1868.

Cooper, Thomas and McCord, comps. *The Statutes at Large of South Carolina*. Columbia, SC: A. S. Johnston, 1836–1841.

Cox, LaWanda Cox and John H. Cox, eds. *Reconstruction, the Negro, and the New South*. New York: Harper & Row, 1973.

Cozart, Abram Whitenack. *Georgia Practice Rules as Laid Down By The Supreme Court and Court of Appeals of Georgia*. Atlanta, GA: Harrison Company, 1918.

Davis, Sidney Fant. *Mississippi Negro Lore*. Jackson, TN: McCowat Mercer, 1914.

Dembitz, Lewis N. *Kentucky Jurisprudence in Four Books*, Book 2. Louisville, KY: John P. Morton & Company, 1890.

Douglass, Frederick. *The Frederick Douglass Papers*. New Haven, CT: Yale University Press, 1980.

Dowd, Jerome. *Sketches of Prominent Living North Carolinians*. Raleigh, NC: Edwards & Broughton, Printers, 1888.

DuBose, John Witherspoon. *Jefferson County and Birmingham Alabama: Historical and Biographical*. Birmingham, AL: Caldwell Printing Works, 1887.

Du Bois, W. E. B. "Race Relations in the United States, 1917–1947." *Phylon* 9:3 (1948): 234–237.

Du Bois, W. E. B. *The Souls of Black Folk*. 1903. Reprint, New York: Dover Publications, 1994.

Duffie, J. S. & W. F. Hill. *The Arkansas Justice: A Treatise on the Powers and Duties of Justices of the Peace, Embraced in their Civil and Criminal Jurisdiction in the State of Arkansas*. St. Louis, MO: Gilbert Book Co., 1888.

Eastman, Crystal. *Work-Accidents and the Law*. New York: Charities Publication Committee, 1910.

Fleming, Walter L., ed. *Documentary History of Reconstruction*, Vol. 2. Cleveland, OH: Arthur H. Clark Company, 1906.

Franklin, John Hope, ed. *John Roy Lynch: Reminiscences of an Active Life: The Autobiography of John Roy Lynch.* Chicago: University of Chicago Press, 1970.

Grice, Warren. *The Georgia Bench and Bar: The Development of Georgia's Judicial System,* Vol. 1. Macon, GA: J. W. Burke Company, 1931.

Gwathmey, John H. *Legends of Virginia Courthouses.* Richmond, VA: Dietz Printing Company, 1933.

Hallum, John. *The Diary of an Old Lawyer or Scenes Behind the Curtain.* Nashville, TN: Southwestern Publishing House, 1895.

Hopkins, John L. *The Law of Personal Injuries and Incidentally Damage to Property by Railway-Trains: Based on the Statutes and Decisions of the Supreme Court of the State of Georgia.* Atlanta, GA: Foote & Davies Company, 1902.

Hopkins, John L. *The Law of Personal Injuries and Incidentally Damage to Property by Railway-Trains.* Atlanta, GA: Harrison Company, 1912.

Hopkins, John L., Clifford Anderson, and Joseph R. Lamar. *The Code of the State of Georgia.* Atlanta, GA: Foote & Davies Company, 1896.

Hopkins, John L., Clifford Anderson, and Joseph R. Lamar. *The Code of the State of Georgia.* Atlanta, GA: Foote & Davies Company, 1911.

Jacobs, Harriet. "Incidents in the Life of a Slave Girl." In *I Was Born A Slave: An Anthology of Classic Slave Narratives, 1849–1866,* Vol. 2., edited by Yuval Taylor, 533–682. Chicago: Lawrence Hill, 1999.

Laws of the State of Mississippi Passed at a Regular Session of the Mississippi Legislature Held in the City of Jackson, October, November and December 1865. Jackson, MS: J.J. Shannon & Co., State Printers, 1866.

Kennedy, Stetson. *Jim Crow Guide to the U.S.A.: The Laws, Customs and Etiquette Governing the Conduct of Nonwhites and Other Minorities as Second-Class Citizens.* 1959; Reprinted, Tuscaloosa: University of Alabama Press, 2011.

Meigs, Return J. and William F. Cooper. *The Code of Tennessee Enacted by the General Assembly of 1857–'8.* Nashville, TN: E.G. Eastman and Company, State Printers, 1858.

Minor, John B. *Institutes of Common and Statute Law,* Vol. 1. Richmond: Printed for the Author, 1882.

Minor, Raleigh Colston. *The Law of Real Property.* University of Virginia: Anderson Bros., Publishers, 1908.

Moore, Bartholomew F. and Asa Biggs. *Revised Code of North Carolina.* Boston: Little, Brown and Company, 1855.

Northup, Solomon. "Twelve Years a Slave: Narrative of Solomon Northup." In *I Was Born a Slave: An Anthology of Classic Slave Narratives, 1849–1866,* Vol. 2., edited by Yuval Taylor, 159–318. Chicago: Lawrence Hill, 1999.

Oberdorfer, A. Leo. *Oberdorfer's Alabama Justices' Practice.* Charlottesville, VA: Michie Company, Publishers, 1905.

O'Neall, John Belton. *The Negro Law of South Carolina.* Columbia, SC: John G. Bowman, 1848.

Parker Jr., Roy. *Cumberland County: A Brief History.* Raleigh, NC: Division of Archives and History, 1990.

Parton, James. *General Butler in New Orleans.* Boston: J. E. Farwell & Co., 1864.

Powdermaker, Hortense. *After Freedom: A Cultural Study in the Deep South.* New York: Viking, 1939.

Reed, John C. *American Law Studies; or, Self-Preparation for Practice in The United States: A Course of Instruction, Reading, and Exercises for Students and Young Lawyers, By Which They Can Thoroughly And Rapidly Train Themselves For Legal Business.* Boston: Little, Brown, and Company, 1882.

Reed, John C. *Conduct of Lawsuits Out of and in Court: Practically Teaching, and Copiously Illustrating, The Preparation and Forensic Management of Litigated Cases of All Kinds.* Boston: Little, Brown, and Company, 1885.

Reese, William M. *A Manual for Ordinaries, Executors, Administrators, and Guardians, in the State of Georgia.* Boston: Little, Brown and Company, 1860.

The Revised Code of the Statute Laws of the State of Mississippi. Jackson, MS: E. Barksdale, state printer, 1857.

Samito, Christian G. *Changes in Law and Society During the Civil War and Reconstruction: A Legal History Documentary Reader.* Carbondale: Southern Illinois University Press, 2009.

Seghers, Julien A. and Patrice Leonard. *The Louisiana Magistrate and Parish Officer's Guide Containing Copious Forms and Instructions,* 2nd ed. Parish of Plaquemines, LA: Office of the Empire Parish Register, 1870.

Smith, John W. *A Treatise on The Law of Frauds and The Statute of Frauds.* Indianapolis, IN: Bobbs-Merrill Company, 1907.

Smith, Wilford H. "The Negro and the Law." In *The Negro Problem: A Series of Articles by Representative American Negroes of To-day,* edited by Booker T. Washington. New York: James Pott, 1903.

Smith, William L. *The Practice in Proceedings in the Probate Courts.* Boston: Little, Brown and Company, 1868.

Stephenson, Gilbert Thomas. *Race Distinctions in American Law.* New York: D. Appleton and Company, 1910.

Taylor, Alrutheus A. *The Negro in the Reconstruction of Virginia.* Washington, DC: Association for the Study of Negro Life and History, 1926.

Thirty Years of Lynching in the United States, 1889–1918. New York: NAACP, 1919; reprinted Clark, NJ: Lawbook Exchange, 2012.

Thompson, Charles. "Court Action the Only Reasonable Alternative to Remedy Immediate Abuses of the Negro Separate School." *Journal of Negro Education* 4, no. 3 (July 1935): 419–426.

Tocqueville, Alexis de. *Democracy in America,* Vol. I. New York: Knopf, 1945.

Watson, Archibald Robinson. *A Treatise on the Law of Damages for Personal Injuries Embracing a Consideration of the Principles Regulating the Primary Question of Liability, As Well as the Measure and Elements of Recovery After Liability Established.* Charlottesville, VA: Michie Company, Publishers, 1901.

Wells, Ida B. *Crusade for Justice: The Autobiography of Ida B. Wells.* Chicago: University of Chicago Press, 1970.

Williams, W. T. B. "Court Action by Negroes to Improve their Schools a Doubtful Remedy." *Journal of Negro Education* 4, no. 3 (July 1935): 435–441.

Williamson, Hugh P. "Document: The State Against Celia, a Slave." *Midwest Journal* 8 (1957): 408–420.

Secondary Sources

Abbott, Martin. *The Freedmen's Bureau in South Carolina, 1865–1872.* Chapel Hill: University of North Carolina Press, 1967.

Aldrich, Mark. *Death Rode the Rails: American Railroad Accidents and Safety, 1828–1965.* Baltimore: Johns Hopkins University Press, 2006.

Alexander, Adele Logan. *Ambiguous Lives: Free Women of Color in Rural Georgia, 1789–1879.* Fayetteville: University of Arkansas Press, 1991.

Alexander, Michele. *The New Jim Crow: Mass Incarceration in the Age of Colorblindness.* New York: New Press, 2010.

Alexander, Roberta Sue. "North Carolina Faces the Freedmen: Race Relations During Presidential Reconstruction, 1865–1867." Ph.D. diss., University of Chicago, 1974.

Alexander, Shawn Leigh. *An Army of Lions: The Civil Rights Struggle Before the NAACP.* Philadelphia: University of Pennsylvania Press, 2012.

Anderson, James D. "Aunt Jemima in Dialectics: Genovese on Slave Culture." *The Journal of Negro History* 61, no. 1 (1976): 99–114.

Arnesen, Eric. "Reconsidering the Long Civil Rights Movement." *Historically Speaking* 10, no. 2 (2009): 31–34.

Ayers, Edward L. *The Promise of the New South: Life After Reconstruction.* New York: Oxford University Press, 1992.

Ayers, Edward L. *Vengeance & Justice: Crime and Punishment in the 19th-Century American South.* New York: Oxford University Press, 1984.

Balleisen, Edward J. *Fraud: An American History from Barnum to Madoff.* Princeton, NJ: Princeton University Press, 2017.

Bardaglio, Peter W. "Rape and the Law in the Old South: 'Calculated to excite Indignation in Every Heart.'" *The Journal of Southern History* 60, no. 4 (1994): 749–772.

Bardaglio, Peter W. *Reconstructing the Household: Families, Sex and the Law in the Nineteenth-Century South.* Chapel Hill, NC: University of North Carolina Press, 1995.

Barkley Brown, Elsa. "Negotiating and Transforming the Public Sphere: African American Political Life in the Transition From Slavery to Freedom." In *Time Longer Than Rope: A Century of African American Activism, 1850–1950,* edited by Charles M. Payne and Adam Green, 68–110. New York: New York University Press, 2003.

Barkley Brown, Elsa. "To Catch a Vision of Freedom: Reconstructing Southern Black Women's Political History, 1865–1880." In *African American Women and the Vote, 1837-1960,* edited by Ann Gordon et al., 66–99. Amherst: University of Massachusetts Press, 1997.

Barnes, Kenneth C. *Journey of Hope: The Back-to-Africa Movement in Arkansas in the Late 1800s.* Chapel Hill: University of North Carolina Press, 2004.

Behrend, Justin. *Reconstructing Democracy: Grassroots Black Politics in the Deep South After the Civil War.* Athens: University of Georgia Press, 2015.

Bell, Derrick A. "*Brown v. Board of Education* and the Interest-Convergence Dilemma." *Harvard Law Review* 93 (1979–1980): 518–533.

Berlin, Ira. *Slaves Without Masters: The Free Negro in the Antebellum South.* New York: Vintage Books, 1976.

Berlin, Ira. *Many Thousands Gone: The First Two Centuries of Slavery in North America.* Cambridge, MA: Harvard University Press, 1998.

Berlin, Ira. *Generations of Captivity: A History of African-American Slaves.* Cambridge, MA: Belknap Press of Harvard University Press, 2003.

Berlin, Ira, Barbara J. Fields, Steven F. Miller, Joseph P. Reidy, and Leslie S. Rowland. *Slaves No More: Three Essays on Emancipation and the Civil War.* Cambridge: Cambridge University Press, 1992.

Berry, Mary Frances. *Black Resistance/White Law: A History of Constitutional Racism in America.* Revised edition. New York: Penguin, 1995.

Berry, Mary Frances. *The Pig Farmer's Daughter and Other Tales of American Justice: Episodes of Racism and Sexism in the Courts from 1865 to the Present.* New York: Vintage Books, 1999.

Blackmon, Douglas A. *Slavery By Another Name.* New York: Doubleday, 2008.

Blassingame, John W. *Black New Orleans, 1860–1880.* Chicago: University of Chicago Press, 1973.

Blight, David W. *Race and Reunion: The Civil War in American Memory.* Cambridge, MA: Harvard University Press, 2001.

Blumenthal, Susanna. "Of Mandarins, Legal Consciousness, and the Cultural Turn in U.S. Legal History." *Law & Social Inquiry* 37 (Winter 2012): 167–183.

Blumenthal, Susanna. "The Deviance of the Will: Policing the Bounds of Testamentary Freedom in Nineteenth-Century America." *Harvard Law Review* 119 (Feb. 2006): 959–1034.

Bodenhamer, David J. and James W. Ely, Jr. *Ambivalent Legacy: A Legal History of the South.* Jackson: University Press of Mississippi, 1984.

Bourdieu, Pierre. "The Force of Law: Toward a Sociology of the Juridical Field." Translated by Richard Terdiman. *Hastings Law Journal* 38 (July 1987): 814–853.

Boyle, Kevin. *Arc of Justice: A Saga of Race, Civil Rights, and Murder in the Jazz Age.* New York: Holt, 2004.

Brooks, Peter and Paul Gewirtz. *Law's Stories: Narrative and Rhetoric in the Law.* New Haven, CT: Yale University Press, 1996.

Brown, R. Ben. "The Tennessee Supreme Court During Reconstruction and Redemption." In *A History of the Tennessee Supreme Court*, edited by James W. Ely, Jr., 100–131. Knoxville, TN: University of Tennessee Press, 2002.

Brown, Robert T. *Immigrants to Liberia, 1843 to 1865, An Alphabetical Listing*. Philadelphia: Institute for Liberian Studies, 1980.

Brown-Nagin, Tomiko. *Courage to Dissent: Atlanta and the Long History of the Civil Rights Movement*. Oxford: Oxford University Press, 2011.

Brundage, W. Fitzhugh. *Lynching in the New South: Georgia and Virginia, 1880–1930*. Urbana: University of Illinois Press, 1993.

Brundage, W. Fitzhugh. "White Women and the Politics of Historical Memory in the New South, 1880–1920." In *Jumpin' Jim Crow: Southern Politics from Civil War to Civil Rights*, edited by Jane Dailey, Glenda Gilmore, and Bryant Simon, 115–139. Princeton, NJ: Princeton University Press, 2000.

Burbank, Jane. *Russian Peasants Go To Court: Legal Culture in the Countryside, 1905–1917*. Bloomington: Indiana University Press, 2004.

Burke, W. Lewis, Jr. "The Radical Law School: The University of South Carolina School of Law and Its African American Graduates, 1873–1877." In *At Freedom's Door: African American Founding Fathers and Lawyers in Reconstruction South Carolina*, edited by James Lowell Underwood and W. Lewis Burke, Jr., 90–115. Columbia: University of South Carolina Press, 2000.

Burin, Eric. "Envisioning Africa: American Slaves' Ideas About Liberia." *Liberian Studies Journal* 47, no. 2 (2002): 1–17.

Burin, Eric. *Slavery and the Peculiar Solution: A History of the American Colonization Society*. Gainesville: University Press of Florida, 2005.

Bynum, Victoria. *Unruly Women: The Politics of Social and Sexual Control in the Old South*. Chapel Hill: University of North Carolina Press, 1992.

Caldwell, Wilber W. *The Courthouse and the Depot: The Architecture of Hope in an Age of Despair: A Narrative Guide to Railroad Expansion and Its Impact on Public Architecture in Georgia, 1833–1910*. Macon, GA: Mercer University Press, 2001.

Camp, Stephanie M. H. *Closer to Freedom: Enslaved Women and Everyday Resistance in the Plantation South*. Chapel Hill: University of North Carolina Press, 2004.

Carle, Susan D. *Defining the Struggle: National Organizing for Racial Justice, 1880–1915*. Oxford: Oxford University Press, 2013.

Carle, Susan D. "Race, Class, and Legal Ethics in the Early NAACP (1910–1920)." In *Lawyers' Ethics and the Pursuit of Social Justice*, edited by Susan D. Carle, 114–119. New York: New York University Press, 2005.

Carter, Dan. *When the War Was Over: The Failure of Self-Reconstruction in the South, 1865–1867*. Baton Rouge: Louisiana State University Press, 1985.

Chafe, William H. *The Unfinished Journey: America Since World War II*, 8th ed. Oxford: Oxford University Press, 2014.

Clarke, Erskine. *Dwelling Place: A Plantation Epic*. New Haven, CT: Yale University Press, 2005.

Clegg, Claude A. *The Price of Liberty: African Americans and the Making of Liberia*. Chapel Hill: University of North Carolina Press, 2004.

Cline, Wayne. *Alabama Railroads*. Tuscaloosa: University of Alabama Press, 1997.

Cottrol, Robert. *The Long, Lingering Shadow: Slavery, Race, and Law in the American Hemisphere*. Athens: University of Georgia Press, 2013.

"Courting Reversal: The Supervisory Role of State Supreme Courts." *The Yale Law Journal* 87, no. 6 (1978): 1191–1218.

Crouch, Barry A. "Black Dreams and White Justice." *Prologue: Journal of the National Archives* 6 (Winter 1974): 255–265.

Dailey, Jane Elizabeth, Glenda Elizabeth Gilmore, and Bryant Simon. *Jumpin' Jim Crow: Southern Politics from Civil War to Civil Rights*. Princeton, NJ: Princeton University Press, 2000.

Davis, Thomas J. "Race Identity, and the Law: Plessy v. Ferguson." In *Race on Trial: Law and Justice in American History*, edited by Annette Gordon-Reed, 61–76. Oxford: Oxford University Press, 2002.

Deen, Braswell D., Jr. and William Scott Henwood. *Georgia's Appellate Judiciary: Profile and History*. Norcross, GA: Harrison Company, 1987.

Degler, Carl. *The Other South: Southern Dissenters in the Nineteenth Century*. New York: Harper & Row, 1974.

de Jong, Greta. *A Different Day: African American Struggles for Justice in Rural Louisiana, 1900– 1970*. Chapel Hill: University of North Carolina Press, 2002.

de la Fuente, Alejandro. "Slave Law and Claims-Making in Cuba: The Tannenbaum Debate Revisited." *Law and History Review* 22, no. 2 (2004): 339–369.

DeLombard, Jeannine Marie. *Slavery on Trial: Law, Abolitionism, and Print Culture*. Chapel Hill: University of North Carolina Press, 2007.

Dorsey, Bruce. "A Gendered History of African Colonization in the Antebellum United States." *Journal of Social History* 34, no. 1 (2000): 77–103.

Downs, Gregory P. *After Appomattox: Military Occupation and the Ends of War*. Cambridge, MA: Harvard University Press, 2015.

Drago, Edmund L. *Black Politicians and Reconstruction in Georgia: A Splendid Failure*. Athens: University of Georgia Press, 1992.

Dray, Philip. *At the Hands of Persons Unknown: The Lynching of Black America*. New York: Random House, 2002.

Du Bois, W. E. B. *Black Reconstruction: An Essay Toward a History of the Part Which Black Folk Played in the Attempt to Reconstruct Democracy in America, 1860–1880*, 1st ed. New York: Harcourt, 1935.

Dumas, Royal. "The Muddled Mettle of Jurisprudence: Race and Procedure in Alabama's Appellate Courts, 1901–1930." *Alabama Law Review* 58 (2006): 417–442.

Edwards, Laura F. *A Legal History of the Civil War and Reconstruction*. New York: Cambridge University Press, 2015.

Edwards, Laura F. "Enslaved Women and the Law: The Paradoxes of Subordination in the Post-Revolutionary Carolinas." *Slavery & Abolition* 26 (August 2005): 305–323.

Edwards, Laura F. *Gendered Strife and Confusion: The Political Culture of Reconstruction*. Urbana: University of Illinois Press, 1997.

Edwards, Laura F. "Status Without Rights: African Americans and the Tangled History of Law and Governance in the Nineteenth-Century U.S. South." *The American Historical Review* 112, no. 2 (2007): 365–393.

Edwards, Laura F. "The History in 'Critical Legal Histories.'" *Law & Social Inquiry* 37 (Winter 2012): 187–197.

Edwards, Laura F. *The People and Their Peace: Legal Culture and the Transformation of Inequality in the Post-Revolutionary South*. Chapel Hill: University of North Carolina Press, 2009.

Elliott, Mark. *Color-Blind Justice: Albion Tourgee and the Quest for Racial Equality From the Civil War to Plessy v. Ferguson*. Oxford: Oxford University Press, 2006.

Elliott, Mark. "Telling the Difference: Nineteenth-Century Legal Narratives of Racial Taxonomy." *Law and Social Inquiry* 24 (1999): 611–636.

Ely, James W., Jr. *The Guardian of Every Other Right: A Constitutional History of Property Rights*. New York: Oxford University Press, 1998.

Ely, James W., Jr. *Railroads and American Law*. Lawrence: University Press of Kansas, 2001.

Ely, James W., Jr., ed. *A History of the Tennessee Supreme Court*. Knoxville: University of Tennessee Press, 2002.

Emberton, Carole. *Beyond Redemption: Race, Violence, and the American South After the Civil War*. Chicago: University of Chicago Press, 2013.

Farrow, Anne, Joel Lang, and Jenifer Frank. *Complicity: How the North Promoted, Prolonged, and Profited From Slavery*. New York: Ballantine Books, Reprinted ed., 2006.

Feimster, Crystal N. *Southern Horrors: Women and the Politics of Rape and Lynching*. Cambridge, MA: Harvard University Press, 2009.

Fields, Barbara J. "Ideology and Race in American History." In *Region, Race, and Reconstruction: Essays in Honor of C. Vann Woodward*, edited by J. Morgan Kouser and James M. McPherson, 143–177. New York: Oxford University Press, 1991.

Fields, Barbara J. "The Nineteenth-Century American South: History and Theory." *Plantation Society* 2, no. 1 (1983): 7–27.

Finch, Minnie. *The NAACP: Its Fight For Justice*. Metuchen, NJ: Scarecrow Press, 1981.

Finkelman, Paul. *An Imperfect Union: Slavery, Federalism, and Comity*. Chapel Hill: University of North Carolina Press, 1981.

Finkelman, Paul. *Slavery in the Courtroom: An Annotated Bibliography of American Cases*. Washington, DC: Library of Congress, 1985.

Finkelman, Paul. "Prelude to the Fourteenth Amendment: Black Legal Rights in the Antebellum North." *Rutgers Law Journal* 17 (1986): 417–450.

Finkelman, Paul. *The Law of Freedom and Bondage: A Casebook*. New York: Oceana, 1986.

Finkelman, Paul. "Not Only the Judges' Robes were Black: African American Lawyers as Social Engineers." *Stanford Law Review* 47, no. 1 (1994): 161–209.

Finkelman, Paul, ed. *Slavery & the Law*. Madison, WI: Madison House, 1997.

Finkelman, Paul. "Thomas R.R. Cobb and the Law of Slavery." *Roger Williams University Law Review* 5, no. 1 (1999): 104–105.

Fischer, Kirsten. *Suspect Relations: Sex, Race, and Resistance in Colonial North Carolina*. Ithaca, NY: Cornell University Press, 2002.

Fisher, James S. "Negro Farm Ownership in the South." *Annals of the Association of American Geographers* 63, no. 4 (1973): 478–489.

Fisk, Catherine L. and Robert W. Gordon. "'Law As . . . ': Theory and Method in Legal History." *UC Irvine Law Review* 1, no. 3 (2011): 519–541.

Flanigan, Daniel J. "Criminal Procedure in Slave Trials in the Antebellum South." *The Journal of Southern History* 40, no. 4 (1974): 537–564.

Foner, Eric. *Free Soil, Free Labor, Free Men: The Ideology of the Republican Party Before the Civil War*. New York: Oxford University Press, 1970.

Foner, Eric. *Nothing But Freedom: Emancipation and Its Legacy*. Baton Rouge: Louisiana State Press, 1983.

Foner, Eric. "Rights and the Constitution in Black Life During the Civil War and Reconstruction." *The Journal of American History* 74, no. 3 (1987): 863–883.

Foner, Eric. *Reconstruction: America's Unfinished Revolution, 1863–1877*. New York: Harper & Row, 1988.

Fox-Genovese, Elizabeth. *Within the Plantation Household: Black and White Women of the Old South*. Chapel Hill: University of North Carolina Press, 1988.

Franklin, John Hope. *The Free Negro in North Carolina, 1790–1860*. 1943; reprinted New York: Russell & Russell, 1969.

Franklin, John Hope. "The Enforcement of the Civil Rights Act of 1875." In *Race and History: Selected Essays 1938–1968*, 116–131. Baton Rouge: Louisiana State University Press, 1989.

Freeberg, Ernest. *The Age of Edison: Electric Light and the Invention of Modern America*. New York: Penguin, 2013.

Friedman, Lawrence. *A History of American Law*. New York: Simon & Schuster, 2005.

Friedman, Lawrence. *Dead Hands: A Social History of Wills, Trusts, and Inheritance Law*. Stanford, CA: Stanford University Press, 2009.

Galanter, Marc. "Why the 'Haves' Come Out Ahead: Speculations on the Limits of Legal Change." *Law & Society Review* 9, no. 1 (1974): 95–160.

Genovese, Eugene D. *The Political Economy of Slavery*. New York: Pantheon Books, 1965.

Genovese, Eugene D. *Roll, Jordan, Roll: The World the Slaves Made*. 1974; Reprinted New York: Vintage, 1976.

Gillmer, Jason A. "Suing For Freedom: Interracial Sex, Slave Law, and Racial Identity in the Post-Revolutionary and Antebellum South." *North Carolina Law Review* 82, no. 2 (2004): 535–619.

Gillmer, Jason A. "Poor Whites, Benevolent Masters, and the Ideologies of Slavery: The Local Trial of a Slave Accused of Rape." *North Carolina Law Review* 85 (2007): 489–570.

Gilmore, Glenda Elizabeth. *Gender and Jim Crow: Women and the Politics of White Supremacy in North Carolina, 1896–1920.* Chapel Hill: University of North Carolina Press, 1996.

Gilmore, Glenda Elizabeth. *Defying Dixie: The Radical Roots of Civil Rights, 1919–1950.* New York: Norton, 2008.

Goldstone, Lawrence. *Inherently Inequal: The Betrayal of Equal Rights By the Supreme Court, 1865–1903.* New York: Walker, 2011.

Goluboff, Risa. *The Lost Promise of Civil Rights.* Cambridge, MA: Harvard University Press, 2007.

Goluboff, Risa. "Lawyers, Law, and the New Civil Rights History." *Harvard Law Review* 126, no. 8 (2013): 2312–2335.

Goodman, Nan. "Law in Popular Culture, 1790-1920." In *The Cambridge History of Law in America,* edited by Michael Grossberg and Christopher Tomlins, Vol. 2, 387–416. Cambridge: Cambridge University Press, 2008.

Gordon, Robert W. "Critical Legal Histories." *Stanford Law Review* 36, no. 1/2 (1984): 57–125.

Gordon, Robert W. "The American Legal Profession, 1870–2000." In *The Cambridge History of Law in America,* edited by Michael Grossberg and Christopher Tomlins, Vol. 3, 73–126. Cambridge: Cambridge University Press, 2008.

Gordon-Reed, Annette. *Race on Trial: Law and Justice in American History.* Oxford: Oxford University Press, 2002.

Gross, Ariela J. "Pandora's Box: Slave Character on Trial in the Antebellum Deep South." In *Slavery & the Law,* edited by Paul Finkelman, 291–327. Madison, WI: Madison House, 1997.

Gross, Ariela J. *Double Character: Slavery and Mastery in the Antebellum Southern Courtroom.* Princeton, NJ: Princeton University Press, 2000.

Gross, Ariela J. "Beyond Black and White: Cultural Approaches to Race and Slavery." *Columbia Law Review* 101 (April 2001): 640–690.

Gross, Ariela J. *What Blood Won't Tell: A History of Race on Trial in America.* Cambridge, MA: Harvard University Press, 2008.

Gross, Kali N. *Colored Amazons: Crime, Violence, and Black Women in the City of Brotherly Love, 1880–1910.* Durham, NC: Duke University Press, 2006.

Grossberg, Michael. *Governing the Hearth: Law and the Family in Nineteenth-Century America.* Chapel Hill: University of North Carolina Press, 1985.

Grossberg, Michael. *A Judgment for Solomon: The D'Hauteville Case and Legal Experience in Antebellum America.* Cambridge: Cambridge University Press, 1996.

Grossberg, Michael and Christopher Tomlins, eds. *The Cambridge History of Law in America,* Vol. 2. Cambridge: Cambridge University Press, 2008.

Hager, Christopher. *Word by Word: Emancipation and the Act of Writing.* Cambridge, MA: Harvard University Press, 2013.

Hahn, Steven. *A Nation Under Our Feet: Black Political Struggles in the Rural South, From Slavery to the Great Migration.* Cambridge, MA: Belknap Press of Harvard University Press, 2003.

Hahn, Steven. *The Roots of Southern Populism: Yeoman Farmers and the Transformation of the Georgia Upcountry, 1850–1890,* updated ed. New York: Oxford University Press, 2006.

Hale, Grace Elizabeth. *Making Whiteness: The Culture of Segregation in the South, 1890–1940.* New York: Pantheon, 1998.

Haley, Sarah. *No Mercy Here: Gender, Punishment, and the Making of Jim Crow Modernity.* Chapel Hill: University of North Carolina Press, 2016.

Hall, Jacquelyn Dowd. "The Long Civil Rights Movement and the Political Uses of the Past." *The Journal of American History* 91, no. 4 (2005): 1233–1263.

Hall, Kermit L. "The 'Route to Hell' Retraced: The Impact of Popular Election on the Southern Appellate Judiciary, 1832–1920." In *Ambivalent Legacy: A Legal History of the South,* edited by David J. Bodenhamer and James W. Ely, Jr, 229–55. Jackson: University Press of Mississippi, 1984.

Hall, Kermit L. *The Magic Mirror: Law in American History.* Oxford: Oxford University Press, 1989.

Hamlin, Françoise N. *Crossroads at Clarksdale: The Black Freedom Struggle in the Mississippi Delta After World War II.* Chapel Hill: University of North Carolina Press, 2012.

Hargis, Peggy G. "For the Love of Place: Paternalism and Patronage in the Georgia Lowcountry, 1865–1898." *The Journal of Southern History* 70, no. 4 (2004): 825–864.

Harris, Cheryl I. "Whiteness as Property." *Harvard Law Review* 106 (1993): 1709–1791.

Harris, John B., ed. *A History of the Supreme Court of Georgia.* Macon, GA: J. W. Burke Co., 1948.

Hartman, Saidiya V. *Scenes of Subjection: Terror, Slavery, and Self-Making in Nineteenth -Century America.* New York: Oxford University Press, 1997.

Hartog, Hendrik. "Pigs and Positivism." *Wisconsin Law Review* 4 (1985): 899–935.

Hartog, Hendrik. "Introduction to Symposium on 'Critical Legal Histories.'" *Law & Social Inquiry* 37 (Winter 2012): 147–154.

Helis, Thomas W. "Of Generals and Jurists: The Judicial System of New Orleans Under Union Occupation, May, 1862–April,1865." *Louisiana History* XXIX (Spring 1988): 143–162.

Higginbotham, A. Leon, Jr. *Shades of Freedom: Racial Politics and Presumptions of the American Legal Process.* Oxford: Oxford University Press, 1996.

Higginbotham, Evelyn Brooks. "African-American Women's History and the Metalanguage of Race," in *History and Theory: Feminist Research, Debates, Contestations*, edited by Barbara Laslett, Ruth-Ellen B. Joeres, Mary Jo Maynes, Evelyn Brooks Higginbotham, and Jeanne Barker-Nunn, 304–327. Chicago: University of Chicago Press, 1997.

Hill, Cecil J. *When the North Carolina Supreme Court Sat In The Capitol.* West Publishing, 1984.

Hinton, Elizabeth. *From the War on Poverty to the War on Crime: The Making of Mass Incarceration in America.* Cambridge, MA: Harvard University Press, 2016.

Hodes, Martha. *White Women, Black Men: Illicit Sex in the Nineteenth-Century South.* New Haven, CT: Yale University Press, 1997.

Hodes, Martha, ed. *Sex, Love, Race: Crossing Boundaries in North American History.* New York: New York University Press, 1999.

Hoff, Joan. *Law, Gender, and Injustice: A Legal History of U.S. Women.* New York: New York University Press, 1991.

Holt, Michael F. *The Fate of Their Country: Politicians, Slavery Extension, and the Coming of the Civil War.* New York: Hill and Wang, 2004.

Holt, Sharon Ann. *Making Freedom Pay: North Carolina Freedpeople Working for Themselves, 1865–1900.* Athens: University of Georgia Press, 2000.

Howington, Arthur F. *What Sayeth The Law: The Treatment of Slaves and Free Blacks in the State and Local Courts of Tennessee.* New York: Garland, 1986.

Huebner, Timothy S. *The Southern Judicial Tradition: State Judges and Sectional Distinctiveness, 1790–1890.* Athens: University of Georgia Press, 1999.

Hunter, Tera W. *To 'Joy My Freedom: Southern Black Women's Lives and Labors After the Civil War.* Cambridge, MA: Harvard University Press, 1997.

Jackson, III, Harvey H. "White Supremacy Triumphant: Democracy Undone." In *A Century of Controversy: Constitutional Reform in Alabama*, edited by Bailey Thompson, 17–33. Tuscaloosa: University of Alabama Press, 2002.

Jeffries, Hasan Kwame. *Bloody Lowndes: Civil Rights and Black Power in Alabama's Black Belt.* New York: New York University Press, 2009.

Johnson, Kimberley. *Reforming Jim Crow: Southern Politics and the State in the Age Before Brown.* New York: Oxford University Press, 2010.

Johnson, Walter. "Review: Inconsistency, Contradiction, and Complete Confusion: The Everyday Life of the Law of Slavery." *Law & Social Inquiry* 22, no. 2 (1997): 405–433.

Johnson, Walter. *Soul by Soul: Life Inside the Antebellum Slave Market.* Cambridge, MA: Harvard University Press, 1999.

Johnson, Walter. "The Slave Trader, the White Slave, and the Politics of Racial Determination in the 1850s." *Journal of American History* 87, no. 1 (2000): 13–38.

Johnson, Walter. "On Agency." *Journal of Social History* 37, no. 1 (Fall 2003): 113–124.

Jonas, Gilbert. *Freedom's Sword: The NAACP and the Struggle Against Racism in America, 1909-1969.* New York: Routledge, 2005.

Jones, Angela. *African American Civil Rights: Early Activism and the Niagara Movement.* Santa Barbara, CA: Praeger, 2011.

Jones, Bernie D. *Fathers of Conscience: Mixed-Race Inheritance in the Antebellum South.* Athens: University of Georgia Press, 2009.

Jones, Jacqueline. *Labor of Love, Labor of Sorrow: Black Women, Work and the Family, From Slavery to the Present.* New York: Basic Books, 1985.

Jones, Martha S. "Leave of Court: African-American Legal Claims Making In the Era of *Dred Scott v. Sandford*." In *Contested Democracy: Politics, Ideology and Race in American History,* edited by Manisha Sinha and Penny Von Eschen, 54–74. New York: Columbia University Press, 2007.

Jones, Martha S. "Hughes v. Jackson: Race and Rights Beyond Dred Scott." *North Carolina Law Review* 91 (June 2013): 1757–1784.

Jordan, Robert H. *Courthouses in Georgia.* Norcross, GA: Harrison Company, 1984.

Kagan, Robert A., Bliss Cartwright, Lawrence M. Friedman, and Stanton Wheeler. "The Business of State Supreme Courts, 1870–1970." *Stanford Law Review* 30, no. 1 (Nov. 1977): 121–156.

Karsten, Peter. *Heart versus Head: Judge-Made Law in Nineteenth-Century America.* Chapel Hill: University of North Carolina Press, 1997.

Kerber, Linda K. *No Constitutional Right to be Ladies: Women and the Obligations of Citizenship.* New York: Hill and Wang, 1998.

Kelley, Robin D.G. *Hammer and Hoe: Alabama Communist During the Great Depression.* Chapel Hill: University of North Carolina Press, 1990.

Kelley, Robin D.G. *Freedom Dreams: The Black Radical Imagination.* Boston: Beacon, 2002.

Kellogg, Charles Flint. *NAACP: A History of the National Association for the Advancement of Colored People.* Vol.1, *1909–1920.* Baltimore: Johns Hopkins University Press, 1967.

Kelley, Blair L.M. *Right to Ride: Streetcar Boycotts and African American Citizenship in the Era of Plessy v. Ferguson.* Chapel Hill: University of North Carolina Press, 2010.

Kennedy, Randall. *Race, Crime, and the Law.* New York: Vintage, 1997.

Kennington, Kelly M. *In the Shadow of* Dred Scott: *St. Louis Freedom Suits and the Legal Culture of Slavery in Antebellum America.* Athens: University of Georgia Press, 2017.

Kilpatrick, Judith. "(Extra) Ordinary Men: African American Lawyers and Civil Rights in Arkansas Before 1950." *Arkansas Law Review* 53 (2000): 299–399.

Kilpatrick, Judith. *Arkansas' Early African-American Lawyers: A Pictorial History.* Fayetteville: University of Arkansas School of Law, 2002.

Kinshasa, Kwanda M. *Emigration v. Assimilation: The Debate in the African American Press, 1827–1861.* Jefferson, NC: McFarland, 1988.

Kirtley, Marjorie D. *Virginia Supreme Court: Biographies, Chronological History.* Richmond, VA, 1969.

Klarman, Michael J. *From Jim Crow to Civil Rights: The Supreme Court and the Struggle for Racial Equality.* Oxford: Oxford University Press, 2004.

Kluger, Richard. *Simple Justice: The History of Brown v. Board of Education and Black America's Struggle for Equality.* 1975; reprinted New York: Knopf, 1976.

Kolchin, Peter. *American Slavery, 1619–1877.* New York: Hill and Wang, 2003.

Konig, David Thomas. "The Long Road to Dred Scott: Personhood and the Rule of Law in the Trial Court Records of St. Louis Slave Freedom Suits." *University of Missouri-Kansas City Law Review* 75 (Fall 2006): 53–79.

Kousser, J. Morgan. *The Shaping of Southern Politics: Suffrage Restriction and the Establishment of the One-Party South, 1880–1910.* New Haven, CT: Yale University Press, 1974.

Kousser, J. Morgan. *Dead End: The Development of Nineteenth-Century Litigation on Racial Discrimination in Schools: An Inaugural Lecture Delivered Before the University of Oxford on 28 February 1985.* Oxford: Clarendon, 1986.

Kousser, J. Morgan. "Why Were There So Many Legal Cases on School Integration in Nineteenth-Century America?." Unpublished Paper Prepared for delivery at the Social Science History Association Convention, Washington DC, Oct.1997 (used with the permission of the author).

Kousser, J. Morgan. *Colorblind Injustice: Minority Voting Rights and the Undoing of the Second Reconstruction.* Chapel Hill: University of North Carolina Press, 1999.

Kousser, J. Morgan. "Strange Career and the Need for a Second Reconstruction of the History of Race Relations." In *Dixie Redux: Essays in Honor of Sheldon Hackney,* edited by Raymond Arsenault and Orville Vernon Burton, 398–416. Montgomery, AL: NewSouth Books, 2013.

Kruse, Kevin M. and Stephen Tuck, eds. *Fog of War: The Second World War and the Civil Rights Movement.* New York: Oxford University Press, 2012.

Landon, Michael de L. *The Honor and Dignity of the Profession: A History of the Mississippi State Bar, 1906–1976.* Jackson: University Press of Mississippi, 1980.

Lavergne, Gary M. *Before Brown: Heman Marion Sweatt, Thurgood Marshall, and the Long Road to Justice.* Austin: University of Texas Press, 2010.

Lebsock, Suzanne. *A Murder in Virginia: Southern Justice on Trial.* New York: Norton, 2003.

Lebsock, Suzanne. *The Free Women of Petersburg: Status and Culture in a Southern Town, 1784–1860.* New York: Norton, 1984.

LeFlouria, Talitha A. *Chained in Silence: Black Women and Convict Labor in the New South.* Chapel Hill: University of North Carolina Press, 2015.

Leslie, Kent Anderson. *Woman of Color, Daughter of Privilege: Amanda America Dickson, 1849–1893.* Athens: University of Georgia Press, 1995.

Levine, Bruce. *The Fall of the House of Dixie: The Civil War and the Social Revolution That Transformed the South.* New York: Random House, 2013.

Levine, Lawrence W. *Black Culture and Black Consciousness: Afro-American Folk Thought From Slavery to Freedom.* Oxford: Oxford University Press, 1977.

Lewis, David Levering. *W. E. B. Du Bois: Biography of a Race.* New York: Holt, 1993.

Litwack, Leon F. *North of Slavery: The Negro in the Free States, 1790-1860.* Chicago: University of Chicago Press, 1961.

Litwack, Leon F. *Been in the Storm So Long: The Aftermath of Slavery.* New York: Vintage, 1979.

Litwack, Leon F. *Trouble in Mind: Black Southerners in the Age of Jim Crow,* 1st ed. New York: Knopf, 1998.

Lofgren, Charles A. *The Plessy Case: A Legal-Historical Interpretation.* New York: Oxford University Press, 1987.

Mack, Kenneth W. *Representing the Race: The Creation of the Civil Rights Lawyer.* Cambridge, MA: Harvard University Press, 2012.

Mangum, Charles S., Jr. *The Legal Status of the Negro.* Chapel Hill: University of North Carolina Press, 1940.

Marable, Manning. "The Politics of Black Land Tenure: 1877–1915." *Agricultural History* 53, no. 1 (1980): 142–152.

Maris-Wolf, Ted. *Family Bonds: Free Blacks and Re-enslavement Law in Antebellum Virginia.* Chapel Hill: University of North Carolina Press, 2015.

Martin, Jonathan D. *Divided Mastery: Slave Hiring in the American South.* Cambridge, MA: Harvard University Press, 2004.

McCann, Michael W. "Reform Litigation on Trial." *Law and Social Inquiry* 17 (1992): 715–743.

McCray, Carrie Allen. *Freedom's Child: The Life of a Confederate General's Black Daughter,* 1st ed. Chapel Hill, NC: Algonquin, 1998.

McCurry, Stephanie. *Confederate Reckoning: Power and Politics in the Civil War South.* Cambridge, MA: Harvard University Press, 2010.

McElya, Micki. *Clinging to Mammy: The Faithful Slave in Twentieth-Century America*. Cambridge, MA: Harvard University Press, 2007.

McGuire, Danielle L. *At the Dark End of the Street: Black Women, Rape, and Resistance—A New History of the Civil Rights Movement from Rosa Parks to the Rise of Black Power*. New York: Knopf, 2010.

McLaughlin, Glory. "A 'Mixture of Race and Reform': The Memory of the Civil War in the Alabama Legal Mind." *Alabama Law Review* 56 (Fall 2004): 285–309.

McLaurin, Melton Alonza. *Celia, A Slave*. Athens: University of Georgia Press, 1991.

McMillen, Neil R. *Dark Journey: Black Mississippians in the Age of Jim Crow*. Urbana: University of Illinois, 1989.

McPherson, James M. *Battle Cry of Freedom: The Civil War Era*. New York: Ballantine, 1988.

Melish, Joanne Pope. *Disowning Slavery: Gradual Emancipation and "Race" in New England, 1780–1860*. Ithaca, NY: Cornell University Press, 1998.

Merritt, Carole. *The Herndons: An Atlanta Family*. Athens: University of Georgia Press, 2002.

Milewski, Melissa. "From Slave to Litigant: African Americans in Court in the Post-War South, 1865–1920." PhD diss., New York University, 2011.

Miller, Randall M., ed. *Dear Master: Letters of a Slave Family*. Ithaca, NY: Cornell University Press, 1978.

Mills, Quincy T. *Cutting Along the Color Line: Black Barbers and Barber Shops in America*. Philadelphia: University of Pennsylvania Press, 2013.

Mitchell, Michele. *Righteous Propagation: African Americans and the Politics of Racial Destiny After Reconstruction*. Chapel Hill: University of North Carolina Press, 2004.

Mitchell, Michele. "Silences Broken, Silences Kept: Gender and Sexuality in African-American History," *Gender & History* 11, no. 3 (1999): 499–513.

Morris, Aldon D. *The Origins of the Civil Rights Movement: Black Communities Organizing for Change*. New York: Free Press, 1984.

Morris, Thomas D. "Slaves and the Rules of Evidence in Criminal Trials." In *Slavery & The Law*, edited by Paul Finkelman, 209–239. Madison, WI: Madison House, 1997.

Morris, Thomas D. *Southern Slavery and the Law, 1619–1860*. Chapel Hill: University of North Carolina Press, 1996.

Muhammad, Khalil Gibran. *The Condemnation of Blackness: Race, Crime, and the Making of Modern Urban America*. Cambridge, MA: Harvard University Press, 2010.

Myers, Martha A. *Race, Labor & Punishment in the New South*. Columbus: Ohio State University Press, 1998.

Nash, A. E. Keir. "Fairness and Formalism in the Trials of Blacks in the State Supreme Courts of the Old South." *Virginia Law Review* 56, no. 1 (1970): 64–100.

Nieman, Donald G. "Black Political Power and Criminal Justice: Washington County, Texas, 1868-1884." *The Journal of Southern History* 55, no. 3 (1989): 398–406.

Nieman, Donald G. *Promises to Keep: African Americans and the Constitutional Order, 1776 to the Present*. New York: Oxford University Press, 1991.

Nieman, Donald G., ed. *Black Southerners and the Law, 1865-1900*. New York: Garland, 1994.

Nieman, Donald G. *The Freedmen's Bureau and Black Freedom*. New York: Garland, 1994.

Nieman, Donald G. "The Language of Liberation: African Americans and Equalitarian Constitutionalism, 1830–1950." In *Black Southerners and the Law, 1865-1900*, edited by Donald G. Nieman, 247–270. New York: Garland, 1994.

Norrell, Robert J. "Law in a White Man's Democracy: A History of the Alabama State Judiciary." *Cumberland Law Review* 32 (2001): 135–143.

Novkov, Julie. *Racial Union: Law, Intimacy, and the White State in Alabama, 1865-1954*. Ann Arbor: University of Michigan Press, 2008.

Oakes, James. *Slavery and Freedom: An Interpretation of the Old South*. New York: Vintage, 1990.

Oldfield, John. "The African American Bar in South Carolina." In *At Freedom's Door: African American Founding Fathers and Lawyers in Reconstruction South Carolina*, edited by James Lowell Underwood and W. Lewis Burke Jr., 116–129. Columbia: University of South Carolina Press, 2000.

Oshinsky, David M. *"Worse Than Slavery": Parchman Farm and the Ordeal of Jim Crow Justice.* New York: Free Press, 1996.

Painter, Nell Irvin. "A Prize-Winning Book Revisited. Review of *Reconstruction: America's Unfinished Revolution,* by Eric Foner." *Journal of Women's History* 2, no. 3 (1999): 126–134.

Painter, Nell Irvin. *Southern History Across the Color Line.* Chapel Hill: University of North Carolina Press, 2002.

Pascoe, Peggy. "Miscegenation Law, Court Cases, and Ideologies of 'Race' in Twentieth Century America." In *Sex, Love, Race: Crossing Boundaries in North American History,* edited by Martha Hodes, 464–490. New York: New York University Press, 1999.

Pascoe, Peggy. *What Comes Naturally: Miscegenation Law and the Making of Race in America.* New York: Oxford University Press, 2009.

Penningroth, Dylan C. *The Claims of Kinfolk: African American Property and Community in the Nineteenth-Century South.* Chapel Hill: University of North Carolina Press, 2003.

Penningroth, Dylan C. "The Claims of Slaves and Ex-Slaves to Family and Property: A Transatlantic Comparison." *American Historical Review* 112, no. 4 (2007): 1039–1069.

Penningroth, Dylan C. "African American Divorce in Virginia and Washington DC, 1865–1930." *Journal of Family History* 33, no. 1 (2008): 21–35.

Perman, Michael. *Struggle for Mastery: Disfranchisement in the South, 1888-1908.* Chapel Hill: University of North Carolina Press, 2001.

Peirce, Paul Skeels. *The Freedmen's Bureau: A Chapter in the History of Reconstruction.* Iowa City: State University of Iowa, 1901.

Pincus, Samuel N. *The Virginia Supreme Court, Blacks and the Law, 1870–1902.* New York: Garland, 1990.

Pitts, Yvonne M. "'I Desire to Give My Black Family Their Freedom': Manumissions, Inheritance, and Visions of Family in Antebellum Kentucky." In *Women Shaping the South: Creating and Confronting Change,* edited by Angela Boswell and Judith N. McArthur, 50–73. Columbia: University of Mississippi Press, 2006.

Price, Edward T. "The Central Courthouse Square in the American County Seat." *Geographical Review* 58, no. 1 (1968): 29–60.

Rabinowitz, Howard N. "More Than the Woodward Thesis: Assessing the Strange Career of Jim Crow." *Journal of American History* 75 (Dec. 1988): 842–856.

Rabinowitz, Howard N. *Race Relations in the Urban South.* New York: Oxford University Press, 1978.

Ranney, Joseph A. *In the Wake of Slavery: Civil War, Civil Rights, and the Reconstruction of Southern Law.* Westport, CT: Praeger, 2006.

Regosin, Elizabeth Ann. *Freedom's Promise: Ex-Slave Families and Citizenship in the Age of Emancipation.* Charlottesville: University Press of Virginia, 2002.

Riegel, Stephen J. "The Persistent Career of Jim Crow: Lower Federal Courts and the 'Separate but Equal' Doctrine, 1865–1896." *American Journal of Legal History* 28, no. 1 (1984): 17–40.

Riser, R. Volney. *Defying Disfranchisement: Black Voting Rights Activism in the Jim Crow South, 1890–1908.* Baton Rouge: Louisiana State University Press, 2010.

Rosenberg, Gerald N. *The Hollow Hope: Can Courts Bring About Social Change?* Chicago: University of Chicago Press, 1991.

Ross, Michael A. *The Great New Orleans Kidnapping Case: Race, Law, and Justice in the Reconstruction Era.* New York: Oxford University Press, 2015.

Rothman, Joshua D. *Notorious in the Neighborhood: Sex and Families Across the Color Line in Virginia, 1787–1861.* Chapel Hill: University of North Carolina Press, 2003.

Russell, Thomas D. "Slave Auctions on the Courthouse Steps: Court Sales of Slaves in Antebellum South Carolina." In *Slavery & The Law,* edited by Paul Finkelman, 329–364. Lanham, MD: Rowman & Littlefield,1997.

Salyer, Lucy E. *Laws Harsh as Tigers: Chinese Immigrants and the Shaping of Modern Immigration Law.* Chapel Hill: University of North Carolina Press, 1995.

Sansing, David Gaffney. "The Role of the Scalawag in Mississippi Reconstruction." PhD diss.,
    University of Southern Mississippi, 1969.

Saville, Julie. *The Work of Reconstruction: From Slave to Wage Laborer in South Carolina, 1860–1870.*
    Cambridge: Cambridge University Press, 1996.

Schafer, Judith Kelleher. *Slavery, the Civil Law, and the Supreme Court of Louisiana.* Baton
    Rouge: Louisiana State University Press, 1994.

Schmidt, Christopher W. "Legal History and the Problem of the Long Civil Rights Movement."
    Law & Social Inquiry 41 (2016): 1081–1103.

Schwalm, Leslie A. *A Hard Fight for We: Women's Transition from Slavery to Freedom in South
    Carolina.* Urbana: University of Illinois Press, 1997.

Schwarz, Philip J. *Slave Laws in Virginia.* Athens: University of Georgia Press, 1996.

Schweninger, Loren. *Appealing for Liberty: Freedom Suits in the South.* Oxford: Oxford University
    Press, 2017.

Scott, James C. *Weapons of the Weak: Everyday Forms of Resistance.* New Haven, CT: Yale University
    Press, 1985.

Scott, James C. *Domination and the Arts of Resistance: Hidden Transcripts.* New Haven, CT: Yale
    University Press, 1992.

Scott, Rebecca J. *Degrees of Freedom: Louisiana and Cuba After Slavery.* Cambridge, MA: Belknap
    Press of Harvard University Press, 2005.

Shick, Tom W. *Behold the Promised Land: A History of Afro-American Settler Society in Nineteenth-
    Century Liberia.* Baltimore: Johns Hopkins Press, 1977.

Shugerman, Jed Handelsman. *The People's Courts: Pursuing Judicial Independence in America.*
    Cambridge, MA: Harvard University Press, 2012.

Smith, J. Clay. *Emancipation: The Making of the Black Lawyer, 1844–1944.* Philadelphia: University
    of Pennsylvania Press, 1993.

Stanley, Amy Dru. *From Bondage to Contract: Wage Labor, Marriage, and the Market in the Age of
    Slave Emancipation.* Cambridge: Cambridge University Press, 1998.

Stauffer, John. *The Black Hearts of Men: Radical Abolitionists and the Transformation of Race.*
    Cambridge, MA: Harvard University Press, 2002.

Stockley, Grif. *Blood in Their Eyes: The Elaine Race Massacres of 1919.* Fayetteville: University of
    Arkansas Press, 2001.

Suggs, Jon-Christian. *Whispered Consolations: Law and Narrative in African American Life.* Ann
    Arbor: University of Michigan Press, 2000.

Sullivan, Patricia. *Days of Hope: Race and Democracy in the New Deal Era.* Chapel Hill: University
    of North Carolina Press, 1996.

Sullivan, Patricia. *Lift Every Voice: The NAACP and the Making of the Civil Rights Movement.*
    New York: New Press, 2009.

Surrency, Erwin C. *The Creation of a Judicial System: The History of Georgia Courts, 1733 to Present.*
    Holmes Beach, FL: Gaunt, 2001.

Surrency, Erwin C. *The Work of the Federal Courts in Georgia Over Two Centuries.* Atlanta,
    GA: Eleventh Circuit Historical Society, 2006.

Taylor, Keeanga-Yamahtta. *From #BlackLivesMatter to Black Liberation.* Chicago: Haymarket
    Books, 2016.

Thompson, Elizabeth Lee. *The Reconstruction of Southern Debtors: Bankruptcy After the Civil War.*
    Athens: University of Georgia Press, 2004.

Tushnet, Mark. *The American Law of Slavery, 1810–1860: Considerations of Humanity and Interest.*
    Princeton, NJ: Princeton University Press, 1981.

Tushnet, Mark. *The NAACP's Legal Strategy Against Segregated Education, 1925–1950.* Chapel
    Hill: University of North Carolina Press, 1987.

Tushnet, Mark. "Brown v. Board of Education." In *Race on Trial: Law and Justice in American
    History,* edited by Annette Gordon-Reed, 160–176. Oxford: Oxford University Press, 2002.

Underwood, James Lowell and W. Lewis Burke, eds. *At Freedom's Door: African American Founding Fathers and Lawyers in Reconstruction South Carolina*. Columbia: University of South Carolina Press, 2000.

Waldrep, Christopher. "Substituting Law for the Lash: Emancipation and Legal Formalism in a Mississippi County Court." *The Journal of American History* 82, no. 4 (1996): 1425–1451.

Waldrep, Christopher. *Roots of Disorder: Race and Criminal Justice in the American South, 1817–80*. Urbana: University of Illinois Press, 1998.

Waldrep, Christopher. *Jury Discrimination: The Supreme Court, Public Opinion, and a Grassroots Fight for Racial Equality in Mississippi*. Athens: University of Georgia Press, 2010.

Waldrep, Christopher and Donald G. Nieman, eds. *Local Matters: Race, Crime, and Justice in the Nineteenth-Century South*. Athens: University of Georgia Press, 2001.

Wallenstein, Peter. "Reconstruction, Segregation, and Miscegenation: Interracial Marriage and the Law in the Lower South, 1865–1900." *American Nineteenth Century History* 6, no. 1 (2005): 57–76.

Ware, Ethel K. *A Constitutional History of Georgia*. New York: Columbia University Press, 1947.

Weiner, Mark S. *Black Trials: Citizenship From the Beginnings of Slavery to the End of Caste*. New York: Knopf, 2004.

Welch, Kimberly. "Black Litigiousness and White Accountability: Free Blacks and the Rhetoric of Reputation in the Antebellum Natchez District." *Journal of the Civil War Era* 5, no. 3 (2015): 372–398.

Welke, Barbara. "When All the Women Were White, and All the Blacks Were Men: Gender, Class, Race, and the Road to *Plessy*, 1855–1914." *Law and History Review* 13 (1995): 261–316.

Welke, Barbara. *Recasting American Liberty: Gender, Race, Law, and the Railroad Revolution, 1865–1920*. Cambridge: Cambridge University Press, 2001.

Welke, Barbara. "Law, Personhood, and Citizenship in the Long Nineteenth Century: The Borders of Belonging." In *Cambridge History of Law in America*, edited by Michael Grossberg and Christopher Tomlins, Vol. 2, 345–386. Cambridge: Cambridge University Press, 2008.

Welke, Barbara. *Law and the Borders of Belonging in the Long Nineteenth Century United States*. New York: Cambridge University Press, 2010.

Wertheimer, John W. *Law and Society in the South: A History of North Carolina Court Cases*. Lexington: University Press of Kentucky, 2009.

White, Richard. *Railroaded: The Transcontinentals and the Making of Modern America*. New York: Norton, 2011.

White, Sophie. "Wearing Three or Four Handkerchiefs Around His Collar, and Elsewhere About Him: Slaves' Constructions of Masculinity and Ethnicity in French Colonial New Orleans." In *Dialogues of Dispersal: Gender, Sexuality and African Diasporas*, edited by Sandra Gunning, Tera W. Hunter, and Michele Mitchell, 132–153. Oxford: Blackwell, 2004.

Wigginton, R. "But He Did What He Could: William Warley Leads Louisville's Fight for Justice, 1902–1946." *Filson History Quarterly* 76, no. 4 (2002): 427–439.

Wilf, Steven. "Law/Text/Past." *UC Irvine Law Review* 1, no. 3 (2011): 543–564.

Wilkerson, Isabel. *The Warmth of Other Suns: The Epic Story of America's Great Migration*. New York: Random House, 2010.

Wood, Amy Louise. *Lynching and Spectacle: Witnessing Racial Violence in America, 1890–1940*. Chapel Hill: University of North Carolina Press, 2009.

Woodman, Harold A. "Post-Civil War Southern Agriculture and the Law." In *Black Southerners and the Law, 1865-1900*, edited by Donald G. Nieman, 447–465. New York: Garland, 1994.

Woodruff, Nan Elizabeth. *American Congo: The African American Freedom Struggle in the Delta*. Cambridge, MA: Harvard University Press, 2003.

Woodward, C. Vann. *Origins of the New South, 1877–1913*. Baton Rouge: Louisiana State University Press, 1971.

Woodward, C. Vann. *The Strange Career of Jim Crow*. New York: Oxford University Press, 1955; commemorative edition 2002.

Woodward, C. Vann, J. Morgan Kousser, and James M. McPherson. *Region, Race, and Reconstruction: Essays in Honor of C. Vann Woodward*. New York: Oxford University Press, 1982.

Wooster, Ralph A. *The People in Power: Courthouse and Statehouse in the Lower South, 1850–1860*. Knoxville, University of Tennessee Press, 1969.

Wright, George C. *Life Behind a Veil: Blacks in Louisville, Kentucky, 1865-1930*. Baton Rouge: Louisiana State University Press, 1985.

Wyatt-Brown, Bertram. *Southern Honor: Ethics and Behavior in the Old South*. New York: Oxford University Press, 1982.

Yarema, Allan. *The American Colonization Society: An Avenue to Freedom?* Lanham, MD: University Press of America, 2006.

Zipf, Karin L. "Reconstructing 'Free Women': African-American Women, Apprenticeship, and Custody Rights During Reconstruction." *Journal of Women's History* 12 (2000): 8–31.

Zipf, Karin L. *Labor of Innocents: Forced Apprenticeship in North Carolina, 1715–1919*. Baton Rouge: Louisiana State University Press, 2005.

INDEX

Page numbers followed by *f* denote a figure and followed by *t* denote a table.